BUFFALO BILL AND SITTING BULL

M. K. Brown Range Life Series

Number Twenty-one

Bobby Bridger

BUFFALO BILL AND SITTING BULL

INVENTING THE WILD WEST

UNIVERSITY OF TEXAS PRESS, AUSTIN

Requests for permission to reproduce material from this work should be sent to
Permissions, University of Texas Press, P.O. Box 7819, Austin, TX 78713-7819.

∞ The paper used in this book meets the minimum requirements of
ANSI/NISO Z39.48-1992 (R1997) (Permanence of Paper).

LIBRARY OF CONGRESS CATALOGING-IN-PUBLICATION DATA
Bridger, Bobby.
Buffalo Bill and Sitting Bull : inventing the Wild West / Bobby Bridger.
p.   cm. — (M.K. Brown range life series ; no. 21)
Includes bibliographical references (p.) and index.
ISBN 0-292-70917-x (hardcover : alk. paper)
1. Buffalo Bill, 1846–1917.   2. Pioneers—West (U.S.)—Biography.   3. Scouts and
scouting—West (U.S.)—Biography.   4. Entertainers—West (U.S.)—Biography.
5. Buffalo Bill, 1846–1917—Relations with Indians.   6. Sitting Bull, 1834?–1890.
7. Indians of North America—Great Plains—History—Frontier and pioneer
life—West (U.S.)   10. West (U.S.)—Biography.   I. Title.   II. Series.
F594.C68 B75 2002
978'.02'.—dc21
2002004974

PECOKAN SUNPI

"'Do you know who this man is?'"
"'Yes, we know him well,' replied one, 'that is Pa-he-haska' (that being my name among the Sioux, which translated means "long hair") 'that is our old enemy,' a great many of the Indians, who were with Spotted Tail at this time, had been driven out of the Republican Country.
"'That is he,' said Spotted Tail. 'I want all my people to be kind to him and treat him as my friend.'"

—William F. "Buffalo Bill" Cody,
describing his meeting with Lakota Chief Spotted Tail
in his 1879 autobiography,
The Life of the Hon. William F. Cody, Known As Buffalo Bill

Perhaps the Lakota custom of wearing the pecokan sunpi, or so-called scalp-lock, has led unnumbered people to believe that the Indian was an inveterate scalp-hunter and that he invited a scalping by wearing his hair in a convenient lock. The Lakota did not wear a braid of hair for this purpose; neither did he always wear this braid at the top of his head.

The men of the Lakota, and most plains warriors, wore the pecokan sunpi, a small circlet portion of the hair which was braided. The term pecokan sunpi means 'a braid' and it never at any time had anything to do with scalping, its purposes being for milder reasons than war. The Lakotas loved feather decorations and used them extensively, not only for their colorful beauty, but for the religious significance and for the further meaning attached to them when worn by scouts and warriors. The men wore their hair long and flowing, and since it was not easy to attach ornaments to loose hair, it was convenient to braid a portion on whatever part of the head the decoration was to be worn. This braid, or so-called scalp-lock, might be at the top of the head, back of the head, at the sides of the forehead, or in the middle of the forehead, depending on the style of the decoration and somewhat on the fancy of the wearer. It was the style with some warriors and braves to wear a braid on each side of the forehead, allowing them to hang to the ears where shell and other ornaments were hung. Then the Lakotas adopted from the Omahas the wearing of the roach to hold it in place. So from time historic the Lakota warrior has worn the pecokan sumpi as a token of his love of decoration and vanity.

Now the Lakota did wear human hair as decoration on clothing, and here again the white man has misjudged motives and infringed on truth, for the custom had its source in love and not in war. There was no such thing as a war shirt, most warriors stripping for a conflict. There was, however, the wicapaha okli, or hair shirt. Upon death of one in a band it was the custom for friends and relatives to cut their hair in mourning; the greater the grief, the shorter the hair was cut. Many of the women had long, lovely braids of which they were very proud and these they gave to male relatives who made a fringe of them for their shirts. The taking of trophies was not an established custom in Lakota warfare, for just as the word of the scout was unquestioned, and it was no more required for one to bring in the fresh scalp of his enemy to prove a conquest than it was for the other to bring in a buffalo chip to prove he had found buffalo. The proof-demanding white man has never, of course, conceded the truthfulness of the Indian, and so another undeserved and ugly characteristic has become attached to him as a race. (*Land of the Spotted Eagle*, Luther Standing Bear)

SCALPING: The custom of cutting off part or all of the scalp of an enemy, not necessarily of a dead one, was practiced in North America by most Indian tribes and some whites and Hispanics. Scalping was a venerable practice, performed not only in North America, but in Europe, Asia, and Africa. Often, as here, it stood for the taking of the entire head of an enemy as a ritual of war and as an insult to the fallen man and his tribe. It was widely performed by native peoples (but not by all tribes) here both before and after white contact. Among some peoples, up to recent times the taking of the entire head remained a more powerful act.

After white contact, the practice spread, partly because of Anglo and Hispanic governments offered bounties for the scalps of native peoples who were causing difficulty. Some whites became scalp hunters, and other whites (for instance, mountain men) took scalps. The popular recent notion that white men corrupted the red man by teaching him to take scalps is a noble exaggeration. (*Dictionary of the American West*, Winfred Blevins)

The Europeans may or may not have introduced scalping to the New World, but the Spanish, French, Dutch, and English colonists made the custom popular by offering bounties for scalps of their respective enemies.

(Bury My Heart At Wounded Knee, Dee Brown)*

This is how they have a victory celebration. They go out to look for [the] enemy, and when they make a kill, they scalp the enemy. When they come back, on the way they scrape the skin thin, then they stretch it across a round hooped stick and hang it up to dry. When they come back, they stop near the camp and all blacken their faces with charcoal. They tie the scalp on the end of stick. On the way back from a kill, the war party gets ready for the celebration. They kill deer and make drums on the way back. They stop a little distance from the camp, then the first kill, the scalper, and the first, second, and third coup (er) get together and the rest stay behind. They gallop into camp and circle around the camp saying, for example: "Black Elk you have said. I met an enemy and I made a kill."

(The Sixth Grandfather, Black Elk's Teachings
Given To John G. Neihardt, Black Elk)*

Of the trophies relating to war, the most prominent were human scalps representing all ages and sexes of the white race. These scalps, according to the barbarous custom, were not composed of the entire covering of the head, but of a small surface surrounding the crown and usually from three to four inches in diameter, constituting what is termed the scalp lock. To preserve the scalp from decay a small hoop of about double the diameter of the scalp is prepared from a small withe which grows on the banks of some of the streams in the West. The scalp is placed inside the hoop and properly stretched by a network of thread connecting the edges of the scalp with the circumference of the hoop. After being properly cured, the dried fleshy portion of the scalp is ornamented in bright colors, according to the taste of the captor, sometimes the addition of beads of bright and varied colors being made to heighten the effect. In other instances the hair is dyed, either to a beautiful yellow or golden, or to crimson. Several of these horrible evidences of past depredations upon the defenseless inhabitants of the frontier or overland emigrants were brought back by the troopers on their return from their scout.

(My Life On The Plains, George Armstrong Custer)*

Pahuska had a strong heart.

(Black Elk Speaks,
as told to John G. Neihardt)

CONTENTS

For Melissa and Gabriel

INTRODUCTION

In the spring of 1973, I sat with my guitars and history books and prepared
to complete the third and final part of my epic trilogy *A Ballad of the West*.
I had selected the life of William Frederick "Buffalo Bill" Cody as my subject and the famous showman's "Indian" name, Pahaska, as my working
title. A Lakota (Sioux) word, *pahaska* means "long hair," and, intuitively assuming a connection between my generation's hirsute rebellion and Buffalo Bill, I felt the word itself would lead me on a direct path to the essence
of William F. Cody.

Aside from his famous shoulder-length locks, Cody had the essential lon-
gevity and nineteenth-century history I needed to complement the lives of
Jim Bridger and Black Elk, the protagonists of Parts One and Three of *A
Ballad of the West*. Vitally important, as Bridger and Black Elk, William F.
Cody also possessed the particular gift for being directly involved with, or
eyewitness to, pivotal moments in western American history. Most significant, in 1857, as an eleven-year-old boy, Cody had met Jim Bridger and Kit
Carson at historic Fort Laramie and spent the winter there soaking up their
influence. Cody's splendid connection with Jim Bridger and the Exploration
and Fur Trade Era provided an eloquent historical symmetry to my trilogy;
it united and completed my original vision of *A Ballad of the West*. In May of
1963, upon having the wild idea of researching the life of American mountain man, Jim Bridger, and developing that research into a long, historically
documented folk song, I was amazed how quickly the idea expanded as I encountered a much different Native America than I had experienced in
movies, television, and textbooks. Suddenly, I became aware that the story
of Jim Bridger would be shamefully incomplete if the positive Native American influence on his life was not presented. Furthermore, upon discovering
the work of Nebraska epic poet John G. Neihardt in 1965, I found myself
increasingly lost in thoughts of combining a narrative group of folks songs
of epic proportions uniting verse, ballads, historical narratives, paintings,
and photographs in order to comprehensively examine the core myth of the
American west from multiple artistic perspectives and disciplines. Twenty
years old in 1965, I naively figured such a work might take ten years to re-

search and complete, yet it seemed a unique and most worthwhile artistic aspiration.

In 1967, legendary studio musician, record producer and executive, Fred Carter, Jr., invited me to come to Nashville, and signed me to my first national recording contract with Monument Records. Simply put, Fred taught me how to write songs and make them into recordings. In 1969, with Fred's steadfast support, I produced my first album of original songs, *Merging Of Our Minds*, and, in 1970, signed a recording contract with RCA Records and publishing contract with Edwin H. Morris Music Publishing in Hollywood. I also relocated from Louisiana to Texas in 1970, and was building a home base in bohemian Austin during the glory days of the genesis of the famous alternative music scene there. In late 1972, as my second RCA album, *And I Wanted To Sing For The People*, faltered and my Hollywood publishing and recording contracts died with the record's failure, I completed *Seekers of the Fleece*. *Lakota* followed immediately in 1973. With the completion of the two epics, however, I had no recording or publishing company to support their release as recordings. Back at "square one" with my career, I decided to return to the studio to make a demonstration recording of *Seekers of the Fleece*.

Jim Inmon, an Austin recording engineer who helped me with the first recordings of *Seekers of the Fleece*, suggested that I take the epics to a theater in town and develop them as musical plays. During the research and writing of the first two parts of the epic I had realized that the finished work would be a marvelous musical and so, acting on Jim's advice, I took the epics to Austin's Creek Theater. Larry Martin, the theater's artistic director, suggested that, rather than developing the works into company musicals, I should perform them myself as one-man shows. Martin agreed to direct me and, after a six-month rehearsal period, I debuted my one-man shows of *Seekers of the Fleece* and *Lakota* in 1973. A feature story about the debut of the work in an Austin newspaper, however, jokingly referred to me as a "misfit in a city full of misfits"; indeed, once I grew my hair down my back and my beard to my chest; donned beaded, fringed, brain-tanned buckskins; and started wearing a coyote headdress to perform a two-hour, historically documented work in Homeric verse, Nashville and Hollywood were forever behind me. In my heart, however, I knew I had chosen the right path, and audience support at the Creek Theater verified my instincts; *A Ballad of the West*, playing to packed houses, ran for fifteen weeks.

Because it is a work of history, time has always been critical to *A Ballad of the West*. Nevertheless, with hopes of creating a "timeless" work of art with my ballads, I sought to remove myself and my work from the trendy demands of popular music while using the genre's songwriting and recording forms and techniques to my own ends. More importantly, the epic, historical span of the story, and the relationship of those historical eras to modern times have provided much of the force driving me to take such an extraordinary course in life. Yet actual performance time was equally important to me from the beginning, for I always intended *A Ballad of the West* to be performed by a single balladeer, or a company of actors, singers, musicians, and dancers. To sing and act a tale narrating documented historical events of the Trans-Missouri of the nineteenth century would not only prove a challenge to most performers, but an extremely unusual request of the most patient and enthusiastic modern audience.

With this concern for my audience, early on I conceived the work as a trilogy. Each part would stand independently of the other two, yet, when united, form a chronological narrative connecting all three pieces into one composition titled *A Ballad of the West*. This structure would allow me to perform Parts One, Two, or Three separately or united in various combinations. If each part was approximately one hour in performance time I believed I might ask audiences to journey with me through at least two-thirds of the ballad as a "normal" two-hour show; on "special" occasions, the full three-hour ballad could be presented in its entirety.

Upon arriving at this general structure, it became a relatively simple matter to devise an infrastructure that would allow me to reconstruct actual historical events into poetic, musical, and historical narratives intertwined and overlaid into one, flowing chronological narrative composition. *Seekers of the Fleece* and *Lakota* had been created following this structure and, in 1973, the completion of *Pahaska* seemed imminent. So, in the spring of 1973, I had completed a year of biographical research on William Frederick Cody in preparation to write *Pahaska*. This research into Cody's life, however, brought with it an unexpected twist: just as research into Jim Bridger's life had opened the door to his critically important relationships with Native Americans, investigation of Cody's life opened my eyes to the need to understand more about classic concepts of heroes and mythology. With the synchronicity that usually accompanies such matters, at this time I also discovered "The Falling Star," or the "Savior/Creation" myth of the Lakota in Neihardt's *When The Tree Flowered*. As many before me, exploration of the life of William F. Cody had led me straight into American mythology.

The need to understand more about classic mythology before attempting to write anything about Buffalo Bill next led me to the work of Carl Jung and from the psychologist to mythologist Joseph Campbell and process philosopher Charles Hartshone. All of these influences suddenly united within the narrative structure of the "epic ballad" I had created for Parts One and Two of *A Ballad of the West*, and a three-hour space fantasy entitled *Aldebaran and The Falling Star* gushed out of me in a six-month writing session. (A psychologist friend suggested I must have needed a break from historical research and "Earth Religion" for a frolic through deep space.)

Then, in 1975, I attempted *Pahaska* again after recording *Seekers of the Fleece* in Colorado with the late, beloved character actor, Slim Pickens; the stalwart Austin musicians, the Lost Gonzo Band; and some guests: the modern mountain man, Timberjack Joe; the legendary Ramblin' Jack Elliott; poet Charles John Quarto; Mike Burton; and Mike Williams. This time focus and creative energy aligned with subject matter; quickly, a theme based upon the unique relationship between Buffalo Bill and Sitting Bull began to emerge. One morning in Austin, however, I was having coffee with a friend and the conversation turned toward my efforts to complete the writing of my epics. Upon hearing my theme with *Pahaska*, my friend asked if I had seen the play *Indians* by Arthur Kopit.

That afternoon I found a copy of the play at the library. On reading it I was stunned by the similarities of theme in *Indians* and *Pahaska*. The similarity was too close; that evening I burned my first draft of *Pahaska*.[1] Depressed and frustrated with two failed attempts to write about Buffalo Bill, I decided it might prove impossible to create anything about the man that had not already been done in triplicate. I consequently abandoned Cody as the principle subject of my third ballad and began a three year research project into the history of a Brule Lakota family with hopes that I would somehow find the chronological thread I needed to carry *A Ballad of the West* into modern times. I learned much about Lakota religion and culture from Godfrey Broken Rope and his family, but could not find the right connections to link a story about them and their history to *Seekers of the Fleece* and *Lakota*. I also could not get Cody out of my mind, particularly the unusual thought of the power of a scene featuring Lakota Holy Man, Black Elk, singing a yet-to-be-written song entitled, "Pahaska Had A Strong Heart."

The idea of the "Holy Man Aria" first came to me upon reading Neihardt's *Black Elk Speaks* and learning that Black Elk traveled to England with Buffalo Bill in 1887, but missed the boat as the Wild West returned to America. Black Elk and three Lakota companions who had also missed the boat somehow found work in a "copy cat" American Wild West troupe following in Cody's wake and headed to Europe with the smaller show. After working his way around Europe visiting the various cathedrals and monasteries and exploring his inherent interest in religion, Black Elk became extremely ill and headed to Paris to recuperate at a girlfriend's home. He was beginning to recover just as Buffalo Bill returned to Europe with the Wild West in 1889.

Upon being reunited with Black Elk in Paris, Buffalo Bill held a large reunion feast in the Holy Man's honor. Afterwards, Cody gave Black Elk money and the option of staying with the Wild West or returning to America. Black Elk told the scout he was extremely homesick and he wished only to return to home on the Great Plains. Buffalo Bill paid the Holy Man's fare home, causing Black Elk to remark, "Pahaska had a strong heart." I immediately felt this story offered important insight into Cody's personal character and his relationship with Indians. I also thought the story would make a very dramatic concept for a theatrical scene and song.

Performing *Seekers of the Fleece* and *Lakota*, however, possessed me now. I was traveling constantly performing the one-man show I created combining Parts One and Two of the proposed trilogy. It was not unusual for me to be away from Austin six months at a time to return only for a couple of weeks before departing for another six months on the road. My travels took me from coast to coast several times over, performing at venues from night clubs to concert halls, from simple Nebraska barns to elegant Manhattan loft apartments, from palatial Beverly Hills mansions to Indian Reservations, international folk festivals, universities, high schools and kindergartens. To complicate matters, I was beginning to work as an actor in other dramas and musicals, and also getting offers to travel abroad with my one-man show. Completion of *Pahaska* became less important to me as most audiences knew nothing of my proposed third part of the work and it was all I could do to maintain the demanding pace of my performance schedule. My older fans, however, familiar with my original vision of *A Ballad of the West*, would always ask about *Pahaska*. Increasingly, I doubted I would ever complete it. Then, in 1988, when I began producing and starring in a full company outdoor musical production of *Seekers of the Fleece* in Cody, Wyoming, what little professional time I had was rapidly consumed. With the synchronicity that often accompanies such matters, my bride,

Melissa, informed me that we were expecting a baby. Gabriel joined us in October, 1989 and, upon his arrival I decided *A Ballad of the West* would have to stand completed in two parts.

Then, in 1993, as *Seekers of the Fleece* entered its fourth consecutive summer season as a full-company outdoor musical drama in the Robbie Pow Wow Gardens at the Buffalo Bill Historical Center in Cody, Wyoming, I ran into Gene Ball, former educational director of the museum.[2] In 1977 I had performed *Seekers* as the first artist-in-residence of the Buffalo Bill Historical Center when Gene headed the educational program. Over the years Gene and I had remained friends, staying in loose contact and trusting serendipity to bring our paths to cross again. Gene and I agreed to meet the next morning for breakfast at the Irma Hotel and, after the usual "catch-up" conversation, he asked about the status of *Pahaska*. I immediately went into my standard explanations, citing all the reasons I had failed to complete the trilogy. I did, however, admit that Black Elk's remarks about Cody had stayed with me and that perhaps I would write a song about Buffalo Bill's relationship with Indians based on that historical footnote. *[Author's Note: The full-company musical of *Seekers of the Fleece* debuted in June 1988 in Cody, Wyoming in a little "sweat-box" on 12th Street just north of the Irma Hotel. The drought that plagued Wyoming that summer resulted in the historic Yellowstone Fires, which turned Cody into a "ghost town" and caused the production to suffer major losses. In 1989 the production moved outdoors to the Robbie Pow Wow Gardens at the Buffalo Bill Historical Center and ran each summer there until 1994.]

"You should read the essay your friend Vine DeLoria, Jr. wrote on Buffalo Bill's relationship with Indians," Gene popped back immediately. "The museum commissioned him to write it back in the 70s."

I was stunned. Vine DeLoria, Jr. had been my best friend for the past two decades. He was the editor of my hardback and paperback editions of Parts One and Two of *A Ballad of the West*, had written a wonderful essay, "The Healing Spirit," to introduce the work's initial publication in *Four Winds Magazine*, and written the foreword to the paperback edition. Furthermore, Vine had honored me by asking me to contribute essays to anthologies he created and edited in tribute to distinguished western literary "lions" John G. Neihardt (*A Sender of Words*) and Frank Waters (*Frank Waters: Man and Mystic*). In the twenty years I had known Vine I had probably spent a couple of years visiting at his house, living with his family. He had known about *Pahaska* and my struggle to find a unique theme upon which to base a telling of Buffalo Bill's story for all those years, yet somehow I knew nothing of this essay. Vine usually recommended I read authors other than himself, however, and, given the prolific outpouring of books, essays, and lectures from his old electric typewriter, and my aforementioned hectic travel schedule, this oversight was easy to understand. It was, as most things, simply a matter of context. We just rarely talked much about "Bison William," as Vine always called Cody.

"If you ask for a copy at the museum library I'm sure they'll run one off for you," Gene laughed.

Upon reading Vine's brilliant essay, "The Indians," I immediately realized my old friend had once again, albeit indirectly and unwittingly, led me to my path. Globally recognized for never pulling any historical, cultural, or religious punches, DeLoria's wit and intelligence, unique perspectives, eloquence, and charm have devastated many American icons, institutions, and disciplines. The Buffalo Bill Historical Center, fully realizing the rising tide of "revisionist" historians emerging in the early 1970s, bravely asked the country's foremost Indian spokesman how modern Indians might view Buffalo Bill. "The Indians" was the key to discovering how to write something different and new about Buffalo Bill. Most people of my "politically correct," counterculture generation, while enjoying the fruits of our great-great-grandfathers' "winning of the west," were anxious to toss out all those old western heroes such as Cody as embarrassing relics of the theft of Native America. Moreover, as the result of many cowardly efforts to debunk Cody and lay claim to fragments of his legend during the first few decades after his death in 1917, our grandfathers had become equally anxious to dismiss Cody as a hack and "carnie" who made up most of those outrageous dime novel stories about himself. Based on Kopit's play, *Indians*, Robert Altman and Paul Newman's atrociously antiheroic 1970s film, *Buffalo Bill and The Indians, Or Sitting Bull's History Lesson*, completed the demythologizing of Cody in the recent collective memory of the public, and most modern Americans became presumptuously misinformed of Cody's mythic contributions and his unique relationship with Indians. When pressed for a simple point of view on the man, most late-twentieth century Americans viewed Buffalo Bill as a kind of blowhard drunk: at best a great buffalo hunter and showman, and, at worst, an Indian killer. Since Cody had been the standard for the American hero for over one hundred years, however, I became curious as to how this negative perspective evolved in our modern collective consciousness. Vine's insight to search through what had been written about him for what had not been written about him suddenly made a lot of sense—particularly Cody's unique relationship with Plains Indians.

Once again ideas started rolling through my head. This sudden burst of enthusiasm soon slipped into old behavior patterns, however, and, though not as distant as before, *Pahaska* faded as I continued working as a road musician and I failed to write a word.

Then, in September, 1995, I returned to Texas from another summer performing *Seekers of the Fleece* in Wyoming to discover a letter from Paul Fees, Senior Curator at the Buffalo Bill Historical Center. Paul wrote to remind me that 1996 would mark the Sesquicentennial anniversary of Buffalo Bill's birth, and the centennial of the town of Cody. Paul asked about the status of *Pahaska*, suggesting politely that a debut of the work would be a wonderful way to celebrate Cody's life and the town that is his legacy.

Paul's letter let me know it was time to complete *Pahaska* and, consequently, my original vision of a trilogy. After a few days of soul-searching, I called Paul and told him I would have *Pahaska* ready for a debut at the Buffalo Bill Historical Center in the summer of 1996.

I completed writing the epic ballad of *Pahaska* in May, 1996, exactly thirty-three years after stumbling on the idea of a trilogy of western epic ballads. My one-man show of *Pahaska* opened July 8, 1996 in Coe Auditorium in the Buffalo Bill Historical Center and ran through August 2. I did two, sometimes three, shows a day of the ninety-minute epic, which I must admit, took every ounce of energy I could muster. As most performers will confirm, however, using one's energy in performance strengthens rather than depletes vitality, and I probably could have done twice as many shows before becoming exhausted. Also, in performing Cody's life story, one cannot avoid being swept up in his epic, optimistic energy. More importantly, writing and debuting the epic ballad of *Pahaska* at age fifty-one, I came to understand why I could not write the work in my twenties, thirties, or even in my forties: I had to age and get some gray in my beard; I had to crisscross the landscape of the American West in order to understand that the Trans-Missouri region gave birth to Native American mythology long before it gave birth to the "American Dream;" I had to spend thirty-three years obsessed with red and white culture's past, present and future in western America in order to present both perspectives with any degree of objectivity; I had to spend twenty-five years performing all over the world in a coyote headdress, beaded-brain-tanned buckskins and moccasins in order to understand Buffalo Bill the performer and the enduring legacy of the American West he gave to the rest of the world; I had to spend twenty-five years in musical theater in order to comprehend Buffalo Bill's everlasting contribution to American theater and show business; I had to spend ten years producing outdoor musical drama in Wyoming—losing over $50,000 the first year—in order to have a tiny glimpse into the challenge and physical strain Buffalo Bill faced producing a daily touring exhibition that, at its peak, numbered over 600 individuals with livestock numbering over 800 head; I had to research Plains Indian culture and religion for over thirty years in order to understand that an extremely complex relationship—the unique bond of true face-to-face, hand-to-hand warriors—existed between Cody and the Lakota and the Cheyenne; and, after shaving my beard into a handlebar mustache and goatee in order to approximate Cody's well-known image for my one-man show, I had to learn to be comfortable with the expansive range of odd circumstances one encounters looking like a Victorian icon from western America come back to life at the turn of the millennium.

With these few examples of my admiration for the man, I humbly offer *Pahaska* with obvious profound respect for William Frederick Cody. It is a rare occurrence when one continues to dig into a person's life history and finds more good than bad. After all these years of prying into Cody's life and times, and retracing much of the landscape upon which most of his fantastic story was created, I find myself believing Cody rose to such glory because he was truly and simply a good man. He became a global treasure because he was able to synthesize the very best of both the Native and the Euroamerican cultures, and, in doing so, brought positive change and everlasting impact to each.

Pahaska is, finally, an epic ballad of the life of Will Cody, child and man of the great migration of humanity into the mythic environment of the nineteenth-century Trans-Missouri. It is the tale of a unique hero who, after participating in western historical events, reenacted these original historical events in a theatrical arena encompassing the entire world. As living legend, Buffalo Bill rode into the spotlight of celebrity and taught us how we create mythology. It is most important, however, to keep in mind that the mythology created by Will Cody was deeply rooted in reality; Cody's depiction of the "wild" West was an affectionate attempt to bring the essence of the western reality he loved to the rest of the world. Understanding this aspect of Cody's creation is, I believe, vital to understanding the man behind the myth; otherwise, one quickly becomes lost in the netherworld Cody himself created between fantasy and reality. Acceptance and understanding of Cody's attempt at theatrical recreation of real history also brings one to a new awareness of the fact that his reality was set in the nineteenth century Trans-Missouri and will forever remain intertwined with the Plains Indians and the buffalo of that time and landscape. Perhaps Cody's greatest contributions are yet to come as Plains Indian religion and culture continues to heal, mend, reunite and revitalize, while buffalo numbers rejuvenate. We shall see.

BUFFALO BILL AND SITTING BULL

PROLOGUE

"As a child one has a dream about life. As one grows up and out into life one tries to make the dream come true," she once said. "All of life is this endeavor to live that life of the dreaming child. What do we know of this strange and wonderful journey, from what to where?" Whatever her dream and journey, if she ever knew it, it may have begun with the Yellow Indian.

She saw him when she was taken by her nursemaid to Buffalo Bill's Wild West Show at the Crystal Palace. Trembling with excitement, she watched the doors of the arena open. Out rumbled the stagecoach behind its galloping horses. Then came the pursuing Indians, whooping and yelling, firing their guns, feathers in their warbonnets streaming as they raced around the arena. One of them, bareback on a pinto horse, rode at first sight into her undying memory. Seventy, eighty years later, she could still vividly recall his naked, slim young body painted bright lemon yellow. A creature of the wild, of limitless space and untrammeled freedom, he flashed everywhere like a lightning streak of lemon yellow before her. Like an archetypal image emerging from her dark unconsciousness to constellate the dream-image she was to pursue for a lifetime.[1]

At the end of a wonderfully prolific and highly celebrated literary career, the late Frank Waters drew a striking portrait of the indelible impression a young Lakota warrior made in 1887 on the life and creative vision of his longtime friend, and sometimes neighbor, Lady Dorothy Brett. In his last book, *Time and Change*, published posthumously in 1998, Waters lovingly captures this seminal event in Lady Brett's life and, in doing so, offers a treasure trove of insight into the comprehensive impact of Buffalo Bill Cody's Wild West, particularly the dramatic, everlasting impressions made by Native Americans.

A cultural cross-pollination of mythic proportions occurred in 1887 when Buffalo Bill took center stage as part of Queen Victoria's Golden Jubilee in London. An unprecedented congregation of European royalty had gathered to celebrate Victoria's half-century reign as the supreme sovereign of the British Empire. No one then could have predicted it would also be the last such gathering of global monarchies. Anxious to impress such an important assemblage and attract business, however, an aggressive group of American and British entrepreneurs organized a trade exposition from the United States to coincide with the Queen's celebration. Acutely aware of the romantic attraction of the European to the American West, these businessmen wisely chose to use Buffalo Bill's Wild West as the centerpiece of their exposition. Their efforts met with success when the Prince of Wales, later to become King Edward VII, attended a performance and so thoroughly enjoyed himself that Cody promptly received notice ordering a command performance for the Queen.

Since the death of her companion, Prince Albert, twenty-five years earlier, Queen Victoria had not ventured beyond Buckingham Palace. If the Queen wanted entertainment, or anything else, it was brought to her at Windsor Castle. The Queen became intrigued, however, when it was explained to her that Buffalo Bill's Wild West was so massive a production that it could not be moved in its entirety to Buckingham Palace. Something then motivated Victoria to surprise everyone by suddenly deciding to break her quarter-century precedent and travel to Earl's Court arena to see for herself what had so impressed the Prince of Wales.

That spring afternoon was magnetically charged with historic occurrences and the lemon-yellow Lakota warrior struck like lightning, imprinting five-year-old Dorothy Brett, as Buffalo Bill and his Sioux companions rolled past like thunderheads that gather to bring terrifying, yet fascinating, electrical shocks from the heavens. Cody had choreographed his Wild West to begin with racing horsemen proudly circling the arena presenting the "Star-spangled Banner" in a "Grand Entry," a tradition that continues in rodeo today. Cody's colorful commencement of his Wild West made history on the afternoon of May 11, 1887. As Cody's cowboys raced past Her Majesty presenting "Old Glory," the supreme sovereign of the British Empire stood, and with a simple elegant bow, saluted the American Flag for the first time in history.

The Queen had a wonderful time and immediately requested a meeting with the Indian people in Cody's show. Black Elk later commented that the Queen addressed the Lakotas and told them they were the "best-looking people she had ever seen."[2] The fact that the Queen immediately asked for a meeting with the Indians after the performance is an important indication of the magnetic attraction of the Lakota people in the Wild West. More importantly, however, the request to meet with the Lakota implies they were the Queen's favorite part of the presentation and the Queen's personal blessing that day instantly made Buffalo Bill's Wild West more than a mere American phenomenon; the success Cody enjoyed that afternoon introduced his Wild West as the world's premiere entertainment attraction. Another command performance was promptly arranged in early June for the Queen's guests. The Queen's command performance of the Wild West was attended by more members of royalty than had ever gathered for a commercial entertainment event. The audience included the king of Belgium; the king of Saxony; the king of Greece; the king of Denmark; the crown prince and princess of Germany (he would soon become Kaiser Wilhelm ii); the crown prince of Sweden and Norway; Crown Prince Rudolph of Austria; Prince George of Greece; the prince and princess of Saxe-Meiningen; Prince Louis of Baden; Princesses Margaret, Sophie, and Victoria of Prussia; the Prince and Princess of Wales; Princes Albert Victor and George of Wales (Prince George became King George v); and Princesses Victoria, Maude of Wales, Marie Victoria, and Alexandria of Edinburgh.[3]

Cody had experience with royalty. His historic 1868 buffalo hunt with Russian Grand Duke Alexis and Lakota Chief Spotted Tail had taught him that European aristocrats loved a good thrill, particularly a vicarious thrill that involved Indians. In London, Cody loaded the Kings of Denmark, Greece, Belgium, and Saxony, and also the Prince of Wales on the Deadwood Stage and personally drove the coach around the arena as painted Sioux warriors chased behind whooping and shooting their rifles. Dorothy Brett was not the only child swept away that magic afternoon. The result of Cody's bold action was that the monarchs of Europe soon began to line up like little giggling children seeking carnival excitement riding the Deadwood Stage. Buffalo Bill had touched the child in the heart's of the sovereigns of Europe, thereby insuring his Wild West's success on the global stage for the next two decades.

Dorothy Brett was a precocious and impressionable five-year-old child in the midst of all this royal entertainment. Frank Waters details her impressive family lineage:

> Her paternal grandfather was Viscount Esher, Lord Chief Justice of the Court of Appeals and Queen Victoria's Master of the Rolls. Her maternal grandfather, a Belgian, put Leopold i on the throne and be-

came his ambassador to the Court of St. James. Her own father, Reginald Baliol Brett, the second Viscount Esher, was Queen Victoria's personal advisor and was believed to be the power behind the throne of Edward VII. Her younger sister, Sylvia, became Lady Brooke, the Ranee of Sarawak. Without going into other ramifications, we can let the Ranee sum up the situation: "Being a child of the brilliant Reginald was like being related to the Encyclopedia Britannica."[4]

The electric vision of the yellow Lakota warrior chasing Buffalo Bill as he drove the Deadwood Stage triggered something deep in young Dorothy's aesthetic instincts and she rebelled against the luxury and privilege in which she found herself and demanded to be allowed to become an artist. Ignoring the unspoken rule that forbade people of her aristocratic class from seeking artistic instruction, little Dorothy insisted upon being taught how to paint. Her inherent resolve eventually led her to training in Britain's Slade School of Art and the establishment of her own studio in Earl's Court. Brett's studio soon began to attract other painters, artists, writers and "free-thinkers" such as Aldous Huxley, Bertrand Russell, Virginia Woolf, and D. H. Lawrence. Brett's association with Lawrence would prove to be an important one: the writer put Brett's feet soundly on the spiritual and artistic path she began as a five-year-old child in the audience at Buffalo Bill's Wild West.

Believing western civilization to be doomed in materialism, American socialite, publisher, and "visionary colonist" Mabel Luhan Dodge had enticed D. H. Lawrence and other artists and philosophers to come to Taos, New Mexico, to explore the creation of an alternative artistic community in the tiny mountain village. Mabel Dodge had married a Taos Pueblo Indian, Tony Lujan, and the pair were actively attracting artists and thinkers to the ancient pueblo in order to seek new, alternative visions, which they hoped would rise from the ashes of the decline of western civilization. Lady Brett followed Lawrence and his German wife, Frieda, to Taos in 1924. Over the next fifty-three years in Taos, generally not recognized or appreciated in the trendy art world, often nearly penniless, using outdoor "facilities" and hauling her own water from a creek, Dorothy Brett evolved into one of America's finest painters of Native American people. Indeed, Frank Waters, himself a mystic and scholar with a broad knowledge and understanding of the native cultures and religions of the Southwest, Mexico, and Central and South America, believed that Brett's paintings of ceremonial dancers at the Taos Pueblo create a body of work deeply concerned with the mysteries of the "other world," and that her highly developed artistic sensitivity and insight perfectly coincided with a mystical Indian perspective that remained vital during the time in which she painted, but has long since passed into history. Waters maintains that Brett's work captured the spiritual essence of that era in Taos at the precise moment of its passing.[5] The Yellow Lakota's thunderbolt presence had somehow dramatically struck, imprinted and inspired five-year-old Dorothy Brett that May afternoon in 1887, mysteriously imbuing her with the promise of the perpetuation of significant Native American religious ceremony half a world away and nearly a century later.

With Buffalo Bill's Wild West as an intriguing connection, the story of Lady Dorothy Brett's evolution as a painter might be viewed as a curious parallel to that of Lakota Holy Man Black Elk and the archetypal vision he experienced as a child on the plains of South Dakota. Where Buffalo Bill's Wild West inspired Lady Dorothy Brett to leave European royalty and journey to North America to encounter and paint the religious ceremonies of Pueblo Indians, however, Black Elk's childhood vision led him to join Buffalo Bill's Wild West in order to travel to Europe to meet royalty and learn about the religion and culture of the *wasichu*, or white man. He returned to the Great Plains in 1890 to survive the Massacre at Wounded Knee and to begin the promethean process of fusing Christianity and the *Lakol wicoh' an*, or Lakota "way of life" into a new American religion.[6]

Black Elk and Lady Brett are but two lives profoundly influenced by William F. Cody. Born into a quintessential American family of the migration across the Great Plains, Cody's destiny was, and forever remains, at the heart of western history; truly, few individuals have affected world culture and history and left such an indelible imprint on mankind as Buffalo Bill. As the horse and buffalo culture of the mystic warriors of the Great Plains vanished under the initial industrial onslaught of our modern technological society, Will Cody was uniquely gifted and, with deft historical timing, able to hold the past, present, and future in his hand for an evanescent, epochal moment. Cody used his abundant natural talents, charisma and command of the moment to create an exhibition of the immediate transition of eras in western American history, preserving something of their essence while entertaining the masses and virtually creating the twentieth-century concept of celebrity out of thin air. Before Buffalo Bill, individuals were merely famous or infamous; the well-known were royalty, military heroes, outlaws, or villains. After Buffalo Bill, we had "stars."

Pahaska is a Lakota word that means "long hair." As did most of the scouts of the American West of the nineteenth century, "Buffalo Bill" Cody wore his hair long. Cody, "Wild Bill" Hickok, and other famous scouts of the era were civilians conscripted and hired by the Army because of their intimate understanding of Plains Indian people and culture and for their working knowledge of the land itself. Pragmatically, politically, and stylistically emulating the mountain men and plainsmen such as Jim Bridger and Kit Carson who preceded them into the heart of North America, Cody and other scouts preferred beaded buckskin costumes and wore long hair in deference to native plains people who preferred not to cut theirs. The Plains Indian custom of wearing long hair initially had nothing to do with martial prowess; by the time young Will Cody appeared among the Lakota and Cheyenne in the 1850s, however, the "scalp-lock"—in the non-verbal, highly visual, and symbolic language of the warrior cultures of the Great Plains—had evolved into a badge that indicated an honorable and dangerous opponent, one who would willingly offer his proud mane to anyone powerful enough to take it in battle. Long hair was the victor's trophy. Lakota people started calling Will Cody *Pahaska* early in his preadolescent career on the Great Plains as he was interacting with them at Fort Laramie and Fort Bridger and had already begun to grow his hair long. Thereafter and throughout his life, Cody spoke with great pride of his Indian name and the showman even named his retreat in the Absaroka Mountains of Yellowstone Country "Pahaska's Tepee."

I believe the name *Pahaska* offers special insight into William Frederick Cody; it reveals his unique bond with the Plains Indians, fused long before the fame and celebrity of "Buffalo Bill" swept him away. Similarly, the name offers a glimpse into the Plains Indians' friendly, personal relationship with young Will Cody, as with other non-Indians, before the invasion of the cultures of the world into North America's heart so devastated them. Peaceful relations between native people and immigrants then were often accompanied by a sense of shared goals and purposes. The death of his father created circumstances that forced young Will Cody to go to work before he even reached adolescence. Working on bullwacker freight wagon trains, Cody crossed the Great Plains three times before his twelfth birthday. Because of the unusual circumstances of his youth, most of Cody's actual boyhood companions and playmates were the Lakota children he met at places like Fort Laramie in the heart of the Oglalas' traditional hunting lands. Some of these boyhood companions, such as Rain-In-The-Face's sons, became lifelong friends. The fact that these friendships endured and survived the Indian Wars, when their friendship suddenly spun them around and cast them as mortal enemies, reveals an unusually powerful relationship. I believe Cody's enduring friendly relationship with Sioux people and his subsequent rise to international fame strongly suggests Lakota mysticism and prophecy at work.

Lakota philosopher Vine DeLoria, Jr. writes:

In tribal religions there is always an open expectation that revelations will and can be received. Much of this expectation is a result of the ceremonies which produce visions or dreams that provide information and predictions about the future. When the universe is conceived as one in which interspecies communication becomes possible, and is probable given the proper set of circumstances, revelation is a major part of religious practice. Within the tribal setting, however, revelation is not regarded as an unusual situation and so it does not suggest the correction of doctrine or the promulgation of any new belief, or the adjustment of the existing understanding and experience of cosmic reality. It at best clarifies the meaning of life and religious experience for individuals who have undertaken to open themselves to receive whatever messages are intended for them which deal with social responsibilities they must assume, powers of healing and prophecy they must demonstrate, or vocations they must follow.[7]

Cody shared a destiny with the buffalo and Plains Indians; indeed, one cannot utter William F. Cody's immortal alliterated sobriquet without conjuring buffalo. Indians and buffalo are symbiotically related both metaphorically and in reality. Buffalo Bill, Lakota Indians, and buffalo are forever linked in American legend and mythology. The world generally recognizes the fact that Cody's Wild West had a dramatic and abiding influence on the shape and character of American mythology through his imaginative creation of the concept of the theatrical form of the "Western." Indeed, most of us now readily accept the fact that the west we love to romanticize is largely, as historian William Goetzmann recently referred to it, "the West of the imagination." The west, however, has always been about the imagination—and spirit. Certainly one of humanity's greatest epics revealed itself in North America as the imagination and spirit of the European reacted dramatically different to the environment than did the imagination and spirit of the Native American. William F. Cody's Wild West, blending the imagination and spirit of both cultures, constructed a unique bridge between the Native and Euroamerican, and, in doing so, created mythology. Nevertheless, it is vitally important to differentiate between Cody's creation of the genre of the Western, the "West of the imagination," and the West of historical fact. It is historical fact that the "Wild West" Cody presented was indeed a meticulous physical recreation of actual historical events. Cody, sharply defining and separating his production from carnivals and circuses, refused to refer to his creation as a "show"; instead, he proudly considered himself unique, a master historical reenactor. Cody carefully and lovingly recreated western events that had only recently passed or were passing into history at just that moment. Thus, ironically, Cody's contribution to American mythology was based more upon historical reality than romantic imagination. This dichotomy presents only a tiny bit of the complexity one encounters when attempting to pigeonhole William F. Cody according to modern standards for mythology, history, war, human rights, environmentalism or anything else. Nonetheless, most today are quick to dismiss Buffalo Bill as a somewhat important relic from an embarrassing and shameful era in our history. For example: In modern ahistorical, yet sentimentally romantic America, it has become socially and academically accepted to view Buffalo Bill's Wild West as exploitative of Indians. This uninformed perspective is a sad indictment of many remaining negative aspects of Euroamerican collective guilt concerning anything that happened between our ancestors and Native Americans. Understanding the unique relationship between Plains Indians and Will Cody, however, could prove to be the beginning of healing some of this confusion. Assuming that Cody was exploiting Indians, one fails to take into account the words and actions of many important, eloquent Lakota leaders such as Holy Man, Black Elk, and philosopher Luther Standing Bear, who were an integral part of Cody's production and who articulately recorded their high personal opinion of Buffalo Bill's character in books and essays they wrote. Even more significant, however, is that in assuming Cody was exploiting Indians, one loses the ability to understand the important contribution of Indians to American show business. To some, this contribution to show business may appear to be a dubious honor; yet I imagine these same cynics would readily concede the enduring artistic impact of the western genre on cinema. Without Native American contributions to the genesis of the form in Cody's Wild West, western movies simply would not exist. Most seriously, however, in assuming Cody was exploiting Native Americans, one also fails to gain a basic knowledge of the fundamentally significant roles

Indians played in the creation of an important design in the fabric of American mythology.

If, on the other hand, one assumes that Cody and the Lakota were cocreating the Wild West, an entirely different perspective presents itself, and some intriguing aspects of Cody's life begin to reveal themselves. For example, for many years, I wondered how on earth Cody, a military scout, was able to convince Lakota warriors, who had only recently been his mortal enemies on the battlefield, to come together time and time again in order to recreate their combat in minute detail in an arena before an audience of thousands of people. Considering what we now understand about post–traumatic stress syndrome, or what folks called shell shock from the time of the First World War up through the Vietnam conflict, Cody's ability to recreate battlefield situations with the actual participants indicates almost superhuman abilities to inspire and lead men. When one reconsiders Cody's relationship with Plains Indians from the perspective of an active cocreation of the Wild West, however, one also begins to reexamine Cody's lifelong relationship with the Lakota and a new perspective of Buffalo Bill emerges.

As we approach a new millennium, "politically correct" hindsight reveals the irony that a man renowned for killing buffalo for the Kansas Pacific Railroad in the 1860s was also a vital part of the visionary team responsible for preserving and restoring buffalo in the 1890s when fewer than five hundred remained. At that nadir, a vital genetic reservoir of buffalo were well-cared for in the Wild West when Cody's good friend, Buffalo Jones, began using animals from the showman's herd as breeding stock to begin a serious restoration plan. As a result of Buffalo Jones and Cody's inspired restoration efforts, most of the major buffalo herds that remain in America today were spawned from the healthy animals in Buffalo Bill's Wild West at the turn of the century.

Considering Cody's reputation as an "Indian fighter," examination of history reveals yet another intriguing irony: Cody was indeed a scout for the famous Fifth Cavalry at various times from 1868–76, and he killed several important Indian leaders during this time of intense conflict. Yet from the beginning of the "Reservation and Reconstruction Era" in Native and Euroamerican relations in the early 1880s, Buffalo Bill's Wild West offered a paradoxical sanctuary for those "incorrigibles" who resisted as traditional Plains Indian religion and culture were being systematically dismantled and destroyed. Indeed, from its inception in Omaha on May 19, 1883, until it was auctioned into history in Denver on July 21, 1913, Buffalo Bill's Wild West became the major, if not the only, defender of the inherent sovereign rights of Indian people.

I do not believe these ironic occurrences happened by accident. Having spent thirty-five years exploring the culture and religion of the native western tribes in order to write *A Ballad of the West*, I have personally experienced the amazing powers of precognition some Lakotas possess. Carefully combing through the known history of William F. Cody's life for important patterns of possible "occult" interaction with Indians, one begins to recognize that the man's entire life was shaped by mysterious, yet pragmatic, connections with Indians. Complicating the mystery, as his contemporary Plains Indian warrior friends and foes, Cody seems to have flourished in some inexplicable way from man-to-man, hand-to-hand, mortal conflict. As his Lakota and Cheyenne counterparts, Cody's early career military victory brought the immediate reward of superior horses. Yet, of paramount importance, victory also brought with it honor and respect. This intriguing bond through mortal combat between Cody and Plains Indians becomes very important when considering the fact that thirteen months after the Battle of Little Big Horn he was able to hire Oglala Lakotas from Pine Ridge to travel to Rochester, New York, to be in his fall melodrama. At first glance, this information seems incongruous. Crazy Horse's Oglala Lakota forces had been the leaders of the Plains Indian Confederacy and its most violent resistance to the military invasion by the U.S. government. Especially considering the brief period of time following the major conflict of Native and Euroamerican forces in history, one would suspect the Oglala Lakotas to be the very last people in the world that Buffalo Bill would seek to act in a melodrama. Nevertheless, unlike Sheridan, Crook, and other military leaders of the United States War Department, Cody had spent his entire life living with the Lakota. As a victorious warrior, Cody knew he could go to Pine Ridge and be greeted honorably. That he also knew he could cast Indians for his melodrama reveals the absolute faith he had in the lifelong bonds he had established and nourished with the Lakota. Earning the respect of Lakota warriors, however, would never insure any Oglala's agreeing to be in a melodrama with Buffalo Bill; the fact that the Oglalas willingly went to participate in the show with Cody implies either the skill of a master salesman, or complete Lakota confidence in a trusted friend. It is unlikely that a people who were willing to die to defend their land and who had walked away from the best hagglers the United States could send to negotiate treaties would fall victim to a master salesman. Something other than show business was clearly going on between Buffalo Bill and the Lakota. If, during and after the years of the Indian Wars, Cody won the faith and trust of any Lakota, it would have to have been on a spiritual level. Clearly, the Lakotas either knew on a spiritual level that Cody had their best interests in mind, or they knew what Cody planned for them would ultimately prove to be for the spiritual good of their people and nation.

Physical needs also had to be met for the Lakota people to continue. In hiring and defending Indians, Cody helped them gain an understanding of the white man's economic concept of employment, working for wages, and learning how to manage their money. He also provided the Indians with a rare alternative to their Christian and military overseers' deadly plan for assimilating them into the Euroamerican world: The Wild West allowed the Indian to enter the white man's world on his own terms. Furthermore, as Plains Indian leaders such as Sitting Bull and Black Elk visited the economic capitals of western civilization and met the general public as well as socialites, religious leaders, and monarchs, Buffalo Bill presented them as the respected Chiefs and Holy Men they were. As a result of Buffalo Bill's insistence that Indians be granted this simple respect and courtesy, leaders were able to leave profound impressions of their inherent dignity and intelligence with Euroamericans and return to their people with a much more realistic understanding of the culture of their temporary conquerors. More importantly, as missionaries and military and government agents rapidly went about their insidious work of attempting the destruction of Plains Indian civilization with religious conversion and reconstruction, Buffalo Bill's Wild West also became the unlikely vehicle from which those same essentials of Plains Indians' religion and culture were able to survive and endure. Only the Indians rivaled Cody for space in the programs. Since the Indians in Buffalo Bill's Wild West were leaders of their people, their very presence brought prestige to the show. The names of Indian leaders, such as Iron Tail, Curly, Red Shirt, and American Horse, had been in the newspapers often enough for the public to have heard of them. Cody also used his programs in an attempt to educate whites to the true nature of Indians. In 1893 Cody had an insert placed in the Wild West program pleading for the humane treatment of Indians. In the insert he defended them as good soldiers, farmers and citizens when given a chance.[8]

It is important here to emphasize that many of the Indians in Buffalo Bill's Wild West were leaders of their people. There was a physical reason that Indian military, social, religious, and political leaders, who were prisoners-of-war, were in Buffalo Bill's Wild West: Red Cloud, Kicking Bear, Short Bull, Sitting Bull, Rain-In-The-Face, and other "troublemakers" were encouraged by Indian agents and missionaries to join the Wild West in order to get them out of the way of the conversion and reconstruction process. With the leaders out of the way, the people incarcerated on reservations were more easily manipulated. While depicting their traditional "vanishing" culture in the Wild West exhibition, however, Cheyenne and Lakota leaders were able to imprint many fundamentally important aspects of their culture's spiritual essence into mainstream Euroamerican society while relatives on reservations were forming secret, underground versions of sacred ceremonies to reunite and renew themselves. Modern stereotypes and cliched images of American Indians such as tepees, peace pipes, Eagle-feather warbonnets, and the general accouterments and icons of Plains Indian culture reveal the enduring cultural imprint these Native American leaders created and presented in Buffalo Bill's Wild West. The resurgence of Plains Indian religion and culture in the past half-century is yet another silent testament to the powerful legacy of these people's preservation efforts during the reconstruction era.

After Sitting Bull and Red Cloud, perhaps the most significant of these "incorrigibles" was the Lakota Holy Man Black Elk, who, as mentioned here earlier, was able to return from the Wild West with the broadened perspective needed to help his people make the transition into white, Christian culture with the essential values of the Plains Indian religion intact. The Holy Man's important childhood vision of a reunification of the world's sacred hoop, presented to him by six omnipotent Grandfathers, has so risen in stature in the past seventy years that modern Indians have come to view *Black Elk Speaks* as a religious representation of reunification of Indian people themselves. In the introduction to a reprinting of Neihardt's book in 1979, Vine DeLoria wrote:

> If any great religious classic has emerged in this century or on this continent, it must certainly be judged in the company of Black Elk Speaks. . . . The most important aspect of the book, however, is not its effect on the non-Indian populace who wished to learn something of the beliefs of the Plains Indians but upon the contemporary generation of young Indians who have been aggressively searching for roots of their own in the structure of universal reality. To them the book has become a North American bible of all tribes.[9]

As the Wild West concluded its tour of England in 1887, however, Black Elk and several Lakota companions missed the boat and were left behind. One of the stranded Lakotas spoke a little English, and the group managed to get themselves to London and employed in a little western show that had sprung up to capitalize on the Wild West's success. Captain Mexican Joe Shelley, inspired by Buffalo Bill's success in London, had organized a "copy" show to compete with the Wild West. In July, 1887, "Mexican Joe's Wild West" departed for England. Somehow the little copy show ended up in Europe before it eventually broke up, leaving Black Elk stranded. Always curious, Black Elk visited western civilization's grand cathedrals and monasteries to begin his personal study of Christianity and the other classic religions of the world. During his European sojourn, as he encountered the many diverse people and religions of the world, Black Elk finally began to understand the enigmatic voices he had been hearing all his life. In Europe, Black Elk started to understand the meaning of the power vision he received as a boy; he began to understand more of the reasons for the conflict his people had endured; and, looking toward the survival of his people, their culture and their religion, he began the process of assimilating all the world's religions into his Plains Indian religion. Buffalo Bill returned to Europe in 1890 and, after a bit of searching, found Black Elk ill in Paris and helped nurse him back to health before giving the holy man a reunion feast and the money to return home.

Black Elk returned to the Great Plains at an extremely tumultuous time. On the reservation, the Lakota were starving and facing the complete destruction of their race. Incarcerated and confused, the Lakota were at the mercy of overseers who, at worst, deemed them subhuman, and, at best, cold statistics in a cruel evangelical effort. As a result of such desperate times, the Ghost Dance religion emerged throughout Indian Country. It is important here to emphasize that the Ghost Dance rose only three years into the reconstruction efforts of missionaries and government agents on reservations. It is equally relevant that the Ghost Dance movement was a prophetic movement; a "Messiah" was prophesized! The fact that the Ghost Dance is so obviously inspired by a desperate, and ultimately deadly, attempt by Native America to embrace the white man's Christianity only makes the massacre at Wounded Knee more tragic.

Since the beginning of relations between Native and Euroamericans, there had been two major factions—military and religious—leading the imperialistic thrust of western civilization into the heart of the North American continent. With the murder of Crazy Horse, and with Sitting Bull in exile in Canada, armed resistance against the United States by Native American forces truly ended in 1877. When Sitting Bull returned to the United States in 1882 and surrendered his rifle, the military faction finally claimed victory over the Sioux. The conquest of the Lakota by the United States War Department was complete when defeated Plains Indians were herded onto reservations. The success of the military faction incarcerating Indians on reservations provided the religious faction with the evangelist's dream: a captive audience. Christian missionary efforts were shifted into high gear with the ultimate objective of completely disassembling and obliterating any vestiges of Indian religion or culture in North America. Well-intentioned but callous zealots, the missionaries proposed to convert Native America into assimilated Christian farmers and businessmen within one generation. The children and grandchildren of abolitionists, many "friends of the Indian" were Quakers, Catholics, Episcopalians, or members of other Christian denominations; after their forefathers freed the slaves, these missionaries viewed the protection of Native Americans from the United States military as the continuation of a social burden they had inherited. Emerging from the Civil War, many Christian leaders had had their fill of death and suffering; these survivors exercised considerable diplomatic political influence, albeit futile, as the Indian Wars escalated toward Little Big Horn. Their time of influence returned, however, when Indian reconstruction began on the reservation. Missionaries were sent to the reservations to begin the process of converting Indians into Christians and farmers. During this time, many Indian children were taken into white society to be educated. Luther Standing Bear wrote in 1933:

> When I had reached young manhood the warpath for the Lakota was a thing of the past. The hunter had disappeared with the buffalo, the war scout had lost his calling, and the warrior had taken his shield to the mountains and given it back to the elements. The victory songs were sung only in the memory of the braves, and even they soon went unsung under a cruel and senseless ban of our overseers. So I could not prove that I was a brave and would fight to protect my home and land. I could only meet the challenge as life's events came to me. When I went East to Carlisle School, I thought I was going there to die; nevertheless, when father confronted me with the question, "Son, do you want to go far away with these white people?," I unhesitatingly said, "Yes." I could think of white people wanting little Lakota children for no other possible reason than to kill them, but I thought here is my chance to prove that I can die bravely. So I

went east to show my father and my people that I was brave and willing to die for them. I was destined, however, to return to my people, though half of my companions remained in the east in their graves. The changes in environment, food, and clothing were too sudden and drastic for even staunch bravery to overcome.[10]

The Carlisle School, which Standing Bear went east to attend, was created by Captain Richard Henry Pratt. From 1875–78, Captain Pratt had been in charge of seventy-two Cheyenne, Kiowa, and Comanche prisoners-of-war interned at Fort Marion, Florida. During the confinement Pratt created an educational program for the Indians and, after their release, seventeen of his prisoners/students enrolled in Hampton Institute. Created by General Samuel Chapman Armstrong, who had risen through the ranks during the Civil War commanding a Negro brigade, Hampton Institute had been established in Virginia as a vocational school for Negroes. In April, 1878, Pratt's seventeen core students at Hampton Institute constituted the genesis of a national Indian educational program. Later, with 82 students recruited from Pine Ridge and Rosebud reservations to a deserted army barracks in Pennsylvania, Pratt created the Carlisle School for Indians. Indian children were gathered up in the Dakotas and shipped off to Pennsylvania, where they were stuffed into white man's clothes, had their hair cut, and were not allowed to speak their native language. For many the drastic change in clothing, custom, diet, and environment was too much to tolerate and they fell victim to disease and died.

Some might say Pratt's Carlisle School succeeded at great human costs in becoming a bridge between the two cultures. Others might say such a massive undertaking always extracts a great human toll. In the final analysis, however, many brilliant Indian people, such as the Lakota philosopher Luther Standing Bear, received a first-class education at Carlisle Indian School. Through their education into the Euroamerican world at Carlisle, these Indian thinkers have been able to build their own bridge between our cultures.

Many altruistic missionaries such as Elaine Goodale also traveled to the reservation to educate Indians during this time. Some of these missionaries were true servants of spirit, humanitarians genuinely concerned that the Indian people, their religion, and culture continue to exist. Those with compassion in their hearts found themselves undergoing great change on the reservation, however, and Miss Goodale, and many others like her, essentially converted to the Plains Indian culture. Miss Goodale married a

Lakota, Dr. Charles Eastman, and dedicated her life to the service of Indian people on the reservation. She became known as a "Sister to the Sioux."[11]

In summary, however, the military faction of the Euroamerican thrust into the heart of the continent was poised for complete genocide if the reconstruction efforts of the religious factions failed to assimilate Indians. So, with the final destruction of Native American culture and religion ironically in the hands of United States religious leaders, it appeared the Euroamericans' victory was complete. As Native American culture and religion faced resolute obliteration, however, one man stood squarely between these two destructive forces. That man was Buffalo Bill.

Indian performers in Buffalo Bill's Wild West were literally prisoners-of-war. As the "humanitarian" reconstruction of Indians into Christian farmers and businessmen intensified on the reservation, Cody was forced to jump through increasingly difficult bureaucratic hoops created by these same Christian and political humanitarians. Only Cody's enduring and trusted relationships with the most powerful men in the War Department allowed him to win permission to continue employing Indians in his Wild West. During most of the history of the Wild West, Christian politicians viciously fought Cody, bitterly accusing him of exhibiting the savage, war-like aspects of the Indian, thereby contradicting and belittling the progressive advances made by the Indian into Euroamerican religion and culture. In 1893 these "humanitarian" forces succeeded in preventing Cody's Wild West from being staged within the main grounds of the Chicago World's Fair. Cody simply rented a nearby location and he and the Lakotas outdrew the World's Fair.

Reconsidering Cody and Plains Indians as cocreators of the Wild West, and recognizing Buffalo Bill's unique role defending Plains Indians and buffalo when both faced extinction, led me to an intriguing, new perspective on Buffalo Bill: What if William F. Cody rose to international fame as Buffalo Bill as part of a broader knowledge and understanding of future events by Lakota prophets? Could Buffalo Bill have been part of Lakota prophecy, and, if so, might he have risen to his unique fame in order to stand heroically between violent, destructive forces and Native Americans and buffalo at the precise historical moment for them to have time and sanctuary to survive and endure? As mentioned earlier, the Sioux possessed a mysterious ability that was accepted as normal *Lakol wicoh'an*, or the traditional way of life to Lakota people. Where this ability was considered normal to a nineteenth century Lakota, modern, empirical thinkers rarely consider, eagerly dismiss, or fail to explore the documented Lakota ability to see into the future. Luther Standing Bear writes, "There were some who had the power of *'wakinyan'*—the power of great intuition and ability to foretell events." Standing Bear proceeds to tell a story of a friend named Walk Ahead who possessed such *wakinyan* powers. Walk Ahead offered Standing Bear a gentle warning not to return to England for a second trip with Buffalo Bill. Ignoring the admonition, Standing Bear departed Pine Ridge for Rushville to sign up with the Wild West and catch the train headed east. In Rushville, based upon his previous experience with the Wild West, Standing Bear was placed in charge of the Lakota people joining the troupe. Soon two young Lakota men who, having already signed on, came to Standing Bear to ask him for permission *not* to go with the show. As most young Lakota men were eager to go with the Wild West, Standing Bear was naturally curious as to why these young men had decided not to go. The young men then spoke of a concurrent dream they both had of a terrible crash. The dream startled and awakened them both simultaneously from a sound sleep. The dream had been so real both young men were shocked to emerge from their tepee to discover a quiet, starlit prairie night. They promptly interpreted the dream as an omen not to go with the Wild West. Standing Bear excused the young men and promptly signed on two others who were eager to quickly take their place. One of these young replacements later died in the accident prophesized in the young men's dream. In the east, as the Wild West train stood still, it was rammed by another train moving at full speed. The car containing the Lakotas was horribly torn and mangled and many Indian people were killed or terribly injured. Standing Bear himself was so badly injured that he nearly died. Star Wild West performer, Annie Oakley, never fully recovered. Afterwards, Standing Bear returned to the reservation and politely acknowledged Walk Ahead's warning.[12]

Those Lakota with *wakinyan* power received it directly from the *wakinyan* spirits themselves. The *wakinyan*, "Thunder Beings," are spirits that hold one of the most revered places in Lakota mythology and religion. The Thunder Beings dwell in the ethers and manifest themselves in the magnificent, electric thunderheads and hailstorms of the Great Plains. According to Black Elk, the Thunder Beings possess the omnipotent power to "make live and destroy." Indeed, the Thunder Beings are the divine initiators of the central religious ceremony of the Lakota—the Sun Dance. As part of the Lakota creation myth, a selfish chief, a man who did not know how to share with the people, had his arm stolen and hung in the stars by the *wakinyans*. The chief's daughter announced that she would only marry the man who can return her father's arm. "Falling Star," a divine being recognized as the "Savior" of the Lakota, appeared, and, accepting the daughter's challenge, went on a successful quest to return the chief's arm. Ceremoniously reenacting the intercommunication between the divine and humans, the Sun Dance Ritual evolves from this creation myth as the Dancers emulate the Falling Star's heroic quest to return fertility and charity to the people.[13]

Black Elk himself was granted his great intuitive powers by the *wakinyan*. All his life Black Elk lived in great fear that the Thunder Beings were disappointed and angry with him for not responding to their calls and fulfilling the prophecy of his childhood power vision. Throughout his youth, Black Elk wrestled with voices calling him from the spirit world to gradually introduce and educate him to his precognitive abilities. As mentioned earlier in this prologue, Vine DeLoria's remarks about *Black Elk Speaks* evolving into an "American Indian Bible" suggest that such important spiritual matters present themselves to men in their own time and circumstance. This inherent understanding of spiritual matters unfolding in the course of time is also very much a characteristic of *Lakol wicoh 'an.*

Dr. Charles Eastman, a Lakota separated from his people to be educated during the reconstruction era, was graduated from Dartmouth University in 1887. Dr. Eastman received a medical degree from Boston University in 1890, becoming one of the very first American Indian doctors. His first assignment was the Pine Ridge Reservation. Eastman arrived at Pine Ridge in December, 1890, just in time to witness the horror of the final bloodletting of the Indian Wars at the Massacre at Wounded Knee. As Black Elk returned from Paris in time to be nearly killed defending women and children at Wounded Knee, Eastman returned to his people to become the doctor attempting to save the wounded and dying brought into the church near the site of the massacre. After experiencing the horror of Wounded Knee, Black Elk, who possessed the *wakinyan* power "to make live and destroy,"[14] turned away from the power "to destroy" and toward the power to "make live" through the creation of a new religion. Equally impacted by the horror of the massacre, Dr. Eastman published eleven books, all with the fundamental goal of bringing Native and Euroamericans together. He published his first book, *Indian Boyhood*, in 1902 and, as the first major Native American author, went on to become one of the most respected Native Americans in the country. In his 1911 book, *The Soul of the Indian*, Eastman wrote:

It is well known that the American Indian had somehow developed occult power, and although in the latter days there have been many imposters, and, allowing for the vanity and weakness of human nature, it is fair to assume that there must have been some even in the old days, yet there are well-attested instances of remarkable prophesies and other mystic practice. A Sioux prophet predicted the coming of the white man fully fifty years before the event, and even described accurately his garments and weapons. Before the steamboat was invented, another prophet of our race described the "Fire Boat" that would swim upon their mighty river, the Mississippi, and the date of this prophecy is attested by the term used, which is long since obsolete.[14]

Once, upon learning I had written a song about Red Cloud, a young man from South Africa exclaimed, "Ain't he the one that was bulletproof?" perfectly proving my point of the general global awareness of the Plains Indians' knowledge of the occult. Indeed, libraries are full of well-documented accounts of Plains Indian leaders such as Crazy Horse, Sitting Bull, and Roman Nose and their inexplicable powers to avoid being shot in battle. Both Indian and non-Indian people have eloquently recalled in detail how these and other Lakota and Cheyenne leaders would often announce that they could not be harmed by bullets before racing alone unscathed into and through a hail of rifle fire by well-trained American soldiers. Even though I think this ability suggests an occult talent somewhat different from prophecy, it nevertheless represents an inscrutable mystical ability of the Plains Indian to control physical events.

In a lifetime of amazing demonstrations of precognitive ability, Sitting Bull prophesized a phenomenally accurate description of the Battle of the Little Big Horn only days before the actual event occurred. In constant communication with animals, particularly birds, Sitting Bull told his followers in Canada in 1882 that a meadowlark prophesized his death at the hands of his own people. Sitting Bull was murdered by his own people on December 15, 1890. Stanley Vestal offers this glimpse into the medicine man's prophetic ability: Having been out searching for enemy camps for several days, some chiefs ordered scouts to intensify the search. As they waited for the scouts to return, some of the Lakotas grew impatient and, aware of Sitting Bull's prophetic powers, went to the Hunkpapa and asked him to divine what was going to happen:

Sitting Bull said, "I will try to find out something."

He walked away from the crowd some distance, and walked up and down singing. They could hear him singing, but he was too far away for his words to be understood. After a while he came back. They had a pipe ready to light waiting for him.

Sitting Bull lighted the pipe and smoked. When he had finished, he said, "In the smoke I see a battle within two days. Many enemies and several Sioux will be killed." After a few moments, he added: "When I was out there singing, I saw a little ball of fire—a spark— coming toward me. But it disappeared when it reached me." The warriors all knew what the spark meant: it was a sign that Sitting Bull was going to be wounded.[15]

The medicine man was shot through the arm by an arrow in the battle he prophesized. Where this story divulges the accuracy of Sitting Bull's precognitive abilities, it also implies that all Lakota warriors had a fundamental understanding of the symbols of prophecy. Yet, most importantly, the story reveals the powers Sitting Bull communicated with constantly and the way his companions sought his assistance with mystical prophecy. Indeed, any examination of the life of Sitting Bull forces one to open one's eyes much wider to the possibility of mystical prophecy.

The same could be said of Jim Bridger or any of his companions who became known as mountain men. Early white visitors to the heart of Native America learned quickly to accept and seek the assistance of Indian prophets. Bridger's belief in Indian medicine men was so devout that the word *superstitious* is associated with most of his biographies even today. Yet most of the mountain men often sought the advice of medicine men, and, finding them to be amazingly accurate in their premonitions, returned frequently for answers to all sorts of dilemmas on the Plains and in the Rockies. Cecil Alter recounts the winter of 1825–26 when some of the young men destined to become the most famous of the mountain men consulted a Snake Indian prophet:

> The Snake Indians at the Ogden-Weber encampment constructed a medicine lodge that winter, a kind of tabernacle in the wilderness— a habitation for the Great Spirit—in which religious services were conducted, [James]Beckworth tells us. The medicine man was a high priest, his utterances sacred. When his presentiments were verified, confidence in the prophet exceeded all belief. Similar supernatural

proclamations were made for prominent whites worthy of the shaman's attention.[16]

Alter continues to relate a tale in which the Snake Medicine Man predicted in minute detail important immediate forthcoming events in the lives of Jim Bridger, James Beckworth, William Sublette, and Thomas "Broken Hand" Fitzpatrick. Each of the men witnessed the prophecy and personally experienced the medicine man's predictions coming true for themselves as well as for each other. As a result of such powerful interactions with Indian prophets, most mountain men turned to them for advice before any major undertaking. I believe this practice of mountain men interacting with medicine men offers a glimpse into the power of the medicine men: Believing everything to be related and connected, these *Wichasaha Wakon*, or holy men, were so spiritually attuned to the most miniscule detail of everything around them that everything became significant. Truly understanding that they were related to everything and that everything was related to them, these highly evolved beings were able to forecast the future by understanding the slightest change in anything going on around them. These enlightened ones were particularly attuned to sorting through their dreams for visions of coming events. The Lakota Duck Dreamers, for example, knew to be on the lookout for the appearance of ducks bringing prophecy in their dreams. Similarly, whether awake or asleep, Stone Dreamers paid special attention to stones and rocks. There were Fox Dreamers, Elk Dreamers, Thunder Dreamers, and so on. Every Indian, male or female, old or young, was taught by such Holy Men from the cradle to the grave to be spiritually attuned, whether awake or asleep, to everything around them. Through a lifetime of positive interaction with Indian people, mountain men gained a little understanding of this way of life. For example, in 1865, after forty-three years on the Great Plains and in the Rocky Mountains, Jim Bridger had become so finely attuned to nature and dreams that the mountain man had obtained a bit of the gift of prophecy himself. Late in his career, Bridger had been conscripted into serving as scout and guide for General Patrick Connor's military expedition into the Powder River Country to "punish" hostile Lakotas. Having been pressured into accepting the job with great misgivings, Bridger soon found himself in a situation brimming with "bad medicine." Once the expedition reached Lakota territory, the omens appeared. As the expedition marched out of Laramie, thousands of big gray buffalo wolves surrounded its nightly camps. Their incessant howling soon began to have a demoralizing effect on the troopers, but Jim Bridger found their singing reassuring; where wolves were plenty, Indians were scarce. He slept undisturbed through their evening concerts, for the wolves had sung him to sleep nearly every night for forty years.

Soon, however, Jim heard a howl which woke him from a sound sleep and sent chills up his spine. Sitting up in his blankets Jim noticed his fellow scouts had also been awakened by distinctive howling. Staring at each other with troubled eyes, they all recognized the howling of a "medicine wolf."[17]

The old mountain man knew the medicine wolf's howl meant that trouble was imminent. Jim also knew that hearing the medicine wolf meant one should leave the present location as quickly as possible. Bridger went to General Connor and suggested they immediately break camp and get out of that territory.

One can imagine how Connor reacted to being awakened in the middle of the night to be informed by his chief of scouts of a "medicine wolf" suggesting he retreat as quickly as possible. Jim's attempts to reason with Connor about a medicine wolf that night might well serve as a perfect metaphor to some for my efforts here to suggest that perhaps Buffalo Bill and his Wild West were part of Lakota prophecy. As one might expect, however, Jim's warnings to General Connor fell on deaf ears. Vestal continues:

> But the General had no ears for Jim's "absurd" proposals. In fact, he did not know what the old scout was talking about. Connor had not spent forty years on the lonely mountains and the teeming Plains, living in the open at all seasons like the wary redskins—sensing what they sensed, feeling what they felt. The delicate balance of wild nature was unknown to him.
>
> He was unaware of that sensitive living network covering the earth in which any disturbance is felt and expressed in some way by every creature touched by its widening circles of influence.[18]

With Connor's refusal to listen to him, Bridger and his group of scouts, knowing trouble was certainly coming, packed up and moved a half mile down river. Vestal continues, "From that hour one disaster after another plagued the expedition, until it collapsed in total defeat and the disgrace of its commander."[19]

Twelve-year-old Will Cody spent the winter of 1857 at Fort Bridger in the presence of fifty-three-year-old Jim Bridger, fifty-year-old Kit Carson and twenty-year-old Wild Bill Hickok. Cody's father had been dead a little over a year and he certainly must have found in the two wizened mountain men surrogate fathers. His playmates during this time were the sons of Rain-In-The-Face and other Oglala Lakotas who lived near Fort Laramie. During this time Cody earned his Lakota name *Pahaska*. I believe he also could have been recognized as a part of Lakota prophecy when he appeared at Fort Laramie as a youth.

I include within the text of my epic ballad of *Pahaska* an imagined "prophecy" by the Lakota Rain-In-The-Face concerning the future of young Will Cody. This "prophecy" is included purely as a dramatic, theatrical device and springs entirely from my imagination. This use of artistic license is employed to draw attention to documented Lakota powers of prophecy and also to emphasize my theme of a co-creation of the Wild West by Buffalo Bill and Plains Indians. In Chapter Three of this historical narrative, however, I present Cody's actual account of what happened between him and the Lakota war party in that cave on the Republican River in Kansas in 1860. Throughout *Buffalo Bill and Sitting Bull*, I have followed a somewhat traditional empirical approach to documenting the actual life of William F. Cody. Nevertheless, as an international icon for nearly 150 years, Cody has been the subject of scores of biographies. Most of these biographers have simply rewritten and paraphrased source material, essentially creating countless versions of the same book. With this in mind, I have used the words of Cody himself often, extensively quoting from his 1879 autobiography to approach my subject in a manner similar to documentary filmmakers, letting Cody himself recreate his own "historical" account of his life. In employing the term "documentary," I mean I have used existing biographical materials freely to create a historical narrative. Further, I mean to acknowledge that, as one of the most thoroughly examined lives in American or world history, Cody's story has been told and retold from numerous perspectives for over five generations. Rather than simply re-paraphrase what has been paraphrased for over one hundred years, I am allowing Cody's autobiographical account of his life to furnish a documentary narrative within my narrative. This technique is particularly important when examining the controversial "duel with Yellow Hand." For example: Rather than join the argument that has persisted for over 120 years concerning what actually happened between Yellow Hand and Buffalo Bill on Warbonnet Creek, in *Buffalo Bill and Sitting Bull* I let Cody himself tell the story in order to present the dramatic effect the theater had on his retelling, indeed, recreation of historical events. In Chapter Three, *The Pony Express*, I use the words of Mark Twain and Will Cody freely to create a portrait of the notorious murderer and prototype western villain, Jack Slade.

Believing his work to be masterfully extensive, I also quoted Don Russell's *The Lives and Legends of Buffalo Bill* profusely in order to flesh out this documentary approach. Hopefully, placing the life of Buffalo Bill in a deep context of Plains Indian culture will create new perspectives for interpreting their cocreation of the Wild West. In exploring the Plains Indians' role as a cocreator of the Wild West, however, one must also reconsider their abilities, which have been thoroughly documented in such acclaimed works as *Black Elk Speaks* and *Land of the Spotted Eagle*, to foresee events. Hopefully, the notion of Buffalo Bill being part of Lakota prophecy will draw new attention to the fact that Cody and Lakota and Cheyenne leaders consciously cocreated the Wild West; that without Indian performers, there could have been no Wild West. Whether the embodiment of Lakota prophecy or cosmic coincidence, I hope to present the idea in *Pahaska* that Cody's Wild West rose to prominence at a critical time in American history to provide a unique sanctuary for both Native Americans and buffalo.

I have also used these unconventional techniques to draw attention to the important parallels, coincidences and patterns in the life of William F. Cody and the "twilight" years of the horse and buffalo cultures of the Great Plains. For this reason, with great debt to Dee Brown's masterpiece *Bury My Heart At Wounded Knee*, George Hyde's comprehensive *Red Cloud's Folk*, and George Bird Grinnell's equally extensive *The Fighting Cheyenne*, I have entwined a superficial history of the Lakota and Cheyenne throughout the historical narrative of *Buffalo Bill and Sitting Bull*, to serve as a unifying thread on which one might explore the intriguing possibility that Plains Indian prophecy was at work throughout Cody's life. At minimum, including a perfunctory parallel history of the Lakota and Cheyenne, *Buffalo Bill and Sitting Bull* allows the juxtaposition of the overlapping careers of several important Native and Euroamerican icons of the nineteenth-century American west, and emphasizes the importance of their coming together in Cody's Wild West. For example, considering the precognitive powers of some Lakota and the prolific manifestation of these powers documented throughout the life of medicine man Sitting Bull, the coming together of Buffalo Bill and Sitting Bull in 1885 becomes historically and mystically intriguing. Considering the "showman and the shaman" from a prophetic, mystical perspective, Buffalo Bill's failed attempt to rescue the Medicine

Man in November, 1890, becomes especially emotionally poignant; as the Ghost Dance controversy swirled around the old chief, the meadowlark's prediction of 1882 in Canada came true; Sitting Bull's own people killed him, triggering the events that led to the Massacre at Wounded Knee. In order to juxtapose the lives of Sitting Bull and Buffalo Bill and the impact the two men had on American mythology. I also borrowed heavily from Stanley Vestal's definitive biography, *Sitting Bull, Champion of the Sioux*. Joseph Manzione's *I Am Looking To The North For My Life, Sitting Bull 1876–1881* offers an in-depth glimpse of the time that Sitting Bull and his followers were in exile in Canada and I owe that manuscript a debt of gratitude.

L. G. Moses's *Wild West Shows And The Images of American Indians, 1883– 1930* also informed much of the latter part of *Pahaska*. Moses' comprehensive research concerning American Indians and the early days of show business has defined the previously unexplored impact of the Lakota and Cheyenne people in the development of Buffalo Bill's Wild West and all the productions that followed in its wake, while also clarifying the behind-the-scenes political tactics of the missionary movements and the government to resist the use of Native Americans in Wild West shows.

Reflecting also on the positive effect Cody had on the lives of Holy Man, Black Elk, and the philosopher, Luther Standing Bear, and on the critical impact these two important Lakota men had on twentieth century perceptions of Native America and the revitalization of interest in *Lakol wicoh'an*, one realizes that, minimally, the Wild West created the unique environment that allowed these important thinkers to discover and express themselves for future generations of Indians. If *Buffalo Bill and Sitting Bull* does nothing but contribute to the continuation of this process it will have succeeded.

Chapter One

THE RAINBOW TRAIL

Oh Shennydore, I long to hear you
Away you rolling river!
Oh, Shennydore, I can't get near you
Away, I'm bound away,
Across the wide Missouri

—"Across The Wide Missouri," Benard DeVoto

THE title of eminent American historian Bernard DeVoto's book, *The Year of Decision: 1846*, emphasizes the temporal, cultural, and global significance of the Euroamerican migration of North America in our collective consciousness and mythology. The movement of 500,000 people across the Trans-Mississippi from 1840–70, a seminal event in American history, began to swell dramatically that very year—the year of William Frederick Cody's birth. The Great Potato Famine in 1846 certainly contributed to the phenomenon as thousands of Irishmen fled starvation to become citizens of the United States. This massive infusion of people only added to the growing restlessness Americans were already experiencing as James K. Polk, campaigning with promises to bring California, Oregon, Texas, and the Great Southwest into the Union, was elected President in 1844.

Polk's expansionist policies had been inspired by America's growing superficial knowledge of the Trans-Mississippi and by the popularity of a national political movement demanding that the United States extend its boundaries from the Atlantic to the Pacific Ocean. Since the War of 1812 with Great Britain, Boston textbook publisher, empire aficionado and political lobbyist, Hall Jackson Kelly, had kept the question of the United States' annexation of the "Oregon Country" before Congress and the American people. In 1818, when the United States signed a joint occupation treaty with Great Britain concerning the Oregon Territory, Kelly remained undaunted and only intensified his populist effort to force the United States to annex the region. By 1823, when President James Monroe issued his famous doctrine concerning colonization in the western hemisphere, the question of the Oregon Country had become a decisive factor in American politics. The year after Polk's election New York journalist, John Sullivan, coined the phrase "Manifest Destiny" in an attempt to define the issue and rationalize and reconcile the morality of the concept with the theft of Native American property.

The Euroamerican migration across the Great Plains did indeed alter the destiny of the continent and its people. More than any single person of the epic era, William F. Cody would come to poetically manifest the Euroamerican's heroic crossing of the continent. As "Buffalo Bill", Cody would also come to epitomize the blending of the Plains Indian and European into the most unique mythological crossbreed America ever produced—the Plainsman.

The emigration era also produced the indelible image of the peoples of the world swarming into the heart of the North American continent seeking the "Promised Land." While this image is generally a true one, most immigrants were indeed fourth, fifth, or sixth generation Americans as the great "wagon train" migration across the Great Plains was essentially a continuation of preceding migrations that crossed the great eastern mountain ranges to homestead in Ohio, Indiana, Illinois, Kentucky, Tennessee, and Missouri. In 1846, in *The Oregon Trail*, Francis Parkman, Jr. wrote of meeting Daniel Boone's grandsons at Fort Laramie heading west with the migration. Boone and his restless sons left Kentucky for Missouri, and his grandsons were simply moving on with western expansion.

Succinctly describing the unique cultural phenomenon that occurred as a result of the movement of so many people into the unknown regions of the North American continent, however, DeVoto also wrote, "History is the social expression of geography and western geography is violent."[1] Perceptively linking the cataclysmic geophysical history of western North America with the violent social expression destined to reveal itself with the migration, DeVoto is of course stunningly accurate. As the Euroamerican entered the Trans-Mississippi, geography began to have an emphatic and profound physical and psychological impact on the social expression of North American and world history. The second half of the nineteenth century would prove to be the time that the Euroamerican would test his revolutionary new system of government and law, his spiritual and humanitarian development, his technological knowledge, and his martial mettle against the pristine western landscape, its native inhabitants and nature herself. This process would unleash one of the most brutal epochs in world history. One would have to search long and hard to find a time period to equal the chaos, death, and destruction of the decades beginning with the Emigration Era in the 1840s, extending through the Civil and Indian Wars and the Reservation/Reconstruction Era, until the Massacre at Wounded Knee in 1890. American literature from 1840–90 eloquently and profusely expresses moral outrage and bewilderment at mankind's capacity for violence during this tragic era.

Certainly primitive, "wilderness" conditions had influenced the character and lifestyles of immigrant Americans as they began their westward journey from the Atlantic to the Mississippi River. Beyond the great river, however, the North American continent changed radically. Nevertheless, the desolation and danger of the Great Plains and Rocky Mountains was ultimately something migrating farmers intended to endure crossing to eventually reach an idealized, fertile, and cheap region of the Pacific coast, where they planned to put down new roots, grow new crops and create new opportunities. As the migration across the Great Plains and Rocky Mountains began, Euroamericans had accumulated two-hundred years of "pioneer" experience, skill, and craftsmanship. As important as these talents were, however, they could never have prepared the immigrants for the unique and extraordinary conditions of space, terrain and climate they encountered west of the Mississippi. Moreover, on entering the North American West, immigrants soon realized that these unfamiliar conditions of climate and space dramatically shifted from sector to sector as the land itself changed. The scorched desert brought with it a different circumstance than the vast prairie grasslands, high mountain plains, or alpine precipice; adapting to one region did not necessarily prepare one for the others. East of the Mississippi, the immigrant encountered environmental conditions not unlike those of his ancestors in Europe; west of the Mississippi he encountered the vast, majestically spiritual space of the native plainsman. East of the Mississippi the Euroamerican had timber, water, and land to support his agrarian lifestyle. Out on the Great Plains, however, water became increasingly scarce as timber disappeared and the Euroamerican was forced to come into a new relationship with the land. Neither would ever be the same.

It is often said that the journey is more important than the destination. Never was this remark more true than in describing the Euroamerican migration across the Trans-Missouri. Here, a dramatically diverse, alien people collectively searching for a new identity entered the ephemeral, mystical west—between the Missouri River and the High Sierras. Since time immemorial this sacred region had given birth to the mythology of count-less nations of Native Americans. Here, ironically, the first true European myth since the middle ages was born. The heroic elements of the epic peri-ods, legends and tales of the Trojan War, the Arthurian or Robin Hood Cycles, Song of Roland and Biblical Eden and Exodus all came to life again as a huge section of society cut itself away from "civilization" and moved across the strange, unfamiliar geography of the Trans-Missouri. Here, on DeVoto's violent, catastrophic landscape, opportunity shimmered over the western horizon.

While thousands were part of the endless stream of Conestoga wagons rolling into the Oregon and California sunset, however, thousands of oth-ers pursued a more circuitous, zigzag path west. Often a couple would travel to one place, adapt to the new region and homestead a few years be-fore moving on. Isaac Cody and Mary Ann Leacock married in Ohio and quickly moved to Scott County near LeClair, Iowa to homestead and begin a family. William Frederick was born on February 26, 1846, the fourth of eight children. There is a legend that the place near Davenport where Cody was born was the site of the last war dance performed by the Sac and Fox tribes before they went on the warpath in a doomed attempt to resist removal that is known as the Blackhawk War.[2] Will, as he was called by his family, had an older brother, Samuel; two older sisters, Mar-tha and Julia; a younger brother, Charlie; and three younger sisters, Eliza, Helen and May. In 1852 tragedy struck the family as a horse reared and fell back on Samuel crushing him.

The loss of his oldest son contributed to Isaac's restlessness but, as most men of the migration era after 1849, he also had gold fever and planned to migrate to California. Yet after selling the Iowa farm, Isaac became appre-hensive of a California journey and, in 1853, headed to Kansas Territory just across the Missouri River from Weston, Missouri, where his brother Elijah owned a general store. Weston lay squarely in between Indepen-dence and St. Joseph at the vibrant confluence of the massive flow of hu-manity migrating west.

Isaac intended to eventually continue moving on to California but de-cided to homestead about twenty miles from Leavenworth on the rich prairie in the Salt Creek Valley. On the way to the homestead location Isaac and Will, then seven years old, visited Fort Leavenworth and the boy saw the cavalry pass in revue on the parade grounds, his first Indians, and the western vagabond adventurers and characters of the day. The cavalry particularly imprinted the boy with a love of choreographed horseback maneuvers.[3] Although the experience made a terrific, unforgettable impression on the lad, national and family tragedy would continue to affect him more profoundly than anything else.

Moral and constitutional arguments concerning the abolition of slavery had been present since the creation of the Union. In 1819, however, the issues of slavery and western expansion clashed violently when Missouri sought admission to the Union as a state in which slavery would be allowed. This request for statehood set off dramatic debate in Congress between lawmakers for or against slavery. The conflict was eventually diplomatically appeased with Henry Clay's famous Missouri Compromise, which allowed "slave state" Missouri and "free-state" Maine to enter the Union simultaneously, prohibited any new slave states from emerging from the Louisiana Territory, and set the official government formula for slave and free territories to enter the Union as states.

In 1821 a Quaker named Benjamin Lundy, inspired by early abolitionist efforts of fellow Quaker John Woolman, began to publish a periodical in Baltimore titled, *The Genius of Universal Emancipation*. By the 1830s, however, the abolition movement had become much more aggressive, ignited by the rhetoric of Lundy protégé William Lloyd Garrison and his Boston publication, *Liberator*. Garrison's pen, denouncing churches that would not declare themselves in favor of unequivocal abolition, rallied many religious denominations such as Baptists and Methodists to join the movement. These arguments intensified in America, especially after 1833, when, after years of perseverance, the British Abolitionist Society was successful in outlawing slavery throughout the British Empire. Many well-known personalities of the day such as the Quaker poet John Greenleaf Whittier and philosopher Ralph Waldo Emerson became outspoken members of the abolition crusade, and soon the movement was spreading from its New England stronghold westward throughout states north of the Ohio River. Theodore Weld was probably the most effective organizational abolitionist; Weld worked to create religious societies in New York, Pennsylvania, and Ohio. Through Weld and Garrison's efforts nearly 2,000 abolitionist societies with a collective membership of 200,000 existed in America by the late 1830s.[4]

The town of Leavenworth, although in reality hardly more than a few tents, a sawmill, and a steam engine, was growing rapidly as hundreds of settlers like the Codys passed through the area daily. The passionate issue of slavery had entered mainstream culture, increasingly dividing the population into hostile factions. In 1854, when President Franklin Pierce signed the Kansas-Nebraska Act into law, violence erupted at the threshold of the road of the immigrants—the Codys' backyard, Leavenworth, Kansas. The Kansas-Nebraska Act repealed the Missouri Compromise and divided the Louisiana Territory into two separate new territories. The act also introduced the explosive aspect of "popular sovereignty" to the issue of western expansion by allowing citizens of these two large new territories to vote whether they wished to enter the Union as a "free" or a "slave" state. Kansas Territory rapidly became a tumultuous harbinger of the civil unrest destined to rip the United States of America apart, as abolitionist leaders from northern states and pro-slavery southern forces rushed into the region prepared to fight for their cause. To complicate matters, the lure of land and opportunities for quick fortunes, as well as the phenomenal numbers of people migrating west had also attracted gangs of border hoodlums, ruffians, ne'er-do-wells, lawless rogues and criminal adventurers to the territory. These desperate, volatile energies combined to make Kansas an increasingly perilous place. "Govern Kansas?" Wilson Shannon, the second territorial Governor of Kansas exclaimed, "You might as well have attempted to govern hell!"[5]

Stacking the election to decide the issue with thousands of illegal votes, pro-slavery elements quickly gained control of Leavenworth in 1855 as vigilantes terrorized the region lynching, killing, and tar and feathering abolitionists. The intimidation and violence forced many like Isaac Cody into silence or hiding.

Isaac was against slavery. He also believed that, to avoid violence amidst the turmoil, Kansas should be a "white" state, and that Negroes, free or slave, should not be allowed to enter the new state. Isaac skillfully kept his opinions to himself and avoided the Saturday night political rallies that invariably developed into drunken mobs prowling for trouble. On the fateful day of September 18, 1854, however, Isaac, with nine-year-old Will along, attended a political rally at Rively's grocery store in Leavenworth.

Pro-slavery neighbors had erroneously assumed for a year that Isaac, along with his openly pro-slavery brother Elijah, was one of "theirs." Rumors had begun to surface that Isaac was a talented public speaker and some among the crowd even regarded him as a potential leader of the pro-slavery cause. His appearance at the rally brought forth a clamor for him to step to the rostrum and make what all assumed would be an impassioned pro-slavery speech.

After failing his attempt to avoid addressing the mob, Isaac stepped up on the soapbox and stated bravely and precisely that he had no quarrel with anyone there, but that he was morally opposed to slavery and would go so far as to lay down his life to prevent its seed from taking root in Kansas. The dumbfounded mob went instantly silent. Just as quickly, a unanimous roar of rage erupted. A scoundrel named Charles Dunn leapt from the crowd and stabbed Isaac twice in the back with a Bowie knife.

Cody fell and Dunn and the crowd assumed he was dead. There would have probably been another assault on Isaac if Rively had not acted and hurriedly assisted young Will and carried Isaac to his home. As there was no doctor nearby, Isaac requested that he be carried to his brother Elijah's home in Weston, Missouri. Soon Mary Ann joined him there and dressed his wounds.[6]

Isaac never fully recovered from the stabbing. His convalescence was exacerbated by gangs of pro-slavery desperadoes who, upon learning Isaac was still alive, relentlessly persecuted the Cody family in repeated efforts to locate him and finish their murderous work. Isaac would often dress as a woman and work disguised in the fields, or hide in the attic to avoid the sudden appearances of his tormentors. Finally, he had to be smuggled out of the area in order to stay alive and try to heal. Nevertheless, the pro-slavery hoodlums continued to terrorize Mary, attempting to intimidate her into telling them where her husband was hiding. Occasionally Isaac would sneak home only to have the vigilantes learn he was back and return to the family's house to threaten Mary and the children as he hid or fled. Still suffering from the knife wounds, Isaac was somehow able to build a sawmill in Grasshopper Falls, thirty-five miles west of Leavenworth.

Throughout this ordeal Isaac began to work with Kansas abolitionist leaders spearheading efforts to encourage anti-slavery immigrants to migrate into the territory. Around this time agents were being sent east to induce immigrants to locate in Kansas and Isaac Cody was sent to Ohio as one of these agents.[7]

Isaac Cody took a steamboat and train to Cleveland, Ohio where he visited his brother Joseph and attempted to recuperate from the stabbing. Eventually the Cody brothers traveled to Chicago to attend a Republican Party gathering, where they met with Abraham Lincoln to discuss the problems in Kansas Territory. Isaac stayed with Joseph about two months and upon his return to Kansas was delighted to discover tensions there had abated. It would prove to be the calm before the storm.

During this brief, tranquil time in Kansas, fate brought Will Cody into contact with a trio of men destined to shape not only his life, but the future of the Trans-Missouri and America. As with most major events in Cody's life, the meeting had to do with horses. During the later part of the summer, as Isaac delivered a hay contract at Fort Leavenworth, Cody met a man who would have a profound impact on his life. As his father worked in the hay fields the boy passed the time riding in the country with William Russell, who introduced him to many wagon-masters, hunters and teamsters. These men also taught the boy the business of handling cattle and mules.[8]

William Russell was born in 1812 in Vermont yet moved to Missouri while in his teens. He had been a storekeeper in Lexington, Missouri and his business flourished from the fur trade commerce along the Santa Fe Trail. In 1847 he entered the freight business shipping goods to Santa Fe. The success of this venture led to major government freight contracts during the Mexican War.

Russell's partner, Alexander Majors, grew up working on the frontier and, as Russell, prospered in the freight business. Born in 1814, Majors was from Kentucky but migrated to Missouri as a child. He was, by nature, a frontiersman who preferred working alongside of the wagon masters, yet he was also a righteous Presbyterian who forced his employees to sign the following pledge:

> While in the employ of A. Majors, I agree not to use profane language, not to get drunk, not to gamble, nor to treat the animals cruelly, and not to do anything incompatible with the conduct of a gentleman. I agree if I violate any of the above conditions to accept my discharge without any pay for my services.[9]

The third man of the partnership was William B. Waddell. Like Russell, Waddell had succeeded as a merchant outfitting immigrants in Lexington, Missouri. Born in 1807 in Virginia, Waddell's family moved to Kentucky in 1815. Then, as a young man, Waddell relocated to Illinois before finally arriving in Missouri. In 1855 he merged his fortunes with Alexander Majors and William Russell creating the largest shipping enterprise in the West.

Recognizing that they had dramatically different temperaments, the three men divided their responsibilities wisely and effectively and became immensely successful. Russell's principle activity was representing the firm to the east—primarily government and banking connections. Majors managed all freight traffic, supervising routes and working with the wagon masters and bull-trains. Waddell handled bookkeeping, finances, purchases, and managed the home office. Russell, Majors and Waddell employed eight thousand men and ran two-hundred and fifty trains, composed of 6,250 wagons and 75,000 oxen. The partnership transported supplies to all the government frontier posts in the north and west and also carried freight as far south as New Mexico.[10]

Working with Russell, Majors and Waddell was an excellent school for Cody and he quickly acquired a fundamentally invaluable, practical understanding of the logistics of moving large animals, supply wagons and men across the Great Plains—knowledge which would prove fundamental to almost every other occupation he would have in life.[11]

The situation in Kansas, however, was beginning to attract much more national attention as news of violence there spread throughout the nation. In northern states immigrant aid societies moved into action, helping families with strong abolitionist sentiments migrate to Kansas. Rifles and ammunition also started to be shipped in to abolitionist forces to help them defend themselves. Perhaps the strongest indication of change, however, was the creation of an abolitionist newspaper in Leavenworth. The proslavery territorial legislature countered by passing laws allowing them to throw people in jail for reading such newspapers. Violence was soon erupting again.

Pro-slavery forces attacked the "free-state" stronghold in Lawrence with a cannon, burning most of the town. In a precursor to his infamous action at Harper's Ferry in Virginia in 1859, abolitionist John Brown went berserk in retaliation at Pottowatomie Creek, massacring and mutilating a group of pro-slavery sympathizers. At this point the U.S. military entered the argument and a military governor was appointed. A strained peace came to the region and Isaac Cody finally came home.

During his journey east, however, Isaac had invited the immigrants he recruited to make his home in Leavenworth their headquarters. By spring the house was overflowing and tents had been set up in the yard. Scarlet fever and measles promptly broke out in the Codys' immigrant campground, causing four deaths. Struggling to help with the outbreak, Isaac suffered a chill working in the rain. On March 10, 1857, he died.[12]

Sadly, the Codys' troubles were only beginning. Mary herself was very ill with consumption.

Alexander Majors had known and liked Isaac Cody and Will was certain, with his mother's blessing, the freight contractor would give him a job. After thinking the situation over, Mary saw the wisdom in her boy's thinking and soon she and Will went into Leavenworth to see Mr. Majors.

The businessman was initially concerned about the boys' age but quickly became impressed with Will's manners, confidence and maturity. Will commented to Mr. Majors that he had often run horse races in the Salt Creek Valley with his partner William B. Russell. After consulting with Russell and considering the Cody family's situation, however, Majors and Russell agreed to hire the boy. He was to be a "boy-extra," a mule-back courier carrying messages seven miles to and fro between the Russell, Majors and Waddell office and the telegraph office in Leavenworth. He would be paid forty dollars a month plus food; the salary would be delivered to his mother. Nevertheless, after two months a wagon master named John Willis, having become fond of the boy, requested Will's help herding oxen.

During this period Mary Cody's financial situation, although far from rosy, had stabilized somewhat with the creation of a boarding house in the family home. Her health improving with her finances, Mary's next important goal became to get her children into school.

In July, 1856, Mary enrolled Will in school. Ten-year-old Will promptly entered into a feud with a twenty-year-old classmate named Steve Gobels. The simmering hostility intensified over the affections of a certain young lady and came to a boil as the older lad challenged Will to a fight. Realizing the situation of a fight with a boy twice his age was desperate, Will brought along a knife hidden in his trousers to even the odds.

Quickly overpowered by his older opponent and, intending to frighten the older boy, Will stabbed him in the leg. Although mildly wounded, the lad screamed and the crowd of schoolchildren rushed in closer, stunned with the sight of blood and Gobels' screams. Apparently Will, as everyone else, thought he had injured Gobels worse than he had intended; once the schoolmaster arrived at the scene, Will fled. The headmaster shouted threats at Will as he ran.

As he raced down the road from the schoolyard, Will ran into wagon master John Willis. The bullwacker pulled the boy onto the back of his horse and, upon learning what had happened at the school, rode up to the schoolhouse and challenged the headmaster and Will's opponent to come out and fight. The tables were turned; now the teacher and Gobels fled the scene!

That evening Mary Cody received a note from the schoolmaster telling her that Will would no longer be welcome at the school. Shortly thereafter, Mary was visited by deputies from Leavenworth along with Steve Gobels' father. After searching in vain for Will the authorities departed. Later, as Willis and Will rode in a wagon toward the Cody home, the posse approached them. Willis instructed Will to hide in the wagon and refused to let the deputies search for the boy. Once the posse left, the pair rode on to the Cody farm. Willis promptly offered Mrs. Cody a solution to the problem; he advised her to give Will permission to accompany him on a bull-train that he was taking to Utah.

Mary realized the authorities would be after Will for awhile but, since the young man Will stabbed had not been seriously injured, the matter would probably fade away in a few months. With this reality in mind, Mrs. Cody consented to allowing her son to join Willis on the Utah trek. The boy, however, was embarking on a journey that would change his life forever. He was entering the world of the bullwacker; he was committing to a life of movement on the edge of the frontier; he was entering the world of massive logistics requiring fundamental knowledge of men, animals, and wagons.

Each of these wagons was driven by a man known as a "bullwacker." Named for the sound of the cracking bullwhip used to drive an ox team, the bullwackers were wily, tough characters by necessity as their work was hard and often dangerous. A typical bull train consisted of twenty to thirty wagons, each drawn by teams of twelve oxen yoked into six pairs. A train of this size would have a herd of twenty to thirty additional oxen in case of emergency, cavallard drivers to herd the loose cattle, and sundry extra hands, all under the supervision of a wagon master. On the journey west with loaded wagons the bull train traveled about twelve to fifteen miles a day. Empty wagons on the return trip would average twenty miles a day. The J Murphy freight wagons used by Russell, Majors, and Waddell were very large and very strongly built. Each wagon was capable of carrying seven thousand pounds of freight and was very spacious, being as large as the room of an ordinary house. Each wagon was covered with two heavy canvas sheets to protect its cargo from rain.[13]

Moving a bull train was a highly organized, logistical task requiring efficient planning and discipline. One mistake could cost lives. Each man of the operation was required to function at his peak at all times within the structure or trouble would quickly follow. Confusion caused delay; delay could bring death. Will, and the other "boy-extras," carried messages from wagon to wagon on muleback, keeping the operation in constant communication and moving in a coordinated, smooth flow.

The endless, pristine horizon of the Great Plains must have sung like a siren to the eleven-year-old boy. The call of adventure on the prairie must have eased the pain of losing his father, and, subsequently, the loss of mother's hearth. His boyhood behind him, Will Cody was now an active participant in the great migration west. No one would ever have to remind him that danger lurked constantly, coiled like a rattlesnake ready to strike. At a tender age experience had already shown him the wickedness in some men; how to spot it, and—most essentially—to keep his composure in the face of danger. He had learned that in order to survive he would have to be cool-headed, clever, and creative. Resourceful beyond his years, Will also knew instinctively that opportunities awaited him and he would need to develop extraordinary talents in order to create and meet those opportunities to succeed. In the middle of the muddy immigrant's road a boy had discovered his shining rainbow trail.

Chapter Two

THE SCOUTS

I'm a lonely bullwacker
On the Red Cloud Line.
I can lick any son of a gun
That will yoke an ox of mine.
And if I can catch him
You bet I will or try,
I'd lam him with an ox-bow
Root hog or die.
It's out on the road,
With a very heavy load,
With a very awkward team
And a very muddy road,
You may whip and you may holler,
But if you cuss it's on the sly;
Then whack the cattle on, boys—
Root hog or die.

"The Bullwacker," Author Anonymous
(*Cowboy Songs*, Ed. John Lomax)

"Root hog or die" is certainly a succinct, poetic phrase capturing the sagacious philosophy of the diverse, rough and rugged, buckskin-clad bullwackers. Most had survived terrific ordeals in life and become instinctively pragmatic and skilled at enduring hardship and peril. Considering this, it is difficult to imagine how strenuous and dangerous a bullwacker's life must have been for an eleven-year-old boy. During peak years of the migration era the highest number of fatalities were children. Diseases such as cholera attacked children on wagon trains with a special vengeance, but more children—and adults—died in accidents than any other way. Mishaps with firearms were more deadly than accidents with animals, weather, terrain, or hostile Indians. Any situation could change rapidly, however, and become life-threatening in an instant. The weather, for example, might become lethal within moments as it is not unusual for temperatures on the Great Plains to rise or fall fifty degrees in under a half-hour span of time. With deadly celerity, a tornado with hundred–mile-an-hour winds, rain, and hail might appear. Cattle stampedes, downed oxen, broken axles, and swollen streams all posed dangers to the bullwackers' daily trek. And the supplies they carried placed them in constant jeopardy of an attack by Indians or bandits. Enduring all these possible calamities, there was the reality of days upon days of trudging through sometimes calf-deep mud after a raging thunderstorm only to emerge on a stark, sun-baked alkali flat praying for rain.

The bullwackers apparently became quite fond of Will Cody immediately. They admired the fact that a boy his age had gone to work to support his family. They also grew to respect the way he worked, taking on whatever task assigned him with enthusiasm and quickly maturing skill. Even at age eleven Will was exhibiting special equestrian talents—usually on a mule. Hired as a dispatch courier, Will's job was to ride from wagon to wagon delivering messages, linking the communications of the operation of the freight teams together as a synchronized train.

Will's first teacher in the equestrian arts was his cousin Horace Billings. In 1853 Billings made a vivid impression on six-year-old Will when he suddenly appeared on the prairie near the Cody farm in Kansas with a herd of 400 wild mustangs he and seven companions had driven from California. Buffalo Bill described the meeting:

> ...my father called me to come and see a genuine western man; he was about six-feet two inches tall, was well-built and had a light, springy and wiry step. He wore a broad-brimmed California hat and he was dressed in a complete suit of buckskin, beautifully trimmed and beaded."[1]

Upon engaging in introductory conversation, all present soon realized they were experiencing a serendipitous moment; in sharing each other's personal history they learned Billings was Isaac Cody's nephew! He had run away from home as a boy and gone to sea. In the Hawaiian Islands Billings joined the circus and became famous as a trick-rider. As most men of the age, Billings caught gold fever and left the circus to seek his fortune in the California gold fields. Before ever attempting prospecting, however, he found his true calling as a *bocarro*—a man whose livelihood was capturing and breaking wild mustang horses. Billings and his companions had crossed the southwest from California to Kansas with the herd of wild horses to sell them to immigrants at the head of the immigrant's road.

After a few moments of small talk concerning the amazing coincidental way the family had "reunited" on the Kansas prairie, Billings immediately commented he had observed young Will was in possession of an unbroken horse and promptly offered to do the job. Within moments Isaac and Will watched spellbound as Billings mounted the wild horse and proceeded to expertly control the animal until the bucking pony surrendered and was mastered. The boy watched Billings' every movement, internalizing the fundamental equestrian skills which would serve him throughout his life.[2]

Isaac convinced his nephew to stay awhile at their farm and help him saw logs for the Cody home in Salt Creek Valley. During this period Billings taught young Will trick-riding as well as many other pragmatic western skills. Billings became a hero to the young boy and soon Cody wanted to do everything that the older man did. As a result of many wild horse races over the prairie, Will made rapid advances as an equestrian. Billings even taught the boy how to use the lasso.[3]

Billings, however, was not the type to stay in one place long, and he departed the young boy's life almost as suddenly as he had appeared; one day he and Isaac quarreled and the *bocarro* quickly left the farm. Nevertheless, his impression and training remained, as Will had learned valuable skills from Horace Billings—lessons that he would need to survive on the Great Plains.

Mary Cody also gave her son a practical tool for his first journey across the plains. Will carried an old muzzle-loading flint-lock rifle that had belonged to his grandfather. The boy used it with enough skill not to shoot himself or anyone else.

Upon his return from the two-month round-trip journey to Fort Kearney, John Willis referred Will to wagonmaster Frank McCarthy, who was heading back to Fort Kearney with a bull-train. In his autobiography Cody described his initial trek with Willis as "uneventful"; his return to Fort Kearney, however, would be anything but uneventful.

In Nebraska the immigrant's road followed the Platte River directly through Pawnee territory. In 1857 the Pawnee, and most Plains Indians, were growing less tolerant of the increasing movement of whites through their lands. To complicate matters, the Lakota and Pawnee were old enemies and Sioux war parties were often in the region. A treasure trove of twenty supply wagons and livestock would be even more tempting than

Pawnee scalps and horses to a Lakota war party. Bull trains traveling through Pawnee territory on the Platte always considered the possibility of an Indian ambush.

Twenty miles west of Fort Kearney, on a tiny tributary that emptied into the Platte, the freight wagon train stopped to prepare for dinner on the banks of Plum Creek. Everything appeared normal and the members of the train went to work at their assigned tasks preparing the meal, corralling the livestock, and making camp.

Suddenly gunshots rang out, echoed by the screams and yells of an Indian attack. Startled, the bullwackers were unable to prevent the Pawnee from stampeding the cattle herd, adding to the pandemonium and calamity tearing madly through the camp. Experienced in such emergencies on the prairie, however, the bullwackers rallied and were able to organize and fire enough shots to hold off the first murderous wave of the hostiles' attack. This quick defense only allowed them to see just how critical their situation was: Outnumbered ten to one with more Indians arriving rapidly at the scene, the bullwackers' only option was to retreat to a high bank of the creek. They fled under a shower of arrows which reduced their numbers dramatically.

The bullwackers scrambled to the creek bank, and, temporarily shielded behind the sandy barricade, were able to fire a second volley of gunshots driving the Pawnees back. Here, they ascertained their only option for survival, hopeless as it appeared, was to make a desperate run for Fort Kearney. They fired one last round as a ruse and fled, carrying and dragging their wounded down the Platte River. The Pawnee quickly saw through the bullwackers charade and pursued. Only the bullwackers' superior firepower was able to halt them once more.

Realizing this plan of retreat was deadly, the bullwackers stopped long enough to build a small raft onto which they loaded the wounded. Because of his age, Will was offered a spot on the raft, which he declined, maintaining he could manage for himself. Yet, brave as he was, the boy could not keep up the pace of the older men and quickly fell one-hundred yards or so behind the main party as the bullwackers walked, waded and floated downstream, fleeing the Pawnees.

Night fell. As the moon rose Will spotted an Indian preparing to ambush the unsuspecting bullwackers. Without thinking, the boy raised his grandfather's old flint-lock and fired, killing the warrior. Wagon master Frank McCarthy rushed back to discover Will struggling to pull the dead Pawnee from the Platte River. Will wanted to stop and bury the body, and it took quick convincing by McCarthy to persuade the boy to leave. As they returned to the main group, McCarthy called out to the group, "Pards, little Billy has killed his first redskin!" Even though the announcement brought forth cheers, the boy, in shock having just killed a man, thought the cheers disrespectful and out of place.[4]

The bullwackers miraculously escaped the Pawnee and the weary survivors dragged into Fort Kearney with the dawn's light. The next day a small party of armed troops accompanied McCarthy and a few of the bullwackers to the remains of their burned-out train. The teamsters recovered and buried their dead comrades. Suddenly empty-handed and afoot, the survivors had no choice but to walk back to Kansas.

Will's arrival in Leavenworth was greeted with the first of a lifetime of newspaper headlines and stories: "The Boy Indian-Slayer!" It is a great testament to Will Cody's youthful character that he seemed genuinely saddened by the entire matter and embarrassed by what he considered improper attention.

Mrs. Cody did not have her boy home for long. Russell, Majors and Waddell negotiated a contract with the U.S. Army to supply troops under the command of General Albert Sidney Johnston as the government readied for the war over the "Mormon insurrection" in Utah. The religious sect had become increasingly violent and Brigham Young's militia, which he called "Avenging Angels," had been responsible for a heinous massacre of immigrants in June, 1857. Mark Twain best describes the "Mountain Meadow Massacre" in his classic, *Roughing It*:

> A great emigrant train from Missouri and Arkansas passed through Salt Lake City, and a few disaffected Mormons joined it for the sake of the strong protection it afforded for their escape. In that matter lay sufficient cause for hot retaliation by the Mormon chiefs. Besides, these one-hundred and forty-five or one-hundred fifty unsuspecting immigrants being in part from Arkansas, where a noted Mormon missionary had lately been killed, and in part from Missouri, a state remembered with execrations as a bitter persecutor of the saints when they were few and poor and friendless, here were substantial additional grounds for lack of love for these wayfarers...a revelation from Brigham Young, as Great Grand Archee or God, was dispatched to President J.C. Haight, Bishop Higbee, and J.D. Lee (adopted son of Brigham), commanding them to raise all the forces they could muster and trust, follow those cursed Gentiles (so read the revelation), attack them disguised as Indians, and with the arrows

of the Almighty make a clean sweep of them, and leave none to tell the tale.[5]

Brigham's "angels" carried out their deadly mission to the letter; none were left to tell the tale! Furthermore, Johnston's first military encounters with the Mormons were not promising; Young's militia ambushed and burned all the general's supply trains, forcing him to retreat. Thousands of miles from the nearest settlements, General Johnston was in serious need of the supplies Russell, Majors, and Waddell's bull trains carried over the plains.

Upon returning to Kansas and learning of the large supply train heading to Utah, Will asked Mr. Majors to re-hire him. Wagonmaster Lew Simpson, having heard of Will's reputation as a "boy Indian-slayer," teased the boy about his fame. Nevertheless, Simpson was genuinely impressed with and fond of the eleven-year-old and hired him immediately.

During the first week or two out on this trek Cody became well acquainted with a man destined to become a life-long and intimate friend. His real name was James Butler Hickok, known to the world as Wild Bill.[6]

Perhaps the best description of Hickok was written by none other than General George Armstrong Custer:

> Wild Bill was a strange character, just the one which a novelist might gloat over. He was a plainsman in every sense of the word, yet unlike any other of his class. In person he was about six feet one in height, straight as the straightest of the warriors whose implacable foe he was; broad shoulders, well-formed chest and limbs, and a face strikingly handsome; a sharp, clear, blue eye, which stared you straight in the face when in conversation; a finely shaped nose, inclined to be aquiline; a well-turned mouth, with lips only partially concealed by a handsome moustache. His hair and complexion were those of the perfect blonde. The former was worn in uncut ringlets falling carelessly over his powerfully formed shoulders. Add to this figure a costume blending the immaculate neatness of the dandy with the extravagant taste and style of the frontiersman, and you have Wild Bill, then as now the most famous scout on the plains. Whether on foot or on horseback, he was one of the most perfect types of physical manhood I ever saw.[7]

Wild Bill was born into a Presbyterian family in Troy Grove, Illinois, and reared to be a preacher. This background imbued Hickok with a high sense of morals and justice evidenced by the fact that he initially came to Kansas to join the abolitionist "Red Leg" militia. A man of Hickok's talents with a firearm was much needed by the abolitionists in Kansas. Of Hickok's legendary marksmanship it was said he once shot a rock an angry man had hurled at him. He was also said to have stood between two telegraph poles with a pistol in each hand, firing simultaneously and hitting bull's eyes marked on each of the poles. He cut a chicken's throat at a distance of thirty paces and, at fifty paces, hit a dime.[8]

In his deathbed interview with Chauncey Thomas of *Outdoor Life* in 1917, however, Buffalo Bill offered a different perspective of his life-long friend:

> Bill was only a nickname we gave him you know . . . we got to calling him 'Wild Bill' because when we were all boys together there were four Bill's in the wagon train and we had to sort them out somehow. Jim Hickox was always popping away at everything he saw move when on guard at night over the stock, so we sort of got to calling him 'Wild Bill' and that's how the name came to him. . .Bill was a pretty good shot but he could not shoot as quick as half a dozen men we all knew in those days. Nor as straight either. But Bill was cool and the men he went up against were rattled I guess. Bill beat them to it. He made up his mind to kill the other man before the other man had finished thinking, and so Bill would just quietly pull his gun and give it to him. That was all there was to it. It is easy enough to beat the other man if you start first. . . . that's how he did it. But he was not the quickest man by any means. He was just cool and quiet, and started first. Bill Hickox was not a bad man as is often pictured. But he was a bad man to tackle. Always cool, kind, and cheerful, almost, about it. He never killed a man unless that man was trying to kill him. That's fair.[9]

In his autobiography Cody described the incident that led to the life-long bonding between himself and Hickok:

> The circumstances under which I first made his acquaintance and learned to know him well and to appreciate his manly character and kindheartedness were these. One of the teamsters in Lew Simpson's bull-train was a surly, overbearing fellow, and took particular delight in bullying and tyrannizing over me, and one day while we were at dinner he asked me to do something for him. I did not start at once, and he gave me a slap in the face with the back of his hand, — knock-

ing me off an ox-yoke on which I was sitting and sent me sprawling on the ground. Jumping to my feet I picked up a camp kettle full of boiling coffee which was sitting on the fire, and threw it at him. I hit him in the face and the hot coffee gave him a severe scalding. He sprang at me with the ferocity of a tiger, and would have undoubtedly have torn me to pieces, had it not been for the timely interference of my new found friend, Wild Bill, who knocked the man down. As soon as he recovered himself, he demanded of Wild Bill what business it was of his that he should "put in his oar." "It's my business to protect that boy, or anybody else, from being unmercifully abused, kicked and cuffed, and I'll whip any man who tries it on," said Wild Bill; "and if you ever again lay a hand on that boy— little Billy there—I'll give you such a pounding that you won't get over it for a month of Sunday's." From that time forward Wild Bill was my protector and intimate friend, and the friendship thus begun continued until his death.[10]

Only days after the fight with the bullwacker young Will was to get his first glimpse into the power of the monarch of the plains as the train was besieged by a stampeding herd of buffalo—the first the boy had ever seen. 500 buffalo crashed pell-mell, through the wagon train. Some of the wagons were turned completely around, as terrified oxen attempted to run to the hills with the heavy wagons attached to them. Others broke the wagons' tongues off, while all the teams got entangled in their gearing, and general pandemonium reigned. One big buffalo bull got himself entangled in one of the heavy wagon chains, and, in his frantic efforts to free himself, snapped the strong chain in two, broke the ox-yoke to which it was attached, and fled toward the hills with the chain swinging wildly from his horns. When the stampede finally subsided the wagon train was broken, crippled and scattered, forcing the bullwackers to create a camp in order to spend a day regrouping and repairing everything they could.[11]

Surviving a buffalo herd stampede only set the stage for the next mishap to befall Simpson's bull-train. As the wagons entered Mormon territory Simpson ordered a noon halt and, with his assistant George Woods and young Will, drove the cattle a mile and a half to Big Sandy Creek, a tributary of the Green River. Returning to camp, the trio was intercepted by a group of twenty men with their guns drawn; the bull-train had been seized by Brigham Young's "avenging angels"—the same bunch responsible for the Mountain Meadows Massacre earlier that year.

Simpson was somehow able to convince the Mormon leader, Major Lot Smith, to allow his party one wagon, oxen to pull it, and even some weapons. Smith later commented that Simpson was the bravest man he ever met. The event, however, was a most important one in the life of young Will Cody; as a result of the ambush he was destined to spend the winter at Old Fort Bridger. Don Russell informs us,

> Simpson's crew in their single wagon went on to Fort Bridger and spent the winter there with the troops of the Army of Utah and remnants of old wagon trains personnel. Bill Cody's presence there is confirmed by Trooper Robert Morris Peck of the First U.S. Cavalry, who wrote in his reminiscences for the *National Tribune* in 1901. Trooper Peck said Cody was then a boy of 11 or 12 years old, employed by Lou Simpson, a bull-train wagon boss, as an extra hand or cavlyard driver, or something of that kind.
>
> He gave no visible signs then of future fame, and only impressed me as a rather fresh "smart-ellick" sort of a kid. The bull-wackers had made quite a pet of him and one of them informed me that Billy was already developing wonderful skill at riding wild horses or mules, shooting and throwing a rope, etc. I had almost forgotten that I had ever seen the little dirty-faced bullwacker when just after the war, I heard the name of Buffalo Bill mentioned frequently in connection with frontier affairs. I thought at first it was another nickname that had been conferred on "Wild Bill," whom I had known on the plains by several sobriquets, as "Injun Bill" and "Buckskin Bill," but on asking an old comrade who had been with me in Utah, "Who is this Buffalo Bill I hear so much about?" he answered, "Why don't you remember that smart little fellow that was in Lew Simpson's bull-train as an extra hand?" my recollection was revived.[12]

That winter was particularly brutal even by Rocky Mountain standards. The unusual numbers of men at Fort Bridger put a severe strain on supplies, making the situation even more stressful. As the winter wore on, near starvation conditions arose. Once again we must remember that Cody was still in his preadolescent years. A great many troops were present in addition to around four-hundred of Russell, Majors and Waddell's employees. To insure order the men were organized into militia companies officered by the wagon masters. The lucky ones were able to live in cabins, but most lived in tents. Aware their supplies would run short during the winter, the men at the fort were initially put on three-quarters rations. Before long, however, this was reduced to one-half, and, eventually, one-quarter. Worn-out cattle, so poor they had to be propped up to be shot down, were killed for beef. When the cattle were gone they ate their mules.[13]

Located on the prairie fringe of Wyoming's Red Desert, Fort Bridger's wood supply was as drastically sparse as was the food store. In order to obtain wood men had to travel to the distant Uinta Mountains. Having slain and eaten horses, mules, cattle and oxen, the men had to haul the wood themselves; ropes were tied to wagons and twenty men, acting as a team, pulled the wagons loaded with wood from the Uintas to the fort.

In the spring of 1858, as soon as the bullwackers could travel, Lew Simpson ordered his group to head home to Kansas. They headed due east to historic Fort Laramie and their first square meal since losing their train to Mormons. The legendary post, built in 1834 by fur trader Robert Campbell and originally named Fort William, had served as a center of commerce for traders, trappers, Indians, missionaries, military expeditions, and immigrants since its inception. With the beginnings of the immigration era in 1839, the post moved to a new location, became known as Fort Laramie, and began its evolution into a walled, self-sufficient city. Outside the adobe walls several thousand Indians camped in a perennial symbiotic village—the origins of the Plains Indian "slang" tribal name *Hangs-Around-The-Fort-People.*

Will would soon have ample opportunity to test all his youthful training and experience as a scout and plainsman. Before departing Fort Laramie Lew Simpson had been assigned two large bull-trains with a company of four-hundred men. Upon leaving the fort, Simpson had the trains running about fifteen miles apart and was dividing his time between both trains as they followed the North Platte southbound for Fort Leavenworth. One morning Simpson ordered his assistant, George Woods, and Will to saddle their mules and ride with him to visit the head train.

About halfway between the two trains the trio was ambushed by a large Indian war party galloping rapidly toward them from less than a mile away. The experienced Simpson immediately acted. He knew that it would be impossible to escape running on worn-out mules. He jumped from his mule and ordered Will and George to dismount. He then shot all three animals and cut their throats as they fell to the ground. Simpson jerked the dead and dying animals into a triangle and ordered his comrades inside the fleshy stockade. Simpson performed all of these actions before the hostiles were within three hundred yards.[14]

Soon arrows and bullets flew in the first volley of the attack. Most of the

Indians were armed with bows and arrows and, though severely outnumbered, Simpson, Woods and Cody were each armed with Mississippi Yager rifles and a pair of Colt .45 revolvers. The bullwackers' superior firepower prevailed and the war party's attack was repelled. Undaunted, the war party withdrew to a safe distance and began to circle and pelter the mule barricade with arrows. An arrow hit Woods in the left shoulder; Simpson dressed the wound with a tobacco poultice, and soon Woods was ready to fight again. Finally, the hostiles pulled away to hold a council and to strategize. The respite was not long, however; the war party soon charged the mule–fort again. Having had time to reload and prepare themselves for a siege, the trio's firepower reduced the numbers of their enemies greatly during the second charge and forced the hostiles into a two-hour council.

The bullwackers used the lull in the fight to dig in, literally shoveling dirt over the mules as they deeply entrenched themselves into a more secure fort. Having an ample supply of ammunition, they prepared themselves for a long siege. As night fell the war-party set a prairie fire to attempt to burn the trio out of their fortification. The buffalo grass was too short to create much of a blaze, but the acrid smoke was an effective shield to conceal sniper archers. All through the night the trio kept watch for yet another attack. The dawn's light brought the anticipated assault. Once again the bullwackers' weapons were able to halt the war party's advance; the Indians retreated and, erroneously assuming the trio to have been part of only one train—the one that had passed ahead of them the day before—prepared to sit and starve the bullwackers into submission. Soon, however, the second train's bullwhips could be heard cracking like rifles in the distance. The war party made one last charge at the mule fort and finally vanished onto the prairie. Miraculously, the trio had survived.

Upon his return to Kansas Will discovered his mother had become very ill. Still, the boy only stayed home for a month before departing on yet another crossing of the Great Plains to Fort Laramie, this time with a wagonmaster named Buck Bonner. When the train arrived at Fort Laramie in November, Will left Russell, Majors and Waddell and joined a group of trappers planning an expedition on the Chugwater and Laramie Rivers. This adventure lasted about two months and was made difficult by increasing Lakota hostilities in the area.

Upon learning his mother's tuberculosis had become worse, Will made his way back to Kansas in February, 1859, and, at his mother's insistence, re-entered school. It would prove to be the longest period of time Cody spent in school in his life—two-and-a-half months. Nevertheless, with spring's arrival the lure of adventure attracted Will again, magnetically tugging him west.

Actually it was the tug of gold. The Pike's Peak gold frenzy was raging at the time and everyone was rushing to claim a share of the diggings. Cody joined a party bound for the spanking new town of Auraria, later to be re-named, Denver, in honor of the then-governor of Kansas. Arriving in Auraria, on Cherry Creek, the mining party pushed on to the gold streams in the mountains. Cody went with them and prospected for two months. As many before him, Cody learned one needs to know a thing or two about the science of mining before undertaking prospecting for gold. Soon Cody and several of his dis-heartened friends headed back eastward for home.[15]

Upon arriving at the Platte River the failed prospectors had the idea to construct a raft to speed their journey home to Kansas. Near Julesburg, in Nebraska territory, the raft hit troubled waters and tore apart, depositing the crew and all their possessions in the river. After pulling themselves out of the Platte, Will and his companions headed on foot to the town of Julesburg, which was already becoming a famous spot along the road of the immigrants.

A rough frontier town near Fort Kearney, Julesburg was an important station on Russell, Majors, and Waddell's Overland Stage route. The station was created and managed by a burly French Canadian agent named Ole Jules Reni, who was as notorious and unscrupulous as the wild and suspicious characters who frequently assembled at Julesburg to take advantage of the flow of humanity through the region. Julesburg had risen to prominence as a station on the Oregon Trail as a result of the Colorado gold strike. With the towns of Denver and Auraria growing rapidly, Julesburg became an important "fork-in-the-road" as some immigrants headed to the Colorado gold fields.

Will had a date with destiny at Julesburg. There he met another old acquaintance. George Chrisman, Russell, Majors, and Waddell's head wagonmaster, had purchased Julesburg, which was to soon become a station for a new business the shipping firm had started—the Pony Express.

Chapter Three

THE PONY EXPRESS

In a little while all interest was taken up in stretching our necks and watching for the "pony-rider"—the fleet messenger who sped across the continent from St. Joe to Sacramento, carrying letters 1,900 miles in eight days! Think of that for perishable horse and human flesh and blood to do!

The pony-rider was usually a little bit of a man, brimful of spirit and endurance. No matter what time of the day or night his watch came on, and no matter whether it was winter or summer, raining, snowing, hailing or sleeting or whether his "beat" was a level straight road or a crazy trail over mountain crags and precipice, or whether it led through peaceful regions or regions that swarmed with hostile Indians, he must always be ready to leap into the saddle and be off like the wind!

There was no idle-time for a pony-rider on duty. He rode 50 miles without stopping, by daylight, moonlight, starlight, or through the blackness of darkness—just as it happened.

He rode a splendid horse that was born for a racer and fed and lodged like a gentleman; kept him at his utmost speed for ten miles; and then, as he came crashing up to the station where stood two men holding fast a fresh, impatient steed, the transfer of rider and mailbag was made in a twinkling of an eye, and away flew the eager pair and were out of sight before the spectator could get hardly the ghost of a look.

The stagecoach traveled about a hundred to 125 miles a day (24 hours), and pony-rider about 250. There were about 80 pony-riders in the saddle all the time, night and day, stretching in a long, scattered procession from Missouri to California, 40 flying eastward, and 40 to the west, and among them making 400 gallant horses earn a stirring livelihood and see a great deal of scenery every single day in the year.

We had a consuming desire, from the beginning, to see a pony-rider, but somehow or other all that passed us and all that met us managed to streak by us in the night, and so we heard only a whiz and a hail, and the swift phantom of the desert was gone before we could get our heads out of the windows. But now we were expecting one along every moment, and we would see him in broad daylight. Presently the driver exclaims: "Here he comes!"

Every neck is stretched further, and every eye strained wider. Away across the endless dead level of the prairie a black speck appears against the sky, and it is plain that it moves. Well, I should think so! In a second or two it becomes a horse and rider, rising nearer—growing more and more defined—nearer and nearer, and the flutter of the hoofs comes faintly to the ear—another instant a whoop and a hurrah from our own upper deck, a wave of the rider's hand, but no reply, and man and horse burst past our excited faces, and go winging away like a belated fragment of a storm!

So sudden is it all, and so like a flash of unreal fancy, that but for the flake of white foam left quivering and perishing on a mail-sack after the vision had flashed by and disappeared, we might have doubted whether we had seen any actual horse and man at all, maybe. (*Roughing It*, Mark Twain)

"Gold is where you find it; mail is when you get it," was a popular remark throughout the west during the 1850s. Much of the essence of the era is captured in the deceptively simple comment as the search for gold during the decade after the California gold rush brought hundreds of thousands of immigrants pouring into remote regions throughout the west. In California especially, population mushroomed, accompanied by increasingly organized pleas for efficient mail service.

In 1859 gold was discovered in Colorado while silver was also discovered in Nevada. Prospectors rushed into these territories, compounding the acute problems with mail services already being experienced in California. As populations in California, Nevada, and Colorado proliferated with the territories' growing wealth and political influence, clamors for competent mail service grew exponentially. The situation rapidly progressed from a simple inconvenience to a political necessity as more intrepid entrepreneurs attempted, yet failed, to organize delivery to these isolated regions. Arguments concerning secession had intensified throughout the nation complicating the issue, yet, with civil war looming on the horizon, potential military/geographic control of the west became increasingly important to northern and southern concerns. The rush to Colorado and Nevada exacerbated the situation greatly, however, because both terri-

tories were hundreds of miles from both major mail lines; neither the Butterfield Route nor the Central Overland Route was of much use to these
isolated miners.

Created by upstate New Yorker John Butterfield and controlled by Wells
Fargo, American, and National Express, the Butterfield Route was sometimes referred to as "the Ox-Bow Route." The government paid Butter-
field $600,000 annually to deliver mail to stations along his stagecoach line,
which ran from St. Louis to Memphis before heading west to Fort Smith,
Arkansas. Butterfield's route departed Fort Smith and headed southwest
through "Indian Territory" to Fort Fillmore near the Mexican border at El
Paso. From El Paso, Butterfield's route proceeded through the desert to
Fort Yuma, Arizona. At Fort Yuma, the line headed west and north to San
Diego and Los Angeles before ending up in San Francisco. The route was
2,800 miles long and took 25 days to deliver mail from St. Louis to San
Francisco.[1]

Russell, Majors and Waddell's shipping firm naturally got into the business of delivering mail to stations along their stagecoach line that followed
the immigrant's road to Salt Lake City. The firm had no government contracts and received no financial assistance from Washington to deliver
mail, but quickly realized it could profit from such an enterprise; rich,
lonely miners would pay almost anything for the most mundane news from
home.

William Russell quickly became deeply involved in the Colorado gold
rush by investing in the Denver City Town Company, a land speculation
developed by his friend from Leavenworth, General William Larimer. The
investment bought Russell thirty acres of land in what Larimer projected
would become the capital of Colorado. Russell next approached his partners with a vision of mail service to Colorado's growing population of isolated mining camps. Unable to convince his partners Majors and Waddell
that their firm should create a mail line to the region, Russell formed a
separate partnership with John S. Jones and the pair created the Leavenworth and Pikes Peak Express Company and bought the government mail
contract between the Missouri River and Denver from J. M. Hockaday. By
the fall of 1859, however, the Russell and Jones company was bankrupt
from the high starting costs of extending the line from Julesburg to Auraria. At this point, Russell's loyal partners bought his defunct company in
order to save him the embarrassment of financial ruin. It had finally become obvious even to Russell that financial assistance from the government was the only way mail service to the isolated populations could work.

Russell had always been the "promoter" of the shipping partnership; Majors and Waddell relied on his political and financial connections for government shipping contracts from Washington. Frustrated with his efforts in Colorado, Russell went to Washington to attempt to obtain a substantial government mail contract.

In the nation's capital, Russell met with California Senator William McKeendree Gwin, who held an important position on the Senate Committee on Post Offices and Post Roads. Gwin was a medical doctor from Tennessee who, after being appointed Grand Marshall of Mississippi by President Andrew Jackson, had been elected to Congress from Mississippi. Gwin relocated to California when the territory entered the Union in 1850 and was elected Senator from the new state in 1854.

Gwin had his own dilemma with mail service. As his constituency in California exploded in numbers demanding more efficient mail delivery, Gwin had been unable to gather enough support in Washington to appropriate funding to deal with the problem. It did not help that Congress was torn with dissension and arguments of secession. Powerful southern forces in Congress preferred the Butterfield Route, as it originated and ran through the southern section of the frontier and would prove an important military asset should civil war erupt. Northerners in Congress, faced with the fact that the Central Overland Route was inoperative nearly half the year because of hazardous weather, had no option; unless a swift, dependable service could be created along the Central Route, the Butterfield Route would remain the quickest way to communicate between the coasts.

Gwin believed he had a bold solution to the problem. The idea was not his; ironically, it was a concept originating from the superintendent of operations for Russell, Majors, and Waddell—Benjamin F. Ficklin. As superintendent of the largest transportation organization in the west, Ficklin was arguably the most knowledgeable man in the field of shipping logistics in the nation.

After his election to the U.S. Senate in 1854, Gwin had traveled on horseback from San Francisco to Washington. Ben Ficklin rode with Senator Gwin along the Central Overland Route of the immigrant's road. As the pair casually chatted along the way, Ficklin offered a possible solution to the mail dilemma. After giving the matter considerable thought, Ficklin believed swift mail delivery could best be achieved with a racing relay team of master equestrians, riding the swiftest horses in the country over landscapes the riders knew from personal, firsthand experience.

William Russell was fascinated with Ficklin's idea from the moment

Senator Gwin presented it. He proceeded quickly back to Leavenworth and enthusiastically presented the vision to his partners.

Neither Majors nor Waddell believed a "pony express" would work. The firm had sustained major losses during the Mormon Wars and both partners were deeply concerned about money. The pair was also concerned that the Colorado gold rush might prove to be short-lived and, if so, the firm would be financially committed to running a mail line to ghost towns. In order to run a mail line to California, the firm would have to create many more stations; the most expensive horses in the country would have to be purchased; and the best riders would have to be hired. Waddell estimated the cost of putting the venture together at $100,000 plus $30,000 a month to maintain. But, motivated by patriotism and a genuine desire to develop a "Union Mail Route," the pair agreed with great reservations to back their enthusiastic partner. Russell, Majors, and Waddell began to construct stations every fifteen miles along the route and hired W. W. Finney as superintendent of the western line and Bolivar Roberts as his assistant. Both men were highly respected individuals and excellent choices to lay the foundation for the Pony Express; Finney was one of the best judges of horses in the country, and Roberts was equally skilled at selecting the finest young men to become riders.[2]

To establish the Pony Express required $100,000 in gold coin to establish and equip the line. It also required 500 of the best blood American horses and one hundred and ninety stock stallions for changing the riding stock. Two hundred station tenders were required to care for the horses and have the horses saddled and prepared for the incoming riders. Naturally, each of the stations had to be supplied with hay and grain for the horses and food for the tenders. The Pony Express also required 80 lean fool-heartedly brave boys who could ride like the wind.[3]

Russell, Majors, and Waddell's financial future would ride on furious, bone-rattling speed; nimble, unburdened lightness; epic equestrian endurance; geographic dexterity; youthful bravura; and, plain, old-fashioned luck. Each horse's load would be rigidly restricted to 165 pounds. With twenty pounds allowed for the mail and twenty-five pounds allowed for saddle, bridle and bags, the rider's maximum weight was a strict 120 pounds. A special light-leather rectangular sheet called a *mochila* was designed with a hole for the rig to fit snugly over the saddle horn. At each corner of the *mochila* was a leather pouch called a *cantinas*. Three of the cantinas were locked with a brass key held only at the principal stations of the route: Fort Kearney, Fort Laramie, Fort Bridger, Salt Lake City, and

Carson City. The fourth pouch contained mail to be picked up or dropped at regular stations. Letters were written on the finest tissue paper and cost $5 (in gold coin) per half once. At such expense most letters were urgent messages. In 1860 Finney and Roberts placed the following ad in San Francisco newspapers:

> Wanted—young, skinny, wiry fellows, not over 18. Must be expert riders, willing to risk death daily. Orphans preferred. Wages $25 per week".[4]

Soon Roberts had more riders than he could hire.

Within two months the Pony Express was ready to ride. On April 3, 1860, a twenty-three-year-old former sailor named John William Richardson raced out of St. Joseph headed west. His counterpart, Sam Hamilton, sped out of San Francisco headed east. For the next nineteen months, eighty riders were in the saddle constantly, each riding three blazing fifteen-mile races a day. Each rider was required to cover fifteen miles in an hour's time. After a short rest, the horseman would repeat his ride, returning to his original station.

When Will Cody and his group of failed prospectors arrived at Julesburg, George Chrisman, Russell, Majors, and Waddell's head wagonmaster, had just purchased the station from "Ole" Jules Reni. Aware that Cody had been spent his life in the saddle, Reni immediately hired Cody as a Pony Express rider with a forty-five-mile route broken into three fifteen-mile relays. Cody wrote to his mother, who tried in vain to discourage her son from the job. In spite of his mother's objections, however, the boy stayed with the Pony Express two months before learning that his mother had become ill again and returning to the Salt Creek Valley.[5]

At Salt Creek Will helped his mother until she recovered. With his mother's recuperation, Will and a friend named David Harrington decided to try their luck as trappers. The boys obtained a yoke of oxen, filled a wagon with provisions, and headed to Prairie Dog Creek on the Republican River near Junction City in northwestern Kansas. The young trappers prospered and were very successful trapping beaver and otter. Bad luck was looming, however, as one of their oxen slipped on ice and dislocated a hip, forcing the boys to have to shoot the beast. Without a team the boys would be forced also to remain on Prairie Dog Creek until spring; this delay would necessitate constructing a shelter to last them throughout the winter. The pair decided to dig out a cave from the side of a hill. This task done, they floored the dugout "cabin" with logs and walled its interior with grass, brush, and mud. A fireplace and chimney were constructed with large stones and the wagon became a fourth wall covering the opening of the cave. Outside, the boys built a corral for their three remaining oxen.

The first night in their new home Will and Dave were awakened by a riotous commotion in the corral. A bear had attacked the oxen and already had one of them down on the ground when Will and Dave arrived at the scene. Dave reached the corral first and fired, wounding the bear. Enraged, the bear turned and charged Harrington; the boy turned to run but slipped and fell on ice. Will shot and killed the bear, saving his partner's life. Two weeks later, Harrington was presented with a situation in which he would return the favor. Once again ice was the culprit.

While hunting elk, Will slipped on ice and broke his leg. Harrington set and bound the broken bone and carried Will to the cave. The boys were now suddenly faced with an emergency situation requiring a mature plan of action; obviously, Dave would have to go for help. It was decided that he would return 125 miles to the nearest settlement to borrow a yoke of oxen to come back for his friend. They determined that the rescue effort would take twenty days, so Dave chopped an appropriate amount of firewood, rigged up a rope and pulley system with a can for Will to get water from melted snow, placed all provisions and utensils within Will's reach, and departed. Cody wrote in his autobiography:

> On the twelfth day after Harrington left me I was awakened from a sound sleep by someone touching me upon the shoulder. I looked up and was astonished to see an Indian warrior standing at my side. His face was hideously daubed with paint, which told me more forcibly than words could have that he was on the warpath. He spoke to me in broken English and Sioux mixed, and I understood him to ask what I was doing there, and how many were with me.
>
> By this time the little dug-out was nearly filled with other Indians, who had been peeping in at the door, and I could hear voices of still more outside as well as the stamping of horses. I began to think that my time had come, as the saying is, when into the cabin stepped an elderly Indian, whom I readily recognized as old Rain-In-The-Face, a Sioux chief from the vicinity of Fort Laramie. I rose up as well as I could and showed him my broken leg. I told him where I had seen him, and asked him if he remembered me. He replied that he knew me well, and that I used to come to his lodge at Fort Laramie to visit him.[6]

Cody says he was taught the Siouan language by the sons of this chief, including the son who succeeded to the name of Rain-In-The-Face, and who years later, it is asserted, killed General George A. Custer. Recent studies, however, discredit stories that Rain-In-The-Face killed either General Custer or his brother, Captain Tom Custer.[7]

Will asked Rain-In-The-Face if the war party intended to kill him, and the old man bluntly answered, "Yes!" The Lakota continued, however, commenting that he would intervene on his young friend's behalf. In a few moments, the group went into a private council.

After talking the matter over, the group decided to spare Will's life as he was still only a boy. Nevertheless, several in the war party made it clear that they wanted Will's rifle and revolvers. Will pleaded with the Lakota to leave him at least one weapon with which to defend himself. The boy realized quickly, however, this was not going to happen and decided to let the matter be; he was, after all, escaping with his life. Soon the war party was digging through his provisions and cooking a meal. Famished, they cooked most of the boy's supplies. Before leaving him with very little provisions, however, they did leave him some of the food they cooked.[8]

Two days after the war party departed, a fierce blizzard set in, rapidly encasing the cave in snow. After three relentless days the blizzard covered the cabin floor with several feet of drifts while snow completely blocked the door. Will's fear grew with the deepening snow as most of his firewood was now covered and extremely difficult for him to get to with his broken leg. He was also painfully aware that the blizzard certainly would delay Dave and his rescue and worried if his partner might have fallen victim to an accident or Indian war party similar to the one that recently visited.

Will had kept track of the days by marking a stick, and upon the arrival of the twentieth day he became very depressed and extremely concerned when Dave failed to show. Adding to his desperate situation, a pack of wolves gathered around the boy's shelter and began to scratch and dig in the snow attempting to get inside.

Days and nights passed in this manner, forcing the boy to become despondent. He was without a fire, eating frozen, raw meat and melting snow in his mouth for drinking water. As each day passed, he became more convinced that Dave was not going to return. On the twenty-ninth day, however, Will heard Dave's voice shouting to the oxen as he headed them up the creek toward the dugout.

After a joyful reunion, Will discovered Dave had indeed suffered through a harrowing ordeal himself. The blizzard had held him snow-bound for three days only to make travel nearly impossible once he finally could start moving again. He had risked his life many times to return for his friend.

Dave immediately retrieved the boys' cache of beaver and otter pelts that the Indian war party had overlooked, and emptied the snow from the wagon. Harrington then proceeded to transfer Will's bedding from the cave into the back of the wagon. Once Will and the traps were loaded into the wagon Dave headed the team toward the settlements. After nearly two weeks of sludging through the snow and muck, the boys arrived at the farm where Dave had borrowed the ox-team. They gave the owner of the team $60 worth of beaver pelts for the use of his cattle and allowed them to keep them until they reached Junction City. The farmer sent his son along with Dave and Will to return with the cattle. Arriving in Junction City, the boys sold their wagon and furs and returned to Leavenworth with a government mule train in March, 1860.[9]

It was not long before Will grew restless again. By summer he arranged for a man to help his Mother, sisters, and brother with the farm, and proceeded to Leavenworth to ask his old employers Russell, Majors, and Waddell for a job.

Arriving in Leavenworth, Will immediately met his old friend Lew Simpson, who was loading a bull-train bound to Atchison with supplies for Russell, Majors and Waddell's Overland Stage Company. Simpson implored his young friend to make the run out to Fort Laramie and beyond with him, but Will had another job in mind; he wanted to return to the Pony Express.

Simpson encouraged Will to ride as far as Atchison with him where he could meet with Mr. Russell to ask him for a job as a Pony Express rider. Encouraged with the idea, Will went home and informed his mother of his intentions. Mrs. Cody was very ill and Will had great difficulty obtaining her consent. After finally convincing her that he would be of no use on the farm and he could make more money on the plains, Will gave his mother all the money he earned trapping, kissed her good-bye and set out for Atchison.[10]

In Atchison Will met with William Russell and asked to be re-employed on the Pony Express line. Russell gave the boy a letter-of-introduction to one Joseph Alfred "Captain Jack" Slade, whom the company had recently hired as agent of the Julesburg station.

Slade was one of the most notorious characters in early American western history. It could be argued that Mark Twain's vivid description of Slade in his classic *Roughing It* immortalized him as the archetypal, cold-blooded, murderous western villain; Slade's deleterious nature became cliché in thousands of early western melodramas and Hollywood films—a stereotype that continues even today.

Twain, while riding Russell, Majors and Waddell's stagecoach line in 1861, introduces us to Jack Slade:

> Really and truly, two-thirds of the talk of drivers and conductors had been about this man Slade, ever since the day before we reached Julesburg. In order that the Eastern reader may have a clear conception of what a Rocky Mountain desperado is, in his highest state of development, I will reduce all this mass of overland gossip to one straight forward narrative, and present it in the following shape:
>
> Slade was born in Illinois of good parentage. At about twenty-six years of age he killed a man in a quarrel and fled the country. At St. Joseph, Missouri he joined one of the early California-bound immigrant trains, and was given the post of train-master. One day on the plains he had an angry dispute with one of his wagon drivers, and both drew their revolvers. But the wagon driver was the quicker artist and had his weapon cocked first. So Slade said it was a pity to waste life on so small a matter, and proposed that the pistols be thrown on the ground and the quarrel settled by a fist fight. The unsuspecting driver agreed, and threw down his pistol—whereupon Slade laughed at his simplicity, and shot him dead! [11]

Twain's fascination with Slade is obvious: the author saw richly manifested in Slade the free, "lawless" society of the American west in diabolical conflict with the "over-civilized," "European-influenced" American east. Yet probably more to the point, Twain knew a good story and Slade's notoriety among the "drivers and conductors" indicated to him a villain he knew readers would love to hate. Nearly two full chapters of Twain's *Roughing It* are devoted to describing Slade's murderous character and escapades.

Slade was reputed to have killed twenty-six men although the name and address of only one is known: Ole Jules Reni was believed to be fronting and sheltering a gang of outlaws who, armed with the former station manager's inside information, were preying on the line. Benjamin F. Ficklin, now route superintendent of the Pony Express, sent Slade to Julesburg to get rid of Ole Jules. Slade ousted Jules but the ousted station manager hid and ambushed Slade with a double-barreled shotgun. Ficklin later caught Jules and hanged him, but his outlaw comrades cut him down and revived him. When Slade recuperated, he stormed the outlaw compound near Rocky Ridge and captured Jules.[12]

Twain continues the tale in *Roughing It:*

> . . . Slade's myrmidons captured his ancient enemy Jules whom they found in a well-chosen hiding place in the remote vastness of the mountains, gaining a precarious livelihood with his rifle. They brought him to Rocky Ridge bound hand and foot and deposited him in the middle of the cattle-yard with his back against a post. It is said that the pleasure that lit Slade's face when he heard of it was something fearful to contemplate. He examined his enemy to see that he was securely tied and then went to bed, content to wait til morning before enjoying the luxury of killing him. Jules spent the night in the cattle-yard, and it is a region where warm nights are never known. In the morning Slade practiced on him with his revolver, nipping the flesh here and there, and occasionally clipping off a finger, while Jules begged him to kill him outright and put him out of his misery. Finally Slade reloaded, and walking up close to his victim, made some characteristic remarks and then dispatched him. The body lay there half a day, nobody venturing to touch it without orders, and then Slade detailed a party and assisted at the burial himself. But first he cut off the dead man's ears and put them in his vest pocket, where he carried them for some time with great satisfaction.[13]

Slade's headquarters were thirty-six miles west of Fort Laramie at a place called Horseshoe Station. Will Cody traveled with Lew Simpson's bull-train to Horseshoe Station and, in his autobiography, describes meeting Slade:

> Almost the very first person I saw after dismounting my horse was Slade. I walked up to him and presented Mr. Russell's letter, which he hastily opened and read. With a sweeping glance of his eye he took my measure from head to foot and then said:
>
> "My boy, you are too young for a Pony Express Rider. It takes men for that business."
>
> "I rode two months last year on Bill Trotter's division sir, and filled the bill then; and I think I am better able to ride now," said I.
>
> "What! are you the boy that was riding there, and was called the youngest rider on the road?"
>
> "I am the same boy," I replied, confident that everything was now right for me."

"I have heard of you before. You are a year or so older now, and I think you can stand it. I'll give you a trial anyhow, and if you weaken you can come back to Horseshoe Station and tend stock."[14]

Soon Cody was assigned a regular route from Red Buttes on the North Platte River to Three Crossings on the Sweetwater River—a distance of seventy-six miles. The route was a lonely and hazardous path including one particularly dangerous crossing of the North Platte; when rain-swollen the normally shallow stream would become over 12 feet deep raging with rapids.

On one run Cody galloped into his home station at Three Crossings only to discover the rider scheduled to replace him had been killed in a drunken brawl the night before. Cody continued the ride to Rocky Ridge, delivered the mail, and the made the same ride back to Three Crossings, covering a distance of 322 miles. While the legend of the murderous Captain Jack Slade spread throughout the west, the gunfighter was genuinely impressed with the young Cody and made sure the lad received extra pay for his amazing ride of endurance. Cody maintained that even though he was a dangerous man, in the two years he rode for the Pony Express, Slade was always kind and never spoke an angry word to him.[15]

Twain was equally seduced by Slade's deceptively charming, "dual" personality when he described him as

The most gentlemanly-appearing, quiet, and affable officer we had yet found along the road in the Overland Company's service was the person who sat at the head of the table, at my elbow. Never youth stared and shivered as I did when I heard them call him Slade.

Here was romance, and I was sitting face to face with it—looking upon it—touching it—hobnobbing with it, as it were! Here, right by my side, was the actual ogre who, in fights and brawls and various ways, had taken the lives of twenty-six human beings, or all men had lied about him. I suppose I was the proudest stripling that ever traveled to see strange lands and wonderful people.

He was so friendly and so gentle-spoken that I warmed to him in spite of his awful history. It was hardly possible to realize that this pleasant person was the pitiless scourge of the outlaws, the raw-headed and bloody-bones the nursing mothers of the mountains terrified their children with. And to this day I can remember nothing remarkable about Slade except that his face was rather broad across the cheek-bones, and that the cheek-bones were low and the lips pe-

culiarly thin and straight. But that was enough to leave something of
an effect upon me, for since then I seldom see a face possessing these
characteristics without fancying that the owner is a dangerous man.[16]

Murderers such as Slade were a reality of the times in the west, yet
Pony Express riders were accustomed to facing a different danger on each
ride. Fortunately, Alexander Majors' old "Presbyterian Code" rode with
the boys. Pony Express riders were instilled with Majors' "code of conduct"
to be strictly observed in the service of delivering the mail. Corny as it
might appear to modern readers, the code's discipline probably saved many
young riders' lives.

Riders completely understood that prompt mail delivery was their primary objective, and they were encouraged to deal with any assault, whether
from desperado or Indian, with superior speed. Each rider was confident
that no enemy's horse would ever be able to match the speed of his mount.
Initially an unwitting target, riders wore a uniform costume of a bright red
shirt and blue trousers, yet pragmatism prevailed, and soon most riders
converted to traditional western buckskin attire. Originally riders were also
given a horn to blow when they approached the station to alert the stock-
tender to his arrival. This proved to be too heavy and bulky and was soon
cast aside as most agents could see the dust of the rider's horse approaching as a warning signal of his arrival. Riders were assigned Colt revolvers
and a rifle and instructed to use them strictly as a last resort when faced
with conflict.

Nevertheless, riders did occasionally make irresistible targets for some
Indians—usually younger men in search of honor within their tribe, men
also for whom a swift horse would bring respect and standing in the community. Still, such a swift rider was nearly impossible to catch; only one
rider and one mail bag was lost in the Pony Express's nineteen month history. The total number of riders was never more than 120, yet these boys
collectively raced over 650,000 miles in the saddle, delivering the mail
without ever being "caught" by Indian or outlaw.

Isolated Pony Express stations, however, presented a much more vulnerable and inviting target for Indians and bandits. There, these swift
horses were corralled, and grain and supplies stacked and stored, usually
with only a handful of men stationed to protect the operation.

Buffalo Bill tells the story of one of his famous rides in which these vulnerable characteristics of the Pony Express riders and stations are made
quite clear:

As I was leaving Horse Creek one day a party of fifteen Indians jumped me in a sand ravine about a mile west of the station. They fired at me repeatedly, but missed their mark. I was mounted on a roan California horse—the fleetest steed I had. Putting spurs and whip to him, and lying flat on his back, I kept straight on for Sweet-water Bridge—eleven miles distant—instead of trying to turn back to Horse Creek. The Indians came on in hot pursuit, but my horse soon got away from them, and ran into the station two miles ahead of them. The stock-tender had been killed there that morning, and all the stock had been driven off by the Indians, and as I was there-fore unable to change horses, I continued on to Plontz's Station— twelve miles further—this making twenty-four miles straight with one horse.[17]

During the Pony Express era, Euroamerican relations with Indians worsened generally throughout the west. In the decade following the Cali-fornia gold rush Plains Indians witnessed the Great Migration with both curiosity and suspicion. It was becoming obvious to them that the change coming with the incredible numbers of immigrants was not going to be good for them. In 1849 immigrants brought disease with them. Asiatic Cholera, carried up the Missouri River on steamboats and out onto the plains with the immigrant's migrations, had devastated the Lakota. Ulti-mately worse than disease, however, in 1849, the U.S. government bought Fort Laramie, initiating a completely new era in the relationship between the Indian Nations of the Trans-Missouri and Washington. Prior to the purchase of the fort the nearest military outpost was 700 miles to the east; suddenly, Fort Laramie, the largest multi-cultural "city" of the Great Plains, was garrisoned with U.S. Infantry.

In 1851 the tribes of the Rockies and Northern Plains met with United States representatives at Fort Laramie to forge a treaty. In the spirit of good faith, friendship and peace, the tribes agreed to allow the United States to establish roads and military posts across their lands.[18]

Initially, the Lakota welcomed the soldiers; the Fort Laramie Treaty misled them into thinking that the troops were coming to help them pro-tect their land from the destruction they were witnessing stemming from the immense numbers of immigrants passing through their country. Inci-dents of trouble between immigrants and Lakotas remained rare and iso-lated until 1854 when trouble erupted between Indians, immigrants, and troops.

In June, 1853, the Sixth Infantry, under the command of Lieutenant

R.B. Garnett, was stationed at Fort Laramie. Also at the fort that summer were the usual large numbers of Cheyenne and Sioux waiting for distribution of government annuities. A large camp of Oglala and Brule Lakotas had set up camp across the river from Fort Laramie.

One day a Minniconjou Lakota visitor to the Oglala/Brule camp fired a shot at an enlisted man crossing the river in a ferry skiff. Immigrant eyewitnesses blamed the trooper for the incident, swearing they had seen the soldier treat the Lakota very rudely by refusing to ferry the Indian over in the skiff. Furious, the Minniconjou fired a "warning" shot at the racist trooper, igniting the controversy.

Five soldiers promptly rode into the Oglala/Brule camp intent on arresting the Minniconjou shooter. Someone fired at the group of soldiers and a spontaneous firefight erupted in which five Lakotas were killed. Four days later Indians retaliated, attacking a small immigrant camp near the fort, killing a family of four; soldiers quickly extracted revenge by killing Lakotas wantonly.

Only the experience of Indian Agent Thomas "Broken Hand" Fitzpatrick was able to calm the situation. A veteran of thirty years in the Trans-Missouri, Fitzpatrick was a former partner of Jim Bridger in the Rocky Mountain Fur Company. Like other mountain men, Fitzpatrick had hard-won, life-long relationships with many Indian leaders. Unfortunately for Indians, these men's diplomatic wisdom was generally ignored from the beginning by the U.S. military. While Fitzpatrick was Indian Agent at Fort Laramie, relationships with Plains Indians went smoothly. Then Washington sent troops. Fitzpatrick first thought it amusing that the government sent infantry to deal with perhaps the greatest equestrian warriors the world has ever known.

Using all his diplomatic skills, Fitzpatrick counciled with chiefs and war leaders to prevent the situation from erupting into a major slaughter; Indians did, after all, greatly outnumber the immigrants and soldiers in their country at the time; nearly 5,000 Lakota camped at Fort Laramie in 600 lodges. The Sixth Infantry was a skeleton garrison of 50 troopers at peak. In returning to peace, however, the Lakota had learned that soldiers were not in their country to protect them.

Then, in the summer of 1854, a Mormon train was passing Fort Laramie when a cow strayed away from the immigrants and into a large camp of Brule and Minniconjou Lakotas. The Mormon owner, afraid to pursue his cow into the Indians' camp, fled after his train, deserting his animal. A Minniconjou immediately shot and butchered the cow.

Second Lieutenant J. L. Grattan, already tugging at his leash after the incident with the ferry skiff, viewed the situation as a certain route to advance his military career. Fresh out of West Point and eager for a fight, Grattan proceeded to upscale the situation from a simple stray, abandoned cow into a dangerous military incident. The second lieutenant called for volunteers for a hazardous mission and selected 29 men to proceed to the Lakota village to arrest the cow-thief.

An arrest order for a Lakota warrior in 1854 was tantamount to a death sentence. No Lakota man would allow himself to be arrested; a Lakota warrior could only find honor dying properly—fighting. The chiefs among the Lakota, fully realizing soldiers with Howitzer guns were marching upon them, could not convince the man responsible for butchering the cow to surrender. Grattan would not wait. He ordered his men to fire upon the combined villages of Brules and Minniconjous. The Lakota fought back fiercely, killing Grattan and all twenty-nine of his men.

Now only the wisdom and experience of James Bordeaux, the French trader who had been at Fort Laramie since 1839, was able to prevent the angry Lakota from attacking the vulnerable fort. Tragically, however, Indians had learned the U.S. military was their enemy. They had also learned to view U.S. treaties with cynicism and caution.[19]

Soon news of "hostile" Lakota began to spread like a prairie fire across the plains. By November Brules began attacking mail wagons near Horse Creek on the immigrant's road; next, they raided a trading post west of Fort Laramie. Soon-to-be-famous Brule Warrior Chief Spotted Tail took part in these mail-wagon raids, an offense for which he later bravely surrendered himself to avoid military retaliation upon his people. Spotted Tail was taken to Fort Kearney where he spent two years as a prisoner of the military.

Nevertheless, the pattern had been set in motion; an isolated incident would create intense misunderstandings to which the military usually responded with force, eliciting violent retaliation by Plains Indians; indeed, it was not long before an incident nearly identical to the one with the stray Mormon cow occurred with the Cheyenne, who picked up some stray horses from an immigrant train passing through their country. Once again, foiled arrest attempts led to military violence and killing, which prompted Indian retaliatory raids and created situations calling for more troops to be sent into Cheyenne territory.

Complicating matters, thousands more immigrants poured into the territory annually. Throughout the decade following the California gold rush

500 wagons a day passed Fort Laramie. By 1857 the Missouri River lands were settled as far upriver as Sioux City with twenty-three steamboats running regular service from St. Louis to that city. Increasingly, tribes that refused to move out of the way of the traffic or who resisted the encroachment of immigrants onto sacred ancestral lands were considered "hostile."

By the time the Pony Express began in 1860, Plains Indians, although initially friendly and helpful to immigrants, were indeed hostile. Angered by broken treaties, repetitious lies, theft of their properties and lands, and the ruthless, often wanton, killing of their people, tribal people of the Great Plains, Rocky Mountains, and high deserts were all beginning to experience terrific hardships caused by the rapid changes being brought by these new people.

When the Paiutes went on the warpath only a month after the Pony Express began operations, matters became serious. With Paiute raids in Utah and Nevada's high deserts and Sioux and Cheyenne raids on Pony Express stations on the Great Plains increasing, nearly all 2,000 miles of the Pony Express route was through "hostile" territory. In only a couple of months of operation Waddell estimated the firm had lost $75,000 to Indian raids.

This escalation of Indian raids on Pony Express stations and riders forced Russell, Majors and Waddell into a situation that demanded action or, more accurately, nonaction. Alexander Majors announced that without military protection along the Pony Express route he would close down mail service. As expected, Washington ignored Majors's ultimatum and, on May 31, 1860, the Pony Express stopped all service.

San Francisco newspapers echoed the public's outrage that the government would not help the Pony Express. After a decade of isolation, the speed of communication the Pony Express offered had become greatly important to the citizens of California and, many argued, to the future of America. In contrast, the government argued that by interrupting mail service, Russell, Majors, and Waddell had proved that the venture was not ready for a federal subsidy. Men of action have a difficult adjustment to idleness; Pony Express riders were not likely to sit out such an impasse. The Indians had become so brazen and had stolen so much stock, however, that Russell, Majors, and Waddell decided to discontinue the Pony Express for at least six weeks and to run the stages only occasionally during that period; indeed, it would have been impossible to even continue the enterprise much longer without restocking the line.

While idle, a party was organized to go out and search for stolen stock. The party was composed of forty well-armed and mounted stage drivers, express riders, stock-tenders and ranchmen brewing for a fight with any number of Indians.

"Wild Bill," who had been driving stage on the road and had recently come down to the division, was elected captain of the company. The group immediately decided that the stolen stock had been taken to the head of the Powder River and vicinity. Cody's party spurred their horses toward the Lakota hunting grounds.

At the head of Horse Creek, about twenty miles from the Sweetwater Bridge, the posse of plainsmen found an Indian trail running north toward Powder River, and could see by the tracks that most of the horses had been recently shod and were undoubtedly their stolen stock.[20]

The party quickly headed further north into Powder River country. Near a tributary of Powder River called Crazy Woman's Creek, the trail the Pony Express vigilantes followed indicated the Indian war party had merged with another, larger group—within a day's time.

With each mile the party was not acutely aware that they were now in the heart of the hostile country and might at any moment be ambushed. So they advanced with more caution and kept a sharp lookout. Approaching Clear Creek, another tributary of Powder River, three miles in the distance on the opposite side of the creek, they saw horses grazing—a sure sign the Indians were there.

Never before having been followed so far into their own country by white men, the Indians, thinking themselves in safety, had neglected to put out any scouts. Wild Bill immediately scouted the camp layout and held a council to plan how to attack it.

The posse knew very well they would be outnumbered at least three to one. Wild Bill suggested they wait until dusk and then creep as close as possible to the camp. Then they would storm the camp and surprise the Indians by stampeding the horse herd.

Hickok's plan was executed to perfection and the Indian camp was totally overcome by the surprise charge. Bewildered, the Indians did not recover from the shock until the company of plainsmen had stampeded the horse herd and gotten away with the Indians' herd of ponies as well as their stolen stock.[21]

The Pony Express "war party" returned four days later with a herd of one-hundred captured Indian ponies as well as their own horses. Several days of celebration followed with the victorious group taking control of the Sweetwater Bridge store for a spree of drinking, gambling, and fighting. After the drunken binge had gone on for three days Slade arrived.

Having heard the news of the recovered horses, the gunfighter rode in to take part in the fun. He soon got into a quarrel with a stage driver and shot and killed him.[22]

William Russell was not about to let Indian troubles stop him. On June 26 the Pony Express resumed operations with service increased from weekly to semi-weekly. Russell seemed determined to get a government subsidy or go bankrupt in the effort.

Meanwhile, impressed with young Cody, Captain Jack Slade invited the boy to his headquarters at the Horseshoe Station. Slade suggested Cody should come to work for him and that he would only send him out to ride when necessary. Aware Slade's offer would give him more time to hunt in the region, Cody jumped at the chance. Soon he was able to explore one of the grandest hunting grounds of the North American continent.[23]

At sunset on one of these hunts Will stumbled upon a gang of desperadoes hiding in a cave in the mountains. Entering the group's hideout, the boy recognized two of the men as former teamsters from old friend Lew Simpson's bull-trains—men Cody knew to be wanted for the robbery and murder of a rancher. Immediately discerning he had fallen into a den of murderers and thieves, Will breathed a little easier when he realized the former teamsters did not recognize him. In order to explain his sudden appearance, Will began by telling the gang the truth—that he had stumbled upon their camp while hunting. Calmly, the boy bought time for himself asking if he might stay with them for the night. The leader of the gang agreed that this was the best plan. Will next offered to leave his rifle as "security" while he went down the creek to retrieve his horse and supplies. The suspicious gang leader agreed, but sent two men with Will as insurance, throwing a kink in the boy's plan to flee and desert his rifle.

As the trio walked down the rocky creek bed toward Will's horse the boy knew he had to think quickly. Remembering he had killed two sage hens earlier in the afternoon, Will hatched a new plan. The boy immediately took control of the situation and engaged the men in conversation, casually mentioning that he had killed two sage hens only moments before finding their camp; soon the men were planning how to cook the birds.

Once the trio got Will's horse and the sage hens they turned back toward the hideout; Will knew then that he must act fast! One man led his horse while the other followed behind the boy. It was becoming dark so Cody decided to make his move. He dropped one of the sage hens and called out to his captors that he had lost the bird. As the outlaw behind him searched the ground for the hen, the boy pulled his Colt revolver and struck the man on the head, knocking him senseless. He turned quickly, only to discover the second outlaw facing him. Cody instantly shot the man and fled on horseback down the mountain.[24]

The outlaws quickly emerged like angry hornets from the dugout and raced to the sound of the gunshot. Discovering their dead comrade, the mob then ran on foot in hot pursuit of Will. Being on foot actually helped the desperadoes, as Will's horse was having a hard time negotiating the declivity in the dark. The gang finally came so near that Will wisely decided to abandon the horse, hoping the outlaws would follow his pony. The mob fell for the ruse and Will was able to give them the slip. Will walked the twenty-five miles back to the station, arriving at dawn.

Slade himself was there and at once organized a posse to go after the horse thieves. At daybreak twenty well-armed stage-drivers, stock-tenders, and ranchmen galloped in the direction of the dugout.[25]

The desperadoes had fled, leaving behind a freshly dug grave. Slade's posse located their trail heading toward Denver but decided not to follow. Nevertheless, theft of horses in the region dropped dramatically with the rustlers' departure.

As might be expected, Slade was not destined for a long life with a peaceful end. His drinking and violent behavior continued to become dangerous for everyone around him. After a drunken spree of gunplay in which he shot up the post canteen at nearby Fort Halleck, Russell, Majors, and Waddell fired him.

Slade then traveled to Virginia City, Montana, to take advantage of the opportunities springing up there from a gold strike. Slade's drinking became much worse, however, and he and his band of thugs repeatedly shot up Virginia City. The situation became so violent that storekeepers would close their doors and people would hide when Slade and his gang rode into town. Slade was frequently arrested and, when sober, usually politely paid his fines and offered sincere apologies. One fateful morning, however, when Sheriff J. M. Fox went to arrest Slade, the desperado tore up the warrant and threw it at the lawman's feet. The act was a declaration of war, as the miner's court had grown weary of tolerating Slade's violent behavior. He was arrested by vigilantes and hanged on March 10, 1864.

Upon learning of Slade's tearful gallows lamentations begging for his life, Mark Twain, presenting a question that Americans have yet to answer concerning its obsession with violent antiheroes, closed the book on the archetypal western villain with this insight:

There is something about the desperado nature that is wholly unaccountable—at least it looks unaccountable. It is this. The true desperado is gifted with splendid courage, and yet he will take the most infamous advantage of his enemy; armed and free, he will stand up before a host and fight until he is all shot to pieces, and yet when he is under the gallows and helpless he will cry and plead like a child. Words are cheap, and it is easy to call Slade a coward (all executed men who do not "die game" are promptly called cowards by unreflecting people), and when we read of Slade that he "had so exhausted himself by tears, prayers, and lamentations, that he had scarcely strength left to stand under the fatal beam," the disgraceful word suggests itself in a moment—yet in frequently defying and inviting the vengeance of banded Rocky Mountain cutthroats by shooting down their comrades and leaders, and never offering to hide or fly, Slade showed that he was a man of peerless bravery. No coward would dare that. Many a notorious coward, many a chicken-livered poltroon, coarse, brutal, degraded, has made his dying speech without a quaver in his voice and been swung into eternity with what looked like the calmest fortitude, and so we are justified in believing, from the low intellect of such a creature, that it was not moral courage that enabled him to do it. Then, if moral courage is not the requisite quality, what could it have been that this stout-hearted Slade lacked?—this bloody, desperate kindly mannered, urbane gentleman, who never hesitated to warn his most ruffianly enemies that he would kill them whenever or wherever he came across them next! I think it is a conundrum worth investigating.[76]

In spite of ruthless desperadoes, Indian raids and under-financing, the Pony Express continued. Tensions between opposing factions in government worsened, however, until Southern leaders announced they would secede from the Union if Republican presidential candidate Abraham Lincoln was elected in November, 1860. In a narrow victory Lincoln received 40%, a minority, of the popular vote, yet drew 180 electoral votes to win. Once the votes were tallied the results were telegraphed to St. Joseph, whereupon Pony Express riders raced 1,800 miles to Fort Churchill, where the next telegraph office tapped the news to San Francisco. Only twelve days after election day San Francisco newspapers printed detailed stories of Lincoln's victory.

Swift accounts of the presidential elections were critical to California remaining in the Union. Political lines-in-the-sand had been drawn in the

United States for over fifty years over the issue of the abolition of slavery, and the nation had become completely polarized. Some California factions even called for the state to secede from the Union to create a separate republic. Vast ideological chasms separated opposing regional economic and cultural lifestyles and formal debate over constitutional interpretation had only widened the canyon; indeed, blood had been shed on the floor of Congress as senators and representatives came to blows in legal argument. It had become obvious to everyone that civil war was eminent.

During this period in American history, as now, presidential elections were held in November. Inaugurations then, however, took place four months later—in March. In the interim after Lincoln's election, as political ultimatums became much more numerous and serious, "Lame Duck" President James Buchanan did little to attempt to hold the Union together. Half-hearted compromise only served to set the stage in Washington for subterfuge and deception as many Southerners, soon to deflect to the Confederacy, held high offices in the United States government. Spies and counter-spies set traps for one another in the intriguing, duplicitous pre-war environment.

Southern states were good to their word concerning Abraham Lincoln's election. Shortly after the November election, South Carolina called a convention in which delegates voted unanimously to secede from the Union. Georgia, Alabama, Mississippi, Florida, Louisiana, and Texas quickly followed South Carolina and withdrew from the Union. In early 1861 delegates from these seceding states met in Montgomery, Alabama to draft a constitution for the Confederate States of America.

Lincoln was inaugurated on March 4, 1861; perhaps the crowning achievement of the Pony Express was the swift delivery of Lincoln's inaugural address. On March 17, only 13 days after Lincoln's being sworn in as sixteenth President of the United States, San Francisco newspapers published his address. On April 12, 1861, Confederate forces shelled Union troops at Fort Sumter in Charleston, South Carolina. The Civil War had begun.

The final sad chapter in the otherwise sterling history of the Pony Express is tragically tainted with a major scandal nurtured in this treacherous pre-war environment. Ironically, it involved Indian Affairs bonds—money belonging to Indians obtained through land transactions, and held in trust by the U.S. Government.

The U.S. government owed Russell, Majors and Waddell a large sum of money. Since the late 1840s, the firm had built its empire shipping freight to army outposts throughout the frontier. By 1858 the Department of Interior owed the shipping firm $500,000, which it could not pay. With the Civil War looming on the horizon the situation became even more strained because military personnel in the west were being transferred to the east to prepare for conflict. Fewer troops required less shipping of supplies; consequently, Russell, Majors and Waddell were experiencing major financial reversals. Furthermore, Majors and Waddell's financial forebodings concerning the Pony Express were coming painfully true; each letter was costing the partnership seventeen dollars to deliver, yet the company only received five dollars to deliver it. Waddell estimated the partnership was losing over $50,000 a month on the Pony Express.

Russell's intrepid efforts to win government financial support for the Pony Express had failed to secure a subsidy. In the months previous to the Civil War a bill had been presented in Congress to proclaim the Central Overland Route as the U.S. government's official mail route, but President Buchanan offered no support for the legislation and it died on the floor. With sharply decreasing fortunes in his shipping business and the Pony Express, William Russell was forced to go to Washington and demand restitution.

In the late 1850s, Russell had convinced Secretary of War John B. Floyd to issue "acceptances" to his firm in lieu of the $500,000 the department owed, but could not pay because of lack of funds. These "acceptances" were formal documents that acknowledged the existence of the debt while simultaneously promising to reconcile the debt at some later date—a "governmental i.o.u." As for Russell's end of the bargain: He promised not to call for the notes to be paid on the due date; rather, he agreed to use them as collateral with New York bankers.

Between March 25, 1858, and October 1, 1860, Secretary of War Floyd issued over five million dollars worth of these acceptances to various firms. Russell, Majors, and Waddell held $861,000 worth of these acceptances.[27] Between October 1, 1860, and Christmas Eve, 1860, a Department of Interior clerk named Godard Baily, who was married to a niece of Secretary Floyd, withdrew $870,000 worth of Indian Affairs bonds and turned them over to William Russell. This transaction was announced on December 24, 1860, and Russell was arrested and held for $200,000 bail.

When Russell tried to use the acceptances he had received as security for loans, the New York bankers refused to take the acceptances. Consequently, the Secretaries of the Interior and War had to do something to get Russell out of his predicament. Their solution was to make the government bonds available to Russell so that he could use them for collateral to get a loan. Presumably acting on orders from his superiors, Baily gave Russell $870,000 worth of the abstracted Indian Affairs bonds and received the acceptances of a like amount as security for the bonds.

That all this activity was performed in secrecy implies that the people involved knew they were breaking the law. On the other hand, Russell seemed not to have had any consciousness of guilt. His obvious intention was to pay off his loan, retrieve the bonds and return them to the government. In doing so, he would have relieved himself from his most demanding financial obligations and the government would get its bonds back.[28]

Russell's scandalous arrest served to flush John B. Floyd's true allegiances from concealment; his covert dealing revealed, the Secretary of War was forced to flee to his native Virginia and into open service of the Confederacy. Meanwhile, the scandal brought Russell's friends forward. Having had to empty his deep pockets before the scandal broke, Russell had to borrow a large sum of money from his old friend, stage-coach mogul, Ben Holladay. Bolstered with Holladay's loan, Russell was encouraged when he returned from the east as western leaders—including some governors—expressed their united support with a testimonial ball. Russell never claimed to be a victim of subterfuge. Although his methods were questionable, Russell defended himself with the argument that the government owed him a very large amount of money and he was acting within his legal rights to recoup it.[29]

Secretary of Interior Jacob Thompson resigned in January, 1861 as southern states seceded en masse. He later became Governor of Mississippi and after Lincoln's assassination was accused of complicity and fled to Europe. Fred Reinfield sums up this sad chapter in Pony Express history:

> The fact that Gwin, Floyd and Thompson were all strong supporters of the Confederacy lends some color to the speculation that they took part in varying degrees in an intrigue to deprive the north of the mail routes by discrediting Russell. Nevertheless, this must remain in the realm of speculation.
>
> On the other hand, if Russell was a dupe, he was a willing dupe, rendered desperate, no doubt, by his pressing financial difficulties. It is hard to believe that in the matter of the bonds he emerged with completely clean hands. A sorry story, in painful contrast to the heroism and devotion of the Pony Express riders. Regardless of what the underlying facts were in this scandal, the fate of the Pony Ex-

press was sealed. The company would never get a mail contract from the government.[30]

Pronouncing the Pony Express "primarily an advertising venture," Don Russell concludes:

The story of the Pony Express is also that of a race with a telegraph line moving both westward and eastward towards a junction. The lines were joined on October 24, 1861, providing thorough service from New York to San Francisco. The last run of the Pony Express was on November 18. Russell, Majors, and Waddell failed to get the mail contract they sought for their Central Overland, California, and Pike's Peak Company, last of their numerous business organizations. The Pony Express was run at a loss—that was expected. But the failure to get the mail contract, added to all their other troubles, caused the downfall of the partnership in all its ramifications. The triumph for which they are remembered bankrupted them.

Why is it remembered? It was spectacular and it had much contemporary publicity, yet a recent historian notes that almost nothing was written about it for half a century after its brief existence. Undoubtedly, the Pony Express owes much of its continuing glamour to one of its riders, William F. Cody. For three decades a representation of the Pony Express was a spectacle at every performance of Buffalo Bill's Wild West. No other act was more consistently on its program. It was easy to stage, and it had the interest of a race, as well as re-creating a romantic episode. It is highly unlikely that the Pony Express would be so well remembered had not Buffalo Bill so glamorized it; in common opinion Buffalo Bill and the Pony Express are indissolubly linked.[31]

Shunned by Eastern bankers and financiers as a result of the scandal, William Russell became a broken, forgotten man. He lived with his son for the last years of his life and died in 1872. Also financially ruined, Waddell was never able to get back into business and his last years were filled with a series of misfortunes. He lost his son in the Civil War and his home was raided numerous time by Union soldiers before he was forced to sign an oath of loyalty to the United States. He was also dogged by continual lawsuits and forced to sell valued property to pay taxes. In the end, his friends turned against him, and he died in his daughter's home a few months before Russell in 1872.

Majors, however, fared better than his partners and remained in the freighting business. By 1867 he had relocated to Salt Lake City and became involved in the construction of the Union Pacific Railroad before dying in 1900.

Fred Reinfield perfectly sums up the relationship between Buffalo Bill and his first employers: "Russell, Majors and Waddell had put on the first Wild West show with the Pony Express. Everyone applauded—but no one paid at the gate."[32]

DESTINY

Chapter Four

Come all you bold robbers and open your ears,
Of Quantrell the lion-heart you quickly will hear,
With his band of bold raiders in double quick time
He came to burn Lawrence just over the line.
They came to burn Lawrence, they came not to stay
Jim Lane he was up at the breaking of day;
He saw them a-coming and got in a fright,
Then crawled in a corncrib to get out of sight.

—"Quantrell," Author Anonymous (*Cowboy Songs*, Ed. John Lomax)

WILL Cody left the Pony Express at Horseshoe Station upon hearing that his mother's fight with tuberculosis had taken a turn for the worse. He arrived in Leavenworth in June, 1861. The Civil War, which was now two months old, had taken a unique expression peculiar to the "border" region of Kansas and Missouri; guerrillas and hoodlums of both Confederate and Union persuasion terrorized normal citizens on either side of the border. Not unlike the tradition of Indian warrior societies of the Great Plains who regularly sent out war parties into enemy territories, frontier militia groups, not enlisted in the regular Union or Confederate armies, yet purely for territorial dominance and revenge and to carry on their own tradition of acrimonious raids upon one another, robbed and pillaged each other's villages. Kansas raiders called themselves "Jayhawkers" and Missourians referred to themselves as "Bushwackers."

Admitted to the Union as a free state in 1861, Kansas was frequently raided by a notorious character named William Clarke Quantrell. Quantrell was from Ohio and had left a trail of murder and graft behind him as he headed west. A shrewd political opportunist, Quantrell often secretly aligned himself with both sides of opposing factions, a practice which eventually led to his being run out of the town of Lawrence. Quantrell fled to Missouri where he initiated frequent murderous raids over the border in Kansas.

Two men who stood in direct opposition to Quantrell were James H. Lane and Dr. Charles R. Jennison. Lane, who later became a U.S. Senator, was a veteran of the Mexican War. Appointed Brigadier General by President Abraham Lincoln, Lane recruited three regiments of men to serve under him in Kansas. A devoted disciple of the militant John Brown, Dr. Jennison considered every Missourian an enemy. As the leader of the outlaw "red leg militia" Jennison took perverse pleasure burning houses, stealing horses and cattle and terrorizing the border region. He boasted that "Missouri mothers hush their children to sleep by whispering the name of Doc Jennison."[1]

Fifteen-year-old Will Cody returned to violent Kansas in 1861 intending to join the Union army. Although fifteen might seem young to modern readers, a large percentage of Civil War volunteers were under age eighteen; drummers' and fifers' legal age to serve was sixteen. Will's mother, although an adamant Union supporter, would have nothing to do with his youthful wishes to fight in the war. Tuberculosis had beaten her health into a fragile state and, playing upon this, she begged Will to wait to join the fight. Always the dutiful son, Will agreed. Will, however, anxious to avenge his father's horrible treatment at the hands of pro-slavery Missourians, became involved in an "embarrassing" episode. Leavenworth being an important outfitting post for the west and southwest, a large number of troops were garrisoned by the old fort. There in Leavenworth, Cody met several men who, like himself, had been victimized at the hands of the Missouri Bushwackers. Seeking vengeance for the way his family had been treated, Cody joined with Chandler's Jayhawkers to raid Missouri.[2] This ignominious period in Cody's life is so contemptible that the mention of it in his autobiography indicates it is truthful.[3]

Chandler launched a raid into Missouri to steal horses—an operation at which his band of thieves met with great success. Ashamed of his participation, Cody goes to great lengths in his autobiography to explain his "horse-thieving" actions in the name of war, yet the entire enterprise of raids to steal horses seems a trait common to the Great Plains of the nineteenth century, when horses and war party raids dictated much of everyone's existence. A cornerstone of Plains Indians' reality was regularly raiding enemy camps to steal horses and generally reek havoc upon their neighbors; indeed, raiding and horse theft was the path to honor rather than dishonor; most of an Indian's wealth and community standing came from noble horse theft and plundering. The paradoxical perspectives concerning the ethics of horse theft reveal perplex, contradictory philosophies separating ironically shared traditional cultural similarities between Native and European Americans. This horse-stealing "game" was also the basis of a great portion of initial social interaction between Native and Euroamericans—particularly traders and mountain men. Friendly plains and mountain tribes would often playfully announce to trapper acquaintances that they intended to steal their horses; sometimes they would even tell the mountain men the night they intended to raid in order to make the "game" more fun for all involved. This is not to suggest people did not get killed playing this "game" of horse theft; rather, it implies diametrical perspectives revealed in similar traditions of Native and Euroamerican frontier culture. It also reveals the unique blending occurring naturally between Native Americans and Euroamericans on the fringes of their separate cultures. Indeed, Cody had already been on a retaliatory horse-stealing raid while serving as a Pony Express rider. Rather than being ashamed of his behavior in this situation, however, Cody was proud of recovering the stolen Pony Express horses as well as stealing a large number of the Indians' horses. The "white" war party's success is cause for a massive celebration of drinking and gambling of the horses stolen from Indians. It was one matter to steal Indian horses and yet another to steal horses from whites. Before long government officials heard of Chandler's operations and put detectives on his trail. Soon thereafter several of Chandler's guerrillas were arrested. Will's mother learned he was involved with Chandler's jayhawks and severely scolded him for such dishonorable behavior. Will agreed and quickly abandoned guerrilla warfare.[4]

Not long after abandoning Chandler's band of jayhawks Will was delighted to run into his old friend Wild Bill Hickok again. Hickok had returned from the mountains with an empty bull-train which he was taking to Rolla, Missouri. Wild Bill immediately offered Will a job and soon the pair was off to Rolla, where they loaded the wagons and delivered them to Springfield, Missouri. Arriving in Springfield, Hickok and Cody heard of the autumn horse races in St. Louis and, since Wild Bill had brought a marvelous horse down from the mountains, the pair decided they would try their luck participating in the races. The boys decided that Cody would ride the horse and confidently proceeded to wager everything, including the horse, on the race. They lost.

St. Louis was the largest city either Hickok or Cody had ever seen and, intimidated and depressed, the pair went looking for work. Being older and experienced on the frontier, Hickok quickly found employment as a government scout. Next Wild Bill borrowed enough money to buy Will a steamboat ticket to Leavenworth; the friends said good-bye and Hickok departed for Springfield. Several weeks later in Springfield Hickok got into an argument one night over a watch won from professional gambler Dave Tuffs in a poker game. Tuffs and Hickok challenged each other and the next morning Wild Bill killed Tuffs in a pistol duel on the streets.

Meanwhile, Will continued to stay close to his mother as her health deteriorated, yet he also accepted jobs which took him out on the Kansas plains. In the spring of 1862 he was a scout for the Ninth Kansas Volunteers on an expedition into Kiowa and Comanche territory on the Arkansas River. He still apparently harbored ideas of avenging his father's death; in the fall Will returned to Leavenworth, enrolled in school, and joined the "Red Legged Scouts." The concept of Brigadier Generals Thomas Ewing and James C. Blunt, the "Red Legged Scouts" was organized early in the war. The organization had originally included a number of "Jennison's Jawhawkers," but most had joined Colonel Charles R. Jennison in forming the Seventh Cavalry in October, 1861. "Redlegs" were, however, described by some more as indiscriminate thieves and murderers rather than "jayhawkers."[5]

In 1863 the guerrilla wars in Kansas/Missouri intensified while Will served as wagonmaster for some merchants and led a small train to Denver, arriving in September, 1863. News preceded Will's arrival on August 20, 1863. Quantrell invaded Kansas with a force of 300 men and attacked and burned Lawrence, killing two-hundred people in four hours. Family tragedy was, however, of more immediate concern to Will than Bushwacker raids. Will's sisters soon wrote to him in Denver summoning him home; their mother was dying! Will barely made it back to Kansas in time; Mary Cody died November 22, 1863.

Even as a pre-adolescent boy cast out upon the Great Plains with bulltrains, bullwackers, Indian raids, Pony Express bandits, and gun-slinging murderers, Mary Cody remained a stabilizing force in Will's life. After her death Will lost his direction and entered a dolorous period of grief. Fortunately, his older sister, Julia, had married a gentleman named J. A. Goodman. The marriage was timely as Mr. Goodman moved into the Cody household to watch over the family—a responsibility always keenly felt by Will.

Grieving his mother's death, however, Cody headed into Leavenworth and embarked upon a prolonged period of drinking and carousing with

gamblers and bums. After about two months of this behavior Will was becoming a self-described "hard case" when the Seventh Kansas Regiment
returned to Leavenworth from the war. Among them Will met quite a few
men who encouraged him to enlist and go back to the war with them. One
day "under the influence of 'bad' whiskey," Will awoke to discover he had
joined the Seventh Kansas.[6]

Even if Cody enlisted in a drunken stupor his attitude promptly became
heroic when he sobered. In February, 1864, as Sherman began his march
through the heart of the South in Mississippi, the Seventh Kansas regiment, known as "Jennison's Jayhawkers," was reorganized at Fort Leavenworth and sent to Memphis, Tennessee, to join General A. J. Smith's
command.[7]

General Andrew Jackson Smith was preparing to engage rebel forces in
southern Tennessee as part of a major Union thrust into the heart of the
Confederacy. Throughout the spring Generals Ulysses S. Grant and
Robert E. Lee had been fiercely locked in continuing epic battles in Virginia while General William T. Sherman had begun his historic advance
from Chattanooga to Atlanta. With no Confederate forces to attack the
northern rear of these maneuvers, Sherman planned to divide Dixie and
march to the sea.

Generals Grant, Sherman and Sheridan experimented with environmental warfare during the Civil War. Grant had ordered Sheridan to turn
Virginia's beautiful Shenandoah Valley into a barren waste. Sherman would,
of course, employ this "scorched earth" military tactic, tearing through the
south. Later, the same three men would use environmental warfare with
great skill in the west to destroy Plains Indian culture as they methodically
attacked the buffalo herds.

Nevertheless, as he tore into the heart of the Confederacy, a major
problem existed for General Sherman on the western perimeter of his attack. In order for his campaign to succeed, Sherman would need clear, un-
hampered communications with his western rear. The Confederate cavalry
leader, Nathan Bedford Forrest, however, had a small command whose repeated successful attacks created major communication problems for Sherman's rear. About the time Cody was enlisting, Forrest had defeated the
cavalry column of Brigadier General William Sooy Smith at Okaloma,
Mississippi, and had driven it back to Memphis. In March, while the Seventh Kansas was advancing toward the front, Forrest seized Fort Pillow,
killing most of its garrison of Negro troops. Having been soundly defeated
by Forrest at Brices Crossroads, Brigadier General Samuel D. Sturgis was

retreating when advance forces of the Seventh Kansas arrived at Col-
liersville on the Memphis and Charleston Railroad in June just in time to
save him.[8]

General Sherman was so frustrated by General Forrest's brilliant resistance on his flanks he ordered his men to hunt him down, "if it costs ten
thousand lives and bankrupts the federal treasury."[9]

Will Cody was part of the Union effort to render General Forrest inef-
fective. Cody's outfit pulled into Memphis about the time General Sturgis
was defeated by the brilliant Confederate general. General Smith quickly
reorganized Sturgis's broken forces and proceeded deep into Mississippi in
pursuit of Forrest. Near Tupelo Smith engaged and defeated Forrest. Soon
after Forrest's defeat Cody became a non-commissioned officer and was
assigned as a scout.[10]

Later, in Cape Girardeau, Cody was acting as a sort of "scout/spy" and
attempting to gather information on Confederate troop movements in
southwest Missouri, when he ran into an old friend. As part of his reconnaissance Will was dressed in a gray Confederate uniform when he rode up
to a Missouri farm and entered the house. Once inside, Will noticed a man
in a Confederate uniform sitting at a table enjoying a bowl of bread and
milk. "He looked up as I entered," Cody continues,

> and startled me by saying:
> "You little rascal, what are you doing in those 'secesh' clothes?"
> Judge of my surprise when I recognized in the stranger my old
> friend and partner, Wild Bill, disguised as a Confederate officer.
> "I ask you the same question sir," said I without the least
> hesitation.
> "Hush! Sit down and have some bread and milk, and we'll talk it
> all over afterward," said he.[11]

Having not seen each other since parting in St. Louis after losing the
horse races, the two scouts, coincidentally disguised as Confederate officers, soon secretly reminisced about life out on the Great Plains. Wild Bill
was able to give Cody important information concerning Confederate
troop activity in the region as well as a packet of letters to deliver to Major
General Alfred Pleasanton and Brigadier General John McNeil. Don Russell explains: "Although the spy papers and the disguise are melodramatic
fare, such things actually went on during the Civil War. The most fantastic
part of the story is Wild Bill and Cody sitting down with bowls of bread
and milk."[12]

Later, Cody witnessed an incredible scene in Wild Bill Hickok's Civil
War history: Near Fort Scott, Kansas Union and Confederate armies faced
each other on the battlefield preparing to charge in mortal combat. Suddenly two horsemen broke from rebel ranks galloping toward Seventh
Kansas lines. Confederate marksmen quickly reacted and began firing at
the fleeing horsemen, killing one of the riders; the survivor proved to be
Wild Bill. He had waited for days—at times at great peril of being discovered as a spy—until the right moment to make a run for it. The information which escaped with him changed General Pleasanton's and General
McNeil's battle strategies and allowed them to drive Confederate General
Price's forces back into Arkansas.

Don Russell offers an interesting conclusion to Wild Bill and Buffalo
Bill's Civil War adventures:

> Cody says that at the end of the Price campaign, he "returned to
> Springfield, Missouri for a rest and for supplies, and Wild Bill and
> myself spent two weeks there in 'having a jolly good time,' as some
> people would express it." He makes no mention of their having bread
> and milk on this occasion . . . Cody served one year, seven months
> and ten days with the Seventh Kansas Cavalry. During his year of ac-
> tive service with his company, the regiment did considerable fight-
> ing and campaigning . . . Cody missed no battle, campaign, or skir-
> mish credited to the regiment during his seven months of detached
> service, his company being in garrison during that entire period.[11]

During the winter of 1864–65, Will mustered out of the Seventh
Kansas and was dispatched to St. Louis for hospital duty. While serving as
a hospital orderly Will met and began a courtship with a beautiful French
girl named Louisa Frederici. In 1865, as the Civil War was ending, the
young couple fell in love and Miss Frederici accepted Will's marriage proposal. Louisa accepted with a condition, however; she demanded that Will
abandon his life on the frontier and settle down. It was agreed that Will
would get work in Kansas in order to save enough money for the wedding
and then attempt a more "domestic" lifestyle.

Preparing to embark upon an entirely new experience, Will left Louisa
in St. Louis and returned to Leavenworth and took a job driving a stagecoach for the famous, flamboyant stagecoach tycoon Ben Holloday. Coincidentally, the line Cody was assigned was between Kearney and Plum
Creek, the location of his first Indian battle as an eleven-year-old boy.

As most young men in love, however, Will did not want to wait to get married and, after only a brief period of time separated from Louisa, grew increasingly lovesick; it was not long before he abandoned the frontier and raced to St. Louis to be with Louisa. The couple married March 6, 1866.

The newlyweds planned a honeymoon trip on the *Morning Star,* a Missouri River steamboat that ran from St. Louis to their new home in Leavenworth. Their happiness was soon interrupted, however, when a small party of people boarded the *Morning Star* in Lexington, Missouri, and immediately began to treat the Codys insolently; the group started to rudely point directly at Will while whispering among themselves. Will eventually asked a gentleman from Indiana to please tell him what the party was saying about him. The gentleman responded that the party were Missourians who said Will was a "Kansas Jayhawker and one of Jennison's houseburners."[14] Will, never denying his involvement with the militia group, proceeded to inform the gentleman of his family's treatment at the hands of the Missourians in the early days in Kansas Territory.

The second day after the steamboat left St. Louis the *Morning Star* stopped to gather wood cut and stacked strategically along the banks of the river for fuel. A large band of horsemen suddenly emerged galloping from the forest, firing upon the Negro deckhands loading wood on the steamboat. The deckhands raced to the boat, pulled in the gangplank and soon the steamboat raced out of range of the ambushers' bullets. The horsemen rode along the banks of the Missouri and began to shout to the steamboat, angrily inquiring, "Where's the black-abolition "jayhawker"?, and, "Show him to us and we'll shoot him."[15] A group of Union Army veterans began to assemble on board in support of Cody as the captain rapidly ordered the riverboat into full-steam and left the angry mob cursing on the shoreline.

Apparently, some of the party of Missourians who boarded the *Morning Star* at Lexington recognized Will from his brief, ignominious career as one of "Jennison's Jayhawkers" and telegraphed ahead alerting Confederate comrades to his presence on the steamboat. Will's bride, naturally emotional, became so overwrought during part of the ordeal that she fainted. Chagrined, and not wishing his bride to think she had married a murdering renegade, Cody telegraphed ahead to Leavenworth to arrange a welcoming party for himself and Louisa, and, with the cordial welcome and affectionate testimony of Will's friends, Louisa began to warm somewhat to Kansas.

The marriage, however, was a disaster from the beginning. Will and Louisa were a classic case of opposites attracting; two people could not have possessed more diametrical personalities; whereas Will was a flam-

boyant, gregarious, nomadic child of the west, Louisa was a native urban-
ite, reclusive, manipulatively inconspicuous, domestic, and demanding. A
brilliant dressmaker who created many of Buffalo Bill's early theatrical costumes, Louisa was also selfish and spoiled, reared in the French community of St. Louis to expect a life of upper-class privilege, sophistication, and
refinement. She intensely disliked Will's raw, unpretentious frontier
friends and was violently jealous of his love for the plains and mountains.

Will attempted to change to meet Louisa's domestic requirements. He
vowed to his bride that he would abandon his career on the plains and
rented a hotel in Salt Creek Valley. (Ironically, the same hotel his mother
ran after being widowed.) Will named the hotel The Golden Rule House
and gave the venture a wholehearted effort, yet, ultimately, he was a failure
as an innkeeper. Flamboyantly gregarious, Will was hospitality manifested
on earth. It did not take long for the reputation of his generosity to spread
over the territory and soon travelers without money would go miles out of
their way to stay free at The Golden Rule House. Will was a social success;
needless to say, however, the hotel quickly went deep into red ink.[16]

Louisa faced terrific problems attempting to transform Will from
plainsman to boniface. Possessed of supreme self-confidence in his ability
to make money Cody never knew what it was to be "thrifty." As most of
the men of his day, Cody considered money to be for pleasure and it was to
be spent quickly with great joy. For Cody to not be gregarious and generous was to deny his basic nature and when Louisa tried to discipline him
and mold him to her desires he became restless and depressed.[17]

Where Cody was the very essence of the frontier, Louisa was completely void of pioneer spirit. Afraid of the Great Plains, Louisa had absolutely no inclination to explore or understand the west. Only her hatred
of show business surpassed her lack of empathy for the western frontier
and the people who loved it. As a result, separations were long and frequent for Will and his bride. In his entire married life it is unlikely that
William F. Cody stayed home with Louisa for longer than six consecutive
months.[18]

Will's failure in the hotel business was a turning point in his life. The
Great Plains were calling and, once again, Will was listening. Much to her
credit, Louisa quickly realized Will should return to his career on the frontier. Perhaps money motivated her more than anything else; after six
months in the hotel business the financial books proved Cody to be a magnificent host and a terrible businessman. They both soon agreed Cody was
better at earning money on the prairie than losing cash in the hotel busi-

ness. Will let The Golden Rule House go and headed to the end of the Kansas Pacific Railroad line to look for work. En route Will stopped in Junction City and ran into Wild Bill, who was working as a government scout. Hickok encouraged his old friend to accompany him to Fort Ellsworth where Will was immediately hired as a scout.

During the winter of 1866–67 Cody scouted between Fort Ellsworth and Fort Fletcher. In the spring of 1867, he was at Fort Fletcher when General George Armstrong Custer came there to go on an Indian expedition with General Hancock. Scouting in the vicinity of Fort Hays, Cody and Custer had their first and only ride together. Custer, with an escort of only ten men, had come up from Fort Ellsworth to Fort Hays. The flamboyant general sought a guide to pilot him to Fort Larned, sixty-five miles across the plains.[19]

A mouse-colored mule marked the initial meeting of western legends Cody and Custer, who had at the time only recently been named Lieutenant Colonel of the newly organized Seventh United States Cavalry. Will, as many plainsmen and mountain men, often rode a mule and was mounted upon one when he arrived to guide General Custer to Fort Larned.

Custer was not impressed and condescendingly suggested to Will that he might consider a different mount. Cody assured the general that the mule would be able to match the pace of the horses; apprehensively and with great disdain for his scout's judgment, Custer ordered the trek to Fort Larned to begin.

It seems odd that Custer, a cavalryman, knew so little about the speed and endurance of mules. Perhaps because he was so accustomed to thoroughbred cavalry horses, he had little actual experience with mules. Army mules, however, are legendary and Custer must have spent some time around them in the cavalry. Perhaps Custer revealed a bit of his infamous "blind-sightedness" in this meeting with Cody?

Custer rode a "frisky, impatient and ambitious thoroughbred steed" which Cody paced for the first fifteen miles of the journey. Custer repeatedly told Cody that the mule was no good and implied that he should have had a good horse. Once the party arrived at the Sand Hills, however, Cody let the mule have his head and even "put the persuaders to him" and was easily outdistancing Custer and his fatigued horses.[20]

At the end of the journey Custer was so impressed with Cody that he offered to hire him at any time he needed employment as a scout. Nevertheless, the journey from Fort Ellsworth to Fort Larned would prove to be

Cody's only active service with the famous general. Ironically, Lakotas began to call Custer by the same name they had given Will as a boy — *pahaska*—as Custer, early in his career on the plains, began to emulate a scout's appearance, wearing his hair long and adopting buckskin clothing.

Scouts were rapidly becoming essential to the U.S. military in the west at the time Cody and Hickok were beginning their careers in the profession. West Point graduates and Civil War veterans, officers such as Custer were educated and experienced in classic military warfare. On the western frontier, the textbook method of battle was practically useless in conflict with sagacious and fierce guerrilla enemies in an environment alien to their formal training. Mountain men, bullwackers, trackers, and hunters—anyone with a working knowledge of Plains Indians—were hired for their intimate knowledge of the language, culture, and religion of native people. Perhaps more important, however, scouts were hired for their knowledge of the terrain and how to find Indians rather than how to fight them. Scouts, guides, and several other kinds of civilian employees such as teamsters and packers were hired by the month and were under no obligation to stay beyond that term, nor were they guaranteed future employment. Hired by the Quartermaster Department of the Army, usually through a post or regimental quartermaster, their pay ranged from $60 a month to $150, or even more for especially dangerous missions. An expedition might be authorized to employ a number of scouts, and usually the most dependable of them was appointed chief of scouts and was paid accordingly. Even though they were not hired primarily for fighting, scouts usually did fight. Indians were hired both for scouting and fighting, and at one period one troop of each cavalry regiment was made up of Indian scouts.[21]

Scouts shared the unique distinction of being a bridge between the two cultures. Often a scout's background included living among the plains tribes for long periods of time. Frank Grouard, for example, was a mail carrier who stumbled into Sitting Bull's hands on the prairie. Grouard probably thanked his lucky stars for his Polynesian mother who saved his life that day. The Hunkpapa Lakota Chief, recognizing Grouard's Polynesian features, ordered the man's life spared and adopted him. Grouard was given the name "Sitting With Hands Upraised" and taken into the Lakota leader's home. Later, acting as a scout for the military, Grouard led soldiers to Hunkpapa camps at Slim Buttes resulting in a Lakota massacre. Other scouts, such as Cody, adopted Indian costume and appearance as a personal style and as pragmatic attire. As the mountain men before them, scouts learned the practical wisdom of buckskin clothing on the Great Plains and in the Rockies and their very appearance was a blending of Native and European American costume. Indians traditionally wore their hair long as a matter of personal taste and style yet, over time, the custom became a symbol to challenge and offer their opponent a worthy trophy should they fall on the battlefield. Scouts adopted this and many other Indian customs. Paul Fees, Senior Curator of The Buffalo Bill Historical Center in Cody, Wyoming, in his essay, *The Flamboyant Fraternity*, writes of the scouts:

> Because they were civilian employees of the army and employment was spotty, scouts remained largely independent. They were well-paid because they were highly skilled and possessed insider's knowledge of Indian culture. They asserted their special status by donning eccentric or splendid attire, by growing their hair to the shoulders, by wearing nicknames as "titles." And why not? Theirs was an uncertain and extremely hazardous profession. Many of Buffalo Bill's confreres— among them, California Joe Milner, Buffalo Chips White, and Medicine Bill Comstock—died violently during the Indian Wars.[22]

Shortly after Will's return to Fort Hays in August 1867, he became involved in one of the most dangerous Indian fights he ever experienced in his career as a scout. A large Indian war party raided nearby, killing several men and stealing a large number of horses and mules. Will was assigned as scout and guide to the Tenth Cavalry, a Negro regiment, to pursue the hostiles. On the second day of the expedition the regiment was ambushed by a very large war party.

Armed with a Howitzer cannon, the officer in charge, Major Arms, positioned his cannon on a little knoll and galloped to fight the Sioux. Suddenly, the troops were surprised by an attack from the rear by a force of over one-hundred Indians. Major Arms returned and drove the Indians away from the Howitzer and ordered his men to take positions there.

The fight lasted over two hours in which several men, including Major Arms, were wounded. The major then had to rely on his scout to negotiate a retreat to Fort Hays. Calling upon his boyhood experience with the McCarthy brothers on the Platte, Will led the retreat through the night as the Tenth Cavalry fled the Sioux.

During the retreat several men were killed. But when night came the group was able to make headway in the darkness. The exhausted party pulled into Fort Hays at dawn only to discover that cholera had broken out at the fort during their absence; five or six men were dying daily. Suddenly, fighting Indians out on the prairie became preferable to facing cholera within the walls of the fort.[23]

Cody was beginning to exhibit signs of his ambitions as a community builder even as he began his career as a scout. Will had been sent with dispatches from Fort Hays to Fort Harker. In the nearby town of Ellsworth Will met a contractor for the Kansas Pacific Railroad. William Rose had been hired by the railroad to do some grading near Fort Hays. Rose had his stock stolen by Indians and, as a result, had been forced to buy more in Ellsworth. Once the pair engaged in conversation, Will discovered Rose was planning to lay out a town about a mile from the fort where the railroad was surveyed to cross. Soon Rose offered Will a partnership in the venture and Cody felt the opportunity was too good for him to let pass.

Within days the entrepreneurs purchased store inventories, hired a railroad engineer to survey the town, staked out fifty-dollar lots, and romantically christened their creation Rome. At the end of the first month of Rome's existence the community amazingly blossomed with two-hundred frame and log houses, three or four stores, several saloons, and a hotel.[24]

Cody and Rose, rightfully so, thought they had quickly become millionaires. Soon, however, the "founding fathers" of Rome were paid a visit by Dr. W. E. Webb, a prospector/agent for the Kansas Pacific Railroad. Without bothering to mention his position with the railroad, Webb complimented Cody and Rose on their flourishing community and boldly asked to be included in their partnership. Both Cody and Rose agreed that they had no need for a third partner, at which point Webb divulged his job with the railroad; He was a prospector/agent who selected town sites to be developed by the railroad. Rose and Cody had usurped the commercial sacrosanctity of the almighty railroad!

Rose maintained he and his partner had saved the railroad much time and money creating Rome, yet Webb politely reminded them that the railroads made money selling lands and creating towns and businesses along their lines. Next, Webb coolly suggested that he might have to create another town very nearby to compete with Rome. Undaunted and feeling supremely confident their little town had already taken root, Cody and Rose invited the competition.

Webb quickly went to work and the next day staked out a new town which he named Hays City. Rumors soon were flying around Rome that Hays City was the place the railroad would locate and within three days Rome packed up and moved to Hays City. Cody and Rose's dreams were shattered.

The entire "Rome" episode graphically presents the absolute power railroad companies welded over the fledgling community system struggling to develop in the nineteenth century Trans-Missouri, while it also reveals the incestuous roles played by these same companies and the U.S. government in manipulating Native and European-Americans into conflict in the heart of the continent. If one wishes to trace the origin of the modern American phenomenon President Eisenhower dubbed the "military-industrial complex," one needs to look no further than Abraham Lincoln's Railroad/Homestead Acts of 1862. With little forethought to the ramifications of encouraging the industrial revolution and world's population to rush into the Great Plains, these two legislative acts set into motion the slaughter of the buffalo and the Indian Wars while simultaneously initiating and creating the prototype for government and industry to unite in order to create new, awesome military power.

Not all the communities that blossomed in the wake of the railroad were so "well-organized" or "preplanned" as Rome or Hays City. Further north along the Platte River, as the Union Pacific inched across the Great Plains, a sordid, symbiotic community, appropriately referred to as "Hell on Wheels," followed violently in tow. Populated with nefarious adventurers, murderers, reprobates, illegal whiskey- and gun-runners, professional gamblers, confidence men, and petty thieves, "Hell on Wheels" existed solely for the vile, parasitic purpose of relieving railroad workers of their money and often their lives. When track was laid and the railroad men moved on, "Hell on Wheels" rolled along with the work force; amusement parlors, saloons, casinos, and whorehouses—in reality, little more than tents or log cabins with canvas roofs—would load up and follow. Many modern western cities such as Cheyenne, Wyoming, were originally "Hell on Wheels" communities that managed to somehow remain, survive, and clean up on the plains after the debauchery moved on with the railroad workers.

These transient railroad towns certainly earned their name; fistfights, brawls, knifings, shootings, and killings went on at all hours of the day. Most icons of "desperado" western mythology originated during this lawless period in American history, yet one cannot claim the communities to be purely "American," for one might have heard nearly every language of the world spoken in "Hell on Wheels." Words and phrases such as "boothill," "died with his boots on," and, indeed, "Hell on Wheels" originated during this period of American history as the Union Pacific crossed the continent.

Will and his partner, severely humbled by their fall from wealth, secured a contract to do grading for the railroad as it ran westward through
the location of their former town site. During this time Will became
friends with Dr. Webb and the two started hunting buffalo together. On
one of these hunts Will and Dr. Webb were about ten miles from town
alone on the prairie when a war party of Indians appeared on the horizon.
A race ensued when it became apparent that the band was attempting to
place themselves between the two white men in order to cut them off from
town.

Often these kinds of episodes occurred on the plains simply to break the
monotony and to have a little fun; Indians and whites chased each other
often with no hopes of catching each other. Cody and Dr. Webb raced
back into town well ahead of the Indians.

During this period of his life, Cody rode Brigham, the horse he claimed
was "the fleetest steed I ever owned." Purchased from a Ute Indian who
named the horse in honor of Brigham Young, this horse was destined to
play a pivotal role in Cody's future. Brigham was a natural-born buffalo
horse—perhaps the best instinctive buffalo pony history ever recorded.
Brigham had been reduced to work horse on a scrapper crew as Will recovered financially from the fall of Rome, yet soon after the playful afternoon race with the Indian war party the horse and his master were destined to ride into history as the best buffalo hunting team that ever lived.

Chapter Five

THE INDIAN WARS

Only the Earth Lasts! It is a good day to die! Hoka Hey!
—Lakota Battle Cry

ONE would find it extremely difficult to chronicle William Frederick Cody's extraordinary life without including the broad, colorful strokes; detailed, intimate shading; and rich, deep texture of Native America culture. It is simply impossible to comprehend Cody without coming first to some fundamental understanding of the history of the Plains Indians of the nineteenth century. Cody's life, character and vision of the world was dynamically shaped and indelibly patterned by experiences with Native America. As previously mentioned in this text, Cody was already socially engaged with the Lakota at Fort Laramie and Fort Bridger during his preadolescent years. Furthermore, Cody's boyhood heroes, Jim Bridger and Kit Carson, were mountain men who, after thirty years of living and fighting with most of the tribes of the Trans-Missouri, had evolved into cultural hybrids—members of a small, unique society of men, not Indian, but certainly no longer totally Euroamerican. These men were comfortable in either world because they were truly masters of their own incomparable realm—the Great Plains and Rocky Mountains. In seeking the freedom possessed by Bridger and Carson, Will Cody set his destiny in motion while still a child; one cannot enter the world of the mountain man without entering the world of the Indian. It is significant that young Cody met "Ole Gabe" and Kit at the same time that he met Rain-In-The-Face and other Lakota families at Fort Laramie; his boyhood companions were Lakota children he met at the fort. It is meaningful that, aside from his sisters and the few children Will encountered in the brief period of his schooling, his only childhood playmates were Indian boys at Fort Laramie.

Upon meeting the veteran mountain men and Lakota families that summer on the North Platte, Cody embarked upon a major life path to become a scout. It is no coincidence that Lakotas started calling Will "Pahaska" at Fort Laramie; he was Pahaska long before the fame of "Buffalo Bill" swept him away. Will wore his hair long, imitating Plains Indians. As Bridger; Carson; his first teacher, Horace Billings; and most of the men Will viewed as role models, he had started to dress in beaded buckskins. Perhaps because of the tragic death of his father and being forced to an early life of surviving by his wits, Will intuitively understood the mystical, warrior attributes of the Plains Indians for, like them, he was a child of the prairie. Will confidently met Plains Indians—initially, as a friend and companion, and later, as a worthy enemy; he won their respect and honor as a man and a warrior. Aside from the death of his father and the influence of Russell, Majors, and Waddell's freight company, nearly every major, pivotal event in Cody's boyhood was attended and shaped in some way by experiences with Plains Indians. Henry Sell and Victor Weybright elaborate:

> To understand the west which Cody loved and eventually portrayed, one must know how it came about that the winning of the west by the white man was so tragic an affair that ever after his final victory the white man has been trying to recapture the unspoiled atmosphere of the primeval plains as they were before he despoiled them. Cody—the buffalo hunter and Indian fighter—became a conservationist, game-preserve exponent, and, above all men of his time, a friend of the Indian. He adopted his half-Indian costume of fringed buckskin, and the long hair that challenged scalpers, to set himself apart as a scout—not a uniformed soldier—without quite knowing at the time the reason for his white version of an Indian chief.
>
> As he grew older he saw the contradictory nature of his duel role as the destroyer and the reincarnation of the west. But not even his Wild West Show could ever reflect the deeper drama of American history in which he was conspicuous. Hence, a glimpse at the highlights of the Indians, especially the Indians of the Plains is essential to understanding Cody and his west.[1]

One must also understand Cody's career as a military scout in order to develop a perspective of the "deeper drama of American history in which he was conspicuous"—the Indian Wars Era. This requires a perception of the historical background of the Lakota and Cheyenne in order to realize that the period of conflict on the Great Plains with these nations and the United States did not occur overnight; decades of peaceful relationships eventually broke under the strain of the massive numbers of immigrants il-

legally seizing control of Indian property, particularly after the end of the
Civil War, the period in which Cody entered manhood and began his career as a scout.

Upon returning to the plains after failing as an innkeeper and community developer, it was inevitable that Will Cody would become involved in
the Indian Wars as a scout. Anyone with the skills Will Cody possessed was
conscripted into such service, yet he was naturally attracted to the life anyway. As a child of the Great Plains migration, Will had spent his entire boyhood and young manhood training to become a scout. If the Civil War was
the defining event of the American nation in the nineteenth century, the
Indian Wars served the same purpose in Will Cody's life. Where the Civil
War pitted brother against brother, the Indian Wars pitted tribe against
tribe and Indian against Indian. On some occasions Will became involved
fighting people he had known since boyhood. In Will's situation this predicament was natural; a scout's occupation inherently placed him between
the two opposing cultures. Indeed, scouts often disagreed with the military
actions and treatment of Indians because of decades of such trust and
friendship. This is not to say Cody did not lead the military to Indian en-
campments or that he was not in the business of killing Indians; he was very
much a man of his times, a white warrior in the service of his people and
country. Before entering the scouting profession, he spent most of his youth
and early manhood in life-or-death encounters with Plains Indians. The
most remarkable adventure tales of his early life on the plains involve amazing horse races with Indians which, if conditions had been only a fraction
different, would have ended his life. Cody always said, "I never killed an
Indian except when my life was in danger."[2] He killed only to keep from
being killed. When considering this aspect of Cody's life it is most important to remember that he also spent his middle and elderly years in a circus troupe traveling the world with many of these same Lakota and
Cheyenne people. The reality of their reenacting their earlier days of mortal conflict each day for thirty years in a thousand cities throughout North
America and Europe for royalty and street urchins will forever remain an
understated, yet extraordinary remark of the depth of their trust and respect for one another. This profound respect and trust was earned over the
course of a lifetime.

Indeed, most of Will Cody's life was spent with Lakota and Shyela Indi-
ans. The Lakota, with their loyal ally/cousins, the Shyela, dominated the
Great Plains and eastern slopes of the Rocky Mountains. The "Sioux" and
"Cheyenne," as the French called them, ranged from Minnesota territory

of the northern Mississippi River Valley in the east; across the Great
Plains, beyond the Black Hills to the Big Horn Mountains in the west; to
Kansas' Republican River in the south; into Canada in the north. French
traders from St. Louis established commerce with the Lakota in the beginning days of the fur trade era and the earliest recorded Euroamerican accounts of their history originate with these interactions. Nevertheless,
Lakota oral and "winter-counts" pictorial history plumb the depths of antiquity and we are only now beginning to comprehend the untold eons implied in recent tribal astronomers' revelations of their ancient "star-knowl-
edge"; indeed, the latest revelations and implications of Lakota stellar
history are so broad and profound that a new field of study—ethnoastron-
omy—has risen to process the phenomenal information coming forth
now. The day approaches when traditional "classical" western science will
accurately date the earliest Lakota memory in North America based upon
fixed placement of ancient stellar constellations.[3]

Initial Euroamerican historical interaction with the Lakota was, however, dominated by French traders employed by the American Fur Company. In 1792 Jacques d'Eglise ventured upriver as far as the famous
Arikara villages in the Great Bend of the Missouri. Ancient enemies of the
Lakota, the Arikara had become powerful with horses and weapons from
trade with the Spanish and had prevented the Lakota from migrating
across the river onto the Great Plains for generations. Nevertheless, trading activity with the French brought guns to the Lakota and, after smallpox devastated the Arikara, Sioux warriors ran rampant over their weakened enemies.

The Lakota quickly came to dominate the plains as fierce, feared warriors. Guns brought them military prowess, yet securing horses introduced
them to remarkable new powers: mobility allowed them to hunt buffalo,
and, succeeding in the hunt, their population began to grow exponentially.
Conservative Euroamerican estimates indicate Lakota population—beginning with several thousand people tallied by Lewis and Clark as part of
their expedition in 1804—doubled every twenty years, indicating a collective community of approximately 20,000 when war with the whites erupted
in the early 1860s. With mobility, food, and a healthy, growing population,
the Lakota began to forcibly seize new territory on the Great Plains in all
directions driving such neighboring tribes as the Omaha and Ponca further
south from their traditional lands along the Niobrara and Missouri Rivers
in Nebraska. To the west and northwest the Lakota pushed the Crow,
Kiowa, and Shoshone Nations away from the Powder River Country of

the Big Horn Mountains. The Cheyenne and Arapaho tribes belonged to a mixed camp of trading Indians—Kiowa, Comanche, and Apache—who ran a continuous traffic in horse herds north and south on the plains along the eastern slope of the Rockies. The Cheyenne and Arapaho Nations formed lasting alliances with the Lakota from the beginnings of their interactions trading horses at Horse Creek, near the present Wyoming/Nebraska border.

As Euroamerican fur traders began to ascend the Missouri River in greater numbers, well-established, seasonal trade routes, hunting expeditions, and tribal warfare kept the Lakota people constantly on the move from location to location. Recent revelations from the aforementioned Lakota stellar history indicate the nomadic Lakota were also following the constellations of the night sky in order to create important religious ceremonies at specific locations and at equally specific times of the year. Evidently, the Lakota were following stars long before they began to follow buffalo.

In 1823, in his second historic ascension of the Missouri River with the party of men soon to become known as "mountain men," General William Ashley stopped at the Arikara villages to trade for horses. The Arikara, without warning or provocation, attacked Ashley's trading party killing thirteen men before the group was able to retreat to the safety of their armed comrades and barges on the Missouri River. Fortified on his barges, Ashley sent a distress call up and down the river to all white traders and trappers; he also sent an urgent message requesting military assistance with the Arikara.

Traders and trappers quickly responded by visiting the friendly Teton Lakota camps and drawing together a sizable force to fight their hated Arikara enemies. By the time Colonel Henry Leavenworth arrived on the upper Missouri with a small force of infantry, Lakotas had amassed an army of over 1,100 Oglala, Minniconjou, Brule, Yankton, and Teton warriors prepared to overwhelm and destroy the Arikaras.

Besieged and outnumbered two to one, the Arikara bravely came out from their barricaded villages on horseback to meet their enemies. The Tetons swarmed upon them and, after a very hard fight, the Arikara were driven back behind the fortifications of their village.

The traders and trappers had bragged about the military might of the whites and the Lakota were anxious to see this power demonstrated upon their enemies. With this in mind, after soundly whipping the Arikara warriors and driving them behind their barricades, the Lakota withdrew and, having done their job, expected Leavenworth's forces to invade the Arikara village and complete the victory.

Colonel Leavenworth cautiously made no assault. He methodically surrounded the villages instead, and, although he clearly had the Arikaras outnumbered and outgunned, decided to sit them out. This impotent, ambivalent action puzzled and disgusted the Lakota warriors. To further provoke and antagonize their enemies, and, to occupy themselves and blatantly display their scorn, the Lakota invaded the Arikara's famous cornfields and began a great, roasting feast while Leavenworth indecisively shifted from one military position to another.

Shortly thereafter, traders and trappers, and even a few of Leavenworth's hungry troops joined the disgruntled Lakota in the cornfield. Exasperated with Leavenworth, the Lakota loaded their ponies down with Arikara corn, stole several of the Colonel's horses, and left with nothing but contempt for the white "warriors."

After several attempts to negotiate pipe ceremonies with the Arikara, Leavenworth finally decided to attack the villages. Much to his surprise and embarrassment, however, the Colonel raided an empty community; the Arikara had slipped away during the night.

This initial ignominious campaign against the Arikaras filled the Sioux with scorn and contempt for the *wasichus'* soldiers, yet the expedition's military might had frightened the Arikaras badly enough to convince them to desert their villages, which were then partially burned. When the Arikaras returned, the Sioux, encouraged by the rancorous traders, badgered them more than ever before. When drought destroyed their crops, the Arikaras made the inconceivable decision to move to Nebraska and rejoin their kinsmen, the Skidi Pawnees.[4]

The Arikara exodus from the mouth of Grand River at the Great Bend of the Missouri opened the way for large numbers of Lakota who lived east of the Missouri to migrate onto the Great Plains to join their kinsmen. Hunkpapa and Blackfeet Sioux quickly crossed over the Missouri and occupied Arikara lands. With each wave of migration the Lakota became more powerful and, as their numbers increased greatly, so did their command of the plains.

By 1825 the Lakota signed their first treaty with the United States. The Atkinson Expedition ascended the Missouri in a steamboat, stopping at various important locations along the river in order to obtain a simple peace/friendship treaty with the Lakota. Nevertheless, when whites came to communicate with the Lakota all interactions translated through French traders whom the Sioux had long trusted. From 1825–35 the American Fur Company monopolized all trade with the Sioux from the mouth of Bad River at Fort Pierre. The American Fur Company initially obtained furs by setting up outposts along the Missouri River in order to tempt Indians with tobacco, guns, powder, lead, whiskey, blankets, cloth, beads and other trade goods. Tried and true, the trading post system had worked well for the French and the Indians.

Arriving on the Upper Missouri in 1823, Ashley's Expedition discovered the Indians of the region no longer were trading with whites. The General was then forced into a radical plan: he ordered his partner Major Andrew Henry to send his men into the Rockies to find friendly tribes with which to trade and to also trap beaver themselves. "Ashley's Hundred" left the river outposts and went on foot and horseback deep into the mountains. These "mountain men" revolutionized the fur trade exploring deep into the heart of the Trans-Missouri searching for beaver and friendly Indians. Their success made Ashley extremely wealthy while such men as Jim Bridger, Jedediah Smith, Hugh Glass, Kit Carson, Thomas "Broken-Hand" Fitzpatrick, Joe Meek, Big Bill Williams, William and Milton Sublette, David Jackson, Robert Campbell, and Jim Beckworth were destined to become western legends as a result of Ashley's making "explorers" of them.

He made businessmen of them as well. Ashley got in and out of the fur trade quickly, selling his interest in the fur company to William Sublette, David Jackson, and Jed Smith. Soon, Tom Fitzpatrick, Milton Sublette, Henry Fraeb, and Jim Bridger joined the partnership to form the Rocky Mountain Fur Company.

While the Rocky Mountain Fur Company was pulling in tremendous profits, the American Fur Company attempted to organize similar competitive trapping brigades. Their efforts were, however, in vain. In creating a new trapping and trading system, the Rocky Mountain Fur Company also had the advantage of having initiated peaceful commercial relationships with the tribes of the Upper Rockies and high plains. These tribes, the Crow and Shoshone, were also bitter enemies of the powerful Lakota. So, largely as a result of these commercial/political relationships in the Upper Rockies and high plains with the Crows and Shoshones, the French-dominated American Fur Company continued to monopolize trade with the Lakota and Cheyenne.

In 1834, Rocky Mountain Fur Company entrepreneurs Robert Campbell and William Sublette, having miscalculated routes and schedules to

Rendezvous, arrived too late and lost their contract to supply trade goods for the annual event. Sublette had taken the Santa Fe route to avoid Indian trouble, while Campbell pushed across the plains to arrive at the mouth of the Laramie Fork of the Platte River. At this location, Campbell constructed a small log stockade and christened it Fort William in honor of his partner. Ensconced at Fort William, Campbell waited for Sublette to join him.

Campbell was acutely aware that he and Sublette would have to figure out a way to trade the inventory of goods they brought for Rendezvous or go bankrupt. Realizing that most of his Rendezvous customers would have been Indians, Campbell then came up with the idea to attract the Lakota from the Black Hills down to his fort on the Platte in order to trade the goods he had failed to move at Rendezvous. Also fully aware that buffalo ran in abundance year round through that country on the Platte, Campbell sought to entice the Lakota to move their tribes to live near his post; he hoped that Fort William might become a central point for trade with the Lakota and their Cheyenne cousins.

Campbell's dream bore fruit when a Lakota chief named Bull Bear broke relations with the American Fur Company and moved 100 lodges of Oglalas to the North Platte to trade. In spite of this success trading their inventory and creating a perennial clientele, Campbell and Sublette decided to sell the entire stockade to their partners in the Rocky Mountain Fur Company. Later, when the Rocky Mountain Fur Company realized that the post was losing money, they sold Fort William to the American Fur Company; suddenly, the Oglala Lakota were realigned commercially with their old French companions. Born in the spirit of political/commercial interaction and alliances on the Great Plains, however, a central trading post for the "wild" western Lakota and Cheyenne had taken root at the mouth of Laramie Creek. The Trans-Missouri and the western tribes would never be the same.

In 1842 the stockade was relocated and renamed Fort John. Log picket fortifications were replaced with adobe walls and the fort began to become a small city. In 1846 Francis Parkman, Jr. described Fort Laramie as

> . . . one of the posts established by the "American Fur Company," who well-nigh monopolize the Indian trade of this whole region. Here their officials rule with an absolute sway; the arm of the United States has little force; for when we were there, the extreme outposts of her troops were about seven hundred miles to the eastward. The little fort is built of bricks dried in the sun, and externally is of an ob-

long form, with bastions of clay, in the form of ordinary blockhouses, at two of the corners. The walls are about fifteen feet high, and surrounded by a slender palisade. The roofs of the apartments within, which are built close against the walls, serve the purpose of a banquette. Within, the fort is divided by a partition; on one side is the square area, surrounded by the storerooms, offices, and apartments of the inmates; on the other is the corral, a narrow place, encompassed by the high clay walls, where at night, or in presence of dangerous Indians, the horses and mules of the fort are crowded for safe keeping. The main entrance has two gates, with an arched passage intervening. A little square window, quite high above the grounds, opens laterally from an adjoining chamber into this passage; so that when the inner gate is closed and barred, a person without may still hold communication with those within, through this narrow aperture. This obviates the necessity of admitting suspicious Indians, for the purposes of trading, into the body of the fort; for when danger is apprehended, the inner gate is shut fast, and all traffic is carried on by means of the little window. This precaution, though highly necessary at some of the Company's post, is now seldom resorted to at Fort Laramie; where though men are frequently killed in the neighborhood, no apprehensions are now entertained of any general designs of hostility from the Indians.[5]

When the government bought the fort in 1849 it was renamed Fort Laramie and had become the vital hub of activity along the Oregon Trail as immigrants joined the blend of Lakota, Cheyenne, French and American traders and trappers who populated the site.

During these years of trade wars between rival fur companies the most reliable weapon in both camps' arsenal was whiskey. Lakota leaders had long viewed whiskey as a destructive force among their people, yet remained powerless to halt its insidious flow. Before the arrival of whiskey murder was practically unheard of among the Lakota. With the arrival of liquor, however, murders rose rapidly among the tribes. Since the days of the Fur Trade Era whiskey was diluted and "doctored" as it worked its way from settlements to Rendezvous. During the Fur Trade Era traders usually drank more than half the contents of a whiskey keg en route to Rendezvous. Water, tea, coffee, and even kerosene and gun powder were then added to the remaining liquor to sell, giving the Indian term *firewater* a much more graphic meaning. The unusually high incidence of violence among "drunken Indians" led to the traders' practice of adding laudanum to the liquor as "humane" treatment; the opiate would dull the senses and prevent rather than incite violence.

The whiskey runners were usually French traders with Lakota wives and numerous half-breed children. Deeply involved in Lakota and Cheyenne culture, these men had long abandoned white society and were often considered as important tribal members. As immigrants entered the picture, these traders became much more important characters as interpreters and guides, yet many wagon train people, churlishly religious, found these men and their lifestyles reprehensible. Thinly veiled behind each necessary interaction, pious immigrant perspectives viewed these men as living in sin with "heathens" and "savages"; indeed, priggish immigrant women could barely hide their contempt for these "squawmen," these "white-Indians" who lived in open "sin" and flaunted their vile disregard for traditional Christian institutions and conventions. Nevertheless, the travelers were forced to interact with these traders and with Indians, particularly at Fort Laramie. The introduction to the business-at-hand was always conducted with presents and gifts, a tradition when initiating contact with plains and mountain tribes since the days of Lewis and Clark. The gift of whiskey rapidly became as important as guns, powder and lead, horses, and tobacco during the Rendezvous era of 1823–34, which was the period in which the Euroamerican established commerce with the tribes of the Upper Great Plains and Rockies. Annual trade fairs, dubbed "rendezvous," attracted thousands of Indians to trade with mountain men. Whiskey remained a vital ceremonial introduction to trading during the immigration era.

Whiskey led to a feud between two Lakota chiefs in the early 1840s. Bull Bear, who led his Oglalas down to the North Platte and Fort Laramie from the Black Hills, began to believe rumors that Smoke, the leader of the Oglalas who camped around Fort Laramie, was his rival. Bull Bear went to Smoke's lodge and challenged him to come out and fight. When Smoke refused to come out, Bull Bear went to the old chief's corral and stabbed and killed his favorite horse. Insulted and dishonored, Smoke still did not have the courage to fight Bull Bear alone, yet he had a loyal group of warriors who quickly concocted a plan to extract revenge.

They soon had an opportunity when Bull Bear and a small group of followers rode into Smoke's camp as French traders were selling whiskey. Both groups began to drink and an argument erupted. Bull Bear ran out of his lodge to see what was happening and was shot and killed. Most Lakotas give credit for the assassination to Red Cloud ("*Makhpiya-Luta*"), the Oglala destined to soon lead the Sioux into war against the U.S. government.

After Bull Bear's assassination, the Lakota remained divided into small bands who occupied specific regions such as Powder River, the North Platte, and the Black Hills throughout the 1850s, yet by the 1860s these bands were beginning to organize under important leaders such as Sitting Bull (*Ta Bloh Kah E Yo Da Kah*), High Back Bone (*Hump*), Red Cloud, and Spotted Tail (*Sinte Gleska*).

From the beginnings of the white migration into their country, the Lakota became increasingly aware that the increased traffic was destroying the valley of the Platte. Whereas helpless immigrants initially needed, and readily accepted, valuable Lakota assistance, they had come to view the Indians as an "inconvenience" to be tolerated while venturing through their "desolate" country. The Lakota learned from their French interpreters the way the immigrants really felt about them. Understanding the prejudice immigrants held for French traders, one can only imagine the biased and vengeful filter through which the Lakota received information concerning immigrants.

As early as 1841, a group of Lakota and Cheyenne stopped a train of immigrants on the Sweetwater, west of Independence Rock; later that summer over 500 Sioux, Cheyenne and Arapaho warriors attacked a large party of trappers and announced they were hostile to continued white encroachment onto their land. The Lakota began to argue among themselves, however, and failed to amass any unified force against the immigrants. Still, these types of incidents arose because the white migration dramatically effected the Lakota as buffalo and other game's natural patterns and rhythms were being altered by the massive numbers of immigrants traveling along the Platte.

With the initial appearance of U.S. military at Fort Laramie and Fort Kearny in 1849, a pattern of confusion and conflict begins to emerge. From 1849 through 1860, however, aside from the Grattan incident, and General W. S. Harney's brutal retaliation on peaceful chief Little Thunder, most conflict was dealt with through masterful diplomacy and brinkmanship in both Native and European American camps.

Then, in 1862, as the Civil War raged, trouble erupted in Minnesota with the uprising of the Santee Lakota. In a decade 150,000 settlers had poured into Santee territory causing major disruption to their way of life. According to provisions in two separate treaties, the Santee were promised by the U.S. government annuities and, as a result of strained finances due to the Civil War, their government agent, Thomas Galbraith, withheld their provisions stored in a warehouse until money arrived from Washington to pay for them. Hungry and unwilling to understand Galbraith's decision, the Santee stormed the warehouse and began to remove sacks of flour. Troops were called in, yet, their leader, Thomas Sheehan, sympathized with the Santee and persuaded Galbraith to issue provisions to the Sioux. The Santees, however, refused to leave the warehouse until Galbraith agreed to also issue provisions to fellow tribal members thirty miles downriver at Redwood.

When Galbraith failed to keep his promise to issue provisions to Santees at the Lower Agency at Redwood tensions mounted. An emergency meeting was called between the Santee, Galbraith, and the four traders in charge of distributing annuities. Santee chief Little Crow rose and eloquently spoke of his people being hungry and starving and demanded that his people be given what was promised. Trader Andrew Myrick responded: "So far as I am concerned, if they are hungry let them eat grass or their own dung."[6]

Even the most peaceful among the Santee were enraged with Myrick's callously stupid remark and it was not long before raids on white settlers began; they started with trader Myrick's place; twenty men were killed, ten women and children were taken captive. Forty-seven people barely escaped with their lives before the Santees emptied the warehouse of its provisions and set the compound ablaze. Trader Myrick was found dead with his mouth stuffed with grass.

After a fierce regional war, the "Santee Uprising" resulted in the deaths of many settlers and the Lakota before its tragic conclusion with the hanging of thirty-eight Lakota on December 26, 1862. The intervention of President Abraham Lincoln clearly prevented the execution of even more as the military had initially requested 303 "hostiles" to be hanged and held nearly 2,000 more Santee men, women, and children as prisoners. Lincoln, after long deliberation, ordered the thirty-eight men to be executed. The Santee prisoners sang Lakota death songs on the gallows and were hanged. Some newspapers referred to the event as "America's greatest mass execution."

After the executions fear quickly stalked the plains. Frightened Santees fled to join their Lakota relatives on the Great Plains as paranoid settlers spread rumors of "Indian massacres" and rushed to larger communities for protection. Some concerned citizens gathered militia troops to raid and harass friendly neighboring tribes. Western newspapers began to print sensational, alarmist headlines accusing Indians of all sorts of imagined mischief while an increased military force was put on alert and war loomed along the North Platte. As the Santee joined their cousins on the Great Plains, the "wild" bands of Lakota were gradually drawn into the fray.

Red Cloud's remark that "the white soldiers always want to make a war" reveals the simple truth of the beginning of the Indian Wars in 1864. Life at a frontier post was a very boring, tedious affair, and there is ample documentation that most of the soldiers and the younger officers, anxious to relieve the monotony of garrison life, were brewing for any excuse to fight Indians. This was true of the regular troops on the Upper Platte in 1852–54 and it was equally true of the cavalry officers who came to the region ten years later.[7]

The South Platte was no different; indeed, conditions were perhaps even worse. Like those before and after, the treaty of 1851 was useless to the Cheyenne and Arapaho once gold was discovered in Colorado in 1859. The valley of the Platte, which once overflowed with buffalo, now was overrun with settlers rapaciously dividing Cheyenne and Arapaho lands while creating new white settlements. Only ten years after the Fort Laramie Treaty of 1851 and Colorado Territory was on the verge of appealing for statehood. All of this activity led to a separate treaty between these Cheyenne and Arapaho Nations and the U.S. government. The "Fort Wise Treaty" was a controversial agreement between all parties involved. As most treaties with Plains Indians, the signing parties constituted neither a majority of tribal leadership nor a majority of popular tribal opinion. This practice led to most treaties being entered into halfway and required constant renegotiations or, in most cases, the proposal of an entirely new agreement. This practice also invariably led to the bungled agreements being broken, causing the unbelievable tangle of confusion that exists to this day. At minimum, the practice led Indians to not trust the process itself as Washington would enter into one agreement only to return several years later to request a new one. The Fort Wise Treaty did, however, set the tragic stage for the Indians Wars Era.

Cheyenne and Arapaho, as all Indian people, learned of the Santee uprising in 1862 in Minnesota and realized major trouble was coming. Two Cheyenne chiefs—Lean Bear and Black Kettle—visited Washington and President Abraham Lincoln to obtain assurances their people would not be harmed by the growing numbers of military troops in their homeland. Commissioner of Indian Affairs, Colonel A. B. Greenwood, presented Black Kettle with a United States flag and instructed him to fly it over his village. Greenwood promised that no soldiers would fire upon Black Kettle's people as long as he flew the American standard over his lodge. Lean

Bear and Black Kettle were also given peace medals cast to commemorate their visit to Washington.

Nevertheless, by the spring of 1864 tensions along the North and South Platte erupted as soldiers attacked the Cheyenne. Black Kettle and Lean Bear decided to flee north to the protection of Lakota and Cheyenne relatives on Powder River, in the Big Horn Mountains and the Black Hills. Unfortunately, the retreating camps were overtaken by the military and, after a brief council, Lean Bear, wearing the peace medals given him by President Lincoln, and, carrying official papers from Washington which verified him to be "friendly" to the United States, was selected to go seek a parley with the soldiers; a group of warriors rode at their chief's side.

About 30 yards from the troops, Lean Bear extended a friendly hand to greet the officers in peace. Suddenly the troops opened fire, killing Lean Bear and another warrior-chief named Star. A terrible fight ensued and the Cheyenne, enraged by Lean Bear's cold-blooded murder, pursued the troops in a running fight, chasing them all the way to Fort Larned.

One can easily trace the origins of the Indian Wars to such hostile, inept military leadership in the Trans-Missouri. George E. Hyde elaborates on the field commanders of the Great Plains in 1863:

> . . . there was nothing judicious in the conduct of the military men who were in control in the west. Major General S. R. Curtis, who commanded the troops on the Platte and Arkansas Rivers, was a pompous man who knew nothing about Indians but imagined himself an authority on the subject. Brigadier General James Craig, who commanded along the Overland Road on the Platte in 1862, knew nothing about Indians when he came west and made no attempt to learn. Brigadier General Robert B. Mitchell, who succeeded Craig on the Overland, was a good-hearted, easy-going man, but he did not understand Indians and frankly said so. Lieutenant Colonel H. M. Chivington of the First Colorado Cavalry was a frontier product of the best Indian-hating type. He looked on the Indians as wild beast, to be hustled out of the way of progress, and to be killed if they resisted. Lieutenant Colonel Wm. O. Collins, who commanded the Eleventh Ohio Cavalry along the North Platte, was by far the best commander in the plains in 1863. He knew nothing of Indians when he came out, but he learned quickly; he honestly desired peace, made friends with the principal chiefs, and never missed an opportunity to learn more of the tribes, their location, numbers, and disposi-

tion. Just when he was equipped to do splendid service he was re-lieved of command and ordered east."[8]

Unfortunately, the end of the Civil War exacerbated the growing tensions on the Great Plains. The war had forced the Transcontinental Railroad project to be halted. The railroad, now seen as a monumental meta-phor symbolizing the reuniting of the American people and the power of their "Industrial Revolution," suddenly took on mythological cultural significance. The Railroad and Homestead Acts of 1862 offered never-before seen hopes of renewal and future prosperity to people torn by years of horrendous conflict and loss. These two legislative acts served as a powerful attraction to the American public seeking their future west of the Mississippi River. As never before, the Indian's home became the Eu-roamerican's "frontier." Rapidly increasing strained situations made it easy for Washington to think first of military solutions. There is ample evi-dence that the incredible numbers of professional military men remaining in the service after the Civil War contributed greatly to the Indian Wars. In the spring of 1866 the United States Army was absurdly overstaffed with hundreds of senior officers with up to four years of battle experience, many of them still young men with West Point training.[9]

This abundance of highly trained and experienced professional "war-riors" was a formula for disaster on the plains. Many of these "West Point trained" soldiers viewed continuing warfare and "glory" on the western frontier as a direct avenue to power, fame and wealth. Indeed, in only a few years, as the Indian Wars raged, one of their own, Ulysses S. Grant, sat in the White House, a drunken role model.

Dee Brown elaborates on the beginnings of the Indian Wars:

At Freemont's Orchard north of Denver, a band of Dog Soldiers was attacked by a patrol of Colonel John M. Chivington's Colorado Vol-unteers who were out looking for stolen horses. The Dog Soldiers were herding a horse and a mule picked up as strays, but Chiving-ton's soldiers opened fire before giving the Cheyennes an opportu-nity to explain where they had obtained the animals. After this en-gagement Chivington sent out a larger force, which attacked a Cheyenne camp near Cedar Bluffs, killing two women and two chil-dren. The artillery soldiers who had attacked Black Kettle's camp on May 16 were also Chivington's men, sent out from Denver with no authority to operate in Kansas. The officer in command, Lieutenant

George S. Eayre, was under orders from Colonel Chivington to "kill Cheyennes whenever and wherever found."[10]

As troubles mounted in Cheyenne/Arapaho country, William Bent, or "Little White Man," as the Cheyenne called him, served as an important diplomat. Having arrived in territory 30 years earlier, Bent built the famous "Bent's Fort" and was married to a Cheyenne named Yellow Woman. The couple had three sons, Robert, George and Charlie, and were highly regarded by both the Native and European Americans of Colorado.

When Governor John Evans ordered all Cheyenne and Arapaho to come in to Fort Lyon, William Bent encouraged the tribes to comply with the order. Black Kettle needed a peaceful white ally. The chief's hands were full attempting to convince younger leaders such as Roman Nose and Tall Bull to stop war-party raids throughout the territory. The "Hotamitanio," or Dog Soldier Societies of the Cheyenne, were enraged by the unprovoked attacks on their people, and especially by the cold-blooded killing of Lean Bear and Star. The Dog Soldiers had begun sending war parties on retaliatory raids, terrorizing white settlers and wagon trains. Absolutely aware that the thought of women and children being held captive by Indians drove white men crazy, the Cheyenne became particularly adept at this practice. As might be expected, however, taking white women and children as prisoners caused the situation to explode rapidly.

By late August Governor Evans opened season on Indians calling upon the citizens of Colorado to "kill and destroy as enemies of the country wherever they may be found, all such hostile Indians."[11] With this blanket authorization friendly, peaceful Cheyenne and Arapaho people did not even know how to comply with Evans' initial order to come to Fort Lyons without putting themselves in extreme danger.

Black Kettle called an emergency peace council through William Bent. The two men were able to arrange the release of several white captives as a gesture of Cheyenne good will. When asked how he had been treated as a captive of the Cheyenne, a young boy indicated that he would have preferred to remain with the Indians. If he had known what fate awaited Black Kettle's people, the boy would have reconsidered.

Nevertheless, through Black Kettle and William Bent's peaceful efforts a young Army Major came over to their side. Major Edward W. Wynkoop—"Tall Chief" to the Cheyenne—arranged a meeting for them in Denver with the governor.

Governor Evans made it clear that he wanted nothing to do with the

Indians until they had been punished: "What shall I do with the Third Colorado Regiment if I make peace?" he asked. "They have been raised to kill Indians, and they must kill Indians." General Samuel Curtis threw the gauntlet of war on the ground with his reaction to Wynkoop's peace commission, flatly admitting, "I want no peace till the Indians suffer more."[12]

Evans and Curtis' blatant hostility toward Black Kettle's peace efforts revealed their ultimate intentions; that Wynkoop was reprimanded for taking Cheyenne and Arapaho chiefs to Denver without authorization, for "letting Indians run things at Fort Lyon,"[13] and relieved of his command at Fort Lyon makes it painfully obvious that the military did not seek peace. Major Wynkoop was replaced by Major Scott J. Anthony—the "Red-Eyed Chief" to the Cheyenne/Arapaho. Anthony was an officer in Colonel Chivington's regiment of Colorado Volunteers, and, upon taking command of Fort Lyon, immediately ordered the Arapaho to surrender their arms.

Soon after Major Anthony's arrival, Black Kettle and Arapaho Chief White Antelope decided to attempt a meeting with him to discuss peace. Anthony assured them that they were safe and encouraged Black Kettle to camp at Sand Creek, forty miles northeast of Fort Lyon. He even suggested that Black Kettle might send a group of young men on a buffalo hunt to secure meat for his people until rations might be approved from Washington.

Colonel J. M. Chivington had been anxious to "pitch into them" for some time, and, viewing Curtis and Evans' remarks as a mandate to murder Indians, seized the opportunity. He quickly proceeded to Fort Lyon with a force of over 600 men, surrounded the post, and forbade anyone to leave under punishment of death. Simultaneously, twenty cavalrymen surrounded William Bent's house and issued similar threats to anyone attempting to enter or leave.

When Chivington, who was also a former Methodist preacher, announced his intention to destroy Black Kettle's camp at Sand Creek, several young, conscientious officers reminded him that such an act would violate the promise of safety given the chief by both Wynkoop and Anthony. The gigantic Chivington flew into a violent rage and screamed, "Damn any man who sympathizes with Indians! I have come to kill Indians, and believe it is right and honorable to use any means under God's heaven to kill Indians."[14] The young officers were duty-bound to follow Chivington's orders; still, they made a secret pact not to fire unless first fired upon by Indians.

Chivington proceeded to conscript mountain man Jim Beckworth as a guide to Sand Creek. A mulatto, Beckworth was sixty-nine years old and a living legend in the west. He was considered a chief among the Crows, having lived with them for most of his life. When Beckworth refused to lead Chivington on his murderous mission, the Colonel said coldly, "I haven't had an Indian to eat for a long time. If you fool with me, and don't lead us to that camp, I'll have you for breakfast."[15]

En route to Sand Creek it became apparent to Chivington that Beckworth's age was indeed a problem. The Colonel stopped at a ranch and ordered the owner dragged out of bed to lead them to Sand Creek. Ironically, the man was William Bent's eldest son Robert. Bent's other sons George and Charlie and his son-in-law Edward Guerrier were camped at Sand Creek with Black Kettle.

Chivington arrived at Sand Creek at dawn and surrounded Black Kettle's camp. The chief immediately ran his American flag of protection up the towering lodgepole of his village. In order to make his military disposition absolutely clear, Black Kettle flew a white flag of truce immediately under "Old Glory." Soon, hundreds of women and children began to gather under the assumed protection of the flags. Seventy-five-year-old Arapaho Chief White Antelope walked out to greet the troops and was shot to pieces as the massacre began. Black Kettle's family quickly pulled him away and fled or he would have met a similar fate. Charlie Bent was taken captive and would have been killed if Ole Beckworth had not recognized and saved him.

The 105 women and children and twenty-eight men killed were horribly mutilated, their corpses violated by Chivington's bloodthirsty volunteers. Men and women's private parts were cut from them; pregnant women were killed, their unborn children ripped from their womb and thrown upon the ground; children lay dead under white flags of truce. No one had ever before seen anything so savage and brutal on the plains.

The few survivors crawled out of their hiding places and managed to gather for a desperate march to join relatives fifty miles east at Smoky Hill. Concerned not to alert the troops to their presence, the Cheyenne and Arapaho silently marched through the bitterly cold night; blood froze over their wounds. Wounded in the fight, George Bent joined the trek to Smoky Hill. His Cheyenne mother, Yellow Woman, left William Bent and joined the hostiles; she said she could never live with a white man again.

The Sand Creek Massacre tore unions such as Little White Man and Yellow Woman's apart while also it created new alliances. Those Cheyenne and Arapaho who had followed Black Kettle's peaceful path had paid a terrible price; now there would be no peace; every Cheyenne and Arapaho knew they were fighting for their lives. A war-pipe went north to their cousins and allies—the Lakota. Oglala Warrior-Chief Red Cloud smoked that pipe. Hunkpapa Warrior-Chief Sitting Bull smoked that pipe.

Upon hearing of the carnage at Sand Creek Jim Bridger predicted a swift and terrible revenge from the Cheyenne and their Lakota allies. He also realized that everyone in the west would be affected by that revenge. He was right. Soon Bridger himself would be in the thick of it.

Red Cloud's Oglala Lakotas were ready to fight the wasichus, as they called the whites. Gold prospectors were pouring through the Powder River country hurrying to Virginia City, Montana, and the gold strike there. Surveyor John Bozeman laid a trail from Fort Laramie to Montana which quickly became known as the "bloody Bozeman" as a result of Red Cloud's attacks on whites traveling the trail.

Still, the wasichus continued to come. In an effort to halt Red Cloud's attacks upon travelers through the Powder River country, General Patrick E. Connor led a three-pronged expedition north into Lakota country in the summer of 1865. Connor's orders to his officers reflected his orders from Washington: "You will not receive overtures of peace or submission from Indians, but will attack and kill every male Indian over twelve years of age."[16]

General Connor's campaign destroyed one Arapaho village and established Fort Connor (later Fort Reno) in the Powder River country. Nevertheless, Connor was not fully prepared for the fierce resistance of Red Cloud's warriors, who drove him out of the Powder River territory.

Later that autumn the government sent representatives with peace treaties and the old pattern of obtaining agreements with friendly, "hangs-around-the-fort-Indians" was tried again. The men who really represented the tribes refused to have anything to do with the wasichus; indeed, Red Cloud had declared war on every living thing west of the Missouri River. These ill-conceived "treaties" proved deadly for the next wave of immigrants who ventured into hostile Sioux territory, assured by the government that the region was now safe for travel. Red Cloud stopped all traffic on the road. Why the government allowed—even encouraged—its citizens to travel along the "Bloody" Bozeman Trail becomes apparent when examining the military's behavior with all the region's tribes from 1864–66; if enough people were killed along Powder River a war could be provoked in Indian country.

The government had another serious motive in provoking the Sioux in the Powder River territory: It was broke. In 1865, after four years of Civil War, the United States Treasury was virtually bankrupt. Gold—and lots of it—was urgently needed to resolve the massive interest of the soaring national debt. For this reason the government was vitally interested in a direct route to the Montana gold fields. Washington financed a survey for a direct route from Sioux City via the Niobrara River.[17]

This route cut through the heart of Lakota territory on the Great Plains. Colonel Henry Beebe Carrington followed on General Connor's heels, striking deep into the sacred Powder River country of the Big Horn Mountains. There, sixty-two miles north of Fort Reno, he built a stockade which he named Fort Phil Kearny, in honor of the one-armed Civil War hero killed at Chantilly. Upon completion of Fort Phil Kearny, Carrington's orders from Washington called for the construction of yet another fort even deeper in the Big Horn Mountains—Fort C. F. Smith. Within weeks locations were being scouted for the final of the three forts planned along Bozeman's Trail from Fort Laramie to Virginia City.

The construction of military forts in the Powder River Country was tantamount to a declaration of war to the Lakota. On the prairie foothills of the Big Horn Mountains, Fort Phil Kearny could not have made a more aggressive statement of Washington's intention to invade the Lakotas' last refuge. The "wild" Lakota were enraged and immediately set out to destroy Fort Phil Kearny. They relentlessly attacked Carrington's troops with constant deadly harassment as they cut timber from the nearby Big Horns to haul the wood out to the fort's location on the prairie. Nevertheless, Carrington persisted and in July completed the stockade. In August Carrington divided his command and, initiating the second phase of his orders, sent a unit of men to begin construction on Fort C. F. Smith. By November Red Cloud's forces constantly surrounded Fort Phil Kearny and attacked anyone entering or leaving the stockade. Red Cloud declared his intention was to starve the inhabitants until they had to leave and then to kill every last one of them and burn the fort to the ground.

Colonel Carrington was a small man, given to intellectual maneuvering rather than military action. Yale educated, Carrington had served as Washington Irving's personal secretary. After his job with the famous author Carrington became a professor to pay his way through Yale law school. Upon beginning a law practice in Columbus, Ohio, Carrington's partner, William Dennison, was elected Governor just as the Civil War erupted.

Carrington spent most of the Civil War in Ohio and Indiana as a titular commander of the 18th Regiment.

While Colonel Carrington was commander of Fort Phil Kearny he wisely chose the most experienced white man of the Rocky Mountains and High Plains as his trusted advisor. Sixty-two years old, no white man knew the Big Horn Mountains and the Powder River country better than Jim "Ole Gabe" Bridger. At ten dollars a day, the mountain man's salary was more than Carrington's, but he was well worth every penny. Blessed with the gift of geographic memory, Ole Gabe had explored and trapped every stream and mountain range of the territory for over forty years. Equally important, Bridger had lived with or fought against most of the tribes of the High Plains and Upper Rockies, understood their culture and individual traits and made his knowledge available to anyone who sought his advice.[18]

Carrington sought Bridger's counsel before making most important decisions. Bridger was particularly important to Carrington's reconnaissance; the mountain man's experience and intimate relationships with the Crow and Shoshone provided the colonel with vital information concerning Red Cloud's warriors' movements and possible future strategies.

Not everyone wanted to ask Jim Bridger's advice about the Lakota. There could be no better example of the type of highly trained, heroic— yet fatally arrogant—military man involved in the Indian Wars than Captain William Judd Fetterman. Dee Brown describes him:

> While Carrington as nominal commander of the 18th Regiment had remained in Ohio and Indiana through most of the Civil War, Fetterman had been winning honors in combat. In the spring of 1862, Fetterman commanded Company A of the 2nd Battalion during the siege of Corinth; later that year he was cited for gallantry at Stone's River after thirty-six hours of continuous fighting. As commander of the 2nd Battalion he fought throughout most of Sherman's Georgia campaign of 1864—Resaca, Kennesaw Mountain, Peach Tree Creek, Jonesboro, the siege of Atlanta . . . Brilliant as his record was, Fetterman knew nothing of Indian warfare, and was boastfully contemptuous of the savages' ability to withstand attacks from trained soldiers of the United States Army.[19]

Where Carrington was perfectly suited to administrating an army base he was clearly not a "fighting man." The colonel's perspective on his assignment in Powder River country was absolutely defensive; he was ordered to build forts rather than mount offensive military strikes against the Sioux. Fetterman, in contrast, was the type of man who seemed to need military conflict. He was a descendant of generations of professional soldiers and eager to advance through the military as had his antecedents. Further complicating matters, before being assigned to Fort Phil Kearny Fetterman had been led to believe that in an eminent increase of U.S. military strength in Powder River country he would replace Colonel Carrington as commander of the fort.

Soon after arriving at Fort Phil Kearny Captain Fetterman became increasingly critical of Carrington's policy concerning Indians. Fetterman and a small group of Civil War comrades began to insolently taunt Carrington with remarks such as: "With eighty men I could ride through the Sioux Nation."[20] Fetterman's indignant harassment made life inside the fort as uncomfortable for Carrington as Red Cloud's siege made it outside. Carrington's every decision was condescendingly questioned and critiqued militarily by Fetterman and his small group of enthusiastic supporters. Somehow Carrington maintained control of the situation throughout the problems with Fetterman. Nevertheless, Red Cloud's forces outside the walls made life increasingly difficult for the military as well as travelers along the Bozeman Trail. Bridger's reports of massive gatherings of Indians in the Big Horns only made matters worse.

Almost four thousand warriors had gathered only fifty miles north of Fort Phil Kearny on the Tongue River. Dull Knife and Roman Nose and their Cheyenne Dog Soldiers as well as Little Chief and Sorrel Horse of the Arapaho had joined Red Cloud's forces; many young warriors were beginning to become well-known leaders among the Lakotas as well.

One young Oglala warrior in particular had developed age-old decoy tricks with which to ensnare the *wasichus*; his name was *Ta Shon Ka Witko* — Crazy Horse! Throughout the fall he and other warriors had experimented with drawing the soldiers into a trap and were coming increasingly closer to major success with each attempt.

On the morning of December 21, 1866, a Lakota war party attacked a train of wagons hauling wood to the fort from the Big Horn Mountains. Carrington reluctantly agreed to allow Fetterman to rush to rescue the train with these orders: "Support the wood train. Relieve it and report to me. Do not engage or pursue Indians at its expense. Under no circumstances pursue over the ridge, that is, Lodge Trail Ridge."[21] The last time anyone saw Fetterman alive was the moment he and his command of

eighty men disappeared over Lodge Trail Ridge in pursuit of a small party
of Indians.

A Lakota named Fire Thunder describes what happened on the other
side of Lodge Trail Ridge:

> There were many of us there. Red Cloud was over all of us but the
> chief of our band was Big Road. We started out on horseback just
> about sunrise, riding up the creek toward the soldiers' town on the
> Piney, for we were going to attack it. The sun was about half way up
> when we stopped at the place where the Wasichu's road came down a
> steep, narrow ridge and crossed the creek. It was a good place to
> fight, so we sent some men ahead to coax the soldiers out. While
> they were gone, we divided into two parts and hid in the gullies on
> both sides of the ridge and waited. After a long while we heard a shot
> up over the hill, and we knew the soldiers were coming. So we held
> the noses of our ponies that they might not whinny at the soldiers'
> horses. Soon we saw our men coming back, and some of them were
> walking and leading their horses, so that the soldiers would think
> they were worn out. Then the men we had sent ahead came running
> down the road between us, and the soldiers on horseback followed,
> shooting. When they came to the flat at the bottom of the hill, the
> fighting began all at once . . . There were many bullets, but there
> were more arrows—so many that it was like a cloud of grasshoppers
> all above and around the soldiers; and our people, shooting across,
> hit each other. The soldiers were falling all the while they were
> fighting back up the hill, and their horses got loose. Many of our
> people chased the horses, but I was not after horses; I was after Wa-
> sichus. When the soldiers got on top, there was not many of them
> left and they had no place to hide. They were fighting hard. We were
> told to crawl up on them, and we did. When we were close, someone
> yelled: 'Let us go! This is a good day to die. Think of the helpless
> ones at home!' Then we all cried, 'Hoka Hey!' and rushed at them. I
> was young then and quick on my feet, and I was one of the first to
> get in among the soldiers. They got up and fought very hard until
> not one of them was alive. They had a dog with them, and he started
> back up the road for the soldiers' town, howling as he ran. I did not
> shoot him because he looked too sweet; but many did shoot, and he
> died full of arrows. So there was nobody left of the soldiers.[22]

Fetterman, two other officers, seventy-six enlisted men and two civilians died that morning. In less than forty minutes Red Cloud had become

the first Indian to win a declared war against the United States government and had altered the course of the Indian Wars.

All inside Fort Phil Kearny were stunned. After an afternoon of palpable dread and tension Carrington sent a detachment to retrieve the bodies; that evening wagons brought in forty-nine naked, frozen, mutilated bodies. No one slept in Fort Phil Kearny that night; there were only 398 men with approximately 20 rounds of ammunition per man remaining in the post.

The following morning Carrington called a meeting of his officers and found them frightened and making excuses for not going out to retrieve the remaining thirty-two bodies. When finally asked, Bridger curtly reminded the wasichus that the Indians always managed to retrieve their fallen warriors.[23] Colonel Carrington showed his courage and leadership abilities in this situation refusing to submit to fear; he declared:

> I will not let the Indians entertain the conviction that our dead cannot and will not be rescued. If we cannot recover our dead, as the Indians always do, at whatever risk, how can you send out details for any purpose? That single fact will give them an idea of weakness here and would only stimulate them to risk an assault.[24]

Jim Bridger led the expedition to retrieve the bodies.
Dee Brown concludes:

> The Fetterman Massacre, made a profound impression upon Colonel Carrington. He was appalled by the mutilations—the disembowelings, the hacked limbs, the "private parts severed and indecently placed on the person." He brooded upon the reasons for such savagery, and eventually wrote an essay on the subject, philosophizing that the Indians were compelled by some paganistic belief to commit the terrible deeds that remained forever in his mind. Had Colonel Carrington visited the scene of the Sand Creek Massacre, which occurred only two years before the Fetterman Massacre, he would have seen the same mutilations—committed upon Indians by Colonel Chivington's soldiers. The Indians who ambushed Fetterman were only imitating their enemies, a practice which in warfare, as in civilian life, is said to be the sincerest form of flattery.
>
> The Fetterman Massacre also made a profound impression upon the United States government. It was the worst defeat the Army had suffered yet in Indian warfare, and the second in American history

from which came no survivors. Carrington was recalled from command, reinforcements were sent to the forts in the Powder River country, and a new peace commission was dispatched from Washington to Fort Laramie.[25]

Red Cloud had halted the invasion of his country. He kept his promise and burned Fort Phil Kearny to the ground.

Chapter Six

PAHASKA BECOMES BUFFALO BILL

Mene-Seela consulted an extraordinary oracle to instruct him where the buffalo were to be found. When he and the other chiefs sat down on the grass to smoke and converse, as they often did during the march, the old man picked up one of those enormous black and green crickets, which the Dahcotah call by a name that signifies "They who point out the buffalo." Holding the bloated insect between his fingers and his thumb, the old Indian looked attentively at him and inquired, "Tell me father, where must we go to-morrow to find the buffalo?" The cricket twisted about his long horns in evident embarrassment. At last he pointed, or seemed to point, them westward. Mene-Sela, dropping him gently on the grass, laughed with great glee, and said that if we went that way in the morning we should be sure to kill game.

(*The Oregon Trail*, Francis Parkman)

As the Indian Wars raged in the Powder River country and along the North and South Platte, Will Cody's reputation as a scout and buffalo hunter began to emerge in Kansas. In 1867 the Great Plains were becoming more densely populated with soldiers, while the fringes of the frontier were also laced with tiny railroad companies heroically competing with Union Pacific in its colossal race to meet the Central Pacific after it crossed the High Sierras. The Kansas Pacific Railroad, which later merged into the Union Pacific Railroad, brought about Cody's failure as a hotel manager and real estate entrepreneur, yet also ironically introduced his unique talents as a plainsman to the attention of the world.

As the railroad grading crews penetrated the heart of Kansas buffalo country, twelve hundred men arrived to lay track across the prairie. The

Kansas Pacific Railroad contracted the firm of Goddard Brothers to feed and board these workers. Consequently, Goddard Brothers hired Cody, paying him $500 a month to kill twelve buffalo a day to feed these men. This was a healthy salary in 1867 yet it was really a bargain for the railroad company as they would have gone to much more trouble and paid quite a lot more money for beef. Cody's unusually high salary was also warranted because of the unique skills he possessed and the danger involved—both from animals and Indians—in securing buffalo meat. With the Indian Wars spreading throughout the west, even normally generous tribes were becoming less willing to share the bounty of the great buffalo herds. Complicating matters, as the railroads reached deeper into the prairie the mechanical commotion combined with ever growing numbers of people and made all game animals increasingly scarce. Along the Platte and Powder Rivers, Lakota Holy Men said the buffalo were being driven away by the smell of blood. Perhaps they were right. Tom McHugh informs us:

> ". . . the herd . . . would gather around her [a slain cow] and stupidly 'mill'—which means poke her with their horns, strike her with their hooves, and just generally lose their heads when they smelled her blood;" or; "They cluster around the fallen ones, sniff at the warm blood, bawl aloud in wonderment, and do everything but run away;" or, "Sometimes the smell of the blood from the wounded or dying would set the bulls crazy. They would run up and lick the blood, and sometimes toss the dead ones clear from the ground. Then they would bellow and fight each other, sometimes goring one another so badly they died. The great bulls, their tongues covered with blood, their eyes flashing, and tails sticking straight up, roaring and fighting, were terrible to see."[1]

Whatever the reason, game was sparse and, as a result, Indians were hungry and angry. This compounded Cody's danger hunting; in exploring the countryside searching for buffalo he was apt to become the hunted rather than the hunter. Nevertheless, having been reduced from town owner to grading laborer had humbled Cody and $500 a month could not be turned down. Buffalo Bill explains how he came to be known by his famous moniker:

> Leaving my partner, Rose, to complete our grading contract, I immediately began my career as a buffalo hunter for the Kansas Pacific

Railroad, and it was not long before I acquired considerable notoriety. It was at this time that the very appropriate name of "Buffalo Bill" was conferred upon me by the road-hands. It has stuck to me ever since, and I have never been ashamed of it.

During my engagement as hunter for the company—a period of less than eighteen months—I killed 4,280 buffaloes; and I had many exciting adventures with the Indians, as well as many hair-breath escapes . . .[2]

Cody's claim of 4,280 buffalo in eighteen months stood for decades until Buffalo Bill biographer Don Russell correctly noted that the scout's math was off; in killing 12 buffalo a day for eighteen months Cody would have killed 6,570 animals. Russell's research also concludes that Cody, because of other recorded events in his life, could not have hunted for eighteen months for Goddard Brothers but, in all likelihood, hunted for eight months delivering approximately 2,928 buffaloes—exceeding his contract by five or six animals a day. Cody's historical relevance should not be evaluated by numbering exactly how many buffalo he killed; the Kansas Pacific Railroad workers themselves immortalized the significance of his buffalo hunting when they sang:

> Buffalo Bill, Buffalo Bill
> He never missed and he never will
> Always aims and shoots to kill
> And the company pays his Buffalo Bill.[3]

Brilliant natural athletic talents and all the skills acquired as a youth on the Great Plains united in a magnificent display of unique abilities as Cody chased and killed buffalo. Cody's intrinsic talent as a hunter blended with his acquired gift for selecting horses—particularly Brigham, the Indian-trained horse he rode to fame as Buffalo Bill. Indeed, as a result of Cody's propensity to deflect credit from himself by praising others—especially his horses—Brigham became nearly as famous as Buffalo Bill himself in the early days of his career as a buffalo hunter. Newspaper headlines of the day mentioned Brigham as frequently as Cody.[4] In praising Brigham, however, Cody also reveals much of his own personality and his capacity to surrender the moment to absolute intuition. In his autobiography, Cody comments on his technique of hunting buffalo while riding Brigham "Indian-style," that is, with no saddle or bridle:

Brigham knew nearly as much about the business as I did, and if I had twenty bridles they would have been of no use to me, as he understood everything, and all that he expected of me was to do the shooting. It is a fact, that Brigham would stop if a buffalo did not fall at the first fire, so as to give me a second chance, but if I did not kill the buffalo then, he would go on, as if to say, "You are no good, and I will not fool away time by giving you more than two shots." Brigham was the best horse I ever owned for buffalo chasing.[5]

Cody's explanation starkly reveals the essence of his success as a buffalo hunter; in surrendering himself over to the instincts of his horse Cody not only rode and hunted like an Indian, he thought like an Indian! Unlike most Indians, however, Cody was armed with a weapon he called a "needle gun." To most frontiersmen, anything that had a needle-like firing pin that went through the powder to strike a primer at the front end of a cartridge was referred to as a "needle gun." When converted to breechloading, the .50 caliber Springfield rifle was commonly referred to as a needle gun. Probably getting the idea from Victor Hugo's drama *Lucretia Borgia; or, The Poisoner,* which he may have seen in St. Louis, Cody named his deadly weapon after the play.[6]

Aside from the combination of an extraordinary horse and powerful weapon performing in concert with his own exceptional natural talents, Cody developed a unique procedure for killing buffalo. The method Cody created reveals a sagacious awareness of Plains Indian buffalo hunting techniques and a penetrating insight into fundamental buffalo nature as well.

Bringing down buffalo was dangerous work. Previous descriptions of the bulls' reactions to the blood of fallen members of the herd is but a small sample of the peril involved. Because of the danger, Plains Indians brought buffalo down anyway they could. They were not morally opposed to setting fire to the prairie and running a herd of buffalo over a cliff in order to enjoy the plunder; developing another tactic, courageous Indian men who were also good swimmers would take advantage of the water and attack the buffalo herds as they crossed rivers. Indians intensely studied buffalo behavior in order to find any circumstance in which the animal might become vulnerable to their attack. Plains Indians simply tried anything to kill buffalo; they were essentially involved in a never-ending, absolutely pragmatic quest for meat, hides, bones, and sinew. Once Plains Indians gained greater numbers of horses, however, an astonishing equestrian spectacle evolved as they raced on ponies into the massive buffalo herds. The artist George

Catlin described a Hidatsa hunt in 1832:

> . . . the hunters were galloping their horses around and driving their
> whizzing arrows or long lances to the hearts of the noble animals,
> which in many instances, becoming infuriated with deadly weapons
> in their sides, erected their shaggy manes over their blood-shot eyes,
> and furiously plunged forward at the sides of their assailants' horses;
> sometimes goring them to death at a lunge, and putting their dis-
> mounted riders to flight for their lives. Sometimes the dense crowd
> was opened, and the blinded horsemen, too intent on their prey,
> amidst a cloud of dust, were hemmed and wedged in amongst the
> crowding beasts, over whose backs they were obliged to leap for se-
> curity, leaving their horses to the fate that might await them in this
> wild and desperate war. Many were the bulls that turned upon their
> assailants, meeting them with desperate resistance; and many were
> the warriors who were dismounted, saving themselves by the supe-
> rior muscles of their legs. Some who were closely pursued by the
> bulls wheeled suddenly round, and snatching the half of a buffalo
> robe from around their waists, threw it over the horns and eyes of
> the infuriated beast, and darting by its side, drove the arrow or lance
> to its heart. Others suddenly dashed off upon the prairies by the side
> of the affrighted animals which had escaped from the throng, and
> closely escorting them for a few rods, caused their hearts' blood to
> flow in streams, and brought their huge carcasses to the ground.[7]

Mounted Plains Indians were the best buffalo hunters in the world.
Their skill, as Will Cody's, sprang from peerless horsemanship and deadly
marksmanship. Again the concept of the circle permeated Plains Indian
thinking. Riders circled the buffalo herd and, signaling a charge, called out
"Hoka Hey!" Soon a great cloud of dust appeared and the hunters, all
nearly naked except for their arrow-filled quivers, raced in among the
herd. Hunters would ride up beside the buffalo and shoot him just behind
the left shoulder. If the hunter was an expert shot and the arrow hit no
bones the shaft might pass straight through the animal. If this happened
the rider would pull the arrow the rest of the way through and use it for yet
another kill.[8]

Francis Parkman, Jr. presents a spectacular description of mounted
Lakota buffalo hunting methods and the danger involved:

> . . . each hunter, as if by common impulse, violently struck his horse,
> each horse sprang forward convulsively, and scattering in charge in

order to assail the entire herd at once, we all rushed headlong upon the buffalo. We were among them in an instant. Amid the trampling and the yells I could see their dark figures running hither and thither through clouds of dust, and the horsemen parting in pursuit. While we were charging on one side, our companions had attacked the bewildered and panic stricken herd on the other. The uproar and confusion lasted but for a moment. The dust cleared away, and the buffalo could be seen scattering as from a common centre, flying over the plain singly, or in long files and small compact bodies, while behind each followed the Indians, lashing their horses to furious speed, forcing them close upon their prey, and yelling as they launched arrow after arrow into their sides. The large black carcasses were strewn thickly over the ground. Here and there buffalo were standing, their bleeding sides feathered with arrows; and as I rode past them their eyes would glare, they would bristle like giant cats, and feebly attempt to rush up and gore my horse.[9]

As Indians hunted buffalo with spears and arrows, all killing had to be done at close range. This method of killing buffalo not only required superb horsemanship and impeccable accuracy but also required nerves of steel; one does not get a second chance at anything while racing through a rampaging herd of wounded and terrified buffalo. Inept hunters found death quickly in a buffalo herd. Indeed, it is a supreme irony that a buffalo nearly ended General George Armstrong Custer's career on the Plains nearly a decade before Little Big Horn.[10]

Taking into consideration that Plains Indians, who would be galloping without saddles or bridles, regarded an arrow passing completely through a buffalo a "clean" kill, one begins to glean an understanding of the unification of mental and physical skills involved killing buffalo in the traditional Indian style. Luther Standing Bear's description of his first boyhood buffalo hunt is perhaps the best presentation of the balance of danger and moral values involved in the Plains Indian style of buffalo hunting:

I rode right up alongside the buffalo, just as my father had instructed me. Drawing an arrow from my quiver, and holding to my pony with all the strength of my legs, I fitted the arrow and let drive with all my strength. I had expected to kill the buffalo right quick, but the arrow went into the neck—and I thought I had taken such good aim! But the buffalo only shook her head and kept on running. I again caught up with her, and let another arrow loose, which struck near the heart. Although it was not fired with sufficient strength to kill at once, I saw that she was fast weakening and running much slower. Then I pulled my third arrow and fired again. This went into the heart. I began to think that buffalo had all the nine lives of a cat, and was going to prove as hard as a cat to kill, when I saw blood running from her nose. Then I knew she would have to drop pretty soon. I shot my fourth arrow into her, and she staggered and dropped over on her side, and soon was dead. So I had killed my first buffalo.

When I examined the fallen animal and noted that I had shot five arrows into her, I felt this was too many arrows for just one buffalo. Then I recalled that my father had once killed two buffalo with only a single arrow. He knew he had hit the first one in the right spot, as the arrow penetrated very deeply and he simply rode up alongside, drew the arrow through, pulled it out again and used it to kill the second one.

As I stood there thinking of this, it made me feel ashamed of my marksmanship. I began to think of pulling all the arrows out but one. In fact, I had started to do this, when a remark that my father had once made to me came into my head. It was, "Son, always remember that a man who tells lies is never liked by anybody." So, instead of trying to cheat, I told the truth; and it made me feel happier.[11]

The virtuous buffalo hunter earned his honorable reputation racing alone on horseback in focused, gleeful abandon among the thunderous herd.

Cody clearly adhered to the Plains Indian ethic of buffalo hunting. Expanding upon the Plains Indians' technique, however, blessed with Brigham's training and speed, and a state-of-the-art .50 caliber rifle, Cody raced to the front of the herd, darted close into the stampede and shot the lead bulls first. In observing buffalo behavior, Cody had learned that when the dominant bulls fell the stampeding herd would suddenly begin to run to the left until they spiraled in a leaderless circle, which allowed him, much like a wrangler with a herd of cows, to ride the edges of the circle and shoot as many animals as he could kill. Furthermore, Cody's clever hunting technique created a fortunate placement of his fallen prey that kept the slain buffaloes in a relatively contained area while also making the butchering and loading of the meat a much simpler process. Cody and Brigham were nothing if not efficient. Otherwise, Buffalo Bill never could have killed and brought in so many animals.

It is important here for the modern reader to realize that the buffaloes Will Cody was killing were being fed to men rather than slaughtered for sport. Most all of the slain animal was eaten or used; aside from the meat, non-Indians enduring a Kansas winter had the same need for buffalo robes as Indians. The Kansas Pacific Railroad quickly realized the advantage of Buffalo Bill's growing fame and began to mount the heads of the buffalo he killed and use them as promotional gifts in advertising campaigns. Later in life, Cody commented that he often saw the mounted heads of buffalo he ·had killed for the Kansas Pacific Railroad on display in restaurants, hotels, and saloons as he traveled the world as a showman.

It is most significant for the modern reader to remember that Cody was hunting buffalo in the style of Native Americans. On any day the buffalo could have won; Cody might have been killed and the world never would have known his name.

Furthermore, in considering Cody's career as a buffalo hunter, it is also important to bear in mind that there were still millions of buffalo on the Great Plains when he rose to fame as Buffalo Bill. William Frederick Cody's entire career as a buffalo hunter, like the hunting careers of untold thousands of Plains Indians who preceded him, had absolutely no effect on the astounding numbers of buffalo still on the prairies in the 1860s. The wanton slaughter, which so catastrophically reduced their numbers, was instigated by President Grant, General William Tecumseh Sherman, General Philip Sidney Sheridan, and the War Department only a few years later in the 1870s.

The War Department's style of buffalo hunting was a completely different matter. This shamefully arrogant military tactic was savage environmental warfare—a skillfully conceived and brilliantly orchestrated, hypocritical, killing-for-the-sake-of-killing—often from a moving train, or from a strategically safe distance with a powerful weapon. By the mid-1870s—as Sherman and Sheridan's War Department wrestled control of the Indian Bureau away from eastern Christian and humanitarian organizations—European royalty, wealthy Americans, patriots, and general thrill-seekers were inspired and goaded by revered government officials in such speeches as this one by General Philip Sheridan:

> Buffalo hunters have done in the past two years and will do more in the next year to settle the vexed Indian question, than the entire regular army has done in the past thirty years. They are destroying the Indians' commissary, and it is a well-known fact that an army losing its base of supplies is placed at a great disadvantage. Send them powder and lead, if you will; for the sake of a lasting peace, let them kill,

skin and sell until the buffaloes are exterminated. Then your prairies can be covered with speckled cattle and the festive cowboy, who follows the hunter as a second forerunner of an advanced civilization.[12]

This purely militaristic and imperialistic thinking was radically different from the lifestyle or logic of Cody or any plainsmen or buffalo hunter of the 1860s—Indian or non-Indian. Truly, aside from the necessity of food, buffalo hunting was ethical sport for the Plains Indian and white buffalo hunter alike in the 1860s. Prior to the senseless carnage of the 1870s, Indian and non-Indian hunters took only the annual increase in the herd with each year's hunt.

Ranging in the west up and down the spine of the Rocky Mountains from Alaska to the Gulf of Mexico and on the prairies as far east as Pennsylvania, the great North American buffalo herds—by some accounts originally numbering 80 million—fed some Indian tribes at all times. Early European descriptions of the numbers of buffalo stagger the imagination. A typical herd was variously estimated by some to number half a million, but it would not be an exaggeration to estimate a normal herd size at 200,000.[13]

Nathaniel Langford, the first superintendent of Yellowstone National Park, offers this amazing description of the sizes of buffalo herds:

> Our trip across the plains in 1862, after crossing the Red River of the North, buffaloes abounded everywhere. We thought the herds of 5,000, 10,000 or more, very large herds, until we got beyond the second crossing of the Cheyenne River, where the herds increased in size...I well recall the day when we camped for the night. The sky was perfectly clear, when we heard a distant rumbling sound, which we thought was thunder but our guide, Pierre Botineau exclaimed, "Buffalo!" and as we could see no sign of them, he said they were a few miles away . . . Soon we saw a cloud of dust rising in the east, and the rumbling grew louder and I think it was about half an hour when the front of the herd came fairly into view. The edge of the herd nearest to us was one-half to three-quarters of a mile away. From an observation with our field glasses, we judged the herd to be 5 or 6 (some said 8 or 10) miles wide, and the herd was more than an hour passing us at a gallop. They were running as rapidly as a horse can go at a keen gallop, about 12 miles an hour . . . the whole space, say 5 miles by 12 miles, as far as we could see, was a seemingly solid mass of buffaloes . . .[14]

Colonel Richard Irving Dodge described the way the massive herds gathered:

Early in the spring . . . the horizon would begin to be dotted with buffalo, single or in groups of two or three, forerunners of the coming herd. Thicker and thicker, and in larger groups they come, until by the time the grass is well up, the whole vast landscape appears as a mass of buffalo, some individuals feeding, others lying down, but the herd moving slowly; moving constantly to the northward. . . . Some years as in 1871, the buffalo appeared to move northward in one immense column, often times twenty to fifty miles in width, and of unknown depth from front to rear.[15]

Until the 1870s, when they became the target of the U.S. military's wrath, the reappearance of the continually migrating buffalo herds would be greeted with merry calls not unlike the whaler's cry "thar she blows," at which time plainsmen of all colors, shapes and sizes would race for their bows, arrows spears, guns and horses. The traditional Plains Indian style of hunting, however, as in the initial non-Indian hunters that followed, was motivated first by the reality of necessity. The buffalo hunters inspired by Sheridan were seeking a less noble kind of glory. It certainly was not sport.

Nevertheless, with the growing numbers of immigrants encountering such incredible numbers of buffalo, it was inevitable that other "Buffalo Bills" would be found on the plains in the 1860s. Perhaps the most outspoken person to claim the title was William Mathewson. According to Wild West press agent, Frank Winch, in 1911 William F. Cody received a letter from Mathewson in which the old-timer chastised him for claiming he won the title from Bill Comstock. Moreover, Mathewson claimed Cody knew he was known by the name of "Buffalo Bill" before he ever went to work for the Kansas Pacific Railroad. Mathewson finished his letter telling Cody that when he brought his Wild West show to Topeka he intended to confront him and tell him to his face that he had no claim to the name.[16]

Winch said that Cody accepted Mathewson's claim and sent him to find the old-timer. Winch discovered that Mathewson was having a such a hard time financially that he had recently been forced to sell a treasured rifle. Winch found and bought the rifle and returned it to Mathewson as a gift

. . . to "the original Buffalo Bill" in Cody's name. That broke the ice, and when the show arrived, Winch brought Cody and Mathewson to-

gether. The quarrel evaporated and Mathewson was an honored guest
at the afternoon performance. Characteristically, Cody arranged to
take care of Mathewson's needs unknown to the recipient. Winch
arranged with a newspaperman to "buy" (with Cody's money) weekly
installments of Mathewson's life story.[17]

Perhaps the most famous "William" competing for the title of "Buffalo
Bill," however, was the man Mathewson mentioned in his threat to Cody,
Billy Comstock, post guide and interpreter at Fort Wallace. Comstock was
part Cheyenne and had served as General George Armstrong Custer's
chief scout in Kansas in 1867. As many scouts of the period, Comstock was
not destined to enjoy a long life and was killed in an ambush by Cheyenne
Indians in the summer 1868, not long after his famous contest with Will
Cody.

The contest between Comstock and Cody ignited Buffalo Bill's fame
and is one of the most celebrated events in American frontier history.
Comstock enjoyed a reputation as a buffalo hunter similar to Cody's, particularly among the soldiers at Fort Wallace. These military men were anxious to arrange a shooting match between the two Bills in order to gamble
on which man would win. Cody was always anxious to enter into any kind
of contest—especially a horse race or a shooting match—and jumped at
the chance to meet Comstock on the field. "We were to hunt one day of
eight hours," Cody writes,

> beginning at eight o'clock in the morning, and closing at four o'-
> clock in the afternoon. The wager was five hundred dollars a side,
> and the man who should kill the greater number of buffaloes from
> on horseback was to be declared the winner.
>
> The hunt took place about twenty miles east of Sheridan, and as it
> had been pretty well advertised and noised abroad, a large crowd wit-
> nessed the interesting and exciting scene. An excursion party, mostly
> from St. Louis, consisting of about a hundred gentlemen and ladies,
> came out on a special train to view the sport, and among the number
> was my wife, with little baby Arta, who had come to remain with me
> for a while.
>
> The buffaloes were quite plenty, and it was agreed that we should
> go into the same herd at the same time and "make a run" as we called
> it, each one killing as many as possible. A referee was to follow each
> of us on horseback when we entered the herd, and count the buf-
> faloes killed by each man. The St. Louis excursionists, as well as the

other spectators, rode out to the vicinity of the hunting grounds in wagons and on horseback, keeping well out of sight of the buffaloes, so as not to frighten them, until the time came for us to dash into the herd; when they were to come up as near as they pleased and witness the chase.[18]

Cody won the first of the three runs killing 38 buffaloes to Comstock's 23. Nevertheless, Cody proudly points out that Comstock's buffalo were "scattered over a distance of three miles, where mine lay close together. I had 'nursed' my buffaloes, as a billiard-player does the balls when he makes a big run."[19]

After a brief champagne break, another herd was spotted and Cody and Comstock went after them in a flash; Cody killed eighteen buffalo to Comstock's fourteen. After this quick run the contestants broke again for champagne and lunch. After eating the group had to search for three miles in order to find another herd and resume the contest. This accomplished, Cody, exhibiting the panache that would soon distinguish him as a showman, decided to demonstrate a bit of his mastery of the sport for the audience: Well aware that he was far ahead of Comstock as they approached the last round, Cody removed Brigham's saddle and bridle, raced back among the herd and promptly killed thirteen buffaloes. Then, spotting a single buffalo, Cody directed the animal straight for the audience and shot him so that he would collapse at their feet. It was his sixty-ninth buffalo to Comstock's forty-six.[20] From that day forward, Will Cody was Buffalo Bill.

Not long after the famous contest the Kansas Pacific Railroad reached its destination in Sheridan, putting Cody out of work. Tensions spreading from the Indian Wars in the Powder River country and along the North and South Platte River had grown much more violent in northern and western Kansas, where the powerful Cheyenne/Lakota alliance was drawing other Plains Indians into the fight. The Arapaho, Comanche, Kiowa, and Wichita, as the Cheyenne and Sioux Nations, were experiencing fundamental changes in their country as the emigration swelled. Anxiety soon exploded into depredations as settlers' homesteads and mail-wagons in the region were attacked with increasing regularity by powerful Cheyenne forces.

Meanwhile, Red Cloud's success on the battlefield in the Powder River wars had major political impact in New York and Washington. The Indian's Friends and other such humanitarian and Christian organizations— many fanatically inspired by the success of the American abolitionist movement in freeing slaves—gained control of the Indian Bureau. In the winter of 1864–1865, many of these church associations and idealists had lobbied Congress demanding that military force should be abolished as a method of dealing with Indians and that such aggressive tactics be replaced with "Christian" attitudes and policies. As these organizations gained more political power in Washington, General Sherman, being accused of creating a "war of extermination," succumbed to pressure to negotiate with the western tribes rather than continue fighting them. Defending himself, Sherman remarked,

As to extermination, it is for the Indians to determine. We don't want to exterminate or even to fight them. At best it is an inglorious war, it is not apt to add much to our fame or our personal comfort; and as for our soldiers, to whom we owe our first thoughts, it is all danger and extreme labor, without a single compensating advantage. To accuse us of inaugurating or wishing such a war, is to accuse us of want of common sense. . . . The injustice and frauds heretofore practiced on the Indians as charged, are not of our making; and I know the present war did not result from any act of ours.[21]

In the summer 1867 General Sherman formed the commission of Taylor, Henderson, Tappan, Sanborn, Harney, and Terry to structure a peace plan. The commissioners selected were heavily influenced by the ideological pressure of humanitarian politicians and such slogans as, "Don't fight the Sioux—feed them!"

Sherman had surrendered to political pressure yet made his true feeling known in a letter to commissioner Tappan:

Either the Indians must give way or we must abandon all west of the Missouri River and confess that forty million whites are cowed by a few thousand savages. . . . I have stretched my power and authority to help them, but when they laugh at our cordiality, rape our women, murder our men, burn whole trains with their drivers to cinders, and send word that they never intended to keep their treaties, then we must fight them. When we come to fight Indians, I will take my code from soldiers and not from citizens.[22]

The peacemakers' dreams were doomed. The warriors on both sides were polarized and had drawn daring lines in the sand. Nevertheless, the peace commission was first sent to deal with the powerful tribes of the southern plains at Medicine Lodge before traveling north to negotiate the famous Fort Laramie Treaty of 1868 with Red Cloud.

Sixty miles south of Fort Larned, in a beautiful grove of trees, the site of Medicine Lodge was chosen for a location for the Southern Plains peace conference. On October 16 as many leaders from the various tribes as could be encouraged to attend arrived at Medicine Lodge. Over 4,000 Indians arrived. The Comanche and Kiowas were promised a reservation of three million acres, while the Cheyenne and Arapaho were promised 4,300,000 acres. They were also promised annuities such as beef, flour, sugar, and coffee. They were also promised farm implements as well as guns and ammunition.

Even though it was inspired and motivated by noble principles, the absence of true tribal leadership doomed the negotiations. With men such as Roman Nose and Tall Bull of the Cheyenne avoiding the conference, the Medicine Lodge Treaty Commission succumbed to the old government pattern of negotiating with tribal members who were not authorized to speak for the people. Sadly, the Medicine Lodge Treaty became yet another muddled, superficial communication which resulted in a strained peace that produced nearly as much tension in Washington for General Sherman as it did anxiety for the Cheyenne, Arapaho, Comanche, and Kiowa leaders on the Kansas prairies.

Henry Sell and Victor Weybright offer a synopsis of the War Department's troublesome situation:

> The problem of the U. S. Army on the western frontier in the years immediately after the Civil War was staggering. General Phil Sheridan's command, the Department of the Missouri, included an area of about 150,000 square miles in western Kansas, eastern Colorado, Oklahoma, and New Mexico. Most of this territory had been mapped by military expeditions, but was known in detail only by Indians and trappers. To patrol the whole area Sheridan was allowed 2,600 men: 1,200 cavalry and 1,400 infantry. The cavalry was the Seventh and Tenth (Negro) Regiments; the infantry the Third and Fourth Regiments, and four companies of the Thirty-eighth Regiment. With these he had to garrison twenty-six army posts at great distances from each other. He was also expected to furnish troops quickly when any of the settlements were attacked.[23]

Sheridan arrived at Fort Leavenworth in the spring of 1868 to discover

Indians extreme dissatisfaction with the Medicine Lodge Treaty of the preceding year. In his memoirs, Sheridan wrote:

> This grumbling was very general in extent, and during the winter found outlet in occasional marauding, so, fearing a renewal of the pillaging and plundering of an early day, to prepare myself for the work evidently ahead the first thing I did on assuming permanent command was to make a trip to Fort Larned and Fort Dodge, near which places the bulk of the Indians had congregated on Pawnee and Walnut creeks. I wanted to get near enough to the camps to find out for myself the actual state of feeling among the savages, and also to familiarize myself with the characteristics of the Plains Indians.[24]

General Sheridan headquartered himself at Fort Hays in order to direct the campaigns from a central location. Almost simultaneously, Cody coincidentally rode into Fort Hays seeking employment as a scout.

Scouting was dangerous business—particularly for horses. Mounts frequently took bullets intended for their riders and, since a man on foot is easier to hit than a rider, were often themselves the target. Since he had no place to keep Brigham, and could not bear the thought of getting him killed in battle, Cody decided to sell his remarkable horse. Reluctant as he was to part with the beloved horse that had often saved his life while also providing him with a livelihood, Cody knew he had to let Brigham go. The clamor over the horse was so great that Cody offered him in a raffle of ten chances at thirty dollars each. A gentleman named Ike Bonham won Brigham and took him to Wyandotte, Kansas. Cody kept himself informed concerning Brigham's whereabouts for several years, noting in his autobiography that his old horse won several big races against thoroughbreds for Bonham. Cody eventually lost contact with Brigham only to rediscover his old friend years later while performing in Memphis. Will reunited with Brigham and, at the publication of his autobiography in 1879, visited the old horse every time he performed in the city.

After selling Brigham Cody was hired as a scout and guide at Fort Larned. He set his family up in a home in Leavenworth and promptly returned to the Kansas prairie to report for duty. The summer of 1868 was the last period of Cody's history which remains obscure. Since the army did not encourage the employment of scouts except during times of active campaigning it is likely that Cody was unemployed during this time. While there were no active campaigns, the Medicine Lodge Treaty had only succeeded in bringing an uneasy peace to the plains. Although Indians had promised to go to reservations, they made no move toward them. This caused a delay in ratifying the treaty in Congress, and affected the paying of annuities promised by the government.[25]

Cody was assigned to Brevet Major General William B. Hazen at Fort Larned. Hazen, who had long made his sympathies with the Plains Indian known, had the near-impossible task of carrying out the provisions set forth in the Medicine Lodge Treaty of 1867. As superintendent of Indian Affairs for the Southern Plains, Hazen's hands were tied at Fort Larned. He could not issue goods until the treaty was ratified and the delay was not making the three hundred lodges of Kiowa and Comanche Indians camped nearby very happy. Complicating matters, in July the Cheyenne began a series of murderous raids, making the general reluctant to issue arms and ammunition promised to the Kiowa and Comanche in the treaty. The Kiowa and Comanche protested, maintaining they had been assured by the treaty that they would be given either arms and ammunition to hunt buffalo, or cattle. Several of the chiefs requested a conference with Brevet Brigadier General Alfred Sully and satisfied him that the depredations were the acts of but a few renegade warriors and he risked angering the entire populations of both tribes by withholding guns and ammunition. General Sully intervened and arranged a meeting with General Sheridan. The Indians thought Sheridan looked like a bear in a bad mood. When he threatened them with death if they used the arms to go on the path of war one of the Indians retorted: "Let your soldiers grow long hair, so that we can have some honor in killing them."[26]

Sully issued arms to the Kiowa and Comanche. By August, however, the general experienced the consequences of his decision; Cheyenne, Arapaho, and Lakota war parties hit settlers hard in a series of violent raids along the Saline Valley and Solomon Rivers.

General Sheridan immediately ordered his assistant inspector-general Brevet Colonel George A. Forsyth to hire fifty first-class hardy frontiersmen to be used as scouts against the hostile Indians and, within five days, had filled all the positions. By mid-September, Forsyth embarked to the headwaters of the Solomon and encountered Cheyenne War Chief Roman Nose and nearly 1,000 warriors.

As Red Cloud led the Lakota, so Roman Nose ("*Woquini*") led the Cheyenne. Roman Nose had refused to sign Medicine Lodge Treaty and his recalcitrance assured the failure of the subsequent treaty. Over 4,000 Indians attended the conference. Still, so few of Roman Nose's Cheyenne were present the treaty was essentially an agreement negotiated with friendly Kiowa, Comanche and Arapaho representatives who—for the promise of the right amount of presents—would agree to whatever the "Great Father" wished. Roman Nose had continued on the warpath after the treaty was signed. During the winter of 1867 most all the Cheyenne had camped south of the Arkansas River near Fort Larned. As spring approached, however, bands began to slowly stream north toward their traditional hunting grounds near Smoky Hill. Along the way the young warriors began raiding settlers again and by mid-summer the entire region was engulfed in a bloody war. As autumn 1868 approached most Cheyenne north of the Arkansas River were gathered along the Arikaree Fork of the Republican River.

Roman Nose, as many Plains Indian warriors, possessed magic abilities which prevented his being killed by bullets. Nevertheless, when Forsyth's expedition arrived at the Arikaree Fork the Dog Soldier's magic power had been tarnished only days before in a feast with Sioux allies in which a Lakota woman had unknowingly used an iron fork to prepare fried bread for the warrior-chief. Unaware of the fact that any metal touching the chief's food would take away his power—his *medicine*—the woman had served Roman Nose and he had eaten the bread before discovering the bread had been prepared with iron. When alerted by Tall Bull and other Dog Soldiers that Forsyth's scouts had discovered his camp, Roman Nose was undergoing purification ceremonies attempting to restore the magic which protected him from bullets. Without his bulletproof power, Roman Nose painted his face for battle realizing that the fight he was about to enter with Forsyth would probably be his last.

The fight took place at Beecher's Island, which was named for a lieutenant among the slain, on the Arickaree Fork of the Republican River. The mounted Indians charged the frontiersmen's tiny force there repeatedly, only being turned back by the scouts' firepower and marksmanship. Forsyth's scouts fired volleys with their Spenser repeating carbines until Indian forces swarmed their fortifications. Then they fought hand to hand with the Cheyenne warriors. The scouts were under siege from September 17-25, when they were rescued by a detachment of the Tenth Cavalry. Roman Nose was killed in the fight.[27]

Roman Nose's death stunned the Cheyenne yet Tall Bull quickly assumed leadership of the Dog Soldiers and retreated to council. Meanwhile, as the Indian Wars erupted with the Cheyenne in Kansas, Cody had a dangerous encounter with Kiowa Chief Santana which reveals the scout's shrewdness as well as his luck. After escorting General Hazen the thirty miles between Fort Larned and Fort Zarah, Cody was returning to Fort Larned. About halfway between the forts Cody was "jumped" by forty Kiowas—men he had seen at Fort Larned earlier that day—men who had suddenly painted their faces for war. As the Kiowa rushed upon him with hands extended, however, Cody's immediate impulse was to shake hands with them, even though the war paint and rowdy manner of the Indians clearly indicated their intention was not friendly. An Indian grabbed Cody's hand and drew him and his mule in so close that he was quickly surrounded by the forty Kiowa warriors. The shouting Indians seized his guns and he was suddenly nearly knocked unconscious by a numbing blow from a tomahawk to his head. Just as quickly, the mob quirted their ponies and Will's mule into a run and headed out across the prairie.

The war party soon arrived at a large encampment and Cody immediately realized the Kiowa were no longer at peace; when he was presented before a group of chiefs, including Santana, Cody figured he would soon be departing this realm. A giant man with jet black hair flowing over enormous shoulders, Santana had thickly muscled arms and legs. Confident of his power, the Kiowa chief liked to laugh, eat, drink, ride, and fight hard and even enjoyed his enemies.[28] Eventually, after what seemed hours to Cody, Santana addressed the scout, asking where he had been.

While Santana and his warriors counciled, however, Will had time to structure a plan of action. Cody realized the Kiowas had been without meat for several weeks because of the delays ratifying the Medicine Lodge Treaty. He also knew the Kiowas had been promised cows and had been expecting a large herd of cattle for days. Cody told the Chief that he had been looking for the Kiowas' cattle herd.

This naturally piqued the old man's interest and he began to pepper Cody with a series of questions as to the whereabouts of the cows. Upon responding to the Chief, Cody led Santana to believe General Hazen had sent him out ahead to tell the Kiowas that the cattle had finally arrived, and that a large body of soldiers accompanied the herd. The scout then saw his opportunity to divert Santana's full attention from the ruse, and indignantly asked why Chief Santana's warriors had treated him so disrespectfully. Knowing the incident would jeopardize his receiving the cattle, Santana responded that his warriors were merely teasing and testing Cody's bravery as a joke. Aware Santana was lying, Cody decided to use the ruse to his advantage and played up his rough, insulting treatment at the hands of the chief's warriors. The wily Kiowa chief figured with a large group of soldiers about to arrive momentarily it would be wise to release the scout and get the cattle peaceably.[29]

Santana soon freed Cody, admonishing him not to be angry with his treatment at the hands of the young warriors. When the chief obsequiously inquired if the scout needed assistance with the cattle, Cody convinced Santana it would be best if he went alone to find the herd. Cody reasoned with the chief that the soldiers could then proceed to Fort Larned while he brought the cattle on to the Kiowa village by himself. The scout knew that he had laid out a pretty thin story and hoped to buy himself as much time as possible in order to make a run for it. To his amazement, Santana agreed to let him leave alone, yet, as Cody suspected, a group of ten or fifteen warriors followed him and he knew the race would soon begin. Giving them a little slip, Cody put a bit more distance between the Kiowas and himself and spurred his mule into a run. The warriors promptly saw what Cody was up to and quirted into quick pursuit.

The race across the prairie was a good one. Even though Cody was mounted upon a fast mule, the Kiowas' swift ponies were steadily gaining on him; the leaders of the war party were soon less than a quarter of a mile behind!

As was the case throughout his entire life, luck rode alongside Will Cody. Fort Larned finally came into sight. The scout was even more relieved, however, to see soldiers approaching in a wagon. Cody galloped his mule up to the wagon and hurriedly announced there was a war party on his heels. The group quickly hid the wagon in the trees, took cover and waited for the Kiowa warriors to appear.

They did not have to wait long. The Kiowa war party raced into the clearing and were caught in a deadly ambush. The tables turned, the Indians whirled, scrambling for their lives. After scalping the two dead Kiowas, taking their weapons and catching their ponies, Cody and the soldiers headed to Fort Larned. Drummers and buglers, having heard the nearby gunshots, were calling troops to arms. All inside thought Santana was attempting to capture the fort. Once inside Fort Larned, Cody learned an amazingly coincidental story concerning Santana's behavior earlier that very day.

Not long after Cody and General Hazen left Fort Larned Santana had arrived at the fort in his ambulance, which was a recent gift from the U.S. government. The chief had stormed into the commanding officer's quarters and demanded an explanation as to why General Hazen had left without giving him the cattle the government had promised. The commanding officer, Captain Parker, assured the chief that the general had no ulterior motives in leaving the fort and told him he did not know why the cattle were late, but they were expected to arrive soon.

Santana was furious and threatened to take the fort by force. Nevertheless, the young Captain refused to be intimidated by the old chief and Santana left in a huff. The Kiowa leader proceeded to the sutler's store and sold his ambulance. Next, he took some of the money from his sale and bought some illegal whisky and headed on horseback to his village.

Santana returned in less than an hour and surrounded the fort with nearly 800 warriors. Cody claimed Santana was "on his ear," but felt the chief intended to carry out his threat of seizing the fort.[30]

"On his ear" or not, Santana's posturing had served his purpose of diverting the soldiers as the tribe prepared to move the village. Once the village was moving, the warriors abandoned Fort Larned and lashed their horses in pursuit of the departing tribe. "On their way thither," Cody continues,

> they surprised and killed a party of wood-choppers down on the Pawnee Fork, as well as some herders who were guarding beef cattle; some seven or eight men in all, were killed, and it was evident that the Indians meant business.
>
> The soldiers with the wagon—whom I had met at the crossing of Pawnee Fork—had been out for the bodies of the men. Under the circumstances it was no wonder that the garrison, upon hearing the reports of our guns when we fired upon the party whom we ambushed, should have thought the Indians were coming back to give them another "turn."[31]

With the Kiowa and Comanche on the warpath it became imperative to get word to General Sheridan at Fort Hays sixty-five miles away. A storm was brewing and the heavens had become ominously dark; consequently, scouts at Fort Larned were afraid of making the treacherous ride and getting lost on the trail. Adding to the peril, it was known that a large war party of Indians was camped in the middle of the most direct route to Fort Hays. No one would volunteer to make the ride to present dispatches to General Sheridan.

Fellow scout Dick Curtis came to Buffalo Bill and, arguing that Cody knew the territory better than anyone else, tried to persuade him to make the ride. Cody initially declined the request, reminding Curtis of his adventures with Santana earlier that day. Curtis persisted. Cody finally relented, saying he did not mind the ride through the storm, but the war party concerned him. Nevertheless, he agreed to make the ride if provided with a good horse.

Cody was given the best horse in the company and, pausing long enough to eat lunch and fill his canteen with brandy, saddled up, rode out into the storm and headed for Fort Hays. He realized that the pitch black night was actually to his advantage; Indians would not be able to see him. The darkness, however, presented yet another danger; his horse might step in a hole. Preparing for such an occurrence, Cody took precautions and tied one of the reins to his belt. His apprehensions were warranted; less than three miles into the run his horse stumbled in a prairie dog hole, throwing him. The tied bridle soon retrieved the horse and Cody was quickly back in the saddle and riding.

As Cody approached rougher terrain he wisely let the horse find his own way through the corrugated gullies of the Kansas landscape. Soon, however, the scout topped a small hill and suddenly discovered himself in the midst of a herd of Indian horses. The intruder's presence was quickly reported and the war party immediately sprang into action. In a flash, there was a furious horse race across the prairie through the pitch black night.

Cody was mounted on a swift horse and, after several narrow escapes, managed to elude an Indian war party for the second time in one day. He rode into Fort Hays as the bugler played "Reveille." Within a few minutes he was introduced to General Philip Sheridan. It would become one of the most important relationships in Cody's life and it would begin with the general immediately asking the scout to perform an even more courageous feat than his accomplishments of the preceding day and night. Sheridan offered this account of the circumstances of his introduction to Buffalo Bill:

> This intelligence required that certain orders should be carried to Fort Dodge, ninety-five miles south of Hays. This too being a particularly dangerous route—several couriers having been killed on it—it was impossible to get one of the various "Petes," "Jacks," or "Jims" hanging around Hays City to take my communication. Cody learned of the strait I was in, manfully came to the rescue, and proposed to make the trip to Dodge, though he had just finished his long and perilous ride from Larned. I gratefully accepted his offer, and after four or five hours' rest he mounted a fresh horse and hastened on his journey, halting but once to rest on the way, and then

only for an hour, the stop being made at Coon Creek, where he got another mount from a troop of Cavalry. At Dodge he took six hours' sleep, and then continued on to his own post—Fort Larned—with more dispatches. After resting twelve hours at Larned, he was again in the saddle with tidings for me at Fort Hays, General Hazen sending him, this time, with word that the villages had fled to the south of the Arkansas. Thus, in all, Cody rode about 350 miles in less than sixty hours, and such an exhibition of endurance and courage was more than enough to convince me that his services would be extremely valuable in the campaign, so I retained him at Fort Hays till the battalion of the Fifth Cavalry arrived, and then made him chief of scouts for that regiment.[32]

The illustrious Fifth Cavalry had been organized in 1855 as the Second Cavalry. In 1861 the Civil War ripped the Second Cavalry apart as such extraordinary officers as Robert E. Lee and Albert Sidney Johnston departed to join the Confederacy, while exemplary leaders like George H. Thomas and George Stoneman, Jr. remained with Union forces. As a result of the divisive upheaval the Second Cavalry was re-organized as the Fifth Cavalry.

While Cody waited at Fort Hays for the battalion of Fifth Cavalry to arrive he spent time with the survivors of General Forsyth's battle and siege under Roman Nose's powerful Cheyenne forces. The battalion arrived on October 3 but Sheridan did not allow the Fifth much time to rest and prepare for its next expedition. The general planned to mount a major expedition of the Fifth Cavalry in pursuit of the Cheyenne Dog Soldiers. On October 5, led by its new chief of scouts, the battalion headed toward the Republican River country.

In rapid succession Will Cody had gone from hotel manager to real estate entrepreneur, railroad grader, buffalo hunter, military courier and scout. The swift transition of occupations leading to his becoming chief of scouts of the celebrated Fifth Cavalry now placed him in the white-hot center of the Indian Wars. The Hotamitanio, or Cheyenne Dog Soldiers, whom he was to locate for the U.S. military, were among the elite warrior societies of the great tribes of the western plains. They were the finest warriors of the Cheyenne Nation, bonded by severe discipline into a mystical fraternity. They were superlative horsemen, masters of guerrilla warfare, fearless, fierce, enraged, looking for a fight, and sworn by blood to defend their country at all costs.

Chapter Seven

CHIEF OF SCOUTS

These damn paper-collar soldiers.

—Jim Bridger, Chief-of-Scouts, Powder River Expedition, 1865
(*Jim Bridger, Mountain Man*, Stanley Vestal)

ALL the skills acquired in his youth on the Great Plains blossomed into maturity as Will Cody became chief of scouts for the Fifth Cavalry. Few on the prairie could shoot a rifle or pistol better than Cody. The requisite stamina and hardy education of the Pony Express had enabled him to endure and survive several courageous horseback adventures to deliver important military dispatches; his intimate understanding of Plains Indians and nimble, levelheaded thinking had saved his own life and the lives of others in the dangerous early days of the Indian Wars; and his extensive knowledge of Great Plains terrain and weather and his logistical experience of moving large numbers of men, livestock, wagons and freight for Russell, Majors, and Waddell served him well as he skillfully led the Fifth Cavalry over the rolling plains of Kansas. Cody felt proud as he admired the procession of the famous regiment behind him. He must have fondly recalled the day he and his father visited Fort Leavenworth and he saw cavalry maneuvers for the first time. The seventy-five six-mule wagons, pack mules and ambulances of the expedition rolled in an impressively long, winding file over the prairie as the regiment headed north toward the Beaver Creek country of the Republican River. Prior to the expedition's departure, General Sheridan had introduced Cody to the Fifth Cavalry's commanding officer, Colonel William Royal, and the other officers of the regiment. From Missouri, Colonel Royal had entered the army during the Mexican War and risen through the ranks to become brevet colonel during the Civil War. Either Royal's background triggered some of Cody's old mistrust of Missourians from his boyhood survival of the antebellum border wars in "bleeding Kansas," or Royal harbored some envy of Cody's fame, but the two personalities definitely clashed upon meeting.

Civilian scouts occasionally disagreed with U.S. cavalry officers and were even sometimes fired. Most were rehired in a few days, however, after tempers subsided. Cody was never fired, but that was not because he did everything according to regulations. His education as a Great Plains bullwacker and his experience in the Union Army during the Civil War had prepared him for dealing with differences of opinion within a traditional military chain of command in a more tactful manner than most, yet Cody was not above defying authority if common prairie sense suggested he could do a job better his way. Shortly after he assumed the position of chief of scouts for the Fifth Cavalry, such a situation arose. Whereas General Sheridan, having interacted with him in serious emergencies, had already been impressed with Cody before selecting him to lead the famous regiment, Colonel Royal would rudely demand an exhibition of Buffalo Bill's abilities.

After a couple of days of marching, Royal ordered Cody to find some buffalo to kill and feed the troops. Cody happily obeyed Royal's orders and routinely requested a couple of wagons in order to bring in the meat. Only slightly aware of Cody's talent through rumor, Royal insolently informed the scout that he intended for him to kill the buffalo first; when the buffalo were killed, he would send wagons for the meat. Exhibiting his characteristic grace, Cody said nothing and politely went about obeying his orders. After a short time, Cody returned and asked for wagons for the six buffalo slain just over the hill from the base camp.

The next afternoon Royal again requested that Cody bring in some fresh buffalo meat. Cody did not bother to ask the colonel for wagons this time. Instead he rode out on the prairie and found a small herd of buffalo, cut out seven brutes from the herd and stampeded them straight for the encampment. Rather than shooting the animals outright, however, Cody ran them full speed straight into the middle of the camp, shooting all seven buffaloes in rapid succession. Royal witnessed the entire proceedings and ran up to the scout, furiously demanding an explanation. Cody calmly responded that he decided to let the buffalo provide their own transportation rather than bothering him by asking again for wagons. The colonel saw Cody's point immediately and gave him no more trouble when he asked for wagons.[1]

Well fed by Buffalo Bill, the Fifth Cavalry continued the search for hostile Cheyenne only to discover them more elusive than expected. Soon, the regiment would learn the Cheyenne were as adept at military tactics as they were mysteriously evasive. Colonel Royal established a base camp on

Prairie Dog Creek and promptly ordered Cody and several detachments out to scout for the Dog Soldiers. While the scouting parties were gone, Tall Bull's warriors attacked the base camp, killing several soldiers and stealing sixty horses before vanishing into thin air.

After the stunning attack the battalion continued to search in vain for Tall Bull's band. Having been out on the prairie for eighteen days, however, the regiment abandoned its pursuit of the Dog Soldiers and headed toward the Kansas Pacific Railroad lines to resupply and to unite with its new commanding officer. On October 22, Brevet Major General Eugene A. Carr arrived at Buffalo Tank along the railroad lines to take command of the regiment. Senior Major of the Fifth Cavalry, Carr was perhaps the most experienced "Indian Fighter" in the U.S. military.'

General Carr brought Forsyth's Scouts with him. As a result of the fight and siege with Roman Nose's Cheyenne Dog Soldiers, Forsyth's Scouts were becoming well-known in the region. The general also brought another, more famous group with him: Major Frank North's Pawnee Scouts. Bitter adversaries of both the Lakota and Cheyenne, the Pawnee mercenaries were already renowned for leading the U.S. military to their enemies' villages.

In 1864, when Major General Samuel R. Curtis marched up the Platte River in a campaign against the Sioux and Cheyenne, Frank North was working as a clerk at the Pawnee Agency's traders' store near Genoa, Nebraska. The general requested a company of Pawnee scouts to lead him to the Sioux and Cheyenne. North and an associate promptly raised the outfit. Curtis was so impressed with North that he asked the clerk to raise a second company of Pawnee scouts in 1865.

On July 28, 1866, when Congress passed legislation authorizing the enlistment of Indian scouts, Frank North was prepared to mount the best group of Pawnee scouts possible to locate and engage the Lakota and Cheyenne. There were no provisions for officers in the new legislation so North and his scouts followed the same procedure as Cody and other scouts and enlisted through the Quartermaster's Department. North, however, had been commissioned captain during the Civil War and, as a result, entered service with that rank. He quickly was promoted to Major and by 1866–67 led a battalion of four companies of Pawnee scouts protecting construction of the Union Pacific Railroad. Around this time his brother, Luther H. North, who had served alongside Frank in the Civil War, enlisted as captain of company A of the battalion of Pawnee scouts.

The Lakota and Cheyenne had been at war with the Pawnee for generations. Dating back to 1830 when the Pawnee ambushed and killed an entire Cheyenne war party, the hostilities between the Cheyenne and Pawnee were especially rancorous. After the traditional year-long mourning of the Plains Indian tribes, the Cheyenne, who were accompanied by their faithful allies, the Lakota and Arapaho, painted themselves for war and boldly rode into Pawnee country intent on bloody revenge.

At Loup Fork on the Platte River, the invaders surprised and attacked the Pawnee villages. A Cheyenne medicine man took the nation's sacred medicine arrows into the battle tied to the head of a lance. Coincidentally, a Pawnee warrior who was very ill and wished to die in battle wandered out between the opposing forces to sit and wait for a noble death. The medicine man charged the sick Pawnee with his lance, but the ailing warrior took hold of the weapon and jerked it from the Cheyenne's grasp. Suddenly in possession of the great power bundle, Pawnee warriors rallied and rapidly swarmed the demoralized Cheyenne forces with such fury that the shamed invaders fled, losing their sacred tribal medicine to their enemy in the process.

The loss of the Cheyenne medicine arrows drew the Lakota into the conflict to ease the opprobrium felt by their kinsmen and allies. The nearby Brule Lakota in particular attacked the Pawnee with a vengeance, driving them from their ancestral lands at Loup Fork on the Platte River. From this retreat and their dispersion on the prairie, the Pawnee entered into a lengthy period of continual movement, prodded by steady harassment at the hands of either the powerful Lakota-Cheyenne-Arapaho alliance or the increasing presence of the U.S. military along the Platte.

Compounding the misfortune of their thirty-year war with the powerful Sioux and Cheyenne, the Pawnee had the historic and geographic predicament of being directly in the middle of the "road of the immigrants." From the beginning days of the migration across the Great Plains, the Pawnee had haggled, squabbled, and fought with overlanders over equitable fees to charge travelers crossing the vast space of their ancestral homelands. When the Mormon migration began in Council Bluffs, the Pawnee were waiting at nearby Shell Creek to charge the saints tolls for their first major ferry crossing; at one point in time, the traffic was so heavy the Pawnee even hired a white man to charge overlanders fifty cents a wagon to ferry Shell Creek. Yet, because of their position in the direct route of the phenomenal numbers of immigrants, the U.S. government was forced to come quickly to terms with the Pawnee. By 1848 the United States had arranged a treaty with the Pawnee which pledged them to refrain from molesting or depredating Americans traveling through their country, and paid the tribe $2,000 for 600 square miles around Grand Island. The ensuing establishment of Fort Kearny in the heart of Pawnee Territory along the Platte plunged the U.S. military presence deeper into the Trans-Missouri than ever before, while it also insured future immigrant travel on the major trails to Oregon and California. Moreover, it made allies of the Pawnee and the U.S. military only a year before the announcement of the discovery of gold in California would attract more immigrants across the continent in one year than all the years of the previous decade combined. Subsequently, when the government bought Fort Laramie in 1949, the military thrust deep into the heart of the powerful western Lakota-Cheyenne-Arapaho country was complete. The Pawnee alliance with the U.S. military presence at these two forts silently spoke volumes to the Lakota-Cheyenne-Arapaho federation. Once this alliance was structured, it became obvious to the Lakota-Cheyenne-Arapaho Confederacy that the U.S. military was their enemy. Whatever future overtures of peace the "Great Father" might offer would be filtered through this alliance with the hated Pawnee. They were right to be so suspicious; nearly twenty years later, General Patrick E. "Star Chief" Connor used the Pawnee mercenaries to great advantage in launching a major "punishment" campaign into the Lakota-Cheyenne-Arapaho stronghold in their sacred Powder River Country.

It began in January, 1865, when Jim Bridger's friend, General Grenville Dodge, summoned the sixty-one-year-old mountain man from his farm in Westport, Missouri, and into service as Chief of Scouts for the Powder River Expedition to be commanded by General Connor. The Montana gold fields had attracted prospectors directly through the heart of Lakota buffalo country and tensions exploded into war along the Bozeman Trail. As Commander of the Department of the Missouri, General Dodge was ordered to punish the Sioux and to overawe the hostile Powder River resistance forces into submission with a bloody display of U.S. firepower. As the engineer in charge of constructing the Union Pacific Railroad, Dodge had another motive in sending Connor and Jim Bridger into the Powder River country: he was exploring the feasibility of routes through the Big Horn-Yellowstone country. In order to pacify and, ultimately, deceive the Lakota-Cheyenne-Arapaho federation, the U.S. government had sent Jesuit Priest, Father Jean Pierre De Smet to meet with Lakota leaders to explore the possibilities of peace.

Bridger thought it strange of the government to attempt to make peace with the Sioux while at the same time secretly launching a murderous strike into their heartland. Experience taught him that it was better to make open war with Indians than to try the underhanded duplicity the government was now attempting. Still, Dodge was his friend and the general felt Bridger's experience was vital to the mission in order to prevent Connor's stepping into any traps the Lakota might lay for him. Reluctantly, Bridger took the job. The mountain man immediately found himself disgusted with the character of the officers he was asked to assist.

Bridger arrived at Fort Laramie in July to discover the old post swirling with controversy. Two Lakota warriors had brought in two white women captives to the fort expecting to be paid the reward offered for their safe return. Instead of rewarding them, however, post commander Colonel Thomas Moonlight publicly hanged the Indians. Exhibiting savage indifference, Moonlight let the two Lakotas' bodies hang in chains for several days before he was relieved of command because of his barbaric behavior. Bridger prophesied that "this hanging would lead to dreadful consequences later on the trails."[3]

Moonlight would not be the only officer Bridger disagreed with over tactics. As previously mentioned, "Star Chief" Connor believed Indians north of the Platte "must be hunted down like wolves." "You will not," the general ordered, "receive overtures of peace or submission from Indians, but will attack and kill every male Indian over twelve years of age."[4]

Still, on July 30, the expedition departed Fort Laramie and headed north on the Bozeman Trail. Shortly thereafter, the mountain man led the expedition to the trail which bore his name as a result of his 1864 attempts to lead immigrants to the Virginia City gold fields through friendly Shoshone Territory in the Big Horn Basin, thereby avoiding the Lakota hunting grounds of the eastern Big Horn slopes. Following the "Bridger Trail," on August 14, Bridger led Connor to a well-wooded site on the Powder River. The mountain man told the general the location was "the point where the various Indian tribes meet to fight their battles."[5] There the general established Fort Connor (later Fort Reno). While the axes were ringing, falling trees for the stockade, Connor marched the regiment on to Peno Creek and sent his Pawnee scouts in search of enemies.

The Pawnee quickly found, attacked, and killed a small party of twenty-five Cheyenne. One of those killed and scalped was Yellow Woman, the estranged wife of William Bent. Most of the Cheyenne were wearing or carrying immigrant clothing, which indicated they had recently raided settler wagons or camps. Returning to the base camp with bloody Cheyenne scalps tied to sticks, the Pawnee danced for two nights celebrating their victory until, tired of fielding enlisted men's complaints, Connor finally ordered North to make them stop.

Meanwhile, Bridger and Captain H. E. Palmer ascended the ridge between Powder and Tongue Rivers. Later, Palmer wrote,

> The old Major was sitting upon his horse, his eyes shaded with his hands. . . . "Do you see those 'ere columns of smoke over yonder . . . by that saddle . . . fifty miles away?" For the life of me, I could not see any columns of smoke, even with a field glass.
>
> The atmosphere appeared hazy . . . but there were no columns of smoke. When the General [Connor] came up with his staff, and was informed of the smoke, the General raised his field glass and scanned the horizon carefully. . . . He then remarked, there were no columns of smoke to be seen.
>
> The Major quietly mounted his horse and rode on. . . . To satisfy curiosity, and to give our guides no chance to claim that they had shown us an Indian village, and we would not attack it, Captain Frank North and seven men were dispatched to reconnoiter.
>
> I galloped on and overtook the Major; and as I came up to him, I overheard him remark about "These dam paper-collar soldiers," telling him there were no columns of smoke. . . . It afterward transpired that there was an Indian village in the immediate locality designated.[6]

On August 29, Connor's advance scouts discovered an Arapaho village in the Tongue Valley. Before Connor could even order an attack, however, his troops broke ranks and tore pell-mell into the village and a terrific battle ensued. Arapaho men, women, and children engaged Connor's forces in vicious hand-to-hand combat defending their village. Nevertheless, General Connor was vastly outnumbered and the Arapaho warriors quickly rallied and forced him to make a hasty retreat. Before retreating, however, Connor killed sixty-three warriors, took 1,100 horses and captured and burned the entire Arapaho village. J. Cecil Alter continues Captain Parker's description of the events following the destruction of the Arapaho village:

> The soldiers, after cremating their own dead to prevent mutilation, tramped toward Fort Connor, possibly not without disturbed consciences. Ever since we left Fort Laramie our camp had been surrounded with thousands of wolves that made the nights hideous with

their infernal howling; but not until tonight have we heard the "Medicine Wolf," which Old Bridger claims to be supernatural.

Bridger, Nick Janisse, and Rulo [guides], being very superstitious, were so frightened at this particular howling that they took up their blankets and struck out for a new camp, which according to their theory, was the only way of escaping from impending danger; they went down the river about a half a mile and camped in the timber by themselves.[7]

Afterwards, Connor wrote, "Harm rather than good was done, and our troops were . . . driven from their country by the Indians."[8] Indeed, the only Sioux or Cheyenne killed in the Powder River Expedition were slain by Pawnee Scouts and because of the failure of his campaign the general was relieved of his command. Connor had, however, initiated the "Red Cloud Wars" and stirred the hornet's nest which led to Captain Fetterman's destruction at Fort Phil Kearney in December 1866 and the Fort Laramie Treaty in 1868. Most important, however, is the fact that General Dodge, convinced by what only his trusted scout, Jim Bridger, could have told him, decided that he would concede the Indians' claim to the Powder River, Big Horn, and Yellowstone country and focus his energy with the Transcontinental Railroad across faraway southern Wyoming.[9]

Another result of Connor's defeat in the Powder River country was Sherman and Sheridan's shift of U.S. attack forces to the southern plains. Since his first observations of the behavior patterns of the Plains Indians Sheridan had theorized that the way to quickly defeat his enemy was to punish him in relentless winter campaigns. Needless to say, the general's theory was controversial. Jim Bridger led the opposition, leaving his Missouri farm and traveling at his own expense to Kansas to attempt to personally persuade Sheridan to give up such a preposterous idea. The old mountain man told Sheridan, "You can't hunt Indians on the Plains in the winter, for blizzards don't respect man or beast."[10] Nevertheless, Sheridan had witnessed too many experienced soldiers such as Patrick Connor and William Fetterman find themselves humiliated, disgraced or killed chasing and fighting Indians. He thought too much of his hard-won reputation to fall victim to a similar fate. The winter campaigns would soon begin on the southern plains.

In spite of the U.S. military's disaster launching an offensive against the powerful Lakota-Cheyenne-Arapaho alliance in the Powder River Territory, the Pawnee Scouts had proven themselves to be extremely successful at locating their hereditary enemies. General Carr knew he could rely on Major North's scouts to find Tall Bull's Cheyenne in Kansas as well. The day after General Carr arrived at Buffalo Tank, he ordered the Fifth Cavalry to move out toward Elephant Rock on Beaver Creek of the Republican River.

On the second day of General Carr's march the regiment arrived at the south fork of Beaver Creek and discovered a fresh trail which promptly led to a very large group of Indians. General Carr ordered an immediate attack. Cody describes the battle in his autobiography:

> The Indians kept increasing in numbers all the while, until it was estimated that we were fighting from eight hundred to one thousand of them. The engagement became quite general, and several were killed and wounded on each side. The Indians were evidently fighting to give their families and village, a chance to get away. We had undoubtedly surprised them with a larger force than they had expected to see in that part of the country. We fought them until dark, all the while driving them before us. At night they annoyed us considerably by firing down into our camp from the higher hills, and several times the command was ordered out to dislodge them from their position and drive them back."[11]

At daybreak the next morning General Carr ordered the Fifth to prepare to attack Tall Bull's fleeing Cheyenne village. From the appearance of the abandoned campsite the village was estimated to be around 500 lodges; Carr pushed the cavalry to double time, quickly following the Cheyenne trail toward Prairie Dog Creek.

Later that afternoon the regiment spotted the retreating village. Simultaneously, Cheyenne warriors raced toward them in order to engage the "long knives" in battle and to protect their women and children as they fled. Next, the Dog Soldiers set the prairie on fire on all sides of the battle in order to create a smoke screen to shield the fleeing village as well as an obstacle for General Carr's advancing troops. The combat lasted all afternoon with the Cheyenne continually attempting to divert the soldiers' attention from the retreating village. By nightfall the Cheyenne village had broken into smaller groups and scattered over the prairie, yet the Indians were still easily tracked by the kettles, robes, furs, lodge-poles and heavy items discarded in flight. From childhood Indians had observed the way various animals and birds elude predators by either allowing themselves to be seen and chased or pretending to be wounded in order to distract the pillager from the young or the nest. When being pursued by the U.S. Cavalry, the tribes would fan out into smaller groups with each leaving an obvious trail of discarded items. This tactic was expensive yet effective; by the time military scouts realized they were following a splinter group rather than the entire village, the Indians had eluded them. Sometimes warrior-chiefs would allow the village to be seen fleeing in order to entice the pursuing military officer to divide his command and leave his supply wagons behind for the sake of speed. Once the command was divided the Indians would circle around and destroy the regiment's supply wagons.

The next morning General Carr's scouts picked up the Cheyenne trail again only to discover Tall Bull had been leading them in a clever, deceptive circle. Nevertheless, Tall Bull's retreat, and Fifth Cavalry's pursuit, continued throughout the second day until the regiment spotted them once again late in the afternoon. By sunset the Cheyenne warriors returned on horseback to engage Carr yet again. This intense battle lasted until dark when, exhausted, both sides camped.

That evening General Carr decided that the Cheyenne had been punished enough and, since he had successfully driven them north from the Republican River country, his mission was completed. The next morning the general ordered Cody to lead the Fifth Cavalry south toward the headwaters of Beaver Creek. The regiment had not been traveling long before General Carr informed Cody that one of his lieutenant's group of scouts had told him they were concerned about the direction in which they were being led.[12]

Cody defended his choice of routes to the general, maintaining he knew exactly where he was headed. He told the general that Beaver Creek had more water near the head than below, and assured Carr that he would find beaver dams strong enough to support a crossing of the stream by the entire regiment as well as all the water he needed. As promised, Cody led the regiment to a lovely little unnamed, spring-fed tributary of Beaver Creek. General Carr promptly named the stream Cody Creek, a not-so-subtle gesture for Buffalo Bill's jealous fellow scouts.

The following morning General Carr ordered the regiment to cross Beaver Creek. Cody rode out ahead of the advance guard to scout for a safe place to ford the stream. As he came around a bend of the creek, a shot rang out and Cody's horse fell. The scout struggled to disentangle himself from the dead horse and use him for cover and quickly noticed two Indians approaching. Cody opened fire on the Indians, wounding one of their horses.[13]

Cody soon found himself under heavy fire from Indians on the other side of the stream also and was considering whether to make a run for it or stand his ground when the regiment's advance guard arrived at the scene with guns blazing. General Carr ordered Lieutenant Brady and Company 1 to pursue the hostiles and Cody went with him. Within minutes they were engaged in another running fight with the Cheyenne.

After several hours of conflict with the fleeing Cheyenne in which they were able to capture some of the Indians' horses and lodges, Cody and Lieutenant Brady's Company returned to the command. Nearly a week later, following three or four more "lively skirmishes" with hostile Indians along the Republican River, the regiment rode into Fort Wallace to resupply and rest.

Cody immediately made use of his time off at Fort Wallace to hunt buffalo. One day he was asked to organize a buffalo hunt for a small party of new soldier friends and comrades at the fort and shortly thereafter the group headed out on the prairie. The hunters were soon attacked by a war party of around 50 Indians. The fight became severe and lasted at least an hour before Cody's party of excellent marksmen were able to drive the Indian forces back, killing four warriors.[14]

The Fifth Cavalry was not to remain long at Fort Wallace. General Sheridan's winter campaigns were intended to create havoc with the Plains Indians' normal routines, destroy the tribes' ancient seasonal patterns, break their resistance, and confine their nomadic wanderings within a policed territory. Sheridan ordered General Carr to proceed to Fort Lyon to link with Brevet Brigadier General William H. Penrose. General Sully had departed Fort Dodge with a battalion of the Third Infantry and the Seventh Cavalry under Major Joel H. Elliott. General Sully and Major Elliott moved slowly and cautiously and found no Indians; indeed, Sheridan was so disgruntled with Elliott's leadership that he petitioned the Secretary of War to remit Custer's suspension and return him to duty.[15]

In 1867 Custer was found guilty of unauthorized absence from his command and suspended from military service for a year. Sully's campaign from Fort Dodge marched south from Fort Dodge through the western part of Indian Territory and it began about the time Cody delivered General Hazen's emergency dispatches from Fort Larned to General Sheridan. At the beginning of hostilities the Cheyenne fled from Fort Larned and the region to the headwaters of the Red River. The purpose of Sully's campaign was to locate and destroy those villages. Sheridan himself accompanied a column composed of Custer's Seventh Cavalry, Crawford's Nineteenth Kansas and five companies of infantry. As Crawford's cavalry arrived at the assembly point the trail of a returning war party was discovered and Custer was ordered to follow it. The trail Custer followed led him down a path that would cloud the rest of his career as a warrior and resulted in the only real fight of Sully's campaign: the Battle of the Washita. Elliott, chagrined and reacting to Sheridan's distrust, charged into a group of Indians proclaiming, "Here goes for a brevet or a coffin," and was killed with nineteen under his command.[16]

Custer's forces annihilated Black Kettle's Cheyenne village, killing 103 warriors (including Black Kettle) and capturing fifty-three women and children and 875 horses. Faced with being unable to move swiftly through the treacherous weather and terrain with the horses, Custer commanded the Cheyenne women to pick a mount before ordering his troops to shoot the horses. Aside from the guns, powder, and lead taken Custer ordered the rest of the village burned; 1,100 buffalo robes and hides and over 1,000 pounds of tobacco were burned with lodges, saddles, bridles, blankets, and anything else of value. As this destruction was ordered, the general observed that the tables had turned and he and his 700 troopers had become surrounded by Indians drawn to the sounds of the earlier battle; Arapaho and Comanche forces peered down from the hills which encircled the now smoldering site of Black Kettle's village. The Battle of the Washita had taken place in a valley in which many of the tribes of the southern plains wintered. Custer had indeed stirred the hornet's nest.

After several tense moments, Custer boldly marched his regiment out of the valley and the situation and, exhibiting extreme concern for the Cheyenne women and children prisoners, the Arapaho and Comanche held back from any attack. Custer escaped the wrath of the Indians that day but, in doing so, the general sealed his doom at Little Big Horn. It is apparent that he made his name known to the Plains tribes; from that day forth, he was referred to as "the wolf of Washita" and vengeance was sworn by many grieving relatives of Black Kettle's people. Perhaps of even greater importance, however, was the fact that in his haste to depart the scene of the Battle of the Washita Custer failed to make a proper effort to locate Major Joel Elliott and the nineteen troopers under his command. Instead, General Sheridan found Elliott's mutilated party himself. Sheridan headed down the Washita River in pursuit of fleeing Indians. Two miles south of Black Kettle's village Sheridan's party stumbled upon the butchered bodies of Elliott and his troops. They had fallen in a circle where they had fought to the last. At the moment Sheridan looked down upon the bloody spectacle of Elliot's last valiant stand, a grisly, ironic prophecy of the grander scale Custer himself would present at Little Big Horn in only eight years, the impetuous general lost forever the trust of his most important ally in the military establishment.[17]

Captain Frederick W. Benteen, later to become famous at Little Big Horn, was so outraged that he wrote a bitter account of Major Elliott's death in the *St. Louis Democrat*. The newspaper story caused a feud between Benteen and Custer which nearly caused a fistfight between the two officers. In short, Custer never fully regained the confidence of his military peers after the affair with Major Elliott at the Battle of the Washita.

Meanwhile, the Fifth Cavalry arrived at Fort Lyon on November 20 and discovered Penrose had departed three weeks earlier with a force of three hundred men and pack mules. General Carr was ordered to follow with supply wagons and overtake Penrose as soon as possible. Cody was as anxious as General Carr to catch up with Penrose. His old pal Wild Bill Hickok was one of the general's scouts. After three days of tracking General Penrose, however, the Fifth Cavalry received the full effect of General Sheridan's winter campaign and was caught in a terrific blizzard in a place most appropriately named "Freeze-Out Canyon." The ground being completely covered with snow, it became impossible to track Penrose and necessary for the regiment to camp and wait out the storm.

General Carr sent for Cody and ordered him to select a small group of scouts and continue pressing on through the storm in order to pick up Penrose's trail. After pushing through the blizzard for twenty-four miles Cody and his four companions reached a tributary of the Cimarron River and, upon scouting up and down the stream, finally located one of Penrose's old campsites. Here, as evening approached, the group took shelter from the blinding storm, made a camp and prepared a hardy meal of venison. Replenished with the warm meal, Cody rode out into the storm again to bring General Carr a report on the discovery of Penrose's trail.

Carr was much relieved to hear the news Cody brought at midnight. Early the next morning the general ordered the regiment to begin the difficult march toward the Cimarron. The expedition faced a formidable trek; high snowdrifts filled the canyon, forcing the regiment's teamsters to have to shovel a path for the wagons. General Carr reached the Cimarron after a day's march and realized that, unencumbered by wagons, Penrose was marching on the more rugged terrain of the western side of the river. Cody discovered a suitable wagon route on the eastern side of the river and, assuming that Penrose would continue to follow the river's western banks, General Carr elected to follow his chief scout's trail.

In order to make headway with the wagon train they had to leave the river and get out on the divide. Finding a road allowed them to travel easily for some distance until they discovered they were on a high table land overlooking a lovely creek that lay winding far below in the valley. High in the foothills of the Sangre de Cristo Mountains of the New Mexico/Colorado border near modern-day Raton, the problem they faced was how to get the wagons down the steep slopes.

When Carr asked Cody's advice the scout told the general to just busy himself picking out a beautiful spot for his campsite and to trust him to get the wagons down the bluffs.[18]

General Carr took Cody for his word and went immediately to the task of dismounting the cavalry in order to lead the horses down the steep slopes. Cody waited for the wagons while the regiment negotiated the declivity.

Needless to say, the teamsters were not happy with the prospects of descending the slopes with their wagons. Nevertheless, Cody was in his element, particularly with bullwackers. When one of the drivers asked how they were going to get down the slopes, Cody writes, he responded, "Run down, slide down or fall down—any way to get down."[19]

Cody ordered the chief wagonmaster, to bring the lead wagon to the edge of the slope. Next, he took chains and locked the wagon's wheels on each side. Then, carefully, they started over the brink and slowly down the slope. Upon reaching the bottom of the hill the wagon started moving faster and pushed the mules so intensely that they broke into a full gallop with such power that the wagons nearly flipped from the force. Nevertheless, after performing the exciting engineering feat, the scout eventually succeeded in bringing all four supply wagons safely into camp. Afterwards it was learned that Cody's skillful descent of the severe slope had gained the regiment precious time; Penrose had marched his expedition along the western banks of the river until they arrived at a wall so steep that he was forced to backtrack, losing three days each way. The time Penrose lost was disastrous; his men were reduced to starving conditions.

Meanwhile, the Fifth Cavalry, loaded with four wagons of provisions, was ironically enjoying the land's bounty; the location General Carr selected for a campsite was literally teaming with wild turkeys. Cody describes the soldiers killing four or five hundred turkeys and cooking the birds in nearly every way imaginable. For the next couple of days after departing "Camp Turkey," General Carr had no problems following Penrose's trail as he headed southeast toward the Canadian River. One afternoon Cody was scouting in advance of the regiment along San Francisco Creek when he found three deserters from Penrose's Tenth Cavalry and they informed Carr of the expedition's being at the point of near starvation. General Carr promptly ordered Major William H. Brown and Cody into action and the pair set out with two companies of cavalry and a train of fifty pack mules loaded with provisions. Three days later they located Penrose on Paloduro Creek. The command was indeed in dire straits; over two hundred horses and mules had died of fatigue or starvation.

The first person Cody saw upon riding into Penrose's starving camp was his old friend Wild Bill. There were many "jolly reunions" at the evening campfires as the provisions Major Brown and Cody brought obviously saved the lives of many in the regiment.

General Carr, outranking General Penrose, quickly arrived to take command of the troops. His first act was to empty all the wagons and order the teamsters to return to Fort Lyon to resupply. Having established a base supply camp, the general next selected 500 of the healthiest men and horses to march south toward the Canadian River in Texas. Both Cody and Hickok accompanied General Carr on this forty-mile expedition as scouts. As the expedition arrived at the supply camp on the south fork of the Canadian River, Cody and Hickok learned from other scouts that a bull-train loaded with beer was soon scheduled to arrive.[20]

Mexicans living near Fort Union had made the beer and were taking it to Fort Evans to sell it to the troops. The beer never reached the fort; Cody and Hickok intercepted and hijacked the Mexicans' wagons and saved them the trouble of hauling their cargo the remaining twelve miles to Fort Evans. The beer was sold to General Carr's troops in pint cups; the happy soldiers heated their picket-pins until they were red-hot and dipped them into the cold beer to heat it. Cody pronounced the occasion "one of the biggest beer jollification's [sic] I ever had the misfortune to attend."[21]

The beer party ended and General Carr returned to the tasks at hand. Important dispatches needed to be sent to Camp Supply and General Sheridan. "General Carr records that 'during the winter of 1868,'" Don Russell writes,

we encountered hardships and exposure in terrific snow storms, sleet. etc. etc. On one occasion that winter, Mr. Cody showed his quality by quietly offering to go with some dispatches to General Sheridan, across a dangerous region, where another principal scout was reluctant to risk himself.' Cody tells of Hickok's carrying dispatches under similar circumstances, but does not mention his own trip—another exasperating instance of his failing to take credit where he has supporting evidence.

After scouting along the Canadian without results, Carr returned to his supply camp. There occurred a ruckus so little to the credit of either Cody or Hickok that Bill's version may be accepted as authentic.[22]

There were fifteen Mexican scouts in Penrose's command. A competitive feud had arisen between these Mexican scouts and the American scouts in the regiment. When Carr took command of the expedition and absorbed Penrose's forces into the Fifth Cavalry he made Cody chief of all the scouts. This action intensified the feud raging between the Mexican and American scouts with the former group threatening to whip the latter in a fistfight. After several failed attempts to organize a fight, the two groups finally had a severe bout with the Mexicans getting themselves badly beaten up. General Carr investigated the incident and called Cody and Hickok into his quarters to reprimand them for instigating the row. Upon questioning the pair, Carr determined the Mexicans were as much to blame as Cody and Hickok, although Cody admitted that he and Wild Bill had "had been partaking too freely of 'tanglefoot' that evening."[23]

General Carr wisely decided to put the boys to work to occupy themselves and to keep them out of trouble. Besides, he needed Cody's special talents as a hunter; the sergeant who commanded the hunting party of twenty wagons, drivers, a wagonmaster and twenty infantrymen reported later that scurvy had attacked many in the regiment and fresh meat was essential.

Cody marched the party for four days before locating a buffalo herd. The scout killed fifty-five buffalo by stampeding them into a snow-filled arroyo. The next day Cody exhausted two horses in killing forty-one buffalo; his right shoulder and chest were so bruised and swollen from the recoil of his rifle that he needed assistance just putting on his coat. It took two days for the troops to gather the buffalo meat.

The Fifth Cavalry rode back into Fort Lyon in late February, 1869. General Carr had accomplished what Sheridan expected of him: he prevented any of the renegade tribes from migrating westward while Sully and Custer swept through them from the east. The results brought the Kiowa and Comanche to the treaty table, and by March, these two tribes had signed a treaty of peace. Arriving at Fort Lyon in March, Carr ordered the regiment to take thirty days off for rest and recuperation; Cody headed home to see his wife and daughter. Along the way, however, the scout got himself involved in a very confusing situation.

Cody had been given permission by General Carr to take a horse and pack mule as far as Sheridan. There, Cody was supposed to leave the animals with the quartermaster at Fort Wallace. Nevertheless, instead of leaving the horse and mule with the quartermaster as he was instructed, Cody left them with a hotelkeeper and went on to St. Louis. While Cody was in St. Louis, the quartermaster's agent at Fort Wallace reported that the scout had sold a government horse and mule to the hotel owner and fled the country. The horse and mule were promptly seized and returned to Fort Wallace.

Cody returned to Sheridan and the hotelkeeper told him what had happened. The scout was furious and vented his anger on the quartermaster's agent administering, "just such a thrashing as his contemptible lie deserved."[24] Next, Cody went to the fort and demanded the horse and mule be returned to him—he was, after all, responsible to the quartermaster at Fort Lyon for the government stock. Both Brigadier General Henry C. Bankhead, commanding officer of Fort Wallace, and the Quartermaster, Captain Samuel B. Lautter, after heated exchanges, ordered Cody off the reservation. Furious, Cody returned, beat up the quartermaster's agent again, and told him to get out of town. The frightened man hurried to Fort Wallace and informed General Bankhead that Cody had threatened his life. Later that evening an old friend of the scout's, Captain Israel Ezekial, brought his Negro regiment to arrest Cody. Personal friends with most of the soldiers at the post, Cody was allowed to sleep in a sergeant's bunk rather than being locked in a cell.

The next morning Cody prepared a telegram for General Sheridan, but the operator took the message to General Bankhead instead. Bankhead tore the telegram up. Cody soon learned of the fate of his message and demanded to be taken under guard to the telegraph office to send his message to General Sheridan. Bankhead backed down and allowed Cody to take the horse and mule back to Fort Lyon provided that he agreed to leave the quartermaster's agent alone.

Cody returned to Fort Lyon with his horse and mule. Don Russell closes the book on the incident with these remarks:

Bill's heedlessness of army procedures is characteristic. His occasional formidable outbursts of temper such as caused his beating up of the quartermaster's agent were less so, for this is one of few cases recorded where he resorted to violence—and to his credit be it noted that there was no gunplay. That the charge of horse stealing should be credited so near his usual haunts indicates that even yet his reputation had not traveled far.[25]

That would soon change; once again Will's destiny was calling.

Chapter Eight

THE TRAIL TO SUMMIT SPRINGS

> They had no way of knowing, of course that the soldier-chief who looked like an angry bear, Sheridan, was planning a winter campaign below the Arkansas.
>
> (*Bury My Heart At Wounded Knee*, Dee Brown)

GENERAL Sheridan's winter military campaign against Plains Indians brought immediate results. Since antiquity, Plains Indians followed deeply ingrained routines of behavior dictated by nature. Aside from the never-ending quest for food, clothing, and shelter, each season brought specific religious ceremonies designed to involve and bond each member of the tribe individually and collectively in the grand scheme of the universe. As mentioned previously, the nomadic movements of Plains Indians were the result of the requirement to create and perform religious ceremonies which would place them in spiritual alignment with the celestial movements of stars as well as the migratory movements of the great buffalo herds and other large game animals. There is considerable evidence that the Lakota were walking from sacred site to sacred site to perform earth and stellar rituals long before they had horses. Indeed, in observing the migratory patterns of animals and humans living on North America's Great Plains, one might draw the conclusion that there is something inherent in the incredible space of the sky and landscape which encourages constant movement; both Native and immigrant Americans responded to the vastness in a nomadic manner. Whatever the subliminal compulsion might be, each season brought different animal and plant harvests and took the Great Plains tribes to distinct regions and sacred sites where ancient, specifically detailed ceremonial rituals were to be performed. "Most Lakota activities were time-factored," ethnoastrologer Ron Goodman writes:

There was a proper time to gather "cansasa" [dried willow bark used to smoke in a sacred pipe], to sew tipi covers, to tell certain stories, to make the buffalo hunt, etc. There is no Lakota word for "religion." While it is true that certain Lakota behaviors—rites and rituals—have (to non-Indians) a recognizably 'religious' character, to the Lakota themselves these are rather the intensification of daily activities all of which must be lived in a sacred manner. The whole "Lakota way of life" or "Lakol Wicoh' an" is their religion.[1]

Nevertheless, the Lakota "way of life," as all Plains Indians patterns, was unfortunately obvious and predictable—a vulnerable trait to a wizened, predacious genius such as Philip Sheridan.

The spring and summer hunts brought Plains Indians the bounty of the buffalo and other game animals they required; in summer and autumn, they harvested various wild crops of fruits, grains, and tubers and prepared for the colder weather. The brutal Great Plains winter was the time to focus on quiet chores such as making new clothing, tools and utensils and the usual long-needed repairs to the lodge. Winter was a time of healing and rejuvenation, purification, meditation, and preparation. As Plains Indians had no written language, winter was also the vitally important time of continuing the ancient oral tradition of the culture. Essential tribal, family, and individual stories needed to be told and retold; individual, family and tribal histories needed to be painted on hides and robes. Sheridan's relentless winter pursuit of the tribes threw all these ancient patterns into chaos. The result was disastrous to the harmony and unity of the Plains tribes.

There has perhaps never been a more pure form of socialism on the planet than that practiced by the Plains Indian. Every single minute aspect of tribal religion, lifestyle, and culture focused the energy and efforts of men and women in the prime of life absolutely toward the care, nourishment and welfare of the sick, the elderly, and the children. Yet, in spite of the selfless devotion to community required within tribal social structure, the individual spirit was also affectionately nourished, encouraged, and supported to blossom by the full spectrum of society through such religious experiences as solo vision quests and sun dancing. Nevertheless, the individual could only come into great wealth, fame, or honor by contributing to the overall good of the tribe. The outcome of this rearing was a highly disciplined, mature tribal member, fiercely individualistic, while also devoutly dedicated through personal integrity to the nourishment of the greater society. A chief became a chief because he earned the right to accept the responsibility. Stanley Vestal explains a few of those responsibilities:

A chief (I-tan-chan) was supposed to be greathearted, magnanimous, generous, and above all personal spite of selfishness. For this reason, few men were willing to undertake the responsibility. It was asking too much to forgive everything, never lose one's temper, and continually to give and share with those who could never by any chance repay benefits. Most men had not enough of the father in them to be father to a whole tribe. Famous warriors—like the Cheyenne Roman Nose—sometimes declined chieftaincy—not feeling themselves fit for it. Among the Sioux, men were sometimes made chiefs for their lovable, gentle qualities, even though they were hardly warriors at all. Black Eagle of the Sans Arc Sioux, is an example. Great warriors sometimes lacked the kindly qualities demanded of a civil chief.[2]

Yet in spite of the magnanimity required of chiefs and the equally demanding, selfless devotion expected of all tribal members, the warrior nature of the Plains Indian also produced intense, often fatal, disagreements; the highly developed, arduously independent nature which encouraged each tribal member to think and act for themselves could become extremely dangerous when perspectives clashed. The great Lakota Warrior Chief Red Cloud rose to power as a youth during such a power struggle among the Oglala around Fort Laramie when he took part in the assassination of Chief Bull Bear. After assuming leadership of the Oglalas during a time of intense, radical change, Red Cloud was forced to wield his power with a delicate blend of assertiveness and diplomacy in order to maintain control of his people as staggering numbers of overlanders and immigrants invaded and populated Lakota country and brought increasing disruption of their way of life.

Most of the disagreements sprang from an ancient love-hate relationship apparent from the beginning of Native and immigrant American interaction. From the day Columbus set foot on North American soil, the two cultures have been simultaneously attracted to and repelled by one another. Consider Columbus's remarks in his journal describing his initial contact with Native Americans to the King of Spain:

They are so affectionate and have so little greed and are in all ways so amenable that I assure your Highness that there is in my opinion no better people and no better land in the world. They love their neighbours as themselves and their way of speaking is the sweetest in the world, always gentle and smiling. Both men and women go naked as their mothers bore them; but your Highness must believe me when I say that their behaviour to one another is very good and their king keeps marvelous state, yet with a certain kind of modesty that is a pleasure to behold, as is everything else here. They have good memories and ask to see everything, then inquire what it is and what is it for.[3]

Yet in spite of his sincere appreciation of the inherent innocence and sweetness of these people's nature Columbus' narrative quickly reveals his true mission and spiritual condescension:

They should be good servants and very intelligent, for I have observed that they soon repeat anything that is said to them, and I believe that they would easily be made Christians, for they appeared to me to have no religion. God willing, when I make my departure I will bring half a dozen of them back to the Majesties, so that they can learn to speak.[4]

The deadly pattern of relations between the Native and Euroamerican was set in motion as Columbus, fascinated though he was with these "affectionate" people of the "New World," ultimately sought only to make slaves of them in his efforts to find gold for the King and Queen of Spain. Columbus's triumphant return to Spain, however, was like sand shifting through his hands. Even though he had become a bridge between the two hemispheres, bringing aspects of both worlds together, he had set in motion a pattern of tragedy and misunderstanding which continues to this very day. Two subsequent voyages to the "New World" found him descending into madness, while the desperate, criminal characters he left behind to colonize paradise had already begun to rape and pillage. One finds traces of this attitude of awkward attraction and enchantment, diabolically underscored with the belief of cultural and spiritual superiority, laced throughout most subsequent relations between immigrant and Native Americans. The only result this thinking could possibly have is violence. This love-hate relationship intensified dramatically as immigrants struggled out onto the Great Plains. Overwhelming evidence shows that in the early days of transcontinental migration, most travelers would never have survived the trek without the ongoing support and vital assistance of Plains Indians, yet most Americans still accept the stereotypical perspective of violent Indian resistance to the settlers in wagon trains. John D. Unruh, Jr., describes immigrant reaction to Plains Indians, the obsessive fascination most overlanders felt for Indians, and immigrants' eagerness to view Native Americans as "savages," which clouded their ability to recognize Native Americans' good samaritanism:

> For virtually all over landers the western Indians were akin to the buffalo in symbolizing danger and adventure. The first trail encounter with Indians invariably resulted in a long diary entry or a lengthy paragraph in the next letter home, complete with an analysis of Indian character, demeanor, apparel, and customs, and rife with speculation on the nature of future encounters. While fascinated immigrant diarists were not always condemnatory in their attitudes toward the Indians, they rarely acknowledged the positive Indian contribution to overland travel. On examination, however, the much-maligned 'savage Indians' of folklore prove to have been of considerable assistance to passing over landers, particularly during the 1840s before the boom in supportive facilities set in. That Indian begging and thievery were traveling nuisances cannot be denied, but it is also clear that the extent of Indian attacks on overland caravans has been greatly exaggerated. In fact, there is considerable evidence that the fatal trail confrontations which did occur were usually prompted by immigrant insults and disdain for Indian rights, as well as by indiscriminate and injudicious chastisement meted out by the U.S. Army. Notwithstanding the fact that nearly 400 emigrants were killed by Indians in the first twenty years of overland travel, Indian tribes provided over landers with information, foodstuffs, clothing, equipment, horses, canoeing and swimming skills, traveling material, and other assistance.[5]

Immigrants were, after all, with the very act of crossing the Great Plains, poaching on the rights of Indians. Some early immigrants clearly understood and respected this aspect of the relationship, yet, as the numbers of Europeans increased, resentment of the situation increased exponentially for both Native and immigrant Americans. This lust for Indian property and the resentment of being forced to confront the situation with the fairness and honesty demanded by the ethical, moral, and legal standards immigrant Americans set for themselves is the source of most of the love-hate aspect of the Native and immigrant American relationship. Immigrant resistance to deal ethically and economically with the Plains tribes eroded the initial positive interactions between the two peoples and evolved into pronounced immigrant righteous indignation concerning the Indian ownership of the land. This ill will gave birth to hostilities and violence.

Ulruh continues:

. . . the overland emigrations quickened, and perhaps made inevitable the military conquest of the western Indians. Almost from
the very first, the perceptive plains Indians had recognized the threat
the overland caravans represented to their way of life. Therefore,
one of their first responses was to demand tribute of the passing
trains. This tactic was employed at least as early as 1843. An 1845
overlander, speculating on the origin of this Indian tax, believed the
practice to have begun with frightened emigrants willing to promise
almost anything to travel safely. But it seems clear that tribute demands, which were most widely experienced by over landers during
the gold rush period, were grounded in more than simple repetition
of a previous chance success. Emigrants continually reported that
the Indians who came to demand tribute explained also why they
were requesting the payments. The natives explicitly emphasized
that the throngs of over landers were killing and scaring away buffalo
and other wild game, overgrazing prairie grasses, exhausting the
small quantity of available timber, and depleting water resources.
The tribute payments, which occasionally were in specie but usually
in provisions, were demanded mainly by the Sac and Fox, Kickapoo,
Pawnee, and Sioux Indians—the tribes closest to the Missouri River
frontier and therefore those feeling most keenly the pressure of
white men increasingly impinging upon their domains.[6]

Plains Indians were equally fascinated with immigrants and eagerly
sought out cultural communication and economic trade. Unfortunately,
Indian leadership was fatally divided over how to deal with the resulting
intercourse and such interaction frequently created even wider divisions
within the tribe. The terrific negative impact of the whiskey trade on the
Great Plains tribes was previously discussed in this text, yet the inability of
Indian leadership to inspire a unified people while also assembling an organized, inter-tribal military resistance against the invasion of their country was perhaps even more detrimental. As tragic as the Euroamericans'
lust for Native American property was, the Indian leadership's inability to
cope with the dramatic changes brought by the European culture was
equally disastrous. Sadly, it tore the leadership apart rather than bringing it
into stronger unity.

Shortly after Red Cloud's military success in the Powder River Wars,
internal bickering began among the Lakota leadership. Brule Lakota

leader Spotted Tail had long separated himself and his band from the wild
Oglalas led by Red Cloud and Crazy Horse and the Hunkpapas led by Sitting Bull. In 1854, which was around the same time Red Cloud rose to
leadership among the Oglalas, Spotted Tail and other young Brule warriors had participated in an attack on a mail-wagon on the road below Fort
Laramie and made off with over $20,000, which was never recovered.
Later, when General William S. Harney demanded the culprits surrender
to avoid a general punishment of the tribe, Spotted Tail and the other warriors involved rode bravely into Fort Laramie singing their death songs, as
they fully expected to be executed when they turned themselves in to white
authorities. Instead, Spotted Tail and the other men were taken to Fort
Kearney, where they spent two years as prisoners. During this time, the
Brules were never confined but were used instead as scouts. While among
the whites, Spotted Tail came to believe that to resist their awesome numbers and advanced weaponry was futile. Spotted Tail spent the rest of his
life attempting in vain to diplomatically mend the torn unity of his own
people, all the while struggling to peacefully resolve the differences between the Lakota tribes and the newcomers. Needless to say, this diplomatic behavior brought Spotted Tail few friends in the warrior-oriented
societies of the Lakota; half of his Brule followers abandoned his leadership to join their cousins in Red Cloud's, Crazy Horse's, or Sitting Bull's
camps. Spotted Tail's efforts toward peace with the whites eventually led to
his assassination by one of his own people in 1881.

The same fractures of unity were quickly evident in the Cheyenne-Ara-
paho camps. In the spring of 1869, immediately following Sheridan's first
major winter campaign, Arapaho leader Little Robe violently quarreled
with Cheyenne Chief Tall Bull over the situation in which the tribes found
themselves. Little Robe accused Tall Bull and his warriors of causing all
the troubles the Arapaho people were suffering because of Sheridan's ruthless winter assaults. Enraged, Tall Bull retorted that Little Robe was weak
and cowardly to surrender his honor by collapsing so easily to the white
man's demands. Furious, Little Robe ordered Tall Bull to immediately
leave the Cheyenne reservation; Little Robe threatened to join forces with
the whites to drive Tall Bull away or kill him if the Cheyenne chief refused
to leave.

Soon, over two hundred Dog Soldiers and their wives and children
joined Tall Bull as the chief embarked on the long and dangerous march
north to join Lakota-Cheyenne-Arapaho friends, relatives and allies in the

Powder River country. As the larger body of the Cheyenne Nation, along with the Kiowa and Comanche, had signed the March, 1869, peace treaties, Tall Bull and his Dog Soldiers had become a splinter, or renegade, band of refugees which attracted other "hostiles" fleeing their homelands to join their relatives and allies on the eastern slopes and high prairies of the Big Horn Mountains.

Meanwhile, Buffalo Bill, having recently been exonerated of stealing government horses, was, ironically, spending his time chasing horse thieves for General Carr. Cody was commissioned "United States Detective" and tracked down several notorious thieves and recovered four mules and eight horses—one belonging to General Carr. This type of activity, however, was clearly interim work to occupy Cody while the military went through a reorganization. Once western military forces were restructured, however, the Fifth Cavalry departed Fort Lyon on May 1 and headed to Fort Wallace. There, Cody and General Bankhead met again, apologized to each other over the embarrassing horse-theft episode, shook hands and "buried the hatchet." From Fort Wallace, the regiment traveled to Sheridan; from Sheridan to Beaver Creek. On May 13 the search intensified as Cody discovered the fresh trail of a large number of Indians. Carr ordered Cody to accompany Lieutenant Edward E. Ward and a small group of troopers to investigate. Shortly, Cody and Ward crept to the top of a small hill and saw a very large village less than three miles in the distance. Buffalo hunters were coming into the village from all directions, indicating the Indians were unaware of the military's presence in the area. Ward hurriedly scribbled an emergency report and gave it to a trooper to rush to General Carr. Soon after the messenger was sent, flying gunshots were heard in the distance; within moments the rider reappeared with a small party of Indians hot on his trail. Only a direct charge from Ward's small detachment of troops could force the Indians to retreat. Acutely aware that the gunshots would alert the village that soldiers were nearby, the scouting party also instantly realized theirs was now a "life-or-death" situation. Simply, they had to get to General Carr very quickly. Cody immediately volunteered to make the ride.[7]

Cody arrived at General Carr's command post in less than one hour. Instantaneously, "Boots and Saddles" blared and the entire regiment retraced Cody's trail and galloped toward the Indian village. After traveling only a short distance, however, the cavalry ran into Lieutenant Ward coming slowly toward them. He had encountered a small party of Indians and become involved in a skirmish in which he killed one warrior and had one of his horses wounded. The regiment quickly charged on in the direction of the village and was soon met by a very large force of Indians on their way to fight the soldiers. In an obvious attempt to give their village a chance to escape the soldiers, Cheyenne warriors formed a straight line of defense. Carr, wanting to attack the village, ordered his troops to charge through the middle of the line. On his left flank, however, Carr immediately experienced trouble; one of his lieutenants misunderstood the order and, breaking the focused attack thrust by the cavalry through the middle of the line of Indians, charged into the warriors on his own volition. Five hundred warriors promptly surrounded the company, forcing Carr to abandon the charge in order to rush to the lieutenant's rescue. The result was a general melee.

The fight went on all afternoon, taking up valuable time. With night coming on, the Indians were fighting desperately to keep the pony soldiers from reaching their village. Indian couriers informed the village of developments on the front and the people started packing up and fleeing. Fierce mounted warriors forced the troopers to fight for every inch they moved toward the village.[8]

Having left orders for the supply train to follow with two companies of men, Carr became worried when the wagons failed to appear. Since he could not allow the regiment's supplies to fall into the hands of the Indians, Carr abandoned the fight in order to search for the wagon train.

Much to the regiment's relief, the train was located that evening. The next morning, however, when Carr returned to search for the village, the Cheyenne had vanished. The prairie where the village had been was littered with personal items abandoned by the Cheyenne in their desperate retreat. General Carr ordered everything burned and sent Cody and his scouts to pick up the Cheyenne trail.

The trail led to the Republican River. There, aware that he was slowly catching up with the tribe, the general ordered a halt and, in order to gain even more time on the retreating Cheyenne, divided his command, sending the supply wagons on to Fort McPherson. Traveling lighter, the cavalry began to get close enough to see the fleeting Indians from time to time on the horizon. The chase intensified and quickened. While crossing a ravine later that morning, however, the Fifth came under a surprise attack by about 300 Cheyenne warriors. After another lively skirmish, Carr was able to rally and drive the Indians back. The Cheyenne retreated and, once again, Carr pursued. Don Russell informs us:

Their trail was followed for three days. At noon on May 16 the advance guard of forty men under Lieutenants John B. Babcock and William J. Volkmar of Company M with Cody as guide were surrounded at Spring Creek by two hundred Indians. The troopers dismounted and formed a circle, holding their horses while firing and falling back to the main body, three miles away. Said General Carr in 1878, "They all, to this day, speak of Cody's coolness and bravery.... Reaching the scene we could see the Indians in retreat. A figure with apparently a red cap rose slowly up the hill. For an instant it puzzled us, as it wore the buckskin and had long hair, but on seeing the horse, I recognized it as Cody's 'Powder Face' and saw that it was Buffalo Bill without his broad-brimmed sombrero. On closer inspection I saw his head was swathed in a bloody handkerchief, which had served not only as a temporary bandage, but as a chapeau—his hat having been shot off, the bullet plowing his scalp badly for about five inches. It had ridged along the bone and he was bleeding profusely—a very 'close call' but a lucky one."[9]

Where Cody's luck was holding, however, Tall Bull's was running out. Once again, however, the regiment began to notice the prairie littered with nearly every type of Indian possession as the Cheyenne discarded everything they had in order to escape Carr's advance. Eventually, even worn-out horses began to appear. Finally, the trail scattered in scores of directions indicating the village had virtually disintegrated. Carr ordered his men to gather the Indian horses and property. Once again, the general ordered everything burned. As the command was out of rations, General Carr sent Cody to Old Fort Kearney, sixty miles away, to get supplies.[10] General Carr, detailing Cody's courage and stamina, expressed the mission very differently. Carr, says Cody,

> decided it was best to undertake the job himself—a point characteristic of him as he never shirked duty or faltered in emergencies.... Cody made the ride of fifty miles during the night, arriving at Fort Kearney at daylight. He had chased and fought Indians all day, been wounded, and when, through his rare frontier instinct, he reached us he had been almost constantly in the saddle and without sleep for forty hours.[11]

The regiment arrived at Fort McPherson on May 20 and spent ten days resting and resupplying. During the time at Fort McPherson General Carr recommended Cody to become Chief of Scouts of the Department of the Platte. At Fort McPherson Cody also finally met Frank North.

Where others might have viewed North as a rival, Cody welcomed him as a comrade-in-arms, appreciated his expertise, and respected his abilities; indeed, North would become another of Cody's lifelong friends; the two eventually became partners of Scouts Rest Ranch in Nebraska and North and his Pawnee Scouts were destined to become a fixture of the Wild West in twenty years. The Pawnee scouts, thoroughly acquainted with the Republican River and Beaver Creek country, had earned a reputation for themselves fighting against their bitter enemies, the Sioux. When it came to scouting for the government, Cody was always pragmatic and was pleased they joined the expedition.[12]

In his deathbed interview with Buffalo Bill, *Outdoor Life* reporter Chauncey Thomas asked the scout, "Who was the best revolver shot you ever knew?" Cody replied, "Frank North, the white chief of the Pawnees. He was the best revolver shot, standing still, in the air, from horseback, or at running animals or men, that I ever saw."[13]

In 1917, as he prepared himself for death, Cody could have perhaps been considered the last best judge of nineteenth-century western marksmanship. As he was always ready to enter any kind of shooting contest, Cody had personally faced many of the best shots of the era in the west in matches so he spoke from personal experience. When he worked as a scout Cody faced many excellent military marksmen also. Such a contest arose during the Fifth Cavalry's ten-day pass at Fort McPherson in 1869. Cody befriended Lieutenant George P. Belden, known as the "White Chief." An hour after their introduction, Belden challenged Cody to a rifle match and soon rules were drawn and a match arranged. Cody won the first round of shooting, but Belden won the second and the match ended.[14]

Within days the command marched toward the Republican River once again. Near the mouth of Beaver Creek Indians were heard yelling and shooting off guns near where the regiment's mule herd had been taken to water. Soon one of the wranglers came staggering toward the camp with an arrow stuck in him. Cody instinctively jumped upon his horse bareback and took off after the stampeding herd of mules. The scout was surprised and impressed to arrive at the scene and discover, like himself, the Pawnee scouts had not waited like soldiers to assemble and receive orders to investigate. Instead, they had also jumped bareback and bridle-less onto their horses, held their ponies' lead ropes in their teeth and raced toward the vicinity of the shots. As Cody, the fifty Sioux warriors attempting to make off with the mules were shocked to be overtaken and suddenly fiercely attacked by the Pawnee. The Lakota warriors had miscalculated they had plenty of time to get away clean before the soldiers could gather themselves and mount a chase.

Yet a chase was what the Lakota war party got that day. The running fight went on for fifteen miles. Cody was mounted on a swift horse which kept him out in front of the Pawnee party pursuing the Lakotas. Suddenly a Pawnee rider galloped past him like he was standing still. Admiring the large buckskin horse, Cody immediately decided, if possible, he would get possession of the animal.[15]

As soon as the group returned to the base camp Cody approached Major North to inquire about the big yellow horse. North immediately recognized the steed of Cody's inquiry. The major informed Cody that the horse belonged to the government and he might trade for him. Nevertheless, Major North warned Cody that the Pawnee who rode him was quite fond of the animal and would be reluctant to let him go.

It took several days of persuasion and many presents, but Cody eventually wore the Pawnee down and convinced him to trade the horse. As the horse was government property, Cody could not trade for legal ownership, but merely traded for the right to ride him in military service. In 1879 Cody wrote:

> I gave him the name "Buckskin Joe," and he proved to be a second Brigham. That horse I rode on and off during the summers of 1869, 1870, 1871, and 1872, and he was the horse that the Grand Duke Alexis rode on his buffalo hunt. In the winter of 1872, after I had left Fort McPherson, Buckskin Joe was condemned and sold at public sale, and was bought by Dave Perry, at North Platte, who in 1877 presented him to me, and I still own him. He is now at my ranch on the Dismal River, stone blind, but I shall keep him until he dies.[16]

Horse trading aside, General Carr soon went back to the business of pursuing Tall Bull. Nevertheless, after twenty days searching on Prairie Dog and Beaver Creeks and several "skirmishes" with small Lakota war parties, the regiment returned to the Republican River and created a base camp. Here, Cody and Frank North arranged a buffalo hunt with the Pawnee scouts.

Cody had learned that Buckskin Joe was a good horse for buffalo and he wanted to show off his skills for the Pawnee. After noticing the Pawnee scouts "surround" a small herd and rush in among the stampede to kill thirty-two buffaloes, Cody asked if he could have the next herd that appeared all to himself. Anxious to test the white man's mettle, the Pawnees readily agreed.

Cody killed thirty-five buffalo, dropping each less than fifty feet apart in under a half-mile run. The Pawnee were astonished. From that point forward they held Cody in the highest respect, considering him a chief among them.

Not long after the Pawnee buffalo hunt, Cody, under Colonel Royal's command, was scouting with Major North and two companies of Pawnee scouts. Late one afternoon after the scouting party had made camp for the evening, a party of Indians was observed galloping over the prairie toward them. Assuming the band to be Lakota, the scouting party raced to find their weapons to prepare for an immediate fight until they realized the Indians were a group of their own friendly Pawnee allies. Captain Lute North quickly noticed the Pawnee were behaving the way they would if they had participated in a fight. Indeed, they had.

The Pawnee scouts had stumbled upon a band of Sioux who had themselves recently survived a rough fight. Many wounded were being carried in travois and the Lakota were caught totally unaware as the Pawnee ambushed them. The Pawnee had killed four Lakota in the skirmish and were celebrating the victory.

Within days General Carr's scouts were discovering signs indicating the regiment was rapidly gaining on the fleeing tribe of Indians. They also began to notice a woman's shoe print from which they drew the conclusion that at least one captive white woman was among the Indians. The possibility of female captives forced General Carr into more urgent action and he ordered the fastest horses and best riders in the regiment forward; next, the general ordered the supply wagon train to keep up as best possible and the remaining regiment to a forced march. Cody was ordered to select a handful of the best of the Pawnee scouts and to move out in advance of the regiment in order to find the village and present the strongest attack position to the general when he arrived. Moving with extreme caution, Cody's scouting party moved into the sand hills area of the South Platte River in what is now the state of Colorado. There they discovered the Indian village and sent word for General Carr.

Enabled by the supreme sacrifice of the warriors he sent to face General Carr, and by breaking his village apart and scattering on the prairie, Tall Bull had barely managed to escape the Fifth Cavalry. After a few days, however, he reassembled his village and led his warriors on a revenge raid in the Smoky Hill region of Kansas. The Dog Soldiers tore up two miles of railroad track and attacked several small settlements, killing as they went. As Custer had taken Cheyenne women and children captive at Wachita, Tall Bull took two white women prisoners in revenge. Both women, Maria Weichel and Susannah Allerdice, were Swiss/German, and no one in the Cheyenne camps could understand anything either of them said. Most Cheyenne considered the two white women to be more trouble than they were worth and would have just as soon let them go or killed them and be rid of them.

Tall Bull had faced considerable obstacles to avoid General Carr's pursuit, but at Summit Springs high water would lead to his end. The chief had hoped to cross the Platte at Summit Springs, but usually high water had forced him to set up a temporary camp. He had ordered some of his young men to explore the river in order to find the best place to ford the stream. The young men had just returned from placing sticks in the river to mark the depth to better facilitate the tribe's crossing.

Acting on Cody's suggestion, General Carr circled to the north, agreeing with the scout that Tall Bull's scouts would probably be expecting an attack from the direction from which they fled: the south. Soon, the Fifth Cavalry completely surrounded the unsuspecting Cheyenne village and Carr ordered the bugler to sound the charge. The bugler became so excited that he forgot the notes. Carr repeated the command and still the bugler was dumbfounded. The quartermaster riding near the general grabbed the bugle from the bugler's hands and sounded the charge. As the troops raced into battle the old veteran tossed the bugle, drew his pistols and was among the first to enter the village.[17]

That day the Fifth Cavalry made one of the most famous charges in its illustrious history, catching Tall Bull's village totally unaware. The Cheyenne had practically no time to react, grab their weapons and horses and return fire. Instead, the stunned people fled in panic as the cavalry tore through their village. A large number of warriors had been mounted and were preparing for fording the Platte when the attack broke. These warriors rushed back to face the cavalry's charge, yet quickly realized the futility of such an effort and fled with the women and children to the surrounding hills.

General Carr had ordered all the regiment to be on lookout for the white women he suspected to be among the Cheyenne. Soon after the capture of the village the two women were discovered. One of the women was dead and the other was severely wounded. Evidently both had been attacked by Tall Bull's wife when she realized the village was about to be taken by the pony soldiers.

The attack on the Cheyenne village lasted only a short time and the Indians were driven several miles away. Soldiers next started gathering in over 800 horses and mules, which had fled during the attack. Surveying the results of the attack, it was determined that one hundred forty warriors had been killed and one hundred twenty women and children had been taken prisoner. The village had been very prosperous, numbering over two hundred lodges.[18]

Once again General Carr ordered everything stacked and burned. A grave was dug and Mrs. Allerdice was buried. While all this activity was taking place Cody noticed the warriors had recovered from their surprise and returned to engage in battle around the camp. There Cody noticed an Indian riding a large bay horse and shouting commands in Cheyenne. Understanding Cheyenne, Cody heard the Indian telling his comrades they had lost everything and were ruined so they should fight until death. Coveting the Indian's horse, Cody determined he would kill the man and take his horse as a battle trophy.[19]

Cody noticed the Indian was passing a ravine each time he rode up and down the skirmish line shouting orders to his warriors. The scout got off his horse and crept to the ravine to find a strategic location to ambush the Cheyenne warrior. When the Indian passed within thirty yards of Cody's hideaway the scout fired, killing the warrior instantly. Instead of returning to the Indian lines, however, the horse continued running toward the cavalry lines, where a young officer in the fight caught him. Realizing Cody would want them, the young lieutenant raced forward and took the fallen warrior's war bonnet as well as the rest of his accouterments. Cody raced to join his comrades and to lay claim to the magnificent horse. He wrote,

Little did I think at the time that I had captured a horse which, for four years afterwards was the fastest runner in the state of Nebraska, but such proved to be the fact. I jumped on his back and rode him down to the spot where the prisoners were corralled. One of the squaws among the prisoners suddenly began crying in a pitiful and hysterical manner at the sight of this horse, and upon inquiry I found that she was Tall Bull's wife, the same squaw that had killed one of the white women and wounded the other. She stated that this was her husband's favorite war-horse, and that only a short time ago she had seen Tall Bull riding him. I gave her to understand that her liege lord had passed in his mortal chips and that it would be sometime before he would ride his favorite horse again, and I informed her that henceforth I should call the gallant steed 'Tall Bull,' in honor of her husband.[20]

Chapter Nine

DIME NOVELS

When Bill Cody is with a command I sleep easy; he has always been
successful on the trail and victorious in battle. A guide's duties are to
prevent disaster and avoid the halo of glory attending a soldier's re-
quiem. Buffalo Bill's preeminence and fame lies in the fact that he is
living—for a dead scout is not worth a damn.

—General Philip Sheridan (*Buffalo Bill, Myth and Reality*, Eric Sorg)

THE Battle of the Washita and the Battle of Summit Springs drew intense media attention as eastern newspapers proclaimed the U.S. military
had driven hostile Indians from the middle of the continent and eliminated
the threat of warfare on the Great Plains from the Arkansas to the Niobrara Rivers. Yet every headline declaring the military's success in the west
was met with an impassioned retort, usually inspired by Christian or humanitarian organizations, condemning the War Department's policy of
winter "punishment" campaigns in which Indian women and children were
being killed. The voice of compassion had measurable impact; the period
writings of Generals Sherman, Sheridan, and particularly Custer frequently refer to such opposing viewpoints as being naively proposed by
"tender-hearted peace commissioners," indicating the military leaders
were more than casually aware of fellow Americans protesting their actions
toward Indians. Nevertheless, only months before the two landmark battles on the southern plains, the famous golden spike had united the Union
Pacific and Central Pacific Railroads at Promontory Point in Utah, and
most of the citizens of the United States were caught up in the euphoric
celebration, congratulating themselves upon the successful completion of
the colossal dream of connecting the Atlantic and Pacific coasts. As the
War Department did, the vast majority of Americans believed that Indians
stood in the way of the progress of civilization. During these nationalistic
times, the eastern media continued its obsession with frontier political issues, while western newspapers, seeking to encourage growth in their

fledgling communities, called for even more aggressive military actions against Indians. Equally fueled by the publicity machines of the Union Pacific Railroad, which was eager to sell seats on trains and acreage in the communities rapidly springing up along railroad lines, and the White House, which was anxious to heal the wounds of the Civil War through a nationally united western expansion, the salesmen and propagandists offering the romantic, wide-open spaces of the American West found willing customers in the vainglorious European royalty, wealthy eastern American "sportsmen" seeking a final exotic thrill from the rapidly vanishing frontier, and the working-class masses who felt the suffocating effects of the factory-driven industrial revolution. If there is a single man who might be considered an ironic impresario for the era Mark Twain sarcastically dubbed the "Gilded Age," certainly Philip Sheridan would be a leading contender for the title. Sheridan's important behind-the-scenes involvement with two men qualifies him as the one man responsible for much of the legend of the late nineteenth-century American west. The general's loyal support of George Armstrong Custer during the Indian campaigns and his introduction of Buffalo Bill to eastern society most definitely altered the course of American history. As a military comrade and political ally, Sheridan naturally depended on Custer's impetuous gallantry and love of a good fight to viciously attack Indians and mercilessly hound them into submission on the plains. In Cody, however, the general found the perfect flamboyant character to personify the romantic frontier west for the movers and shakers of post–Civil War American culture. Buffalo Bill was the real deal.

The early 1870s were pivotal years in Cody's life. Although he was often broke and looking for a job during this critical time, he was also discovering his unique path in life and becoming increasingly aware of where his talents might lead him. It was during this time that Cody first began to realize the power of his fame as a plainsman and evolved into a genuine celebrity. Trained as a seamstress and adding greatly to the flamboyance that would set her husband apart from the crowd, Louisa now skillfully tailored his beautiful buckskin jackets. A jealous and nagging wife, however, Louisa was increasingly threatened as Cody gathered more and more attention. Beautiful women had begun to chase Cody, but Louisa was equally threatened by the men who eagerly sought her husband's companionship. Men wanted to befriend Cody because he knew no fear of Indians, outlaws, or wild horses. He could outdrink them all without getting drunk, play cards all night, and wake them all up in the morning fresh and ready to ride. Few could outshoot him and none could outride him. He was the Wild West personified.[1]

Where Cody had come to exemplify the Wild West, however, Sheridan had charmed his way into a realm vastly different from the frontier. Ensconced in the upper-class parlor society of the east coast, the general easily waltzed from President Ulysses S. Grant's White House to the chief executive's summer retreat in fashionable Long Branch, New Jersey; from his military headquarters in Chicago as Commander of the Department of the Missouri to Europe as a distinguished observer of the Franco-Prussian War. Interestingly, as graft engulfed the Grant Administration, Sheridan diplomatically managed to remain very close to the president while at the same time distancing himself from the shady characters who increasingly surrounded the chief executive. Along the way, Sheridan acquired a taste for high society as readily as he had for the military. He was a glorified Civil War hero, a bachelor who attracted the attention of social matchmakers, and was in constant demand in the east while he was simultaneously engaged in the Indian campaigns. General George Crook, referring to Sheridan's love of the sweets and pastries of upper-crust society, once joked about his comrade's "bloated little carcass." Crook, as almost every other career military peer of Sheridan's, easily recognized the general's tactics courting social favor. To Crook and others Sheridan had earned his fame and simply sought to exploit and enjoy it. In spite of the considerable historical impact of his own military career in the Civil War, his stronghanded military tactics supervising Reconstruction in violently recalcitrant post–Civil War Louisiana, or his masterful martial control of the chaos surrounding the Great Chicago Fire in 1871, however, Sheridan's brutal success in the Indian Wars won him the most romantic adoration with eastern power brokers and with European royalty; then, as now, people were quixotically fascinated with Indians and the American West. Hungry for lionization in high society, the general quickly made use of his intricate web of connections and, no doubt to reinforce his own frontier credibility, began the process of acquainting his personal friend Buffalo Bill with eastern "dudes" so that the scout might subsequently introduce them to the American west. Some even argue that the modern western tourist trade was born when Sheridan began to court eastern upper-class society through his relationship with Buffalo Bill; indeed, in later life, Cody would be given credit for creating the first "dude ranch" in the American West.

Yet even as Sheridan began to realize the social impact of the romantic west and the charismatic power of Buffalo Bill in eastern power circles, another, equally important character was about to enter Cody's life. As if to somehow mystically precede and perfect the mythological transition of Buffalo Bill's career from plainsman and Army scout through his first major entrances at the center of a global stage, Cody was destined to meet Edward Zane Carroll Judson, and, through him, enter the ancient world of the theater. Judson was also known as "Ned Buntline," an alias by which he had become famous as an author, playwright, actor, temperance lecturer, and dime novelist. Where Sheridan was connected with the upper classes of American society, Buntline was acutely attuned to the ebb and flow of the everyday lives of the normal American public; he earned his living depending upon his developed sensitivity and intimate knowledge of what the "common man" wanted and needed to feed his physical and psychological desires; indeed, one cannot become a "temperance lecturer" without first arriving at some understanding of what stimulates the masses; it is essential to understand what inspires people in order to motivate them. Moreover, Buntline certainly had to have his finger on the pulse of the everyday man in order to make a comfortable living selling plays and dime novels. His experience in the theater, particularly with melodrama, had absolutely acquainted him with the art of creating dramatic, heroic characters specifically designed to appeal to the average man. Working with ancient theatrical axioms and guidelines drawn from the never-ending struggle between good and evil, Buntline knew exactly how to use the process of the theater to evoke mankind's deepest fears and longings. Where Sheridan began the process of mythologizing Buffalo Bill through royalty and powerful media moguls, Buntline began the process of mythologizing Buffalo Bill to the man on the street.

Judson had served for two and one-half years as a private in New York's "Mounted Rifles" during the Civil War. Don Russell explains,

> . . . he fought in no battles but did spend some time behind bars for desertion. He claimed to have been "chief of scouts with the rank of colonel," a dime-novel formula that Cody's press agents were to make familiar. He had acquired the name of Ned Buntline more legitimately by signing it to an enormous amount of printed matter and by editing "Ned Buntline's Own Magazine," which sunk and refloated on his precarious financial seas a number of times. He was not the originator of the dime novel, but he took advantage of the successful innovation of Beadle and Adams as an able and prolific storyteller and boasted that he wrote as many as six novels a week.

He was reputed to have made as much as $20,000 a year, and he supported half a dozen wives, several of them simultaneously.[2]

Buntline had a very colorful background, having even once been hanged in Nashville after shooting a jealous husband in a duel; he was saved when the rope broke. He was prone to instigating political riots and was often indicted or, when he failed to flee the law, jailed for such behavior.

Buntline arrived at Fort McPherson in July, 1869, to deliver a temperance lecture at the same time that Will Cody was ordered by General Carr to accompany Major Brown on an expedition from the fort in pursuit of a war party which had attacked O'Fallon's Station on the Union Pacific Railroad lines, killing several men and stealing some stock. Brown informed Cody that the expedition would be accompanied by the famous novelist Ned Buntline. Buffalo Bill describes the meeting:

> Just then I noticed a gentleman, who was rather stoutly built and who wore a blue military coat, on the left breast of which were pinned about twenty gold medals and badges of secret societies. He walked a little lame as he approached us, and I at once concluded that he was Ned Buntline.[3]

Cody, revealing the stark perspective of a man deeply involved in the life-or-death struggle of warfare, commented to Major Brown that all the medals on Buntline's breast made a good target for a marksman. Later, however, Cody gained respect for Buntline as the writer, jumping at the chance to accompany the expedition, seemed to be more interested in participating in a fight than writing about one. Cody was also impressed that while he had initially apologized for his horsemanship and explained that he had not ridden in years, Buntline quickly proved himself in the saddle and had been the first to swim his mount across the dangerously rain-swollen South Platte River.

Cody soon discovered the trail of the war party and concluded that it was a small group traveling north. Major Brown pursued the Indians as far as the North Platte before deciding to return to Fort McPherson. The major then ordered Cody to accompany Buntline back to Fort Sedgwick. During the short ride Buntline asked Cody a great many questions about his background on the plains. Cody even let the writer ride Powder Face.[4]

As Cody made no further mention of Buntline in his autobiography it is assumed that the novelist failed to obtain permission to accompany another expedition and continued his journey to the east coast. Nevertheless, the seeds of the future had been planted. Upon returning to New York Buntline went to work. On December 23, 1869, the first installment of Ned Buntline's serial *Buffalo Bill, the King of the Border Men*, appeared in the *New York Weekly*. Buntline had discovered the alliterative magic of the name of Buffalo Bill.[5]

Meanwhile, after delivering Buntline safely to Fort Sedgwick and getting paid, Cody was about to participate in one of his favorite pastimes: racing horses. Cody arranged a race matching Tall Bull with a horse ridden by a young lieutenant and won three hundred dollars. Next, Cody bet all his winnings on another race in which Tall Bull outran the best of the Pawnee Scout's horses. Having won over $700, Cody was unable to get anyone to bet against Tall Bull so he arranged a race for Powder Face, pitting him against one of Luther North's horses. Once again Cody's horse won; the scout was making more money racing horses than risking his life searching for hostile Indians! Considering Cody's growing abilities as a marksman and horseman, he probably could have made a nice living just traveling around the west arranging shooting matches and horse races. He would, however, soon find himself returning to the prairie tracking Indians.

With General Carr on a leave of absence, Colonel Royal assumed command of the Fifth Cavalry and, with Cody as scout, ordered the regiment to march to the Republican River in search of Indians. At Frenchman's Fork of the Republican, the expedition spotted a fleeing Indian village and immediately began pursuing the tribe. The Indians quickly outdistanced the cavalry, leading them into the sand hills area of western Nebraska before Royal decided to abandon the chase. Cody tells a story that has intrigued every paleontologist who ever heard it:

> While we were in the sand hills, scouting the Niobrara country the Pawnee Indians brought into camp, one night, some very large bones, one of which the surgeon of the expedition pronounced to be the thigh-bone of a human being. The Indians claimed that the bones they had found were those of a person belonging to a race of people who a long time ago lived in this country. That there was once a race of men on the earth whose size was about three times that of an ordinary man, and they were so swift and powerful that they could run along-side of a buffalo, and taking the animal in one arm could tear off a leg and eat the meat as they walked. These giants denied the existence of a Great Spirit, and when they heard the

thunder or saw the lightning they laughed at it and said they were greater than either. This so displeased the Great Spirit that he caused a great rain-storm to come, and the water kept rising higher and higher so that it drove those proud and conceited giants from the low grounds to the hills, and thence to the mountain, but at last even the mountain tops were submerged, and then those mammoth men all drowned. After the flood had subsided, the Great Spirit came to the conclusion that he had made man too large and powerful, and that he would therefore correct the mistake by creating a race of men of smaller size and less strength. This is the reason, say the Indians, that modern men are small and not like the giants of old, and they claim that this story is a matter of Indian history, which has been handed down among them from time immemorial.[6]

Cody finishes the story lamenting that the bones had to be left on the prairie as the regiment had no wagons and they were too large to carry. Later, in 1870, eminent Yale University professor and American originator of the then-new science of paleontology, Othniel C. Marsh, having heard stories of the discovery of the gigantic bones, visited the region. Actually, Marsh was returning to the prairie, having initially visited the Great Plains in 1868 to discover a treasure trove of prehistoric fossil horses near Antelope Station, Nebraska. The discovery and Marsh's stunning reconstruction of the horse "all the way from the three-toed Protohippus of the Pleistocene down to the modern, hooved variety"[7] empirically demonstrated the horse's existence in North America predated the Spaniards. The professor had attempted to continue his research, but the Indian Wars prevented his return to the region; indeed, Marsh's involvement with Cody upon his return in 1870 was more to provide the scientist's safe passage through hostile Indian territory than to scout for fossils. William Goetzmann explains:

> In 1870, however, with support from Sherman, Marsh led an elaborate entourage of Yale graduate students of the first of a series of Western expeditions. Armed with pistols, fine rifles, hunting knives, and great quantities of camping paraphernalia, the Yale contingent left New Haven on the last day of June, 1870. They proceeded out across Nebraska to Fort McPherson, near the railroad town of North Platte. There they picked up a military escort of veteran cavalrymen, two Pawnee Indian trackers, and the celebrated scouts Major North and Buffalo Bill.[8]

Cody, characteristically confusing dates, continues the story in his auto-biography:

During the summer of 1871, Professor Marsh of Yale College, came out to McPherson, with a large party of students to have a hunt and to look for fossils. Professor Marsh had heard of the big bone which had been found by the Pawnees in the Niobrara country, and he intended to look for that as well as other bones. He accordingly secured the services of Major Frank North and the Pawnees as an escort. I was also to accompany the bone-hunters, and would have done so had it not been for the fact that just at that time I was ordered out with a small scouting party to go after some Indians. . . . However, I had the opportunity to make the acquaintance of the eminent Professor, whom I found not only to be a well-posted person but a very entertaining gentleman. He gave me a geological history of the country; told me in what section fossils were to be found; and otherwise entertained me with several scientific yarns, some of which seemed too complicated and too mysterious to be believed by an ordinary man like myself; but it was all clear to him. I rode out with him several miles, as he was starting on his bone-hunting expedition, and I greatly enjoyed the ride. . . . After having been absent some little time Professor Marsh and his party came back with their wagons loaded down with all kinds of bones and the Professor was in his glory. He had evidently struck a bone-yard and 'gad!' wasn't he happy! But they had failed to find the big bone which the Pawnees had unearthed the year before.[9]

In 1874 Marsh narrowly escaped being killed by the Sioux, but the scientist continued expeditions into the Dakotas for years, eventually becoming friends with Red Cloud. Marsh took the story of Red Cloud's mistreatment at the government's hands back to Washington, and provoked a scandal in the Department of the Interior. Cody says it was Professor Marsh who first made him aware of the possibilities of a community in the Yellowstone Country. Whenever the Wild West played New Haven, Buffalo Bill, in all his regalia, called at the home of Yale College's eminent scientist.[10]

On July 10, 1871, Brevet Major General William H. Emory arrived at Fort McPherson and established the location as the official regimental headquarters of the Fifth Cavalry. General Emory assured Cody that he would build a log house at the fort for his family so Will sent for his wife and baby daughter in St. Louis to join him.

Cody enjoyed himself at Fort McPherson; the region abounded with the type of game the scout loved to hunt, and he continued to win horse races with both Tall Bull and Powder Face. Nevertheless, as his horses' reputations spread it became increasingly harder for Cody to find someone to race against. During this time Buffalo Bill's showmanship began to emerge. Cody made a bet that Tall Bull would beat another horse in a mile-long race. The scout, however, obviously having well-rehearsed the stunt, proposed that he would ride Tall Bull bareback and jump on and off the horse eight times over the course of the race. Holding on to Tall Bull's mane, Cody performed the feat and won the race.

Soon the scout would lose part of his fledgling act, however, as Powder Face was stolen in a raid by a Sioux war party. With Cody along as scout, a young lieutenant and a company of the Fifth Cavalry immediately began in hot pursuit of the Indians. By nightfall Cody had led the outfit to the war party and, after deciding to rest themselves and their horses, a dawn ambush was quickly planned.

The next morning the lieutenant ordered the attack to begin just as the war party was mounting their ponies to start out on the prairie; a race immediately began. Yet a creek lay between the cavalry and the fleeing Indians. This natural barrier prevented the military from catching the war party even though over thirty horses were captured. Cody promptly went through the herd of Indian horses vainly searching for Powder Face. Then, on a distant ridge, Cody spotted an Indian riding Powder Face. After a blazing race across the prairie in which Cody shot two of the fleeing Lakotas, Powder Face pulled way ahead of Cody and the scout gave up the chase.[11]

Realizing he had seen the last of Powder Face, Cody returned to the fallen Lakota warriors and took possession of their war bonnets and accouterments while he also "gently 'raised their hair.'"[12] Returning to the Indian camp, Cody and the hungry troopers found enough dried buffalo meat to satisfy their needs and remained in the camp for two days, resting themselves and their horses before heading toward Fort McPherson.

Not long after Cody arrived at Fort McPherson, however, another expedition was organized to head to the Republican River country to search for war parties. Major Frank North and his Pawnee scouts, having mustered out of service after the winter campaigns of the late 1860s, returned to action with this expedition. Cody had become fond of North and the Pawnee and was delighted to see them again. One day near Prairie Dog

Creek, which was near the cave where Will as a fourteen-year-old boy had spent a month while his broken leg healed, Cody and Major North were busy searching for a spot to camp after a successful day of hunting buffalo. Having separated from North to find a suitable campsite, Cody became alarmed when he heard shots in the distance. Within a few moments, North appeared in a full gallop, pursued by a war party of fifty Indians. Cody fired a few shots at the war party yet soon was himself mounted and fleeing with North from the angry Indians. The warriors came so close that Cody's quirt was shot from his hand while bullet holes were shot through his hat. Very soon, however, Cody and North were saved by Lieutenant William J. Volkmar's troops who, having heard the shots, were racing to the rescue. Upon seeing his allies North began to race his horse in a circle, indicating to his Pawnee comrades to ignore any other orders and rush immediately into the war party. As the fight raged one of the Sioux war party raced back to the nearby village to warn the tribe to flee.

Later, it was learned that the war party was part of Pawnee Killer's Oglala Lakota band. Pawnee Killer, having resisted immigrant encroachment for over a decade, was a seasoned veteran of the Indian Wars. An ally of Roman Nose, Pawnee Killer had participated in the siege at Beecher's Island in which the Cheyenne Chief was killed and been involved in skirmishes from the Arkansas to the North Platte Rivers over the years. In Sheridan's initial winter campaigns, Pawnee Killer had first met with Custer in friendly parley, only to later elude the general and his Seventh Cavalry's deadly pursuit all over the southern plains. Indeed, Custer credited Pawnee Killer with the brutal massacre of ten troopers of the Second United States Cavalry; their leader, Lieutenant Kidder; and his Lakota scout, Red Bead. Only days before his attack on Cody and North, Pawnee Killer had massacred a surveying party. The military pushed Pawnee Killer's war party back across the Platte before returning to Fort McPherson.

Upon returning to the fort, Cody received some good news. In his absence, Louisa had given birth to a son. Lulu had waited for her husband to name the boy and Cody preferred Elmo Judson, in honor of Ned Buntline. Upon hearing this name, the officers and scouts at the fort objected until a Major Brown suggested the name Kit Carson Cody and that name was selected.[13]

Not long after the birth of his son, however, Cody discovered he was flat broke. Always confident of his ability to come up with money quickly, Will soon remembered that after winning the race with Lieutenant George

F. Mason, the officer had offered to buy Tall Bull. Cody found Mason and sold Tall Bull to him.

Suddenly without both of his fast horses and unable to race, Cody continued to scout for the military. Unwittingly beginning yet another of his careers as a plainsman, he started to act as a guide for the increasing numbers of hunters coming into the region. By the winter of 1870–71 he was guiding hunts for an English gentleman named George Watts Garland and was leading other expeditions searching for big game in Pawnee Territory in the Loupe region of the Platte River. Cody also guided for The Earl of Dunraven in 1871. The Earl's trip was arranged by General Sheridan, whom the noble had met when he was a correspondent for the Daily Telegraph and the general was a military observer during the Franco-Prussian War of 1870–71.

Don Russell describes the initial meeting between Buffalo Bill and the Earl:

> Dunraven was met at the station by Buffalo Bill and Texas Jack [Omohundro]. His descriptions of them before they became show men indicate what the scout of the plains considered proper attire. "Bill was dressed in a pair of corduroys tucked into high boots, and a blue flannel shirt. He wore a broad-brimmed felt hat, or sombrero, and had a white handkerchief folded like a little shawl loosely fastened round his neck, to keep off the fierce rays of the afternoon sun. Jack's costume was similar, with the exception that he wore moccasins, and had his lower limbs encased in a pair of comfortable greasy deer-skin trousers, ornamented with fringe along the seam. Round his waist was a belt supporting a revolver, two butcher knives, and in his hand he carried his trusty rifle, the "Widow."
>
> Jack, tall and lithe, with light brown close-cropped hair, clear laughing honest blue eyes, and a soft and winning smile, might have sat as a model for a typical modern Anglo-Saxon—if ethnologists will excuse the term. Bill was dark, with quick searching eyes, aquiline nose, and delicately cut features, and he wore his hair falling in long ringlets over his shoulders, in true western style.[14]

Around this time, as the need for some attempt at legal order was rising rapidly with the numbers of settlers in the region, General Emory suggested that Cody should become Justice of the Peace. Will, protesting his ignorance of the law, resisted but Emory was adamant and had the county commissioners appoint the scout to the position anyway. One of Buffalo

Bill's most enduring stories also springs from this period. One evening Cody was asked to perform a wedding ceremony for a sergeant who served at the post. The groom happened to be a friend of Cody's and, as a result the wedding party, including the Justice of the Peace, had started the celebration early and were "braced up" for the occasion; in modern words, they were drunk. Being in such condition the wedding party and honorable justice failed to locate the marriage ceremony in the statutes. Upon failing to find the actual ceremony, Cody winged it:

> "Do you take this woman to be your lawful wedded wife, to support and love her through life?"
> "I do" was the reply.
> Then addressing myself to the bride, I said, "Do you take this man to be your lawful wedded husband through life, to love, honor and obey him?"
> "I do," was her response.
> "Then join hands," said I to both of them; "I now pronounce you to be man and wife, and whomsoever God and Buffalo Bill has joined together let no man put asunder. May you live long and prosper. Amen."[15]

Whether in a wedding ceremony or a horse race, the natural showman in Cody's personality was emerging more clearly with each passing day. Much of Cody's transformation certainly took place when he came to the realization that as the Indian Wars wound down he would soon have to create another occupation for himself. More historically important, however, is the fact that Cody also realized that the defeat of the Indian Nations simultaneously marked the end of the west that he loved and depended upon to earn a living; indeed, the collapse of the Indian Nations was a resounding, yet mostly subconscious signal to all immigrant Americans that everything they once considered "wild" about North America would be forever changed. Since the days of Lewis and Clark, the immigrant American concept of the west had undergone several major transitions. Initially considered the "Great American Desert," trappers and missionaries had opened immigrants' eyes to a vision of the west as a pristine "promised land," a "second Eden" waiting to be reclaimed by God's chosen people. The epic migration across the Great Plains to the Pacific coast, combined with the crowning completion of the Transcontinental Railroad, left little doubt that the transplanted, mostly European, culture would soon come to dominate everything once considered "wild" in North America. Cody, however, re-

alized this historic transition from a position of awareness—a heightened
sensitivity that people would want to know about the vanishing "wild"
West; he knew that as the "wild" was vanishing the public would become
hungry to experience it. Intuitively, he knew he was born to bridge the gap
between the "wild" and the "civilized" American West.

By the fall of 1871, much of Cody's new direction would become apparent when word was received at Fort McPherson that General Sheridan and
a group of his friends from the east were coming west on a grand hunt. Sheridan's group planned to arrive at Fort McPherson and to hunt the plains all
the way to Fort Hays. This was no ordinary expedition, since it included
General Sheridan; his brother, Colonel Michael Sheridan; Colonel Daniel
Henry Rucker, the acting quartermaster general; Henry Eugene Davis, a
major general of volunteers in the Civil War; General Anson Stager of the
Western Union Telegraph Company; James Gordon Bennett, the editor of
the *New York Herald*; editor of the *Chicago Evening Journal*, Charles L. Wilson; and many other powerful eastern businessmen.

Sheridan had met James Gordon Bennett 11 at President Grant's summer home in Long Branch, New Jersey just before the gentleman was to
inherit his father's newspaper. General Sheridan, aware of the newspaper's
extensive coverage of the Indian Wars, had entertained Bennett with stories of his adventures in the campaigns. Nevertheless as a result of the *New
York Herald*'s coverage of the Indian Wars, particularly the Battle of Summit Springs, Bennett had heard about and was most interested in Buffalo
Bill. Learning this information, Sheridan proposed a buffalo hunting expedition with Buffalo Bill as leader and the publisher jumped at the opportunity.

The group left New York by rail and traveled to Chicago where Sheridan entertained them at his mansion and his brother Michael joined the
expedition. In Chicago the group also visited the Lincoln Park Zoo to have
a look at a real buffalo and study their quarry and better prepare for the
hunt. Continuing on to Omaha by rail, the expedition boarded the Union
Pacific lines, even riding part of the way on the locomotive's cowcatcher.
Along the way they decided to offer two trophies on the hunt—one for the
first elk and one for the first buffalo.

General Emory met the expedition at the lonely North Platte station.
The station's dwindling population was a clear indication of the impact of
the railroad and Army on the Great Plains. Upon completion of their work
there, the Union Pacific workers had moved on down the line; General
Carr had taken most of the Fifth Cavalry to Arizona after receiving orders

from Sheridan to make certain that Buffalo Bill remain to scout for the expedition. The tone of the expedition would indicate the immediate future for the region.

Sixteen wagons, including one just to carry ice, were required to simply carry the group's baggage, supplies, and incidentals; three four-horse ambulances were needed to carry the expedition's guns; linen, fine china, and glassware were brought for the multi-course meals which would be prepared by French chefs and served by waiters in evening dress; five greyhounds were brought to chase antelope and jackrabbits. For years afterwards, people on the plains could locate the hunting parties' former campsites by the numbers of empty, discarded champagne bottles.

That Cody's fame was spreading quickly is implied in the first dispatch sent to the *New York Herald* when the party arrived at Fort McPherson on September 22, 1871:

> General Sheridan and party arrived at the North Platte River this morning and were conducted to Fort McPherson by General Emery [sic], commanding. General Sheridan reviewed the troops, consisting of four companies of the Fifth Cavalry. The party starts across the country tomorrow, guided by the renowned Buffalo Bill and under the escort of Major Brown, Company F, Fifth Cavalry. The party is expected to reach Fort Hays in ten days.[16]

Cody knew this was an important moment in his life and was prepared to dazzle the easterners. He dressed in a new suit of light buckskin trimmed along the seams with fringes. He also wore an "ornamented" crimson shirt and a "broad" sombrero and rode a snowy white horse.[17]

In his pamphlet detailing the experiences of the hunt for the expedition's participants, *Ten Days On The Plains*, General Davies vividly describes the impression Cody made on the group:

> The most striking feature of the whole was the figure of our friend Buffalo Bill riding down from the Fort to our camp, mounted on a snowy white horse. Dressed in a suit of light buckskin, trimmed along the seams with fringes of the same leather, his costume lighted by the crimson shirt worn under his open coat, a broad sombrero on his head, and carrying his rifle lightly in his hand as his horse came toward us on an easy gallop, he realized to perfection the bold hunter and gallant sportsman of the plains.[18]

Cody did more than impress the easterners with his clothing and posture; soon he had to design and construct a bridge capable of supporting the group's heavy wagons as they crossed a stream. Upon successfully crossing the creek Cody had to double-up the horse team's to overcome the steep grades on the rolling plains. Performing with poise and confidence, Cody gained more of the hunting party's respect and admiration with each exhibition of his unique prairie talents and skills. Sell and Weybright offer this very important point:

> He, in turn, seemed to grow in stature as he achieved a new conception of himself, in the mirror of their admiration. They constituted a new and strange audience for him, wonderfully appreciative and responsive. Their comradely feeling of social equality and frank acknowledgment of his leadership supported his self-confidence. He saw himself through their eyes in a fresh vision of self-recognition.[19]

Each night Cody entertained the party with stories around the campfire until finally the buffalo herd he sought was spotted. After charging into the herd and killing several animals a halt was called to the hunt in order to break out the champagne to celebrate the expedition's success. Cody had only tasted champagne once before in his life; he had an immediate liking for the bubbly. Lawrence R. Jerome, the oldest member of the entourage, became fond of Cody's government issued horse, Buckskin Joe, and persisted asking until the scout agreed to let him ride the horse. As soon as the group came upon the herd, Mr. Jerome dismounted in order to get a better shot. Buckskin Joe fled the scene and did not return to Fort McPherson until three days later.

The party hunted for 194 miles along Medicine Creek. They crossed the Republican River and its branches, and then swept along Beaver Creek and the Solomon and Saline Rivers. More than six hundred buffalo and two hundred elk were killed.[20]

Sell and Weybright offer an interesting perspective in conclusion to the impact of Sheridan's buffalo hunt on the career of Buffalo Bill:

> The whole excursion was so delightful that the dudes invited Buffalo Bill to visit them in New York. Cody probably learned as much from the dudes as they did from him. They discovered the Great West; he discovered the potentialities of Buffalo Bill. The outlines of his new role grew clearer and stronger. The easterners returned with a pow-

erful impression of a vivid, unique personality, a favorite topic of
their conversation for years afterward as their anecdotes about him
grew with the telling. The clubsmen reassured their fellow members,
"That Cody fellow is all they say he is and more. Let me tell you
about . . ." And thus the stories multiplied.[21]

Chapter Ten

MAGICIANS FROM MYTHOLOGY

> . . . myth, that most basic expression of the human spirit which has served all civilizations and which, when destroyed, has left pathology and death in its stead.
>
> *(Beyond Geography: The Western Spirit Against the Wilderness,*
> Frederick Turner)

I N autumn, 1871, a squadron of the Russian Imperial Navy sailed into New York harbor escorting a most important twenty-six-year-old man. The visit of Russian Grand Duke Alexis, third son of Alexander II, Czar of Russia, captured all of America's attention as friendly, diplomatic international relations between the United States and Russia soared. For months the American press had been expressing genuine appreciation of Czar Alexander II's recognition and support of the government of the United States in the international community. Of particular importance in light of the Civil War and the confusing image the conflict projected to the rest of the world, Alexander II's recognition of the United States was timely and essential in healing international misconceptions of an American nation torn by internal strife. Using his influence to prevent Britain and France from lending their support to the Confederacy during the Civil War, Alexander II had further demonstrated his friendship to America by selling the Alaska Territory to the United States in 1867. As a result of the Czar's prestigious diplomatic support, pro-Russian, pro-Romanov articles had filled columns of American newspapers for weeks as the people of the United States expressed their heartfelt regards to the Czar and Russia. In order to further contribute to the mutual goodwill, the emperor, in a warm, personal gesture, arranged through the White House for his son

Alexis to tour the United States and on September 26, 1871, the Russian battle fleet steamed out of Falmouth, England, bound for North America.

While the majority of New York newspapers devoted most of their space to articles covering the Grand Duke's visit, Buffalo Bill's name was also rapidly gaining recognition in Manhattan. News articles and photographs of Sheridan's great buffalo hunt with Buffalo Bill and eastern businessmen were prominently placed in major newspapers while those same powerful businessmen were singing Cody's praises at such prestigious places as New York's exclusive Union Club. Throughout Manhattan, boys barked Buffalo Bill's name on street corners as Ned Buntline's dime novels were quickly becoming best-sellers. With shocking synchronicity Buffalo Bill was simultaneously becoming a hero to the man on the street and the man in the ivory tower. Even so, the drama had only begun.

The artist Albert Bierstadt had written to Sheridan earlier, recommending that Alexis be offered a buffalo hunt as the most American adventure he could possibly have. It was only natural that Sheridan would offer Buffalo Bill as a guide for such an expedition. Alexis promptly accepted the general's offer. Almost as soon as he began making arrangements for the hunt, however, General Sheridan was called to emergency military action. Chicago, the general's home city, was burning! The president declared the city under martial law and General Sherman ordered Sheridan to supervise military control of the panic and calamity surrounding the Great Fire. With Sheridan involved in the disaster, General Sherman took control of the Grand Duke's tour and notified the Army that the hunt was to take place in January and to plan accordingly.

Even with his Chicago headquarters destroyed in the conflagration, Sheridan immediately put his staff to work planning the hunt. General George Forsyth, Major W. H. Brown and Lieutenant Edward Hayes were told to spare no expense on supplies, food, or personnel in creating the expedition. Buffalo Bill was officially requested as head scout and Generals Custer and Fitzhugh were invited to accompany the party. Unbeknownst to the scout, Sheridan had a most important mission which he knew only Buffalo Bill could accomplish; as a special added attraction for the Grand Duke's pleasure, and, as a diplomatic gesture to the Lakota, Sheridan wanted Buffalo Bill to arrange for the famous Brule chief Spotted Tail to bring one hundred Sioux warriors to join in the hunt and perform a war dance.

Early in January the first of Sheridan's staff began to arrive at Fort McPherson. The hero of the Beecher's Island fight with the Cheyenne,

General Forsyth, and the expedition's official surgeon (Brevet Major) Dr. Morris Asch, immediately asked Buffalo Bill's advice concerning the best location from which to base the hunt and the scout suggested they establish "Camp Alexis" sixty miles south of Fort McPherson on Red Willow Creek. Next, Forsyth and Dr. Asch informed Cody that General Sheridan requested he locate Spotted Tail's camp and ask the chief to join in the hunt. Cody expressed little surprise to Forsyth or Asch upon receiving Sheridan's bold request and kept his misgivings about the mission to himself. After selecting a location for "Camp Alexis" in the Red Willow Valley, Cody said good-bye to Forsyth and Asch as they returned to Fort McPherson.

In searching alone for any Lakota camp Cody was undertaking extremely hazardous duty; he was a mortal enemy of many Sioux warriors in Spotted Tail's village; indeed, the Fifth Cavalry's Chief of Scout's hair would be major trophy adorning any Lakota's lodge pole. He was, however, aside from the serious personal danger, taking the first, most important action in the future direction of his life, while simultaneously creating a seminal moment in history; in seeking to include Spotted Tail and the Lakotas' participation in the international diplomatic event which was about to take place, Cody was also, truly as an ambassador, creating a new era in the future of the American west. European royals had shown a fascination with the American west since the discovery of the "New World." Jim Bridger and other mountain men acted as guides leading European aristocracy on "safaris" in the American West. Buffalo Bill was nevertheless bringing Indians, buffalo, and royalty together for the first time as a diplomatic and political gesture, and, in doing so, creating much of the formula he would use for the next forty years when respectfully requesting and securing Indian participation in his "Wild West." Indeed, many of those four decades of reenacting history would, ironically, be for audiences of European royalty. In spite of the importance of the mission, however, the journey would not be a pleasant one; the weather was extremely cold and stealth compelled Cody to travel light.[1]

Upon successfully locating Spotted Tail's village, Cody wisely decided to wait until night before placing a blanket over his head Indian-style and riding unobserved into the camp. Will rode straight to Spotted Tail's lodge, dismounted, opened the flaps to the chief's tent, and requested permission to enter.

Spotted Tail recognized Cody immediately and invited him to enter his lodge. Inside, the scout was surprised to discover luck was on his side: Todd Randall, an old frontiersman who was also Spotted Tail's agent, sat by at the chief's side. The old man had lived with the Lakota for many years and spoke Lakota fluently and was able to act as an interpreter for the meeting. Through Randall Cody readily communicated his mission to Spotted Tail.[2]

Ever the visionary diplomat, Spotted Tail immediately enthusiastically agreed to take part in the hunt and informed Cody that he would gather the tribe the next morning to select the people to accompany him on the expedition. Upon discovering how Cody had entered his village, Spotted Tail agreed that the scout had indeed acted wisely in being so cautious as many in his camp did consider him an enemy. Still, an important moment in the history of the relationship between Native and immigrant Americans had been reached in the parley Cody, Spotted Tail and Randall conducted that evening. Considering the future global impact of the bonding of Buffalo Bill and Native Americans to perform historical re-enactment as international arena entertainment, the moment might also be considered of fundamental importance in the history of the modern American entertainment industry. Cody continues the story of how it all began:

> Next morning the chiefs and warriors assembled according to orders, and to them was stated the object of my visit. They were asked:
> "Do you know who this man is?"
> "Yes, We know him well," replied one, "that is Pa-he-haska," (that being my name among the Sioux, which translated means "Long Hair") "that is our old enemy," a great many of the Indians, who were with Spotted Tail at this time, had been driven out of the Republican country.
> "That is he," said Spotted Tail. "I want all my people to be kind to him and treat him as my friend."
> I noticed that several of them were looking daggers at me. They appeared as if they wished to raise my hair then and there. Spotted Tail motioned and I followed him into his lodge, and thereupon the Indians dispersed. Having the assurance of Spotted Tail that none of the young men would follow me I started back for the Red Willow, arriving the second night.[3]

On January 12, 1872, General Sheridan and Buffalo Bill met the Grand Duke at North Platte and, after welcoming ceremonies filled with military pomp and circumstance, the hunt was ready to begin. Don Russell elaborates:

The party moved immediately to the camp at Red Willow. That night the Indians put on the war dance Bill had arranged for, to the great admiration of the visitors. Cody says that Alexis paid much attention to a handsome redskin maiden and that General Custer carried on a mild flirtation with one of Spotted Tail's daughters— Custer in his own writings is so open in describing his interest in Indian girls that the "mild" may be accepted as literal. Mention is also made of Cody's prowess as a yarn spinner. A New York Herald headline referred to "Buffalo Bill as Guide, Tutor, and Entertaining Agent."[4]

In reference to Alexis and Custer's "flirtations" with Lakota maidens, it should be noted here that throughout his book, *My Life On The Plains*, Custer's interest in beautiful Indian women is quite thinly veiled; he carried a pretty young Indian woman captive all over the southern plains as part of his command during Sheridan's 1868–69 winter campaigns. The woman spoke little or no English, yet the general explained her presence by claiming she was needed as an "interpreter."[5]

Cody and Alexis enjoyed each other's company. The Grand Duke was only a year older than Cody and obviously brimming with the vitality and enthusiasm the scout respected in a man. As the evening wore on, the Grand Duke asked Cody question after question concerning the proper weapons and techniques for hunting buffalo. When the Grand Duke decided that he would hunt with a pistol rather than a rifle, Cody arranged for him to ride Buckskin Joe in order to make certain the young man would be properly mounted; Will knew that his horse would run straight in among the herd and guarantee Alexis a close pistol shot.

Early the next morning the herd was spotted and, as the purpose of the expedition was for Alexis to kill a buffalo, the royal was placed close to Cody as the group of men charged into the herd. When Cody helped the Grand Duke negotiate himself to within twenty feet of the herd, the young man emptied his six-shooter without hitting an animal. Cody promptly rode up beside the Grand Duke and exchanged pistols with him. Alexis fired six more shots without hitting a single buffalo. Moving quickly to prevent the herd from escaping, Cody rode close to Alexis again, offered "Lucretia," and yelled for the Russian to follow his lead. Instantly, Cody struck Buckskin Joe with his quirt and the horse instinctively raced up alongside of a big bull buffalo. Cody shouted to Alexis to shoot and the big bull fell in his tracks.[6]

The Grand Duke jumped from his horse and began to wave his hat in the air; immediately, Cody and Alexis were surrounded by royal attendants, all speaking excitedly in Russian. Just as rapidly, the champagne bottles were popped open and the festivities began with toasts to Alexis, the mighty buffalo hunter. Sheridan immediately wired Secretary of War W. W. Belknap and soon headlines in New York, Philadelphia, Boston, Washington, and Chicago sang of the Grand Duke's successful hunt with Buffalo Bill.

The Grand Duke was having the time of his life and Cody was also enjoying himself, particularly the numerous champagne toasts after each of the eight buffaloes Alexis shot. Will genuinely enjoyed the experience of showing Alexis such a good time and personally skinned the hides and took the heads of the slain animals for the Grand Duke's trophies.

Next, the Grand Duke wanted to see how Indians hunted buffalo. Spotted Tail ordered some of his best warriors to surround a herd and race in among them with bows, arrows and lances. The Grand Duke was instructed to follow closely on the heels of a Lakota named Two Lance as the warrior enjoyed the reputation of often shooting an arrow completely through a buffalo. Two Lance lived up to his reputation and the arrow he shot completely through the buffalo he killed was given to the Grand Duke as a souvenir of his hunt with the Lakota on North America's Great Plains. Following Two Lance's remarkable feat the Lakota also gave the Grand Duke a demonstration of the art of killing a buffalo with a ten-foot lance. The skill required the hunter to single out a buffalo and race toward him with incredible speed, and plunge the lance deep into the animal, while simultaneously releasing the spear's shaft at precisely the right moment to avoid being pulled from his horse. The Grand Duke was amazed at the skill of the warriors.

Buffalo Bill was the consummate showman even until the end of the Grand Duke's expedition. As the party was traveling the six miles back to the railroad, Alexis and General Sheridan rode in an Irish dogcart drawn by four spirited cavalry horses. The Grand Duke expressed admiration for the driving of the stagecoach driver who had brought the party to camp. When Sheridan informed Alexis that Cody was also a stagecoach driver, the Russian immediately wanted a demonstration, and the scout took the reins. With Sheridan's encouragement, Buffalo Bill let out the horses more than he had intended. When they began descending a hill Cody could not hold the horses in, so there was nothing to do but let them go. The team virtually flew down the hill and Cody believed they covered the six miles in three minutes.[7]

Upon completion of the hunt, the Grand Duke attempted to give Cody a thick roll of money for his services and invited him to visit Russia. When the scout explained that he would not accept any money for the hunt, the Grand Duke gave him a tiny jeweled box, a Russian fur coat, and a purse of gold. Later, when the Grand Duke returned to New York, he hired a jeweler to make Cody a set of cuff links and a scarf pin studded with diamonds and rubies in the shape of a buffalo's head. The Grand Duke's presents, however valuable, were the least important reward for Cody's services; the Russian had presented him with the opportunity to perform his first Wild West exhibition.[8]

Cody completed his duty with the royal buffalo hunt at North Platte while Sheridan and the Grand Duke's party moved on to Denver. From Denver, General Custer escorted the Grand Duke to New Orleans, where a Russian warship met him. As the excursion with the Grand Duke ended, however, Buffalo Bill was only beginning to move into the public eye. Before departing for Denver, General Sheridan reminded Cody that James Gordon Bennett II had invited him to come to New York for a visit and urged him to take advantage of the opportunity to travel east as the guest of the newspaper heir. Upon persuading Cody to make the journey, Sheridan arranged for a thirty-day pass for the scout and contacted Bennett; the publisher sent $500 for Cody's expenses to New York and General Anson Stager secured railroad passes for him.

Will arrived in Chicago in February, 1872, and was met at the Union Station by General Sheridan's brother, Colonel Michael Sheridan. The general had instructed his brother to entertain Buffalo Bill in Chicago until he arrived and the younger Sheridan made certain he did exactly as his brother ordered. The first thing Colonel Sheridan did was take the scout to Marshall Fields to have him fitted for a suit of clothes. Upon seeing himself in a suit for the first time, Will thought he should cut his long hair but was finally convinced by Colonel Sheridan to leave his locks flowing down over his shoulders. Cody also declined a silk hat in favor of his Stetson.

Chicago was another important step in Cody's future. It was in the "windy city" that Buffalo Bill first interacted with the elite of American society on their intimidating turf. Even as his initial experiences entertaining socialites on the Great Plains had revealed to him the uniqueness of his personality, however, in Chicago Cody began to get a deeper glimpse into the pure social power of his personal charisma. He also started to realize a few of the delicate challenges involved in the direction in which his life was heading. General Sheridan arrived and took Buffalo Bill to a ball in Chicago's aristocratic Riverside suburb. There, in the midst of a "throng" of beautiful socialites, Cody became embarrassed and admitted that it was more difficult for him to greet a throng of lovely ladies than an Indian war party. He was also very uncomfortable being "stared at" and answering "hundreds of questions."[9]

Cody visited Niagara Falls and his future home of Rochester before arriving in New York City, where he was met by J. G. Hecksher and promptly whisked away to the prestigious Union Club. There, James Gordon Bennett, Leonard Jerome and others from Sheridan's buffalo hunt planned a reception and dinner in Cody's honor. Hecksher disapproved of the clothes Cody bought in Chicago and along the way took the scout to his personal tailor to be fitted for a new suit. Hecksher also took Cody to the Niblo Gardens Theater that evening to see *The Black Crook*. Will was particularly impressed with "viewing the many beauties" in the cast. Upon experiencing a taste of the New York nightlife, Cody quickly sought to get away from the staid gentlemen of the Union Club and kick up his heels. In his mid-twenties, the scout must have also been more than a little intimidated by the elite, elderly company in which he found himself. Perhaps that might explain why he immediately sought a different, more reckless type of personality: Soon the scout went looking for his old friend Ned Buntline, whom he quickly found. Within days Cody was dividing his time between the Union Club and Buntline's quarters.[10]

This resolution to the problem of the number of people demanding his attention quickly put Cody in a most embarrassing social situation; he became so confused by the numbers of invitations he was receiving that he completely forgot to attend a dinner given in his honor by James Gordon Bennett. When Cody arrived at the Union Club the day after the failed event Lawrence Jerome politely asked where he had spent the evening. The old gentleman explained that Bennett had meticulously planned a "splendid reception" in Cody's honor and everyone had waited until past nine o'clock before leaving in great disappointment. Cody's obvious surprise and embarrassment was followed with profuse apologies and explanation, prompting the banker August Belmont to step in and diplomatically arrange for another elaborate dinner. James Gordon Bennett was among the guests at the Belmont affair and, upon meeting Cody, promptly accepted the scout's apologies by inviting him to the Liederkranz masquerade ball. Bennett suggested to Cody that he forego the fancy city duds and wear his buckskins. Cody not only wore his own costume to the ball; he showed the party-goers some enthusiastic "backwoods steps" before departing the dance floor when the "artistic dancing" began.

Having spent his entire life dancing between the world of the Indian and the white man, Cody was now learning to dance between two more worlds. Buffalo Bill's charisma grew even stronger as he jumped and stomped, swirled and twirled adroitly through New York, entertaining elite sophisticates, while also letting his more frisky nature run free with the spirited Ned Buntline. Don Russell writes,

> It has been intimated that Ned Buntline had something to do with inviting Cody to New York, on the assumption that the dramatization of "Buffalo Bill: King of the Border Men" was about to have its premiere. Of course this is incorrect, for General Davies had seen the play before the 1871 buffalo hunt. Obviously Ned Buntline had been in and out of too many riots and jails to have been an intimate of any of Bill's hosts. Moreover, Ned was living at the Brevoort with his fourth wife, Anna, whom he had married the previous October 3, much distressing his third wife Kate, who did not get around to divorcing him until the following November 27. His second wife, Lovanche, was less troublesome and agreed to forget the whole thing for a cash settlement. But in New York's better social circles in those days, three wives were regarded as excessive.[11]

Russell believes Buntline had lost interest in Buffalo Bill until Cody sought the novelist out in Manhattan. The biographer also believes that, upon realizing the impact of Buffalo Bill himself being in New York, Buntline quickly arranged for Fred Maeder's script of his dime novel to be revived. Whatever the reason, a production titled *Buffalo Bill*, staring J. B. Studley, was mounted at the Bowery Theater. Studley was a popular actor who worked constantly in Manhattan. Having received raves from the critics for his portrayal of Buffalo Bill, Studley was playing to packed houses. Henry Sell and Victor Weybright ask,

> What might have been in Buffalo Bill's mind as he saw himself portrayed on the stage? It must at first have seemed like an incredible nightmare that such a distorted version of his life should be the subject of a play and that such a drama would appeal to New York audi-

ences. He had seen in print the first of the romances which Ned
Buntline had concocted about him. He could hardly visualize what
effect this dime novel—and others which he knew were to follow-
would have upon him, his career, or his fortune, but he had fervent
hopes that such stories would aid him financially. He needed such
help badly. Not only did he have a wife and daughter to support; he
now also had a son . . ."[12]

The audience, discovering that Buffalo Bill was in the house, roared with
applause that demanded Cody's acknowledgement. The theater manager
escorted Buffalo Bill to the stage. For the first time in his life Cody found
himself behind the footlights, in front of an audience. He was petrified.[13]

Cody shyly and stiffly attempted to utter a few remarks but could not
manage to make himself heard beyond the footlights. Nonetheless, upon
beating a "hasty retreat" to the wings Cody was met by the theater manager, who offered him five hundred dollars a week to take the part of Buffalo Bill in the production. Incredulous, especially considering his painful
exhibition of stage fright only moments before, Will thought the man was
surely joking. When the theater manager was able to convince Cody that
he was serious, the scout suggested "that he might as well try to make an
actor out of a government mule."[14]

Buffalo Bill had been in New York City for twenty days when General
Sheridan finally arrived. Naturally curious about what he had set in motion, the general asked how Cody was enjoying his adventure in the big
city; the scout informed him it was the "best camp he had ever seen" and
requested that his leave of absence be extended for ten more days. Sheridan granted Cody's request, but reminded him that he would soon be
needed with an expedition of the Third Cavalry from Fort McPherson to
Arizona.

Cody spent most of his extended leave in the company of Ned Buntline.
The journalist took Buffalo Bill to the Chestnut Street Theater to see
Peril; or, On the Beach at Long Branch and to a meeting of a fraternal order
for which Buntline served as an organizer. Buntline also accompanied
Cody on a visit to Philadelphia to meet the scout's relatives in the suburbs
of Westchester; Buntline, already acting as Cody's press agent, arranged to
interview Buffalo Bill for the *Philadelphia Public Record* to present the
scout's impressions of the hunt with Russian Grand Duke Alexis. Anxious
to capitalize on the widespread publicity of the Grand Duke's buffalo hunt
and Cody's trip to New York, Ned Buntline barely waited for Cody to

leave the city before beginning a second dime novel based on Buffalo Bill. On March 25, 1872 *Buffalo Bill's Best Shot; or, The Heart of Spotted Tail* started running serially in the *New York Weekly*. From July 8 through October 14 he serialized *Buffalo Bill's Last Victory; or, Dove Eye, the Lodge Queen.*[15]

Sell and Weybright conclude,

> Ever since he had guided those fashionable hunting parties he had been a man waiting for a miracle, and this trip to New York seemed to be such a miracle. It was incredible enough to see himself the hero of a printed book; to see himself dramatized an unbeatable hero on the stage was even more astonishing.
>
> Whatever his contemporaries may have said about Buffalo Bill, all agreed that he was intensely practical—not about saving his money, but about getting ahead, about getting out of predicaments. A man had to be practical and realistic to survive in the frontier world. Money was not easy to earn, but men all about him were trying, by get-rich-quick schemes, by gold prospecting, by land speculation, to make money easily. It was part of a western tradition, and very much a characteristic of Cody, to spend money recklessly. But he always had an eye for the main chance, and a new faith that opportunity would turn up on the other side of the next hill.[16]

When Cody arrived in New York he was clearly searching for that miracle "on the other side of the hill." Ironically, Buffalo Bill was facing the same predicament his idols Jim Bridger and Kit Carson faced in the 1830s: The west he depended upon to earn a living was rapidly vanishing before his very eyes and, as Bridger and Carson before him, Buffalo Bill knew that he would have to find another livelihood. Unlike Bridger and Carson, however, who lived most of their boyhood years in urban areas before entering the west and the fur trade in their late teenage years, Cody was in his mid-twenties and had spent his entire life working odd-jobs on the Great Plains. In gaining vital frontier experience in a broad variety of occupations such as bullwacker, Pony Express rider, stagecoach driver, innkeeper, railroad crewman, buffalo hunter, and Army scout, however, Cody had failed to find a lasting occupation. Cody had, as Bridger and Carson before him, maintained a positive belief that the transitory nature of working on the frontier was natural and the land would continue to provide a livelihood. The major difference in the three men's vocational dilemma, however, is that when the fur trade ended and Bridger and Carson went to work, either for the government as scouts, or as independent entrepreneurs, the west of the late 1830s was not remarkably different from the west of the 1820s. Where the west was still largely pristine at the end of the Fur Trade Era when Bridger and Cody faced major shifts in their occupations, however, the situation Cody faced in 1872 was profoundly different. For over thirty years, hundreds of thousands of people had crossed the continent to settle the west coast. This colossal immigrant westward experience had caused much of the collective public perception of the west as "the Great American Desert" to vanish and be replaced with a new vision of the west as the "Promised Land." Moreover, this major population shift had inflicted quick, profound, and permanent change upon the face of the continent: Indian resistance to the white encroachment upon their land, for all intents and purposes, was quickly dissolving under the relentless onslaught of the military; moreover, the continent had been linked through the telegraph service and the intercontinental railroad, insuring rapid communication to an increasingly mobile culture obsessed with gaining wealth from the heartland of North America. As a result of these profound changes, it was obvious to even the most unobservant that the west would never be the same. At this moment, Will Cody certainly must have realized the important part he had played in the subjugation of the land and, consequently, the elimination of the lifestyle he so dearly loved. This realization must have put him in a walking state of shock. Furthermore, much like Red Cloud or any of the Lakota leaders who had been brought to New York from the Great Plains, Cody must have also experienced acute culture shock when visiting the urban metropolis. Before visiting Chicago, St. Louis was the largest city Cody had seen in his life. The realization of his role in the destruction of the West combined with the shock of visiting the most elite social circles of eastern American culture certainly gave birth to Buffalo Bill's consideration of a career in show business.

"Now, in 1872," Henry Sell and Victor Weybright write,

> he was suddenly transported to cities, to the East of the Gilded Age, to the New York of Jim Fisk and Boss Tweed, to the world of Barnum and Broadway. Most amazing, most miraculous of all, here was he, Will Cody, now glorified as Buffalo Bill, in the very center of this theatrical world. It was a kind of magic, the kind of experience the young frontiersman had never seen or imagined—but, and in this he was only human, he enjoyed the 'spotlight.' Nothing it would seem, could be farther from his tastes and talents, for here was a universe of intangibles. Everything suddenly became a fantasy, created by the imagination and not by nature.[17]

Cody possessed a vivid imagination; his boyhood had been spent sitting at the feet of the frontier masters telling tall tales around a campfire and he could yarn with the best. Still, it took little imagination to recognize that in New York he had been offered as much money for a week of "playacting" as himself as he had earned in a month in his most successful occupation— hunting buffalo. From his youth and the days when William Russell first assisted him and his family, Cody understood the relationship between himself and older, powerful gentlemen. Throughout his life, he had directly sought the help of older men with more authority than himself. He had served under strong men his entire life and through experience well understood the natural routes to be taken to accept power from these men and to hold and wield such power himself. The men Will met in New York were simply a more wealthy, sophisticated version of the forceful men who preceded them in influencing his life: men such as his father, Isaac, Horace Billings, William Russell, Alexander Majors, Lew Simpson, Bill Hickok, Jim Bridger, Kit Carson, Rain-In-The-Face, Jack Slade, General Sheridan, and scores of others unknown to us now. In fact, Cody had always been around men of great wealth and power. The gentlemen in Manhattan, however, opened Cody's eyes to a world of fabulous luxury—a world which he never before could have imagined. Will realized that money opened the door to this new world and was also smart enough to realize that if Buntline and others were making money exploiting his name then perhaps he could do the same for himself. Before leaving New York Cody made a deal with Buntline to meet him in Chicago in the fall to do a stage production with some real Indians.

Chapter Eleven

TRODDING THE BOARDS

He watched the seats fill in keen anxiety, and the moment the curtain rose and his father appeared on the stage, he would make a trumpet of his little hands, and shout from his box, "Good house, Papa!"

—Helen Cody Wetmore, describing her five-year-old nephew Kit Carson Cody (*Buffalo Bill, Last of the Great Scouts*, Helen Cody Wetmore)

TALES of Buffalo Bill's adventures in New York preceded his return to the Great Plains and a group of his friends, unable to contain their excitement awaiting his arrival, traveled to Omaha to meet his train and organize a welcoming celebration. Once the reunion party began, the group of men, no doubt heavily fueled by a multitude of champagne toasts, demanded to see the scout in his complete wardrobe of fancy evening attire. Eager to accommodate his "ole pards," Cody went to his room at the Paxton Hotel and put on his new suit—complete with silk top hat. With his long hair tucked up under the stovepipe hat, Buffalo Bill's friends hardly recognized him. The scout's novel appearance brought forth cries for even more rounds of toasts, which culminated in Cody leaving his suitcases, trunks—and buckskins—in Omaha. The scout arrived at Fort McPherson adorned in evening apparel. The comical situation immediately became complicated, however, as the expedition, under the command of Brevet Major General J. J. Reynolds, colonel of the Third U.S. Cavalry, had moved out and left fellow scout Buffalo Chips White behind to guide Cody. Buffalo Bill had little choice but to mount Buckskin Joe in formal evening dress and report for duty.

After a few very awkward moments with General Reynolds, the humor of the situation prevailed and everyone had a good laugh before settling into yet another celebration to welcome Cody back to the plains. Texas Jack Omohundro, Buffalo Chips White, and fellow scouts accompanying the expedition rummaged through their gear and pulled together a set of buckskins and a Stetson for Cody and he was soon mounted and ready to ride.

Cody's field preparation was not a moment too soon. A small party of Indians had raided the McPherson Station about five miles from the fort, killing several men while also getting away with a large herd of horses. Cody was ordered to pursue them as scout for Company B of the Third Cavalry under the command of Captain Charles Meinhold and First Lieutenant Joseph Lawson. Meinhold and Lawson were Civil War veterans and career military men, the former a German immigrant who had been commissioned first lieutenant while serving in Kit Carson's New Mexico Volunteers, the latter a Kentuckian who had spent his entire military career in the cavalry. Buffalo Chips White was one of Buffalo Bill's oldest friends and he had known Texas Jack Omohundro since the two met on the plains immediately after the Civil War. Like Cody, Omohundro wore his hair long; unlike Cody, he was accustomed to wearing Indian scalps on his belt. Buffalo Chips was fated to be killed at Slim Buttes while scouting for General Crook; Texas Jack was destined to trod the theatrical boards with Buffalo Bill and Ned Buntline.

Arriving at Loup Fork two days after leaving the fort April 24, the scouts discovered the Indians' trail had scattered. Meinhold ordered the expedition to camp and sent Cody, under the command of Sergeant Foley and a detail of six men, on a scout to search for the war party. Cody discovered the Indian camp less than a mile away from Meinhold and his men. Since the war party was small, Cody determined to charge them with his six men rather than returning to the command. He polled the men and all replied they would follow wherever he might lead. The scouting party moved forward.[1]

Cody figured the odds were two to one. Nevertheless, the scout soon gave the signal and the small group of men roared into the Indian camp with guns blazing. Once the Indians started returning fire Cody discovered himself in a most unusual, and dangerous, situation: Mounted upon Buckskin Joe, Cody thought nothing of jumping the camp's creek to engage Indian reinforcements as they approached the big fight. Cody's horse, however, was better than most; his companions could not force their horses to make the leap! Before the soldiers could dismount and ford the stream to assist Cody, two mounted warriors circled him, firing at close range. Cody immediately took one of the warriors out with a shot from his rifle. Instantly, however, the scout noticed blood streaming down his forehead; quickly running his hand through his hair, Cody realized he had been wounded; one warrior had shot Cody as the scout simultaneously killed his comrade. Upon seeing his companion fall, the surviving warrior fled. Cody whipped Buckskin Joe forward and soon caught and killed the Indian warrior who wounded him. After the fight ended Cody discovered that he had received a scalp wound and Buckskin Joe had also been wounded—shot in the breast.

Meinhold's official military report states,

> Mr. Cody had guided Sergeant Foley's party with such skill that he approached the Indian camp with fifty yards before he was noticed. The Indians fired immediately upon Mr. Cody and Sergeant Foley. Mr. Cody killed one Indian; two others ran toward the main command and were killed. . . . While all this was going on, Mr. Cody discovered a party of six mounted Indians and two led horses running at full speed at a distance of about two miles down the river. I at once sent him, in the beginning of the chase, gained a little upon them, so that they were compelled to abandon the two lead horses, which were captured, but after running more than twelve miles at full speed, our jaded horses gave out and the Indians made good their escape . . Mr. William Cody's reputation for bravery and skill as a guide is so well established that I need not say anything else but that he acted in his usual manner.[2]

On May 22, 1872, as a result of Meinhold's report, Cody was awarded the Medal of Honor. Nevertheless, on June 16, 1916, only six months before his death, Cody's name was stricken from the rolls. In the 1870s, the Medal of Honor was much more commonly offered than today. The Medal of Honor was the only award given to American heroes—soldiers or civilians—and the 1916 Act of Congress removed the names of all civilian winners of the Medal of Honor from the rolls.[3]

Cody continued to scout throughout the summer with the Third Cavalry. He was out for over thirty days with Major Alick Moore before departing with Major James Curtis, with whom he followed a war party from the South Platte to Fort Randall on the Missouri River in the Dakotas. On the return trip to Fort McPherson, Major Curtis' expedition ran out of supplies and had to survive for fifteen days on whatever game they could bring into camp. Will returned to Fort McPherson to learn that on August 15, 1872, Louisa gave birth to their third child—a girl, Orra Maude.

A few weeks after Orra's birth, the Earl of Dunraven returned to the Great Plains for a six weeks' hunt. The Earl brought three friends along and was also escorted by Brevet Lieutenant Colonel Anson Mills, captain of the Third Cavalry. The Earl brought a letter from General Sheridan requesting Buffalo Bill's services as scout for his hunting expedition. Cody considered the Earl a "thorough sportsman and excellent hunter" and spent several weeks hunting with him. While out with the Earl, however, a group of Cody's friends from Chicago arrived at Fort McPherson with a letter from General Sherdian requesting Cody to guide them on a hunt. Having been out for several weeks with the Earl, Cody decided to leave him and accompany the Chicago group.[4]

Upon making his decision Cody went to the Earl and told him he would be leaving him in the capable hands of his friend Texas Jack Omohundro, who would be his guide for the remainder of his hunt. The Earl seemed offended with this news and Cody felt he never forgave him for "going back on him." The entire situation with the Earl of Dunraven, however, indicated Cody's time was becoming less his own with each passing day. Even though he was in demand as a scout and guide, Cody was about to expand his political horizon.

In 1872 some of Cody's friends attended a political convention in Grand Island and nominated him as the Democratic candidate to represent the Twenty-sixth District of the Nebraska Legislature. The Twenty-sixth District being predominately Republican, Cody believed he had no hope of winning the election and made no campaign whatsoever. In spite of the odds, however, Cody won the election by forty-four votes. Even though Cody claimed to be proud of his election, he was apparently more proud of the "Honorable" title that accompanied the victory and failed to show up at the capital to claim his seat in the house.[5]

The election was later contested by Cody's opponent, D. P. Ashburn, who charged that the returns were filed incomplete. The House Committee on Privileges and Elections declared on January 14, 1873, that Mr. Ashburn had indeed won the seat in the Nebraska House of Representatives. The fact that Cody had failed to claim the seat in the first place did not help the scout's case with the committee. In any event, Cody had never taken his political career seriously and had developed more lucrative dreams for his future; he was going to become an actor.

Since returning from New York, Cody had received many letters from Ned Buntline urging him to return east to portray himself on the stage. Buntline's enticing remarks, "There's money in it and you will prove a big card, as your character is a novelty on the stage," magnetically attracted Cody to the theater.[6] Most of Will's closest friends, however, believed Buntline to be a con artist leading him naively down a primose lane. Many even teased Cody and made fun of his thinking he could become an actor. Nothing in these reactions from his friends could have eased the fact that Cody was still stinging from the attack of stage fright he suffered at the Bowery Theater when called to address an adoring audience. Buntline, however, insisted that he could teach him to overcome his fear and face an audience of "five thousand as easily as half a dozen."[7] The novelist insisted that the scout meet him in Chicago where he promised to organize a strong company of actors to perform in a new show with Cody himself in the role of Buffalo Bill.

Many important factors entered into Cody's final decision to accept Buntline's offer, not the least of which was the fact that Louisa wanted to visit her mother in St. Louis. Soon, Cody informed General J. J. Reynolds that he was resigning as Chief of Scouts. The general urged him to reconsider taking such a drastic step. He reminded Cody that he was leaving a comfortable home where he was assured of making a good living and "embarking upon a sea of uncertainty." Cody, however, had made up his mind and nothing would change it.[8]

"Embarking upon a sea of uncertainty," Cody was returning to the intuitive. From his boyhood experiences with bullwackers and Pony Express riders through his career as a buffalo hunter and military scout, Cody had instinctively reinvented himself time after time. If anyone was perfectly trained to become an actor it was Will Cody; in repeatedly recreating himself since childhood while mastering skill upon skill in a colorful parade of difficult and dangerous tasks, he had been training all of his life to enter the world of the theater. As the actor recreates himself in of each of his characters, Cody was experienced in deftly changing from one role into another. His life had often depended upon his ability to transform himself. Moreover, his inherent personality was that of the athletic entertainer, showman and impresario; where one man might consider himself competent if able to ride a horse with enough talent to win races, Cody had taught himself to win races dramatically, gracefully jumping on and off his horse while his opponents remained safely mounted throughout the match. After defeating the competition, Cody competed with himself, revealing a personality constantly striving to improve itself, a highly motivated individual concerned with artistic growth. Furthermore, as the flamboyant mountain men before him, Cody had gleaned his entire unique personal appearance from the most visually stunning and appealing men who ever lived in America—the Plains Indians. Perhaps because of losing his father at such a tender age, Cody had attracted to himself some of the most important Indian and non-Indian men in early American western history, while he had humbly made himself available to learn from them in order to blend the best characteristics of their personalities into his own. Exhibiting exemplary courage and personal moral character, he had lived by his intuition and intelligence, surviving, indeed, flourishing within, while rising above, one of the most violently dangerous eras in American history. Throughout his entire life Will Cody instinctively embraced uncertainty. He had understood since childhood that success or failure in life is based on how one deals with uncertainty. The death of his older brother, Samuel, in a horse accident must have impacted him terrifically with the reality of uncertainty. At the tender age of nine he had witnessed his father's stabbing by a suddenly enraged political opponent. What could be more uncertain than becoming the "man" of the house at eleven years of age? What could be more confirming of life's uncertainty than facing a siege by a blood-thirsty Pawnee war party as a child? Could facing an audience of adoring fans be more challenging than riding with emergency dispatches through a pitch black night in enemy territory? Was venturing onto the stage more intimidating than matching life-or-death wits with Kiowa Chief Santana at the outbreak of a major regional war? Will had every reason to believe that he would succeed in reinventing himself as an actor and make more money than ever before in his life doing it. Besides, he had enough self-confidence to know that if he failed in this theatrical adventure with Ned Buntline that he could return to the Great Plains and re-create himself yet again.

While preparing to leave the fort, one of Cody's fellow scouts, "Texas Jack" Omohundro, asked to accompany him. Cody figured Texas Jack would make "as good a star as myself" and arranged for the scout to accompany him.[9]

Born near Palmyra, Virginia, on July 26, 1846, just five months younger than Cody, "Texas Jack" was John Burwell Omohundro, Jr. Omohundro joined the Confederate Army's Virginia Cavalry about the same time that Cody joined the Union Army's Seventh Kansas. Jack's regiment was part of famous Confederate General J.E.B. Stuart's Cavalry Corps and he served as a courier and scout during the Shenandoah Valley campaigns. After the war Jack headed for Texas, but only got as far as Florida, where he taught school after his leaking ship forced him ashore. His link with Texas is vague, but Omohundro came north on a trail drive and may have been at the signing of the Medicine Lodge Treaty. He knew California Joe and Wild Bill at Fort Hayes, and was employed as scout at Fort McPherson and also by the Indian Service in 1872 when he accompanied Pawnees on a buffalo hunt.[10]

In Omaha, Cody said good-bye to Louisa and his children as they departed for St. Louis while he and Texas Jack headed to Chicago. The two scouts did not find Ned Buntline in the best of moods; in fact, he was furious. Cody had promised to bring ten Indians with him to be in the production and Buntline had placed advertising in the *Chicago Evening Journal* for the opening of *Buffalo Bill* at Nixon's Amphitheater on Monday, December 18, featuring the "real" Buffalo Bill and Texas Jack appearing with ten Sioux and Pawnee chiefs.

The two scouts may have forgotten to bring the Indians, but that was the least of their worries; Buntline had yet to write the play! Complicating matters, Buntline had made production arrangements with the theater owner to divide percentages of the show's expenses and profits. Upon learning the full extent his partner's blithe professional attitude, however, Nixon became furious. Frightened the show was advertised to start in just days, Nixon canceled his contract with Buntline. The irrepressible Buntline next asked Nixon what he would charge to rent him the amphitheater; Nixon offered him the space for $600 a week and Buntline promptly tossed $300 on the table and became the sole producer of his unwritten play. Since it is unlikely that Buntline had that kind of money personally it is safe to assume that Buffalo Bill and Texas Jack probably financed the show themselves.

The theater secured, Buntline rushed to buy pens, ink, and paper and retired to the hotel. Ensconced in his room, Buntline hired all the clerks in the hotel to take dictation and went to work. Less than an hour after he had rented the theater, Buntline was dictating page after page of his script to his clerk/scribes. After four hours he sprang from the table and shouted "Hurrah for the 'Scouts of the Plains.'"[11]

As soon as Buntline finished writing the drama, he assigned Buffalo Bill and Texas Jack the tasks of committing the script to memory. Both men, having absolutely no experience in such matters, scratched their heads in bewilderment; yet, being accustomed to doing what they were told in the military, the two novices went to work attempting to memorize Buntline's new play. After a few hours' work the two scouts were pleased to discover they were actually succeeding in remembering a few of their lines. Nevertheless, when Buntline appeared and asked for a line reading he was stunned to discover his two stars, without a sense of theatrical timing or cues, had no concept of when to stop and start with their individual lines.

When Buntline attempted to explain the fundamentals of the art of acting, his stars grew even more intimidated and frightened that they had undertaken a task that was obviously out of their league. Their confidence deflated, Cody suggested that perhaps he and Omohundro should return to the prairie. Of course, Buntline could have none of that and the playwright put his formidable skill in the art of persuasion to work encouraging the crestfallen scouts to stay with him. Finally, Buffalo Bill and Texas Jack went back to work, reluctantly attempting to overcome their theatrical awkwardness and master the art of acting in forty-eight hours. Buntline sent the stage manager to the hotel to gently coach them, but by opening night the stars were not much better than when they began. Tension was growing thick in the air.

If they were to fail, however, it would be before a full house. Buntline knew how to draw a crowd and was extremely successful doing so in Chicago. Cody and Omohundro's courage began to fail them as they peered through holes in the curtain and watched the theater fill to capacity; facing war parties or wild wounded animals would have been easier for either man. When it came time for Cody to make his entrance he was warmly received with applause, to which he responded with a wooden, petrified bow. Nevertheless, he was instinctively wandering yet again onto his own personal path to destiny. Cody describes it best himself:

> Buntline, who was taking the part of "Cale Durg," appeared, and gave me the "cue" to speak "my little piece," but for the life of me I could not remember a single word. Buntline saw I was "stuck" and a happy thought occurred to him. He said—as if it were in the play:
>
> "Where have you been, Bill? What has kept you so long?"
>
> Just then my eye happened to fall on Mr. Milligan, who was surrounded by his friends, the newspaper reporters, and several military officers, all of whom had heard of his hunt and 'Indian fight'—he being a very popular man, and widely known in Chicago.
>
> So I said:
>
> "I have been out on a hunt with Milligan."
>
> This proved to be a big hit. The audience cheered and applauded; which gave me greater confidence in my ability to get through the performance alright. Buntline, who is a very versatile man, saw that it would be a good plan to follow this up, and he said:

"Well, Bill, tell us all about the hunt."

I thereupon proceeded to relate in detail the particulars of the affair. I succeeded in making it rather funny, and I was frequently interrupted by rounds of applause. Whenever I began to "weaken," Buntline would give me a fresh start, by asking some question. In this way I took up fifteen minutes, without once speaking a word of my part; nor did I speak a word of it during the whole evening. The prompter, who was standing between the wings, attempted to prompt me, but it did no good; for while I was on the stage I "chipped in" anything I thought of.[12]

Trusting his wits and drawing Milligan into the scene by ad-libbing, Cody was resorting to one of his favorite pranks to play on hunting expeditions. Cody would often isolate a man from the party and, in prior, secret arrangement with Indian friends, stage an ambush by a war party. When the attack began Cody would ask the gentleman if he wanted to fight or run. The scout had duped Milligan into thinking he had been attacked by such an Indian war party and Milligan had fled in panic. This prank evolved into a feature of the Wild West in Europe as Cody would invite monarchs aboard the Deadwood Stage and have "wild" Indians chase them in a thrilling race around the arena. Cody and Buntline, forced by necessity to employ the ancient theatrical device of ad lib, had unwittingly stumbled upon a unique formula for presenting the cultural phenomenon of Buffalo Bill: They would encourage Cody to tell the truth, yet embellish it to the scale of dramatic "tall tales" for the stage; through anecdote they would simply allow Cody to really play himself.

This was something Cody understood. In his youth, Will had certainly experienced the most brilliant storytellers of the American west. The mountain men, in glorious, ribald splendor, called it "yarning" and elevated the skill to a campfire art form. Later, upon initially attempting to describe the unbelievable majesty of the American west to incredulous easterners, Jim Bridger and other American mountain men gained the dubious reputation of being grand liars and raconteurs. Realizing most people thought his stories were the result of a fertile imagination, Bridger decided to take a physical reality such as an enormous canyon, and imbue it with his own unique flavor: Describing Utah's Echo Canyon—which he named—the mountain man said each night he would prepare for bed and shout into the rocky gorge: "Jim Bridger, Git out o' them covers!" Ole Gabe claimed the echo would wake him returning promptly eight hours later. Buntline and Cody had innocently discovered how to transpose this colorful form of western oral history and storytelling to the stage. Buffalo Bill's life and times would become the basis for the drama taking place on stage. Rather than acting the scout would simply re-create scenes of his heroic experiences and Buntline would dress it up theatrically.

Baffled as to how he might end the first act of *The Scouts of the Prairie*, however, Buntline signaled to the "Indians" ("actors" Buntline had hired off the street and put in tan-colored costumes) waiting in the wings to make their entrance. They hooted and howled, leapt up and down and pretended to attack the "actors" on stage. Since the script had long since lost importance, the scouts were as confused as the phony Indians concerning what they were supposed to do next. Nevertheless, they followed Buntline's lead and pulled their pistols and filled the phony Indians full of phony lead. Mercifully, the curtain fell and the first act came to a close.

During the intermission, Buntline the director tried desperately to guide his cast back to the script. Cody and Omohundro were over the worst of their stage fright, yet both were still green-horns behind the footlights; when they could remember their lines they could not deliver them with enough vocal power to be heard. Finally, once again in on-stage desperation, Buntline coached the Indians into tying him to a tree with the purpose of burning him alive. The audience howled in delight while the Indians prepared to roast him. Buntline seized the opportunity to fill space with something familiar and launched into one of his temperance lectures. The audience responded with screams and howls to "burn the rascal" to mercifully end his torturous pontification. The curtain came down as the Indians set the wood surrounding Buntline ablaze. The audience went wild with tumultuous applause.

The third act recapped the first two with the exception that the cast found lariats and spent a lot of time roping one another. Buntline's character, Cale Durg, was also reincarnated and killed again. Cody described the play's reviews:

> The next morning there appeared in the Chicago papers some very funny criticisms on our first performance. The papers gave us a better send-off than I expected, for they did not criticise [sic] us as actors. "The Chicago Times" said that if Buntline had actually spent four hours in writing that play, if was difficult for any one to see what he had been doing all the time.[13]

Don Russell confirms the fact that the critics gave Buffalo Bill and Texas Jack good reviews:

> Such was the case in the "Evening Journal," which said: "Nixon's Amphitheater was last night the scene of a most extraordinary character and one in which the audience bore quite as prominent a feature as did the occupants of the stage. The occasion was the first appearance of Ned Buntline's play with the blood-curdling and hair-raising title of 'The Scouts of the Prairie; or Red Deviltry As It Is,' being a descriptive affair of life on the plains and in the mountains of the West, and in which the noted characters 'Buffalo Bill' and 'Texas Jack' in their own original selves were presented, as well as 'Ned Buntline' the author of the play. Last night not less than 2,500 boys and young men crowded the amphitheater to catch a glimpse of their heroes. Mlle. Morlacchi, the Italian danseuese, essayed the part of the Indian maiden Dove Eye with great success . . . largely sustained the dramatic link in the chain of events."[14]

From that review, one might assume Mlle. Morlacchi somehow held the show together. Yet when the *Chicago Tribune*'s critic referred to her character having "an Italian accent and a weakness for scouts," he was accurate and prophetic; within weeks Giuseppina Morlacchi and Texas Jack Omohondro were married. Recognized for introducing the "Cancan" dance to America and having trained primarily in Europe as a dancer, the future Mrs. Omohondro was the most experienced thespian of the cast, causing one to wonder just how she was able to even work herself into the pandemonium passing for a play on the stage. Evidently she danced her way through it all.

Presenting the *Chicago Times* critic's remarks, Don Russell offers important insight into what was really taking place:

> The "Times" did say this: "On the whole it is not probable that Chicago will ever look upon the like again. Such a combination of incongruous drama, execrable acting, renowned performers, mixed audience, intolerable stench, scalping, blood and thunder, is not likely to be vouchsafed to a city for a second time—even Chicago."

No critic was ever more wrong than that. With a reported $2,800 in the till for the first night, Buffalo Bill himself was to bring something almost as bad to Chicago every year for a decade, and from that day to this something very like "The Scouts of the Prairie" was to meet similar condemnation from successive generations of Chicago stage, motion picture, radio, and television critics. The "Times" reporter had witnessed the birth of the Western. It is not surprising that he did not recognize it, for neither did its creator, Ned Buntline. Buffalo Bill, knowing less about the stage, just possibly did.[15]

Buntline's lighthearted, sink-or-swim attitude concerning the theater and playwriting had taught Cody not to take his new occupation too seriously. As a result, Cody was never intimidated again getting in front of an audience. More importantly, however, Cody's naivete allowed him the freedom to continue the process of re-inventing himself and his new form of melodrama on the stage. Where a highly trained actor or playwright might balk at something "below" his skill, or dignity, Cody was only concerned with entertaining his audience by simply being Buffalo Bill.

Whether the show was an artistic success or not, one cannot argue with the bottom line that the production made money. By the end of the week the Chicago production made so much money that Nixon convinced Buntline to let him back into the partnership. The following week the show moved to St. Louis and was such a hit that hundreds of people were turned away, unable to secure seats. December 23, 1872, was a bitterly cold opening night but the St. Louis Grand Opera House was packed in spite of the weather. A St. Louis native, Louisa Cody came with her family to see the show. As previously explained the shows were never the same for two consecutive performances. Moreover, the more extemporaneous the performances, the better the audiences liked it. When Buffalo Bill saw Louisa in the third row he called to her, "Oh Mama, I'm a bad actor!" and the crowd roared in loving approval.[16]

In a matter of days, Cody had mastered the art of being completely honest on stage. He had learned to open himself totally to his audience, exposing the essence of his heart and soul. The world was now gathering around his campfire, eager to hear his tall tales. The full story of his interaction with Louisa on the stage that evening reveals the degree of openness and honesty to which Cody had so quickly evolved as a performer. Upon seeing Louisa and, preceding Bertolt Brecht by a half-century, breaking theater's "fourth wall" by communicating with an audience member over the footlights, Cody asked his wife and the audience: "Honest Mama, does this look as awful out there as it feels up here?" The audience, taken with the scout's actions, began to encourage the terrified woman to join her husband on the stage. "You can't be any worse scared than I am. Come on up." When Louisa refused to climb to the stage Cody playfully remarked: "Now you can understand how hard your poor old husband has to work to make a living."[17]

In exposing himself so casually addressing his wife, Cody adroitly touched every member of the audience; his intimate inclusion made them unconsciously aware that, as silly and "clownish" as his behavior might seem on stage, what he was doing was not as easy as he made it appear. He had innocently allowed the audience to see he was exactly as, indeed, *one* of them; his innocuous "scene" with Louisa also nonverbally revealed simultaneously that, unlike them, he was brave enough to get up on the stage and entertain. He had shown that while he may not be an actor, he was a consummate showman.

In spite of the show's great success, however, Ned Buntline was arrested the day after Christmas. Some might argue the playwright should have been arrested for crimes against good taste, but twenty years earlier Buntline had been a member of the "Know-Nothing" political party and had jumped bail in St. Louis after being jailed for instigating an anti-German riot there.

Between 1845 and 1860, nearly two million Germans immigrated to the United States. Most of these new citizens settled on land in Ohio, Indiana, Illinois, Wisconsin, Iowa, and Missouri. When combined with the incredible numbers of Irish refugees fleeing the Potato Famine at the same time, many "native-born Americans" began to be extremely threatened by the newcomers. As most of the new Irish citizens were also Roman Catholic, the fear of the United States being controlled by the Pope in Rome was stirred into the soup and soon secret sects such as "the Supreme Order of the Star-Spangled Banner" and "the Sons of the Sires of '76" began to emerge on the fringe of the political scene. When asked about their involvement in secret orders, the members would respond, "I know nothing," giving birth to the "Know-Nothing Party." During the late 1850s, the Know-Nothing Party became a very powerful force in American politics, particularly in the heavily populated urban areas where the Irish clans gathered and, through their growing numbers and political clout, threatened the traditional power brokers.[18]

The play's receipts were attached while Buntline awaited trial. Somehow, however, Buntline was able to convince the authorities to let him post bail again. When the troupe moved to Cincinnati the rascal changed the name of the show to *The Scouts On The Prairie* and jumped bail again.

Word quickly spread throughout the country and soon theater owners, managers, and booking agents were contacting Buntline with urgent, lucrative offers to appear in their region. The troupe played one week at the Boston Theater and grossed $16,200; audiences were standing room only in New York and Philadelphia. When they closed the season on June 16, 1873, the tour had been a big success. When he tallied his payday cash, however, Cody was disappointed to discover his share of the profits were only $6,000.[19]

Whatever their profits were, after a season on the stage Buffalo Bill and Texas Jack were both ready to return to the Great Plains and their old way of life. The pair quickly gathered enough businessmen in New York City to put together another major hunting expedition and returned to Fort McPherson. Nevertheless, the scouts had also been bitten by the acting bug and the money they could make in the theater and planned to return to the stage once the summer hunting season ended.

The return to the stage, however, would be remarkably different from the scout's initial outing. Don Russell comments:

> Both he and Texas Jack had gained confidence in themselves, and they decided to dispense with Ned Buntline. No one knows why. Ned was full of great plans; to play "The Scouts on the Prairie" on horseback under canvas, which might have led a little sooner to Buffalo Bill's Wild West; to take the show to London; to open early in August for a long season. Perhaps much of this was talk, and the scouts had been exposed to a lot of it. Ned Buntline must have been difficult to live with, although a view of upstate New York neighbors expressed it as, "For all Ned's dereliction's, he seems to have been a person one couldn't hate; he was utterly irresponsible but not mean or vicious." If the break was violent, "calling each other names not fit to print," as has been stated, neither Cody or Buntline ever gave a hint of it.[20]

Cody alluded to the reason for the split when he complained of only earning $6,000 at the end of the extremely successful financial season; Cody obviously realized that he was due a lot more money than Buntline paid him. After parting ways with Buffalo Bill and Texas Jack, however, Buntline, attempting to return to the formula he created, wrote another play, which was based upon his 1872 dime novel, *Dashing Charlie, the Texas Whirlwind*. Dashing Charlie and Arizona Frank appeared as themselves fighting the already stereotypical war party of Indian villains. Nevertheless, without Buffalo Bill as his star Buntline was never able to get the show to work and he retired from the theater. He wrote another dime novel with Buffalo Bill as his hero, *Buffalo Bill's First Trail; or, Will Cody, the Pony Express Rider*, yet the brief, but important, relationship was over. "Ned Buntline capitalized on Buffalo Bill's reputation much more than he contributed to it." Don Russell concludes, offering a succinct perspective on the impact of Cody and Buntline upon one another:

> He wrote the first dime novel, but failed to make it either contemporary or western. He brought Buffalo Bill to the stage, but failed to understand the value of Cody's showmanship. Ned's translation of dime novel to melodrama suggested a publicity device that served Cody well, but Ned failed to see its possibilities. His greatest failure, however, was in not discovering the Western; after pointing the way, he turned his back on it. Because of his notoriety he came to typify the dime-novel writer in his own day and since. It is commonly assumed that he wrote hundreds about the West. Bibliographers have listed not more than twenty-five or thirty western titles.[21]

Cody hired Hiram Robbins as his manager and turned to Giuseppina Morlacchi's manager, Major John M. Burke, to manage publicity for the second eastern tour. The rotund Burke was spurned when the actress married the handsome Texas Jack and quickly shifted his devotion to Buffalo Bill, idolizing him for over thirty-four years. Henry Sell and Victor Weybright offer this picture of the prototype press agent:

> Burke had the imagination to see the place that Buffalo Bill should occupy in show business. He dreamed of the Wild West Show in a grand style, and he lived to be an indispensable element in attaining those dreams. Near the end of his life Burke wrote in *Billboard* about his first meeting with Cody:
> "For once realization excelled anticipation. Physically superb, trained to the limit, in the zenith of his manhood, features cast in nature's most perfect mold, on a prancing charger that was foaming and chafing at the bit, and in his most picturesque beaded buckskin garb, he was indeed a picture.
> "When he dismounted I was introduced to the finest specimen of God's handiwork I had ever seen, and felt that for once there was that nearest approach to an ideal human, a visual interpretation given to the assertion that man was indeed a replica of His Maker."[22]

With such essays, it is no wonder that Don Russell says of Burke:

> In his writing he was a master of the adjective to the exclusion of
> other parts of speech, and he seldom constructed an intelligible sen-
> tence, although he so entangled flowers and figures of speech that
> the lack of a mere verb was unnoticeable. However, he was at his best
> in getting someone else to do the writing—and make it favorable to
> Buffalo Bill. A good storyteller, jovial and friendly, he was welcome
> in every newspaper office, and almost without seeming to, he always
> got what he was after. He was one of the founders of the art of press-
> agentry, and to him goes much of the credit for making the name of
> Buffalo Bill a household word. It is also possible that the subsequent
> deterioration in the reputation of Buffalo Bill is due to Burke's exag-
> gerations, in inconsistencies, his flagrant misquotations, and his lazy
> carelessness.[23]

Burke may have cost Buffalo Bill credibility in the twentieth century,
yet he was perfect for what Cody needed in the 1870s as he created his new
career. Anyone with minimum theatrical experience understands that a
good press agent is essential to financial success. No one did more to contribute to the creation of the enduring myth of Buffalo Bill than "Arizona"
(as he was soon dubbed) John Burke. He had begun his own career as an
actor and had done just about every job a person can do in the theater.
When he could not find work acting he would hustle jobs writing for
newspapers and, as a result, knew most of the newspapermen in America's
urban centers. Most importantly, however, Cody and Burke agreed on procedure; Buffalo Bill had quickly learned from Buntline that a "star" was
equal to receipts at the box office in the theatrical world and Burke completely shared that opinion; both men realized the public was much more
interested in seeing a "star" than any particular actor or play. Unwittingly,
the two were creating the concept of "celebrity" in American show business; prior to Cody, no one earned their living simply from being famous.
With that important point in mind, as they began their second theatrical
tour, Burke, Buffalo Bill, and Texas Jack began to imagine how they might
replace Buntline onstage and attract a larger audience. Deciding that Wild
Bill Hickok would be an excellent choice to replace Buntline, they wrote to
him in Springfield, Missouri, and offered him a large salary to join them
that winter.[24] Wild Bill, warning Cody that he would never make an actor
of him, surprised his friend and accepted his offer to join the troupe in

New York. Hickok was ready for the east, but was the east ready for Hickok?

Cody's ole pard had been severely wounded by an Indian's lance in a fight in 1869. Wild Bill returned to his home in Troy Grove, Illinois, to recuperate from the wound and, as Buffalo Bill and other period scouts, began experimenting with creating work from which he might capitalize upon easterners' fascination with the American West. While recuperating from the lance wound Hickok was hired by future vice president of the United States Henry Wilson to guide his family on a sight-seeing tour of the west. On the return to Troy Grove the Wilson family excursion stopped in Hays City, Kansas only days after the sheriff had been killed; the city fathers soon convinced Hickok to accept the job.

Hickok was a born peacemaker and immediately upon accepting the appointment began his rise to western legend as a lawman. He quickly became the Marshall, as well as the Sheriff of Hays City, and, by 1871, was the Marshall of Abilene, Kansas. Both communities were dangerous with wild cowboys herding cattle north from Texas to Union Pacific railheads to meet United States treaty obligations with Plains Indian nations entering reservations. Hickok reached his prime on the dusty streets of those Kansas prairie towns.

Ironically, Hickok had already experimented in the east with a prototype "Wild West" show which predated Cody's idea by twelve years. In 1870, after he left Hays City to become City Marshall of Abilene, Kansas, Wild Bill traveled along the Republican River and somehow managed to corral six buffaloes. Upon trying to figure out what to do with his buffalo, Hickok had the notion to take them to Niagara Falls and hold a "buffalo chase." He soon hired a few Comanche Indians and headed to New York. Wild Bill was so inexperienced in the art of show business, however, that he had no idea how to present the extravaganza outdoors and charge admission; he failed to construct a fence in order to charge his audience to enter for the show. A harbinger of the future popularity of Cody's Wild West, Hickok's buffalo chase drew five thousand people. Calamity loomed, however; the buffalo herd managed to get away from the Indians and stampeded through the streets of Buffalo, New York, with a pack of barking dogs and laughing children following in its wake. To add to the comic hysteria during the pandemonium, a bear Hickok had brought along in a cage for the show managed to also free itself from its railroad car and went after a vendor's sausage wagon. Citizens were eventually able to herd the buffalo into a dead-end street and subdue them. Hickok had to sell the herd and bear and pass the hat in order to raise the money for his Indian friends to return with him to the Great Plains.

In spite of Hickok's failure as an impresario, Cody, Texas Jack, and Burke were on to something by approaching their fellow scout to join them. Like Cody, Hickok was a part of a very elite group of living western legends. He certainly met their celebrity criterion as a "star" personality. Additionally, as his friend Buffalo Bill, Hickok intuitively knew the essentials concerning personal appearance and theatrics; anyone who ever saw him was impressed with his colorful costume, handsome features, and charismatic personality; and, could anything could be more dramatic than facing a man in a life-or-death pistol duel? Drama is the reason the image of two men meeting at high noon on an abandoned street in a frontier town worked so well in melodrama on stage, screen, and television that it became an American cliche; Hickok's reputation as a gunfighter contributed greatly to the creation of the icon. Yet Hickok, even though obviously as brave as any man who ever drew breath, could not overcome his fear of the audience and make himself heard beyond the footlights. Hickok insisted that the trio were making fools of themselves and that they were the laughing stock of the people.[25]

To complicate matters, Hickok was a prankster who was constantly playing jokes on members of the cast. He developed a particular fondness for tormenting the actors portraying Indians, or "supers," as they were called in the theatrical jargon of the day. The script usually called for Hickok to shoot several Indians; once he shot them with blanks and they fell to the floor, Hickok would walk close to their prone bodies and, pretending to "finish" them off, shoot his pistol at such close range that he would powder-burn their legs. Soon the frightened actors would refuse to "die" on stage out of concern that they might actually perform the act in reality if Hickok was allowed to continue his harassment. Cody spoke to his friend about his behavior and pleaded with him not to hurt the extras and Hickok agreed to stop. Soon, however, the gunfighter returned to his old ways of giving the actors a few extra shots to make sure they stayed dead. Cody and Burke tolerated Hickok's behavior and occasionally giggled to themselves when he gave the supers a hard time.

Hickok also had a knack for disturbing whatever theatrical consistency and atmosphere Cody and Omohundro were able to establish as they sought to learn how to put on a professional show. On one occasion, the scouts were performing a campfire scene, telling stories and passing a bottle of "whiskey" around. Tasting the cold tea in the whiskey bottle, Hickok tossed the bottle and shouted, "You think I'm the worst fool cast of the Rockies. I can tell whiskey from cold tea. I can't tell my story unless I get real whiskey." The amused audience enjoyed Hickok's breaking character, but his behavior had a demoralizing impact on the cast. Cody attempted to appeased his old friend with real whiskey, but after a few shots of the real thing Hickok's amorous nature took center stage and he would break character to pursue the ladies on stage.[26]

Hickok was a handful offstage as well as on. Nevertheless, some might argue that Cody should have foreseen the problems he would face with his old friend Wild Bill from the very start. Instructed by Buffalo Bill to take a cab to the Brevoort Hotel when he arrived in Manhattan, Hickok had also been warned by Cody not to pay more than two dollars for the ride. Upon arriving at the hotel, the driver demanded five dollars for the fare. Hickok refused and the cab driver threatened to take the fare out of Wild Bill's hide. Hickok's fists quickly convinced the cabdriver he had provoked the wrong man.

During Hickok's first performance that evening the lighting director thought it would be amusing to keep the spotlight on Hickok as he moved about the stage. When Hickok mistook the audience's laughter, he assumed he was the butt of the joke and threw his pistol at the spotlight and smashed it.

It was perhaps inevitable that the company would attract violence once Wild Bill joined the production. In Titusville, Pennsylvania, while the troupe was registering in their hotel, the manager warned them not to go in the billiard room as a group of men from the oil fields was on a drinking binge and had bragged that they had stayed over in town to "clean out the Buffalo Bill gang." The manager pleaded with Cody to avoid any trouble as he did not want any fights in his fancy hotel. Having been in the hotel business himself, Cody was most sympathetic and called a meeting of the troupe to explain the situation. Wild Bill immediately wanted to head to the billiard room to engage the group by himself, but Cody was able to convince his friend to hold his temper. Will came up with a plan which would allow his group to avoid the toughs altogether; they would enter and exit the hotel through a door which connected to an adjoining building. Before Cody had time to implement his plan, however, the hotel manager came running up to him out of breath screaming that Wild Bill was having a fight in the billiard room. Cody describes the inevitable brawl best:

It seemed that Bill had not been able to resist the temptation of going to see what kind of mob it was that wanted to test the pluck of the Buffalo Bill party; and just as he stepped into the room, one of the bruisers put his hand on his shoulder and said:

"Hello Buffalo Bill! we have been looking for you all day."

"My name is not Buffalo Bill; you are mistaken in the man," was the reply.

"You are a liar!" said the bruiser.

"Bill instantly knocked him down, and then seizing a chair he laid out four or five of the crowd on the floor, and drove the rest out of the room. All this was done in a minute or two, and by the time I got down stairs, Bill was coming out of the bar-room, whistling a lively tune. "Well!" said he, "I have been interviewing that party who wanted to clean us out."

"I thought you promised to come into the Opera House by the private entrance?"

"I did try to follow that trail, but I got lost among the canons, and then I ran among the hostiles," said he; "but it's all right now. They won't bother us anymore. I guess those fellows have found us." And sure enough they had. We heard no more of them after that.[27]

The changing era was clearly reflected in the increasing strain on Cody and Hickok's relationship. Even though nothing could interfere with their tried and true friendship, Cody obviously recognized times were quickly changing and the west that he and Hickok loved would soon be forever gone. More importantly, however, Cody realized that people—Indian and non-Indian—wanted desperately to hold on to some vestige of the untamed west which was departing North America. Conversely, Hickok was still part of the untamed west and, as everything else truly "wild," would soon be departing himself. In contrast, Cody would spend the next three years with a boot in both worlds, wintering in the theater and summering on the Great Plains. Where Hickok's wild spirit simply could not function in the city or on the stage, Cody's had evolved with the changes. Where Hickok mocked "civilization," Cody, in an action which indicated he was fully prepared to embrace a new way of life, bought property in Rochester, New York, and intended to move Louisa and his children there.

As fate would have it, the show was booked in Rochester not long after Wild Bill's incident with the ruffians in Pennsylvania. Cody was anticipating a packed house of prospective new neighbors and pleaded with Wild

Bill not to return to his on- or off-stage antics. Hickok promised he would mind his manners and not harass the "supers."

The theater was packed in Rochester and Cody was pleased to see the first act run smoothly without incident from his old pal Wild Bill. The second act was too much for Hickok to stand, however; when it came his time to shoot the "supers" he could not resist singeing the actors legs with pistol fire. Of course, as soon as the act ended the frustrated actors ran to Buffalo Bill to complain of Hickok's actions. Cody was furious with his friend and told him he must stop hurting his fellow performers or leave the production. Cody wrote:

> He made no reply, but went to the dressing-room and changed his buckskin suit for his citizen's dress, and during one of my scenes I looked down in front and saw him elbowing his way through the audience and out of the theater. When I had finished the scene, and had retired from the stage, the stage carpenter came up and said: "That long-haired gentlemen, who passed out a few minutes ago, requested me to tell you that you could go to thunder with your old show."[28]

It was the last time Cody and Hickok performed on the stage together. Of course, the friendship had weathered too many hard times to let a little spat come between them. After the play was over Cody went to Hickok's favorite watering hole and found the scout waiting for him. Having had a few minutes to cool off, Hickok, exhibiting his normal friendly attitude, welcomed Cody. He told his old pard that he had decided to quit the theater and return to the west. Cody pleaded with him to remain at least until the end of the season so that they could return together but it was to no avail; Hickok wanted to go home. Burke paid Hickok the money due him and Texas Jack and Buffalo Bill gave him $1,000 for traveling money as well.

The next day Hickok departed for New York City to prepare to head west. In Manhattan, however, the gunfighter promptly lost all his money in a card game and was forced to accept a theatrical producer's offer to "star" him in a show much like the one from which he recently retired. The show was a failure and, after a few days, Hickok left it. Nevertheless, the promoter continued to tour the production, advertising Wild Bill Hickok as the star and continued the charade to the point of hiring an actor to portray the gunfighter off-stage as well.

When Hickok learned of the deception he sent word to the producer to immediately stop impersonating him. Naturally, the producer ignored the scout's request and continued to tour with his show. Hickok was never one to shy away from conflict; he obtained the play's touring schedule and showed up at a performance. Wild Bill took a seat close to the stage and waited until the imposter made his entrance. The gunfighter then leapt to the stage and knocked the actor through the set. The stage manager, attempting to defend the befuddled actor, ran onto the stage to confront the enraged Hickok. Wild Bill took the man by the shoulders and tossed him over the footlights into the orchestra pit. As the actors on stage began to shout "Police!," the audience assumed the fight to be a scene in the play and howled with laughter until Wild Bill departed the stage, returned to his seat, and instructed the actors to proceed with their show. Buffalo Bill tells what happened next:

> A policeman now appearing, Bill was pointed out as the disturber of the peace; the officer tapping him on the shoulder, said: "I'll have to arrest you, sir."
> "How many of you are there?" asked Bill.
> "Only myself," said the policeman.
> "You had better get some help," said Bill. The officer then called up another policeman, and Bill again asked:
> "How many of you are there now?"
> "Two," was the reply.
> "Then I advise you to go out and get some more reinforcements," said Bill, very coolly.
> The policemen thereupon spoke to the sheriff, who was dressed in citizen's clothes. The sheriff came up and said he would have to take him into custody.
> "All right, sir," replied Bill, "I have no objections to walking out with you, but I won't go with any two policemen." At court the next morning Bill stated his reasons for having acted as he had done, and the judge fined him only three dollars and costs.[29]

Within months James Butler "Wild Bill" Hickok would be dead, shot in the back of the head as he played cards in Deadwood, South Dakota. As Hickok entered the everlasting mythology of the American west, his murderer, Jack McCall, was tried and hanged in Yankton, South Dakota.[30]

At the end of the 1874 season, Cody returned to the Great Plains to guide Englishman Thomas P. Medley on a hunt. Medley was an extremely wealthy gentleman who had heard of Cody and offered him $1000 a month for his services. Upon completing his hunt with Medley Cody hired out as a military scout again, departing for the Powder River and Big Horn Country with Lt. Colonel Anson Mills and the Third Cavalry. Cody was happy to return to his old stomping grounds. He fondly recalled riding the Pony Express and driving the Overland Stage through the region fifteen years earlier; he remembered the expedition Wild Bill had led into the region to retrieve stolen Pony Express horses from the Lakota. After being out for a month and driving Little Wolf's band of Arapahos into the reservation, however, the regiment was ordered to return to Fort McPherson. As Texas Jack was hunting in the Yellowstone Country with the Earl of Dunraven, Cody immediately returned alone to the east to organize his company for the 1875 season. After his first, extremely successful solo season in the theater Cody also spent his first summer in the east in Rochester with his family before beginning his 1876 tour. While performing in Springfield, Massachusetts, on April 21, 1876, Cody received a telegram just as he was about to take the stage. His son, his "greatest pride," Kit Carson Cody was severely ill with scarlet fever. Cody completed the first act and left for Rochester, leaving John Burke in his part for the remainder of the show. He arrived in Rochester the next morning, finding his little boy near death and unable to speak. The child did recognize his father, however, and put his arms around Cody's neck and tried to kiss him. Little Kit died in his arms.[31]

Chapter Twelve

THE DUEL WITH
YELLOW HAND

As I pen these lines I am in the midst of scenes of bustle and busy preparation attendant upon the organization and equipment of a large party for an important exploring expedition, on which I shall start before these pages reach the publisher's hands. During my absence I expect to visit a region of the country as yet unseen by human eyes, except those of the Indian—a country described by the latter as abounding in game of all varieties, rich in scientific interest, and of surpassing beauty in natural scenery.

—General George Armstrong Custer,
commenting on his 1874 Black Hills Expedition
(*My Life On The Plains*, George Armstrong Custer)

THE Spanish conquistador Cortes, in perhaps the most poetically succinct description of the fundamental difference between Native and immigrant Americans, explained to Aztec King Montezuma: "I and my companions suffer from a disease of the heart which can be cured only with gold."[1] As psychologically revealing as Cortes's remark might appear, the sad truth is that most Indian people wish that gold was all the invaders needed to cure this "disease of the heart"; the French, English and Dutch, following their intrepid Iberian neighbors into the "New World," wanted game, forests, rivers, lakes and land; they wanted everything. By the 1870s, however, after 400 years of deception and conflict, everyone—Indian and non-Indian—understood clearly the ramifications of the war on the Great Plains; the fight there was for nothing less than the final domination of North America.

The Lakota consider *Paha Sapa*, as they refer to the Black Hills, not only the heart of the North American continent, but the center of the universe.

A holy place of individual, family, and tribal continuity, *Paha Sapa* is to the Sioux first and foremost a living, sacred shrine to renewal; ancient ceremonies and rituals born, taught, learned, and performed there were intended to be perpetually recreated by the Lakota for the purpose of spiritually aligning with earth and heaven, the temporal and the eternal, in order to rejuvenate all forms of life; the core Lakota belief in the interconnectedness of all life—*mitakuye oyasin*—was realized and nourished in ceremony within *Paha Sapa*. The traditional nomadic Lakota returned to *Paha Sapa* at specific seasonal intervals in order to relax and reunite with relatives and friends while replenishing their sense of family and community as well as their foodstores. Spiritually, however, as previously mentioned in this text, the Lakota returned to perform vitally important religious ceremonies, as the Black Hills were specifically mirrored by stellar constellations which brought the people themselves into seasonal religious union with heaven and earth. The region's pleasant summer climates, mysterious nooks, crannies, and spirit gave birth to the body of Lakota mythology, religion, and culture as surely as its plentiful game and pine forests provided food, clothing, and shelter. Adolescent boys became warriors, holy men, and chiefs seeking visions, purpose and direction in the canyons and on the cliffs and peaks of the rocky cathedrals of *Paha Sapa*. Young women proudly shaped the history of the community as they matured into the dignity of matriarchal power and standing in the tribe, annually creating and participating in seasonal religious and cultural ceremonies in *Paha Sapa*; it was these women and children and such holy places as *Paha Sapa* that Lakota warriors would fight to their death to defend.

When the United States entered into the Laramie Treaty in 1868, ending over two decades of violent incidents, skirmishes, battles, and war with the powerful tribes of the Great Plains, it considered the Black Hills worthless, forfeitable property. Succumbing to the increasingly powerful forces of liberal eastern Christian and humanitarian organizations, the United States government was willing to promise the region to the Lakota for "as long as the grasses grow and the rivers flow." Even the "wild" Lakota were promised their freedom forever in the Powder River country along the eastern slopes and high plains of the Big Horn Mountains.

Forever lasted four years. After that brief interval, the "disease of the heart" Cortes so accurately described in Mexico in the 14th century returned like a plague in the nineteenth century; the Euroamerican's episodic relapse into this particular sickness was soon evident as rapacious prospectors began to trickle into the most sacred regions of the Plains Indians. By

1874, however, as Buffalo Bill was establishing a career on the stage in eastern urban centers, rumors of gold in the Black Hills had become so strong
that the U.S. government, strapped for capital to cope with the great economic depression which followed the Civil War, and, in overt defiance of
the 1868 Laramie Treaty which required Indian permission to enter reservation lands, authorized an illegal reconnaissance into the Black Hills. General George Armstrong Custer's Seventh Cavalry headed an expedition of
over one thousand soldiers, scientists and entrepreneurs from Fort Lincoln
across the prairie and into *Paha Sapa*. Some say this violation of the integrity of the 1868 treaty and his subsequent report of gold from the grass
roots down sealed Custer's fate two years later on the dusty plains at Little
Big Horn. Whether cosmic retribution or simply the trigger of fatal historical coincidence, Custer's defiling of the 1868 treaty reopened hostilities between the Lakota-Cheyenne-Arapaho alliance and the U.S. Government and a state of war was reignited on the Great Plains. The fact that
Custer's mission was sanctioned by Washington, however, makes the War
Department's ultimate intention painfully clear; the government was initiating a military solution to the "Sioux Problem."

By the early 1870s, the inherently conservative War Department found
itself increasingly frustrated and in sharp conflict with the prominent liberal Christian and humanitarian organizations who proposed spending
even more massive amounts of money to "buy" peace with the Sioux.
Heavily influenced by the high ideals of such organizations, the Laramie
Treaty of 1868 called for annuities to be paid to the Lakota in the form of
cattle, arms and ammunition, food, clothes, utensils, blankets, etc. The argument being that it was better to spend a million dollars feeding the Sioux
than five million going to war, Christians and humanitarians felt they had
achieved a great spiritual victory with the Laramie Treaty. Even more important to the proselytizing Christians, however, was the fact that as the
great western tribes were being herded onto the reservations an extraordinary opportunity to evangelize the "savage" presented itself; all Americans
knew, upon finally subduing the hostile factions, the government intended
to "dole out" the various tribes to the major Protestant and Catholic denominations for the purpose of "reconstruction" and assimilation. A united
Christian task force of Episcopalian and Catholic missionaries would be
charged with the glorious responsibility of totally dismantling and destroying the Plains Indians' religion and culture while also converting them
from pagan buffalo hunters to God-fearing farmers in one generation.

The missionaries, however, as the military tacticians, were about to get a lesson in plot twist. Upon entering into the 1868 treaty with the United States the Lakota and Cheyenne fell into a pattern of behavior which caused great confusion and concern to the War Department and the humanitarian organizations while it also threatened to disrupt the delicate balance between war and peace: Lakotas would show up to gather their annuity payment only to promptly return to their former "wild" way of life—off the reservation. As a result, it became impossible for the government to determine whether a Lakota or Cheyenne was a "hostile" or "agency" Indian. To be fair, however, Indian people also never knew whether or not the government was friendly or hostile; sometimes the U.S. military would come with outstretched arms, sweet words and gifts, yet at other times they arrived on horseback with sabers drawn. In reality, Indians, as the soldiers, were sometimes in both camps. When the Lakota began killing prospectors with government issued weapons, however, the volatile situation escalated.

By the spring of 1875, government agents estimated over 1,000 miners were trespassing in the Black Hills. Considering the fact that so many prospectors were there in flagrant disregard of Indian rights guaranteed by the United States government makes Lakota restraint seem near angelic. More accurately, however, Lakota constraint indicated the power Oglala leader Red Cloud and Brule leader Spotted Tail wielded over their "friendly" Lakota bands of "agency" Indians. Both chiefs had been granted agencies by the government and, having visited the east and realized the military strength and sheer massive numbers of the *wasichus*, advocated diplomacy and encouraged their followers to continue believing Washington would honor the 1868 treaty, intervene on their behalf, and drive the invaders from their country. At the two chiefs' insistence, the government did finally send troops into the region and some prospectors were even arrested. Nevertheless, as soon as the culprits were processed on minor charges and released, they would simply return to the Black Hills to work their claims. This lack of respect and support for the two chiefs' diplomatic efforts brazenly revealed the government's contempt for Indian people in general; "the great white father's" diplomatic indifference served to undermine the very power the U.S. government had superficially sought to invest in Red Cloud and Spotted Tail. This behavior also reveals the duplicity used by the U.S. government in order to manipulate the goodwill and trust of the Lakota in all interactions. The government clearly manipulated Red Cloud and Spotted Tail as long as they were needed and then discarded them. If the government had wanted a peaceful resolution to the problems it could have easily approached one diplomatically through the relationship it had cultivated with Red Cloud and Spotted Tail. Instead, the government did nothing and inflicted great damage to the personal esteem of both great chiefs. Thereafter, realizing the loss of control over the situation through the impotence of these two great chiefs, the Lakota began to refer to the prospectors trail from the Missouri River to *Paha Sapa* as the "thieves road," as miners took increasing amounts of gold from the region. Cries for armed resistance began to mount as many Lakota remained loyal to Red Cloud and Spotted Tail while others fled the reservation to join the "wild bands," or "hostiles," led by Sitting Bull and Crazy Horse. The resistance movement grew even stronger, however, when the United States government, adding insult to injury in an act revealing remarkable disrespect and arrogant lack of understanding of the Lakota people, religion and culture, began making overtures to buy the Black Hills.

The Fort Laramie Treaty required the signatures of three-fourths of all adult male Lakotas to sell the Black Hills. Nevertheless, the government persisted in its effort to buy *Paha Sapa* in spite of the fact that everyone on both sides knew securing that tribal consensus was impossible. Hungry for gold, however, and displaying incredible diplomatic ineptitude, the government continued to haggle. The final offer was four hundred thousand dollars a year for the mineral rights. If the Sioux wished to sell the hills outright, however, the price would be six million dollars payable in fifteen annual installments. Considering that one Black Hills mine alone yielded more than five hundred million dollars in gold, this was indeed a bargain.[2]

Whatever fee offered, the divisive effect of the United States offering to buy the Black Hills was multilayered: Perhaps most fundamentally damaging, it absolutely undermined any Lakota belief in the basic integrity of the United States government; to the Lakota the act of offering to buy what had only recently been promised in perpetuity proved beyond any doubt the whites were untrustworthy opportunists who showed no respect for sacred obligations; and, even more damning, it revealed the United States could not be trusted in any future negotiations. Furthermore, in continuing to allow unprosecuted prospectors to trespass on their land, the government was sending a not-so-subtle message that their ultimate goal was to deceive the Lakota with hollow treaties and promises all the while plotting to take what they wanted through chicanery. It is little wonder that so many angry Lakota people deserted the reservation leadership of Red Cloud and Spotted Tail in order to flock to the free Lakota leadership in the Powder River country. Neither Sitting Bull nor Crazy Horse had ever lived on a reservation or accepted any gifts from the U.S. government. As a result of their steadfast refusal to allow themselves or their followers to become dependent upon the U.S. government, both chiefs had come to power as increasingly important spiritual and military leaders during the 1860s. Of the two, Sitting Bull actually had more face-to-face, personal experience dealing with whites. Where Crazy Horse was first and foremost a warrior, Sitting Bull was a warrior/statesman. The first written Euroamerican accounts of Sitting Bull's words came from the famous Jesuit Priest Pierre Jean De Smet, who bravely sought a peace council with the "wild" Lakota bands in the Powder River country in the spring of 1868. In what would prove a forerunner to the Fort Laramie Peace Conference, the "Black Robe" had proceeded wisely, slowly, and carefully with proper introductions and a sincere desire to communicate honestly with leaders of the free Lakota. Sitting Bull, when told the priest had a hundred little children praying for his mission everyday, responded warmly and greeted the Jesuit to hear what he had to say. The Hunkpapa and the priest formed a diplomatic friendship but, when the subject of hostilities arose the Lakota warrior made it clear to De Smet that he had never sought a fight with the United States government but was instead defending his country from invasion. With brilliant diplomatic articulation, Sitting Bull informed Father De Smet that he only fought the whites because his people demanded that of him as their leader. Sitting Bull also made De Smet aware that he favored peace and only wanted the whites to leave him and his people alone. De Smet gave Sitting Bull a crucifix and the conference ended. The impact of Father De Smet's first "recording" of Sitting Bull's words, however, thrust the chief to center stage in the white man's world; from that point forward he would be recognized in the international media as the leader of the "hostile" factions of the Lakota. With the Industrial Revolution's crowning achievement, the Transcontinental Railroad, now linking the continent with fluid communications, the same emerging media forces that catapulted Buffalo Bill from a frontier scout and buffalo hunter to front page American celebrity would now begin to nourish the fame of the Lakota medicine man/warrior chief.

Born in March, 1831, on the Grand River (a tributary of the Missouri) and originally named "Slow," Sitting Bull was from a family of respected Hunkpapa Lakota warriors and medicine men. As his father, Returns Again, Slow was blessed with the power to understand the animal's language. Not long after Slow's birth, Returns Again had been visited by a buffalo spirit and given four sacred names: Sitting Bull, Jumping Bull,

Bull-Standing-With-Cow, and Lone Bull. Even though his name was that of an honored warrior who, having already won honor, returned to the fight, Returns Again, upon receiving this vision, chose Sitting Bull for his new name and reserved the remaining three names for future heirs.[3] From the beginning of his life, Sitting Bull's son was deliberate and ponderous, and because of these traits was known affectionately by the name "Slow." In spite of his inquisitive, premeditative nature, however, at age ten Slow thought nothing of impulsively following his father and a war party of Hunkpapa men to fight their Crow enemies. Armed only with his little boy's bow and bird arrows, Slow initially drew the serious concern of the other warriors in the group; all respected Slow's youthful courage, but allowing a tagalong boy to participate in a battle might endanger the lives of every man involved. Nevertheless, Sitting Bull was proud of his youngster and, rather than attempting to turn the boy away, or to replace his little boy's bow and bird arrows with the unwieldy weapons of an adult, decided instead to allow his son to go into battle only with a coup stick.

In the 1840s, the Plains Indian warrior's greatest honor on the field of battle was to "count coup," or touch an enemy. The honor of counting coup required numerous eyewitnesses and was awarded in degrees; whether the enemy was alive and fighting, or whether the enemy was wounded, dying, or dead determined the level of honor accorded to the warrior counting coup. Coups honors were recorded with notches cut into highly decorated sticks and feathers and were necessary if one aspired to any advancement in the warrior society of the Lakota.[4]

Traditional Lakota believed it was better to die honorably on the battlefield than to grow old and be a burden on the people. Slow had, in spite of his few years, been trained his entire life to believe this to be the proper behavior of a male Lakota—regardless of his age. His father saw no reason to stop training him in this belief that day. If his son was so eager for honor it would be better for him to win it or die young. Stanley Vestal informs us,

> Plains Indian warfare, as practiced in those days, was probably the finest sport ever known in this world. No man who loves horseflesh and the bright face of danger but must long to have shared its thrilling chances. It had all the dash and speed of polo, informality of a fox hunt, the sporting chance of sudden wealth afforded by the modern horse race, and danger enough to satisfy the most reckless. And it was no game for weaklings, for the Plains Indian seldom gave, and never expected, quarter.

Yet its prime object was not bloodshed or manslaughter. The warrior, unless he was out for loot or revenge for recent injuries, or fighting in defense of his family, made war a grandstand play. He fought not so much to damage his enemy as to distinguish himself. In very early times the Sioux warrior had fought at close range simply because he had no long-range weapons. Later, when he had obtained these, he still regarded hand-to-hand combat as the only manly form of battle. He still felt that a brave man would grapple with his foe. . . . In short Indian warfare on the Plains was simply a gorgeous mounted game of tag. Public honor, social privilege, wealth and the love of women were its glittering prizes: its forfeit, death.[5]

The Hunkpapa war party soon spotted their Crow enemies and an ambush was planned. The Lakota quickly hid themselves and waited for the Crows to step into their trap. Before the ambush could be successfully sprung, however, the Lakota warriors noticed Slow racing alone toward the Crow war party. Eager to gain his reputation and unskilled in the martial art of ambush, Slow caught men on both sides of the impending fight totally unaware. The Lakota, realizing the opportunity of surprise was lost, immediately rushed behind the boy into the fight while the stunned Crows clumsily prepared to meet their attackers. Meanwhile Slow had selected his prey, a single flabbergasted Crow warrior on foot. As the boy rushed toward the Crow the older warrior drew his bow and aimed an arrow at his attacker. Before the Crow could send his arrow flying, however, Slow tapped his arm with his coup stick, deflecting his aim. Slow's pony slammed into the man and sent him tumbling over the prairie; before the Crow could pick himself up, Lakota warriors swarmed him. The Hunkpapa routed the Crow warriors that day and brought home many horses, scalps and honors. That evening Slow's father announced to the tribe's celebratory gathering that he was taking another of the names given him by the spirit buffalo. From this day forward he would be known as Jumping Bull; his son Slow would now be known as Sitting Bull.

Throughout his life, Sitting Bull was respected by the Lakota as much for his songwriting and prophecy as his for his abilities as a warrior and a chief. His family's gift of understanding the language of animals was a particularly strong trait of Sitting Bull's; most all of his recorded visions, dreams, or prophecies arrived through a message from a bird. This pattern began on an afternoon hunt near his home on Grand River not long after he was awarded his father's name. As he entered a wooded area, Sitting Bull grew tired and decided to sit for a rest. As the afternoon sun beamed down on him through the trees, the boy grew sleepy. Just as he was nodding off to sleep Sitting Bull noticed a Yellowhammer sitting on a nearby branch.

Soon the boy was lost in a nightmare. In the dream Sitting Bull heard a grizzly bear tearing through the woods toward him. In the 1830s, particularly along the Grand River, the giant Great Plains grizzly bear dwarfed every other animal of the region. Possessing an unusually fierce and aggressive personality, the Great Plains grizzly particularly despised men and would go out of his way to attack a "two-legged." Preparing to face the bear in his dream, Sitting Bull noticed two distinct thumps on the trunk of the tree he slept beneath. Looking up he noticed the Yellowhammer, who seemed to say, "Lie still."

Next, Sitting Bull was suddenly awakened to discover the dream had come true; a great grizzly towered over him. The bear surrounded him so that it was impossible to even think of escaping. All he could do was remember the warning of the Yellowhammer and lie completely still as the bear came so close Sitting Bull could feel and smell his hot breath. Sitting Bull called upon all of his courage and laid absolutely still. After sniffing around a while the great giant finally lumbered off into the woods. As soon as he felt safe Sitting Bull arose to notice the little Yellowhammer still sitting on his branch. Sitting Bull's life had been saved by the bird and he would never forget it. He composed a song on the spot for the Yellowhammer and from that day forward he would pay special attention to the birds and the messages they brought for him.[6]

Sitting Bull continued to win battlefield recognition among the Hunkpapa until he became one of only two sash-wearers in the elite Strong Hearts Society of the Lakota. In a highly decorated and symbolic uniform, the sash-wearers staked themselves to the ground with a pin or lance through their sash; only a fellow warrior could release them and they could never retreat from a fight unless victorious.

Sitting Bull rose through this mystic society to become the leader of the Midnight Strong Hearts, the elite order comprised of the finest warriors of the Strong Hearts. The men in this society would form the core of Sitting Bull's leadership for the next forty years. Nevertheless, his ascension to the position of military leadership also meant that he was responsible for feeding the tribe. In this obligation, as other Lakota warrior chiefs encountering dwindling buffalo herds in the 1850s, Sitting Bull faced a major dilemma; the massive immigrant migration cut directly through Lakota buffalo country and made it nearly impossible to find and kill enough buffalo to feed the people. This made it absolutely necessary to embark upon wars of conquest on surrounding tribes in order to poach their lands and animals. Thus, in a very real sense, the imperialistic intrusion of the European culture made imperialists of Native Americans also as Indians were increasingly forced to seek hunting territory away from their own traditional regions. This is not to say that some tribes were not given by nature to seeking the bounty of their neighbors' wealth; globally, neighbors have poached one another's property since time began. The violent European intrusion, however, made it imperative to seek food elsewhere and take it by force if necessary. With that in mind, it is a silent testament of Sitting Bull's military genius that once he took control of the Midnight Strong Hearts Order and started seeking new hunting grounds the Lakota drove most of the other tribes from the fringes of the plains far into the mountains. By the 1860s, traditional Lakota enemies such as the Shoshone and Crow were driven to the northern and western slopes of the Rockies; the Lakota and their allies, the Cheyenne and Arapaho, dominated the Great Plains. Tragically, this dominance is what put them in the cross-hair sights of the American military; the stage was set for the dramatic conflict immediately following the Civil War as the Industrial Revolution spilled across the Plains, expanding with its moralistic rationalization of "Manifest Destiny."

From 1865–69 the Indian Wars focused west of the Black Hills and east of the Big Horn Mountains on the high plains of the Powder River Country as prospectors, seeking a quicker way to the gold strike in Montana, flooded through the sacred Lakota hunting grounds along the Bozeman Trail. Even though Sitting Bull had been instrumental in driving General Patrick Connor from the Big Horns in 1865, and young Crazy Horse, who was then twenty-two years old, led the decoy party which set up the Fetterman Massacre in 1866, the Powder River War belonged to Red Cloud as the "Bloody Bozeman" ran straight through his Oglala territory. After Red Cloud defeated the U.S. military on the northern plains and the Laramie Treaty was negotiated in 1868 General Sheridan shifted the focus of the attack to successful winter campaigns on the southern plains. Everyone knew, however, it was only a matter of time before the U.S. military returned to the northern plains to confront the powerful Lakota-Cheyenne-Arapaho alliance.

The Euroamerican had a particularly difficult time with the attitude of the tribes of the Great Plains and this aspect of the relationship may have contributed greatly to the return of hostilities. Frederick Turner offers a series of intriguing psychological possibilities:

Maybe it was the sheer space that seemed so fascinating to the whites. Or maybe it was the style of the Plains culture with its nomadism, its horse herds, hunters, warfare, and apparently aimless, leisurely movement over the land. Or maybe it was the immensely colorful costumes of these people who seemed to play at life with a sort of fierce artfulness. At bottom, maybe it was the sense that was to be gained over and again that the tribes love this life, thought themselves the privileged and elect of all creation to be permitted the gusty, wide-skied joys of their world. This made them seem arrogant to the whites, but it also compelled a kind of admiration that lingers yet in our culture.[7]

United States Indian Inspector E. C. Watkins' November 9, 1875, report to the Commissioner of Indian Affairs emphasizes some of the very language of Turner's insight concerning the psychological differences between the Plains Indian and the Euroamerican. Stanley Vestal explains how Watkins' perceptions of the Plains Indians "attitudes" incited the military's return to the Great Plains:

On November 9, 1875, a United States Indian Inspector, one E.C. Watkins, having just arrived in Washington from a tour of the agencies, reported to the Commissioner of Indian Affairs on the attitude and condition of "Sitting Bull's band, and other bands of the Sioux nation under chiefs of less note, but no less untamable and hostile." He complained of their attacks on friendly tribes, lauded their country as "the best hunting grounds in the United States," and expressed resentment of their lofty and independent attitude and language to government officials. Watkins went on to say that these Indians numbered but "a few hundred warriors and these never all together," and urged that a thousand soldiers, striking the Indian camps in winter would be amply sufficient for their capture or punishment. He also blamed Sitting Bull for the failure of the Indian Bureau to civilize the friendly tribes, when—as a matter of fact—Sitting Bull had done more to tame them than the Indian Bureau ever dreamed of doing. Sitting Bull had forced them to abandon their hunting grounds in the buffalo country, had taken away their arms and their horses, had done to them, in truth, exactly what the War Department would have liked to do to him.[8]

Watkins' report was cause for serious concern in Washington and President Grant called important members of his administration into council.

The results of the conference was a vote by the President; the Secretary of Interior; the assistant Secretary; the Commissioner of Indian Affairs; and, the Secretary of War that the Sioux must go upon the reservation or face the U.S. military and, in Watkins' words, be "whipped" into submission. On December 3, 1875, the Secretary of the Interior wrote the Commissioner of Indian Affairs:

> Referring to our communication of the 27th ultimo, relative to the status of certain Sioux Indians residing without the bounds of their reservation and their continued hostile attitude towards the whites, I have to request that you direct the Indian agents at all Sioux agencies in Dakota and at Fort Peck, Montana, to notify said Indians that unless they shall remove within the bounds of their reservation (and remain there), before the 31st of January next, they shall be deemed hostile and treated accordingly by military force.[9]

Once again the U.S. government was either displaying incredible lack of understanding of the Lakota and the Great Plains region and climate, or intentionally pushing the Sioux into an impossible situation. The order for the wild bands to immediately report to the reservation arrived on December 22 during the record-breaking winter of 1875. Only a month earlier General Sheridan had been forced to suspend operations because of the severity of the weather, yet the government expected runners to seek and find the "hostiles" to order them to return to the reservation in the middle of winter. This situation was further complicated by the fact that the reservation Indians were starving and Sitting Bull and Crazy Horse's camps were full of Lakotas who, simply to have food, had fled the reservation in order to join the free bands. The idea of returning to the reservation, in spite of the government's military threat, held little attraction; off the reservation they could at least feed themselves; indeed, the majority of the Lakota were leaving the reservation rather than coming into the agencies.

On February 1, 1876, the Secretary of Interior notified Secretary of War Belknap that the time given the "hostile" Lakota bands had expired and he was turning them over to his department to deal with as they deemed "proper under the circumstances."[10] On February 7 Secretary of War Belknap authorized General Sheridan to begin a military campaign against the "hostile Sioux": specifically, the bands of Sitting Bull and Crazy Horse. On February 8, General Sheridan implemented his battle plan ordering General Crook and General Terry to the Powder River country to find Crazy Horse.

With absurd irony, no sooner had the government declared war on Sitting Bull and Crazy Horse for not forcing their people to march through the snow from the Powder River to the Missouri and surrender, than the U.S. military thought it advisable to postpone its expedition against the Sioux leader because the snow was so deep and the number of men badly frozen so great. As a result, "Three Stars" Crook, who was prepared for a winter campaign, made elaborate preparations for a winter campaign redirected to attack the renegade hunting bands in the south.[11]

In January, a runner found Sitting Bull's camp near the mouth of the Powder River and informed him of the government's order. The chief politely told the courier that he would consider the ultimatum, but that he would not be coming in before the spring. Crazy Horse, in order to be ready to attack miners in the spring when they attempted to return to the Black Hills, was camped near Bear Butte near where the "Thieves Road" entered Paha Sapa. As Sitting Bull, the Oglala chief also politely replied that he would consider the demand but remain where he was until spring. Meanwhile, the severe winter weather was continuing to present problems for the U.S. military. Brevet Major General Alfred H. Terry, brigadier general commanding the Department of the Dakota, could not gather the Seventh Cavalry because it was divided into outfits at several western posts and unable to march in the snow. Complicating matters, General Custer, scheduled to command the Seventh Cavalry, was called to Washington to testify in a Congressional investigation of the War Department. Custer's willingness to testify concerning graft in his administration angered President Grant to the point that he nearly denied the outspoken general permission to participate in the campaign. Humiliated, Custer had to beg General Sheridan, who was also upset with the impetuous general, to intervene on his behalf. This disgrace certainly affected Custer's attitude as he embarked upon the important campaign. He was fully aware that the quickest way for him to redeem himself would be on the battlefield.

Brevet Major General Crook, brigadier general commanding the Department of the Platte, however, was not one to wait on men or the weather. He went immediately into action. Don Russell writes, describing the first skirmish of the campaign:

> Cody's former commander, General Reynolds, with five companies of the Second Cavalry, five of the Third, two of the Fourth Infantry, and a pack train left Fort Fetterman on March 1. On March 17 the cavalry struck a camp on Powder River assumed to be that of Crazy

Horse but possibly that of Two Moons' Cheyennes. The camp was captured and burned, but Reynolds, under fire from Indians in the hills, "left so precipitously," in the words of General Crook, "that our wounded men were left to fall into the hands of the Indians." Reynolds was tried by court-martial and suspended from command for a year.[12]

Dee Brown describes the Cheyenne perspective of the fight and corroborates the fact that the camp was indeed Cheyenne and that the Indians peppered the soldiers with fire from the mountain:

Without warning at dawn on March 17, Crook's advance column under Colonel Joseph J. Reynolds attacked this peaceful camp. Fearing nothing in their own country, the Indians were asleep when Captain James Egan's white-horse troop, formed in a company front, dashed into the tepee village, firing pistols and carbines. At the same time, a second troop of cavalry came in on the left flank, and a third swept away the Indians' horse head.

The first reaction from the warriors was to get as many women and children as possible out of the way of the soldiers, who were firing recklessly in all directions. "Old people tottered and hobbled away to get out of reach of the bullets singing among the lodges," Wooden Leg said afterward. "Braves seized whatever weapons they had and tried to meet the attack." As soon as the noncombatants were started up a rugged mountain slope, the warriors took positions on the ledges or behind huge rocks. From these places they held the soldiers at bay until the women and children could escape across the Powder.[13]

The surviving Cheyenne made their way to Crazy Horse and Sitting Bull's camps and were taken in and fed while the wounded received emergency aid. Crook and Reynolds' attack, however, would have the opposite effect of what the U.S. military sought; rather than stopping the flight of the discontented from the reservation, the ambush served to encourage even more to flee the reservation to join the free bands. News of the attack forced Sitting Bull to make an important decision. Since the Black Robe Father De Smet had come to visit and smoke with him eight years earlier, he had kept the promise of peace he made with the pipe. As many great fighters before and after, he had remained a patient and gentle man. As a chief he was obliged to take personal attacks in stride, but the *wasichus* had now attacked his people. Now he had a different obligation to his people. Now he was angry. When Lakotas had counciled on Tongue River he had commented that the people were like an island of Indians in a lake of whites. After drawing the analogy the chief had reminded his people that they must now stand together or be rubbed out separately. He was ready to fight.[14]

The attack on Two Moons' camp was the rallying cry for all the plains tribes. Like Sitting Bull, all the warrior chiefs realized the fight was close at hand and began to gather with the free Lakota. Aware that the U.S. military was being loosed upon them, even those not prone to fighting now rushed to join either Sitting Bull or Crazy Horse's camp for protection. By the time the weather warmed the two large bands merged into one very large, growing tribe under Sitting Bull's leadership. Anticipating spring, they began to move north toward the Rosebud Valley in search of food and new grass and along the way even more bands of Cheyenne and Arapaho joined with them. By the time the tribe reached the Rosebud River, however, runners arrived with word that horse soldiers were marching toward them from three directions: "Three Stars" (General Crook) approached from the south; "The One Who Limps" (Colonel John Gibbon) from the west, and "One Star" (General Terry) and "Long Hair" (General Custer) from the east.

The horse soldiers were coming. Ready and waiting for them were perhaps the best mounted warriors in the history of the world. Stanley Vestal, commenting on Sitting Bull's frame of mind and the powerful forces he commanded, writes,

> Sitting Bull was a proud man in those days. And nobody who knows the old-time Sioux, and can realize the competition he had, can blame him. For they were then, as General Frederick W. Benteen said, "good shots, good riders, and the best fighters the sun ever shone on."
>
> Few people realized the strength of Sitting Bull's small army at the time. But military men, though ignorant of the number of his warriors, were fully aware of their splendid efficiency. . . . Read the statement of one of Crook's staff officers, "the finest light cavalry in the world." Read the words of General Charles King, "foemen far more to be dreaded than any European cavalry." Read Colonel Ford's official report, calling the Plains Indians "the finest skirmishers he ever saw." Read the words of General Anson Mills: "They

were the best cavalry in the world; their like will never be seen again." Finally cap all this by the statement of Mr. P. E. Byrne, who made a special study of this phase of history, "the greatest mounted fighters of all time."[15]

Making his admiration for the Plains Indians' equestrian abilities absolutely clear, General Custer wrote:

> The Indians, however, moving at such a rapid gait and in single file, presented a most uncertain target. To add to this uncertainty the savages availed themselves of their superior—almost marvelous—powers of horsemanship. Throwing themselves upon the sides of their well-trained ponies, they left no part of their persons exposed to the aim of the troopers except the head and one foot, and in this posture they were able to aim the weapons either over or under the necks of their ponies, thus using the bodies of the latter as an effective shield against the bullets of their adversaries.[16]

Of course, the image Custer describes evolved from warfare to become a staple of Cody's Wild West, and, from there into a movie cliche, yet it is most important to remember these remarkable feats were not performed by movie stuntmen with actors shooting blanks at them; these Indian riders, shooting under a horse's neck while running at full speed, were riding for life or death. Custer also verifies the Plains Indians' uncanny ability to ride unscathed into a hail of bullets:

> The Indians, being mounted on their fleetest ponies, would charge in single file past our camp, often riding within easy carbine range of our men, displaying great boldness and unsurpassable horsemanship. The soldiers, unaccustomed to firing at such rapidly moving objects, were rarely able to inflict serious damage upon their enemies. Occasionally a pony would be struck and brought to the ground, but the rider always succeeded in being carried away upon the pony of a comrade. It was interesting to witness their marvelous abilities as horsemen; at the same time one could not but admire the courage they displayed. The ground was level, open and unobstructed; the troops were formed in an irregular line of skirmishers dismounted, the line extending a distance of perhaps two hundred yards. The Indians had a rendezvous behind a hillock on the right, which prevented them from being seen or disturbed by the soldiers. Starting out singly or by twos and threes the warriors would suddenly leave

the cover of the hillock and with war whoops and taunts dash over the plain in a line parallel to that occupied by the soldiers, and within easy carbine range of the latter.[17]

As Custer, Terry, Crook, and Gibbon marched toward them, Lakota, Cheyenne, and Arapaho camped on the Rosebud and prepared for the annual Sun Dance. Meanwhile, Buffalo Bill ended his 1876 theatrical season early in order to join the war that was breaking. Colonel Anson Mills had written Cody several times throughout the spring informing him that General Crook wished for him to join his expedition into the Powder River country. When Cody arrived in Chicago, however, he learned that his old regiment, the Fifth Cavalry, was returning from Arizona to join General Crook. He also learned that his old commander, General Carr, was in command of the Fifth, and had written to military headquarters in Chicago inquiring about his whereabouts. Cody immediately gave up the idea of overtaking General Crook and sought General Carr and the Fifth Cavalry instead.[18]

Cody was so eager to join the campaign that he was still wearing the ornate black velvet and gold Mexican costume from his last performance in Wilmington, Delaware, when he arrived in Cheyenne seven days later. Eric Sorg postulates that, suffering severe depression from the loss of his son, Cody was perhaps suffering from a mental breakdown at the time he joined his old regiment to take part in the campaign.[19] Whatever his mental condition, the scout was greeted with cheers upon reuniting with his old regiment. General Carr promptly named Cody chief of scouts and the following morning the Fifth Cavalry departed for Fort Laramie to rendezvous with General Sheridan.

Upon arriving at Fort Laramie, Cody, with a cavalry escort, accompanied General Sheridan to the Red Cloud Agency and back. The Cheyenne had been successfully raiding all along the road between the Black Hills and the Red Cloud Agency and Sheridan ordered the Fifth Cavalry there to scout for hostiles. After two weeks and several minor skirmishes General Wesley Merritt, who had recently been promoted to Colonel of the Fifth Cavalry, took control of the regiment. Cody felt it was wrong for the War Department to relieve General Carr of his command, yet instantly liked and respected General Merritt.

As the Fifth Cavalry joined the other U.S. military forces seeking Sitting Bull and Crazy Horse, the large tribe continued to grow in the Powder River country as the time for Sun Dance grew close. Indeed, the gathering tribes themselves had difficulty estimating the number of Indians gathered on the Rosebud. Nevertheless, all of them realized this would be Sitting Bull's Sun Dance. Having offered himself so often in the ritual, Sitting Bull's breast and back were heavily scarred. Even so, the chief realized this would perhaps be his most important ceremony. He vowed to offer one hundred pieces of his flesh.

The Sun Dance ceremony is the centerpiece of Plains Indian religion. Totally misunderstood by immigrant Americans, who considered the ritual so savage that the government banned it from the 1880s until the 1960s, the Sun Dance was the most important annual event in Plains Indian culture. Lakota Holy Man Black Elk describes the Sun Dance preceding Little Big Horn:

> About the middle of the Moon of Making Fat (June) the whole village moved a little way up the River to a good place for a sun dance. The valley was wide and flat there, and we camped in a great oval with the river flowing through it, and in the center they built the bower of branches in a circle for the dancers, with the opening of it to east whence comes the light. Scouts were sent out in all directions to guard the sacred place. Sitting Bull, who was the greatest medicine man of the nation at that time, had charge of this dance to purify the people and to give them power and endurance. It was held in the Moon of Fatness because that is the time when the sun is highest and the growing power of the world is strongest.[20]

The Lakota sent a Holy Man out to find a cottonwood tree, which was a sacred tree and would stand in the middle of the circle of dancers. Once the tree was located the people would come singing and gather around the cottonwood. Next, the pregnant women would perform a dance around the sacred tree to honor the spirit of fertility. After the women danced, warriors who had won battlefield honors were allowed to approach the tree and strike it, counting coup. Upon completion of this ritual the warriors would go to the poorest in the tribe and offer them gifts. Once this portion of the ceremony was completed a group of singing maidens approached the tree. These maidens had to pass the tribe's most rigorous, intimate ritual to prove their purity and to be worthy of the honor of chopping the tree down. After the tree was felled, the chiefs who were the sons of chiefs were given the honor of carrying the tree as they might a wounded comrade to the location of the dance. They would stop four times en route offering prayers for each season. In camp, the tree was placed in the center of the camp circle and, at a signal, mounted warriors were allowed to charge the tree; it was believed the first to count coup would not die in battle that year. That evening a big feast and dance was held to prepare for the Sun Dance.

The following morning the Holy men would sing songs as they planted the sacred cottonwood in the center of the camp. Once the Sun Dance pole was set in the ground women of the tribe who were nursing would bring their infants and lay them at the base of the trunk. This act was to bless the sons to become brave warriors and the daughters to become the mothers of brave men.

Those scheduled to take part in the dance purified themselves by fasting and praying in sweat lodges. Next, the dancers would be painted by Holy men. Finally, they would lie prone beneath the tree and a Holy man would take a rawhide rope hanging from the top of the Sun Dance pole, cut the flesh on the dancer's breast or back and slip a thong through the skin and tie it. The dancer would then stand and dance to a particular drum beat for as long as the pain could be endured or the flesh tore.

Children had a particularly good time during the Sun Dance. They were allowed to tease the dancers, as they were required to endure humiliation as well as great pain.[21]

Indeed. Having vowed one hundred pieces of his own flesh, Sitting Bull leaned against the sacred pole while his adopted son, Jumping Bull, knelt beside him with a very sharp, steel knife. Beginning near the wrist of the right arm and working upward, Jumping Bull lifted the skin on Sitting Bull's arm and cut a slice of flesh about the size of a matchhead. This process was repeated for thirty minutes until Jumping Bull had worked his way up each of Sitting Bull's arms, taking one hundred pieces of flesh.

The flesh offering complete, it remained for the Hunkpapa leader to Sun Dance. With blood dripping down his arms and off his fingers, Sitting Bull danced throughout that day and all through the night. Around noon the following day he was nearly unconscious and warriors laid him down. Cold water revived Sitting Bull and he whispered in a weak voice to his friend Black Moon.

Black Moon announced that Sitting Bull had received a vision. In the vision the chief heard a voice from above saying, "I give you these because they have no ears."[22] Sitting Bull looked up and saw soldiers falling down like grasshoppers into the Hunkpapa camp. Every Lakota knew exactly what Sitting Bull's vision prophesized; they were going to defeat the *wasichus!* Stanley Vestal writes:

Afterwards Sitting Bull warned the people: "These dead soldiers who are coming are the gifts of God. Kill them, but do not take their guns or horses. Do not touch the spoils. If you set your hearts upon the goods of the white man, it will prove a curse to this nation." Twelve lesser chiefs heard this warning, but said nothing. All the people heard of this, but some of them had no ears.[23]

The Sun Dance ended June 14. On the evening of June 16 Lakota scouts returned to Sitting Bull's camp to report Three Stars's soldiers camped in the valley of the Rosebud River. General Crook had over 1,000 soldiers and nearly 300 Crow, Shoshone, and Arikara scouts.

Sitting Bull was weak from the Sun Dance yet promptly went to work organizing a large war party, leading one-hundred Cheyenne and nearly nine-hundred Sans Arc, Minniconjou, Brule, Oglala, and Hunkpapa Lakota toward Three Stars's camp. Sitting Bull realized he would not be able to fight in his weakened condition. He would be able to encourage warriors and coordinate battle strategy from the sidelines, yet everyone knew this fight belonged to Crazy Horse.

Crazy Horse had been waiting for a long time for the chance to test himself in battle with the Pony Soldiers. Since the Fetterman fight at Fort Phil Kearny, he had studied the soldiers and their ways of fighting. He had retreated into the Black Hills to seek visions and ask *Wakantanka* to help him lead the Oglalas when the Pony Soldiers came again to make war upon his people. Crazy Horse had known since childhood that the world men lived in was only a shadow of the real world and he had learned to dream himself into the real world before going into a fight. There, he could endure anything.

On June 17, 1876, Crazy Horse dreamed himself into the spirit world and showed the Sioux new ways to fight the white soldiers. Instead of rushing forward into the fire of their rifles and sabres when Crook ordered his cavalry in mounted charges, Sioux warriors drifted off to their flanks and attacked the weak places in their lines. Rather than engaging in hand-to-hand combat, Crazy Horse kept his warriors mounted and always moving from one place to another. By noon the mystic warrior had Crook's troops confused and engaged in three separate fights. Accustomed to forming skirmish lines and powerful defensive fronts, Crook's troops were thrown into massive confusion, and Crazy Horse controlled the battlefield.[24]

Crazy Horse had outwitted Three Stars. The Lakota had always fought in the tradition of counting coup or winning individual honors on the battlefield. At Rosebud, however, this fighting technique suddenly changed: Lakota warriors were following Crazy Horse's brilliant, highly coordinated battle plan. Rather than counting coup, or distinguishing themselves with individual battlefield honors, the warriors were intent on killing every soldier in their sights as quickly as possible. Upon befuddling and whipping the bluecoats on the battlefield with flanking movements, Crazy Horse had intended to force Three Stars and his troops into a natural canyon from which there could be no escape, yet, at the very moment Crook began to march into the trap, Colonel Royall was warned by observant Shoshone scouts of the canyons' perfect conditions for an ambush, and rallied his forces from the rear. Crook suddenly countermanded his own order, reversed his direction, and thwarted Crazy Horse's strategy. Miraculously, Crook was able to repulse the Sioux forces. Nevertheless, Crazy Horse had won the day and Crook retreated in defeat.

General Crook later attempted to claim the battle was his victory, maintaining he had driven the Lakota completely from the field. If Crook had been on the defensive, the word *driven* might have accurately described what happened at Rosebud. He was on the offensive, however, his objective being to reach the Lakota camps and win the day. In truth, Crazy Horse stopped him cold. After the fight at Rosebud Crook retreated to his Goose Creek base camp, where he remained for nearly six weeks awaiting reinforcements. The Lakotas had finally been driven from the field, but they returned at dawn in respectable force. They dogged Crook to Goose Creek, harassing every step of his march. They circled his camp until June 20 before suddenly disappearing. In spite of Crook's claims, the true results of the Battle of the Rosebud were that his campaign was ruined and that he was surrounded defending himself in his base camp while the Lakotas were engaged with Custer at Little Big Horn.[25]

Sitting Bull and Crazy Horse's large group of Indians had come to the Powder River country seeking food and, upon defeating Three Stars, rather than even taking time to hold a celebratory dance, they returned to this quest. The great numbers of men and horses in the valley of the Rosebud, however, drove most game from the region and made it necessary to move in search of food. Nevertheless, scouts brought reports of a very large antelope herd on the Greasy Grass and Sitting Bull ordered the tribe to move. As they marched to Greasy Grass, as Lakota call the Little Big Horn, most realized that, as great as their victory over Three Stars might appear, it was not the great victory of Sitting Bull's prophecy; no soldiers had fallen into their camp. Everyone knew something big was yet to come.

Something big came soon enough. In their hunting camp in the valley of the Little Big Horn the women and children were the first to notice the large, rolling cloud of dust from "Long Hair" Custer's forced march of the Seventh Cavalry. The "Wolf of Washita" and the soldiers of Sitting Bull's prophecy were riding straight into the Lakotas' camp. Cody wrote,

> . . . we had started on our way back to Fort Laramie, when a scout arrived at the camp and reported the massacre of General Custer and his band of heroes on the Little Big Horn, on the 25th of June, 1876; and he also brought orders to General Merritt to proceed at once to Fort Fetterman and join General Crook in the Big Horn Country.[26]

The news of the Custer massacre brought the United States into a sudden and shocking realization that the nation was in a state of war in the same Powder River country where wars with the Sioux had been fought in 1865, 1866, and 1867. Crook had misrepresented his fight on the Rosebud as a victory, but the Custer massacre left no doubt that the United States military was in deep trouble. This same military, shamefully defeated on the battlefield, had predicted only a few weeks before that they could easily and quickly drive all the hostiles to the reservation. Suddenly in need of an alibi, embarrassed generals attempted to blame their defeat on the Indian Office. They denounced the Indian Office for misleading reports concerning the number of the hostiles and for allowing warriors to slip away from the agencies to join Crazy Horse and Sitting Bull.[27]

Arriving literally on the eve of America's Centennial Celebration, the news of Custer's annihilation threw a somber blanket over the festivities. Cries for revenge rose over mournful wails in the east, while western newspapers warned that the Indians were so strong entire frontier towns would soon be wiped out by coordinated savage invasions. Panic or not, no one quite knew what to expect after Custer fell. The military had no idea how many Indians were in Sitting Bull and Crazy Horse's camps and even less idea of how to proceed if the debacle at Little Big Horn was immediately repeated somewhere else on the plains. After a decade of losing almost every martial encounter with the Plains Indians Alliance, Custer's defeat certainly was cause for alarm in the War Department, particularly after they had boasted how quickly they could resolve the Indian situation. The military's inability to deal with the mounting hostile Indian forces had been embarrassingly apparent throughout the springtime campaign; following on the heals of this humiliating exhibition of the U.S. military's ineptitude dealing with Sitting Bull and Crazy Horse, the Custer massacre induced near panic.

Meanwhile, complicating the situation for General Merritt, on July 14 Major Thaddeus H. Stanton, the commander at Camp Robinson, reported that nearly one thousand Cheyenne were planning to flee the Red Cloud Agency in order to join Sitting Bull and Crazy Horse in the Big Horns. Stanton's report stated the Cheyenne camp had been the scene of much mourning after the Battle of the Rosebud and the Little Big Horn and he felt this indicated warrior relatives had been involved in both battles. Stanton also stated that there had been a heavy demand for ammunition at the agency with some offering as much as a horse for 30 rounds of cartridges. He strongly advised Merritt to not allow the Indians to get out on the prairie where they would spread out into smaller groups and become impossible to catch.

Merritt realized he had to act to prevent the Cheyenne from joining their relatives and comrades in the Big Horns. Complicating the situation, however, was the fact that the courier who brought news of Custer's defeat also brought General Merritt orders to report to Fort Fetterman, and from there to proceed immediately to join General Crook. Merritt realized he was going to have to break orders so that he could deal with the immediate circumstance of preventing the Cheyenne warriors from reaching Sitting Bull. The general felt his superiors would certainly understand the seriousness of the situation he faced. He sent an emergency dispatch to Fort Laramie to telegraph Chicago and the War Department to inform them of his actions.

In order to intercept the fleeing Cheyenne, Merritt would have to backtrack north, returning over the trail he recently traveled. Initially heading westward, however, would also serve his purpose: it would convince the Indians at the agency the Fifth Cavalry was heading to Fort Laramie and on to join Crook. Merritt felt this would give the Cheyenne a false sense of security and allow him to get ahead of them to establish a surprise out on the prairie. Once the regiment traveled the fourteen miles to Rawlins Creek Merritt ordered the horses watered before the Fifth Cavalry headed northwest toward the Niobrara River.

The regiment faced a forced march in order to head off the Cheyenne; anyone with experience knew it was nearly impossible to catch Plains Indians when they were running from the U.S. military. Merritt was successful in his objective—the regiment marched eighty-five miles in thirty-one hours before reaching Warbonnet Creek. On the morning of July 17,

Cody went out on a scout to explore whether or not the Cheyenne had crossed the creek. Returning to the regiment with a report that the Indians had not crossed Warbonnet Creek, Cody discovered a very large Cheyenne war party, apparently preoccupied with some activity on the western horizon, and sped back to the base camp to get the news to Merritt.

Upon reaching Lieutenant Charles King's outpost, Cody learned the cause of the Cheyenne Dog Soldiers' concern: Lieutenant Hall had pushed the Fifth Cavalry's supply train throughout the night to maintain the pace of the regiment; unbeknownst to him, his wagontrain was about to roll right into General Merritt's ambush, and, in doing so, be ambushed by those same Cheyenne warriors Merritt plotted to surprise. A dangerously complex situation was silently unfolding on the open prairie. The Fifth Cavalry quietly mounted and Merritt ordered them to remain concealed as he, several aides and Cody rode carefully to a hill to get a better reconnaissance. Upon arriving at the summit of the escarpment, Cody and Merritt were able to see the Cheyenne were heading directly toward them. Suddenly, about 20 warriors broke off from the main group and raced their ponies to the west. A closer view through binoculars revealed two mounted soldiers, evidently with emergency dispatches, also heading toward the regiment.

Merritt was now in a major predicament: If he tried to assist the couriers he would reveal the ambush he had laid for the Cheyenne Dog Soldiers. Still, he could not simply ignore the two soldiers' obvious fate. Quickly sizing up the situation, Cody suggested to Merritt that the best plan was to wait until the couriers came closer to the command and to let him take the scouts and cut them off from the main body of Cheyenne coming over the divide.[28]

Merritt gave Cody permission to enact his scheme. Several scouts, including Buffalo Chips White and Tait, moved quickly with several troopers and First Lieutenant Charles King to attempt Cody's plan of cutting the Dog Soldiers off from the main war party. Neither Ned Buntline, Arizona John Burke, nor any other of Cody's silver-tongued press agents were present that day on the prairie. Nevertheless, a military poet was an eyewitness to the events taking place. First Lieutenant Charles King, later a General and a novelist, described the dramatic scene:

> Savage warfare was never more beautiful than in you. On you come, your swift, agile ponies springing down the winding ravine, the rising sun gleaming on your trailing war bonnets, on silver armlets,

necklace, gorget; on brilliant painted shield and beaded legging; on naked body and fearless face, stained most vivid vermilion. On you come, lance and rifle, pennon and feather glistening in the rare morning light, swaying in the wild grace of your peerless horsemanship; nearer, till I mark the very ornament on your leader's shield. And on, too, all unsuspecting, come your helpless prey. I hold vengeance in my hand, but not yet to let it go. Five seconds too soon, and you can wheel about and escape us; one second too late, and my blue-coated couriers are dead men.[29]

Having waited upon nerves of steel, King ordered, "Now, lads, in with you."[30]

Cody had so successfully mastered the art of dramatically blurring reality his autobiographical account of the actual "duel" is a classic example of the effect of the theater on actual historical events in his life. Controversial even to this day, the fight between Cody and the Cheyenne warrior remains one of the great myths of the 19th century American west. The version Cody depicted in his 1879 autobiography was obviously heavily influenced by the need to metaphorically dramatize historical events in romantic, Anglo-Saxon, "knightly" fashion for the stage. Even so, Cody was still basing his mythology in truth: When facing certain death on the battlefield, it was not uncommon for Plains Indian warriors to find a worthy opponent, sing a death song and eagerly greet death with magnificent, even joyful, courage.

Cody wrote in his autobiography:

The two messengers were not over four hundred yards away from us and the Indians were only about two hundred yards behind them. We instantly dashed over the bluffs, and advanced on a gallop towards the Indians. A running fight lasted several minutes, during which we drove the enemy some little distance and killed three of their number. The rest of them rode off towards the main body, which had come into plain sight, and halted, upon seeing the skirmish that was going on. We were about half a mile from General Merritt, and another lively skirmish took place. One of the Indians, who was handsomely decorated with all the ornaments usually worn by a war chief when engaged in a fight, sang out to me, in his own tongue:

"I know you, Pa-he-haska; if you want to fight, come ahead and fight me."

The chief was riding his horse back and forth in front of his men, as if to banter me, and I concluded to accept the challenge. I galloped towards him for fifty yards and he advanced towards me about the same distance, both of us riding at full speed, and then, when we were about thirty yards apart, I raised my rifle and fired; his horse fell to the ground, having been killed by my bullet.

Almost at the same instant my own horse went down, he having stepped into a hole. The fall did not hurt me much, and I instantly sprang to my feet. The Indian had also recovered himself, and we were now both on foot, and not more than twenty paces apart. We fired at each other simultaneously. My usual luck did not desert me on this occasion, for his bullet missed me, while mine struck him in the breast. He reeled and fell, but before he had fairly touched the ground I was upon him, knife in hand, and had driven the keen-edged weapon to its hilt in his heart. Jerking his warbonnet off, I scientifically scalped him in about five seconds.

The whole affair from beginning to end occupied but little time, and the Indians, seeing that I was some little distance from my company, now came charging down upon me from a hill, in hopes of cutting me off. General Merritt had witnessed the duel, and realizing the danger I was in, ordered Colonel Mason with Company K to hurry to my rescue. The order came none to soon, for had it been given one minute later I would have had not less than two hundred Indians upon me. As the soldiers came up I swung the Indian chieftain's top-knot and bonnet in the air, and shouted:

"The first scalp for Custer."[31]

The regiment charged past Cody and into the main body of Cheyenne and soon began to force them to retreat thirty miles to the reservation. Even though the Cheyenne were able to stay ahead of Merritt's forces, the Fifth Cavalry was able to force the Cheyenne back to the reservation. Nevertheless, the troopers were unable to capture or kill any more of the rebels. On the reservation the 800 Cheyenne rapidly blended back into the tribe at the Red Cloud Agency and, once again, the military was unable to determine the rebel Cheyenne from the agency Indians. The Cheyenne effort to join Sitting Bull's forces, however, had been quashed.

Most did notice something noteworthy upon returning to the reservation, however; in spite of—and indeed because of his role in their return to the reservation—the rebel Cheyenne were fascinated with Cody. "One and all they wanted to see Buffalo Bill," General Charles King wrote, "and wherever he moved they followed him with awe-struck eyes."[32] This reaction of the Cheyenne to Buffalo Bill presents an obvious respect for the warrior traditions of the Plains Indian culture; they respected Cody because he fought and won the old Indian way.

At the Red Cloud Agency Cody learned the name of the Cheyenne warrior he had killed was *Hay-o-wai*, or Yellow Hair, so named for the woman's blonde scalplock he wore as a headdress. The first interpretation of Hay-o-wai's name, however, was Yellow Hand and, on Sunday, July 23 the *New York Herald* brought the news of Cody's "first scalp for Custer" to the world with the misinterpreted name and it stuck. Cody wrote to his wife: "We have had a fight. 1 killed Yellow Hand a Cheyenne Chief in a single-handed fight. You will no doubt hear of it through the papers."[33]

Cody continued scouting throughout the summer. General Terry and General Crook's forces, in the maneuver which had originally been intended to wedge the Sioux between them, united under one command. Crook was somewhat chagrined turning his command over to Terry; most, including Cody, considered Crook to be the consummate Indian fighter. Where Crook had trimmed his forces and put them on rations in order to pursue Indians, Terry arrived with full comforts such as wall tents, portable beds, large hospital tents for dining rooms, and even carpets. Crook prepared his own food using a quart cup for coffee and a stick for broiling bacon. Terry's forces, though comfortable, moved slowly. Don Russell observes,

> This may help explain why Custer was eager to cut loose from Terry, to the point of meeting disaster in his effort to follow and fight Indians, and it suggests that Crook might also have had it in mind to go it alone whenever he could.[34]

Alexander B. Adams presents a conversation between the Chicago journalist John Finnerty and Cody in which the author believes the scout defined the exact problem the military faced immediately after the Custer debacle:

> "If they want to find Indians," said he, "let them send a battalion, which I am willing to guide, and I'll engage we'll have our fill of fighting before reaching the little Missouri. The hostiles will never face this outfit unless they [the officers] get it in some kind of hole, and there are plenty of them in this country. Crook ain't going to run into them though. He served in Arizona too long for that."

Cody had summed up the army's problem. The Sioux and Cheyennes were not going to commit suicide by massing a large force and attacking two-thousand well-armed Americans. They could not efficiently move the number of warriors, much less control them during the ensuing battle. On the other hand, they could easily elude a column of that size. It had to march so slowly and its presence was so easily noticeable that they could avoid it without difficulty.[35]

The situation was not much better for the Sioux. Their ability to move freely had been severely cut. The large coalition Sitting Bull had pulled together was as easily located as Terry and Crook's combined forces and next to impossible to feed.

As Cody predicted, the campaign just bogged down and wore itself out. On August 22, believing the fighting to be over, Cody was discharged as Chief of Scouts for the Big Horn and Yellowstone Expedition. It was his last service as a scout for the U.S. Army. Cody explained that he was returning to keep theatrical commitments in the east, yet he, as all "fighting men," realized the campaign was over.

Don Russell explains,

Actually, Cody had no theatrical commitments. When he left the stage in the spring, he ended his partnership with Texas Jack Omohundro, which was never again revived. Texas Jack and Mlle Morlacchi organized their own combination in the fall of 1876, taking with them Major John Burke, so that Buffalo Bill was left with no one particularly interested in his return to the stage save William F. Cody, who occasionally took personal charge of his own destiny.[36]

Cody boarded the *Far West* steamboat and headed down the Missouri to Bismark. Upon arriving in Bismark the scout proceeded by rail to Rochester, New York. His few years of experience in the theater had made him aware of the formula for success on the stage; he knew he needed a writer to create a new show based on the interest stirred in the recent Sioux wars. He would create a completely new show, one in which he would be the single star of his own theatrical combination.

Chapter Thirteen

GRANDMOTHER'S LAND

I am looking to the north for my life, and hope the White Mother will never ask [me] to look to the country I left, although mine, and not even the dust of it did I sell, but the Americans can have it. Those who wish to return to the Americans can go, and those who wish to remain here, if the White Mother wishes to give them a piece of land, can farm, but I will remain what I am until I die, a hunter, and when there are no more Buffalo or game, will send my children to hunt and live on prairie mice.

—Sitting Bull, Wood Mountain, Saskatchewan, 1879
(*I Am Looking To The North For My Life*, Joseph Manzione)

ANYONE with the least knowledge of the history of the Indian Wars could have predicted that the U.S. military could not allow the 1876 campaign against the Plains tribes to end without claiming some sort of battlefield victory. The humiliated War Department had to save face and convince the American public that Custer's death had been properly avenged. Particularly intent on quickly mending his own wounded reputation, General Crook was determined to continue the campaign until his honor was restored. Even as Buffalo Bill's train sped eastward across the continent toward Rochester, New York, and the scout planned the next phase of his career in show business, Crook, seeking vengeance for his and Custer's defeat, trimmed his troops to fighting size and speed and intensified his pursuit of Sitting Bull and Crazy Horse. Crook's experience fighting Apaches in Arizona had taught him much about fighting Indians. The general had learned that it was impossible to catch fleeing Indians with a normal military regiment.

Throughout the history of the Indian Wars, the gargantuan size of military expeditions often doomed their success before even encountering any Indians. Feeding large detachments of troops required a wagon train of supplies to follow the expedition. Supply wagons could not travel as fast as the cavalry, yet left unprotected, the supply train was vulnerable to attack. As a result, the command was spread dangerously out across the plains, often more concerned with protecting essential supplies than chasing hostile and extremely mobile Indians. In his Arizona campaigns, Crook had learned to approach the situation from a different perspective. He allowed his men to wear civilian clothing and did away with the unwieldy supply wagon train; his troops carried minimum rations in their packs. Crook himself, his long beard braided and tied behind his neck, used one can from which he cooked, ate, and drank. Even adopting such an austere lifestyle, however, Crook was on Indian turf; the wily Lakota, needing time to decide what to do next, led Three Stars straight into the muddy gumbo of the Owl (Moreau) River Valley, where his campaign, lean as it was, bogged down in the muck.

The need for food affected both sides during the Indian Wars. Aside from the logistical vulnerability of such a large group of people attempting to elude the U.S. military, it had become nearly impossible for Sitting Bull to locate enough game to feed his large confederacy. The Hunkpapa leader called Lakota, Cheyenne, and Arapaho leaders into emergency council to decide what they must do. Smoke signals had carried the news of Long Hair's demise even more rapidly than the telegraph and everyone in Indian country knew it was no longer advantageous to flee the reservation to join Sitting Bull. Besides, any Indian attempting to join Sitting Bull's followers would have a hard time finding them; shortly after the Custer fight Sitting Bull began planning a retreat into Canada. Since the days of the Santee Rebellion, the Lakota had sought refuge in "Grandmother's Land" and Sitting Bull knew his people would be safe there; only two generations earlier, all the Lakota had been British subjects in Canada.

Crazy Horse, however, felt differently. The Oglala chief resolved that he was staying to fight until the end. Simply put, he was a warrior; his entire life was centered around fighting and it made no sense to him to abandon the fight as it grew most intense. Where Sitting Bull was honor-bound to first seek to provide food for the people, Crazy Horse's only obligation was to fight. He fully realized his days were numbered, yet he was equally aware that the people depended upon him to defend them. He had also sought to hold the confederacy together but it had nevertheless become clear that Crazy Horse and Sitting Bull's grand coalition was going to have to splinter into smaller groups in order to have enough to eat. As Crazy Horse and his band rode toward the Big Horn Mountains Sitting Bull realized he would probably never see the strange young man again. Sitting Bull and nearly one thousand Hunkpapa followers went into camp at Twin Buttes along the Grand River as Crazy Horse led his band of Oglalas to the Powder River country. Iron Shield, who was also known as American Horse, and his forty lodges of Oglala, Brule, and Minniconjou followers camped at Slim Buttes.

About the same time the Lakota forces began to break into smaller groups, General Crook's reinforced troops ran out of rations as they negotiated the bog of the Owl River region. Crook finally managed to emerge from the sludge to start a hungry, forced march to the Black Hills, where he hoped to procure rations from miners. On September 14, 1876, a forward detachment under the command of Captain Anson Mills accidentally stumbled into American Horse's camp at Slim Buttes and attacked. The stunned Sioux somehow rallied and fought Mills' forces back. While Mills was waiting for Crook to join the fight many of the Sioux were able to escape and run to Sitting Bull for help. An alarm soon rang through Sitting Bull's camp that Three Stars was attacking American Horse. The Hunkpapas quickly prepared themselves for battle and raced the thirty miles to defend their relatives and allies.

Most of American Horse's followers managed to escape while Captain Mills waited for General Crook to join the fight. Nevertheless, American Horse, with four warriors and fifteen women and children, fell under siege in a small cave at the dead end of a ravine. When Crook finally arrived at the scene, he ordered his marksmen to strategic positions from which they could fire directly into the cave. Sitting Bull's reinforcements arrived at the fight about the same time as Crook but found themselves outnumbered two to one. Their ammunition severely depleted from the preceding months' battles, the Sioux were driven back into the surrounding hills. Meanwhile, after a firefight of several hours at the cave, Crook sent scout Frank Grouard to speak in Lakota to the besieged American Horse. Grouard, a mixed-blood of Polynesian heritage who had at one time lived with and been adopted by Sitting Bull, told the chief his people would not be killed if they surrendered. Upon receiving this promise, American Horse and his followers emerged from the cavern. The chief had been shot in the stomach and was literally holding his entrails in his hands. A military surgeon examined American Horse's wounds and informed the chief he would not recover. American Horse wrapped a blanket around himself, sat down beside a fire, slipped into unconsciousness and died.

The next morning, as American Horse predicted before dying, Sitting Bull returned to Slim Buttes to attack Crook's forces as they headed toward the Black Hills. Crook's troops, reinforced with ammunition, responded with such heavy fire that the Lakota were forced to pull back. It was a logical retreat. Sitting Bull was convinced Three Stars was abandoning the fight and, being most anxious to aid the wounded and dying at American Horse's ravaged camp, returned to Slim Buttes.

The scene Sitting Bull discovered at Slim Buttes moved him to tears. Crook's forces had extracted their bitter revenge from those most helpless; the majority of the victims were women and children. When a group of released captives brought Sitting Bull a message from Crook that "white men do not make war upon women and children," the irony did not amuse the Hunkpapa leader.[1]

Stanley Vestal describes what Sitting Bull actually discovered after Crook's brutal visit to American Horse's camp:

> There was a woman in the ravine whose whole head had been blown off, clear down to the roof of her mouth; they did not know who she was. And right close by was another woman. The soldiers had shot her through the breasts. Little Wounded, a boy of five years, had seen his mother shot dead; he was wounded in the foot himself. When he told about this tragedy, there were tears in the eyes of his listeners.
>
> But the worst thing of all on that battlefield was what they found where Little Eagle's daughter had tried to run away. She was about to become a mother, and when the shooting began, became frightened, and ran. She dropped her unborn child; it was lying there on the muddy ground, cold as the mud itself. But the mother was a Sioux woman, and hard to kill. She survived.[2]

The young mother may have survived, but, viewing the carnage at Slim Buttes, Sitting Bull quietly worried about the fate of the Lakota. The people had disregarded the admonition of his Sun Dance vision and mutilated the bodies of Custer's fallen men. In their great victory, further ignoring the ominous warnings of their visionary chief, the Lakota had taken the weapons, ammunition, horses, and personal effects of the defeated Seventh Cavalry. At Slim Buttes, the Lakota witnessed the first retribution of their failure to follow Sitting Bull's vision to the most minute detail. This failure deeply concerned the chief. Adding to his disappointment at Slim Buttes, Sitting Bull learned that his former adopted son, Frank Grouard, was the scout responsible for leading Crook's forces to American Horse's camp. This somber revelation only contributed to the mounting perplexity surrounding Sitting Bull as he watched his great alliance splinter into smaller and smaller bands. Only recently, he had been bewildered to learn that even some Cheyenne and Lakota had gone over to the enemy and were assisting the military in locating him. Saddened with the knowledge that he could no longer trust his own people, Sitting Bull realized his last option was to move his most loyal followers north toward Grandmother's Land.

With winter approaching, Sheridan also felt new tactics were needed; he ordered General Terry to build a temporary cantonment at the mouth of the Tongue River on the Yellowstone. From this garrison Colonel Nelson A. Miles, Commander of the Fifth Infantry, reinforced with six companies of the Twenty-Second Infantry, would base his operations in the Yellowstone Valley until spring would allow a revived campaign. Miles, whose wife was General Sherman's niece, had distinguished himself in military service in the southwest and was blatantly hungry for more acclaim. Referring to his nephew's ruthless ambition, Sherman once commented sarcastically in a letter to General Sheridan that the only way he could make Miles happy would be to give him absolute control of the military. Acutely aware that he might find the military success he so eagerly sought on the plains of Montana, the colonel focused all of his unwavering ambition on capturing Sitting Bull. By late September Miles' soldiers had constructed crude barracks from wood and mud, roofed with sod and canvas. As summer faded into autumn, the Sioux were also busy preparing for winter. Once their preparation was complete, however, they raided the cantonment's mule herd, making off with 47 mules and even managing to put several bullets through Colonel Miles' tent. Next, Sitting Bull began hitting the supply wagons en route to Miles' garrison. On September 15 Lt. Colonel E. S. Otis, escorting eighty-six wagons, was attacked at Spring Creek. Otis soon entrenched his forces in a natural depression on the prairie as Lakota snipers attempted to pick his men off one by one. Within hours, Otis received an ultimatum from Sitting Bull which stated:

> I want to know what you are doing travelling on this road. You scare all the buffalo away. I want to hunt on the place. I want you to turn

back from here. If you don't I will fight you again. I want you to leave what you have got here, and turn back from here.

I am your friend,
Sitting Bull
I mean all the rations you have got and some powder. Wish you would write as soon as you can.

Otis replied that he "intended to take the train through to Tongue River, and would be pleased to accommodate the Indians with a fight any time."[3]

Otis had boldly called Sitting Bull's bluff; the Hunkpapa were weary of fighting. Instead, following the counsel of close Hunkpapa leaders and advisors, Sitting Bull offered a flag of truce to Otis and with it word that the Sioux wanted peace. Sitting Bull's interpreter told Otis the Sioux were hungry and tired of fighting and offered to meet on the open plains. Otis attempted to force Sitting Bull to come talk with him first. Sitting Bull, however, would have none of that; he wanted to talk to the head chief or no one at all. After several diplomatic overtures the meeting between Colonel Miles and Sitting Bull was finally arranged. Following Sitting Bull's original suggestion, the two met between lines of soldiers and warriors on the open prairie on October 22. Because it was a cold day, Colonel Miles wore a long coat trimmed with bear fur and from that day forward the Sioux called him "Bear Coat." Sitting Bull arrived shirtless in buckskin leggings with a breechcloth. He wore a buffalo robe wrapped around his body to shield himself against the cold.[4]

Wizened military leaders, both Miles and Sitting Bull realized they had been afforded a rare opportunity to study each other. Miles described Sitting Bull as a "fine, powerful, intelligent, determined-looking man," adding that in continence the chief was "cold, but dignified and courteous." Though it had been agreed that weapons should be left behind, Sitting Bull's nephew, White Bull, suspected that the soldiers had hidden weapons under their long coats. Miles confirmed in his memoirs that he and his men were indeed armed with revolvers.[5]

There were no brocade introductory speeches, no friendly preliminary smokes of the pipe. The interpreter was Johnny Brughiere, a mixed-blood who fled a murder charge and hid in Sitting Bull's camp. Sitting Bull adopted him and named him "Big Leggins" because of the big cowboy chaps he wore. Brughiere served as an interpreter for Sitting Bull and wrote the note to Lt. Colonel E. S. Otis which initiated the parley between Miles and the Hunkpapa leader. In December, 1879, Miles secured a pardon of the murder charges for Brugiere and hired him as a government scout.[6]

With Johnny Brughiere interpreting, Bear Coat began the parley by accusing Sitting Bull of always being hostile toward the ways of the white man. Sitting Bull readily admitted that he did not like the ways of the whites, but countered that, left alone, he was not their enemy. Then Miles foolishly demanded to know what Sitting Bull was doing in the Yellowstone country. Sitting Bull politely replied that he was hunting buffalo to feed and clothe his people. Bear Coat brought up the subject of a reservation for the Hunkpapas, but, informing Miles he would winter in the Black Hills, Sitting Bull rejected it. The talks ended with nothing resolved, but the two men agreed to parley again the next day.[7]

At the meeting the next day Miles immediately became hostile, accusing Sitting Bull of having an arrogant attitude. Puzzled by the white man's behavior, the Hunkpapa responded by asking Bear Coat why he had changed since the first meeting. His own dander rising, Sitting Bull asked Miles why he was angry and marching through his country. Miles replied that the Grandfather had ordered him there. The sudden stormy tone of the meeting alarmed advisors on both sides and Sitting Bull's young warriors also noticed Miles' troops preparing for a fight. When informed of this, Sitting Bull began to lose his temper, but not before suggesting the talks should come to an end. Miles warned Sitting Bull that refusal to surrender would be considered an act of hostility and the stage was set for a fight.

About the time Sitting Bull returned to his warriors, Miles began his attack. The Lakota managed to avoid casualties only because they were so scattered over the prairie. They quickly rallied and got themselves out of range of Miles' cannons and marksmen. The fighting continued the next day until Sitting Bull ordered his camp abandoned and, easily outdistancing Miles' infantry on their horses, the Hunkpapa vanished on the plains.

Even while the fight between Sitting Bull and Bear Coat was being waged on the Montana prairie, commissioners and agents in Washington were initiating the policy of starving the reservation Sioux into signing the Black Hills away. The general American public had little sympathy for Indians. Alexander B. Adams succinctly describes the reality of the Euroamerican population's impact on the Great Plains in the 1870s:

> Iowa, one of the states west of the Mississippi, was one of only thirteen out of a total of thirty-eight that had a population of more than

a million persons. It was bigger than all but five of the original thirteen colonies, almost as big as the heavily populated state of Massachusetts, with its factory towns and the emigrants disembarking at its ports.

Nebraska, only admitted to the union in 1867 . . . had a population of 122,993, not large by today's standards, but at the time only about three thousand short of the population of the much older state of Delaware. On its plains, the white men were grazing 47,000 horses and 73,000 oxen and other cattle, many more than in the states of Delaware and Rhode Island combined.

Minnesota, where the Santee Sioux had staged their futile uprising just a few years ago, now produced multimillion-dollar crops of wheat, as well as large harvests of oats. Kansas produced far more corn than all of the New England states taken together and fed more hogs than either South Carolina, New Jersey, or Kentucky.

These figures, arranged by the government's statisticians in dull-looking rows, revealed the westward shift of the nation's energies and forecast the fate of the Indians. The soldiers whom they feared and hated were not the real enemy, for most of them would have welcomed orders calling them back to the more comfortable posts of the East, where the danger and hardship were much less. The real foe was the swelling population of the nation, which had more than doubled since Sitting Bull's birth: thirty-eight million restless men, women and children, most of them with a stake in the development of the West. They owned bonds in Western railroads, they invested in the stock of corporations with Western interests, they worked in businesses that expanded when the west expanded. Even if they did not come West themselves, driving their wagons across the plains or riding more comfortably and swiftly behind the smoking locomotives, they were convinced the future greatness of their country lay in the West, and they were determined to gain control of those lands that were still occupied by the Indians.[8]

Congress ordered that no annuities would be given the Lakota until they signed the contract relinquishing all claims to the Black Hills. The provision of the 1868 Laramie Treaty requiring three-quarters of the male population's signatures to sell any tribal lands was blatantly ignored as agents cajoled and bullied reservation males with promises of food for signing away *Paha Sapa*.

Meanwhile, Sitting Bull's following was becoming even more divided. As they crossed the Yellowstone River on October 24, the majority of the

Lakota wanted to surrender. After an all-night council the camp split as the Sans Arc and Minniconjous bands decided to return to the Cheyenne River agency. Sitting Bull and his Hunkpapa followers continued moving through the Big Horns and Yellowstone River country toward Canada. Meanwhile, Colonel Miles, only slightly delayed by having to deal with the surrender of Bull Eagle's band of 1700 Sans Arc and Minniconjous, continued his pursuit of Sitting Bull. On November 3 the Fifth Infantry returned to the Tongue River Cantonment. Two days later, using a strategy that had worked well for him Texas in 1874 against Comanche, Miles divided his command into three columns assigned to separate, but contiguous operational areas. Throughout November and December, as temperatures dropped below -50° F and gale-force winds whipped the high plains, Miles' columns crisscrossed Montana from the Milk to the Yellowstone Rivers. Ice crystal "fogs" blinded the troops by day and the aurora borealis astounded them at night as blizzards pounded the troops three or four times a week.[9]

On December 6, Sitting Bull learned First Lieutenant F. D. Baldwin was approaching his camp on Porcupine Creek. As Baldwin commanded three companies of infantry Sitting Bull elected to elude the lieutenant and headed across the Missouri River to properly prepare for his attack. On December 18, Baldwin attacked Sitting Bull's camp at the head of Red Water while most of the men were hunting. Baldwin primarily hit the Sioux herd of horses and mules, capturing over sixty head. As the weather became frigid Sitting Bull moved his people south toward the Powder River country before heading upriver in search of Crazy Horse. When Crazy Horse could not be located Sitting Bull turned eastward. On the high plains, the Sioux discovered the wolfers had been shooting buffalo and poisoning the carcasses in order to kill wolves. This seemed to frighten all game away from the region and, once again, the Lakota became hungry. Their options were running out. It had become time to retreat to Grandmother's Land.

General Crook and Colonel Miles meanwhile began an openly competitive effort to bring Crazy Horse to surrender. Both men were absolutely aware of the reputation they would earn by convincing the famous chief to bring himself in to negotiate peace and each eagerly sought the coveted prize. Crook, mindful that Miles was concentrating his efforts on cornering and capturing Sitting Bull, began to focus his energy on Crazy Horse.

In December, 1876, Crazy Horse was camped on the Tongue River, not far from Colonel Miles' winter camp at Fort Keogh. As the intense winter was becoming particularly difficult for the children and old people of Crazy Horse's band, some of his fellow chiefs began to talk to him about the possibility of surrendering to Bear Coat. Crazy Horse characteristically told them to do as they pleased. About thirty chiefs and warriors decided to ride to Bear Coat's fort to explore the possibility of surrendering. Crazy Horse agreed to accompany them part of the way. From a hill not far from the fort, eight chiefs volunteered to ride down to the fort under a flag of truce. As soon as the Lakota were close enough to the fort to be recognized, however, Miles' Crow scouts, ignoring the Lakotas' white flag, rushed out of the fort and fired their weapons directly into the peace party. Five Lakota warriors fell in the attack as the surviving three fled for their lives. Responding immediately to the vicious assault, Crazy Horse wisely sent his remaining force racing to alert the camp to scatter and run rather than attempt to extract vengeance from the Crows; he realized that Bear Coat would immediately respond to the melee with soldiers pouring out of the fort to comb the countryside for Sioux. Miles did not prove him wrong.

Crazy Horse's warriors had so little ammunition with which to defend themselves that they were forced to use their wits against the soldiers yet again. While Crazy Horse and the main body of Lakotas escaped, skilled warriors decoyed Miles' soldiers into an icy canyon. After several hours of slipping and sliding over frozen precipices the colonel gave up the search and ordered his troops to return to the fort.

The winter was brutal. Death took Crazy Horse's only child, a daughter.

By February, as Lakota hunger approached starvation, runners brought news that Spotted Tail was approaching the encampment. Three Stars had put Crazy Horse's uncle in a difficult diplomatic situation. Aware Spotted Tail wished his tribe to remain on their reservation in Nebraska, Crook told the old chief that if he could convince his nephew to surrender he would not have to move his people to the Missouri River agency. Aware of his uncle's diplomatic nature, however, Crazy Horse realized Spotted Tail's purpose in visiting could only be to attempt to convince him to surrender. He told his father to make Spotted Tail welcome in camp and that those who wished could come into the reservation in the spring when it was more advantageous to move. Before Spotted Tail arrived in the camp Crazy Horse had vanished into the wintry white shroud of the Big Horn Mountains.

Spotted Tail was disappointed by his failure to meet with Crazy Horse. Before leaving camp, however, the chief was able to win diplomatic points

to help ease his situation with Crook by convincing Big Foot of the Minneconjous and Touch-The-Clouds of the Sans Arc to pledge to him they
would come in to the reservation in the spring. On April 14, Touch-The-
Clouds, keeping his pledge to Spotted Tail, rode in with a large group of
Minneconjous and Sans Arc Lakota to surrender. Only a few days before
Crook had sent Red Cloud out to find Crazy Horse to promise him that if
he surrendered he would have a reservation in his beloved Powder River
country. The two Oglala leaders met on April 27 and Red Cloud informed
Crazy Horse of Three Star's promise. Crazy Horse's nine hundred follow-
ers were starving, had no ammunition and their horses were mere skele-
tons. The promise of a reservation in the Powder River country was all
Crazy Horse needed to bring him in to surrender at Fort Robinson.[10]

Never defeated on the battlefield, the great warrior-chief brought his
starving band of Oglala's into Fort Robinson and surrendered his weapons
and horses. The "strange young man" of the Lakota may have surrendered
to the soldiers, yet, even surrendering, Crazy Horse remained their unspoken leader. As had been the case even before the Indian Wars, Crazy
Horse's natural charisma brought the failings of older chiefs to the surface.
Crazy Horse's gaunt, ascetic appearance nonverbally revealed to the people how the older chiefs had become fat from the *washicus'* life on the
reservation. This situation did not help his political problems with Red
Cloud. When Red Cloud surrendered to the United States government
and agreed to visit Washington, the natural rivalry between the two
Oglalas intensified. Red Cloud's power over the war-loving Oglalas diminished dramatically as he was forced by circumstance to become a statesman
rather than a warrior, and, as Crazy Horse took command of the recalcitrant Oglalas, the older chief became jealous of his young rival. Crazy
Horse's terms for surrender, which demanded an agency of his own exactly
like Red Cloud's, clearly indicates that Crazy Horse was also jealous of his
former warrior-chief. As competition between the two chiefs reached its
peak with the surrender of Crazy Horse, however, news of Chief Joseph's
Nez Perce rebellion in Washington arrived at Fort Robinson, unleashing a
tragic series of events which would bring the rivalry to an end.

The Nez Perce alliance with the Crows cast them as enemies of the
Lakota. Aware of this, government officials began enlisting young men
from Crazy Horse's band to serve as scouts against the Nez Perce revolt in
the Northwest Territory. Crazy Horse was very outspoken against Lakotas
fighting other Indian people. In spite of his admonitions, however, some of
his Oglala followers signed on to help the government scout against the

Nez Perce. This angered Crazy Horse so much that he announced that he intended to gather any who would follow him and return to the old ways in the Powder River country.

When Crook learned of Crazy Horse's declaration to flee Fort Robinson, he ordered the chief arrested. Crazy Horse was nevertheless warned of the approaching soldiers and ordered his Oglalas to scatter and hide while he raced—alone—to the sanctuary of Touch-The-Cloud's camp at the Spotted Tail agency.

The soldiers found him there and placed him under arrest. The chief was then taken back to Fort Robinson for an audience with Three Stars.

When the party arrived at the fort, Crazy Horse was told that it was too late to visit with Crook. The Oglala chief was then turned over to Captain James Kennington and Indian agency policeman Little Big Man. The presence of Little Big Man must have grieved Crazy Horse in much the same way that Sitting Bull had been saddened at the awareness of Frank Grouard and other Lakotas aiding the military against their own people. Little Big Man had been a trusted Lakota warrior. He had been among the first to stand and challenge the theft of the Black Hills by government negotiators. He had fought alongside his chief, Crazy Horse, but now he was a government policeman charged with arresting him.

Kennington and Little Big Man told Crazy Horse they were taking him to a place to stay for the night before visiting with Three Stars the next morning. The chief walked between the pair the short distance from headquarters to a nearby small wooden building. Upon entering the building and seeing the barred windows and prisoners in leg irons, Crazy Horse realized it was a jail. The warrior resisted, pulled a knife from under his blanket and a violent struggle ensued. Little Big Man grabbed one of the chief's arms while Captain Kennington grabbed the other. As Little Big Man and Captain Kennington held the chief, the guard on duty, Private William Gentles, plunged his bayonet deep into Crazy Horse's back. The warrior stumbled out of the jail and fell to the ground.

A crowd gathered around the fallen chief and, for a moment, everyone thought he had only swooned from fasting and collapsed. Then, as the Oglalas realized what had happened, a dangerous tension surrounded the scene. Lakota leaders urged everyone to remain calm and the chief was taken to the officer's headquarters as runners were sent to bring his mother and father. That night, September 5, 1877, the greatest Lakota warrior died. He was thirty-three years old.

The next morning Crazy Horse's mother and father put their son's body in a casket on a travois and took it to the Spotted Tail agency. There the chief's remains were placed on a burial scaffold for mourners to pay their respects. While Crazy Horse was being mourned at Spotted Tail's agency the sad news arrived: the reservation was being moved from Nebraska to the Missouri River. As the Lakota were being herded toward their new reservation, however, small groups began to slip away from the tribe to head north to join Sitting Bull in Canada. Crazy Horse's parents joined one of these groups. They took their son's remains to the sandy white hills alongside Wounded Knee Creek and buried him in a place known only to them. Afterwards, they rejoined the group of Lakotas heading to Grandmother's Land to join Sitting Bull.

Entering Canada on May 7, 1877, Sitting Bull's retreat had unwittingly stirred an international hornet's nest. The United States' northern neighbors were, of course, members of the British Commonwealth. Relations between Canada and the United States were friendly enough, yet, since Great Britain's surreptitious support of the Confederate states during the Civil War had been exposed, a contemptuous diplomatic tension existed between the nations. Sitting Bull's presence in Canada produced a unique international situation which had the potential to explode into major political conflict if left untended. As Canadian Indians and the refugee American Lakota would now be vying for the same land and game, the competition created a complex predicament for Canadian officials: Sitting Bull's Lakota people were entitled to political asylum, yet not at the expense of Canadian Blackfeet, Cree, or Ojibway Indians. If the American Lakota were to be given asylum, sovereign Canadian Indians demanded compensation. The situation became more complicated when Sitting Bull's position was explained to officials in Ottawa. Canadian authorities promptly interpreted that the chief had acted entirely according to international rules of war and was entitled to full political protection. Canadian legal experts then found themselves in a precarious political situation which would require utmost caution and diplomacy to avoid an international incident between themselves, the United States and Great Britain. When made aware of the complicated situation in western Canada, however, diplomats in Great Britain took full advantage of the opportunity to point out the U.S. government's duplicitous political policies concerning Native Americans. British statesmen were quick to remind the United States government that it had provoked the war with Sitting Bull by breaking the 1868 Laramie Treaty with the Lakota and illegally invading the Black Hills. Hence, Great Britain, and consequently Canada, took the position that Sitting Bull and the Lakota were diplomatic refugees of war and chastised the United States for breaking their own treaties and not being able to contain internal rebellions within their boundaries.

The Canadian government meanwhile sent Royal Canadian Mounted Police Superintendent Major James M. Walsh to meet with Sitting Bull to make certain the chief fully understood the terms of his unique status. As superintendent of the fledgling organization, Walsh had been charged with important diplomatic and legal responsibilities in the western provinces of the Dominion. Created in 1874, the paramilitary police force had been dispatched to western Canada to remove foreign legal interlopers and set up a system of law and order among Indian and non-Indian populations. The "Mounted Police" had successfully dismantled much of the illegal American/French fur trading networks, arresting and deporting those who did not cooperate with the law. In spite of Walsh's efforts, however, the *Metis*, a large group of French-Indian mixed-bloods, exerted broad influence in Alberta and Saskatchewan. The American Lakota, with many relatives living among the Metis, had been buying arms and ammunition from them throughout the Indian Wars and obviously intended to continue dealing with them upon arrival in Canada.

After searching through the many Lakota refugee camps that were forming around Wood Mountain near Frenchman's Creek on the international boundary, Walsh found Sitting Bull. The Mounted Policeman minced no words with the Hunkpapa leader. He explained to Sitting Bull that if he or any of his people crossed back over the international border—whether simply to hunt or to raid American settlements—their political sanctuary would be voided. Walsh urged Sitting Bull to return to the United States where a reservation—and government annuities—awaited him. Responding to this suggestion, the Hunkpapa leader expressed serious concern that if he returned to his home the U.S. government would have him assassinated.

He was probably right. Crazy Horse's murder was still fresh in his memory. The diplomatic interaction with Walsh was, however, new to Sitting Bull. He was embarking on a bold new adventure with the Canadian. Sitting Bull, out of necessity, was about to learn to trust a white man for the first time in his life. Finding a receptive ear, Sitting Bull opened up to Walsh and described at length his people's suffering at the hands of the U.S. military. As the talks progressed Sitting Bull also expressed concern that the U.S. military would attempt to follow him over the international border in order to attack and kill his people. Having few arms and little ammunition

Sitting Bull asked if the Canadians would supply them with enough weapons to defend and feed themselves. Walsh assured the Lakota that the Canadian government would never allow the American military to cross the border to attack the Sioux. He did, however, agree that the Lakotas would need ammunition and arms to feed themselves and, to prevent their dealing with the Metis, promised to do what he could in Ottawa to procure enough materials for the Sioux to hunt. Sitting Bull had indeed found his first white friend in Major James Walsh. The Hunkpapas began to call the superintendent "Long Lance." During Sitting Bull's seven years in Canada, "Long Lance" was often the only person standing between the Lakota and starvation. Sitting Bull also knew his enemy well. As the friendship between Sitting Bull and "Long Lance" grew on the Saskatchewan plains, Great Britain and Canada's official policy concerning the Lakotas' political asylum did not win any friends in Washington. When informed that Sitting Bull would be protected in Canada, Colonel Miles became so enraged that he wanted to defy Great Britain and lead troops into Canada to arrest Sitting Bull. General Sherman had to use all the restraint at his disposal to prevent Miles from escalating the issue into a full-blown war with Great Britain. Undaunted, Miles took his campaign to the media; his cohorts in the major western newspapers editorialized that Sitting Bull was using the protection of the British government to amass an even greater force than had been present at Little Big Horn. Furthermore, the editors maintained, Sitting Bull was breaking the terms of political asylum and crossing the international boundary to make raids in the United States and returning to sanctuary in Canada.

Meanwhile, as international controversy swirled around them, Sitting Bull and his followers were attempting to find a new life in Grandmother's Land. His understanding of the rules regarding his Canadian sanctuary was soon put to the test. Joseph Manzione writes,

> In late May Assistant Commissioner A. G. Irvine was vacationing in Fort Benton, the only sizable settlement within a few days ride of Fort Macleod and Fort Walsh. When news arrived of Walsh's visit with Sitting Bull, Irvine immediately set out for Fort Walsh. Arriving at the fort several days later, he learned that Walsh was temporarily away. Six Sioux representatives from Sitting Bull's camp were waiting for his return. Irvine rode out to greet them, and introduced himself as Walsh's "chief." The Indians told him that the Sioux were holding three Americans at Wood Mountain until the Mounted Po-

lice could arrive. One of the Americans was a "Black Robe," a Catholic priest.[11]

Walsh returned later that evening. The next morning he joined with Irvine, two other Canadian agents, and the six Lakota warriors to make the 140 mile trek east to Sitting Bull's camp. Sitting Bull welcomed his visitors and promptly introduced them to his American prisoners. They had followed him across the border all the while attempting to convince him to return to the United States. Sitting Bull stated openly that if Walsh had not taught him Canadian law that he would have immediately killed the two assistants and personally squired the priest to the border.

The priest, one of the more active Catholic missionaries from the Missouri River reservations, was Reverend Abbot Martin Marty. Carrying letters of introduction from the Catholic Commissioner in Washington, D.C. and the U.S. Commissioner of Indian Affairs, Reverend Abbot Marty claimed his visit was "official," and he was instructed to find Sitting Bull and offer him terms of surrender and convince him to return to the United States and the reservation. The abbot acted surprised to see the Mounted Police and claimed not to know he was in Canada.[12]

With little regard for Christians, Sitting Bull had no reason to trust Father Marty, especially when considering the reverend's companions. The priest's scout was Johnny Brughiere, who was the same Johnny Brughiere who had found solace in Sitting Bull's camp after fleeing a murder charge in the settlements; the same man who had acted as interpreter during the disastrous miscommunications at the initial conference between Sitting Bull and Bear Coat; and the same traitor who later had deserted Sitting Bull to become a scout for General Miles. The reverend's interpreter was Joseph Culbertson, another Lakota mixed-blood who was known to be an alcoholic and a liar. It is a silent testament of Sitting Bull's extraordinary patience and respectful understanding of his situation in Canada that he showed such diplomatic restraint concerning the fate of the three men, especially Brughierre and Culbertson. The chief's wisdom and openness was likewise evident when later pressured by Reverend Marty to reconsider returning with him to South Dakota. Even though he remained adamant that he intended to stay in Canada, Sitting Bull agreed to a general council meeting to discuss the issue. The next day the council began.

Marty opened the council by committing a serious error: He insisted that he had come to Grandmother's Land as a messenger of God to convince the Sioux to do the right thing, and now he demanded a decision.

Aware that members of his band had relatives on the reservation with Catholic affiliations, Sitting Bull may have been threatened by Marty. Now, however, either through ignorance or by design, the abbot had challenged his authority as a chief. According to Stanley Vestal, Sitting Bull angrily turned to Irvine and said:

> "God is looking at me now, and you know it. If he has a treaty to sign no one can destroy it but by God's will. [a reference to the loss of the Black Hills]. God told me that if anyone came from the East, to eat with him just the same. It is no use. God made me the leader of the people and that's why I'm following the buffalo. God told me, if you do anything wrong your people will be destroyed, and that's why I came here. I was afraid."
>
> Turning back to the abbot, he said:
>
> "You told me you came here as the messenger from God. What you told me is not good for me. Look up, you will see God. Look up, as I am looking. You came and told me, as God's messenger, what to do, but I don't believe it. I have nothing but my hands to fight the white man with. I don't believe the Americans ever saw God, and that is the reason they don't listen to me. You know, as the 'messenger of God' that they tried to kill me. Why did you wait until half my people were killed before you came?"[13]

Father Marty was obviously not up to the challenge of Sitting Bull's intellect. Confused and befuddled as the chief proceeded to expose his true secular motives, and, failing logically to convince Sitting Bull, or any of the Canadian officials, that he was indeed on a "divine" mission, Marty began to stumble and fall ever deeper into the analytical hole he dug for himself. Sitting Bull quickly and shrewdly spun the priest's own argument into a circle which revealed to everyone, including Marty, that the abbot contradicted himself. Humiliated and soundly defeated, Marty finally completely reversed himself and told the council he thought the Lakota were better off in Canada. The council ended and the Americans were released to return to the United States.

Sitting Bull's intellectual dexterity in his debate with Father Marty made a profound impression on Irvine, Walsh, and the other Canadian officials present at the council. Experiencing Sitting Bull's brilliant logical dismantling of Marty's arguments made them absolutely aware of the Hunkapapa leader's abilities. The chief's performance revealed a razor-sharp intellect; one that it would be impossible to manipulate with bureaucratic games. They did not want to appear to the Americans to be cooperating with their enemy; indeed, they wanted the Sioux to return to the United States. As mentioned previously, they had their own predicament with Native Canadians which were exacerbated by the presence of the Sioux in the western provinces. The issue was especially complex concerning the Canadian Blackfeet, who were ancient enemies of the Sioux. The Blackfeet had become increasingly more vocal in expressing their unhappiness over the Lakota "invasion" of their country. Irvine and Walsh realized clearly that, aside from the potential problems between Great Britain and the United States, the dangerous political situation between Native Canadians and the Lakota required their immediate attention. Witnessing Sitting Bull's dazzling unraveling of Father Marty's arguments, however, made them aware they had to be completely honest in all their dealings with the Hunkpapa leader. Irvine and Walsh's objective, nonjudgmental stance during the council indicated the official policy the Dominion would assume concerning the Lakotas in Canada: The refugees would be allowed to remain protected in their country, but they would receive no assistance whatsoever from the Canadian government.

This policy was a double-edged sword for Sitting Bull. One side of the blade afforded him the amnesty he sought from the persecution of the United States military; the other cut directly to his oldest and always most immediate problem: food. Philip Sheridan's solution to "the Indian problem" was having its catastrophic effect on North America's buffalo herd by the late 1870s. Beginning with the hide hunters at the inception of the decade, the multifaceted destructive consequence of the Industrial Revolution was making itself tragically clear. Advances in weaponry had wrought unprecedented death and destruction during the Civil War. Even more deadly after a decade of refinement, the guns the hide hunters brought to assault the herds allowed marksmen to shoot with even more accuracy, rapidity, and power. What had once been one great herd had first divided into a northern and southern herd as a prophetic effect of the initial decade of the massive migration of people and equipment across the Great Plains. After twenty more years of escalating dramatic intrusion and impact, the Indian Wars of the 1860s had taken place in the very middle of both the northern and southern herds, further confusing and diminishing the normal migratory and growth patterns of the species. Then, as it was conceived, created, and intended from its advent, the railroad brought the military to the very heart of the West, which was the core of the northern and southern herds. With General Sheridan's military came the most destructive force of his arsenal: the hide hunters. Where just a few years earlier white buffalo hunters such as Will Cody had hunted only for the purpose of securing food and clothing, these hunters sought only the hides of the animals and the wanton destruction of the Indians' foodstore. Encouraged by Sheridan, they proceeded to rapidly assault the herd with their powerful new weaponry. The effect was catastrophic. Acting alone, the hide-hunters would have exterminated the massive herds within a short period of time, yet following closely on the heels of the hide-hunters, railway excursion/package deals, sold by the robber barons of the "Gilded Age," worked in tandem with the hide-hunters and completed the wholesale slaughter. The celerity of the extermination caught even the whites unaware. Yet, completely cognizant of the fact that the buffalo was being exterminated from the earth, the railroad owner's emotional advertising sales pitch was for the public to "experience the west before it was gone forever," encouraging people to hurry and shoot a buffalo from a moving train while there was still one to shoot.

The Canadian herds were diminishing as rapidly as the herds on the plains in the United States. Everyone was becoming aware that it was only a matter of time before Indians would not be able to depend on the buffalo hunt for survival. The Canadian government was keenly aware that in a few short years their own indigenous people would not have any buffalo to hunt. The rapid downward spiral of the buffalo population made it clear that the days of the "monarch of the plains" were numbered. Canadian officials realized when the buffalo became extinct that humanistic programs would become essential in order to prevent the western tribes from starving. Canadian officials recognized the day was rapidly approaching when they would be forced to create a reserve for Indians, yet, economically it made no sense to become involved with the creation of a reserve for the Lakota so long as they were rejecting the one being offered in their own country.

In spite of the extremely complicated legal and survival questions looming around Sitting Bull's presence in Canada, the Hunkpapas settled into the best existence they could realize from their circumstances. They had somehow emerged from a lengthy exodus from their homeland, fleeing hostile enemy armies, while surviving harsh winter conditions and famine and carrying their old, young and wounded, retreating to Canada. They were in no condition to fight anyone. They were hungry. They needed time to mend and mourn.

Walsh was able to secure arms and ammunition to help them feed themselves and the friendship between the Lakota and the superintendent of the Mounted Police continued to grow. Soon the Lakotas were busy restocking their food caches, repairing lodges and equipment, and healing wounded bodies. Even as they began their convalescence, however, Sitting Bull began to send messengers to American tribes in an attempt to structure new military alliances. This behavior did not escape the authorities and it did not help the chief's bargaining position with Canadian officials or his reputation in western American newspapers. In his defense, however, one must consider the fact that the chief did not know whether he could trust the situation in which he found himself and his people in Grandmother's Land. He had to have contingency plans to exercise in the event he was booted out of Canada. As a further testimony to the ragged condition of the Hunkpapa army, however, authorities did not allow Sitting Bull's attempts to form such alliances to create more than a simple annoyance.

As the Lakota successfully transplanted themselves and healed in Canada, the international political maelstrom concerning them swirled and intensified in London, Ottawa, and Washington. For months, the issue of Lakota exiles in Canada grew more intense as politicians and diplomats continued to argue the legalities of the situation. On August 7, 1877, a Canadian official named David Mills made an unauthorized and unsolicited visit to Washington in a clandestine attempt to resolve the question of Sitting Bull's presence in Canada. Mills was a very intelligent career politician who had become minister of the Canadian Department of Interior and was in charge of Indian relations throughout the Dominion. In the early morning of August 8, Mills went straight to the home of charge d'affaires of the British legation, Frederick Plunkett, and knocked on his door. After overcoming the impropriety of Mills' appearance at his door before breakfast to broach a subject he felt was interfering with the traditional prerogatives of the British legation, Plunkett loosened up and decided to help Minister Mills. Plunkett promptly introduced the Canadian to Assistant Secretary F. W. Steward in the U.S. State Department. Upon hearing Mills' assessment of the problem, Steward ascertained the matter was one for the Department of the Interior and, within hours, Mills was acquainted with his American counterpart, Secretary of Interior Carl Schurz. Secretary Schurz listened with great interest as Minister Mills explained in detail the purpose of his unauthorized visit. After Mills completed his presentation Secretary Schurz invited Plunkett and Mills to accompany him to the White House for a meeting with President Rutherford B. Hayes. In the Oval Office, Mills finally laid the question of the refugee Sioux in Canada directly at the feet of the United States government. Chagrined by the action, President Hayes brusquely assigned General Sherman the task of finding an immediate solution. Within a few days, Sherman, following ancient military procedure by selecting his immediate subordinates, announced that General Alfred Terry and General William McNeil would head a commission to travel to Sitting Bull's dissident camp in Canada in an effort to convince him to return to the United States. Within a few days of the announcement, however, McNeil withdrew his name.

Then, with impeccable historical timing, another extremely dangerous drama appeared as an impromptu plot twist in the Northwest Territory and spilled over to Sitting Bull's international stage in Canada. As General Terry eagerly sought a replacement for General McNeil and prepared to journey to Canada, Chief Joseph's Nez Perce rebellion and subsequent flight through Montana for Canada focused even more attention on the complex legal international issues being raised by Sitting Bull's amnesty.

Chief Joseph's flight began as a misunderstanding over territorial claims of various tribes residing along the Wallowa River in Oregon and near the mouth of the Salmon River in Idaho. Once again misguided treaty negotiations were the culprit.

In 1863 the government negotiated a treaty which established the Lapwai reservation along the Clearwater River in Idaho. In establishing the reservation, however, the government neglected to include the traditional territories of the Nez Perce. In the early 1870s, the government offered proposals to the Nez Perce to modify the situation, but all efforts failed to meet the approval of the tribe. Violence exploded when talks broke down and American officials threatened to force the Nez Perce onto the reservation.[14]

Complicating matters, as the Nez Perce fled into Yellowstone National Park—occasionally taking tourists hostage—the story of Chief Joseph's rebellion began to make headlines in international newspapers. Were the Nez Perce fleeing to join Sitting Bull's forces in Canada? Next, the drama intensified as the Sioux simultaneously disappeared from their camping grounds at Wood Mountain in Canada. Were they racing to join and assist Chief Joseph? General Terry, whom the Lakotas called "Star," was ordered by President Hayes to stand ready in St. Paul, Minnesota, before being instructed to proceed to the Northwest Territories to search for Sitting Bull. If found in the Northwest Territories, Terry was ordered to negotiate the Dakotas' return to the United States. If Sitting Bull was discovered in the

United States, however, Terry was ordered to begin military action against the Sioux. The situation exploded as the Nez Perce, hoping to align themselves with their old allies, the Crow, came to a tragic realization: The Crow were now the allies of the U.S. military! As their one-time fighting comrades were now their aggressive adversaries the Nez Perce had no choice but to make a desperate race to embrace a former enemy. Chief Joseph now was compelled to make a grave and valiant attempt to reach Sitting Bull's amnesty camp in Canada. As the Nez Perce headed northward from the Yellowstone Park region, however, they ran straight into the forces of Colonel Nelson Miles.

Colonel Miles, supported with mounted elements of the Fifth Infantry and the Second and Seventh Cavalry, had intercepted the Nez Perce forty miles south of the Canadian border on the northern fringes of the Bear Paw Mountains. Convinced that Chief Joseph was moving to join Sitting Bull, Miles had quickly led his forces northwest and placed them between the Nez Perce and Wood Mountain. Disturbed by alarming reports that messengers from the Nez Perce had gotten through to Sitting Bull in Canada, at any moment Miles expected the Sioux leader to assault his northern perimeter with more than 1000 warriors. He called for emergency supplies and reinforcements.[15]

Miles was also personally concerned with apprehending Chief Joseph. Bear Coat was worried that General Oliver O. Howard, who had been fighting and pursuing the Nez Perce since the beginning of the rebellion, might convince the Nez Perce to surrender before he could defeat them on the battlefield. Wanting all the glory of Joseph's surrender to himself, Miles was determined to end the flight of the Nez Perce at Bear Paw.

Nez Perce runners made it to Sitting Bull's camp at Wood Mountain with news of the fighting in the Bear Paw Mountains. Arriving with the Nez Perce messengers was a fierce blizzard, which blanketed the entire region with ice and snow. It was as if the Great Spirit froze the situation in order to let it cool long enough for the Sioux to decide what to do. As the snow mounted, the Sioux went into council to contemplate a course of action. Their deliberations were, however, monitored by "Long Lance" Walsh. The superintendent waited patiently as the Hunkpapa refugees spoke in favor of rushing to the aid of their former enemies. Enraged warriors demanded to know how they could stand aside and do nothing when people of their race were being murdered only forty miles away? Some of the wounded Nez Perce had already begun to appear in their camp. Their blood, now spilling on Grandmother's Land, demanded immediate assistance! Walsh then rose to speak, firmly reminding the Sioux that to cross the international boundary to assist the Nez Perce would cost them their amnesty. "Long Lance" told the Sioux chiefs that if they crossed the border they would be prevented from returning to Canada and that their woman and children would be gathered and escorted across the border to join them if they returned to help the Nez Perce.

Walsh's ultimatum swayed the decision of the Sioux. Their circumstance forced them to make a most horrible decision; they could not sacrifice their amnesty to help the Nez Perce.

The Hunkpapa decision sealed the fate of the Nez Perce at Bear Paw. Miles' forces pounded them with no mercy until they were forced to surrender. In spite of the defeat, however, Nez Perce survivors who had managed to escape the carnage began to appear in small groups in the Hunkpapa camps at Wood Mountain. The sight of the bloodied and wounded Nez Perce refugees staggering into the Wood Mountain stronghold broke the hearts of every witness. On October 8 word arrived in camp that the Nez Perce had surrendered.

Once again, unfortunate timing affected international efforts to convince the Sioux to return to the United States. The Nez Perce victims of the U.S. military's actions south of the border were still bleeding and dying in Sitting Bull's camp when General Terry's military "peace" commission arrived at the Canadian Border on October 15. Commissioner of the Royal Canadian Mounted Police James F. Macleod greeted General Terry at the border and the U.S. military escort was released to return to base. Macleod and the Mounted Police accompanied the Terry Commission into Fort Walsh the next day.

As Macleod led General Terry and his team of negotiators into Fort Walsh, "Long Lance" was using all his power to convince Sitting Bull and the Hunkpapas to even come to the council. Considering the Nez Perce people still dying and mending in Sitting Bull's camp, victims of the same U.S. military who now wished him to come to a peace conference, one glimpses the trust Sitting Bull had developed in his relationship with Walsh. Most of the Lakotas were convinced that the commission was an elaborate trap set to lure them into Fort Walsh so they could be taken captive to the United States to be killed.

Upon arrival at Fort Walsh, however, General Terry went right to work. The very next morning his commission met with Sitting Bull and his headmen. Sitting Bull entered the conference and passed the commissioners coldly, implying his disdain for them, while warmly shaking hands with the Mounties. The chiefs and his headmen sat on the floor opposite the commissioners' chairs and demanded the table between them be removed. Finally, he ordered all spectators shut out of the room.[16]

A language structure for the proceedings was established. Eventually, one interpreter was selected along with two Lakota interpreters who would verify his words.

Terry rose and addressed the Sioux, telling them that the "Great Father" only wanted peace between the Lakota and the United States, and had authorized his commission to offer a full and total pardon for any acts in the past—no matter what those acts might have been. The General told the Sioux that the United States wished for all hostilities between them to cease and promised not to punish them if they returned to the United States to live in harmony. He told them it was time for them to learn to support themselves raising cattle instead of hunting buffalo. He informed them that the United States was already bringing cattle herds onto the reservations and providing the reservation Sioux with rations, clothing and shelter until they could learn to produce enough crops and cattle to support themselves. Terry continued warning the Sioux that game in Canada was rapidly diminishing and that in a few short years the Sioux would not be able to feed themselves there. He reminded them that the Canadians would never give them a reserve so long as they denied the one offered them in their own country. He admonished them to remember that if they returned across the international boundary line they would be considered enemies of the United States government. Terry politely concluded, urging the headmen to take time to talk and smoke and take into careful consideration everything he said. He promised to wait patiently until they reached a decision. Stanley Vestal elaborates:

> The General spoke in a kindly, conciliating, if somewhat patronizing manner, apparently under the impression that the Sioux would be glad to come back on such terms, and gain a "pardon" for past offenses. But he very soon had his eyes opened and his ears set burning when Sitting Bull began to talk. That old cripple had a heart full of accumulated indignation. So the Grandfather would pardon him, and suggested that he "march on foot to the reservations"—a thousand miles or so! It is hard to understand how Sitting Bull was able to get along with a language which contains no profanity.
>
> Sitting Bull: "For sixty-four years you have kept me and my people and treated us bad. What have we done that you should want us to stop? We have done nothing. It is all the people on your side that

have started us to making trouble. We could go nowhere else, so we took refuge here. It was on this side of the line that we first learned to shoot, and that's why I came back here again. I would like to know why you came here. I did not give you my country, but you followed me from place to place, and I had to come here. I was born and raised here with the Red River mixed bloods, and I intend to stay with them. I was raised hand in hand with these people, and that is why I shake their hands [shaking hands with the Red Coats]. That is the way I was taught. That is the way I intend to go on doing. See how I live with these people.

Look at me? I have ears. I have eyes to see with. If you think me a fool, you are a bigger fool than I am. This house is a medicine house. You come here to tell us lies, but we don't want to hear them. I don't wish such language used to me, nor any such lies told to me in my Grandmother's house. Don't you say two more words. Go back home where you came from. This country is mine now, and I intend to stay here, and raise people up to fill it. I shake hands with these people [shaking hands again with the Red Coats]. You see me; that's enough. The country that belonged to us, you ran me out of it. I have come here, and I intend to stay. I want you to go back, and take it easy going back."[17]

Sitting Bull ended his talk and introduced several Lakota men and one woman to echo and underscore his remarks. One by one the Lakotas stood and eloquently and passionately voiced grievances to the commission. Each of them spoke of being driven from their country by the relentless persecution of the U.S. military. They spoke of relatives being murdered and lands being lost. Stanley Vestal continues:

It was not overly pleasant for the United States commissioners, to sit and listen to the frank reproaches, almost abuse, of these "savages" whom they had condemned and despised and had come so far to "pardon." More especially, it was unpleasant because all was spoken in the presence of the officers of the British government, with which the Americans were none too friendly in feeling just after the Civil War. Particularly, as both the Americans and the Red Coats knew very well that Sitting Bull's stand was thoroughly justified by the corruption of the Indian Bureau, the unnecessary Indian Wars, the abuses of the Indian trade, and the indiscriminate killing of Indians, including not a few women and children. There sat Terry, who had been in command of the troops when Custer fell, and when thousands of American soldiers could not keep peace on the frontier. And in the same room sat the Red Coats who—with a mere handful of policemen—controlled the Indians of a territory far larger than the country of the Sioux, and without any bloodshed whatsoever. And there sat Sitting Bull, the man whose warriors had inflicted the most complete disaster to American arms in the history of the nation, pointing the difference in the two groups of officials in the most dramatic way, his whole attitude a tribute to the justice of the Red Coats and a proclamation of the corruption and inadequacy of the frontier government of the United States. It must have been a relief to Terry when Sitting Bull rose to leave the council.

However, "Star" spoke once more:

"Shall I say to the President that you refuse the offers that he has made you? Are we to understand from what you have said that you refuse those offers?"

"Sitting Bull: I could tell you more, but this is all I have to say. If we told you more—why, you would pay no attention to it. I have no more to say. This side of the boundary does not belong to your people. You belong on the other side; I belong here."[18]

Having completed his mission, General Terry and his commissioners left the next morning. Within hours diplomatic, analytical tongues were wagging again in Washington, Ottawa, and London. Mounted Police Commissioner Macleod met with Sitting Bull and the Hunkpapas the next day to make certain they understood the ramifications of their actions with Terry. He informed them that the response they gave General Terry prevented their ever returning to the United States with arms and ammunition. He very firmly told them it was his duty to prevent any Lakotas from crossing the border with arms and ammunition and that if any ignored this restriction it made all of them the enemies of the Canadian government. He implored them to reconsider the commission's offer while they still could, reminding them they were now absolutely dependent on hunting buffalo on the Canadian side of the border. He did not have to remind the Sioux that buffalo numbers were rapidly dwindling. They already knew that. They also knew the Americans were lying to them.

Sitting Bull responded to Macleod by reminding him that the Americans' past behavior proved them totally untrustworthy. He was perplexed by the fact that they forced him out of the country only to go to such lengths to attempt to persuade him to return. The chief was convinced the only reason they could have in wanting him to return was to kill him. He assured Macleod that he would obey the Grandmother's rules. He also told the commissioner that the only reason his people even agreed to attend the commission was out of respect of the conciliatory efforts of "Long Lance" Walsh.

The die had been cast. Yet, as bleak as their predicament was, in their flight to Canada Sitting Bull and his followers had created an unprecedented international legal dilemma and, following that, successfully negotiated an equally unique circumstance of diplomatic immunity at least a quarter-century before Euroamerican legal minds began to envision anything as civilized as a League of Nations. Newspapers in the western portion of America still maintained the Sioux were using Canadian sanctuary to protect them as they continued to hunt and raid in the United States. A surprising number of eastern newspapers, however, editorialized that, considering the sad history of our interaction with Indians, the Sioux had little reason to trust us. The eastern humanitarians began to become more vocal again. Diplomats continued to debate the legal consequences of the exiled Sioux.

Meanwhile, as debate over their Canadian exile escalated in the world's capitals, the power structure of Sitting Bull's center of leadership slowly began to crack under the prolonged stress. Rival chiefs, taking advantage of Sitting Bull's weakened position, became more bold and led small groups south to surrender at the border. The Hunkpapa leader's camp then consisted mostly of older people. The young warriors, adventurous and eager to prove themselves with challenges, were the first to go in to face the government. The elders, although "pathetically" eager to return to their homes, remained loyally devoted to Sitting Bull. The chief had led them through war, famine and exile and they would remain with him until the end; only he could decide their fate.[19]

Sitting Bull may have also had a falling out with James Walsh and the Mounted Police. Rumors were circulating that the two had an argument over food stores at Fort Walsh and that Walsh had publicly humiliated Sitting Bull by bodily picking him up and tossing him through an office door. Whether the rumors were true or not, in reality, Walsh's attitude had changed. What began as sympathy for Sitting Bull's band of refugees had changed to tolerance and that toleration had become contempt. Long Lance had struggled to maintain positive relations with Sitting Bull's refugees, but his compassionate and benevolent behavior provoked distrust among his superiors and compromised his already fragile position.[20]

As Sitting Bull's actual power began to wane in Canada, his legend grew in the United States. Newspaper stories had him kidnapping the governor of Montana Territory, absconding with the chief executive across the border to hold him as a hostage until Chief Joseph was released. When Governor Potts returned to Helena from his farm he was astonished and amused to learn of his kidnapping. Even after such embarrassing episodes exposing the alarmist mentality which surrounded the chief, however, Sitting Bull—Robin Hood style—was often reported seen in several locations, simultaneously buying weapons and ammunition, leading raids, and generally disturbing the peace throughout the territory.

Sitting Bull was indeed crossing the border. As autumn arrived, the need for food became critical as buffalo were becoming harder to find north of the border. By winter the Mounted Police acknowledged that the Sioux had begun to send increasing numbers of hunting parties into Montana seeking game. Sitting Bull led a small hunting party across the border and stayed for a week camping with relatives from the Yanktons on the Montana reservation. When questioned about this by Major Walsh, Sitting Bull promptly acknowledged that he had crossed the border only to prevent the starvation of his people. He assured the superintendent that he believed the Great Spirit would soon pity his people and send the buffalo north again.

As the famine worsened so did the political situation. Returning to Canada from a hunt in Montana, a group of Nez Perce refugees told Sitting Bull that the Crows might soon be joining them in exile in Canada. Rumors were swirling in Crow country that the U.S. government planned to soon disarm them. Realizing a window of opportunity had appeared, Sitting Bull abandoned his submissive, pro-Canadian arguments, and declared in council that the Canadians and the Americans were now allies and the time was approaching when the Mounted Police would allow the American soldiers to come over the border to attack the Sioux.[21]

Sitting Bull next did the unthinkable: He sought an alliance with the most ancient of Lakota enemies—the Crow! Within days a band of Sitting Bull's emissaries were sent to discuss the proposed confederacy with the Crow and the Missouri River Lakota.

Both groups refused Sitting Bull's proposition. Insulted at the rejection of his relatives and enemies, Sitting Bull furiously attempted to organize a war party to cross the border to attack the Crows. While this mission was being planned, however, a Crow war party crossed the Canadian border and stole several horses from the Lakota at Wood Mountain. About this time Major Walsh, having caught wind of the mounting problems with the Crow, decided to pay Sitting Bull a visit. Meeting with his old friend, Sitting Bull told Long Lance that the Americans had sent the Crows to raid his camp in Canada and demanded that the Mounted Police protect him. Walsh assured the chief that he would complain about the Crow raid to American authorities but that he believed that his attempt to create a rebellion in Crow territory forced the Crows to retaliate. Sitting Bull admitted to Major Walsh that he had sent emissaries with a proposal of a military alliance with the Crow. Walsh countered the headman's argument, maintaining that the Sioux were afforded protection by the Canadian government and there was no need for any more war alliances. In spite of the friendship the two had nourished, Walsh failed to convince Sitting Bull that he need not concern himself with building anymore confederacies to fight the Americans.

Once the Sioux's only friend, after speaking with Sitting Bull, Walsh lost faith in them. He predicted in his report to Irvine that Canada would be blamed for any trouble the Sioux might create. His report also expressed concern that the Dominion would be blamed for allowing the Sioux to replenish their arms and ammunition and recruit fresh warriors. He concluded by telling Irvine that the Sioux hated all whites—both Americans and Canadians.[22]

Walsh's remarks reflected the rapidly changing position of the Mounted Police in reference to the Sioux. Assistant Commissioner A. G. Irvine was also beginning to alter his support of the Lakota. In a report to the Canadian Department of the Interior Irvine predicted that Indian competition for food in the western provinces would soon escalate into open violence. Irvine's predictions were accurate. U.S. Secretary of State William Evarts soon wrote a very angry letter complaining vigorously to the British government that American Indians at Fort Peck reported refugee Hunkpapas appearing throughout their reservation killing game and herding horses and buffalo back across the border. Evarts warned that if Britain failed to do anything about the situation the United States would be forced to resort to military action even at the cost of risking endangering relations between the United States, Great Britain and Canada. Secretary Evarts condemned the Sioux, maintaining they had renounced their American rights in accepting asylum in Canada. As Major Walsh had predicted, Evarts blamed Canadian authorities for protecting the Sioux and allowing them to cross the border for the purpose of raiding American settlements and stealing American property. The Secretary of State informed British authorities that the United States now regarded Sitting Bull's Hunkpapas as Canadian Indians and no longer accepted any responsibility for their behavior.

Famine and fragmentation mercilessly attacked Sitting Bull's camp of exiles at Wood Mountain during the bitter winter of 1880. Two of the chief's most loyal lieutenants rode south to surrender to the Americans; Gall and Crow King had endured much and remained devoted to Sitting Bull throughout the Indian Wars, but now even they had departed in order to feed their families. Early in the summer of 1881 Sitting Bull began to explore a way of returning home himself.

Jean Louis LaGare was the principal trader in the Wood Mountain District. Born in France, LaGare was illiterate but a shrewd trader who knew and understood Indians. Aware that there would be a reward for the man who could get Sitting Bull to surrender at Fort Buford, LaGare called a council at his store at Willow Bunch. The Sioux had never heard him talk and they listened.[23]

LaGare urged the Sioux to surrender. He reminded them of their poverty and declared that the Canadians had come to view them as a burden. As everyone before him, LaGare reminded Sitting Bull that the days of the buffalo hunt were now over. He told them that their hunger and poverty would only increase in Canada and that it was time to surrender and go home.

Sitting Bull told LaGare he trusted him but not the Americans. The chief remained convinced that the Americans only wanted to get the Sioux all together in one bunch so that they could kill them all. When made completely aware of Sitting Bull's concern, LaGare offered a way to test the Americans: he would provide rations and supplies to accompany a small band in to discuss surrender; if the leaders of the surrender party were not satisfied with the terms the Americans offered, he would return with them.

Thirty Hunkpapa men were selected to make the journey with LaGare. As the surrender party departed south, Sitting Bull rode northeast to Fort Qu'Appelle to make one last desperate plea to the Canadian government to grant the Lakota a reserve in Canada.

It was not to be. Sitting Bull rode back to LaGare's Willow Bunch store hungry and despondent. LaGare informed him that he would be taking another group in to surrender in two days and suggested the chief come with him. The time to surrender had finally arrived. LaGare rode into Fort Buford with Sitting Bull at High Noon July 19, 1881. Stanley Vestal describes the surrender of the greatest warrior-chiefs of the Lakota:

While the Indians were going into camp, the officers gathered to see the famous chief. Colonel William H. C. Bowen, USA, retired, then a young officer at Fort Buford, writes that Sitting Bull was in plain clothes, no gaudy trappings. He "did not appear to be a well man, showing in his face and figure the ravages of worry and hunger he had gone through. He was getting old. Since the sixties he had been the hero of his race. Giving in to the hated whites and the final surrender of his cherished independence was a hard blow to his pride, and he took it hard. He was much broken.

"It was hard to give up those fast horses which had carried him through so many hunts and fights and endless journeys, but he had to let them go. And when the men lined up to turn over their weapons, Sitting Bull was said to have handed over his own through the hands of his son Crowfoot, then eight years old. Said he, 'My boy, if you live, you will never be a man in this world, because you can never have a gun or pony.'"[24]

THE WILD WEST

We did not think of the great open plains, the beautiful rolling hills, and the winding streams with tangled growth, as "wild." Only to the white man was nature a "wilderness" and only to him was the land "infested" with "wild" animals and "savage" people. To us it was tame. Earth was bountiful and we were surrounded with the blessing of the Great Mystery. Not until the hairy man from the east came and with brutal frenzy heaped injustices upon us and the families we loved was it "wild" for us. When the very animals of the forest began fleeing from his approach, then it was the "Wild West" began.

(*Land of the Spotted Eagle*, Luther Standing Bear)

WHEN Crowfoot surrendered Sitting Bull's rifle and horse at Fort Buford in July, 1881, Buffalo Bill was contemplating leaving what had been a very prosperous career in the theater in order to attempt a bold new adventure. News of the surrender of the last great Sioux warrior-chief was the final evidence that the Euroamerican culture would soon dominate the North American continent and the "wild" west would succumb to civilization. Sitting Bull's surrender was a harbinger of profound change that Buffalo Bill heard loud and clear.

Since a boyhood visit to Fort Leavenworth in 1853, at which time he first witnessed cavalry maneuvers, Will Cody had been fascinated with choreographed horsemanship. From this moment forward Cody began to think more like an Indian than a white man about horses. Learning trick riding from his cousin, Horace Billings, young Will's training perfectly reflected the Great Plains equestrian education of Lakota boys, who were by necessity trained from the earliest age to mount, ride, and dismount ponies with remarkable dexterity in a widely diverse number of circumstances; the childhood game might later save a life in combat. Indian boyhood games included such things as mounting a racing horse by holding on to his tail and running behind long enough to jump onto the animal's back.

Cody's inherent love of horses and his skill handling them led him to the culture of the Plains Indian. As a boy bullwacker and as a teenage Pony Express rider Cody had also learned that a fast horse equaled survival. As his Plains Indian counterparts, he learned that horses equaled mobility and that the unrestricted movement they provided also created opportunity. Recognizing the superior horsemanship of the Plains Indian, Cody wisely sought animals trained by Native Americans because he knew they would best serve him. "Brigham," the Indian-trained steed with a unique, intuitive ability to chase buffalo, was responsible for much of Cody's nascent fame as a hunter. Cody's bold riding with emergency dispatches first drew him into scouting for the U.S. military; Will's subsequent success as a scout had been paralleled and underscored by his continual quest for, and ownership of, swift, highly intelligent horses. This perpetual pursuit of horses was a powerful motivation for Cody in both the Tall Bull fight and the Battle of Summit Springs; he emerged with superior mounts taken from Indians he killed in both skirmishes. As a scout he was not obligated to participate in either battle, yet, spotting horses that caught his fancy drew him into the fight. This behavior would have been perfectly mirrored and admired by any of the Indians Cody ever killed in battle. Only honor could attract a Plains Indian—or Cody—into combat quicker than a trophy horse; honor and horses were synonymous. Aside from buffalo, there is no more vital link between Cody and Plains Indians than horses. Simply, horses allowed the warrior culture of the Great Plains to exist. This magnetic attraction to horses in which honor was at once economically manifested, defined, and distributed through mortal combat is an obvious, nevertheless, enigmatic connection between Cody and Plains Indians. The fact that it is essential to understand this nonverbal, mortal blood bond of warriors with horses before one can truly understand either William F. Cody or Plains Indians underscores the mystic vitality of the link. For example, the resplendent costumes and exquisite regalia of the Plains Indian culture that continue to stimulate aesthetic awe in glass museum cases today once nonverbally indicated tribal, clan, and society affiliations and also battlefield honors and prowess. The highly visual culture of the Plains Indians obviously evolved from the vast, open range, where one can see a hundred miles in any direction. On the Great Plains one could observe another approaching from great distances and both could understand much about each other simply from the colors, designs, styles, and attitudes of the clothing and general accoutrements of the other. The beaded buckskin costume Cody adopted from the mountain men evolved first from this nonverbal warrior tradition of the horse culture of the Plains and Rocky Mountain Indian. Horses, buffalo and space gave birth to the culture. From his earliest days on the plains forward, Cody adopted the costume and horse and buffalo culture of the western tribes.

Cody sought horses that would serve him on the racetrack as well as the battlefield. Will's talent racing horses at western Army posts led to the emergence of the showman in his personality as he was increasingly forced to include a dare-devil performance as part of any contest in order to find anyone willing to compete against one of his fleet ponies. In this sense, Cody rode like an Indian. Where it was normal behavior for Indians to demonstrate their riding skills in tribal ceremonial and recreational events, few white men of this era would even think of including dramatic athletic feats as part of a horse race. It was inevitable that Cody would ride all these fantastic ponies into the theatrical world.

In the 1870s, the American theatrical world was in a state of flux and very much ready for a character like Buffalo Bill. Immigrant Irish and Jewish Americans had laid the foundation of the modern entertainment industry, creating the genesis of Broadway with broad characterizations of the trials and tribulations of their people transplanted in the New World, particularly in Manhattan. Audiences tended to prefer unrefined melodrama with abundant interaction between the audience and the actors and, contributing greatly to the "soiled" reputation of the early entertainment business, prostitutes worked openly in the upper balconies. By the 1870s, an effort to clean up the theater had begun to make entertainment suitable for the entire family and the prostitutes were driven from the balconies. When Cody began his career on the stage the melodramas he acted in were boisterous spectacles created for the entire family.[1]

The great American impresario, Phineus T. Barnum, had been very much impressed with painter George Catlin's early attempts to present elements of Native American culture and the frontier west in New York in 1837 and London in 1840, but the showman's bigotry toward American Indians prevented his being able to present even a slightly realistic portrait of them or their culture in his circus. The few times Barnum attempted to present Indian people reveal the circus master's prejudice: Barnum presented Indians as sideshow "oddities." Cruelly aware they did not understand what he was saying, Barnum insulted Indians and their culture to the audience while smiling and feigning cordiality to the Native Americans. Nevertheless, in 1843, in an attempt to capitalize on Catlin's efforts to explore a western exhibition, Barnum presented a herd of fifteen buffalo in

Hoboken, New Jersey, but the crowd spooked the herd and the animals stampeded into a swamp. The showman never attempted to present buffalo again and lost interest in western exhibitions. Aside from his impatience, racism and bad manners, however, an all-important characteristic separated Barnum and Cody: Barnum was not "of" the west; harkening to the days of the gladiators and Roman exhibitions, his forte was the presentation of exotic wild animals, European acrobats, clowns, and sideshow freaks of nature. In contrast, Buffalo Bill was a bona fide western American hero, a man audiences recognized as having participated in the very events he depicted on stage. Where Barnum created much of the initial interaction involving friendly "public relations" between newspapers and "the show business," Buffalo Bill offered the press its first truly American "star."

The historical timing of Cody's arrival in the theater world in 1872 could not have been more heroically perfect. The wages of fratricide were tragically manifested in a loss of cultural identity and unity of vision as the shattered American nation was still in shock and numbly seeking healing. The Civil War had ended and the Transcontinental Railroad had linked the nation. With peace and technological marvels, however, a wounded country emerged from the war still torn and divided with profound psychic trauma and new socioeconomic ills. Sectionalism, which contributed greatly to the ignition of the conflict, turned upon itself with the vengeance of a plague. The defeated South was economically destroyed yet endured a cruel and politically corrupt "Reconstruction" as it was reintegrated into the United States. With a large portion of its male population either dead or physically maimed, the South's economy was so devastated the region would take a full century to recover. To a region which had more per capita millionaires than any other region in antebellum times, the fall from luxury was long, bloody, and permanent. More destructive than the regional economic abyss, however, losing the war, the South had suddenly and completely lost its sense of cultural continuity within the Union. The aftershocks would ripple for generations. Peace also brought loss of cultural identity and regional confusion to the North. The end of the war brought with it a flood of men returning to the urban labor force and the expanding working class it created was falling under the increasing power and influence of industrial tycoons who would soon be recognized as "robber barons." Morally corrupt men, profiting from the war, the railroad, and the exploding Industrial Revolution, rose to great power and prestige and accumulated massive fortunes by abusing men, women, and children in factories, mines, and sweatshops. Immediately after the war, these plutocrats and their powerful monopolies and corporate trusts created a dangerous American "class structure" bordering on Neo-Feudalism. Complicating the situation, the entire country fell into a great economic depression immediately after the Civil War as the nation faced the financial bill for its self-destructive implosion.

It could be argued that all of this chaos, the Civil War included, was the result of the Industrial Revolution shifting every aspect of society into profound, permanent change with unprecedented, stunning velocity. Nowhere is this argument more obvious than in the inception, creation and completion of the Trans-Continental Railroad and its linking of the Pacific and Atlantic coasts. Considering the 1870 consequences of the "states rights" aspects of Steven Douglas's Kansas/Nebraska Act of 1854, spun in motion and created by political efforts to simultaneously repeal the Missouri Compromise of 1819 and create a transcontinental railroad, the Industrial Revolution, and its impact on the Civil War, takes on a new meaning. With remarkable lack of foresight, politically and racially dividing the old territory of the Louisiana Purchase in order to attract a technological invasion into utopia while simultaneously coordinating a massive migration of immigrants into the heart of the unknown continent, the leaders of the day had unleashed primal, chaotic forces which nearly destroyed the Union. The slavery and expansion issues had collided with terrific force in 1819 as Missouri sought to enter the Union. The clashing of these issues facing the young nation tore the first fissures in the bonds of the nation and made the United States government painfully aware of the looming conflict. The Missouri Compromise created a diplomatic solution by allowing a pro-slavery state to enter the Union only with the balance of a "free" state entering simultaneously. The Kansas/Nebraska Act repealed the Missouri Compromise and created the environment for violence by introducing a "states rights" issue which would allow voters to decide whether to enter the Union as a slave or free state. The act, though intended to open up the public to a Transcontinental Railroad, created the initial bloodshed on the Kansas/Missouri border which exploded into the Civil War.

Immediately following the Civil War, however, with little consideration of the legal rights of Native America, reflection upon the social chaos created by initial efforts to construct the railroad, or concern for the environmental consequences of their actions, the government rushed to implement the assassinated President Lincoln's Homestead and Railroad Acts of 1862, using the construction of the Union Pacific Railroad as a poetic metaphor representing technology and industry reuniting the North, South, East, and West into one American people. Nevertheless, instead of magically reuniting the country, the technological invasion only brought more confusion to this increasingly critical dilemma of shattered national identity. This condition was exacerbated when the populations of the world suddenly began pouring into North America in unprecedented numbers. These new American citizens left their "old country" behind only to form ethnic and cultural ghettos in the exploding urban centers of the east.

As the promise of wealth and freedom in the west emerged in the media, the railroad's ability and financial need to swiftly transport Euroamericans and the U.S. military to the continent's most remote corners attacked the heart of the culture of the Plains Indian with a intensity and mobility never before experienced. The shocks of the Industrial Revolution tore through the fabric of Indian national identity just as surely as the Euroamerican society had been forever altered by the profound and sudden changes occurring in North America. Indeed, the continuing psychic aftershocks of the Industrial Revolution and the Civil War and the massive numbers of immigrants entering the country profoundly affected the future of everyone on the continent. The mammoth undertaking of the Transcontinental Railroad, however, served its purpose and physically connected the country. The effort also succeeded in emotionally uniting the country by encouraging the United States to look west once again to search for healing and a future. The urban European immigrant joined the shell-shocked survivors of the industrial north and agrarian south facing the sunset seeking a vision. Once again major conflict with the Indian Nations loomed on the horizon.

Most of these Civil War–era Americans and European immigrants learned to read and write plodding through the popular dime novels of the day. Through these western fantasies a new romantic vision of the American character was emerging from the chaos. Soldiers from both North and South, seeking escape during the conflict, had made dime novels popular during the war years. The girls these soldiers left behind also read dime novels to romantically flee to the west, where anything was possible, where there was no war.

William F. Cody was knightly heroism literally come to life. Following in the path of his boyhood idol and original hero of the dime novel, Kit Carson, Cody emerged from the Civil War as the driving force of the genre. As the major dime novel hero of the era, Buffalo Bill came to represent to the world what could be accomplished by a free man in the "new world." Cody's success as a romantic dime novel hero served as a symbolic catalyst to reunite and focus post–Civil War America westward again to search for a collective identity, an act which would make it forever impossible to distinguish between the mythic Buffalo Bill and the real William F. Cody. The dime novel, often staged as melodrama, blurred what was "real" and what was "romantic" all the while creating an even greater audience for Cody in the theater.

Each and all of these dynamics came together with unprecedented force immediately following the Battle of Little Big Horn. Cody's theatrical career had prospered from the beginning, yet as the Indian Wars of the mid-1870s raged, Cody's fame soared. Running in direct parallel to Sitting Bull's exile in Canada, Cody's stage career exploded in the press, especially after he returned from the Sioux Wars of 1876 and the international notoriety of Little Big Horn with headlines screaming he had taken "the first scalp for Custer." Consequently, the fight with Yellow Hand launched Buffalo Bill's theatrical career with a force never-before experienced in the relationship between the press and the fledgling world of "show business." This unique connection between the frontier hero and newspapers is arguably the genesis of modern "pop culture"; "celebrity," as we now recognize it, was being created in this unprecedented relationship between Buffalo Bill and the American press. Will Cody was singularly qualified to bring such a concept as celebrity into being because the opening of the American west had, through the catastrophic psychic after-shock of the Civil War, transformed into the metaphor of the great collective Euroamerican Dream. If anyone had become the manifestation of the metaphor, it was Buffalo Bill.[2]

Realizing the strength of his charisma in the press and through his intimate connections with the powerful fathers of the American media such as J. Gordon Bennett, Cody, undoubtedly, consciously helped to create this unique development in American culture. Through his talented press agents, the scout was able to creatively manipulate the press to put even more sparkle on his rapidly expanding fame. Yet even as his legend was being nourished in the theater, Buffalo Bill was becoming less comfortable earning his living as an actor.

Cody's abundant comments on the subject reveal he shared a perspective not much different from his friend Wild Bill Hickok concerning performing on the stage: Hickok thought he was making a fool of himself and, as a result, could not comfortably continue the life of a thespian. Buffalo Bill, however, understood the life he and Hickok once cherished in the West was over. Facing that harsh reality, Cody was able to push his ego aside and continue on the stage in order to create a new livelihood for himself. Unfortunately, Hickok went instead to "Boot Hill" in Deadwood, South Dakota. Nevertheless, as his career in melodrama flourished, Cody continually expressed his frustration and discomfort at being on stage. He confided to Lulu and his sisters that he longed to get out of the business, yet he obviously enjoyed the prosperity his new occupation provided.

Cody may have enjoyed the creative process of show business even more than the money. In the world of the theater, his innately lucid imagination was artistically stimulated and nourished. His beloved West may have vanished, yet Cody had only begun to scout the landscape of his creative dreams. The discovery of his creative personality kept Cody's appetite whetted and allowed him to continue in the theater in spite of his increasing discomfort performing on stage. He had learned how to channel his artistic frustration with melodrama into his newly discovered creative outlets.

This aesthetic process began while Cody was performing in duel careers, working as a scout for the military on the plains during the summer months and returning to the eastern urban centers and performing on the theatrical stage during the winter. In his first theatrical outing with Ned Buntline and Texas Jack Omohundro, Cody had stumbled into the epiphany that he could fill a house and entertain audiences simply by portraying himself; people wanted to see him because he was famous. Expanding upon this concept had proven extremely successful as he began the historic process of reenacting his actual "summer" adventures creatively in his "winter" productions. This success indicated to Cody that, aside from merely seeing a frontier hero, the public was also extremely interested in experiencing western historical events reenacted, while simultaneously being presented with the opportunity to experience and learn about the culture of the west before it was gone. At this point Cody started to take increasingly active roles in developing original melodramas based either upon his personal prairie adventures, or upon western historical events that were in the news at the time. Eric Sorg observes,

> Cody managed to fuse an idealized concept of manhood with the world's positive emotional response to the frontier. Cody was acceptable as a mythic hero because he stood for the values of southern individualism as well as northern industrial pragmatism. He helped the government kill Indians, whose holistic spiritualism did not mesh with the white man's scientific positivism. At the same time Cody didn't offend the Indians, who respected him for always treating

them fairly and not using his influence to persuade them to sign treaties of dubious value.[3]

Cody had always shown signs of an artistic personality; indeed, one must be creative to envision a bustling town on the empty Kansas prairie or to outwit a band of outlaws with murder on their minds. This creative personality allowed him to become a hero and living legend to widely diverse geographic sections of nineteenth-century America. Reinventing himself and parlaying his heroic status to celebrity in the theater had been a relatively simple matter for Cody. Now, however, he was entering a singular realm extending well beyond mere theatrical frontier melodrama. In wedding recent historical events and their actual participants to theater, Cody was creating a cornerstone of American mythology. Although hired writers were creating the plays, Cody was employing, inspiring, and informing the authors. He created the central theme of the drama, related its minute details to the writers, was the star of the production, and personally guaranteed the work's authenticity with his heroic presence in the cast. Audiences trusted him to present them with a "true" western experience even within the ridiculous structure of the melodrama; in spite of the form's restrictions, Cody felt compelled not to betray their trust. Watching Cody reinvent himself on the stage, his audience learned how to reinvent themselves and, in the process, psychically heal. Nevertheless, Cody continually expressed his frustration at having to appear in corny melodramas and this discontent, coupled with the ever-present need to make more money, certainly led him to explore different outlets for his blossoming creative energy.

About this time, encouraged by his success onstage, and inspired by his popularity as a hero of Ned Buntline's dime novels, Cody also began to write books himself. While some cynically maintain Cody's literary efforts were penned by "ghost writers," Don Russell strongly suggests otherwise:

> During the theatrical season of 1874–75 which preceded this burst of literary activity, Cody was going it alone, without the services of Major Burke, who had gone off with Morlacchi and Texas Jack. Burke has never been definitely connected with dime-novel writing, but the fact that Cody was separated from all his publicists at the time he first appears as author lends weight to the theory that he might have written these productions himself. Albert Johannsen, foremost authority on dime novels, has assembled evidence to indicate that this is the case, and maintains that early productions signed Buffalo Bill are not of such literary excellence as to be beyond Cody's capacity.[4]

In 1879 Cody published his first autobiography, *The Life of Honorable William F. Cody*. The book has remained the most comprehensive account of the first thirty years of the life of Buffalo Bill. Once again Don Russell presents a convincing argument that the book was truly penned by Buffalo Bill rather than other writers such as Prentiss Ingraham, Ned Buntline, or Major John Burke:

> Who else but Cody would have mentioned his brief and unrecorded service with the jayhawkers and horse thieves whose leader was killed by federal police action? It is impossible to imagine Ingraham or Burke or Ned Buntline putting in a manuscript intended for publication the fact that Cody volunteered for Civil War while so drunk he did not know what he was doing. Anything any of them wrote about this episode—in fact what they did write—dripped with patriotism. Who else but Cody would have been so uninhibited in relating other drunken incidents.[5]

While the creative aspects of Will Cody's personality were blossoming in the theater, he was becoming increasingly more focused on the actual source of his uneasiness with the stage. He gradually became aware that he was artistically frustrated with inherent structure of the theater. Cody realized that audiences would never fully appreciate the West as he knew it, loved it, and wished to showcase it, as long as real horses could not be used on stage. The inherent exclusion of horses from the theatrical stage indicated to him the venue was entirely too constricting to contain the natural panorama of the American West.

Even before the Sioux wars of 1876, Cody had contemplated leaving the stage in order to attempt to create an outdoor show which would depict the west in a more realistic way. Cody's knowledge of Wild Bill's 1870 failure in presenting an exhibition of the west to easterners indicated a fundamental requirement to success; he needed an arena! Hickok had attracted over 5,000 people in Niagara Falls, New York, to see his buffalo herd and Indians. Wild Bill had not thought out his scheme, however, and had failed to create a structure to isolate his exhibition in order to charge the crowd to enter to enjoy the show. Complicating matters, as Barnum's group in Hoboken before them, the crowd spooked the uncorraled buffalo herd, forcing it to stampede through the streets of Niagara Falls. Hickok's disaster had colorfully revealed the outdoor show would have to take place in an arena in order to be able to sell tickets and control the wild animals.

Such realizations also made Cody completely aware his vision would be extremely expensive and that he would need to continue working in melodramas in order to build a financial and audience base from which he could attempt this broader concept.

As Buffalo Bill was forced by finances to continue working in the theater, however, he was also learning crucial business lessons producing melodrama. He was learning how to create and produce his own shows, manage a budget and complete the season with a profit. Fundamentally important, however, he was learning what type of show to present his audiences. Successful productions involved Indians and frontiersmen, a lost maiden to be rescued, and comic relief. The more shooting, violent dilemmas and absurd coincidences, the better the audiences like them. The prototype for western movies was being born."[6]

Where Cody's original vision for his Wild West began at Fort Leavenworth as a seven-year-old boy, and expanded as he discovered the theatrical arts, much of the core of the concept was inspired by his first and only cattle drive. Upon leaving the military in the late summer of 1876, Cody and partner Frank North bought a herd of cattle in Ogallala, branded and drove them to their ranches on the Dismal River in Nebraska. The cattle drive took most of the summer. Cody wrote in his autobiography:

> After my arrival at North Platte, I found that the ranchmen or cattlemen, had organized a regular annual "round-up," to take place in the spring of the year. The word "round-up" is derived from the fact that during the winter months the cattle become scattered over a vast tract of land, and the ranchmen assemble together in the spring to sort out and each secure his own stock. They form a large circle, often of a circumference of two hundred miles, and drive the cattle towards a common centre, where, all the stock is being branded, each owner can readily separate his own from the general herd, and he drives them to his own ranch. In this cattle driving business is exhibited some most magnificent horsemanship, for the "cow-boys," as they are called, are invariably skillful and fearless horsemen—in fact only a most expert rider could be a cow-boy, as it requires the greatest dexterity and daring in the saddle to cut a wild steer out of the herd.[7]

Don Russell is quick to point out a most important point concerning Cody's remarks describing his first cattle drive: "Writing in 1879, Cody found it necessary to define both "round-up" and "cow-boy" and to put both terms in quotation marks. He was to make both household words."[8]

Upon delivering the herd to their ranches, Buffalo Bill left North in charge of the cattle and proceeded to Red Cloud Agency, where, for the very first time, he hired reservation Indians to perform with him. Notably, less than a year after the Little Big Horn fight, Cody was at Pine Ridge auditioning and signing Lakota Indians to travel with him to Rochester to perform in his 1877–88 theatrical tours. Cody also attempted to incorporate horses and a Mexican burro onstage in the production. He opened his season September 3, 1877, at the Bowery Theatre in New York in a show written by A. S. Burt entitled *May Cody, or Lost and Won*. The show proved to be the most financially successful of Cody's career thus far. Louisa, however, did not like the traveling life of the actor and begged her husband to let her return to North Platte, where she supervised the construction of a home for their growing family.

During this period in Cody's life, his marriage, strained from its inception, began to show signs of severe problems. Personality differences existed from the beginning of the union; moreover, financial problems had come between the couple, since Lulu constantly squirreled money away in order to protect herself from her husband's overspending and getting into debt. This loss of trust compounded the divisions created by the contrary personality traits that naturally existed in the union. Compounding the situation, however, Mrs. Cody surprised her husband in Omaha at the end of his 1877 theatrical season only to discover him bidding an affectionate adieu to the actresses in his company. Mrs. Cody flew into a jealous rage over what she deemed "inappropriate" farewell kisses shared between her husband and the ladies of the cast. Lulu would not speak to her husband for the rest of the summer; later, when asked to sign important business papers, she refused. In a desperate attempt to regain her favor, Cody signed over all the North Platte property to his wife, but the damage had been done. The issue of the farewell kisses in Omaha still held a powerful charge 28 years later in 1905, when it raised its head in court during the Codys' famous divorce trial. Nevertheless, as his marriage continued to disintegrate, Cody continued this pattern of successfully touring with melodramas with hopes of somehow amassing enough money to produce his emerging dream. Cody spoke to his press agent, Arizona John Burke, and close associates about an increasing obsession with doing a massive outdoor show. Fate would soon introduce Cody to someone with a similar vision.

In early 1882 Cody was playing the Grand Opera House in Brooklyn when a well-known entertainer of the era, Nate Salsbury, contacted him. At the time Salsbury was playing nearby at Brooklyn's Park Theater with a stock company he called "Salsbury's Troubadours."⁹ Salsbury, born in Illinois, was nearly the same age as Cody and had become America's most popular comic and song and dance man entertaining Union troops during the Civil War. Salsbury had enlisted in the Union Army at age fifteen and did more than sing his way through the Civil War; he was a veteran of Sherman's march through the South, and, while still a teenager, served seven months as a prisoner-of-war in Andersonville Prison. While enduring the horrors of prison Salsbury discovered his talent entertaining fellow inmates. Surviving the war, Salsbury emerged as the biggest attraction of New York's popular music scene. He founded "Salsbury's Troubadours" and the group quickly became internationally famous. One evening at a supper at the Saturday Night Club in Manhattan, Salsbury overheard honored guest General William T. Sherman offering anecdotes of his Civil War Campaign in Georgia. Richard Walsh and Salsbury's son, Milton, continue the tale and offer a colorful description of what happened that evening:

With astonishment, Nate Salsbury overheard him [General Sherman] saying:

"Passing along the line, I was continually greeted by the familiar, but affectionate greeting of 'Hello, Uncle Billy,' from the tired soldiers, who had marched nine miles that morning under the broiling sun. As we neared the right of the regiment my attention was arrested by a boyish voice spouting imperfectly, 'Hamlet's' soliloquy, a short distance ahead of us, then changing into a rollicking negro melody, accompanied by shouts of laughter that made the welkin ring again. A strange sight met our eyes.

"Standing on top of a decayed stump of a cedar tree, was a young fellow, who could not have been more than sixteen or seventeen years old, in full uniform, except for an old plug hat, that had once been white, that was cocked on one side of his head, after the exaggerated style of the funny men of the minstrel stage, that lent color to the vociferous accents of his vocal efforts. Between the verses of his song he danced a jig to the delight of the lookers on.

"You may think, gentlemen, that this was not so strange a sight after all, but it would have seemed so to you, if you had been there, and realized as I did, that this was an incident in the life of a regiment that had been under fire from the 4th day of May to that 14th day of June."

Colonel Robert Ingersoll interrupted the General by saying, "That must have been a very funny song General. Do you remember the name of it?"

"No," said Sherman, "I wish I could."

At this point Nate Salsbury found his voice and said, "General Sherman, I can tell you the name of the song, and to prove it I will sing you a verse."

And he sang:

"Oh, Susanna, oh don't you cry for me,
I've come from Alabama wid my banjo on my knee."

The General fairly shouted, "That is the song sure enough. How came you to know?"

"Because I was that kid," said Salsbury.[10]

That "kid" was about to meet Buffalo Bill.

In 1877, returning by steamer from an engagement in Australia, Salsbury met circus agent J. B. Gaylord. The two men shared a love of horses and both had attended the Melbourne races and been amazed at the equestrian skills of Australian jockeys. As the pair continued their conversation, Gaylord expressed his opinion that the Aussies were the best horsemen in the world. A veteran and patriot, Salsbury strongly disagreed with Gaylord's remark and the two argued well into the evening with the singer maintaining no horsemen in the world could outride the American and Mexican cowboy.

Salsbury could not let the issue go. As the night passed, he could not go to sleep but instead continued designing in his mind the greatest horse show the world had ever seen. That evening, somewhere on the Pacific Ocean, Nate Salsbury unwittingly merged his destiny with Will Cody. Where a vision of reenacting western history was unfolding in Cody's imagination, however, Salsbury envisioned a bold, new presentation that would embody a comprehensive display of the world's best equestrians. With such similar obsessions it was inevitable that the two men would meet.

Even as the years passed, Salsbury never lost sight of his vision and he resolved to research the different elements of this show. After exploring and considering the matter, Salsbury decided he would need a well-known personage to attract attention to the show and that character was William F. Cody. When they both were working in the Manhattan area in 1882, the pair agreed to meet at a restaurant that adjoined Haverly's Theater.[11]

Cody and Salsbury immediately agreed to unite their visions somehow.

At the lunch, it was decided that Salsbury would go to Europe to explore the possibility of touring the show there as soon as they could structure it. Salsbury did indeed travel immediately to Europe to scout a possible tour. Upon his return, Salsbury advised Cody that it would cost a great deal of money to succeed in creating their dream. Neither man felt they could afford to produce the show themselves so they decided to wait until they had the money and the time was right.

Having signed his North Platte property over to Lulu, Cody had nothing to use as collateral to raise funds. His melodrama career was making money but the signs of change were everywhere. His final years on the melodrama stage were the most unpromoted of Cody's years in show business. The publication of his autobiography brought much-needed publicity to his theatrical tours and Prentiss Ingraham's dime novels were another important boost.[12]

This lack of publicity, however, should not be misconstrued to mean a loss of money. Cody netted $48,000 from his 1880–81 season and his final two seasons were also financially successful. In spite of these profitable seasons, however, the diminishing press interest indicated to Cody that dramatic change was imminent.

Facing the end of an epoch in which he had been a legendary participant, Cody was characteristically reinventing himself to adapt to the rapid change around him in order to greet the next era. The precise historical timing of the arrival of the Wild West, however, would echo the fortuitous timing of Cody's arrival in the theater a decade earlier and indicate that a great deal of thought went into the act of re-creation. Whether the re-creation was intuitive or planned, however, once again Cody's metamorphosis was stunningly accurate. By the 1880s the nation was beginning to heal and emerge from the chaos of the Civil War. L. G. Moses observes:

> . . . when Buffalo Bill Cody created the Wild West show, the generation that had fought the Civil War had bid farewell to its youth. The Union had been preserved and slavery eradicated. The middle-aged veterans, Northern and Southern, protected the traditions of noble sacrifice; but when their organizations shared the battlefields in annual convocation, they exchanged handshakes along with their memories. Americans, once again, looked to the West for truly national myths and legends. Younger Americans perceived the heroic in the lives of the pioneers and soldiers who went west in the years after the Civil War and survived. A newer generation of heroes, and a few

heroines, acquired their fame on the high plains. Although some won renown as lawmen, gunfighters, pathfinders, scouts, soldiers, or hunters, most—whether civilians or soldiers—achieved their celebrity by fighting Indians.[13]

Integrating the mythological and romantic impact of generations of Euroamericans who earned their unique fame, stature, or fortune fighting Native Americans, Moses accurately describes the forces which gathered around the unique relationship and, in doing so, also perfectly supports the concept of a Native American cocreation of both celebrity and the Wild West:

> Indians figured prominently in the self-conscious quest to create a truly American literature and art in the years between the War of 1812 and the Civil War. Cultural nationalism and romanticism sustained the quest. In their search for American themes, writers and artists declared their independence from Europe. They found in the eastern forests and their inhabitants sources for an American literature and art. Romanticism, in overthrowing the neoclassicism of the Enlightenment, extolled indigenous traditions and folk custom, and glorified the national past. Romantic writers and artists replaced rationalism with sentiment and feeling. The eastern woodlands represented immensity and wildness on such a scale as to dwarf anything European. Part of the wildness of the forest came from its very sublimity, the nature of its inhabitants, and the terrors of warfare between Native and Euroamericans. Ambushes, torture, escape, ritual cannibalism, and reprisal aroused emotions of the most romantic kind. The noble and the ignoble savages made ideal subjects for American high culture.[14]

With the demise of the noble/ignoble "savage" as a physical enemy to the Euroamerican, however, the profound mythological need to recreate the image of the powerful yet ultimately vanquished foe surfaced. To enable and sustain this allegoric image, the power of the conquered Native American would need to be romantically presented in direct proportion to the strength of the Euroamerican pioneers, allowing future generations to fully comprehend how their stalwart forebears subdued and conquered Indians and "won the West"; the more powerful the defeated enemy, the greater the victory of the conqueror. Cody's western melodramas, inspired both by his actual historical experiences and the romantic literature of the era, perfectly captured this extremely subtle yet equally important dynamic between Native and Euroamericans and contributed another fundamental ingredient of the Wild West. In order to create drama, a play required "dynamic tension." Since time immemorial, the everlasting struggle between "good and evil" has been the theatrical device that playwrights use to create this dramatic tension. Consequently, the Indian's role in the Wild West was transforming metaphorically and becoming the symbolic "bad guys" as Cody led the heroic Euroamerican's "good guy" forces to hard-won, melodramatic victory. The "Cowboys and Indians" genre was being born in Cody's Wild West at the precise moment the actual warrior culture of the Great Plains was fading.

The enduring popularity of James Fenimore Cooper's classic, *The Last of the Mohicans*, originally published in 1826, clearly reveals the Euroamerican proclivity for romantically viewing the Native American as "vanishing." Tragically, American Indians fit perfectly into the Euroamerican religious disposition to destroy what is charismatically and exotically attractive—and misunderstood—only later to romanticize and venerate it when it is gone. One needs only to call to mind the story of Christ to verify the argument on many different levels. Nevertheless, Sitting Bull's surrender at Fort Buford announced to the world that western civilization would now totally dominate North America and assimilate the Native American into its mainstream culture. In a very real sense, this was part of a Euroamerican "prophecy"; from the beginning of contact between the two cultures the Euroamerican had perceived the Native American's religion, culture, and population as noble, yet inferior, and disappearing under the overwhelming forces of western civilization. Indeed, the nineteenth-century Euroamerican nicknamed the Native American "Lo"—as in "Lo, the poor Indian"—sarcastically implying pathos concerning what they perceived to be his inevitable fate. All of these perceptions, nourished by generations of Europeans and Euroamericans, came rushing together with Sitting Bull's surrender in 1882. It is no coincidence that the horse visions of Cody and Salsbury simultaneously united that same year. Mythological forces—subliminal and conscious—brought the two men together in order for Cody to be able to present the "vanishing" West to the world at the very moment it was passing. The moment had arrived for the birth of the Wild West.

Cody knew that wherever romantic American literature had been successful he could follow. Consequently, the first action Cody and Salsbury decided upon as a team was to explore the concept in Europe. Salsbury's subsequent report of needing great finances to produce the show only made the desire to do it more immediate and urgent. Neither Cody nor Salsbury could produce the show. Cody had nothing to use as collateral, and Salsbury, though a major entertainment attraction himself, was in a similar financial situation. They had reached an impasse.

Then, suddenly in North Platte, in June of 1882, just as the financial dilemma seemed insurmountable, the fates presented Cody with an opportunity to experiment with the grand idea. Cody's fellow citizens in North Platte decided to celebrate the Fourth of July with what they dubbed an "Old Glory Blow-Out" and asked Buffalo Bill to take charge of the production.[15]

Having ridden the old Deadwood Stage in 1876, Cody was impressed with the history of the old coach. Later, Cody discovered an old stage that had been abandoned for three months by the side of the trail after an Indian attack. In a moment of brilliant insight, Cody, aware that everyone in the west knew the history of the Deadwood Stage and would pay to see it, bought it and had it restored. Drawn by six horses, the elegant old coach was capable of seating twenty-one people comfortably even though its history from beginning to end was one of violence. Its first driver was filled with buckshot during a robbery, initiating many such killings and brutal raids at the hands of outlaws or Indians. Traveling between Cheyenne and Deadwood, the old Concord Coach had been robbed by bandits, attacked by Indians, and violently assaulted continually throughout its existence. During one of these famous robberies the driver was shot and killed and a woman named Martha Jane Canary, who was better known as "Calamity Jane," grabbed the reins and drove the old stage into Deadwood.

Using the restored old Concord Coach as a centerpiece of the performance, Cody hired Indians and local cowboys and rounded up a small buffalo herd. Cody was also aware that people were fascinated with expert marksmanship. An expert marksman himself, Cody had also learned to build a show around a cast of charismatic performers; he hired a local sharpshooter, a dentist named W. F. Carver, who was anxious to get into show business. Carver was to have a dramatic influence on the structure of the Wild West. The dentist, who claimed to be part Indian and billed himself as "the evil spirit of the plains," was a phenomenal marksman capable of shooting nickels tossed in the air. Later, of course, Cody improvised upon Carver's idea of shooting nickels, adding the dramatic dimension of shooting glass balls thrown into the air as he raced by on horseback at full speed. Cody directed horse races, rope tricks, sharpshooting matches, and a holdup of the Deadwood Stage, and also presented the various skills of the cowboy in what was later to evolve as the rodeo; the "Old Glory Blow-Out" was a huge success. Bolstered by the North Platte success and a $27,000 investment by Dr. Carver, Cody was now ready to produce the Wild West and immediately began pulling all his various associates together to structure the next production. Plans were drawn to include the dramatic riding and horse exchanges of the Pony Express into the show. Inspired by audience reactions, Cody also designed more exhibits of marksmanship and cowboy skills. Once his production was in place, Cody felt it was time to go back to Nate Salsbury and see if the singer wished to be included.

Believing Dr. Carver to be a charlatan, Salsbury was furious that Cody had moved forward with the production without him. The song and dance man was chagrined and refused to have anything to do with the new creation. Undaunted, Cody had no reason or obligation to wait for Salsbury to cool off. For all he knew, Salsbury was just another man with an idea to capitalize on the fame of Buffalo Bill; Carver, on the other hand, had put up hard cash and the two had cosigned a note at an Omaha Bank making them partners. Cody went ahead with plans for his next Wild West production as well as his fall/winter melodrama season.

A clay pigeon shooter, Captain A. H. Bogardous, Major Gordon "Pawnee Bill" Lillie, and Major Frank "The White Chief of the Pawnees" North joined Cody and Arizona John Burke in organizing the Wild West presentation. They decided to call it "The Wild West, Rocky Mountain and Prairie Exhibition" and booked it at the Omaha Fair Grounds May 17, 1883.

The Wild West was assembled at North Platte during the winter, but it was organized in April at Columbus, Nebraska. "Thus it was launched," Cody said,

> on the spot famed from time immemorial as the dead line between the powerful Pawnees south of it and the Sioux to the north, a place fairly entitled to its appellation of the dark and bloody ground. This nursery cradle was in a section well grassed, watered and wooded, a natural commissary depot, and in all respects suitable for the beginning of such a venture.[16]

Having been a major trailhead of the Oregon Trail and the railhead of the Union Pacific Railroad, the selection of Omaha as the location for the premiere of the Wild West was certainly poetic. More importantly, however, Cody's selection of the Columbus birthplace for the Wild West also indicates his very clear understanding of the Plains Indian contribution to the vision. The choice of an ancient battlefield, a "dark and bloody ground," as a nursery for the Wild West overtly reveals the mystic warrior bonds of mortal combat shared and understood by Cody and the Native Americans in the production.

The original Nebraska cowboys employed in Cody's Wild West offer an interesting glimpse into the wholesome image of the gentleman wrangler that lingers even today. They joined the Wild West willingly but insisted that their gentleness be stressed and did not like to be advertised as wild men or desperados. It was said that the first man advertised as the "King of the Cowboys," Buck Taylor, possessed the pleasant disposition of a child. Taylor, who could easily throw a steer, subdue a bucking bronco, or ride like the wind, imprinted and balanced the rough and rowdy image of the cowboy with his inherent sweet and pleasant nature.[17]

Encouraged by the success of the performances in Omaha, Cody crossed the Missouri to Council Bluffs, Iowa before traveling to Springfield, Illinois, and on to New York and Boston. As they had no lighting, the shows were by necessity afternoon events playing in vacant lots and fairgrounds. Complicating matters, many of the cowboys frequented the saloons and could not be found when showtime arrived. Even worse, the problems of transporting such a group overwhelmed the pair.[18]

Cody and Carver had problems from the beginning. The temperamental dentist, jealous of Cody's fame, was constantly maneuvering himself into the spotlight and exploded into violent rages when he failed to get his way or when technical or logistical problems arose. Complicating matters, Cody was drinking excessively. Associates reported, however, that Carver and Cody's drinking habits were similar with the dentist having a nip as often as the scout. The stress and strain of the massive undertaking to which the partners committed was more than either man had foreseen and contributed greatly to their inclination to hit the bottle. By the time the tour reached Manhattan frayed emotions were ready to snap. Salsbury saw the show in Brooklyn and correctly predicted that the partnership between Cody and Carver would not last much longer.

Salsbury was right. The cowboys and Indians, homesick from the start, quarreled constantly among themselves until they become an unruly mob. By the end of the season Cody and the temperamental dentist were barely speaking to each other. Fortunately for Cody, Nate Salsbury and his Troubadours were performing in Chicago when the Wild West appeared there.

Cody arranged a meeting and, informing Salsbury that he could and would not continue without him as a partner, implored the song and dance man to join him. Carver, equally despondent, announced that he was leaving the show, that no amount of money or success could compensate him for the stress of attempting to manage such an unwieldy troupe of cowboys, Indians, and livestock. Cody and Carver dissolved their tattered partnership by flipping a coin for the property. Cody won the toss, but they nevertheless divided the equipment evenly. With Carver out of the picture, Salsbury happily became Cody's partner and took charge of business management.[19]

The union of Nate Salsbury and William F. Cody was the proverbial marriage made in heaven. Salsbury's business skills surpassed even his extraordinary talent in musical comedy. With Nate Salsbury brilliantly managing the business of the Wild West, Cody was finally free to let his creative energies blossom while also devoting his attention to managing the awesome logistics of such a massive and diverse undertaking. The Wild West administrative and creative team had come together and was poised to make history.

Nevertheless, horrible luck plagued them the first year. Weather refused to cooperate and in Hartford Major Frank North fell from his horse and was trampled. It was to be his last performance in the Wild West. The loss of his old friend certainly disheartened Cody, but it was only one of many tragic occurrences hitting the Wild West in 1884.

Because of the weather losses, Salsbury went back to work with his Troubadours in order to raise cash. It was decided that Cody would head South with the show in search of good weather. New Orleans was hosting a "Centennial Exhibition" celebrating the exportation of cotton from its port and Salsbury and Cody thought this would prove to be the fair-weather drawing card they sought. They loaded the Wild West on a riverboat en route to New Orleans and Cody raced ahead to find a venue for the show. Arriving at his hotel in New Orleans, however, Cody learned the riverboat had sunk in the Mississippi River. The Deadwood Stage, the band coach and some horses had been saved; everything else, wagons, cattle, buffalo, ammunition, and arms were at the bottom of the river.

Cody telegraphed Salsbury in Denver with the terrible news. Salsbury was shaken, but strong and true to the show business adage that the "show must go on." He confidently wired Cody with instructions to proceed with the show and he would come up with the money.

Salsbury was able to raise the money and Cody was somehow able to find the animals and equipment to perform. Frank North, still in critical condition from being trampled by horses, arranged for Pawnees to get to New Orleans to help with the production. A week later, on March 14, 1884, Major North died. In spite of Frank North's death and the tragedy of the riverboat sinking, the Wild West did go on. Unfortunately, the rain did also. It rained for forty-four days straight in New Orleans. The same fate that brought the rains, however, brought two bright stars together in the Crescent City. Even though Cody and Salsbury would lose $60,000 in their first year—much of it in New Orleans—one of their most important performers came to them there in Louisiana. Her name was Annie Oakley.

Annie Oakley was born Phoebe Ann Moses to Quaker parents in Ohio in 1860. The family had run a small Pennsylvania inn until a careless guest caused an accidental fire, which burned the establishment to the ground. Suddenly homeless, the Moses family headed to Ohio in search of better times. A few years later, however, Annie's father, Jacob, died in a blizzard, leaving the family of six in even more desperate straits. Annie's mother, Susan, soon remarried; yet, after adding a seventh child to the brood, this husband also died.

To help feed the family, Annie took her late father's old black-powder 16-bore rifle and started hunting small game for extra food. Soon she was feeding the family regularly on squirrels, rabbits and quail. Because of the need to bring home game as economically as possible, Annie learned to make every shot count. As she was also preparing, cooking and eating the game she was shooting, she learned to aim for the head so as to leave the meat of the animal's body unspoiled. Soon Annie became so expert at shooting squirrels in the eye that she starting selling her surplus harvest to a Cincinnati hotel owner named Jack Frost. Frost became curious about the fifteen-year-old girl who was bringing all these perfectly slain squirrels to his hotel kitchen. When Annie came to Cincinnati to visit her older sister, Frost arranged for a meeting in which he proposed a shooting match between Annie and a well-known professional marksman named Frank Butler. Annie agreed and a match was arranged for Thanksgiving Day, 1875.

Butler was taken aback when he discovered his opponent was a diminutive teenage country girl. He was a street-smart Irishman who emigrated to the United States while still a young boy. He had entertained on the streets of Manhattan in a variety of different "acts," even working as a dog trainer for a while. After a failed marriage, Butler had developed his shooting act to tour variety theaters around the country.

The contest between Frank Butler and Annie Oakley was an old-fashioned pigeon-shoot with each contestant shooting twenty-five live birds. The match was a virtual tie throughout the contest, ending with Annie killing the winning bird. Annie won more than the match, however; she won Frank Butler's heart. A year later they were married, a union which lasted until the devoted couple died within twenty days of one another in 1926.

Early on Butler realized that Annie's was the greater talent and essentially managed his wife's career. Soon after their marriage, however, Annie dubbed the act "Butler and Oakley" and the team began touring variety theaters around the country before finally working their way into the Sells Brothers Circus. The Sells Brothers Circus was booked in New Orleans during the same rainy season of 1884 that the Wild West appeared there. As a matter of professional courtesy, Butler and Oakley arranged a social meeting with Cody and the Wild West troupe. During the meeting Butler suggested that he and Annie join the Wild West.

Cody and Salsbury were very short on cash and with Cody in the show, were not in any particular need of shooting talent. So they were naturally reluctant to consider Butler's offer. Butler was persistent, however, and proposed to put his and Annie's act on trial for three days. Finally, Cody and Salsbury decided to give Butler a chance and the pair were invited to join the Wild West in Louisville. Annie went on to shoot before 17,000 people and Cody and Salsbury hired her in fifteen minutes. Annie later said of Cody:

> I traveled with him for seventeen years—there were thousands of men in the outfit during that time. Comanches, cowboys, Cossacks, Arabs, and every kind of person. And the whole time we were one great family loyal to a man. His words were more than most contracts. Personally I never had a contract with the show after I started. It would have been superfluous.[20]

Annie Oakley quickly became one of the Wild West's most popular performers. Aside from being a marvelous attraction with her shooting, Annie served another extremely important role in the production: Many women of the day, true to ostentatious Victorian etiquette, were committed by strict social stigma to feign frailty and pretend to be afraid to come to the Wild West because of all the firearms and shooting. Suffering more from a sense of false social propriety than an actual fear of being injured, women in the audience were quickly put at ease to see Little Annie Oakley race into the arena to open the Wild West with her phenomenal marksmanship. Relaxed to see a young woman so accomplished at marksmanship, the women were able to drop their pretensions and simply enjoy the show.

Annie Oakley had an even more important role in the Wild West than to allow the women audience members to let down their defenses and relax with the performances. Her presence in the show attracted another vitally important member to the team. Out in the Dakotas, with impeccable mystical timing, historical events were taking place which would draw another man's destiny to merge with the Wild West. This man's impact on the internal structure, immediate success, and future of the Wild West exhibition would equal Buffalo Bill's and Nate Salsbury's. He was the most famous Indian in the world.

Upon surrendering to the United States, the Hunkpapa Holy Man and Chief, Sitting Bull, had fully expected the government to kill him as soon as he crossed the border. Ironically, Sitting Bull's increasingly powerful celebrity saved him; in promoting the medicine man as the mastermind of Custer's destruction, the media had simply made Sitting Bull too famous for the U.S. government to kill him. With Sitting Bull's name alongside General Custer's in all the banners, the Battle of Little Big Horn had created headlines all over the world. The United States would have to answer too many legal questions in the international community if it assassinated Sitting Bull.

Surprised at surviving his surrender, Sitting Bull continued in defeat to act as the leader of the Lakota people. The medicine man, in realizing the media had saved him, also became increasingly aware of the power of his celebrity among the whites and immediately began to use his fame as a weapon in political negotiations as he entered this new way of life.

The treatment of Red Cloud and Spotted Tail, in contrast to that of Crazy Horse and Sitting Bull, reveals yet another divisive technique employed by the government to break the spirit of the Lakota. Upon surrendering both Red Cloud and Spotted Tail had been honored as chiefs and given their own agencies. The government even went so far as to build both chiefs two-story, wood-frame houses in which to live out their days on the reservation. When Crazy Horse came in to surrender he was led to believe that he would be given his own agency in the Powder River country. Instead, he was murdered.

Surviving, Sitting Bull expected his own agency which he hoped would allow his people to live with some of their old ways and their integrity intact. The government had different plans for Sitting Bull, however, and he was immediately taken to Fort Randall as a prisoner of war. Here, after surviving over three decades of mortal combat and five strenuous years of famine and political exile, Sitting Bull would enter a struggle of will with the U.S. government that would last until his death.

The government would not allow Sitting Bull to go unpunished for what it perceived as masterminding the Custer calamity. Perhaps even more significant, however, was the fact that as long as Sitting Bull was revered by the Lakota as their chief and leader he remained dangerous. U.S. authorities feared if Sitting Bull was allowed to continue secure in his leadership he would be a major threat to Indian Reconstruction and potentially a leader of violent revolt on the reservation. With this in mind, on May 10, 1883, Sitting Bull was finally sent to his old home in the Grand River territory—Standing Rock—and introduced to the man who would serve as his warden for the remainder of his life.

Indian Agent James McLaughlin was a Canadian who in 1870 emigrated to Minnesota, where he married a Santee Lakota woman. After a brief stint as a blacksmith, he went to work at the Sioux agency at Devil's Lake in Dakota Territory. When his immediate superior died in 1873, McLaughlin assumed full responsibility as Indian Agent and took the perfunctory title "major" with the job. Major McLaughlin's long career in the Federal Indian Bureau (1871–1923) carried him to the very top of his field; at the end of his years of service, only the Commissioner of the Indian Bureau was above McLaughlin. As Chief Inspector of the Indian Bureau, however, more than anyone else, McLaughlin defined the U.S. government's paternalistic approach to the Reconstruction Era on reservations. As most of the "Friends of the Indian" of this era, McLaughlin believed the Indian should be "individualized," or separated from the authority and security of the tribal system and forcefully assimilated into white, Christian, Euroamerican society. McLaughlin felt the greatest service he could perform for the American Indian was to offer him the culture and religion of western civilization. His strict Catholic doctrine created an extremely complex situation as McLaughlin's approach was to vigorously attack the religious fundamentals of the Lakota way of life. With his Lakota wife informing him of the mystical, religious, and ceremonial workings of the infrastructure, McLaughlin struck at the very essence of the culture. McLaughlin was especially obsessed with dismantling the Lakota system of polygamy and insisted on married "couples only" restrictions for receiving government allotments and services. To a culture that had operated under a system of polygamy for untold generations, being forced into the new way of marriage created confusing and disastrous effects in the immediate family and general social structure for the Lakota. Nevertheless, McLaughlin persisted to assault the fundamentals of what he considered "pagan" customs, rituals, ceremonies, and dances. With economic restrictions attacking their stomachs and verbal assaults eroding their belief system, McLaughlin was forcing the Lakota to give up the old ways and replacing them with the fundamentalist Christian church and rudimental farming techniques.

Perhaps the most poetic description of the conflicting dynamics in the relationship between McLaughlin and Sitting Bull is revealed in their initial meeting. Sitting Bull arrived at Standing Rock expecting to be treated with the dignity and respect of his singularly important position within the Lakota tribe. McLaughlin instead defiantly presented the chief with a hoe and showed him to the garden. From that hostile introduction the lines were drawn in the dirt. McLaughlin was determined to absolutely destroy any credibility Sitting Bull had as an individual or a leader of the Lakota and forced the chief to become more obstinate and recalcitrant than ever before.

This intense contest of wills was made even more complex by Sitting Bull's fame confronting McLaughlin's ambitious ego. When important visitors came to visit Standing Rock it was usually to see the famous chief, Sitting Bull, and not the perpetually chagrined Major McLaughlin. Complicating matters, McLaughlin discovered that the medicine man's presence made it difficult to influence the tribe as Lakota headmen deferred any final major decision to Sitting Bull. Consequently, after a few months of failed attempts to break Sitting Bull's spirit and undermine his leadership, McLaughlin jumped at the chance to get Sitting Bull out of his hair for a while when officials in North Dakota requested the chief's presence.

So, with President Grant and dignitaries arriving to celebrate the opening of the Northern Pacific Railroad, Sitting Bull was sent to Bismarck. Colonel Alvaren Allen had offered the highest bid for the privilege of exhibiting the chief. On September 15, 1884, the chief carried a flag at the head of the procession, sold his autographs from the tail of a wagon and made his first appearance in St. Paul as part a scheduled tour of fifteen American cities. Advertising him as the "slayer of General Custer," Allen misled audiences with false translations of Sitting Bull's words of friendship by interpreting the chief's speeches as a sensational account of the Battle of Little Big Horn.[21]

Sitting Bull agreed to be exhibited on Colonel Alvaren's tour because he was promised he would be able to talk to President Grant. The medicine man hoped to visit with the former President and secure his own reservation so that he could properly take care of his people. In getting the chief off the reservation for a brief period of time McLaughlin had been able to make great progress in manipulating some of the lesser Lakota headmen into his plans for reconstruction. More importantly, in St. Paul Sitting Bull had gone to a theater to see Annie Oakley perform her shooting act. Astonished, the medicine man believed Annie's superior marksmanship revealed a person who possessed a supernatural gift and immediately asked permission to go backstage and meet Oakley. Sitting Bull promptly christened Annie *Wantanya Cicilia*, or "Little Sure Shot," and adopted her as his daughter.

Buffalo Bill first requested permission from Major McLaughlin in 1883 for Sitting Bull to join his Wild West. McLaughlin promptly denied the request, explaining that the removal of such an important chief would confuse the Indians in his charge as they were in a delicate stage of transition into the white world. When Buffalo Bill heard about the Alvaren tour, however, he sent John Burke immediately to McLaughlin to renew his request for permission to employ Sitting Bull in the Wild West. When Sitting Bull saw Annie Oakley's picture in the publicity photographs that Burke had with him, the medicine man immediately agreed to join the Wild West. Having experienced success manipulating and dividing the power base of the Lakota without their leader present, McLaughlin had also finally become receptive to Cody's idea.

Cody immediately wired the Secretary of Interior, Lucius Q. C. Lamar, on April 29, 1885, to request Sitting Bull's presence in his Wild West. The telegram informed the Secretary that Major McLaughlin had sanctioned the idea and granted his permission for the chief to leave with the Wild West in the custody of Buffalo Bill and listed endorsements from Generals Sheridan, Miles, Crook and Terry.

Lamar emphatically refused Cody permission to exhibit Sitting Bull, underlining "no" three times on his handwritten denial. Commissioner of Indian Affairs John D.C. Atkins informed Cody that both he and Lamar were strictly opposed to releasing Sitting Bull, whom they considered a war criminal, to travel with the Wild West. Atkins said he and Lamar believed Indians should not be "roving through the country exhibiting themselves and visiting places where they would naturally come in contact with evil associates and degrading immoralities."[22]

Cody realized he would have to go higher up. He gathered further glowing endorsements from General William T. Sherman and Colonel

Eugene A. Carr and concluded with his own personal statement detailing his life-long relationship with Plains Indians in which he promised the best treatment of Sitting Bull. Secretary Lamar suddenly reversed himself and agreed to let Sitting Bull become part of the Wild West. L. G. Moses writes:

> Sitting Bull and the Hunkpapa Sioux joined the show in Buffalo, New York, on June 12. The 1885 season confirmed the success of Cody's Wild West both financially and artistically. Cody and company toured more than forty cities in the United States and Canada. A part of the show's success is explained by the presence of Sitting Bull.[23]

The phenomenal combination of Buffalo Bill and Sitting Bull was the explosive box office power that launched the Wild West into history. This is not to imply that the Wild West was not destined for greatness before Sitting Bull joined the effort; indeed, Cody and Salsbury's combined energies were themselves historically and artistically unique; with magnetic personalities like Buffalo Bill and Annie Oakley, it was inevitable that the Wild West would bring in unprecedented crowds and handsome profits. Their visions combined to create the basic structure of the Wild West that was to flourish for thirty years and leave an indelible imprint on humanity. In order to create that dramatic structure, however, they needed the dynamic adversary, the majestic force through which its natural fierce resistance would serve to define the mythic character of the newly dominant culture of the immigrant in North America. In Sitting Bull, Cody and Salsbury not only had the manifestation of the magnificent adversary, they had a box office attraction to equal Buffalo Bill himself.

Because of the old military scouting connections of both Major Frank North and Major Gordon Lillie with the Pawnee, members of that tribe were the Indians employed by the Wild West during its first two years. In hiring Lakota leader Sitting Bull and his family, however, Cody risked creating major internal problems within the Indian camps of the troupe; the Lakota and the Pawnee were ancient mortal enemies. Cody's solution to the dilemma communicates Sitting Bull's powerful influence on the Wild West, while also revealing the scout's understanding of the nature of Plains Indians: Hiring Sitting Bull and his Lakota family to perform in the Wild West defined Cody's policy that the only Indians hired were Lakota or their close allies, the Cheyenne. Acutely aware of the ancient traditional

bloody rivalries between various Plains Indian tribes such as the Pawnee
and Lakota and, to avoid constant bickering, Cody made the wise decision
to hire from only one tribe. Aside from the loss of Frank North and his
connection with Pawnee, Cody's decision was also based on box office potential; because of their fierce resistance to the Euroamerican invasion,
particularly at Little Big Horn, the Sioux were the most internationally famous warriors of the Indian tribes and the natural choice to create the
Wild West image of the courageous opposition of the Euroamerican advancing across the continent. Sitting Bull's presence insured the fact that
Lakotas would be the exclusive tribe working in Cody's Wild West during
its critical infancy.

Once the Wild West policy shifted to hiring Lakotas exclusively, Cody's
sign-up trips to Rushville, Nebraska became major events. Five or six hundred Lakotas—mostly Oglala's from Pine Ridge—would travel to
Rushville in order to present themselves to Cody in their finest costumes.
Cody, in a further attempt to create harmonious situations, would hire
Lakota families whenever possible. Ever the leader of the Sioux, facing the
extermination of his people, Sitting Bull had taken one of his only options;
he had led the Lakota into the theater, into the ironic sanctuary of Buffalo
Bill's Wild West.

"When performing," L. G. Moses writes of Sitting Bull,

> he wore his buckskin, paint, and feathers. In the parade of perform-
> ers at the opening of the show, he wore a red tunic. When not in the
> arena, his usual dress included a plush brocade waistcoat, black flow-
> ered pants, a scarlet tie, a printed shirt with its tails hanging down out-
> side his trousers, and beaded, rubber-soled moccasins. He adorned
> himself with jewelry and sometimes wore a crucifix, mostly because
> he liked its design. Introduced to the audiences simply as Sitting Bull,
> the famous Hunkpapa chief, he endured the taunts and boos of the
> crowd who associated him with Custer's death at the Little Bighorn.
> From all reports, he bore the insults impassively—or with greater
> dignity than those who screamed their insults. He made considerable
> money selling his photographs, perhaps gaining some measure of re-
> venge upon the unfriendly crowds.[24]

Cody's decision to present himself, Sitting Bull, and each minute aspect
of the Wild West as historical legend rather than sideshow created a crucial rapport between performers and audience and reveals a brilliant solu-

tion to a complex and potentially violent situation. The fact that Sitting Bull—generally recognized falsely as the man who killed Custer—toured over forty cities in the United States and Canada with the Wild West without a violent incident clearly communicates the subliminal harmony present between performers and audience. The official headline publicity around Sitting Bull and Buffalo Bill was "Foes in '76–Friends in '85." Promoting Sitting Bull in this fashion, Cody wisely chose to make audiences aware through Sitting Bull's publicity that the two had resolved their differences and were now friends. In doing so, he quietly, yet emphatically, empowered the medicine man before the crowds and allowed audiences to vent their misguided hostilities in a "theatrical" format.

The "sanctioned" booing and hissing in the arena released audience hostility, preventing the ever-present possibility of actual violence. Indeed, the entire Wild West performance strongly implied to audiences a major healing had taken place "backstage." Audiences understood that the act of recreating violent events from the recent past with actual participants demanded profound trust and understanding of the performers. This subliminal awareness of healing was as important to the success of the Wild West as was the spectacle of the panoramic passing of an era.

Sitting Bull was willing to participate in the Wild West and endure such audience hostility impassively because he was a chief of the Lakota. As a chief he bravely faced such humiliation because he hoped to meet with the President of the United States in order to plead his people's case. He also needed excursions into the white man's world to learn how to better help his people. He particularly enjoyed walking the streets of American cities in the night when everyone was asleep. Sell and Weybright inform us:

> Canadian newspapers filled pages with stories of Sitting Bull; he achieved more space than Buffalo Bill, who finally made the headlines when he told the press at Toronto, 'In nine cases out of ten when there is trouble between white men and Indians, it will be found that the white man is responsible. Indians expect a man to keep his word. They can't understand how a man can lie. Most of them would as soon cut off a leg as tell a lie.[25]

Cody did not need to make such remarks to sell tickets. On the contrary; such remarks were not likely to endear him to the conservative, expansionist power brokers of either Canada or the United States. The only purpose Cody could have had in saying such things was spiritual; he had become the only white man in the world with the power and prestige to properly and eloquently speak out on behalf of the Plains Indian. Consider the power of Buffalo Bill's remarks to Indian men like Sitting Bull, and other leaders who had been lied to repeatedly while they struggled to finally hold to nothing but the truth in the face of the total destruction of everything they cherished. Cody told the Canadian newspapers:

> The defeat of Custer was not a massacre. The Indians were being pursued by skilled fighters with orders to kill. For centuries they had been hounded from the Atlantic to the Pacific and back again. They had their wives and little ones to protect and they were fighting for their existence. With the end of Custer they considered that their greatest enemy had passed away. Sitting Bull was not the leader of the Sioux in that battle. He was a medicine man who played on their superstitions—their politician, their diplomat—who controlled their emotions through the power of his argument and the vehemence of his speech.[26]

These were unusually strong words from any white man in 1885. Even today Lakotas have to emphasize the fact that they were defending themselves, their wives and children at Little Big Horn. Coming from Buffalo Bill in 1885, however, these words were like manna to the compassion-starved Lakota. Finally, an important white man had appeared to inform the world of their desperate situation. It is no wonder that Sitting Bull felt he had found a friend in *Pahaska*. In words and actions, Buffalo Bill presented Sitting Bull and the Lakota before the American public with all the dignity to which they were entitled. Critically important, however, was the fact that the Wild West provided them with a safe respite from the chaotic forces of destruction suffocating them on the reservation. It is not clear whether or not Sitting Bull enjoyed being exhibited. Naturally gregarious, however, the chief enjoyed meeting new people and was given to pouting when not noticed. He quickly learned how to sign his name in order to sell his autograph on photographs. He also learned that people wanted to purchase his personal possessions and kept a stash of such things as pipe bags.[27]

Stanley Vestal informs us what the chief did with his money:

> Sitting Bull made money, most of which, as Annie Oakley bears witness, "went into the pockets of small, ragged boys. Nor could he understand how so much wealth could go brushing by, unmindful of

the poor." He formed the opinion that the white man would not do much for Indians when they let their own flesh and blood go hungry. Said he, "The white man knows how to make everything, but he does not know how to distribute it."[28]

At the end of the 1885 summer season, the Wild West grossed over a million dollars and showed a profit of $100,000 and by some estimates played to over one million people. As the season drew to a close, Buffalo Bill gave Sitting Bull a size 8 Stetson hat and a white trick horse as a token of appreciation for joining the Wild West. Sitting Bull's trick horse attracted much attention among the Sioux at Standing Rock. At the sound of gunfire the horse would sit down and then raise one hoof. The Chief only wore the hat on special occasions and became angry if anyone else put it on. Of the hat Sitting Bull said: "My friend Long Hair gave me this hat. I value it very highly, for the hand that placed it upon my head had a friendly feeling for me."[29]

In the fall, Cody, successfully making the transition from the theatrical matinee idol to outdoor impresario, returned to the stage and performed his last season as a melodrama star. Sitting Bull's presence in the Wild West obviously contributed greatly to its success and finally presented Cody with the opportunity to leave melodrama and devote his full attention to the recreation of historical events. In early April of 1886, Cody sent John Burke to Standing Rock to visit Sitting Bull and request McLaughlin's permission for the chief to return to the Wild West for a second season tour. McLaughlin, however, was stubbornly opposed to Sitting Bull returning to the Wild West. The agent, maintaining the chief had been corrupted from his experiences the previous season, denied Sitting Bull permission to leave Standing Rock. L. G. Moses informs us:

> The agent complained to Burke, that Sitting Bull had spent the money he earned with Buffalo Bill in trying to secure his position in the tribe. McLaughlin, ever hostile to Sitting Bull, described scenes of profligacy. He wrote that Sitting Bull "is such a consummate liar and too vain and obstinate to be benefited by what he sees." He made no "good use of the money he thus earns, but on the contrary spends it extravagantly among the Indians in trying to perpetuate baneful influences which the ignorant and non-progressive element are too ready to listen to and follow." He spent his money in feasting the Indians. Of the money he had brought back to the reservation the previous fall, not a dollar remained. "I had a great deal of trouble

with him," the agent explained, "and through him with other Indians caused by his own bad behavior and arrogance." A less-hostile observer might have understood that Sitting Bull's gift-giving was nothing more than the altruism expected of a Lakota leader by his people.[30]

Cody realized dealing with the churlish McLaughlin was futile and gave up his effort to bring Sitting Bull back to the Wild West. Instead, he instructed Burke to travel on to Pine Ridge, where the agent signed twenty-nine Oglala men to compose the Indian company for the 1886 summer season.

Acquiescing to McLaughlin was probably the wisest tactic Cody could have taken. Moreover, Sitting Bull himself realized his people needed him more at Standing Rock than in the Wild West. The government had renewed efforts to take even more land from the Lakota and Sitting Bull was completely aware that he alone could lead the people through the troubled times ahead. Besides, like many of the other Lakota performers in the Wild West visiting the eastern urban centers, Sitting Bull was suffering from overstimulation and culture shock. Overwhelmed with the Euroamerican's hurried and noisy lifestyle as well as the multitude of industrial wonders around them, Lakotas often blindfolded themselves and plugged their ears in order to calm themselves through sensory deprivation in the midst of the pandemonium of western civilization. Using such methods to quiet the overstimulation and confusion about them, the Lakota were able to process the rapid change they were enduring as they departed their horse and buffalo culture to enter the white man's industrial age.

Aside from culture shock, however, Sitting Bull had more important reasons for not returning to the Wild West. Failing to win an audience with the President, Sitting Bull had not accomplished his primary goal in joining the Wild West. His secondary goal of visiting the world of the *waschicu*, however, was fully realized. Furthermore, he could accomplish no more with a second trip, especially since he was now needed more at home to resist the next wave of the Euroamerican invasion into his homeland.

Financially solvent after the successful 1885 season, Salsbury and Cody now spared no expense in creating the Wild West according to their vision. By the spring of 1886, as Cody completed his last season on the melodrama stage, the Wild West had its own railroad train. Each of the cars was painted white, with "Buffalo Bill's Wild West" colorfully painted in gold on the side. When the 1886 season opened in St. Louis, the company mushroomed to 240 people organized military-style into crews working under the strict discipline of a single boss. The Wild West now had a sophisticated lighting system, seats, a canvas canopy and a canvas mural depicting the majestic mountain ranges of Wyoming. "Custer's Massacre," a scene depicting the famous battle, was added as a feature of the Wild West with Buffalo Bill arriving just moments after the death of the famous general as the words *Too Late* appeared on a screen.

From St. Louis, the Wild West traveled to Terre Haute, Indiana; Dayton, Ohio; and Wheeling, West Virginia, before arriving triumphantly in Washington. Indeed, the entire 1886 season was a triumph for the Wild West. By the time the show reached New York, its success was firmly established. After a magnificent parade through the streets of New York on June 27, the Wild West settled in at Erastina, a summer resort owned by Erastus Wiman on Staten Island. It ran to capacity crowds there all summer. Over a million people saw the Wild West that summer in New York alone. There, General William Tecumseh Sherman, Elizabeth Custer, Thomas Edison, Mark Twain, and P.T. Barnum were among the many notable Americans who attended and adored the Wild West. The mighty movers and shakers of the day visited the Wild West, but Buffalo Bill also made certain that his Wild West would reach a specific segment of the general public he sought for an audience. Perhaps remembering his own fatherless youth and the tender age at which he went to work, perhaps revealing the influence of Sitting Bull and the Lakota "giveaway" tradition on his life, Cody took out ads in all the New York newspapers announcing that he would give a free ticket to the Wild West to any bootblack or newsboy who came to the ferry going over to Staten Island for the show. Fifteen hundred boys arrived on the arranged date and were greeted with free sack lunches and tickets to the Wild West. That afternoon the Wild West was performed exclusively for these children. After the performance Cody addressed the boys, admonishing them to be good and learn all they could even if they had to work and go to night school. Cody concluded by requesting that if their paths ever cross again that, whatever the circumstance, they re-introduce themselves and tell him they had been there to see the Wild West at Staten Island that afternoon and inform him what they had done with their lives.

Twain, who so eloquently satirized the American society of Buffalo Bill's era, particularly from the perspective of precocious boys, offers us a very clear image of the impact of Cody and Salsbury's creation when he was moved to comment that the Wild West brought back vividly the breezy, wild life of the Plains and Rocky Mountains. It is wholly free from sham and insincerity and the effects it produced upon me by its spectacles were identical with those wrought upon me a long time ago on the frontier. Your pony expressman was as tremendous an interest to me as he was twenty-three years ago when he use to come whizzing by from over the desert with his war news; and your bucking horses were even painfully real to me as I rode one of those outrages for nearly a quarter of a minute. It is often said on the other side of the water that none of the exhibitions which we send to England are purely and distinctly American. If you take the Wild West Show over there you can remove that reproach.[31]

Twain's glowing critique of the Wild West ended with the awareness that it was inevitable that the show would travel to England. Perhaps the most prophetic of the important visitors to Staten Island to comment on the future of the Wild West, however, was the old impresario P. T. Barnum. He simply predicted, "When Salsbury takes this show to Europe it will astonish the Old World."[32]

Chapter Fifteen

GRANDMOTHER
ENGLAND

"Civilization itself consents to march in the train of Buffalo Bill."

The London Times, Summer, 1887 (qtd. in *Buffalo Bill and
the Wild West*, Henry Sell and Victor Weybright)

THE Wild West enjoyed such unprecedented success at Erastina during the summer of 1886 that Cody and Salsbury quickly negotiated with circus producer Adam Forepaugh to help them hold over with a winter exhibition at Madison Square Garden. With nearly 200,000 people attending during one week in July alone, public response to the Wild West throughout the summer indicated that Manhattan would enthusiastically support a winter exhibition. Neither Salsbury nor Cody, however, had the money to risk producing the winter run at Madison Square Garden by themselves. Forepaugh, who made his fortune securing exotic animals for circus companies and foreclosing when they failed to pay, was sought out as a partner. Consequently, the Wild West run at Madison Square Garden was produced with Forepaugh as the sole lessee of the famous venue and Cody and Salsbury as owners and managers of the exhibition.

Once negotiations between Forepaugh, Salsbury and Cody were complete the Wild West would have to be restructured in order to make the transition from an outdoor arena exhibition to an indoor arena spectacle. As this process was begun it was also decided to redesign the Wild West to employ the most modern theatrical technology available. Avant-garde artistic engineers were hired, while state-of-the-art devices such as wind machines and double-moving stages were creatively incorporated into the production to dramatically expand the scope and elevate the realism of the Wild West experience. Steele Mackaye was employed as a dramatist and stage manager and he adroitly restaged the Wild West, transforming it into an indoor arena presentation entitled the *Drama of Civilization*. Wild West audiences in New York would be the first to witness such cutting-edge special effects as a cyclone whirling through Madison Square Garden's arena. With such technological spectacles enhancing the inherent historical pageantry and majesty of the Wild West, in just three years Cody and Salsbury had positioned their dreams to take the center ring in global entertainment.

Buffalo Bill's Wild West opened to phenomenal success on November 24, 1886, at Madison Square Garden. The front page headline of the *New York Herald* on Thanksgiving Day exclaimed: "The Greatest Triumph Ever Known in the History of the City"[1] with subheadlines mentioning thousands being turned away as the Wild West played to over-flowing crowds. By February, 1887, matching the million-plus summer attendance at Erastina, a million people had seen the show in Madison Square Garden. Plans were being structured to take the show to England.

Even as the Wild West was basking in such glorious success, however, forces were gathering which would oppose Cody throughout his career producing western exhibitions. On January 10, 1887, Brooklyn Republican Congressman Darwin Rush James offered a resolution to the House of Representatives which demanded that the Secretary of Interior explain why "wild Indians" had been permitted to leave the reservation to tramp around the country with a traveling circus. Denouncing the Wild West as "the Drama of Savagery,"[2] James insisted that the government explain fully its involvement in releasing Indians, which he viewed as either wards of the state or as prisoners of war, to appear in a circus.

By 1886, the Indian Rights Organization had successfully lobbied the Indian Bureau to regulate Indian employment in exhibitions. A surety bond of $10,000–$20,000 was required to enter into negotiations to employ Indian performers. Contracts were negotiated by the Indian Bureau and required employers to provide food, clothing, shelter, and medical care. Moreover, producers were required to provide show Indians with interpreters and chaplains. Any violation of the contract resulted in forfeiting the surety bond.

Congressman James was clearly motivated more by the need to control Indians than out of any compassionate concern for their well-being. Indeed, most lawmakers were well aware that James's resolution was politically motivated, and he would have never complained if the Wild West had selected his home district of Brooklyn over Staten Island or Manhattan for its location. Many congressmen sarcastically dismissed their colleague's resolution and rushed to Buffalo Bill's defense with glowing testimonials praising the Wild West as grand, educational American entertainment.

Nevertheless, James's actions boldly thrust the issue of the government's role with "show business" Indians into the political arena and drew lines in the sand between Buffalo Bill's Wild West and the influential Indian Rights Organization. Armed resistance by Indians had essentially ended with Sitting Bull's surrender; most Indians had been confined to reservations and subjected to various "Friends of the Indian" missionary efforts to "humanely," yet forcefully, assimilate them into Euroamerican society. This "Reconstruction" effort was in full evangelic fervor on reservations with either the U.S. military or Christian/humanitarian organizations possessing absolute control over the fate of American Indians.

Reconstruction efforts by missionary and government agents on reservations divided Indians into two distinct categories: those who submitted to assimilation were considered "progressive," while those who resisted were considered "blanket" Indians. Blanket Indians defiantly clung—overtly and covertly—to traditional, tribal, "savage," or "pagan" ways even as their basic human rights were systematically ignored and abused with reconstruction, where "progressive" Indians readily surrendered to Christianity, the English language, the Bible, short hair, cloth and wool clothing, leather shoes, and the hoe. Buffalo Bill's exhibition of "wild," "savage" Indians diametrically opposed the "friends'" assimilation policies and was a blatant affront to the representation of the reconstructed "progressive" American Indian's humanitarians wished to parade before the American public. Simply, the "friends" wished to project the chimerical image of the progressive Native American, magically transformed by them and fully assimilated into Christian society in one generation.

To the "friends," Buffalo Bill's Wild West was exactly as Representative James described it—"the drama of savagery." At best, "Victorian" Euroamericans viewed professional show business people as having loose morals, while the most pompous considered them gypsy vagabonds, spiritually corrupt and socially dangerous. Of utmost concern, however, was the reality that near-naked, painted "savages," riding madly, whooping, screaming, pursuing, and shooting at terrified white passengers on the Deadwood Stage represented the antithesis of the Christian goals of the Indians' "friends." The term "savage," used to maximum effectiveness as martial propaganda during the years of the Indian Wars, became an increasingly more derogatory weapon in the reconstructionist's arsenal as Lakota people were confined on reservations. Indeed, in his Annual Report to the Commission of Indian Affairs on October 24, 1881, Commissioner Hiram Price, a prominent Methodist layman, commented, "The greatest kindness the government can bestow upon the Indian is to teach him to labor for his own support. Savage and civilized life," the Commissioner continued, "cannot live and prosper on the same ground. One of the two must die."[3] Price was not necessarily calling for an American Indian genocide; his patronizing scheme was to kill the "savage" Indian and replace him with a Christian Indian. In spite of the noble intention, Price's thinly veiled ultimate objective was to destroy the religion and culture of the Plains Indian.

Luther Standing Bear offers this concise explanation of the negative cultural effects of being referred to as a "savage":

> After subjugation, after dispossession, there was cast the last abuse upon the people who so entirely resented their wrongs and punishments, and that was the stamping and the labeling of them as savages. To make this label stick has been the task of the white race and the greatest salve that it has been able to apply to its sore and troubled conscience now hardened through the habitual practice of injustice.[4]

Standing Bear's perceptive analysis of the "friends'" deadly game of imperialistic semantics draws the horror of 1880s American "cultural reconstruction" into sickening perspective. From this lowest point in Lakota history, however, a completely new perspective of the historical importance of William F. Cody and his Wild West begins to emerge.

Facing extinction, yet faithfully following their great chief Sitting Bull's lead, Lakota people had learned they could safely surrender to playing the role of "savage" in the Wild West in order to escape the subjugation and manipulation of the agents and missionaries on the reservation. Furthermore, aside from merely surviving, this brilliant, nonviolent, last-resort tactic allowed Lakota leaders to have the precious time and protection to council in secret to simply gather their thoughts and plans of action. From this blessed sanctuary, Lakota leaders would be able to visit and experience Euroamerican society on their own terms, under the trusted guidance and faithful protection of their friend Buffalo Bill. Furthermore, the Wild West also permitted all segments of Euroamerican society to experience some of the most regal and majestic people of the Lakota culture, resplendent in their finery, performing their most exciting equestrian skills. The inherent strength and depth of character of the Lakota was most positively revealed as Cody insisted on Plains Indians and their culture at all times being exhibited in the most dignified light. This is not to say that Indians did not most effectively present the requisite "wild" and powerful enemy of the Euroamerican in Cody's exhibition. This role they absolutely relished. With their freedom, horses and guns taken from them, Buffalo Bill's Wild West was the last place on earth for the Lakota to be able to resurrect and enjoy any vestige of their former way of life. The inherent common origins of theatrical ceremony and religious ritual were a spiritual reality Plains Indians understood instinctively. In Cody's exhibition, Lakotas could once again ceremoniously paint themselves for battle and ride and shoot with wild abandonment and glee. Even if the bullets were blanks and the chase was feigned, the Wild West offered the last opportunity to revisit the old way if only for a few hours a day. Offstage, the constant movement of the Wild West from town to town, the breaking, moving and making of Cody's large camp, was the closest they would ever be again to their former way of life and the old Lakota nomadic tradition. Buffalo Bill simply offered those Lakotas of the horse and buffalo culture of the nineteenth century a final chance to be themselves.

Of equal political importance, the American public responded positively to such an honest presentation of Native Americans. Indeed, much of the magnetic appeal of Buffalo Bill's Wild West to Euroamerican society was the fact that it offered a "safe" environment to experience the "vanishing" Native American culture. With Euroamerican fears and hostilities toward Indians being given a secure, "theatrical" outlet for release in the Wild West, Cody's historical exhibition of Native American people concurrently created a vehicle which allowed audiences to freely express their intrinsic attraction to the indigenous culture of North America.

Consequently, Cody's Wild West was increasingly becoming a double-edged sword for the "friends": the greater the success of the "savage" Indians in Cody's Wild West, the more difficult the "friends'" problem of presenting their success with the "progressive" Indian became. Complicating matters, as the show business Indian's success was literally in the spotlight and the "progressive" Indian's success was more subtle, and, by nature more difficult to highlight and emphasize, the "friends" were also more than a little jealous of the Wild West's ability to showcase "savage" Indians. This conundrum was made even more complex by the fact that most Indian agents and missionaries, following James McLaughlin's lead with Sitting Bull, discovered their efforts were dramatically more successful when Lakota social, military, political, and religious leaders—the incorrigibles—were physically removed from their positions of leadership on the reservation. With this in mind, agents and missionaries stumbled upon a unique solution to their problem: When politically convenient, they would encourage the unmanageable Lakota leaders to join the Wild West; those that wished to remain uncooperative could act like wild "savages" in Cody's circus. Meanwhile, employing their upper-level political influence in Washington, the "friends" would continue to harass Cody, making it legally difficult to hire Indians to be in his Wild West. This superficially contradictory yet ultimately pragmatic plan would allow the "friends" to "concede" to Cody's political influence in order to get the Indians they wished out of the way, while using their own considerable political influence to keep most confined in reconstructive isolation and oppression on the reservation.

A tragic irony in American history, these "friends" organizations inherited their roles through decades of morally defending Native Americans from the United States government's superior military capabilities. In 1787, Congress had combined the office of Territorial Governor with that of Superintendent of Indian Affairs and in 1834 created the Department of Indian Affairs in order to employ agents and commissioners to deal with the Indian trade and to cope with illegal whiskey trafficking. Until 1849 all the various Indian agencies were located within the War Department, with the St. Louis superintendent overseeing virtually all the western tribes. In 1849, however, all responsibility for Indian Affairs was transferred to the Department of Interior. Consequently, with the Emancipation Proclamation and the simultaneous Indian Wars era on the Great Plains, the various "friends" organizations rose from humble Quaker beginnings to great ecumenical political influence in Washington in the 1860s, while also becoming the genesis of the powerful Bureau of Indian Affairs developing within the Department of Interior. Many of the leaders of the various "friends" movements had survived the horrific death and destruction of the Civil War and emerged from the chaos sincerely committed to improving America through Christian and humanitarian service. By 1882, inspired by the grassroots leadership of a women's church movement and Helen Hunt Jackson's 1881 expose of corruption in Indian affairs, *A Century of Dishonor*, the Indian Rights Organization was organized in Philadelphia by Herbert Walsh and Massachusetts Senator Henry L. Dawes. Senator Dawes had served on an 1882 Congressional Commission to negotiate with the Lakota for the relinquishment of eleven million acres of land. In 1883, however, a second round of negotiations was required when it was learned that the commissioners, ignoring the 1868 Laramie Treaty requirement of three-fourths of the Lakota men, had used intimidation to deceive the Sioux and secure the land deal. Dawes headed the committee which investigated allegations that similar underhanded tactics were used in the second round of negotiations.[5]

The IRO's initial noble mission was to assist the Indian through lobbying Congress for protective legislation. Many of the various leaders of the IRO had also successfully worked with President Grant's administration to discover and expose improper fraudulent distribution of government annuities on reservations. By 1883, when Board of Indian Commissioners member Albert K. Smiley invited all the various "Friends of the Indians" organizations to his Lake Mohonk Lodge in upstate New York, the political power of the group was beginning to take shape. Each October the well-intentioned but condescending "friends" would gather in what became known as the "Lake Mohonk Conference of the Friends of the Indian." With no differentiation between the diverse religious and cultural spectrum of Native America, the reformers increasingly influenced senators and congressmen and the structuring of the government's official Indian Policy. At the annual Lake Mohonk Conferences, the friends shaped their agenda to address the "Indian Problem" and set out to apply political pressure in Washington through media and public opinion to pass legislation.[6]

Though superficially motivated by the highest of Christian ideals, it is most important here to emphasize that conscious cultural, religious and racial manipulation is the one trait each of these various humanitarian "friends" organizations held in common. The Indian Rights Organization's three ultimate goals eloquently reveal its true motivation and mission: The IRO sought first to completely destroy all tribal bonding and social patterning. In order to accomplish this end, all familial structure and tradition, all religious ceremony, all language—the entire culture of the Indian—had to be obliterated before the Native American could be fully assimilated into Euroamerican society. The reward for making this transformation would be a 160-acre homestead on which they would be taught to farm; secondly, the IRO sought to force the Indian to assimilate into white society, thereby becoming a United States citizen and forfeiting his status as a sovereign power; as assimilated citizens Indians would become subject to the same laws as every other American; and, thirdly, the IRO sought to create a government-assisted program to educate Indians, particularly children, with or without their parents' permission.

Relations between Native and Euroamerican people remain even today tragically infected with this condescending and insidious racial and cultural manipulation. Bitterness toward such self-righteous religious orchestration and social experimentation eloquently voiced itself in 1933 in Lakota philosopher Luther Standing Bear's civilized and logical remarks:

> All sorts of feeble excuses are heard for the continued subjection of the Indian. One of the most common is that he is not yet ready to accept the society of the white man—that he is not yet ready to mingle as a social entity.
>
> This, I maintain, is beside the question. The matter is not one of making-over the external Indian into the likeness of the white race—a process detrimental to both races. Who can say that the white man's way is better for the Indian? Where resides the human judgment with the competence to weigh and value Indian ideals and spiritual concepts; or substitute them for other values?
>
> Then, has the white man's social order been so harmonious and ideal as to merit the respect of the Indian, and for that matter the thinking of the white race? Is it wise to urge upon the Indian a foreign social form? Let none but the Indian answer!
>
> Rather, let the white brother face about and cast his mental eye upon a new angle of vision. Let him look upon the Indian world as a human world; then let him see to it that human rights be accorded to the Indians. And this for the purpose of retaining for his own order of society a measure of humanity.[7]

In 1886, forty-seven years before his friend Standing Bear's visionary remarks concerning human rights, Buffalo Bill was the only white man in the world with the unique, personal compassion and understanding of Plains Indians, and the powerful political connections in Washington to defy the equally powerful influence of the Indian Rights Organization's effort to ignore and abuse the fundamental rights of an entire race of people. Essentially the wedding of government and religion into a "political church," the IRO stood with a pious saber drawn to fulfill western civilization's "supremacist" prophecy by self-righteously executing the coup de grace of the Plains Indian.

At this precise and deadly moment, however, all of Will Cody's personal history with the Lakota came surging forward into sharp perspective. Defending himself against Representative James in an interview in the New York newspaper, *The World,* Cody made his feelings on the matter crystal

clear, and, in doing so, reveals the first glimpse of his true visionary heroism concerning human rights:

> I claim that these Indians, as Americans, have a perfect right to hire
> their services where they please. They earn a good salary here and
> send their money home for the support of their wives and children.
> The "savage" sports are simply their every day form of amusement
> and sport in their own country. All their associations here are elevat-
> ing morally. They visit places of interest and instruction; they have
> attended worship at Dr. Talmage's and Mr. Beecher's churches and
> they have also visited the office of "The World." Not one of them
> out of seventy-five or eighty has ever been know to be drunk since
> they came to New York.[8]

Cody's retort was poetically brief and to the point. It is important to
note here, however, that, in suggesting in 1886 that Indians had rights equal
to other humans, Cody was bravely exposing the oppression of the political
church's patronizing policy of reconstruction. Revealing the hypocrisy of
the political church, Cody's words make four important points that perfectly
reflect the singular and critically important role he held at this tragic nadir
in the history of the Lakota people in 1886.

First, taking the dangerous stance that no politician, religious leader, or
humanitarian of his era dared to take, Cody clearly acknowledges the Indian has rights. He stops short of referring to the Native American as a citizen, but, more significantly to Indians, Cody strongly implies that Indians
possess human rights. Since President Calvin Coolidge did not proclaim
American Indians citizens until June 5, 1924, in stating in 1886 that Indians have the "perfect right" to hire their services where they please, Cody
was nearly forty years ahead of his time in demanding that Indians should
be granted basic human rights, if not the fundamental rights granted all
American citizens.[9] The Indian Rights Organization pretended to be defending Native Americans, while concurrently destroying their religion
and culture.

Secondly, Cody emphasizes that Indians working in his Wild West earn
a good salary and send it home to their wives and children. One cannot
over-emphasize the importance of this opportunity Cody created for
Plains Indians. Buffalo Bill's Wild West was actually employing Indians.
Rather than brutally forcing them to accept abstract religious and socioeconomic dogma through starvation and physical oppression, the Wild

West celebrated the culture and religion of the Plains Indian while offering Indian people the actual experience of employment. Through offering Native Americans work and wages, Cody was also offering them a singularly important opportunity for learning and dealing with the Euroamerican economic system. This vital knowledge of Euroamerican economics and the real money to experiment with it certainly reached those less-fortunate Lakota at home on the reservation.

Thirdly, Cody addresses the pejorative term *savage* with subtle yet articulate language, and, in doing so, forcefully exposes the simple subjective fact that "savagery"—like "beauty"—is in the eye of the beholder. Without mentioning his personal experience in mortal combat with Indians, Cody uses his fame as an Army scout to turn the logic of the reconstructionists' argument on its ear. Yet again quietly revealing his profound warrior-bonding with the Lakota and Cheyenne, and with simple poetic eloquence, Cody poses a finely tuned, logical argument that what the Euroamerican viewed as "savage" combat was to the Plains Indian simple "everyday amusement and sport."

Fourthly, Cody emphasizes that the Indians in the Wild West are "elevated morally" in all their associations, stressing their attendance at church services and abstinence from alcohol. Elevated morally indeed. The Lakota and Cheyenne people Cody was employing in his Wild West were often the political, religious, and social leaders of their nations. They were the very repository of moral values and spiritual ideals of their people. In truth, some of the "friends" were "elevated morally" to associate with the Lakota "show Indians."

Much to the chagrin and disdain of the "friends," as part of the celebration of Queen Victoria's Golden Jubilee, these Lakota performers in Buffalo Bill's Wild West—these "savages"—were destined soon to delight and enchant the largest gathering of European royalty in the history of the world. In an unprecedented historical reunion that would somehow elude the obtuse American political church, these Lakota would soon ironically expedite a profound healing among the peoples of the Anglo-Saxon race. Even while Cody was defending himself against Representative James's congressional resolution, negotiations were in place for Buffalo Bill's Wild West to travel to London as part of the historic event.

Yorkshire businessman John Robinson Whitley had envisioned an extensive exhibition of American "arts, industries, manufactures, products and resources," which would be the first such exposition outside of the United States. Whitley's vision was for the exposition to coincide with

Queen Victoria's Golden Jubilee celebration, but the idea had failed to attract attention until he came up with the idea of booking Buffalo Bill's Wild West.[10]

Nate Salsbury negotiated an agreement with American entrepreneurs Colonel Henry S. Russell and Vincent Applin who, when aligned with Whitley, were able to arrange for Buffalo Bill's Wild West to perform at Earl's Court in London in the spring as Queen Victoria's Jubilee began. All the partners would share percentages of the gate receipts.

On Thursday, March 31, 1887, as the Cowboy Band played "The Girl I Left Behind Me," Buffalo Bill's Wild West departed America for England. Aboard the *State of Nebraska*, backing up Cody's boast of "a company of more than two-hundred," was a menagerie rivaling Noah's: eighty-three saloon passengers, thirty-eight steerage passengers, and ninety-seven Indians, 180 horses, eighteen buffalo, ten mules, ten elk, five wild Texas steers, four donkeys, and two deer.[11]

Stormy seas would plague the Wild West's crossing of the Atlantic. After several days at sea, the *State of Nebraska*'s rudder broke, causing the ship to roll and toss for over forty-eight hours as the crew labored to repair it during a raging storm. Plains Indians, encountering the ocean for the first time, had a particularly strenuous experience with the repair of the rudder while the storm caused the ship to lean, roll and groan with the tremendous waves. One of the Lakota passengers, Black Elk, then twenty-four years old, had decided to join the Wild West in order to visit the land of the *wasichus* so that he could experience the culture and return with knowledge to better serve his people. As the *State of Nebraska* embarked upon a tumultuous crossing of the Atlantic, however, the young Holy Man must have had second thoughts about leaving the Great Plains. As a big North Atlantic storm set in and the ship started to roll from side to side as well as rise and fall, the Sioux passengers' despair swelled and some began to sing death songs. At first the whites mocked the Lakotas, but as the storm grew even worse and battered the ship they also became concerned. As the storm tossed the ship over and down fantastic waves, crewmen brought floatation devices and instructed the Lakotas to put them on. But Black Elk said he preferred to prepare to meet death with dignity, dressed for death joined with other brave Lakotas to sing songs of death.[12]

On April 16, 1887, the *State of Nebraska* finally reached Gravesend at the mouth of the Thames, where a tugboat, flying the American flag, greeted them with a small band aboard playing "The Star-Spangled Banner." William Sweeny hurried the Wild West Cowboy Band to answer with "Yankee Doodle." After a brief quarantine on board, Arizona John Burke led a prestigious welcoming party climbing the rope ladder to the main deck of the *State of Nebraska*. Lord Ronald Gower and the directors of the American Exhibition warmly welcomed the arrival of the Wild West and announced the British government was raising the quarantine and allowing all the animals to enter the country. Lord Gower addressed the company and, inviting them ashore, informed them that Her Majesty Queen Victoria was extending every courtesy to the performers of the Wild West.

From the Royal Albert Docks in London's East End, the Wild West traveled by three trains to Earl's Court in Kensington. There, the producers had spent $130,000 to construct the arena, grandstands, and Wild West livestock stables. With grandstand seating and standing room the facility could hold an audience of 40,000. The three railroad lines serving the massive complex of the American Exhibition at Earl's Court were very important, easing the colossal task of re-creating the landscape of the actual American West. A cadre of workers unloaded seventeen thousand carloads of rock and earth to create the simulated Rocky Mountain landscape. Full-size trees were uprooted and brought in from the midlands to create the imaginary west of Kensington.[13]

Opening was scheduled for May 9. Nevertheless, the Wild West attracted much attention even as it was setting up. Swift, efficient movement of men, livestock, equipment, and wardrobe was a logistical art and science developed by American circuses and exemplified at its top professional level by Buffalo Bill's Wild West. Large crowds gathered to watch the Wild West expertly setting up camp and to get a free show as the performers rehearsed their various routines. Having been in England for months securing pre-publicity for the show, Arizona John Burke moved into high gear promoting the event. Since his days promoting melodramas, Burke learned that attracting distinguished and important visitors to the show succeeded in creating the newspaper headlines he sought to bring in massive crowds. In this sense, England was no different than America to Arizona John. Soon to be knighted as England's most famous actor, Henry Irving assisted Burke greatly in this task. Henry Sell and Victor Weybright explain:

He was then playing in "Much Ado About Nothing" with Ellen Terry. Already he had welcomed the Wild West Show in an article in the London Era: "I saw an entertainment in New York which impressed me immensely," he wrote. "It is coming to London. It is an entertainment in which the whole of the most interesting episodes of life on the extreme frontier of civilization in America are represented with the most graphic vividness and scrupulous detail. You have real cowboys with bucking horses, real buffaloes, and great hordes of steers, which are lassoed and stampeded in the most realistic fashion imaginable. Then there are real Indians who execute attacks upon coaches driven at full speed. No one can exaggerate the extreme excitement and 'go' of the whole performance. It is simply immense, and I venture to predict that when it comes to London it will take the town by storm."[14]

On April 28, two weeks before opening, legendary former Prime Minister William Ewart Gladstone appeared with a small entourage for a preview of the exhibition. Upon reviewing the performance, Gladstone remarked that Americans were much better horsemen than the British, and that he hoped seeing the Wild West would encourage his countrymen to improve their "noble" equestrian skills. After he overheard Lakota Chief Red Shirt (Ogilasa) and Prime Minister Gladstone's conversation, the roving correspondent for the London *Daily Telegraph*'s report perfectly demonstrates the international importance of Plains Indians traveling with Buffalo Bill's Wild West and interacting with the leaders of the *wasichu* world: "Mr. Gladstone asked Red Shirt if he thought the Englishmen looked enough like the Americans to be kinsmen and brothers. Red Shirt wasn't sure about that."[15]

Gladstone may have been motivated to ask such a question by an editorial feature on Buffalo Bill's Wild West in the *London Illustrated News*, which brilliantly emphasized the blood-kinship of the British Empire to the American West; revealed the charismatic, romantic allure of Buffalo Bill's Wild West to the Old World; and drew into sharp perspective the global impact of the massive numbers of English-speaking immigrants invading North America:

It is certainly a novel idea for one nation to give an exhibition devoted exclusively to its own frontier history, a story enacted by genuine characters, of the dangers and hardships of its settlement, on the soil of another country, 3,000 miles away. Yet this is exactly what the Americans will do this year in London and it is an idea worthy of that thorough-going and enterprising people.

We frankly and gladly allow that there is a natural and sentimental view of the design which will go far to obtain for it a hearty welcome in England. The progress of the United States, now the largest community of the English race on the face of the earth, is a proper subject for congratulation, for the popular mind in the United Kingdom does not regard, and will never be taught to regard what are styled "imperial interests"—those of mere political domination—as equally valuable with the habits and ideas and domestic life of the aggregate of human families belonging to our race. The greater numerical proportion of these, already exceeding sixty million, are inhabitants of the great American republic.

It would be unnatural to deny ourselves the indulgence of a just gratification in seeing what men of our blood, men of our own mind and disposition in all essential respects, though tempered and sharpened by more stimulating conditions, with some wider opportunities for exertion, have achieved in raising a wonderful fabric of modern civilization and bringing it to the highest prosperity across the whole breadth of the Western continent. We feel sure this sentiment will prevail in the hearts of hundreds of thousands of visitors to Buffalo Bill's American camp, about to be opened at the West End of London; and we take it kindly of the great kindred people of the United States that they now send such a magnificent representation of the motherland, determined to take some part in celebrating the jubilee of Her Majesty the Queen.[16]

Brits may have been naturally curious about their kinsmen across the Atlantic ocean, but they were captivated with American Indians; everywhere Indians went large crowds followed. In Sitting Bull's absence, the Oglala, Red Shirt, became the most famous of the Wild West's Indian troupe. As spokesman for the Lakotas, Red Shirt also became the most quoted of the Indian company of performers as newspaper and magazine reporters flocked to the exhibition. Red Shirt's handsome features and dignified persona attracted so much attention that, as Sitting Bull before him, his popularity in the Wild West was rivaled only by Buffalo Bill himself.

Plains Indians were equally enthralled with Englishmen and their culture and became enthusiastic and inquisitive tourists in London. Supporting Cody's argument promoting healthy cultural exchange, and his assertion that the Indian performers in the Wild West received religious instruction wherever they traveled, about forty Sioux visited the Congregational Chapel at West Kensington, where they treated worshipers to the hymn "Nearer My God To Thee" in Lakota. Red Shirt and a small party of

Lakotas also attended a performance by Henry Irving of Goethe's *Faust* at the Lyceum Theater. When asked what he thought of the play Red Shirt answered that it "seemed to him like a big dream."[17]

Visiting the tombs of the kings in Westminster Abby with a group of Lakotas, including Black Elk, Red Shirt received a vision. Red Shirt rested his face in his hands as the Anglican minister spoke and heard "soft music and sweet voices" as a great cloud came toward him. Just as the cloud reached him it suddenly opened in a "blaze of light" which further revealed "the girls with wings." Excited, Red Shirt called out to his Lakota companions to come see what he had spotted. They told him he had been dreaming. L. G. Moses elaborates on the importance of dreams to the Lakota:

> Reporters may have scoffed at his vision, believing instead that he had simply fallen asleep for a moment during the ritual. His compatriots knew, however, that he had been "dreaming." One did not have to sleep to receive visions. His friends did not share his dream; but that did not make the dream any less real for the other Sioux. To Red Shirt, the stone angels on the abby's wall had come alive and beckoned him to a greater understanding. As he claimed repeatedly throughout his stay in England, he would share his experiences with his people once he returned home. They might also share his wonder.[18]

The Lakota performers continued to attract attention for the Wild West. Then, on May 5, lightning struck; Edward Albert, the Prince of Wales, later to become King Edward VII, asked for and received an invitation to attend a special preview performance of the Wild West. On May 6 the Prince and Princess of Wales were entertained with the first dress rehearsal of the Wild West, which was, coincidentally, the first complete performance of the Wild West on British soil.

British "mud," however, would describe that afternoon more accurately. Don Russell's account of Cody's thoughts that historic afternoon illustrates the fact that the mud made little difference:

> The ground was muddy and the show ill rehearsed, but when the Indians, "yelling like fiends, galloped out from their ambuscade and swept around the enclosure like a whirlwind, the effect was instantaneous and electric," says Cody, boasting justifiably. "The Prince rose from his seat and leaned eagerly over the front of the box, and the whole party seemed thrilled by the spectacle. 'Cody,' I said to myself,

'you have fetched 'em!' From that moment we were right—right from the word 'Go.' Everybody was in capital form—myself included—and the whole thing went off grandly."[19]

The Prince of Wales became the biggest fan of the Wild West that afternoon. Cody was equally impressed with the Prince. After the show, he immediately requested a backstage visit to greet the performers and get a closer look at the animals from the American frontier. Tramping through the muddy grounds of the arena and mingling with the troupe of performers, a bond developed between Cody and Edward Albert, as the future King of England humbly requested permission to meet Buffalo Bill's twenty-one-year-old horse, "Charlie," a half-breed Kentucky horse that was arguably the most publicized horse of the day. Buffalo Bill claimed Charlie had almost human intelligence and was so fast he had once used him to run down wild horses. Cody also claimed he had won a five hundred dollar bet that he could ride Charlie one hundred miles over the prairie in ten hours. Cody maintained Charlie was so reliable that he had run the actual one hundred miles in nine hours and forty-five minutes.[20]

Horse-talk aside, the friendship between Cody and Edward Albert brought immediate positive results for the Wild West—a command performance for Queen Victoria. As Don Russell informs us, the world would literally never be the same:

The command performance for Queen Victoria, was the high spot to date for Buffalo Bill's Wild West. In more than a quarter of a century since the death of her consort, Prince Albert, the Queen had not attended any kind of public entertainments, although she had commanded some companies to give plays privately at Windsor Castle. However, when it was explained that the Wild West could not feasibly be brought in its entirety to the castle grounds, she agreed to go to the Earl's Court arena. Having broken one precedent, she was ready for another. When the American flag was presented according to the usual Wild West custom, the Queen rose from her seat and bowed deeply and impressively towards the banner, and her entire party joined in the salute, says Cody, "there arose such a genuine heart-stirring American yell from our company as seemed to shake the sky. It was a great event. For the first time in history, since the Declaration of Independence, a sovereign of Great Britain had saluted the star-spangled banner and that banner was carried by a member of Buffalo Bill's Wild West!"[21]

The Queen had attended the performance with the strict understanding
that she must see the entire Wild West within an hour. Nevertheless, Her
Majesty stayed for the fifty-minute show and afterwards commanded that
Buffalo Bill and the featured performers of the exhibition be presented before her. Nate Salsbury, Annie Oakley, and Lillian Smith accompanied
Cody, Red Shirt, and a group of Oglala Lakotas to meet the Queen. Evidently, Black Elk was part of Red Shirt's delegation and said:

> After the show was over they put all of us Indians in a row according
> to size. I was next to the youngest boys and girls. Then Grand-
> mother England came out and shook hands with us. She made a
> speech, saying that she was seventy-five years old. . . . When she fin-
> ished her speech to us, she raised her hand and we all hollered and
> yelled and gave cheers. She did not care much about seeing the white
> men in the show. She only shook hands with the Indians. Then
> about fifty chariots came in and we did not see which one she got
> into, but she got into one and left.[22]

That afternoon, when Her Majesty Queen Victoria attended Buffalo
Bill's Wild West, saluted the American flag, and held court with Lakota Indians, Will Cody synthesized nations and individuals, cultures and eras. As
surely as Columbus's voyages initiated religious, cultural, social, and agri-
cultural cross-pollination between the planet's major hemispheres, that afternoon at Earl's Court Buffalo Bill's Wild West brought the "Old" and
"New" Worlds together and introduced new mythological dialogue and
interaction to the global village. From that day forward the world would
embrace the images of Buffalo Bill's Wild West as the symbolic expression
of the romantic quest of westering mankind.

Meanwhile, the triumph with the Queen prompted an equally important command performance of the Wild West. On June 20, the day before
the great Jubilee ceremonies in Westminster Abby, the crowned heads of
Europe arrived at Windsor Castle for a special presentation of Buffalo
Bill's Wild West. Never in the history of the world were more monarchs
ever gathered together in attendance of a commercial performance. Don
Russell elaborates on the momentous afternoon:

> It was on this occasion, that the Deadwood coach carried four kings,
> those of Denmark, Greece, Belgium and Saxony, along with the
> Prince of Wales, with Buffalo Bill as driver, during the simulated at-

tack by Indians. In 1871, President Grant had appointed General Robert Cumming Schenck as minister to the Court of St. James, and that envoy had conferred upon London society a great boon—a knowledge of the game of poker. The Prince of Wales was speaking as an apt pupil when he said to Cody, "Colonel, you never held four kings like these before."

"I've held four kings," said Cody, "but four kings and the Prince of Wales makes a royal flush, such as no man ever held before."[23]

Cody indeed held a royal flush. Having charmed the monarchies of Europe in one fell swoop, Buffalo Bill's Wild West more than fulfilled P. T. Barnum's prediction that it would "astonish the Old World." Two and a half million people saw the show in London during the summer of 1887. In the autumn, as the Wild West prepared to close and move on to Birmingham and Manchester, John Robinson Whitley's American Exhibition at Earl's Court sponsored a conference of American and British representative's promoting an agenda to create a Court of Arbitration to finally settle differences between the two countries. The conference moved the *London Times* to write:

> Exhibitions of American products and scenes from the wilder phases of American life certainly tend, in some degree at least, to bring America nearer to England. They are partly cause and partly effect of increased and increasing intercourse between the two countries, and they tend to promote a still more intimate understanding. Those who went to be amused often stayed to be instructed. The Wild West was irresistible. Colonel Cody suddenly found himself the hero of the London season. Notwithstanding his daily engagements and his punctual fulfillment of them, he found time to go everywhere, to see everything, and to be seen by the world.
>
> All of London contributed to his triumph and now the close of his show is selected as the occasion for promoting a great international movement, with Mr. Bright, Lord Granville, Lord Wolseley and Lord Lorne for its sponsors. Civilization itself consents to march in the train of Buffalo Bill. Colonel Cody can achieve no greater triumph than this, even if someday he realizes the design attributed to him of running the Wild West Show within the classic precincts of the Colosseum at Rome. . . . Hence it is no paradox to say that Colonel Cody has done his part in bringing America and England nearer together.[24]

Later Cody and his daughter Arta indeed traveled to Rome specifically to research the possibility of the Wild West appearing in the Colosseum. Cody found the ancient structure too unstable and too small as a venue for the Wild West.[25] After closing in London on October 31 the Wild West moved to Birmingham, where it enjoyed another successful run. Immediately after the Birmingham run, the Wild West moved to Manchester and opened on December 17. On January 10, 1888, Nate Salsbury departed England to return to America and plan a summer tour while the Wild West continued its successful Manchester run, ending in early May, 1888. On May 5, the Wild West's final performance in England was given at Hull. On May 6 the Wild West, onboard the *Persian Monarch*, sailed from the Alexandra Dock at Hull.

The *Persian Monarch* sailed without a few of its passengers; Black Elk and a few other Lakotas missed the boat.[26] Black Elk and his Lakota companions managed to get themselves promptly arrested. Being incarcerated, however, was a blessing in disguise; in order to question the Lakotas, the authorities somehow found an interpreter. Upon being absolved of any charges, the interpreter told Black Elk and his companions about another western show from America which might help them get back home. Captain Joe Shelley had been so inspired by Cody's triumph in London that he organized a rival wild west show and departed Baltimore for London in July, 1887. "Mexican Joe" had a troupe of Omaha Indians working in his exhibition and he hired Black Elk and his companions to join them for $30 a month.

"Mexican Joe's Wild West" did one show in London before traveling to France, Germany and Italy. The show eventually returned to Paris, where Black Elk developed a relationship with a woman and moved in with her and her family.

Meanwhile, Buffalo Bill's Wild West was experiencing a milder crossing of the Atlantic on its return voyage. The journey was not without misfortune, however; Cody's old horse Charlie died. The scout led an elaborate funeral service for his old friend, draping the horse's carcass in an American flag and personally delivering an emotional eulogy for Charlie before surrendering him over to the sea. A few days later Cody's triumphant return to America was perhaps best described by the *New York Word*:

> The harbor probably has never witnessed a more picturesque scene than that of yesterday, when the "Persian Monarch" steamed up the quarantine. Buffalo Bill stood on the captain's bridge, his tall and

striking figure clearly outlined, and his long hair waving in the wind; the gayly painted and blanketed Indians leaned over the ships rail; the flags of all nations fluttered from the masts and connecting cables. The cowboy band played "Yankee Doodle" with a vim and enthusiasm which faintly indicated the joy felt by everybody connected with the "Wild West" over the sight of home.[27]

Buffalo Bill was needed at home. Even as Cody was synthesizing global hemispheres and estranged kinsmen, the American buffalo, as the Plains Indian, was precariously close to extinction. The years between 1870 and 1883, which directly paralleled the era during which Cody enjoyed a successful melodrama career, had proved to be the most destructive to the great American herds. Having been slaughtered in numbers exceeding a million a year, after 1875 the massive southern herd no longer existed. The disappearance of the northern herd had come so suddenly that the hide hunters of 1882–83 went out in search of buffalo and were stunned to discover they had vanished. Hide hunters and Plains Indians were not the only people shocked by the sudden disappearance of buffalo: The Smithsonian Institution discovered it had no satisfactory specimens and became concerned the species would completely disappear before any could be secured. In 1886 a Smithsonian expedition was organized and sent to Montana Territory in search of wild buffalo and, fortunately, the expedition discovered enough buffalo to create a comprehensive scientific display. William T. Hornaday's resulting 1887 report to the Smithsonian, *The Extermination of the American Bison*, is credited with being instrumental in saving the buffalo from extinction. Cody's name appears on the first page of Hornaday's report in reference to "Cabeza de Vaca, the prototype of Buffalo Bill."[28]

From herds once so immense that their size could not be fathomed, the remaining buffalo could now be sadly counted in taxidermist Hornaday's report to the Smithsonian Institution. In less than twenty years, Sherman and Sheridan's environmental warfare and the Transcontinental Railroad had wrought a tragic harvest. Facing immediate extinction, the twenty healthy buffalo in Cody's Wild West suddenly became vitally important to the survival of the species. Of particular interest to Hornaday's report was the fact that Cody's herd of buffalo had survived a journey to England and returned, adding four healthy new calves to the herd along the way. Don Russell informs us of the sudden importance of Buffalo Bill's herd of healthy animals:

At the end of 1888, of the 256 buffalo in captivity, only two herds were larger than Buffalo Bill's. S. L. Bedson, of Stony Mountain, Manitoba, was a pioneer in breeding buffalo, and from ten in 1877 he had produced seventy in 1888, when he sold his herd to Charles J. Jones, of Garden City, Kansas, known as "Buffalo Jones."[29]

In 1886, Charles Jesse "Buffalo" Jones began to round up buffalo calves in Texas. Facing enraged mother buffaloes, Jones would rope the healthy calves he wanted and take them for his herd. The calves were nursed by dairy cows Jones dragged in tow on his expeditions. Once weaned, the buffalo calves were taken to Kansas and released in Jones's pastures. Combining his Texas herd with the buffalo he bought from Bedson, Jones's herd numbered 140, making it the largest privately owned herd in existence. "Buffalo Jones" was no Smithsonian biologist or scientist; he was a visionary rancher whose efforts to create a hybrid "cattalo" had inspired him to seek healthy buffalo calves and, in the process, Jones had come to realize the serious need for an emergency restoration program. When Cody lost his herd in 1886, he had been forced to buy two buffalo from the Philadelphia Zoo. Buffalo Jones had provided Cody with the rest of his Wild West herd. There was no place else to turn. Don Russell presents the sad reality that the once unfathomable numbers of buffalo could now be completely itemized:

Charles Allard of the Flathead Indian Reservation in Montana had thirty-five, Charles Goodnight, rancher, had thirteen from the last of the Texas herd in Paloduro Canyon near his home in Clarendon, Texas. At Bismark Grove, Kansas, the Santa Fe Railroad maintained ten buffalo as a tourist attraction. Similarly, John H. Garin had four at a summer resort at Glen Island, near New York. The number in zoos was small: Philadelphia had ten; there were four in Cincinnati; four in Central Park, New York City; seven in Lincoln Park, Chicago; and a pair at the Nation Museum, Washington. Abroad were two at Manchester, England; one in London, one in Liverpool, purchased from Buffalo Bill; two in Dresden, Germany; and one in Calcutta, India. Frederick Dupree of the Cheyenne agency, Dakota Territory, had nine; Dr. V. T. McGillicuddy had four in Rapid City; and fourteen more were held singly or in pairs. The total was 216 kept for breeding purposes and 40 for exhibition. The Yellowstone Park herd was estimated at 200. The estimate of the remaining wild buffalo in the United States was eighty-five—twenty-five in Texas, twenty in Colorado, twenty-six in Wyoming, ten in Montana, and four in Dakota. Adding an estimated 550 in Canada, the survivors of the millions of only a decade before totaled only 1,091.[30]

Buffalo Bill's conquest of England would be for naught without buffalo in his Wild West; he naturally joined Buffalo Jones's restoration efforts. Likewise, as political pressure from the Indian Rights Organization mounted, making it increasingly difficult to hire Plains Indians as performers for his show, he had no choice but to fight them.

The Wild West had become much more than unique, historic international entertainment; Cody's loving reenactment was rapidly becoming a temple for Plains Indians and buffalo—at once a genetic, spiritual and cultural sanctuary and the vessel of living mythology.

Chapter Sixteen

ARROWS OF LIGHT

Confidential Headquarters
Division of the Missouri
Chicago, Ill. Nov. 24, 1890
Col. Cody.

You are hereby authorized to secure the person of Sitting Bull and deliver him to the nearest Commanding Officer of U.S. Troops, taking a receipt and reporting your actions.

Nelson A. Miles, Major General, Comd. Division
(*The Making of Buffalo Bill*, Richard J. Walsh and Milton Salsbury)

Buffalo BILL returned from England as the "hero of two continents" and promptly offered the American public the opportunity to join his triumphant celebration; the Wild West opened on Memorial Day in 1888 at Staten Island and was held over at Erastina until August, when it traveled to Philadelphia, Baltimore, Washington, and Richmond. In the nation's capital, Buffalo Bill and the Lakota performers visited the Senate, the House of Representatives, and the Indian Bureau and were invited by President Grover Cleveland to visit the White House.

Upon meeting the "great father" in Washington, the Lakota performers returning from England with Buffalo Bill's Wild West had experienced the full spectrum of western civilization. Since leaving the Great Plains, these Lakota performers had become a major part of entertainment history. They had contributed greatly to the shattering of attendance records in cities all over America, especially in three separate historic runs of the Wild West in New York. More importantly, however, these Lakota had helped facilitate an important healing in diplomatic relations between the United States and Great Britain. They had crossed the ocean to perform for the queen and future king of England and personally met and socialized with the crowned heads of Europe; they had visited the holy shrines of

Anglo Saxon Christendom, toured world-famous museums to view historic works of art, and been entertained by the greatest British actors of the day who performed classic theatrical works. When these Oglalas crossed the Atlantic a second time and returned home to Pine Ridge, they had visited places, met people, and seen things the likes of which America's upper classes could only dream. Equally important, these Lakota left a splendid, indelible impression of the culture and character of the Plains Indian upon the monarchs, parliamentarians, and power-brokers of Europe, while they also brought home to their own people a much broader comprehension of the world of the wasichu.

Meanwhile, Cody and Salsbury had learned a fundamental show business rule from successfully booking their Wild West to run concurrently with Queen Victoria's Golden Jubilee: whenever possible, they would schedule the Wild West to be performed where crowds were already gathering. With this formula in mind before leaving England, the partners negotiated and signed contracts to open the Wild West in Paris during the Exposition of 1889. All of Europe would be visiting Paris to celebrate the centennial of the French Revolution, and the unprecedented success of the Wild West in England virtually ensured massive crowds in France and throughout Europe.

In spite of the historic success he was enjoying on the international stage, however, the strain of the pace he was keeping was beginning to negatively affect Cody's physical and mental health. Today some might refer to Cody's symptoms as "burnout," but he was obviously suffering physically as well as mentally from the intense pressure of constant movement and performing. It is important to note that Cody's naturally robust health begins to show the first signs of diminishing immediately after his great success at Queen Victoria's Jubilee in London in 1888. England's perpetually wet climate negatively affected the health of all Wild West company members. Cody and all the plainsmen of his troupe were accustomed to the arid climates of the Great Plains and Rocky Mountains, and the continual dampness of England kept each of them sick with colds. Cody suffered from bronchitis throughout the run in Manchester and, because of the additional stress on his health from constantly performing both on- and offstage, he could not allow himself the time to recuperate. For years Cody had possessed unusually powerful physical stamina and could put in the equivalent work of several men during the day, stay up all night carousing, and still greet the first light of the next day fresh and eager for adventure. As he entered his forties, however, the years of pushing himself to extremes began to make themselves increasingly evident. Complicating matters, as a result of the interruption of his regular patterns in diet and exercise brought about by touring constantly, Cody also started putting on weight. He had never made a secret of his drinking, which certainly did not help his health; since the beginning days of the Wild West, however, he had kept his promise to Nate Salsbury not to drink while performing. Still, tales of Cody's drinking adventures when he was not working are the stuff of legend. This lifestyle could only lead to the downward spiral of health which became evident after Cody's greatest triumph. Buffalo Bill was ill with chills and fever throughout the celebratory engagement at Staten Island upon the Wild West's return from England. In letters to his sister Julia, Cody complained frequently of needing rest. Irritable and concerned that his success was being quickly and cheaply copied by imitators, Cody's grumbling was a clear indication that he was burned-out and homesick for the Great Plains.

Indeed, very much like an Indian, Cody became melancholy and exhibited classic signs of being homesick if away from the Great Plains for too long. Cody's homesickness was even more complex than an Indian's, for it was also his nature to seek the greatest success possible; yet the greater his achievement, the further it took him from home. Moreover, his monumental celebrity had begun to increasingly isolate him even as his enormous popularity expanded to encompass most of nineteenth-century western civilization. One of the ways Cody reacted to this paradox of fame was to become obsessed with the minute details of domestic affairs. Divorce being anathema to most Victorians, the Codys' marriage had dissolved into one of convenience. Will and Lulu negotiated a truce in their stormy relationship which allowed both of them to keep up appearances. Since Cody had signed over the property to her, Lulu remained ensconced in the main house, while Cody's development of the North Platte property was managed by his oldest sister, Julia, and her husband, Al Goodman.

Since the death of Mary Cody, Al Goodman had served a very important role for the entire Cody family, particularly Will. Goodman had married the eldest daughter, Julia, and assumed much of the patriarchal role Will inherited prematurely as an eleven-year-old boy. With Goodman there to supervise the immediate family affairs of his sisters, in his mid-teens Will had finally been freed from the social responsibilities of looking after his siblings and soon thereafter began his rapid ascension into Great Plains and world history. From that time forward, Will depended upon Al and Julia to hold the internal Cody family together as he pursued his precarious destiny. As his fortunes increased, however, he longed to be re-

united with his family and to actualize his domestic dreams. His many letters to his sister Julia are filled with fantasies of the Cody siblings all
united, safe, and comfortable in their dotage. As he became more successful and began to make his fortune, Cody depended more and more on Al
and Julia to mind his personal domestic affairs as well as those of his sisters.
Cody wrote Julia and Al frequently as he toured the world, usually sending
money with explicit details of how to implement his ideas at his Nebraska
ranch. When he returned to Scouts Rest Ranch after his success in England, Cody was able to see for himself that with his new prosperity and
Julia and Al's loyal assistance the ranch was indeed blossoming as he had
envisioned.

Cody purchased 3,000 acres on the Platte in the spring of 1870, and he
and Lulu had settled there when he worked as a scout at Fort McPherson.
Nebraska's famous Sand Hills country is still generally considered some of
the finest cattle country in the world, and Cody certainly envisioned creating a prosperous future for himself there as a stockman. As early as 1885,
the *Omaha Herald* described Cody's Scout's Rest Ranch as one of the finest
on the continent:

> The waters of the Great Platte flow through no prettier or more nat-
> ural stock ranch. Nature in all her bounteous gifts or freaks never
> designed a place more fitting. The river skirts along the northwest-
> ern portion for four miles; in the southern portion a small overflow-
> ing creek, fed by a cool, living spring, flows nearly through the cen-
> ter from west to east, dividing it into two parts, and while on the
> south side the rich nutritious buffalo grass grows and furnishes food
> on which cattle grow fat in the summer, on the north side a long,
> juicy wild prairie grass is found which when cut and cured furnishes
> a provender unequalled for cattle in the winter. He has a tract of
> nearly four thousand acres here, the eastern portion adjoining the
> city's limits which the rapid growth of North Platte is making very
> valuable.
>
> Besides the ranch buildings which are three miles from the city,
> he has a residence one mile west of North Platte. Mr. Cody is a great
> lover of fine stock, and moreover a good judge of a horse or cattle as
> well. He takes great pride in his herd of 125 of the best blooded cat-
> tle, composed of Herefords, Shorthorns, Polled-Angus, and other
> high grades. His Hereford bull, Earl Horace, has a pedigree, and was
> imported. Among the herd of 181 horses, most of which are thor-
> oughbred, are some of the best ever brought out west.[1]

After closing the Wild West season in Richmond, Cody was able to use his brief break from touring to return to North Platte and finally rest. He drew great pleasure seeing the huge barn he had designed had been constructed and was housing the fine-blooded livestock he had sent home from Scotland and England to join and expand his herds. He was equally pleased to see that the trees he had planted had survived and were growing. His brief time at Scout's Rest Ranch was one of healing and contentment as he was able to enjoy the fruits of his labor, reflect upon his unbelievable accomplishments, and imagine his future.

Even though he was becoming increasingly preoccupied with developing his Great Plains retreat and entertaining ideas of community building in the Rockies, Cody would never again be able to truly rest there or anyplace else. Because of his success with the Wild West in America and England, he would now be responsible for designing, administrating, and supervising the expeditious and fluid logistical movement of a troupe of people and livestock which was the equivalent of a small town. Aside from the incredible amount of work required to keep the Wild West running smoothly, Cody had also created his singularly unique life as the ringmaster and star of the show. Now that people wanted to see the Wild West, he was obliged to take it to them. He was very well aware that at this moment in his life he truly belonged to the world. Cody soon headed to New York and in May, 1889, once again on the *Persian Monarch*, the Wild West departed for France.

As usual, Arizona John Burke had done his job well. By the time the Wild West arrived on French shores at Havre, the small shops of Paris were filled with trinkets and souvenirs of ceramic bucking horses, buffaloes, saddles, toy cowboys and Indians, cheap bows and arrows, moccasins, and Indian baskets. Burke sent the cowboys and Lakota performers through the streets of Paris in their show costumes and soon the Wild West's ancillary products were flying off shelves and western fashion became the rage; Parisians became the first Europeans to adopt the clothing style of the American West.

On May 19, the Wild West opened in Paris to overflowing crowds. Along with members of his cabinet, French President Sadi Carnot and his wife were honored guests. Several important Americans who were in Paris at the time were able to attend. Whitelaw Reid, the American ambassador to England, and the American ambassador to France, Louis Maclean, were in the audience. Touring France with his wife, Thomas Edison also attended the European debut of the Wild West.

Once again the Deadwood Stage served Cody well; in order to maintain national prestige, the French could not be outdone by the British and were honor-bound to ride in the coach while attempting to outrun the attacking Sioux. The gathering of royalty present at Queen Victoria's Jubilee was a once-in-a-lifetime event; this is not to say, however, that monarchs were not present in Paris to ride in the Deadwood Stage: Queen Isabella of Spain and Shah Naz-er-el-den of Persia climbed aboard as Buffalo Bill drove the coach ahead of the fierce Lakota warriors' attack. Afterwards, the Shah pronounced riding the Deadwood Stage during the Lakota attack the greatest emotional experience of his European sojourn.

The Wild West captured the hearts of Parisians as surely as it had those of the British. Clothing fashion and showmanship aside, however, French fascination with the American West revealed itself most uniquely through paint. The artist Rosa Bonheur became so enamored with the Wild West camp in Paris that she returned frequently to paint portraits of members of the company and the action scenes being created in the arena. Madam Bonheur's portrait of Buffalo Bill, which was painted during this time, is one of the most famous images of the scout. Bonheur's standing in the European arts community quickly brought other avant-garde painters following in her wake. Here again, an important reconciliation was occurring. Where the triumph of the Wild West in London brought about a diplomatic healing between feuding Anglo-Saxon cousins, however, French artists became enchanted with the Plains Indian sense of aesthetics; the French were intrigued with the idea that Lakotas wore paint as costume— often paint being practically the only costume! French impressionist painters involved in the visionary process of liberating paint from traditional representational forms certainly found themselves in creative league with the Lakotas' expressive and personal use of color and design. The Lakotas were themselves moving paintings.

Even more important than artistic appreciation and creative exchange, however, a reuniting of blood relatives was also occurring between the Lakota and the French. The French had been the first Europeans to live among the Lakota on the Great Plains of North America and, as a result, had made an indelible impact on Lakota society—even giving them their slang name, *Sioux*, or "cutthroat." For several generations in the regions of the Trans-Missouri and western Canada, French explorers, trappers, and traders and the Lakota had intermarried and blended the two cultures. Some of the Lakota performers in the Wild West were indeed coming to

France to reunite relative cultures just as surely as Anglo-Saxon performers had in England.

While in Paris, Buffalo Bill and Black Elk were also reunited. The young Lakota holy man had become so homesick in Italy that he had become very ill and could not continue with the "Mexican Joe" tour. His companions had urged him to return to Paris, where he had a girlfriend who could take care of him while he recuperated. Black Elk somehow made his way to Paris, where he located his girlfriend and moved in with her family. At breakfast one morning, however, Black Elk collapsed, to all appearances dead. In a coma-like state, the young Lakota holy man astrally projected himself to the Great Plains to visit home. Hovering over familiar homeland scenes in the Dakotas, Black Elk observed minute details of his former life on the plains before returning, nearly twenty-four hours after collapsing, to his body in France. Black Elk learned upon reviving that doctors had been summoned when his Parisian friends realized his body remained warm even though it appeared lifeless. The doctors arrived and, only detecting an occasional faint heartbeat, pronounced him very near death and instructed his friends to prepare a coffin and funeral. The Indian's sudden revival had at first frightened his caregivers until they finally realized he had not come back from the dead but had merely been in an inexplicable mystic trance.

Black Elk told Neihardt:

A few days after that, these people heard that Pahuska was in town again. So they took me to where he had his show, and he was glad to see me. He had all his people give me three cheers. Then he asked me if I wanted to be in the show or if I wanted to go home. I told him I was sick to go home. So he said he would fix that. He gave me a ticket and ninety dollars. Then he gave me a big dinner. Pahuska had a strong heart.[2]

Pahuska means the same as *Pahaska*; both are aberrations of *Pe-heinska*, or "long hair."

Cody hired a policeman to escort Black Elk to his ship and soon the Holy Man was on his way back to the Great Plains. Black Elk recognized a strong heart in his friend Pahaska, but the signs of physical decline in Cody were already there. The negative effects of show business reveal themselves clearly in his letter to Julia from Paris dated July 5, 1889:

Dear Sister. Thanks for your letter of June 20th. I am always so glad to hear from any of you. I have rec'd three short letters from Al only, But as everything is going on right, I am content. Yesterday was a busy day for me, first I went with the American minister to the Tomb of General LaFayette then to the unveiling of Barthold's Statue, then to a reception & dinner we gave in camp—then the afternoon performance—then to the Legation reception—back for the evening show—then into my evening dress and to Minister Reid's reception, turned in at daylight—and today I am off my feet—I am like you. I can't stand so much as I used to and I am not at all well this summer. Now as we are getting old we must not kick at our breaking down, it can't be helped, but I don't won't to break down until I get out of debt and ahead of the hounds enough to take it easy. Sorry you and Al are not well—but don't worry. Love to you all. Brother Will.

P.S. About getting ahead and not losing it, that's a hard thing to calculate on—as I have to take such awful risks in my business. Brother.[3]

Cody was indeed beginning to take greater risks as his fortune grew, but he had always gambled on his future. His entire life had been based on the belief that opportunity lay just over the horizon. Cody was conditioned from a lifetime of survival on the Great Plains to believe he should pursue his destiny and let fate provide the details. With his tremendous success, however, Cody's risks were now taken on a global stage and held broader multicultural and international ramifications. The dangerous implications of Cody's new status would begin to make themselves obvious as the Wild West ended the successful run in France to began its initial European tour.

The Wild West closed in Paris in October and, from Marseilles in the south of France, the company sailed to Spain. Upon arriving in Barcelona, Arizona John Burke had the Lakota performers pose in front of the statue of Christopher Columbus. As the photographer snapped the picture an unidentified member of the group of Lakotas exclaimed, "It was a damned bad day for us when he discovered America."[4]

Spain proved to be a disaster for the Wild West. The production arrived in the country at the same time that an influenza and typhus epidemic was rapidly spreading throughout the population. The epidemic naturally affected crowds as Barcelona went under partial quarantine. Soon the epidemic reached the camps of the Wild West and many performers became ill. The show's announcer, Frank Richmond, became so ill with the flu that he contracted pneumonia and died. Four Indian performers died;

Annie Oakley nearly died; and seven Lakota performers, desperately ill, were sent home to America. The company hobbled out of Spain in January, 1890, having taken severe financial hits and sustained priceless losses in personnel.

The Wild West headed to Naples by way of Sardinia and Corsica and opened January 26, 1890. A creative Italian criminal printed and sold two-thousand counterfeit tickets for the Wild West's opening in Naples, however, and preshow bedlam reigned as the confused audience fought and argued over seating. Nonetheless, in spite of such a befuddled opening, in Italy the Wild West regained its old spirit. By the time the production arrived in Rome, the prince of Teano, Don Onorio Herzog of Sermonetta, offered a bold challenge to Cody's cowboys: Don Onorio had a stable of wild Cajetan stallions which no one in Italy had been able to ride—let alone tame! The prince challenged Cody's cowboys to attempt to ride and break his stallions. Naturally, the scout accepted the challenge on behalf of his wranglers. The contest was scheduled to take place on March 4.

On the day before the horse-breaking contest, Major Burke, a devout Catholic, arranged for Buffalo Bill and a small group of Lakota performers to travel to the Vatican to meet Pope Leo XIII on the twenty-fifth anniversary of his coronation. His Holiness had to pass through the small Ducal Hall en route to festivities in the Sistine Chapel, so Burke instructed Cody and the Lakotas to wait there for a brief audience. Moments before being introduced to the Lakotas, the pontiff compared the meeting to the return of Columbus to the court of Ferdinand and Isabella.

With customary brief austerity, however, the pope formally greeted Cody and the Lakotas in the hallway and promptly moved on to join the festivities. The fact that the pope, as the "representative of God on Earth" or merely an important leader, was so distant and inhospitable did not sit well with the Lakotas, who felt he did not act with the magnanimous dignity of a chief of their people. They expected a great chief to be extremely gregarious and generous; the pope's magisterial greeting certainly did not meet with their standards of hospitality toward welcoming honored guests. Adding to the complexity of the cultural and religious misunderstanding, the Lakotas returned to the Wild West camp to learn that one of their comrades, thirty-eight-year-old Little Ring, had died in his sleep while they were gone. Little Ring had been left behind because of his illness and, even though an autopsy proved he died of heart disease, Lakota headman, Rocky Bear, logically asked Major Burke why "God's representative on earth" did not protect their brother while they were away to meet with him. Needless to say, they did not receive an answer that met with their approval.

Always promoting, Arizona John Burke did not let the confused papal meeting or Little Ring's death distract him from promoting the horse-breaking contest. Rumors soon flashed through Rome that the prince's stallions were so dangerous that they actually ate people. Accentuating the drama, on the day of the contest, Burke had the horses brought to the arena in chains and erected special barricades to protect the crowds in the event that any of the ferocious beasts should escape. As usual, Burke's outrageous publicity antics worked; twenty-thousand Italians bought tickets to witness the event. The Roman correspondent of the *New York Herald* wrote that even while the wild horses had bucked, kicked, bit, and raced in all directions, within five minutes the Wild West cowboys had captured, subdued, and saddled the beasts. When the cowboys rode the conquered horses around the arena, the crowds went wild.[5] One of the Wild West cowboys later explained that the job was actually easy. The cowboys simply roped the wild horses, tossed them to the ground, and kept them subdued with the ropes. Next, two cowboys on horseback rode up beside the horses as they were released and rose to their feet. Surrounded, the horses promptly learned there was no possible escape and were subdued quickly.

Believing this practice to be a deception, however, the crowd quickly became indignant. They had expected a fierce battle and were wagering that their wild Italian horses would outwit the Americans. But the entire contest was over so quickly that the entire event seemed anticlimactic. Italian pride was insulted, and the American cowboys were booed by the audience. To alleviate the situation, Buffalo Bill challenged the men who had come from southern Italy and brought the wild horses to tame wild broncos from the American West. Italian daredevils were quick to take the challenge and were just as promptly tossed into the air and onto the ground by the wild horses. Next, the colonel even offered to allow the Italians to use their own methods of using irons and chains to break horses, but after they had worked for only a half an hour, Buffalo Bill determined the practice cruel and brutal and put an end to the contest.[6]

Cody's cowboys continued breaking horses for Europeans as they toured the continent. Teddy Roosevelt wrote in his book, *The Wilderness Hunter*,

When Buffalo Bill took his cowboys to Europe they made a practice in England, France, Germany and Italy of offering to break and ride, in their own fashion any horse given to them. They were frequently given spoiled horses from the cavalry services in the different countries through which they passed, animals with which the trained horsebreakers of the European armies could do nothing; and yet in almost all cases the cow-punchers and broncobusters with Buffalo Bill mastered these beasts as readily as they did their own western horses.[7]

The Wild West cowboys were indeed natural marvels at breaking wild horses. Their sense of fair play and justice, however, left much to be desired. Luther Standing Bear describes what actually went on for a while behind the scenes between the cowboys and Indians in the Wild West and, in doing so, vividly reveals Cody's quiet yet forceful way of dealing with racism and his genuine regard for the Lakota performers in his company:

> There were a great many cowboys with the show. There was a chief of the cowboys who had general supervision over both horses and men. When an unbroken horse would be brought in, this cowboy chief would give it to an Indian to ride bareback. After the animal was well broken, it would be taken away from the Indian and given to a cowboy to ride. Then the Indian would be given another unbroken horse. For quite awhile we said nothing about it, but finally it began to be just a little too much to stand. One day one of the Indians came to me just before it was time to enter the arena. His horse was saddled and bridled, but he was leading the animal by the bridle. I asked him what was the matter, and he said it was a wild horse and he was not going to ride it into the arena.
>
> I went to the chief cowboy and said, "I do not think you are doing right. You know our Indian boys have to ride bareback, but you always give them the wild horses to ride. Then, when they have the horse nicely broken, you give it to a cowboy. Why don't you give the wild horses to the cowboys to break in? They ride on saddles, and it would not be so hard for them."
>
> But the chief cowboy only said, "Well, I can't be bothered by a little thing like that. You will have to see Buffalo Bill about the horses."
>
> But I retorted, "You know very well that Buffalo Bill does not know what you do with the horses. He does not know that you give the wild ones to the Indian boys to ride until they are broken in. Give that horse back to that Indian boy or he will not go into the arena today."

That was all—but the boy got his horse in time to enter the arena with the others. Just as I was ready to go back to the Indians, I looked at Buffalo Bill, and he had a twinkle in his eye. After that, we had no more trouble with the horses. Although Buffalo Bill never said anything to me, I knew he had fixed things to our satisfaction.[8]

Standing Bear's personal relationship with Buffalo Bill offers very clear insight into the showman's sincere affinity with the Lakota performers in the Wild West. Standing Bear learned very quickly that he could depend on Cody to protect Lakota people, but more importantly he learned that he need not answer to anyone in the Wild West hierarchy but Cody himself. Cody quietly and consistently empowered the Indian people in his company through actions rather than words.

One morning Standing Bear came into the dining tent and noticed that everyone but the Indians had been served hotcakes. Since Indians never ate much, and were not particularly fond of hotcakes, this did not concern Standing Bear. That evening at dinner, however, he was surprised to discover he and his fellow Lakota had been served hotcakes left over from the other performers' breakfasts. Furious, Standing Bear held his anger inside, quietly left the table and went straight to Buffalo Bill.

When informed that his cook had withheld hotcakes from the Indian performers at breakfast only to attempt to serve them as leftovers for dinner, Buffalo Bill's "eyes snapped" and he quickly rose from his seat and ordered Standing Bear to come with him. With Standing Bear present, Cody confronted the dining room manager and told him he would not stand for the Indian performers to be treated in such a disrespectful manner. Cody went further to inform the man the Indians were the "principal feature of this show, and they are the one people I will not allow to be misused or neglected." He instructed the manager to serve the Indians exactly what they wanted at meal time. Standing Bear said the Indian performers had no more trouble with meals after that confrontation.[9]

The Wild West continued its success in Italy; after closing in Rome, it next traveled north to Venice, where Major Burke set up a photo shoot with Cody and a group of Lakota performers in a gondola. The troupe visited Doge's palace and St. Mark's Cathedral before Burke negotiated the actualization of one of Cody's dreams in Verona: The Wild West performed in an amphitheater built by Diocletian. The attendance for the performance was nearly 50,000.

Bolstered by its success in Italy, the Wild West moved further north

across the Alps and into Germany, where it was greeted by the most enthusiastic crowds in all of Europe. The Wild West played Innsbruck, Tyrol,
Munich, Stuttgart, Frankfurt, Berlin, Dresden, Bonn, and many other
German cities as well as Vienna, Austria. The Wild West was now creating
a major sensation everywhere it played.

Much of Cody's success in Germany might be attributed to the popularity of the author Karl May. Strongly influenced by James Fenimore
Cooper's *Leatherstocking Tales,* May's hero, "Ole Shatterhand," captivated
generations of youthful readers and attracted a wildly diverse audience of
future historical figures such as Albert Einstein, Carl Jung, Albert Schweit-
zer, Henry Kissinger, and even Adolph Hitler when they were schoolboys.
As many young men with fertile imaginations, May got himself into trouble with the law and, having been sentenced twice to prison, began writing
during his second incarceration. In his prison cell, Karl May wrote dozens
of books set in a West he was never to visit. In spite of never being in the
American West, however, May's ability to create novels that appealed to
Germany's romantic notions of the American West led the magazine *Der
Spiegel* to pronounce his influence on the level of Goethe and Mann. The
first of May's novels was published in 1887, three years before the Wild
West's arrival in Germany. The incredible success of May's work certainly
whetted Germans' appetite to see the real thing, literally setting the stage
for the Wild West. Interest in all things western reached fever pitch in
Germany as evidenced by the insatiable demand for western exhibitions;
Cody's old partner, Doc Carver, had also arranged a European tour and the
two companies actually crossed paths in Germany during July, 1890.[10]

Even as Cody was conquering Europe, however, trouble was brewing in
America. On August 4, 1890, Secretary of the Interior John Noble reversed himself and ordered that under no circumstance would permission
be granted to exhibit Indians in Wild West shows in the future. Indian
Commissioner Thomas Jefferson Morgan initiated an investigation into
the Wild West and prepared a list of questions for Cody and his partners,
demanding they provide the government with documented accounts of
their treatment of Indians.

The reported five deaths of Indian performers in Cody's show was all
members of the Indian Rights Organization needed to fan the flames of
discord with allegations of neglect and abuse of Indian performers in the
Wild West. The controversy surrounding the treatment of Indians in
western exhibitions, however, had begun in March, 1890, when Commissioner Morgan informed Pine Ridge Indian Agent Hugh Gallagher that

two Oglala Lakota "show Indians," Swift Hawk and Featherman, were dead. The two Lakotas had been part of the Wild West and had become seriously ill in France. As Swift Hawk and Featherman had been too sick and contagious to travel and the Wild West was moving on, Major John Burke prepaid Conception Hospital in Marseilles for private rooms, physicians, and attending nurses for the Lakota performers as the troupe departed for Barcelona. Swift Hawk later died from influenza and Featherman succumbed to a virulent strain of smallpox.

Then, on April 1, Commissioner Morgan informed Agent Gallagher that four Oglalas from Pine Ridge Agency had appeared destitute at the Cheyenne/Arapaho Agency. Even though these Indians had left the reservation without permission and probably joined Pawnee Bill's exhibition, their returning indigent and in poor health appeared to Commissioner Morgan to represent a pattern of abuse of Wild West Indians. The commissioner issued stern warning statements to the Lakota that admonished them to avoid Wild West shows altogether and to focus themselves instead toward education and farming.

Meanwhile, the State Department informed Commissioner Morgan of the deaths of two more Lakotas from Cody's troupe: Goes Flying, forty-five, died of smallpox in Naples, and Little Ring, thirty-eight, died in his sleep of a heart attack in Rome. Adding insult to injury, the Lakotas John Burke sent back from Barcelona with influenza finally arrived in New York at this time. One of this group, Kills Plenty, failed to improve with medical treatment and died in New York's Bellevue Hospital.

Kills Plenty's death quickly brought the issue of Indians in Wild West shows to headlines in New York's newspapers. Assistant U.S. Superintendent of Immigration of the Port of New York, James R. O'Beirne, a member of the Indian Rights Organization who had done humanitarian service work among the Sioux at Pine Ridge in 1877, clearly saw the circumstance as a way to attack and discredit Buffalo Bill, make a name for himself, and support the reconstruction goals of the IRO on the reservations. O'Beirne took it upon himself to inform the New York press of Buffalo Bill's abuse and neglect of Indians in his Wild West. Kills Plenty's death soon occupied front page headlines as O'Beirne lied, charging that Cody had sent the Lakotas home without even an interpreter when in fact they had been accompanied by Fred Matthews, a veteran stage driver from the Wild West.

Nevertheless, O'Beirne sanctimoniously arranged for six pallbearers to accompany Kills Plenty's coffin home to Pine Ridge from New York. He sent along a pillow of flowers and a note to Agent Gallagher informing him that he intended to lay the matter of Kill Plenty's death and the abuse of Wild West Indians before the government in Washington.

O'Beirne charged that Cody used Indian performers like chattel until their spirits were broken; when spent, he abandoned them or sent them home without their former robust health, money, or even an interpreter. O'Beirne also claimed over one-third of the original group of Lakotas who signed on with the Wild West had been callously cast off from the shows and returned in such pitiful condition.

By August, three more of the Lakotas who returned from Spain and accompanied Kills Plenty's funeral entourage to Pine Ridge were reported to be seriously ill: two with symptoms of heart disease and the other with jaundice. This news brought Secretary Noble to reverse his decision to allow Indians to be exhibited in traveling shows.

When the Wild West arrived in Berlin, Cody and Salsbury received news of the growing scandal and of the government's investigation into their treatment of Indians. The partners immediately put the Wild West into winter camp in Alsace-Lorraine and personally accompanied the Lakota performers in the troupe back to America. Before leaving Berlin, however, Major John Burke went to work cabling the newspapers in New York with the first salvos aimed at O'Beirne and those attacking the Wild West, referring to them as "notoriety-seeking busybodies"—"the forked-tongue of human serpents" attempting "without reason or rhyme, truth or reason to stain a fair record."[11] Burke also cabled Commissioner Morgan telling him that he and Salsbury had decided to accompany the Indian performers in his Wild West to Washington to personally explain their treatment in his company. Burke closed by imploring Morgan to reserve his final judgment in the matter until the Wild West partners had a chance to present their side of the case.

As Commissioner Morgan was touring Indian Agency schools, acting commissioner Robert V. Belt received Burke's cable. On October 1, acting on his own authority, Belt issued a circular to all agents ordering them to warn all Indians under their control against becoming involved with exhibitions and to inform Indians that to leave the reservation to join any Wild West show would be considered an act of defiance of the U.S. government. Next, Belt learned when Cody's ship, the *Belgenland*, would arrive in Philadelphia and arranged for James O'Beirne and Herbert Welsh of the Indian Rights Organization in Philadelphia to accompany the immigration officers to examine the returning members of the Wild West. O'Beirne brought with him Father Francis M. Craft, a Catholic missionary who had spent years with the Lakota and spoke the language. In order to insure their benevolent behavior was properly covered by the press, the trio also brought along a gaggle of reporters as they boarded the *Belgenland* at the Philadelphia navy yard.

John Burke refused to let the group examine the Indians and promptly denounced O'Beirne, Welsh, and Craft before the reporters. The skillful press agent was able to detain the party until Cody and the Lakotas could allude them and sneak off the ship. Then, he informed the trio and reporters that Cody had departed for New York and that he, Salsbury and the group of Indians were leaving for Washington that very afternoon. Salsbury and Burke made a wise decision to send Cody to New York and keep him above the fray. The very next morning Burke and Salsbury arrived at the offices of the Bureau of Indian Affairs only to be chastised by acting commissioner Belt for refusing to allow Welsh to examine the Indians in their care. Burke and Salsbury defended their actions, maintaining that they would have been receptive to an impartial inspection but that General O'Beirne's presence prejudiced the entire idea of a judicious examination of their case. The showmen skillfully argued that O'Beirne had been responsible for creating most of the controversy and any interrogation with him present could not have been impartial. Instead, they had decided to personally bring the Indians in question into the Bureau offices; there, the commissioner could see for himself that they were in good health and the Indians themselves would be able to answer all his questions. Belt was appeased with Burke and Salsbury's logical arguments and a meeting was scheduled for 10:00 A.M. the next morning in the Department of the Interior.

The following morning seventy-nine Indians from Buffalo Bill's Wild West arrived at the appointed time. Belt demanded that Burke and Salsbury remain outside and met alone with the Indians. Their spokesman, Rocky Bear, opened the meeting by reminding those present that he and his companions were expected to meet with President Harrison in the White House at 1:00 P.M. and they needed to bring the proceeding to a halt before that time. Rocky Bear next introduced Chauncey Yellow Robe, a student from Carlisle Indian School who would act as their interpreter. When Belt asked if any in their group had been mistreated in any way, the Lakotas unanimously responded that they had not been abused. Making it quite clear that he was free to make his own decisions, Rocky Bear went further to explain to Belt that if he had been mistreated that he would have left the show. The Lakota explained that he was getting fat working in the show and that when he returned to the reservation he was poor. Noting that he continually sent money home and had three hundred dollars in gold coins in his pockets, Rocky Bear concluded by responding to the charge that performing in Cody's Wild West show demeaned the Lakota: "If the great father wants me to stop, I would do it. That is the way I get money. If a man goes to work in some other place and goes back with money, he has some for his children."[12]

Belt's investigation was uncovering a fundamental aspect of Buffalo Bill's relationship with Plains Indians: Cody truly believed that Indians should be treated like any other person might expect to be treated, that Indians had the basic human right to be whatever or whoever they wished to be. When visiting the great cities of western civilization, Cody did not put Indian performers on a leash, as the Indian Rights Organization might have wished. Cody did not follow his cowboys, sharpshooters, musicians, teamsters, or stage crew around on their time off from work; likewise, he did not believe Indians should be restricted in their freedom of movement and exploration. On the contrary, Cody encouraged Indian performers to explore western society with hopes they would learn and adapt more readily to the changes being forced upon them by their conquerors. This is not to say Cody just allowed the Indians under his charge to go unprepared into the sprawling slums of industrialized urban decay. From the very beginnings of his employment of Plains Indians, Cody taught them to be mindful of their money and to send as much as possible home, and, in later years, the Wild West even set up a system to allow Indian performers to hold back portions of their salary in a savings account. Fundamentally, however, Cody did not believe in interfering with the Indian performers' basic rights to spend their money as they pleased. Cody naturally had to deal with the very real and dangerous problem of alcohol among the Indian performers. Here again, he allowed them to monitor themselves. In accepting the role as a Lakota "chaperone," Luther Standing Bear offers personal insight into Cody's way of allowing Lakota performers to govern themselves as they explored western civilization:

> My relations, you all know that I am to take care of you while going across the big water to another country, and all the time we are to stay there. I have heard that when any one joins this show, about the first thing he thinks of is getting drunk. I understand that the regulations of the Buffalo Bill show require that no Indian shall be given any liquor. You all know that I do not drink, and I am going to keep

you all from it. Don't think that because you may be closely related to me I will shield you, for I will not. I will report to Colonel Cody immediately any one I find drinking.[13]

Cody's concerned trust in Lakota performers continued to reveal itself as acting Commissioner Belt pressed on with his inquiry. Belt was finally won over when the Lakota, Black Heart, rose to counter O'Beirne's charges while also offering the most resonant argument for the right of Indians to work in Wild West shows:

> What [he] has said, that is not to be listened to. What the great father says, that is to be listened to . . . These men [Cody, Burke and Salsbury] have got us in hand. We were raised on horseback; that is the way we had to work. These men furnished us the same work we were raised to; that is the reason we want to work for these kind of men . . . if Indian wants to work at any place and earn money, he wants to do so; white man got privilege to do the same—any kind of work he wants.[14]

In defining the fact that the Lakotas ultimately only needed to listen to the orders of the President of the United States, Black Heart had simply and eloquently expressed to Belt a most astute understanding of the Plains Indians' unique legal status. Of equal importance, however, Black Heart had also succinctly and passionately expressed the natural attraction of the recently "wild" Lakota to the "make-believe" reenactment of the Wild West; these people were raised to ride horses and, in the Wild West, they could still ride and shoot and get paid for it. In closing, Black Heart had punctuated all this with a gentle reminder that the Indian had the same fundamental needs and rights as the white man to earn a living.

Upon hearing Black Heart's defense of his basic human rights, Belt called Salsbury and Burke into the room and exonerated them and Cody of the charges of abusing Indians. Before allowing the Lakotas to leave, however, Belt warned them that upon returning to the reservation they would encounter "some little excitement growing out of the religion of your people."[15]

The "excitement" of which Belt spoke was the messianic movement known as the "Ghost Dance."

Even as Belt issued his warning to the Lakota performers, the Ghost Dance was the cause of major alarm throughout "Indian Country." The

"Messiah Movement" of 1890, however, did not spring up "overnight"; its ancient origins lay deep in the prophetic religious history of both the Native and Euroamerican cultures. The similarities of historic messianic prophecies in both cultures were emphasized and nourished by Christian missionary efforts to convert Indians, particularly as they were herded onto reservations. As whole Indian nations and cultures fell under the European invasion of North America, prophets, much like priests offering last rites, often appeared when doom was evident in order to offer the desperate hope of miraculous relief from oppression. As the malignant effects of the holocaust spread rapidly in the late 1880s, the Ghost Dance had become increasingly important to the Lakota and other plains tribes. Nevertheless, the actual messiah movement began near Walker Lake in western Nevada in 1857 with a Paiute shaman named Tavibo and his mentor, Wodziwob.

Around this time a voice spoke to Tavibo and Wodziwob. The voice told them the earth was worn out and the Great Spirit was going to renew it. This rejuvenation of the earth would be for Indians exclusively. All the Indians who had died would come back to life with this renewal if living Indians would perform a sacred dance for the departed souls—a dance of the ghosts. The Paiutes' vision caught on very quickly with the desperate tribes of neighboring California and Oregon, even contributing to the "Modoc War" of 1872–73 on the border of these two states. Soon after the Modoc War, however, Tavibo suddenly became ill and died and the tribes lost interest in the Ghost Dance and the movement faded away.

Tavibo's death left his fourteen-year-old son orphaned and homeless. A neighboring white ranching family named Wilson adopted Tavibo's son, Wovoka, gave him the name Jack, and raised him with their two sons. Devout Christians, the Wilson family held nightly Bible readings and prayer sessions. From these gatherings, Wovoka gained a fundamental knowledge of Christianity. The curious youth sought more knowledge of the white man's religion from Mormon missionaries who worked among the Paiutes.

Wovoka got the idea for the famous "Ghost Shirts" worn by Ghost Dancers while he was living among the Mormons. Exclusive elders in the Mormon faith were presented with "divine" vestments which promised heavenly protection in this life and celestial glory in the next. Wovoka incorporated the Mormon idea of divinely protected garments into the concept of the "Ghost Shirts."

Wovoka also spent time as a teenager working in Washington and Oregon in the hop fields. There he encountered the "Shakers," or "Shaking

Quakers." The Shakers were ascetic Christians who, as the "Whirling Dervish" sects of Sufi Muslims, believed a heightened state of awareness and prophecy could be obtained through "agitated" or ritualistic dancing. Spiritual, ceremonial dancing and prophecy being an essential trait common to all tribes of Native American people, the Shakers reaching premonitory states of awareness through sacred dancing certainly influenced Wovoka's attempts to reconcile his Pauite spiritual heritage with Jack Wilson's Christian future. Wovoka's desperate effort to hold to the values of his traditional Pauite spiritual heritage reflected every single Indian in North America at the time; all Indian people understood clearly that the final act of their subjugation would be to have their religion taken from them and replaced with Christianity. Having been turned over to Christian missionaries, Indian religious leaders were valiantly attempting to rapidly transpose and translate Christianity to their people through similarities within their own cultural tradition. Facing the annihilation of everything they held sacred, all Indian parents realized that their children would be forced to embrace Christianity in order to survive.

Even though Wovoka came into contact with these various religious influences during his teenage years, he married a Pauite woman and settled into a quiet, normal life. Sometime in 1886, however, this changed suddenly. Wovoka was chopping wood in the mountains when he was overcome with an unusual feeling. Soon, he collapsed and experienced a vision in which he died and was taken to heaven. In heaven Wovoka spoke with God, who issued forth a message to him which was nearly identical to the Ghost Dance visions of his father, Tovibo.

As Tovibo before him, Wovoka started to attract a very small following. Unlike Tovibo, however, Wovoka was unable to immediately gather a sizeable congregation of disciples. This all changed dramatically, however, on January 1, 1889. During a complete solar eclipse occurring on that very day, Wovoka's vision took an entirely new direction; he had been suffering from Scarlet Fever and as the sun "vanished" it appeared to all present that the medicine man died with the darkening of the light. Assuming Wovoka dead, his followers started funeral arrangements. The medicine man's wife would not allow the disciples to bury her husband, however, and, as the eclipse ended, Wovoka miraculously returned to consciousness with return of the sun.

Revived, Wovoka spoke again of ascending into Heaven to receive a prophecy. Now, however, he was returning as the son of God, the messiah, a Christ with control over the fate of the world. Moreover, his earlier prophecies were now expanding: The new prophecy predicted the old, worn-out world would be completely destroyed before eventually being restored as it was before the coming of white men. Now, as the messiah, Wovoka was commanded by God to summons all people to come to him to receive the Great Spirit's new message; his prophecy was for all mankind. The Indian messiah's vision was not unlike the Hebrew messiah's; both simply implored men to love one another and to do right.

As always, the message of peace and love was timely. Soon Indians began flocking to Wovoka'a nightly Ghost Dances until the numbers swelled into the hundreds. Fasting for days, fanatical dancers would continue dancing until they collapsed to the ground exhausted. Then, in their dissipated state they would experience ascending into heaven themselves, visiting with departed loved ones and receiving glimpses and visions of the coming paradise. With growing intensity, Wovoka's disciples began to proselytize the new religion to all surrounding tribes until the Ghost Dance developed into a full-fledged messianic movement throughout Indian Country.

The Ghost Dance flourished in the state of desperation which existed throughout Indian Country after armed resistance ended. Conquered, the Lakota people faced horrific consequences. Aside from the total destruction of their religion and culture, they were defenseless as the U.S. government began its organized efforts to steal their remaining land. In 1882, as soon as Sitting Bull surrendered and was imprisoned at Fort Randall, Newton Edmunds headed a commission comprised of frontier lawyer Peter Shannon and James Teller. Newton Edwards was a former territorial governor of the Dakotas. Dating back to 1865, Edwards had a history of attempting to steal Lakota land. James Teller was the brother of Henry Teller, who was Secretary of the Interior.[16] Reverend Samuel D. Hinman, whose history of duplicity and manipulation with the Lakota went back as far as the Santee uprising, served as interpreter for the commission. Hinman bullied and lied to the Lakota, going so far as to secure children's signatures in a vain attempt to gather the three-fourths majority required by the Laramie Treaty of 1868 to cede land. In spite of the failure to obtain the required majority of legal Lakota males' signatures, early in 1883 Edmunds and Hinman went to Washington with their bogus petition and were successful in lobbying members of Congress to introduce a bill ceding about half of the Great Sioux Reservation to the United States. Fortunately, in spite of Hinman and Edmunds' unethical methods, there were senators who were aware of the requirements of the so-called "Red Cloud Treaty of 1868." These lawmakers quickly pointed out to their colleagues that, even if the petition proved valid, Edmunds and Hinman had failed to obtain the requisite percentage of signatures. The fraudulent legislation consequently failed.

A second commission, headed by Massachusetts Senator Henry L. Dawes, was immediately formed to investigate the questionable methods of the Edmunds Commission. Accompanied by the Honorable John A. Logan of Illinois, the Honorable George G. Vest of Missouri, the Honorable John T. Morgan of Alabama, and the Honorable Angus Cameron of Wisconsin, the Dawes Commission arrived in the Dakotas shortly before Sitting Bull returned from prison at Fort Randall to his ancestral homeland on Grand River at Standing Rock. In an overtly hostile "welcoming" act designed to make his and Sitting Bull's position painfully clear, Indian Agent James "White Hair" McLaughlin had handed the chief a hoe and showed him to the garden. Around the time Sitting Bull had planted his first crops, however, Dawes's illustrious commission arrived at Standing Rock to begin its investigation.

McLaughlin's attempted control of Standing Rock was obvious even as the Dawes Commission began its inquiry. "White Hair" used the situation to attack Sitting Bull's control over the traditionals and belittle the chief's revered position within the tribe by arranging for Lakotas under his control to be in leadership roles in the council. The true leader of the people, Sitting Bull, was ignored and relegated to the role of witnessing the proceedings from the audience while McLaughlin's Lakota "yes" men, led by John Grass, who was known as "Charging Bear" among the Lakota,[17] were honored as the first to be invited to speak.

McLaughlin was able to attract rivals of Sitting Bull at this time because many Lakotas were also deeply concerned about Sitting Bull addressing any commission representing the U.S. government. The chief's history of debating U.S. negotiators such as General Terry in Canada usually resulted with the government's humiliation being spun into fierce retaliation painfully manifested upon the Lakota people. Under the boot of such brutal oppression, many Lakotas were far too weary and fragile to bear the brunt of anymore backfiring ramifications of their chief's speeches. Nevertheless, when he realized the true nature of the commission Sitting Bull could not simply remain a passive witness.

Stanley Vestal perhaps best sums up why Sitting Bull was forced to engage the commissioners:

The report of this Select Committee is one of the funniest docu-
ments in all the files of the minutes of Indians councils—and that is
saying a good deal. It reads like the Trial Scene in "Alice In Wonder-
land." The Senators snapped out one question after another, questions entirely unrelated to the answers previously given, and they
soon had poor John Grass bewildered. The Indians went into their
grievances at some length, and the committee as steadily ignored
their remarks and kept hounding the Sioux as to whether or not they
wished to earn the money (already due them), and whether they
would try to earn it, if the Grandfather ever sent them the tools and
seed and machinery promised them so many years before. It is quite
clear that the committee cared nothing whatever for the Indians or
their troubles, but were merely preparing a document for printing
which would read well on the frontier and whitewash the commission of 1882.[18]

Sitting Bull's very presence created a major problem for the Dawes
Commission: No matter how corrupt, committee members realized they
could not return to Washington without interviewing the most famous living Sioux. Having been sanctioned and charged by Congress to report on
the Indians of the Dakotas and Montana, ignoring Sitting Bull would have
undermined the validity of anything else in their subsequent report. The
chief's fame had worked for him yet again; without uttering a word, the
chief had forced his opponents to come to him as chief. Stanley Vestal
presents the official report verbatim:

> Chairman (to the interpreter): Ask Sitting Bull if he has anything to
> say to the committee.
>   Sitting Bull: Of course I will speak if you desire me to do so. I sup-
> pose it is only such men as you desire to speak who must say any-
> thing.
>   Chairman: We supposed the Indians would select men to speak
> for them. But any man who desires to speak, or any man the Indians
> here desire shall talk for them, we will be glad to hear if he has any-
> thing to say.
>   Sitting Bull: Do you know who I am that you speak as you do?
>   Chairman: I know you are Sitting Bull.
>   Sitting Bull: You say you know I am Sitting Bull, but do you know
> what position I hold?
>   Chairman: I do not know any difference between you and the
> other Indians at this agency.

Sitting Bull: I am here by the will of the Great Spirit, and by His will I am a chief. My heart is red and sweet, and I know it is sweet, because whatever passes near me puts out its tongue to me; and yet you men have come here to talk with us, and you do not know who I am. I want to tell you that if the Great Spirit has chosen anyone to be the chief of this country, it is myself.

Chairman: In whatever capacity you may be here today, if you desire to say anything to us we will listen to you; otherwise we will dismiss the council.

Sitting Bull: Yes, that is all right. You have conducted yourselves here like men who have been drinking whiskey, and I came here to give you some advice. (Here Sitting Bull waved his hand, and at once the Indians left the room in a body.)[19]

Once again Sitting Bull had simply and powerfully demonstrated his mastery over government negotiators while simultaneously exhibiting his obvious leadership of the Lakota Nation. In spite of their respect for their chief, however, the next day several Lakota headmen came to council with Sitting Bull. They expressed concern that these commissioners were visiting with sincere efforts to rectify the abuses of the first committee and that he had insulted and angered them. Swallowing his pride, Sitting Bull acquiesced and the headmen hurriedly reconvened the council with the commissioners. Sitting Bull eloquently apologized to the commission but quickly moved on, presenting a history of the grievances of his people brought about by the U.S. government's consistent string of broken promises in negotiations. Rather than politely accepting Sitting Bull's apology and offering to hear what he had to say, however, the commissioners attacked. Senator John Logan disrespectfully reprimanded the chief for interrupting the earlier council by accusing the committee members of being drunk. Not content to insult the chief by publicly scolding him, Senator Logan attempted a complete humiliation and told Sitting Bull that he was not a great chief, had no following, power, or right to control. Logan went for the throat when he told Sitting Bull:

You are on an Indian reservation merely at the sufferance of the government, your children are educated by the government and all you have and are today is because of the government. If it were not for the government you would be freezing and starving today in the mountains. I merely say these things to you to notify you that you cannot insult the people of the United States of America or its committees. . . . The government feeds and clothes and educates your children now, and desires to teach you to become farmers, and to civilize you, and to make you as white men.[20]

The entire interaction with the Dawes Commission and the Lakota, ending with Senator Logan's acrimonious attempt to denigrate Sitting Bull, vividly reveals the complete and total disregard of the basic legal and human rights of Native America by the American people, their religious community and their Congress in 1883. The Dawes Commission's raw attack on Sitting Bull also indicated to McLaughlin the fact that the government absolutely understood and authorized the necessity of breaking the influence of the chief. Logan, Dawes and the other lawmakers had discovered what McLaughlin had before them dealing with Sitting Bull: No matter how dangerous the threat of reprisal, the people followed their spiritual chief. Consequently McLaughlin's fundamental procedure was to "break" the chief much like one might train a horse. Once a particular chief such as John Grass was "broken," he could be easily reconstructed and useful to further manipulate the tribe. From the beginning of his relationship with Sitting Bull, however, McLaughlin realized he would never be able to "break" Sitting Bull. To his credit, McLaughlin first sought to simply get the chief out of his hair; it is no wonder that "White Hair" jumped at the chance to send him off to St. Paul in late 1883. It also explains why McLaughlin was anxious to release the chief to perform in Buffalo Bill's Wild West in 1885. Likewise, the nefarious tactics used by the Edmunds and Dawes Commissions also make it perfectly obvious why Sitting Bull did not put up a fight when McLaughlin reversed himself and blocked the chief's return to the Wild West in 1886: Sitting Bull realized the Lakota needed his leadership to defend the next wave of land poachers from Washington. Furthermore, Sitting Bull had already accomplished his objective of getting Lakota performers in the Wild West and was well aware of McLaughlin's underhanded tactics of getting him out of the way in order to do his dirty work. "It is bad for our cause for me to parade around, awakening the hatred of white men everywhere," Sitting Bull said, finally declining the Wild West invitation in 1886. "Besides, I am needed here; there is more talk of taking our lands."[21]

The battle of wills between McLaughlin and Sitting Bull intensified dramatically as soon as the Dawes Commission departed and the agent began recruiting all Lakota men who were jealous of the medicine man. McLaughlin decided to employ one of mankind's most ancient tools of conflict—divide and conquer. From the beginning, the agent had the backing of the settlers, missionaries, traders, and the military. From this power base, McLaughlin was able to organize a powerful force of followers comprised of employees, Indian police, and those aspiring to political office. This group allowed McLaughlin to create false chiefs to rival Sitting Bull and erode his power. Sitting Bull's stepson, Gall, was set up as the "conquering hero"; John Grass, of the Blackfeet, the mastermind. In order to win the agent's favor, these chiefs had become obedient, yet, like McLaughlin, were jealous of Sitting Bull's power and fame. Whenever a stranger came to visit Standing Rock the first person they asked for was Sitting Bull. It drove McLaughlin and the subchiefs crazy with jealousy; they worked constantly to win attention and favor while Sitting Bull did nothing and still attracted respect and admiration.[22]

As McLaughlin and the missionaries furthered their control over Standing Rock, Sitting Bull retreated increasingly to his homeland on Grand River. He built a cabin there for his wives and children and began to farm, raise cattle and chickens, and generally attempt to do as McLaughlin and the government wished. Yet even as Sitting Bull attempted to meet McLaughlin's rigid requirements, the agent continued to assemble a police force of Lakotas who were envious of the chief. By 1888, however, yet another government commission attempted to swindle a cession of eleven million acres of Lakota land at a fixed price of fifty cents an acre. Perhaps even worse than the thought of losing the land, however, this act would divide the Great Sioux Reservation into six smaller ones, leaving nine million acres open to settlers. If this cession of land was successful, each of the six smaller reservations would become like islands surrounded by an ocean of whites. Sitting Bull could not bear this thought and he rallied. He quickly consulted with John Grass and Gall and convinced them both to side with him and hold fast. As a result of Sitting Bull's Hunkpapa/Blackfeet Lakota coalition, the commissioners failed yet again to gather the required signatures of three-fourths of the Lakota male population to cede land and the government effort collapsed.

Undeterred, by 1889 the government enlisted General George "Three Stars" Crook into the effort to break up the Great Sioux Reservation. A respected former enemy, Crook had evolved into a negotiator most Indians trusted. Aware that the Lakota considered Crook trustworthy for good reason, government officials first convinced the ethical general that the Lakota were ultimately destined to lose their land and that he would be acting in their best interest to help them negotiate a monetary solution. In May,

1889, Crook accompanied Charles Foster of Ohio and William Warner of Missouri in yet another effort to gather the magic three-fourths majority of signatures from the Lakota and break up the reservation promised by the Laramie Treaty of 1868.

Being a military man, Crook first attacked at the Lakotas' weakest link—Spotted Tail's Brules. Among the Brules Three Stars would use the same ancient tactic as McLaughlin; he intended to divide his opponents into two conflicting camps. Since Spotted Tail's assassination, however, Crook realized his work had already been done for him; the Brules were already divided as evidenced by the political killing. The general worked his way in between the feuding Brules and began negotiations with them. After nine days of discussion he secured the majority of signatures and headed to Pine Ridge. The first signature on the petition was that of Spotted Tail's assassin, Crow Dog.

At Pine Ridge, because of Red Cloud's enduring influence and the several hundred warriors the old chief ordered to surround the proceedings, the commissioners were only able to gather signatures from half the male population. Undaunted, Crook shifted his effort to the smaller agencies to attempt to keep the momentum moving in favor of cumulatively gathering the three-fourths majority of the male population. The tactic worked and the general was successful gathering legal signatures. As fate would have it, by the time Three Star's commissioners arrived at Standing Rock in July, the decision to sell the Great Sioux Reservation lay with the votes of the Hunkpapa and Blackfeet Lakota. If Sitting Bull could hold his coalition together Crook's commission would fail; if it crumbled, the huge reservation would be carved into smaller ones surrounded by settlers. Again in true military fashion, Crook used his lieutenants and ordered Agent McLaughlin to use his power to break Sitting Bull's influence.

McLaughlin went immediately to work on his reconstructed sub-chiefs. He arranged for a surreptitious meeting between himself and John Grass in a secluded stable where the two rehearsed a speech in which the Blackfeet Lakota would reverse himself and urge his followers to vote for selling their land. The two then visited Gall and informed him of the prepared speech John Grass would deliver at the council. Realizing the political tables had turned, Gall shifted his allegiance to Grass and McLaughlin. To further secure his position, White Hair stationed his Indian Police in a four-column formation around the semi-circle formed by the council when it convened. A final underhanded ploy, McLaughlin waited until the very last minute to inform Sitting Bull of the council; when Sitting Bull and his followers arrived late for the proceedings they were unable to make their way through McLaughlin's Indian Police force in time to interrupt the agent's plan. Following the "leadership" of Grass and Gall, Sitting Bull's alliance was broken and, as Grass eloquently delivered his "ghost-written" speech, the Standing Rock Lakota signed the document; the government had finally succeeded in breaking up the Great Sioux Reservation. Dejected, when a reporter asked what Indians thought of ceding their land, Sitting Bull responded: "Indians! There are no Indians left but me!"[23]

Perhaps he was right. With his failure to block the theft of Lakota lands Sitting Bull retreated with his most devoted followers to Grand River. Sensing his vulnerability, and provoked by McLaughlin, Sitting Bull's Lakota enemies became more bold and, like wolves stalking a wounded animal, increasingly circled the chief and began nipping at his heels. With such aggressive and destructive movement succeeding on Sitting Bull's outer perimeters, McLaughlin also intensified his efforts to subvert the chief internally, sending his minions regularly to Grand River to council privately with Sitting Bull and to chip away at his resolve and that of his immediate circle of followers.

During this confusing time a white woman named Catherine Weldon became intricately involved in Sitting Bull's life. A member of the National Indian Defense Association, Mrs. Weldon traveled from Brooklyn with her fourteen-year-old son, Christie, to attempt to help Sitting Bull defeat government efforts to break up the Lakota Reservation. An artist, Mrs. Weldon was in her thirties, rich, erratically eccentric, stubborn, well-dressed, and obsessively impressed with Sitting Bull. Mrs. Weldon and Agent McLaughlin clashed immediately as the wealthy widow supported the importance of Sitting Bull by moving in with him and virtually becoming like one of his wives. The wealthy widow bankrolled most of Sitting Bull's feasts given for his followers at Grand River, an act which reinforced the medicine man's magnanimous reputation and caused White Hair great discomfort. Mrs. Weldon and the Indian Agent withdrew to separate corners, settling into a tense toleration of one another.

Sitting Bull was as confused as anyone by Mrs. Weldon's unusual behavior. In Lakota culture, if a woman was so forward as to pursue a man in such a manner as Mrs. Weldon, it was assumed by everyone she intended to also become his bed-partner. Following the dictates of his culture, the old chief did the honorable thing and proposed to the widow. Rather than being honored by his sincere proposal, however, Mrs. Weldon's righteous rejection bordered on disrespect of the chief. Complicating matters, Sitting Bull's Lakota wives became jealous of the white woman's presence and their husband paying her any attention at all.

McLaughlin immediately capitalized on the opportunity to discredit both Sitting Bull and Weldon and started rumors that the widow had actually married the old chief and bore him a child. Newspaper reporters referred to the widow as Sitting Bull's "White Squaw." Unfazed by the humiliating notoriety, Mrs. Weldon and Christie stayed in a cabin near Sitting Bull's compound on Grand River. She painted Sitting Bull's portrait, washed his clothes, cleaned his cabin and continued bankrolling his many feasts for his followers.

Sitting Bull may have had trouble with women, but much more serious problems were rapidly increasing for his Lakota enemies. As Sitting Bull predicted, the government had no more intention of honoring Crook's treaty than any negotiated in the past. Earnest money promised by the commissioners never was paid. Moreover, rather than increasing the food and clothing rations as promised by the terms of the new contract, annuities were decreased. Adding to the severity, the trusted negotiator of the new treaty, General George Crook, died in the spring of 1890. After Crook's death, the Lakota entered a terrible summer drought which destroyed all attempts at farming. Sitting Bull prophesized the drought of 1890–91. He told his followers that the drought would continue into the winter and that snowfall would be so low that they would be able to continue the Ghost Dance throughout the winter months.[4] Complicating matters, in July the government issued orders that the Lakota could no longer hunt for any game. Forbidden to hunt, as the annuities were held back from distribution all of the agencies began to face starvation and, as epidemics of whooping cough and measles spread throughout Indian Country, children started dying of the lethal combination of disease and malnutrition.

As their situation on the reservation became more deadly, Lakota leaders, like other desperate Indians, sent emissaries to visit Wovoka's camps to explore the talk of an Indian messiah. In June of 1890 three Lakota men—a Minneconjou named Kicking Bear, a Brule named Short Bull, and an Oglala named Porcupine—traveled to Nevada to seek out the messiah. The trio returned in midsummer and began to tell the Lakota of the *Wanekia* and teach them how to perform the new dance. By the end of July the Ghost Dance was spreading rapidly throughout the Pine Ridge and Rosebud Reservations. By August, hundreds were dancing daily. Next Kicking Bear headed to Cheyenne River Reservation to proselytize his own Minneconjou people. There, Chief's Big Foot and Hump enthusiastically joined the movement. Finally, on October 9, Kicking Bear visited Sitting Bull's camp at Grand River to tell the chief about the messiah.

Sitting Bull remarked upon hearing Kicking Bear's account of the messiah's Ghost Dance: "It is impossible for a dead man to return and live again."[25] As mentioned repeatedly in this text, the daily life of the Lakota and religion were one and the same. As Lakota religion was entirely tolerant they were always prepared to try anything once; any prayer that brought positive results was a good prayer. Longing to see departed relatives convinced most to participate in the "moving seance." Sitting Bull feared the troops would prevent their dancing as they had the Sun Dance, but Kicking Bear convinced him the troops' bullets were powerless to stop the dance. Kicking Bear told the dancers to wear sacred tunics painted with the images of the sun, moon, stars, eagles, magpies, and buffalo; these "Ghost Shirts" would provide protection against any bullets.[26]

Kicking Bear, mimicking the inexplicable ability of Lakota and Cheyenne warriors to prevent themselves from being hit by enemy fire, is consequently credited with attributing Wovoka's "Ghost Shirts" with the unique Plains Indian characteristic of being "bullet-proof." Indeed, most of the militant misinterpretation of Wovoka's message of peace and love can be directly traced to the Minneconjou. Kicking Bear can also be credited with translating Wovoka's peaceful message of a resurrected world into the concept of the coming new/old world being predicated upon and born from a massive destruction of the white world brought about through the Ghost Dance.[27] Kicking Bear's dangerous embellishment of the mystical protective power of the Ghost Shirts, however, would prove to be the perfect route past Sitting Bull's natural cynicism concerning a messiah: The medicine man had on several occasions himself sat in an open prairie smoking his pipe as bullets zipped within inches of his body; he had known many Lakota and Cheyenne comrades who possessed such magic powers. Sitting Bull was also desperate to raise the spirits and morale of his followers. As all Indians facing genocide, Sitting Bull was also ready to accept any hope the Great Spirit offered. He therefore invited Kicking Bear to stay at Grand River and teach his followers about the Ghost Dance.

Stanley Vestal astutely observes:

> Thus overnight, Sitting Bull's band became Christianized. Of course the missionaries of long-established sects would not admit that the Ghost Dance was a Christian church. But their claim is absurd. For you cannot believe in the Second Coming of Christ unless you be-

lieve in the First. The Ghost Dance was entirely Christian—except for the difference in rituals. However, it taught nonresistance and brotherly love in ways that had far more significance for Indians than any the missions could offer. No wonder the missionaries became alarmed; they were no longer sure of their converts.[28]

Vestal's insight into the true origins and ultimate mission of the Ghost Dance could not be more obvious than in Sitting Bull's back yard. As soon as Kicking Bear started teaching the new religion and dance to the Hunkpapas at Grand River, arguments insued between two rivals competing for the medicine man's attention. A Christian missionary herself, Mrs. Weldon immediately began ridiculing Kicking Bear's "messiah" and the pair battled so intensely that the widow's forceful arguments backfired and turned the Lakotas against her. Soon even Sitting Bull was convinced that she was plotting against him. As the Ghost Dancing quickly started to become more intense and fanatic, Mrs. Weldon finally started to consider leaving Sitting Bull's compound.

On October 14, McLaughlin sent a dozen Indian Police led by Lieutenant Chatka to eject Kicking Bear from Sitting Bull's camp. The next day Lieutenant Chatka and his police force escorted Kicking Bear to the Moreau River, the southern boundary of Standing Rock Reservation. That night Sitting Bull broke his peace-pipe, according to Lakota custom signifying his being prepared to die. Unfortunately, McLaughlin interpreted Sitting Bull's statement as an eagerness to become a martyr for the new messiah religion. The next day McLaughlin notified the Commissioner of Indian Affairs that Sitting Bull was the real power behind the Ghost Dance frenzy at Standing Rock; hoping to personally bring the chief to submission, he further recommended that Sitting Bull be arrested and removed from the reservation before the movement could be allowed to grow into a full-blown return to hostilities. At this juncture Mrs. Weldon gave up the fight; on October 22 Sitting Bull escorted her to Cannonball, where she and her son boarded a steamboat headed downriver. Christie Weldon stepped on a rusty nail as he was boarding the steamboat, developed lockjaw, and was dead before the boat arrived in St. Louis. Devastated, Catherine Weldon retreated from Indian Country and withdrew into privacy.[29]

By the middle of November Ghost Dancing had become so prevalent throughout the Dakotas that all other activities ceased. Western newspapermen began printing outrageous headlines suggesting that Sitting Bull was urging his followers to take up arms and return to the warpath. Rumors spread through settler communities that the Sioux were preparing surprise attacks with massive numbers of warriors. The intensity of the situation accelerated when a new, inexperienced agent, Dr. Daniel F. Royer, replaced Agent Hugh Gallagher at Pine Ridge. The name given Royer by the Oglalas—"Young Man Afraid Of His Indians"—perfectly sums up his personality. Frightened by the Ghost Dance and rumors of hostilities, Royer telegraphed Washington with the urgent message:

> The Indians are dancing in the snow and are wild and crazy . . . We need protection and we need it now . . . I deem the situation at this agency very critical, and believe that a outbreak may occur at any time, and it does not seem to me safe to longer withhold troops.[30]

On November 14, agents at Pine Ridge, Rosebud, Cheyenne River, and Standing Rock Reservations received telegrams notifying them that the President had directed the Secretary of War to assume military responsibility for suppressing any outbreak of hostilities among the Ghost Dancers. On November 20 the Indian Bureau ordered agents at the same reservations to telegraph the names of the "fomenters of the disturbances"[31] to Washington. This list was forwarded to Chicago to General Nelson Miles, who had become commander of the Military District of the Missouri. When "Bear Coat" saw Sitting Bull's name on the list he immediately assumed that his old adversary was the ringleader of all the trouble.

Miles certainly realized that any attempt by troops to arrest Sitting Bull would be met with fierce resistance and quite possibly initiate a new Indian War. Motivated by this awareness, Miles was forced to consider less aggressive options. This thinking led the general to consider his friend, Buffalo Bill, as a peaceful arbitrator. As one of the only white men whom Sitting Bull liked, General Miles believed Cody might be able to quietly convince the chief to peacefully surrender himself to authorities.

Cody returned from Europe to deal with his own unique problems with Indians and not to become involved in any new U.S. military operations. When he avoided General John O'Bierne, Herbert Welsh and their entourage of reporters and slipped off the *Belgenland* in Philadelphia in October, 1890, Cody traveled to New York and let Nate Salsbury and Major John Burke represent the Wild West before Commissioner Belt's investigation in Washington. Upon arrival at his hotel in New York, however, Cody was handed General Miles' telegram summoning him to Chicago. The scout hurried to Chicago and reported to General Miles a day and a half later. Miles immediately briefed Cody on the developments in the Dakotas but allowed Cody to return to Scout's Rest Ranch in Nebraska on November 15 for a family reunion with all his sisters.

While Cody was in Nebraska tension intensified in the Dakotas as McLaughlin went to Grand River and interviewed the Chief. Sitting Bull disclaimed all responsibility for the dance, which he maintained had been brought in from another agency. The Chief declared it peaceful and harmless, but seeing McLaughlin still was not dissatisfied, offered a logical proposition: The Hunkpapa suggested that he and McLaughlin travel together from tribe to tribe until they discover the tribe where the Ghost Dance began. There, Sitting Bull wisely suggested, if they could not produce the Messiah, he would personally return and tell his people the dance is all a lie. If, however, they did find the Messiah, then McLaughlin would have to allow the dancing to continue.[32]

If McLaughlin had truly wished to bring the Chief in without bloodshed he could not have had a better chance. Sitting Bull himself realized that no one would be able to attempt to arrest him without violence; he could, however, safely leave the compound of his own choice and he offered to do so with McLaughlin. Sitting Bull's offer of a logical and peaceful solution to the Ghost Dance frenzy was particularly meaningful when considering the fact that the chief and his bodyguards were quite aware that McLaughlin was secretly plotting to arrest him. McLaughlin himself had unwittingly made Sitting Bull's camp aware of his covert operation; indeed, McLaughlin had initially sought volunteers from Sitting Bull's own camp. Failing to recruit members of the chief's camp to help arrest him brought a Yankton Lakota named Bullhead into greater importance in the unfolding scenario. Bullhead offered to help McLaughlin assemble a team of Lakotas willing to arrest the chief. A few days later on the prairie a meadowlark sang out to Sitting Bull: "The Sioux will kill you!"[33]

On November 24, General Miles issued Cody orders to "secure the person of Sitting Bull." It is unclear whether or not Cody understood that General Miles intended for him to "arrest" Sitting Bull. Given Cody's history with Sitting Bull, it is very likely that he intended merely to have a friendly talk with the chief and attempt to safely bring him in to peacefully council with authorities.[34] Two days later Cody returned to the same Bismarck rail station from which he had departed the Dakotas after his fight with Yellow Hair fourteen years earlier. Accompanied by his old friends "Pony" Bob Haslam and Dr. Frank "White Beaver" Powell, Buffalo Bill reported immediately to Agent McLaughlin at Standing Rock on November 28. Having laid such elaborate, covert plans to bring about Sitting Bull's destruction, McLaughlin was deeply shocked yet remained silently outraged when Cody presented him with General Miles' orders. White Hair had planned for his Indian Police to arrest Sitting Bull when all Indians came into the agency on a ration day. He was acutely aware that any attempt to arrest the chief with his followers present would end in bloodshed and believed his minions could accomplish a relatively simple arrest when the chief was surrounded by only a few devoted guards. Nevertheless, faced with General Miles' orders, McLaughlin, with steely military obedience, arranged for a span of mules and wagon for his famous guest. Ever devious, however, McLaughlin went immediately into action and telegraphed acting Commissioner Belt in the Office of Indian Affairs in Washington:

> William F. Cody (Buffalo Bill) has arrived here with commission from General Miles to arrest Sitting Bull. Such a step at present is unnecessary and unwise, as it will precipitate a fight which can be averted. A few Indians are still dancing, but it does not mean mischief at present. I have matters well in hand, and when proper time arrives can arrest Sitting Bull by Indian Police without bloodshed. I ask attention to my letter of November 19. Request General Miles's order to Cody be rescinded and request immediate answer.[35]

McLaughlin next plotted with Lieutenant Colonel William F. Drum of the Eighth Cavalry and Twelfth Infantry at Fort Yates to delay Buffalo Bill from his mission until he could receive an answer from Washington. Cody had never scouted with either of these regiments and their officers probably dismissed him only as a showman and dime-novel hero. Ignorance of Buffalo Bill's reputation could be the only explanation for the underhanded method they chose to prevent Cody from getting to his friend Sitting Bull. Assuming that by drinking in relays they could drink the old scout under the table, they invited Cody to the officers club. There, the Colonel's legendary capacity for alcohol was such that it took all the officers of both regiments working in details of two and three at a time to maintain Cody's drinking pace throughout the day.[36]

The next morning Cody slept late before loading the wagon with presents for Sitting Bull and his wives and heading out toward his old friend's cabin on Grand River. Unarmed, "Pony" Bob Haslam, Dr. Frank "White Beaver" Powell, Steve Burke and "Bully" White accompanied Buffalo Bill. That Cody traveled without weapons to visit Sitting Bull amidst such tension indicates much: he was not afraid of Sitting Bull; he was not approaching the medicine man as an enemy; he was approaching an old friend with gifts. The fact that his presents were comprised mostly of candy indicates Cody's intimate knowledge that Sitting Bull was partial to sweets. The scout probably intended to eat candy and chat with his old friend. "If they'd let him alone," Cody's adopted son, Johnny Baker, said later, "he'd have captured Sitting Bull with an all-day sucker."[37] Sitting Bull's closest relative, nephew One Bull, also thought that his uncle would have gone in with Cody.[38]

One must wonder what went through acting Commissioner Belt's thoughts when he received McLaughlin's urgent cable and learned about General Miles and Buffalo Bill's actions with Sitting Bull. Only a few weeks had transpired since his investigation of Cody's treatment of Indian performers; Belt must have been shocked to realize that as his investigation was taking place in Washington, Cody was being recruited by General Miles to bring Sitting Bull into custody. Even though he had been genuinely impressed by Salsbury and Burke's sterling defense of Wild West procedures, and by the Lakota performers themselves, Belt probably harbored some resentment that the famous showman had not appeared at his investigation in Washington. Whatever his motives, Belt wasted no time presenting Agent McLaughlin's cable to President Benjamin Harrison, who quickly ordered Cody recalled from his mission. Ten miles from Fort Yates Cody's party was overtaken by a scout with President Harrison's order to return to the post. Buffalo Bill promptly realized he had been caught in a military/political conspiracy to bring Sitting Bull down and, as angry as he was, could not defy the President of the United States; he obediently returned to Fort Yates. Even though he realized the military personnel who had manipulated him considered him an outsider, Cody did not consider himself as such. He always believed if he had been able to get through to Sitting Bull he could have prevented the chief's murder and the bloodshed that followed at Wounded Knee. Later, Cody said that President Harrison told him that he regretted rescinding Miles' orders and recalling him from his mission.[39]

McLaughlin, of course, felt completely opposite. He boasted, "My telegram saved to the world that day a royal good fellow and most excellent showman."[40]

Successfully eliminating the threat of Cody's mission, however, McLaughlin created for himself a new dilemma: now he had to make good his claim that his Indian Police could bring in Sitting Bull without bloodshed.

This boast was further complicated by acting Commissioner Belt's December 1 telegram instructing McLaughlin to go about his normal educational activities, but also urging him to be aware the military had been assigned to the reservations and to follow their orders. Once President Harrison established martial law McLaughlin's obsession with arresting Sitting Bull truly turned deadly; at this juncture White Hair began to speed up his plan for his Indian Police force to bring in the medicine man. On December 12, Lieutenant Colonel Drum was ordered to arrest Sitting Bull and McLaughlin realized that he had to act immediately. Using his influence with Drum, White Hair protested again against sending anyone but his Indian Police to arrest Sitting Bull, maintaining that any military force would certainly bring bloodshed.

The next decisive move in the unfolding drama belonged to Sitting Bull; the medicine man informed McLaughlin that he intended to visit Pine Ridge to meet with the messiah when he appeared there. McLaughlin immediately interpreted this action as Sitting Bull's thinly veiled attempt to flee the reservation and mobilized a force of forty-three Indian Policemen, led by Lieutenant Bullhead. White Hair ordered Lieutenant Bullhead to bring Sitting Bull in peacefully but authorized him to kill the chief if at any moment it appeared that he might escape. To insure his actions, McLaughlin arranged with Lieutenant Colonel Drum for two troops of the Eighth Cavalry to be posted on Owl Creek, eighteen miles from Sitting Bull's camp.

Lieutenant Bullhead, also known as Afraid-of-Bear, was the worst possible choice to head a party to arrest Sitting Bull. His controversial history with Sitting Bull went back to the time when the chief arrived at the agency after his Wild West tours with Buffalo Bill. Soon after Sitting Bull returned to Standing Rock, the Crow Tribe issued an invitation to his band to travel to their agency at Lame Deer, Montana. This goodwill gesture carried with it the full implication that horses would be given in honor to those Sioux who would make the trip. Horses being increasingly rare at Standing Rock, Sitting Bull was quick to accept his ancient enemy's invitation. Unfortunately, the Crow proposal was also read publicly at a dance and so the subsequent entourage traveling to Lame Deer included a mixture of "progressive," or "reservation," Lakota and Sitting Bull's traditional band of seasoned warriors. When the group stopped en route to collect rations at the Cheyenne River Agency, trouble broke out when a long-time bodyguard of Sitting Bull named Catch-The-Bear and Bullhead had a disagreement over a ration sack. The argument ended with Bullhead seizing the sack, emptying its contents and striking Catch-The-Bear. A veteran of decades of strict self-discipline, war, famine, and diplomacy, Sitting Bull's loyal friend fully realized the tragic implication of losing his temper and destroying one of McLaughlin's prize students. He restrained himself at the moment, but warned Bullhead, "Today you have insulted me, you have struck me. We have always been friends. But now you have made me angry. Look out in the future. I am going to get you."[41]

Sitting Bull was quickly informed of the manner in which Bullhead had insulted his old friend but said nothing. In spite of the medicine man's silence, however, trouble was brewing between the "progressives" and the "blanket" Lakotas as they entered the land of their most ancient enemy, the Crow. At Lame Deer the widening gap in understanding between reservation Lakotas and Sitting Bull's band became even more confused when traditional "bragging" ceremonies occurred. The Crow used the occasion to boast of their military prowess by flaunting their battlefield victories and parading themselves before the great Hunkpapa chief. Sitting Bull, fully aware that to succumb to the taunts of his enemies would grant them victory, remained taciturn, calmly smoking his pipe; he realized that if he could remain unperturbed by the antics of his enemy he would be given many horses as a prize for his victory over his emotions. Unaware of ancient ceremonial warrior customs, however, Bullhead and his younger reservation Lakota comrades interpreted Sitting Bull's reticence as cowardly behavior. They were outraged when finally, "[O]ne of the Crows, Crazy Head, in the heat of his national pride, jerked off his breechcloth, and going over to the place where Sitting Bull sat smoking placidly, stood right in front of him, and thrust the tokens of his manhood almost into the face of the Sioux chief."[42]

Sitting Bull remained unfazed by Crazy Head's insulting behavior. When the Crow section of the ceremony was over, however, and it became time for the Sioux to have their turn to swagger and boast, the Crow rewarded Sitting Bull with thirty beautiful horses for maintaining his dignified restraint and enduring Crazy Head's attempts to humiliate him. Sitting Bull returned to the Lakota camps with his new herd of horses and, ever generous, immediately began to distribute them to his people. As the military had confiscated their horses and most were afoot, the Sioux were all eager to receive one of Sitting Bull's gift horses. Bullhead, apparently thinking that because of his status as a policeman he could take whatever horse he wished, roped a beautiful spotted black and white pony. But Sitting Bull had a different plan; the chief called Catch-The-Bear forward and told him to throw his rope on the beautiful black and white pony Bullhead had roped and claim it.[43] The chief's judicious method for resolving the dispute between the feuding Lakotas would nevertheless only draw him deeper into the quarrel; upon returning to Standing Rock, Bullhead, chagrined and mistaking Sitting Bull's stoicism during the Crow's welcoming ceremonies for weakness, reported to McLaughlin that the chief was a coward. Bullhead's wounded ego, nourished by this deadly false impression of Sitting Bull as a coward, played right into McLaughlin's obsessive plan to personally arrest the chief. Immediately upon returning from Lame Deer, Bullhead had indeed assembled a posse that would "stick," and his group was now ordered by White Hair to arrest Sitting Bull. An hour before dawn on December 15 Lieutenant Bullhead's posse boldly rode into Sitting Bull's compound at Grand River and pounded their rifle butts on his unlocked cabin door, knocking it open. Before the chief's wife could even strike a match, the dark room filled with the sounds of the shuffling feet of men. Sitting Bull arose in the darkness to greet his intruders and was immediately seized from behind by Red Tomahawk, who informed the chief that he would be killed if he resisted.

The lantern's light revealed the people in the cabin: half of the Lakota posse, led by Lieutenant Bullhead, Sergeants Shavehead and Red Tomahawk, Sitting Bull, one of his wives, and the chief's seventeen-year-old son, Crowfoot, stood luminated in the glow. The chief's wife immediately began to taunt and jeer at the posse, calling them cowards for seizing her husband in the night. Crowfoot, like a young colt hiding behind his mother, peered from behind the woman's back.

It was the chief's habit to sleep naked so his captors began to search the dimly lit cabin for clothing. Failing to find Sitting Bull's good clothes, his wife was released to go find them in a nearby cabin. Even so, the Lakota posse was in no mood to wait for Sitting Bull's bodyguards to realize what was happening; they began to hurriedly force the chief to put on whatever they could find in the room. With his captors holding his arms, however, the chief was unable to dress himself and was soon hopping about with one moccasin and one leg in a pair of old leggings. This undignified performance caused Sitting Bull to remind his captors that he was a chief and should be allowed the respect to dress himself properly before being taken in to be presented to White Hair.

As the chief dressed himself in whatever clothing could be gathered around the cabin he realized that he could perhaps stall his captors a bit longer and requested that someone saddle his circus horse—the one given him by Buffalo Bill—to ride in to see White Hair. Bullhead immediately ordered White Bird to begin preparing Sitting Bull's horse. Growing more concerned about bodyguards as the chief stalled, Sergeants Shavehead and Red Tomahawk began pushing Sitting Bull toward the cabin door. As they reached the door Sitting Bull pressed against the frame with his feet and hands and stopped Shavehead and Red Tomahawk from pushing him out into the dawning light of morning. Red Tomahawk, who was holding the chief from behind, kicked the chief's legs free from the door and shoved him out of the cabin.

Sitting Bull's followers, now aroused by the commotion, had begun to gather around the cabin door. Once outside in the cold morning facing the gathering crowd, the captors became even more concerned about Sitting Bull's bodyguards discovering their presence and began to push a revolver into the chief's back urging him through the crowd and toward the corral. Sergeant Shavehead ordered the Indian Police to form a circle around the chief but the crowd was rapidly growing into an angry mob. Surrounded by Indian Police, Bullhead ordered the group to move through the crowd toward Sitting Bull's saddled horse.

Just as Bullhead started to move Sitting Bull through the angry Hunkpapas, his old enemy, Catch-The-Bear, roared around the corner of the cabin, Winchester-in-hand. As commander of the chief's bodyguards, Catch-The-Bear was prepared to defend Sitting Bull at all costs; as Bullhead's sworn enemy his blood was boiling. He cocked his rifle and ordered Bullhead to release Sitting Bull at once.

When Sitting Bull saw what was happening he shouted out, "I am not going. Do with me what you like. I am not going. Come on! Come On! Take action! Let's go!"[44]

At his chief's command, Catch-The-Bear drew his rifle to his shoulder and fired, hitting Lieutenant Bullhead in the leg. As he fell to his back, Bullhead fired his rifle, hitting Sitting Bull in the back as he wrestled with his captors. As the chief stumbled and reeled from Bullhead's bullet, Red Tomahawk shot him from behind. Either of the shots would have proved fatal. Sitting Bull was killed instantly.

As the greatest chief of the Lakota fell to the ground, a terrible firefight broke out among the Lakota people around him. The fighting was so intense that once guns emptied, they became clubs; most were engaged in hand-to-hand fighting.

At the moment the bullets starting singing throughout the compound, the old gray circus horse, hearing all the shooting and understanding the shots as his Wild West show cues, began to do his tricks again. He solemnly sat down in the middle of the bloodbath, and raised his hoof. The horse's act frightened some of the Indian policemen who saw it as an act more dangerous than the bullets buzzing by their heads. They thought the murdered spirit Sitting Bull had entered into the sitting horse! Even more frightening, even though the bullets were flying all around him, the old horse survived the tragedy totally unharmed.[45] The old horse survived the fight and was "stove-up" for weeks after being ridden hard back to Fort Yates with the news of Sitting Bull's murder. Buffalo Bill later bought him back and used him in the Wild West. In the 1893 Chicago World's Fair a rider carrying the American Flag rode Sitting Bull's trick horse ahead of a troop of American cavalry.[46]

Even while the trick horse performed his act, Bullhead ordered his troops to take him and the other dead and wounded into Sitting Bull's cabin. As they moved a mattress to make a bed for Bullhead, the Indian Police discovered Sitting Bull's son, Crowfoot, hiding. The boy began to cry, pleading with his relatives to let him live. So the Indian Policemen went to where Bullhead lay covered in blood and dying. When asked what they should do with the boy, Bullhead answered, "Kill him, they have killed me."[47] Red Tomahawk promptly struck the boy and sent him staggering through the cabin door. Waiting outside, the Indian police shot him dead.

Chapter Seventeen

ABSAROKA

You are carrying a lot of "little" things and a lot of little people in the Big Horn Basin that will eat up every dollar you can get for the rest of your life if you don't get rid of them. When I was in the Big Horn Basin I saw your affairs conducted in a way that made me sick to my stomach, and from what I hear they are in no better condition.

—Nate Salsbury, warning Buffalo Bill (*The Making of Buffalo Bill*, Richard J. Walsh and Milton S. Salsbury)

IMMEDIATELY following Sitting Bull's murder, most of his Hunkpapa followers feared military reprisals and fled ninety miles south to join their Minneconjou relatives in Chief Hump's camp on the Cheyenne River. Even in death, Sitting Bull inspired passionate controversy; Holy Medicine, a relative of one of the slain Indian Policemen, enraged upon discovering the death of his kin, took an old oxen-yoke and brutally attacked the slain chief's corpse until the chin was under the left ear. Indian Police managed to pull the grief-stricken Holy Medicine away from Sitting Bull's corpse, but when it came time to load the bodies of those killed in the bungled arrest into a wagon, another intense argument erupted. Indian Police had been ordered to bring Sitting Bull in dead or alive, yet had only one small wagon in which to carry fourteen bodies, and the surviving Indian Policemen refused to carry Sitting Bull's body in the same wagon as their dead comrades. Red Tomahawk, who upon the deaths of Lieutenant Bullhead and Sergeant Shavehead had become the leader of the Indian Police, resolved the dilemma by tossing Sitting Bull's corpse in the wagon first and then piling the bodies of the dead Indian Policemen on top of the slain chief.

Sitting Bull's mangled remains were delivered to the military at Fort Yates. When consulted, missionaries at the fort determined that the chief was a "pagan" and, as such, required no "formal" Christian burial. Military authorities decided to avoid any possible further conflict and ordered Sitting Bull buried as quickly and quietly as possible. The chief's body was turned over to the post carpenter, J. F. Waggoner, who was directed to construct a simple pine coffin. Waggoner measured and sawed as soldiers, seeking puerile claims to mythic posterity, filed into his shop for the opportunity to hammer metaphorical nails into the wooden box being constructed for the chief. Sitting Bull's violated corpse was finally stuffed inside the coffin and hauled to an open grave in the corner of the military cemetery at Fort Yates. A final degradation, upon reaching the freshly dug grave the undertaker poured five gallons of chloride of lime and muriatic acid—quicklime—into Sitting Bull's coffin, buried him, and marked the gravesite with a simple wooden marker. After sixty years of diplomatic "legal" efforts to have Sitting Bull's remains returned to them, the chiefs relatives were forced to surreptitious tactics in 1953. Led by a nephew named Gray Eagle, Sitting Bull's relations crept into Fort Yates Cemetery at night, exhumed the chief's remains and properly buried him in Mobridge, South Dakota.[1]

Even as the body of the greatest chief of the Lakota was being defiled in death, General Miles, hoping to contain the Ghost Dancers and prevent their forces from combining, ordered the Eighth Cavalry in pursuit of the fleeing Hunkpapa and Minneconjou bands. Next Miles diplomatically sent an old scouting friend of Chief Hump to attempt to convince the headman to bring his followers in to Fort Bennett. Much to everyone's surprise, Hump agreed and even went so far as to promise to use his influence to help bring the fleeing Lakota Ghost Dancers into the forts. Most of Sitting Bull's refugee Hunkpapa band agreed to go in to Fort Bennett with Chief Hump. On December 18, however, a group of seventy Hunkpapa and Minneconjou Ghost Dancers fled in the night to seek Big Foot's band.

Word of Sitting Bull's murder spread fear and panic rapidly through Big Foot's Minneconjou band. Desperate and aware that his name was at the top of the list of "fomenters," Big Foot decided his only option was to head quickly to Fort Bennett and surrender. On December 21, however, before reaching the fort, Big Foot was overtaken and arrested by the Eighth Cavalry.

General Miles had ordered the Eighth Cavalry to deliver Big Foot's band to Fort Meade in the Black Hills, a trek which would now force the soldiers to backtrack the Lakotas through their recently abandoned agency settlement. Upon returning to the deserted settlement, the Minneconjou prisoners immediately rushed into their cabins for shelter and rest, making it difficult for the soldiers to get them back on the trail to Fort Meade. The

situation became even more complicated when more troops arrived at the
Minneconjou agency with new orders; Miles had reversed himself; Big
Foot was now to be delivered to his original destination—Fort Bennett. At
this confusing development Big Foot became convinced that the military
intended to arrest and kill all Ghost Dancers. That night he and his followers eluded the guards, crept out of camp and quickly headed through the
Badlands toward Pine Ridge and the protection of Red Cloud's Oglala
warriors. Notified of Big Foot's escape, General Miles ordered the Sixth
Cavalry to join the Eighth Cavalry in pursuit of the fleeing Indians. Arriving from Fort Riley, Kansas, led by several surviving officers from Custer's
divided command at Little Big Horn, the Seventh Cavalry was also ordered to begin a flanking maneuver from the south to prevent Big Foot's
band from joining with Kicking Bear and Short Bull. By December 25, a
brutal winter storm froze the prairie and forced the Minneconjous to make
camp. Reflecting the plunging temperature, Big Foot's declining health
suddenly collapsed into pneumonia. The following morning, as Big Foot's
condition worsened, Oglala messengers arrived in his camp with word
from headmen at Pine Ridge that Kicking Bear and Short Bull had agreed
to come there to surrender on December 29. The messengers also informed Big Foot that the Pine Ridge headmen suggested that he surrender
on that same day. In order to safely do so, the Oglalas further recommended that Big Foot swing his band far to the southwest to avoid running
into Seventh Cavalry troops, now camped along Wounded Knee Creek. As
he had begun coughing up blood, however, Big Foot decided to take the
most expedient path to Pine Ridge. Unfortunately, that trail led straight
into Major Samuel Whiteside's command. On the morning of December
28, Big Foot's people broke camp for what they hoped would be the final
part of the journey to safety at Pine Ridge. They were several miles east of
Wounded Knee when Big Foot's scouts surprised and captured four scouts
from Major Whiteside's Seventh Cavalry. Two of the scouts were held prisoner while the remaining two were sent back to the troops with a message
that Big Foot was coming into the soldiers' camp in peace to parley.
Whiteside mounted his troops in battle formation and went out to meet
the Indians. Upon seeing the troops prepared for battle, Big Foot's followers began waving white flour sacks and anything else white they could find
as flags of truce. Big Foot then went to meet Whiteside and talk.[2]

A somber omen of the looming tragedy, the flour-sack/truce-flags were
stained with blood from Big Foot's hemorrhaging lungs. As Whiteside demanded and immediately received Big Foot's unconditional surrender,

frozen blood thawed and trickled from the critically ill chief's nose, staining the snow below him pink. Within moments, the Seventh Cavalry surrounded Big Foot's band and ordered them into camp on Wounded Knee Creek. Major Whiteside compassionately offered Big Foot his ambulance and medical assistance, and the chief ordered his followers to do as the soldiers told them. Major Whiteside offered medical mercy to Big Foot, but, once encamped, he also made it absolutely clear to the Lakotas that the Seventh Cavalry's security would be much tighter than the Eighth's; Big Foot's band was surrounded by troops armed with two rapid-fire Hotchkiss cannons. Later that evening Colonel James W. Forsyth, leading Custer's former regiment, arrived and took command of the operation. Forsyth promptly deployed his troops with Whiteside's and added his two Hotchkiss cannons to the artillery and soldiers now strategically encircling the ragged band of Lakotas.

Forsyth's orders were to destroy the Lakotas if they chose to fight; granted that power, he was further ordered to disarm the Lakotas, to take every precaution to prevent their second escape and to bring them into Pine Ridge. Carefully following those orders, the colonel decided it would be best to encourage the Lakotas to relax by feeding them and gaining their confidence before attempting to disarm them. Forsyth was also sincerely concerned about Chief Big Foot's health and assigned him to a tent with a stove and sent a physician to attend him. After taking care of the critically ill chief Forsyth distributed rations to the hungry Lakotas and a cold, tense night settled upon the prairie. Inside his tent, the colonel and his officers opened a jug of whiskey, quietly celebrated the capture of the renegade Minneconjous and Hunkpapas and deliberated the morning's dangerous mission.

Forsyth's officers suspected several Lakota men of having Winchester repeating rifles and everyone realized these men would be most hesitant to relinquish their weapons. Experienced scouts warned Forsyth and his officers that the slightest provocation would certainly unleash a deadly firefight. The colonel nevertheless decided to feed the Lakotas breakfast before attempting to disarm them.

An army bugle announced the dawn of December 29, and breakfast rations were soon dispersed. As the people ate and greeted the unseasonably pleasant day, Colonel Forsyth assembled the wary Lakotas to begin the risky process of taking their weapons. Chief Big Foot had grown too weak to stand or walk without assistance and was helped out of his warm tent and propped against an earthen mound. Several Lakota men and boys sat

in front of their chief, forming a semicircle around him as Forsyth began
to speak through an interpreter. The colonel first assured the Lakotas that
they were now safe and would receive increased rations. He went on to say
that the soldiers were their friends, but that to prevent any possible accidental fights from erupting it would be necessary for them to turn over
their weapons.

Surrounded by heavily armed troops, the Lakotas were naturally quite
alarmed by Forsyth's order. Perhaps even worse, Lakota elders recognized
soldiers from Custer's old regiment and were concerned that these men
held vengeance in their hearts because of the fight at Greasy Grass. Grumbling voices began to spread and rise through the gathered Lakotas. Yet
even as the cries of protest grew louder and more numerous some Lakotas
came forward and hesitantly surrendered their weapons. When no others
came forth the captives announced they had surrendered all their weapons.
Yet even as the Lakota prisoners denied it, Forsyth was not satisfied that all
weapons had been surrendered. He ordered a search of Big Foot's camp;
soldiers went through tepees and personal belongings and produced
butcher knives, tent pegs, hatchets, axes, and about forty very old, broken-
down pistols and rifles.

All this activity naturally caused both the Lakotas and the soldiers to become increasingly more agitated and apprehensive. One of the Ghost
Dancers, a medicine man named Yellow Bird, raised his arms and began to
chant in Lakota and dance. Forsyth ordered Yellow Bird to stop his dance
and, as the Lakota medicine man obeyed and sat down, soldiers simultaneously shouted they had discovered a Winchester under a Lakota's blanket.

Upon detecting the repeating rifle, Forsyth ordered all the prisoners
into two lines from which they were directed to file past inspectors who
would personally search every member of the band. After twenty older
men passed by the inspectors and were proven to be unarmed, two young
Lakota men were discovered in possession of rifles.

At this point, Yellow Bird began to dance and chant in Lakota again, reminding the prisoners that their Ghost Shirts would protect them from
bullets. When Yellow Bird called upon the young men to take action a deaf
Minneconjou named Black Coyote raised his Winchester and yelled in
Lakota that he had paid a great deal of money for his rifle and demanded
compensation if it was to be seized. Two sergeants made their way behind
Black Coyote and grabbed him, forcing the gun to discharge in the ensuing struggle. Immediately, the surrounding troopers panicked and began
firing randomly into the crowd, killing Big Foot and most of the Lakota

men and boys around him instantly. The few wounded Lakota survivors of the initial firefight raced to attempt to protect women, children and old ones, but the Hotchkiss guns on the hills now opened up on the mass of people below them, killing everything in sight. Because of their circular deployment, the hysterical soldiers were even shooting their own comrades caught in the spontaneous crossfire of the melee.[3]

Oglala Holy Man Black Elk had returned from Paris to Pine Ridge as the Ghost Dance frenzy was peaking among the Sioux. His cabin on Wounded Knee Creek was only a few miles west of the site where the massacre was beginning. Upon hearing the gunfire, Black Elk rapidly dressed himself for battle and raced on horseback toward the sound of the shooting. Along the way he met other Lakota warriors galloping from Pine Ridge to defend their kinsmen. Upon arriving at the scene of the fighting the band of twenty warriors immediately saw cavalrymen riding along the hillsides shooting down into the ravines. Instantly, bullets started zipping past them as they raced into the frenzy. Later, Black Elk told the poet John Neihardt:

> We followed down along the dry gulch, and what we saw was terrible. Dead and wounded women and children and little babies were scattered all along there where they had been trying to run away. The soldiers had followed along the gulch, as they ran, and murdered them in there. Sometimes they were in heaps because they had huddled together, and some were scattered all along. Sometimes bunches of them had been killed and torn to pieces where the wagon guns hit them. I saw a little baby trying to suck its mother, but she was bloody and dead.[4]

No one really knows how many people died in the massacre, although it is estimated over 300 Lakota men, women and children perished. A fierce blizzard swept into the region even as mortally wounded women and children attempted to crawl away from the soldiers' bullets. Black Elk, himself nearly killed before the fighting finally ended, spoke poetically of the tragedy when he told John Neihardt: "I did not know then how much was ended. When I look back now from this high hill of my old age, I can see that something else died there in the bloody mud, and was buried in the blizzard. A people's dream died there. It was a beautiful dream."[5]

After President Harrison rescinded General Miles' arrest orders, Buffalo Bill had visited Dr. Frank "White Beaver" Powell in Lacrosse, Wisconsin, where his old friend and new business partner had recently purchased a coffee company. Naturally, Cody was the financial backer. After a few days in Wisconsin, Buffalo Bill returned to Scout's Rest Ranch in North Platte. There, Cody learned of Sitting Bull's murder and the subsequent massacre at Wounded Knee. On November 23, however, before departing on his ill-fated mission to Standing Rock, Nebraska's Governor James M. Thayer had commissioned Cody a brigadier general and aide-de-camp to his staff. Now, after Sitting Bull's murder and the following massacre of Ghost Dancers, all the white settlers of the region were certain a general Indian war would erupt at any moment. In order to protect his constituency, Governor Thayer ordered Nebraska's most famous citizen to "proceed to the scene of the Indian troubles and communicate with General Miles."[6] The Pine Ridge Agency had become headquarters for the military campaign and Cody immediately headed there. He found the agency also buzzing with media; a hive of twenty-five zealous war correspondents were filing hourly dispatches to the eastern newspapers. Cody joined the reporters and sent dispatches of his own to the *New York Herald* and in his editorializing urged immediate attention to the Indians' rights.[7] Even though the historical importance of the proceedings apparently eluded most present at the time it did not escape Don Russell's keen observation:

> On January 16 the Indians formally surrendered, giving some, at least, of their weapons and delivering nineteen leaders as hostages. On that day Buffalo Bill rode with General Miles and his two aides, both notable Indian fighters, Captain Frank Baldwin and Captain Marion P. Maus. General Miles reviewed all the troops present, probably the largest assembly of Regular Army organizations since the Civil War, adding to the review's primary purpose of overawing the Indians. It was midwinter, with snow on the ground, and General Miles found the scene "weird and in some respects desolate," marking the end of the war power of the Sioux, although he did not fully realize that it also marked the end of the Indian wars. It was fitting that Cody should see the finish. It was his last service for the government.[8]

The political and moral ramifications of the slaughter at Wounded Knee spread quickly through the government. Clearly seeking to deflect attention from the military's responsibility for the massacre, eighteen Congressional Medals of Honor were awarded to troopers for their actions in what was now becoming emphasized to the general public as the "Battle" of Wounded Knee. In spite of the military effort to whitewash the mass murders, however, Commissioner of Indian Affairs Morgan blamed General Miles and the military for the massacre, banned the Ghost Dance on all reservations, and initiated his own investigation into the causes and repercussions of the Ghost Dance "uprising." General Miles reacted immediately and removed Colonel Forsyth from command of the Seventh Cavalry and accused him of the massacre as well as the reckless deployment of his troops which caused them to fire upon one another. Forsyth was later exonerated by a military court of inquiry. Agent McLaughlin, finally free of the resistance of Sitting Bull at Standing Rock, began his eventual rise to the powerful rank of Inspector—the second in command of the Office of Indian Affairs. McLaughlin's tenure (1871–1923) and creation of policy in the Indian Bureau fundamentally affected the development and direction of the Bureau of Indian Affairs and remain criticized to this day.

As the Ghost Dance conflict ended, Cody wasted little time recruiting Lakotas for his next tour of Europe and quickly sent Major John Burke to Pine Ridge. Upon his arrival at the agency, the bachelor press agent promptly adopted a boy orphaned at Wounded Knee. Never one for modesty, Burke named his adopted Lakota son "John Burke No Neck." In spite of his unbridled vanity, in adopting the Lakota boy, Burke also made an uncharacteristically non-verbal statement concerning the political position of the Wild West concerning the Wounded Knee Massacre. In fact, Burke's adoption of the Lakota boy more accurately fits behavior characteristic of Buffalo Bill and leads one to suspect that, as was often the case, Cody was at work behind the scenes in the matter. Even so, Burke may have simply been mimicking the conduct of his famous boss. Whatever his true motivation may have been for adopting the boy, Major Burke was also delighted to discover that in the midst of the Ghost Dance troubles, Pine Ridge Agent Royer—"Young-Man-Afraid-Of-His-Indians"—somehow managed to complete the interviews of the Oglalas that acting Indian Commissioner Belt had demanded from those performers returning from Cody's Wild West. The Wild West was vindicated when Royer returned a glowing report to the Commission of Indian Affairs. Royer noted that the Oglala performers who were veterans of the Wild West had remained loyal to the government during the Ghost Dance revolt and even traveled to the agencies where the dancing was most intense in order to encourage their relatives to remain peaceful. As opposed as he was to releasing Indians to Wild West shows, Morgan was forced to concede the positive effect of the expe-

rience on the Oglalas as reported by Agent Royer.[9] Immediately following
the surrender of Kicking Bear and Short Bull, General Miles took the two
disciples of Wovoka and twenty-eight other Ghost Dancers with him to
Chicago as prisoners of war. The general had evidently intended to incar-
cerate and personally interrogate the Ghost Dancers later at Fort Sheridan, Illinois. Before the prisoners could be taken to Fort Sheridan, however, Buffalo Bill, who was en route to Pine Ridge to meet Major Burke to
audition Oglalas for his upcoming European tour, dropped in to visit the
general. The preceding March, acting Commissioner Belt had overruled
the Commission of Indian Affairs' ban on Cody hiring Indians for his Wild
West, and Major Burke had been given permission to hire one hundred
Lakotas for the upcoming European tour. During their visit, however,
Miles proposed to Cody that he should also take any of the "Ghost Dance"
prisoners willing to accompany him to Europe as part of his show. Cody
enthusiastically agreed. Later, Commissioner Morgan, also anxious to remove the incorrigibles and their influence from the reservation, ardently
supported General Miles' proposal. Cody was allowed to hire Ghost
Dancers Kicking Bear, Short Bull, Lone Bull, Mash the Kettle, Scatter, and
Revenge as well as peace-makers Long Wolf, No Neck, Yankton Charley,
and Black Heart.[10] On April 1, 1891, twenty-three of the Ghost Dance prisoners of war joined the other seventy-five Lakotas in Philadelphia and departed on the Red Star steamer *Switzerland* bound for Europe. The Lakotas arrived in Antwerp and joined the Wild West in Strasbourg.

   While Cody had been involved in the Lakota uprising during the Ghost
Dance frenzy, Nate Salsbury had been busy redesigning the Wild West.
The song-and-dance man had been waiting fourteen years to actualize his
vision of a show presenting the world's best equestrians. Now, with all the
pressure from the Indian Rights Organization concerning Native American Wild West performers, Salsbury and Cody were acutely aware that
they had to prepare themselves for the possibility that in the future they
might be prevented from employing Indians. It was consequently time for
Salsbury to act on his idea of the creation of a pageant celebrating the
comprehensive global history of horsemanship. When Cody arrived in Europe with over one hundred Lakotas he discovered Salsbury's equestrian
production also now in place; Cody and Salsbury had created the unique
structure of what would in 1893 be anointed "Buffalo Bill's Wild West and
Congress of Rough Riders of the World." The production had literally become a small nomadic town:

As organized in 1891, Buffalo Bill's Wild West had 640 "eating members." There were 30 German soldiers, 20 English soldiers, 20 United States soldiers, 12 Cossacks, and 6 Argentine Gauchos, which with the old reliables, 20 Mexican vaqueros, 25 cowboys, 6 cowgirls, 100 Sioux Indians, and the Cowboy Band of 37 mounted musicians, made a colorful and imposing Congress of Rough Riders.[11]

As the Wild West reunited in Switzerland and prepared for the 1891 tour, Europe had begun to recognize yet another unique attribute of Cody and Salsbury's production. Whereas the traditional European circus was a "one-ring" production, Barnum's American "three-ring" circus had revolutionized this concept and become internationally renowned for its remarkable aptitude for moving massive numbers of men, animals, equipment, and properties. In its ascension to the pinnacle of the entertainment world, Cody and Salsbury's Wild West had come to personify such ingenious logistics; the pair's combined knowledge and experience moving large groups of people and animals was simply unparalleled. This unique skill began to attract an ironic following throughout the Wild West's 1891 tour of Europe. Annie Oakley wrote in her diary that the Wild West never moved without at least forty Prussian officers in tow. The Germans carried notebooks, taking copious, detailed notes of each performance. The military men made minute notes of how the Wild West pitched camp: the exact number of personnel needed, every man's tasks and position in the work force, and how long it took to pitch and break camp. They were also deeply concerned with how the company boarded trains, packed the horses, and broke camp. Once again, every rope and bundle and kit had to be itemized and cataloged.

More than anything else, however, the Prussians were interested in the Wild West's traveling kitchen. The cooks were interviewed in detail concerning techniques of storing food, preparing it, and having basic foodstuffs ready for use at a minute's notice. The performers suspected that the Prussian officers were attempting to learn how to incorporate the Wild West's culinary logistics into its army; they had no idea, however, that the world would be stunned twenty-five years later by the stories of the German army's traveling kitchens, which served piping hot meals on the road to conquer Brussels. The idea obviously came from the Wild West Show.[12]

Back in Nebraska, Julia Cody Goodman might have also taught the Kaiser a few things about feeding men. As Scout's Rest Ranch grew with Cody's fortunes, Julia was responsible each day for feeding as many as twenty-five working ranch hands as well as entertaining the continual ten to twenty "friends of Buffalo Bill's" arriving every few days from various parts of the country and abroad at the personal invitation of her brother. The dilemma Julia faced each day at Scout's Rest Ranch is also a perfect example of how her bighearted brother eventually lost several fortunes: Will Cody, often to the exclusion of his own personal needs, felt he was responsible for everyone else. Perhaps he came to this self-concept as the result of his being called upon at such a tender age to provide for the Cody family after the loss of their father; Will Cody could hardly remember not being a providing father figure. Equally true, he had most certainly observed the genuine unselfishness of the greatest of the chiefs of the Plains Indians and perhaps aspired to their benevolent approach to leadership. Whatever the source behind Cody's altruism, his inherent generosity combined with his great fame, wealth and charisma to naturally attract anyone who felt they could develop a financial association with him and few were ever turned away. Invariably, however, attracting such a large, competitive retinue, Cody's magnanimity created more problems than it solved and Scout's Rest Ranch was no different from any of his other financial adventures. If Cody had allowed his devoted "mother-sister" Julia and her husband to develop and supervise his bountiful Nebraska property simply as a working ranch it probably would have evolved into a financially self-sufficient and successful operation—one which could have supported all of them later in life. As was the case with all of his business endeavors, however, Scout's Rest Ranch essentially became another vehicle which Buffalo Bill could use to distribute the wealth and power of his position to the never-ending line of needy friends. As a result, money and energy were always going out rather than coming in at Scout's Rest Ranch. Equally serious, with Cody absent most of the time touring and his growing entourage competing vigorously for a bigger slice of the pie, leadership at the home base became increasingly hazy and unfocused as confusion reigned over his business affairs.

Adding to the perplexity at North Platte, Cody's wife, Lulu, also remained a possessive and dangerous thorn in his side, especially as his fortunes grew. In all fairness, Lulu had good reason to fear her husband's dangerous lack of business acumen. Aside from his success with the Wild West, Cody had shown a great talent for spending large amounts of money chasing wild hares. Nevertheless, her meddling into his business at North Platte certainly did not help stabilize Cody's affairs. Lulu was intensely jealous of her husband's loyalty to his sisters, resented his desire to share his wealth with them, and despised the family for never being reluctant to accept his generosity.[13]

In an act which threw the administration of the Nebraska property into a state of serious disorder, Cody's daughter, Arta, married Horton Boal in 1890 and promptly announced that she and her new husband wanted to run the North Platte ranching operation. Encouraged with Lulu's enthusiastic support, Arta and her husband became so aggressive in their efforts to seize the reins of Scout's Rest that Al Goodman, whose health had begun to fail, became fearful that he would lose his position administrating the ranch. Even though he tried to smooth the dangerous rivalry out through letters, Cody was unable to convince Goodman that Arta and Horton were not a threat to his security. Goodman's growing insecurity and declining health threw the administration of Scout's Rest Ranch into mounting disarray. Adding to the perplexity, even as the core of his family unity and North Platte business structure were coming unraveled, Cody was investing heavily in other ventures. Aside from the North Platte ranch, he had bank-rolled his friend Dr. Frank Powell's coffee company in La Crosse, Wisconsin; another sister, Helen, had married Hugh Wetmore, a Duluth, Minnesota, newspaper editor; and Cody had bought Hugh's newspaper and built the operation a new brick building. As "Welcome Wigwam," the original home at Scout's Rest Ranch, had burned, Cody bought Lulu a new home in the rapidly growing community of North Platte. Additionally, Buffalo Bill had paid off the debts of all the five churches in North Platte, paid the salary of each church's preacher for a full year, bought uniforms for the town band, and donated the cemetery and fairgrounds.[14]

Even as Cody invested in the dreams of his family, friends and community and his Wild West was delighting European audiences, the darkening clouds of discontent among the "Friends of the Indians" was gathering into yet another political storm. A Congregational missionary at the Standing Rock reservation, Mary Collins, apparently initiated the protest. Collins had become an outspoken opponent to the employment of Indians in the Wild West shows. Sometimes a friend, but usually an adversary of Sitting Bull, Collins believed that his tour with Buffalo Bill in 1885 had spoiled the Hunkpapa leader's views toward white society and religion. The missionary claimed that Sitting Bull had only seen the corruption and debauchery of Euroamerican society while traveling with the circus and, being a moral man, wanted nothing to do with it. This sense of morality, she postulated, was the reason the chief had fought the civilization programs of the Indian Bureau and become a champion of the Ghost Dance.

Collins blamed the Wild West and the chief's contrary nature for murder at the hands of the Indian Police.[15]

With retired general Oliver O. Howard's assistance, Collins took her campaign straight to the imprisoned Ghost Dancers. Military rivals, General Howard and General Miles had competed fiercely during the Nez Perce Revolt in 1880–81 to bring Chief Joseph to surrender. Upon retiring, Howard became a devoted humanitarian associated with the Indian Rights Association.[1] Howard arranged for Collins to travel to Fort Sheridan for a private meeting. Speaking in Sioux, Collins met with them and, according to her, several of the Lakotas asked her to interfere with Miles' plans to send them to Europe with the Wild West. Fired up with this information, Collins returned to Chicago with hopes of stopping the prisoners from going with the Wild West. As fate would have it, immediately upon returning from Fort Sheridan to Chicago, Mrs. Collins learned from General Howard that Commissioner of Indian Affairs Morgan had come to Chicago to address a meeting of the local Congregational Club the very next evening.

Collins went to the meeting and confronted Morgan, who made his opposition to Indians in Wild West shows clear. More significantly, however, Collins won the support of the Congregational Club and, before the evening ended, had convinced three hundred ministers and business leaders to draft a resolution which protested allowing any Indians to go with Buffalo Bill. This group appointed a committee of three, named Collins chairperson, and sent her to Washington to present the resolution before the President. To add fuel to the flame, Collins recruited eastern Congregational Clubs to initiate letter-writing newspaper campaigns, editorializing the national shame of allowing Indians to be exhibited in Wild West shows. Ever Cody's enemy, Herbert Welsh and the Indian Rights Organization quickly joined Collins's zealous campaign. Soon another political firestorm was raging.

Secretary of Interior Noble, furious with Collins's effort to undermine his office, promptly tossed water on her evangelic arson. When Collins finally received her audience with him, Noble curtly reprimanded her for not simply and quietly approaching him privately rather than inciting and drawing him into a very public media campaign. Noble next directly attacked Col-lins's crusade with the announcement that he supported both Buffalo Bill's Wild West and the employing of the Ghost Dance prisoners in the European tour. He concluded with a final angry slap on Collins's wrist, telling her to take up any further grievances with the Secretary of War.[16]

Meanwhile, Herbert Welsh continued his investigation into the treatment of Indian performers in the Wild West. The head of the Indian Rights Organization sent questionnaires to the agents at Pine Ridge and Standing Rock Reservations inquiring further into the general health and behavior of Lakotas returning from tours with Buffalo Bill. Those questionnaires were forwarded to the Wild West in Europe and Nate Salsbury's response to Pine Ridge Acting Agent Charles Penny precisely reveals the perspective and policies he and Cody held concerning the employment of Indians, as well as the payment structure and general treatment of Indian performers in their production. Most importantly, Salsbury's response reveals the way Cody and Salsbury felt about Indians as fellow humans. Cody and Salsbury did not report on the salaries paid the Omaha and Pawnee during the first seasons, yet, aside from travel, food and lodging, they reported that since 1885 they had paid the Lakotas $74,000. Salsbury wrote Agent Penny:

> You can also add to this sum the cost of a good substantial suit of clothes which we invariably present to each Indian at the close of each season of service with us and which is entirely outside of our contract with them. We give the clothes as sort of premium for good conduct and saving habits. I am sorry that no record has been kept of the money sent home by them. . . . We do not pretend to control the disposition of their wages. In the first place we have no shadow of a right to do so. In the next place, we find that an Indian knows the value of a dollar quite as well as a white man. Of course we constantly urge upon them the value of saving habits and we exercise a constant vigilance that they do not fall into the hands of tradesmen who are sharpers. This is hardly necessary as we find that they have as good a knowledge of relative values as any Jew or Gentile with whom they might come in contact.
>
> They transmit their money home through the various agencies of Post Office Orders, Bank checks, and express companies. And as each man is a free agent in his personal affairs we have no means of knowing what sums they send without direct violation of our rule to treat them with the same personal consideration as we do our white employees. We believe that the application of this rule adds to their self esteem and dignifies the relations between us.
>
> It would interest you, I know, to be present on a pay day to note the careful scrutiny each man gives to his account. They are honorable to a degree in paying their debts and equally careful to get all that belongs to them, some of them going so far as to enquire the

rate of exchange between a foreign coin and the American dollar. I assume that any man who can exercise such judgement is quite capable of choosing his occupation and profiting by it.[17]

Where Cody and Salsbury believed Indians to be intelligent, moral, financially prudent, and generally competent individuals possessing basic human rights, Welsh and Collins continued to cling to the paternalistic—and ultimately racist—role of the political church's strict "Christian" agenda for reconstructing Indians into American society. The pair ignored Salsbury's articulate retort and rushed to the New York newspapers with a statement carefully prepared to emphasize what they viewed as the government's legal role in reconstructing its Indian "wards" into American society. When New York's *Evening Post* printed Welsh and Collins' essay suggesting that participation in the Wild West had nourished Sitting Bull's "inordinate pride" Salsbury fired back, sarcastically and more accurately countering that Sitting Bull was blessed with natural-born confidence and his hatred was inspired and nourished by the white men who had robbed and abused him for years.[18]

Even as the controversy raged in America, the Wild West continued to play to record-breaking crowds across Europe. The show moved into Holland and Queen Wilhelmina attended, evoking memories of the majesty of Queen Victoria's Jubilee. Before leaving the continent the Wild West traveled to Belgium and raised the American flag on the site of the historic Waterloo Battlefield. The Wild West departed western Europe at Antwerp and crossed the North Sea to return to Great Britain. In England Cody decided to leave the show early and return to America to deal with the "religious cranks" who "are jumping on me because I am 3000 miles away and can't defend myself."[19] With the very core of his absentee business falling apart, however, Cody also needed to return to North Platte; Al Goodman had resigned at Scout's Rest Ranch and moved Julia back to their farm in Kansas. Furthermore, Cody complained of "feeling poorly," of the "continual strain" and of becoming increasingly nervous.[20] In spite of the aforementioned complaints, Cody nevertheless admitted that he was shooting better than at any other time of his life. By December the company had created several small troupes to play theaters in various locations around Britain and put the Wild West in winter quarters. Cody finally headed home to deal with his dangerously confused business affairs. Also, after eleven months with Kicking Bear, Salsbury thought it was time for him and some of the other prisoners from the Ghost Dance revolt to return to America with Cody. Salsbury sent General Miles a letter in which he warned him that he considered Kicking Bear to still be hostile and he would very likely create trouble when returned to the reservation.

Wind, rains, and ruined crops eventually forced Julia to flee Kansas to live in Denver with her sons Will and Ed while Al, having become even more ill, struggled valiantly to save their farm. Meanwhile, at North Platte, Cody did not have enough time to properly deal with the situation at home. He merely patched up his business problems and headed back to England, leaving Arta and Horton Boal in naive control of the management of Scout's Rest Ranch.

The Wild West returned to Earl's Court to begin the 1892 season. The return engagement, in spite of Queen Victoria's return to see the Congress of Rough Riders, could never match the uniqueness of the 1887 Jubilee triumph. Buffalo Bill's sobriety made nearly as many headlines as the Wild West itself. As rumors of his vows of abstinence to Nate Salsbury spread to the press, the Salvation Army capitalized on Cody's fame and used his abstention to promote temperance throughout England.[21] While the second command performance for Queen Victoria secured the Wild West's successful future in Great Britain, most of the season in England was spent planning for an important upcoming American event. Cody and Salsbury had made millions using the simple formula of performing where people were already gathering and in 1893 the world would be flocking to Chicago.

Don Russell observes,

There can be little question, however, that Buffalo Bill's Wild West and Congress of Rough Riders of the World hit its high point at the World's Columbian Exposition in Chicago in 1893. The Wild West was ruled off the exposition grounds, but Salsbury with forethought had leased a lot between Sixty-second and Sixty-third streets near the entrance. It is said that there were those who mistook the entrance to Buffalo Bill's Wild West for the entrance to the Columbian Exposition and, after seeing the show, came away well satisfied.

It must not be supposed, however, that Buffalo Bill's Wild West ran away with the Columbian Exposition. Of all the World's Fairs it probably rates the highest in general interest and lasting influence. It was one of a very few that did not run in the red. Of 27,539,041 persons who saw the 'White City' between May 1 and October 30, 1893, admiring the classic architecture or its Little Egypt on the Midway, 716,881 paid admission on one day, October 9, Chicago Day, and that likely still stands as a record for the number of persons buying tickets to a place of entertainment.[22]

Once again controversy over the depiction of Native Americans engulfed the Wild West and Cody and Salsbury were denied a sanctioned location on the exposition grounds. Rather than the political church, however, this time the scientific community had feathers ruffled by the Wild West. Frederick Ward Putnam, curator of the Peabody Museum of American Archaeology and Ethnology at Harvard University, had in 1890 proposed that the stages of development of mankind in the Americas since Columbus's arrival should be demonstrated as a central component of the exposition. To accomplish this mission, Putnam also proposed to create an unprecedented collection of exhibits about Native American religion and culture which would become the core collection of a permanent Chicago museum that he intended to serve as a monument celebrating the 1893 exposition. Putnam and his gifted young assistant, Franz Boas, went about gathering living cultural and religious exhibits from North and South America and the effort quickly became so large that over one hundred people were employed on the project.[23]

As the political church before them, however, Putnam's scientific community had a manipulative agenda concerning the exhibition of Native Americans: Putnam and his colleagues wished to support Darwin's emerging theoretical concepts of evolution in their fledgling field of anthropology. Putnam's "living" exhibition was carefully designed to depict American Indians slowly but steadily progressing into a state of "civilization." Buffalo Bill's Wild West presented a "living exhibition" of Native Americans as threatening to Putnam's "scientific" agenda as it had been to Mary Collins and Herbert Welsh's exploitive desires to present Indians as converted Christian farmers. Putnam's exhibition, as mammoth as it was, depicted a meek and submissive people who had "evolved" very little since the arrival of European colonists; Buffalo Bill's Wild West presented fiercely intelligent Indian warriors, armed and dangerous opponents of the invasion of their land by western civilization.[24]

Salsbury and Cody rose to dominate the world of show business by learning well the behavior of their opponents; anticipating the bigoted attitudes of World's Fair officials, the show business veterans had the foresight to rent a fourteen acre lot literally at the front door of the exposition where they erected a grandstand capable of seating eighteen thousand people. Seventy-four Oglalas were employed to be in the show; Cody, however, out of his own pocket, hired another hundred Lakotas from Pine Ridge, Standing Rock, and Rosebud to perform in the formal opening ceremonies May 1, 1893.[25] Don Russell informs us,

Crowds were turned away from the Wild West on the opening day, a 130,000-attendance day for the Fair. Adam Forepaugh's circus attempted to compete, but made not a dent in Buffalo Bill's business. It had been called the most successful year in outdoor-show history, with profits estimated at from $700,000 to $1,000,000. The Wild West cashed in on a long accumulation of public interest. Since its first invasion of the Old World six years previously, the show had played only one season in the United States, that of 1888. The shows appearances before the crowned heads of Europe, Cody's victory in the controversy over the treatment of Indian performers, and his part in the last of the Indian wars had been widely acclaimed.[26]

While the Wild West was entertaining the masses and shattering attendance records, Putnam's exhibition became increasingly controversial. As the political church before them, the anthropologist's zeal spun back upon them and Putnam's attempts to exploit Native Americans in the name of science imploded. Once the fair began the Indian office aggressively tried to disconnect itself from what was being presented at the midway and today Putnam's "revolutionary" theory of developmentalism appears, aside from being racist, simply not very well thought out.[27]

While Putnam's hegemonic anthropology collapsed around him in failure, the artistically synchronized teamwork of Cody, Salsbury, and Burke performed masterfully and Buffalo Bill's Wild West attracted over two million delighted spectators. When Chicago Mayor Carter Harrison requested that World's Fair officials admit poor children to the fair free of charge and was denied, Cody, Salsbury, and Burke were quick to announce the Wild West would not only admit poor children free, but provide free transportation, candy and ice cream to the unfortunate kids. On the appointed day, fifteen thousand thrilled, happy children swarmed the Wild West for one of the best days of their lives.[28]

Cody's brilliant team also aligned the Wild West with such classic publicity events as a "Thousand Mile Cowboy Race" from Chadron, Nebraska to Chicago. The good citizens of Chadron, in order to beat a French endurance record of fifty horseback miles a day, offered a $1,000 prize to the winning rider. What had originally been envisioned as a simple trail ride quickly evolved into a race to publicize the stamina of the western horse. The rules were simple: each cowboy would start with two horses which he would ride alternately over the course of the race.[29]

Soon after encouraging the race, Cody and Burke were attacked by the s.p.c.a. for promoting harsh treatment of animals. Cody took reporters to his stables, pointed out an ordinary horse, and maintained the animal could endure more vigorous riding than most could imagine. From his years of experience the old scout reminded the reporters that what would kill a thoroughbred only whet a Great Plains pony's appetite. Ever diplomatic, however, Cody offered an extra five hundred dollar purse to the man who brought his horses to the finish line in the best condition.[30]

Appeased by Cody's sweetening of the pot encouraging proper treatment of horses, and the fact that representatives of various humane societies along the route were invited to supervise the race, objections rapidly diminished and, averaging seventy-seven miles a day, half of the contest's ten participants completed the ride in thirteen days. A fellow from Sturgis, South Dakota, named John Berry won the race.[31]

With the astonishing success at the World's Fair, the Wild West was at the very pinnacle of its power. When encouraged to continue the fight to prevent Cody from employing Indian performers, Carlise Institute founder, Captain Richard Pratt, responded, "What's the use?"[32] P. T. Barnum was dead, but the "Circus Era" he created was also at the peak of its influence and fortune and Buffalo Bill's Wild West and Congress of Rough Riders of the World was the act to reap the rewards; simply, the Wild West had whipped all copy-cat competitors both at home and abroad. Reports claimed the Wild West made a cool million-dollar profit at the 1893 World's Fair. Even so, change was on the horizon.

Thomas A. Edison had recently perfected the motion-picture machine and built a producing studio. In fact, two of the first actors to appear before his camera were Buffalo Bill and Annie Oakley. The stars' pictures were shown in nickel-in-the-slot machines. As experiments were being made with projection on a screen for large audiences, the photographs were shown in prototype nickelodeons. Ironically, the visionary Edison discouraged the idea of projecting the photographs on screens. As he was making a healthy profit with his nickel machines, Edison believed the entire United States could be served by only ten screens and that to introduce them would ruin his market for nickel machines and "kill the goose that lays the golden eggs."[33]

As Sitting Bull before him, Cody's celebrity and generosity had turned on him and, with the exception of Salsbury and Burke and a few others, everyone around him seemed to be determined to kill the goose laying the Wild West's golden eggs; increasingly, Buffalo Bill attracted the greedy.

This trait became evident when rumors of Cody's involvement with a young woman emerged. The scandal intensified when Cody knocked a gentleman named Fred May out during an argument in a fancy Washington restaurant. It was later explained that the dispute was over a bottle of wine, but the gossip was that the two were fighting about a woman whom they both had known in London, a beautiful actress named Katherine Clemmons.[34]

After the public fight in Washington Cody had promptly retreated to North Platte to avoid a scandal. With her theatrical career on the rocks, however, Miss Clemmons went to the press and reported that Buffalo Bill had invested over $50,000 to produce the play *A Lady of Venice* for her debut on the American stage. Having met Clemmons during his own debut in London in 1887, Cody had referred to her as the "finest looking woman in the world" so he obviously once held her in high esteem. Upon losing $50,000 on Miss Clemmons, however, Cody remarked that he would "rather manage a million Indians than one soubrette" and, seeking a different type of beauty, fled to the Big Horn Mountains on a bear hunting trip.[35]

Cody's interest in the majestic Big Horn Mountains went back many years. The Big Horns were the treasured hunting grounds over which the Crow and the Lakota battled for generations. Beyond the Big Horns to the west was *Absaroka*, which was the heart of the Crow territory and, specifically, the magnificent Yellowstone Country, one of North America's natural crown jewels. Long before Euroamericans first visited the region, the Crows had been continually forced to defend Absaroka from all directions as aggressive enemies, particularly the Lakota, were constantly nibbling into their extraordinary territory. As surely as Sitting Bull's surrender had indicated the end of Indian resistance to the Euroamerican invasion of North America, however, the Wounded Knee Massacre implied, as Black Elk so eloquently stated, "the end of a people's dream." With the Native American dream dying, the coveted Big Horn Basin and Absaroka lay waiting for the victor. It was natural that Cody would be the first white man to seek to create a community in the wondrous Yellowstone Country. Distinguished by the Crow Indian's sacred Buffalo Heart Mountain, the northwest portion of the Big Horn Basin begins a spectacular ascent from the high dusty plains. Traversing the craggy pass of the Shoshone River canyon between Spirit and Rattlesnake Mountains, one enters the breathtaking Absaroka Mountain Range of the Yellowstone Country. Rapidly descending from the multitude of magical waters flowing in all directions out of Yellowstone, the Shoshone River rushes eastward, falls, roars, races and meanders through the Wapiti Valley en route to the Big Horn Basin and the sea. Cody's sister, Helen, offers her brother's vivid description of the distinctive Wapiti Valley, a magnificent sixty mile watershed in the Absaroka Mountains which is the eastern entrance to modern-day Yellowstone National Park:

> To my right stretched a towering range of snowcapped mountains, broken here and there into minarets, obelisks, and spires. Between me and this range of lofty peaks a long irregular line of stately cottonwoods told me a stream wound its way beneath. The rainbow-tinted carpet under me was formed of innumerable brilliant-hued wild flowers; it spread about me in every direction, and sloped gracefully to the stream. Game of every kind played on the turf, and bright-hued birds flitted over it. It was a scene no mortal can satisfactorily describe. At such a moment a man, no matter what his creed, sees the hand of the mighty Maker of the universe majestically displayed in the beauty of nature; he becomes sensibly conscious, too, of his own littleness. I uttered no word for very awe; I looked upon one of nature's masterpieces.[36]

As most who followed him there, Cody fell in love with Absaroka and the Yellowstone Country. There, where the high plains merge into the Shoshone River's Wapiti Valley, Cody decided to create his town. Once again, Cody was also using the old formula of going where the crowds would be gathering; he knew the world would soon be coming to see Yellowstone. They would be coming from the east and would have to pass through his town on the way to the Yellowstone.

Cody sought more than the beautiful and bountiful land, however; he also hoped his mountain retreat would be his escape from Lulu's increasing meddling into his affairs in North Platte; in Absaroka he would start anew, in control of his own affairs. More importantly, as he had grown extremely weary of show business, he also hoped to retire from the circus life. In Absaroka, he would return to nature and the new West and create a community as a monument to his life's accomplishments. Cody was also in serious need of a place to relax. With $4,000 a day in expenses just to keep their Wild West running, he and Salsbury faced phenomenal pressure to make money. Having based their success on epic scale, Cody and Salsbury had no choice from the beginning but to grow ever larger in size. This process, however, required continually greater success and profits. Simply, the Wild

West peaked in 1893. This reality hit the Wild West hard during the 1894 season. Following the Wild West's most successful year ever, ticket sales could not keep up with the costs of maintaining the mammoth operation. Salsbury, anticipating the problem, had developed a new idea for a comprehensive exposition of Negro life entitled *Black America*, which he hoped would be a hit and create a new cash flow. Following their old pattern, Cody and Salsbury went full bore to create an epic scale production, employing 300 Negro actors, singers, dancers and musicians traveling in a train composed of fifteen cars. Unfortunately, the show flopped and suffered heavy losses.

The strain of the disastrous 1894 Wild West season and the failure of *Black America* was terrific on both partners. Cody, having fainted during a couple of Wild West performances, was indeed growing older and his health declining. Nate Salsbury was also suffering from serious health problems, and, by the close of the 1894 season was a partial invalid, no longer able to tour with the Wild West.

This separation of Cody and Salsbury marks the beginning of the end of the Wild West. Aside from his mother, Mary, no other person was able keep Cody as stable and focused as Nate Salsbury. Artistically, he could match Cody vision for vision, yet, unlike Cody, Salsbury was a brilliant financial manager. Over the years Cody had become dependent upon Salsbury's sage business advice and sound financial direction as the Wild West prospered. Most seriously, Nate's departure from the day-to-day administration of the Wild West necessitated a change which would dramatically accelerate and further complicate the pace and quality of Cody's increasingly confused and harried life. The partner Salsbury brought to the Wild West to replace him was one of the most successful men in the history of American show business: James A. Bailey.

Bailey had indeed revolutionized the circus world. For decades before Bailey's dramatic altering of the basic touring structure, the circus—as the Wild West—would come to town, stay until the crowds faded, and move on. Bailey created the one-day, two-performance stand. With amazing synchronicity the circus would arrive by train, unload, set up, perform a matinee and evening show, strike the sets and tent, reload on the train and depart within a twenty-four hour period. A year younger than Cody and Salsbury, Bailey was an orphan-boy who ran away with the circus. Appropriately, Bailey made up most of his story, claiming to be a descendent of Hachaliah Bailey, the circus pioneer who brought the first elephant to America in 1815. He pulled himself up through circus hierarchy by his bootstraps and before reaching age 30 was half owner of the Cooper and Bailey Circus. In 1880, an elephant was born on his circus lot and Barnum offered him $100,000 for the calf. Bailey immediately went to the press and rented billboards to promote Barnum's offer to buy his baby elephant. Outsmarted, Barnum quickly offered Bailey a partnership in his circus. Adam Forepaugh died in 1890 and Barnum and Bailey promptly acquired the huge Forepaugh and Sells Brothers Circus. In 1891 Barnum died and suddenly Bailey was in control of the two largest circuses in the world. Assuming control of the performance routes of the Wild West, Bailey could now hit his chief competitor, the Ringling Brothers, head-on.

Bailey's capacity for work was legendary in the circus world. Obsessed with work, he never relaxed with any form of social or personal recreation. Acutely aware that his circus routes were absolutely linked with the success of farm products, when reading the morning paper Bailey first sought the commodities page for the prices of potatoes, wheat, butter, and eggs.[37]

Already in deep financial trouble because of his generous over-speculation, Cody had no choice but to submit to Bailey's rigorous schedule of one-day stands. The Wild West played 321 performances in 1895 and Cody did not miss one. Bailey also scheduled the Wild West to travel over 9,000 miles, performing in one hundred-thirty-one towns in one hundred-ninety days.[38] Suddenly Cody's entire life revolved around either being on a train or in the arena.

As hard as it was on Cody physically, the 1895 tour made money. As soon as the tour ended Buffalo Bill returned to Absaroka and his growing community there. He hired Al and Julia's son, Henry, to drive a herd of cattle from North Platte to Hyannis, where the cattle were loaded onto a train and shipped to Sheridan. Cody's nephew then went to Deadwood, where he picked up another large herd. This Black Hills herd, branded TE by Cody's friend Mike Russell, became the origin of the name of Buffalo Bill's TE Ranch.[39]

Meanwhile, Cody went to work on creating the necessary water to nourish his garden:

> In 1895 Cody joined George T. Beck, Bronson C. Rumsey, Sr. and others in the construction of the Cody Canal, a project of the Shoshone Land and Irrigation Company. It had been proposed to name a town at DeMaris Springs for Cody. The company also laid out a townsite, calling it Shoshone, but that name was rejected for a post office because of possible confusion with the Shoshoni Indian

agency. Charles Emery Hayden, engineer, said Beck, Nate Salsbury, Ed Goodman, Charles Gilette, and Hobo Jones then conspired to annex the name of Cody before the DeMaris Springs townsite got around to it. The Cody post office was established in August, 1896, with Ed Goodman, son of Julia, as first postmaster. The water project eventuated in the construction of Shoshone Dam, called the highest in the world, at 328 feet, when completed in 1910. It was renamed the Buffalo Bill Dam in 1946.[40]

Sadly, at the moment he hoped to regain charge of his life, Cody was about to lose control of everything.

Chapter Eighteen

PAHASKA HAD A STRONG HEART

As a fellow gets old he doesn't feel like tearing about the country forever. I do not want to die a showman. I grow very tired of this sort of
sham hero-worship sometimes.

—William F. "Buffalo Bill" Cody, 1897
(*The Making of Buffalo Bill*, Richard J. Walsh and Milton S. Salsbury)

No dime novelist or press agent ever invented for Buffalo Bill a more
courageous act than this—that in his seventy-first year he took up
his rifle again, mounted his horse and shot the glass balls.

(*The Making of Buffalo Bill*, Richard J. Walsh and Milton S. Salsbury)

WHEN Nate Salsbury's health forced him to quit touring with the Wild
West, Buffalo Bill drew his most loyal companions closer and continued
on the road. Arizona John Burke, who had been with Cody since the beginnings of his career in show business, remained a devoted influence;
Cody's adopted sharpshooter son, Johnny Baker, assumed a more important role in his life and in the administration of the Wild West, and his
long-time friendship with Dr. Frank "White Beaver" Powell also deepened.
This trusted and protective circle of faithful friends clustered around their
star as James Bailey's rigorous touring schedule rapidly broke Cody's health
down while simultaneously building him into the most recognized man in
America. In spite of his superficial control of the situation, however, Cody
clearly perceived the profound change he faced in both his health and in
his finances; by 1896, when Cody traveled over ten-thousand miles and
played in one-hundred thirty-two cities, he announced the first of his many
"farewell tours."[1]

Even as Cody's circle of "pards" drew closer attempting to shield and protect him, forces more insidiously destructive than a bone-rattling tour schedule threatened the aging showman. Ironically, these impending ruinous forces originated at the source of Cody's unique power. By the mid-1880s Cody had become acutely sensitive to the fact that as his celebrity grew he proportionately became a parody of himself; indeed, he saw from the beginning that the sensational "image" of Buffalo Bill cannibalized the genuine heroic substance of Will Cody. This inherent parasitic characteristic of celebrity revealed itself simply to Cody in the late 1860s when he became embarrassed at the realization that his friends on the frontier would know the exaggerated exploits and preposterous adventures attributed to him in dime novels were impossible to replicate. A footnote of the industrial revolution, however, modern media had been born as fluid communication and transportation rapidly linked the North American continent. Dime novels fed the immigrant American public's growing need to define a nebulous collective personality and, in doing so, became cash cows for the emerging eastern publishing establishment. As dime novels exploded in popularity publishers and authors found it necessary to make the romantic adventures increasingly dramatic. The result of this process of sensationalizing frontier heroics of course was that the line between reality and legend was forever blurred, and the "winning" of the American west, quietly set in motion when trapper-explorers entered the Trans-Mississippi, rapidly evolved as the foremost of American myth. Will Cody, however, was not merely present at the epicenter of this mythic transition; he was the individual spinning the wheels of change as media's dime novels swirled from the page to the stage, and he was the bona fide hero who mounted and exhibited the epic, historic era in the arena before millions of adoring people in search of a collective "American" identity. As Cody adroitly shifted his career from legendary buffalo hunter to military scout during the Indian Wars and from there to dime novel hero and matinee idol of the melodramatic stage, the conflict between reality and "make-believe" merely troubled him creatively until he solved the predicament by boldly bursting back into the outdoors to attempt a realistic reenactment of history with the creation of the Wild West. The very personal, "dark" side of celebrity struck Cody with numbing psychic force, however, as the buffalo suddenly disappeared at the precise moment that his Wild West was born. When his namesake creature vanished Cody realized that, in accepting the dramatic essence of the "winning of the west" portrayed in his roles in countless dime novels, and continued on the stage and in the Wild West arena, the general public had come to erroneously perceive him as the man most singularly responsible for exterminating the buffalo and the American Indian.

This epiphany shocked Will Cody to his core. He truly cherished America and the role he played in his country's history on the frontier. An orphan of the Great Migration, he believed himself to be the classic example of the fact that anyone could overcome circumstance and rise to wealth and fame when blessed with the freedom America offered. A son of the plains, Cody profoundly cherished the West, particularly the natural American West of the Indian, and could not bear to be perceived historically as the man responsible for its destruction. Moreover, even as an enemy on the battlefield, Cody had somehow maintained positive communication with many Plains Indians throughout the Indian Wars Era and could not allow himself to be remembered as the man responsible for destroying them and their culture. Nevertheless, the sudden disappearance of the buffalo brought with it the inescapable awareness that the essence of America's high-minded Manifest Destiny was the violent destruction of peoples and ecosystems. This painful self-realization certainly triggered Cody's conscientious interest in the preservation and restoration of the buffalo and correspondingly influenced his scrupulous behavior with the Indian performers who traveled with his show. In spite of his personal efforts to restore buffalo, educate the world to the vanished era of the early American West and assist American Indian efforts to preserve their unique culture, religion, and basic human rights, Cody had played his "conquering hero" role far too well and become trapped by the sheer power of his unprecedented, mythic celebrity as a buffalo hunter and "injun killer." His youth was drawn in genuine epic, heroic proportions, yet, when pared down to mere theatrical scale, Cody had paradoxically mushroomed into a parody of himself. Furthermore, as the nineteenth century drew to a close and the era he lovingly depicted rapidly faded, a middle-aged Cody naturally found himself facing the first unavoidable stages of the reality that he was also vanishing. Adding to the complexity of emotions Cody faced as he grew older, Euroamerican guilt, nourished by the continuing efforts of humanitarian and Christian organizations, began to impact society as the twentieth century approached, and the image of the "conquering hero" was beginning to show the beginning signs of wearing thin at society's fringes—and with Cody himself. His prized long hair, once highly sought as a battlefield trophy, came to represent to him a relic of a form of combat which had long-since passed. Richard Walsh writes of Cody telling a caller:

> "Just wait until I put up my hair and I'll go out with you. I do hate long hair, but people have come to identify me with long-hair, so I won't cut it." As he wound a top-knot, pierced it with one silver hair-pin and tucked it under his broad-brimmed hat, he grinned. "Long hair is business and not art with me."[2]

Pahaska, however, as Biblical Sampson, and American Indians, drew mystical strength and spiritual power from long hair. The unknown territory into which Cody now embarked would require him to become truly heroic again, and, as the long-haired Lakota chiefs he had admired and respected since childhood, he would soon be drawing courageously upon all of his powers—physical and mystical—in order to face the unmerciful onslaught of time and change and play out the final act of his life with any shred of dignity and integrity.

While vividly underscoring the fact that the core of Buffalo Bill's image was his shoulder-length hair, Cody's remark about his long hair also reinforces the certainty that this characteristic, when combined with beaded fringed buckskins, was essentially one and the same as the Plains Indian. Nevertheless, where Cody had come to represent the destroyer of the west, he had similarly become the romantic American notion of a "white chief"; where "civilized" society cruelly forced Indians to cut their hair in a symbolic gesture of Christian domesticity, however, public image forced Cody to wear his hair long in order to represent the "wild" in the West. Where the remark sadly reveals that Cody had allowed the very source of his power to become entrapped by his celebrity, it nevertheless reveals that Buffalo Bill understood and accepted with good cheer the role he was required by his public to play. He was a true Plainsman; Pahaska was indeed a wasichu chief—a unique bridge between the Native and Euroamerican. At its peak, the incredible numbers of people and livestock of the nomadic Wild West would approximate the size of any major Plains Indian band such as the Oglalas, or Brules, and Cody's role as the head of the operation demanded the same qualities of him as would be expected of Lakota tribal chiefs. Furthermore, his global success had proved also that, in accepting this unique role as a bridge between Native and Euroamerica, he had risen to become a vital link between the Old and New World. Ever loyal to his public, and himself, Cody's hair—essentially the link between all these disparate cultures—would remain long.

Will Cody realized this important connection to the "wilderness" and "civilization" early in his boyhood and accepted the fact that his destiny was to become a plainsman drawn to the epic scale of the American west. As a child, Cody surrendered himself to the great western migration of humanity and, rising to the pinnacle of this violent and dramatic epic era, became a living legend. When Cody was first forced to come to terms with the negative aspects of his celebrity he was also smart enough to realize that no one could have possessed the spiritual wisdom or physical experience to negotiate the mysterious, uncharted territory he had entered; childhood for Cody was, however, a process of learning to rely instantly, completely, and consistently upon his instincts in order to survive and enjoy the freedom the "American" frontier offered. Moreover, since boyhood Cody had known that the freedom of the American frontier was the ability to create multiple opportunities, and he characteristically approached celebrity from that same intuitive and optimistic perspective. Consequently, Cody instinctively accepted his destiny with celebrity as the North American mythos he reflected, created and manifested expanded exponentially. This process of course naturally resulted in Cody's being drawn into a theatrical career and consequently the creation of the Wild West and the shaping of global history. As the era he so colorfully and lovingly represented actually faded into history, however, Cody was acutely aware that, like his graying goatee and thinning crown, he was not long for this world. Many of his oldest, closest friends were gravely ill or had "gone under"; Nate Salsbury, the man he had relied upon for years for astute business advice and emergency loans, was dying. Even with his eternal optimism, Cody also had certainly come to realize his health was fading fast and his ill-fated investments were demanding more money than he could ever possibly earn. He had never made enough money with the Wild West to quit show business, but he also always made too much money to quit.[3] Now he was so deep in debt that he had no choice but to continue touring to support the massive payrolls of his numerous financial adventures. Nevertheless, even as he continued touring and his health declined, he characteristically held to the hope that he would finally make enough to clear his debts and retire to the Big Horn Mountains and his emerging community of Cody, Wyoming.

Unfortunately, each of these negative aspects of Cody's fame rushed into America's center stage spotlight as the United States prepared to go to war with Spain in 1898. At 52 and suffering from a variety of physical ailments, Cody was certainly well past the age to be expected to charge into battle, yet his image as America's "warrior" forced his multitudes of fans and admirers to anticipate his leading the country into the conflict that loomed on the horizon. By simply continuing to perform in the Wild West, however, Cody encouraged the public to expect such behavior of a man in his middle years and, considering the militaristic aspects of the Wild West, Cody's patriotic flag-waving can only be interpreted as natural. Indeed, the United States government, inspired by the popularity of the Wild West, raised volunteers for the Spanish-American War by exploiting Theodore Roosevelt's boast that cowboy "Rough Riders" would make the best cavalry to fight the Spanish. Uncle Sam's call-to-arms brought cowboys from all sections of the country riding in to volunteer to join the fight.

Even though he admitted in private that his heart was not in the war, Cody was also a true patriot. On April 18, 1898, Cody proposed to raise a company of cavalry scouts; he volunteered a herd of 400 horses and the Wild West's chief cowboy, George Burch, to recruit 2,000 "Rough Riders." Cody's old friend, General Nelson Miles, quickly accepted Cody's offer of his services and appointed him to his staff. Cody shipped two personal horses, "Knickerbocker" and "Lancer," to Washington to be transported later to the front.[4]

Nevertheless, Cody faced a major dilemma as the country drew closer to war with Spain; his public persona required dropping everything and marching off to war, yet the reality of abandoning the Wild West was wholly and completely unrealistic. At the time of the Spanish-American War, the Wild West company consisted of four hundred sixty-seven people, four hundred fifty-three horses and mules, two field pieces and caisson, two prairie schooners, the stage coach, four buggies, thirty-five baggage wagons, two water-tanks, two engines for electric lighting, sixteen flat cars, fifteen stock cars and eight sleeping coaches.[5] Cody simply could not afford to pull the plug on an operation the size of the Wild West and put that many people, himself included, out of work. Money was the reason he could not just quit show business and retire to his mountain retreat, and money likewise prevented his shutting his show down to go running off to war.

The War Department nevertheless moved quickly forward and the United States declared war on Spain on April 25. With the official declaration Major Burke announced to the press that Colonel Cody would remain with the Wild West until he was needed at the front. By early June, as the Navy prepared to clear the way for an invasion, General Miles headed to

Tampa, Florida to lead troops into Cuba. Miles, as mentioned earlier in this text, was extremely ambitious, and his detractors suggested that he was using the Spanish-American War to position himself politically for a run for the presidency. At the last minute, however, in what some suggested was a surreptitious political ploy designed to thwart the general's presidential aspirations, Miles was recalled to Washington on emergency matters, and Major General William R. Shafter sailed in his place with the expedition to invade Cuba. The last-minute recall to Washington was indeed successful in keeping Miles out of the conflict; by July, troops led by Shafter had won the battles of El Caney and San Juan Hill. Roosevelt's Rough Riders had their day of glory when they charged the hill; it was actually a misnomer to refer to the soldiers as "riders" for they fought on foot. Their horses remained in Florida, cared for by four troops. Admiral William T. Sampson's fleet destroyed the Spanish fleet off Santiago on July 3, virtually ending the war.[6] The war was moving quickly without Cody or General Miles. By the time Miles could get to Cuba in early July, the Spanish were already beginning negotiations to surrender. On July 17 the Spanish surrendered and it was all nearly over. Miles rode Cody's horses in a few small, insignificant battles before hostilities officially ended on August 13, but Buffalo Bill had been caught for the first time in the spotlight "talking big and performing little."[7]

The show business axiom that any publicity is good publicity was certainly the case for Buffalo Bill concerning the Spanish-American War. Even though he had been publicly embarrassed by missing the war, the negative publicity packed crowds into the bleachers to see the Wild West. As if to emphasize the fact that Cody's popularity could overcome any negative attack, the scout was also soon to receive one of the greatest honors of his career. The organizers of the Trans-Mississippi Exposition in Omaha had booked the Wild West to return to the very place of its birth fifteen years earlier. On August 31, 1898, only eighteen days after the official end of the Spanish-American War, the Trans-Mississippi Exposition celebrated Nebraska's most famous citizen with "Cody Day." Dignitaries gathered to shower praise on the Great Plains "favorite son"; Nebraska Governor Silas A. Holcomb and U.S. Senator John Thurston were present, as was the man who had helped create Western Union, Edward Creighton.

Cody rode into the arena to the tumultuous applause of twenty-four thousand people. As Cody dismounted his magnificent chestnut stallion, Duke, and climbed the bleachers to the rostrum, Governor Holcomb spoke eloquently of Cody's contributions and welcomed him to the celebration in his honor. An elderly Alexander Majors greeted the scout at the podium with a friendly handshake, turned to the hushed audience, and told them how forty-three years earlier he had given Cody his first job:

> I remember when we paid him twenty-five dollars for the first month's work. He was paid in half dollars, and he got fifty of them. He tied them up in his little handkerchief and spread the money all over the table.
>
> "I've been spreading it ever since," interjected Cody.
>
> "Bless your precious life, Colonel," the old man said when he sat down.[8]

Although delighted by the tender repartee, the audience did not fully realize the truth represented in the affectionate interaction between Majors and Cody. Bankrupted in 1861 by the Pony Express, Russell, Majors and Waddell had folded up its massive shipping and freight operation and the three partners faded into history. Upon making big money, however, one of the first people Cody took under his protective wing was Alexander Majors. For years he had given Majors a regular annual "retainer" and enabled his old boss to live comfortably.[9]

When it came time for Cody to respond to the accolades, he rose and, showing the influence of Arizona John Burke in his language, said,

> The whistle of the locomotive has drowned the howl of the coyote; the barbed-wire fence has narrowed the range of the cowpuncher; but no material evidence of prosperity can obliterate our contribution to Nebraska's imperial progress.
>
> How little I dreamed in the long ago that the lonely path of the scout and the pony-express rider would lead me to the place you have assigned me today. Here, near the banks of the mighty Missouri, which flows unvexed to the sea, my thoughts revert to the early days of my manhood. . . . Time goes on and brings with it new duties and responsibilities, but we who are called old-timers cannot forget the trials and tribulations which we had to encounter while paving the path for civilization.[10]

The subtext of Cody's brocade remarks in Omaha perfectly summarize his self-concept: From the beginning of his career on the plains Cody had seen himself as a cog in the wheel of civilization's optimistic quest for whatever lay over the horizon. To Will Cody the advancement of society depended totally upon the individual's access to abundant opportunity and he had based his entire life upon his ability to manifest good fortune for himself and for others. Where the typical Euroamerican could not envision incorporating the American Indian into this magnificent quest, however, Cody saw the Native and Euroamerican participating equally in the same glorious, evolving dream. Perhaps it had to do with the fact that Cody came into his unique perception of the world at a time when Plains Indians were noted for being extremely open and receptive to sharing the abundance of the land with the wasichus and actually assisted them with their migration. Perhaps it was because he was aware of the Plains Indians' early and indelible influence upon the shaping of his personality and his subsequent success, and fully realized his unique role in aiding their difficult transition into "civilization" as their great horse and buffalo culture was overwhelmed by the Industrial Revolution. Perhaps he had also realized as a child that part of his responsibility would be to educate wasichu society to the merits of Plains Indian culture and religion. At a very fragile age, Cody certainly had experienced the lascivious nature of the wasichu personally and this propensity to unethical and immoral behavior revealed to him that most of his white brethren had quite a way to go themselves before becoming truly "civilized." Conversely, he appreciated from personal experience the inherent moral and ethical integrity of most Indians and throughout his life was outspoken concerning what he saw as the root of all problems between the two races: wasichu lies. Whatever the origin of his belief, Cody did nevertheless perceive his role as one of uniting the Native and Euroamerican in what he envisioned as the "march of boundless opportunities."

Once promoter James Bailey entered the picture, however, Cody's self-perception of his role in a historical reenactment of the march of civilization quickly became more of a circus complete with sideshows. The 1898 Wild West program included Bailey's additional offerings of Japanese magic, a snake enchantress, a boy giant, midgets, a king of cards, a fire king, a sword swallower, a juggler, a Kaffir warrior, some Venetian glass blowers, and a couple of mind readers.[11] This new carnivalesque lifestyle eroded Cody's spirit and his sense of being at the forefront of civilization as much as the pace he was being forced to keep broke down his physical health. A month after the Cody Day celebration in Omaha, he fainted three times during a performance. Various veiled explanations, which ranged from a simple cold to a nervous breakdown, were offered to hide

Cody's obvious and advancing serious illness. It was even suggested that he was heartbroken because Katherine Clemmons was in love with Howard Gould.[12]

By 1900, the Wild West had evolved into a eclectic blend of carnival, circus and military revue, traveling Bailey's rigorous circuit of one-night-stands. Cody enjoyed taking the Wild West on a series of "farewell" tours through his old stomping grounds in the Great Plains region as the performances brought out many of his oldest friends. In October, 1901, however, fate dealt Cody a full plate of troubles. On October 21, his longtime partner/brother-in-law, Al Goodman, died. Then, as Cody and his family were still mourning Goodman's passing, disaster struck: On October 28, 1901, as the Wild West train left Charlotte, North Carolina for its last engagement of the season at Danville, Virginia, its second section had a head-on collision with a freight train. Several Lakota people were indeed killed in this crash. This is the train wreck prophesized by Walks Ahead, the Lakota mentioned by Luther Standing Bear in this work's Prologue. One hundred ten horses were killed and Annie Oakley suffered severe internal injuries which would terminate her career with the Wild West; never again would she run joyfully into the arena to open the Wild West. After several operations, she finally recovered, but it was more than a year before she was able to return to show business, opening November 12, 1902, in *The Western Girl*, a melodrama written by Langdon McCormick. White-haired after the train wreck, her once strong vitality never fully returned, but she was eventually able to regain her shooting skill. In 1912, she toured with the Young Buffalo Bill Wild West and Col. Commins Far East Combined Show.[13]

With characteristic professionalism, the Wild West quickly mended and continued after the train wreck. In March, 1902, Cody wrote his widowed sister, Julia, describing the details of his plan to build a first-class hotel in Cody and urged her to leave North Platte and run the hotel. Naturally, Julia accepted her brother's offer and moved to Cody.[14] When the 1902 season ended in November Buffalo Bill had traveled coast-to-coast and logged more performances than any other year in his career. Will hurried to Cody, Wyoming, and the official November 18 opening of the Irma Hotel, named for his daughter. Bailey's pace still dogged him, however, and after only a few days in the Big Horn Basin, Cody headed to England to prepare for a winter "farewell" tour of Europe.

Nate Salsbury died on Christmas Eve, 1902. True to the fundamental dictum of show business and Nate Salsbury's wishes, the Wild West opened in London on schedule the day after Christmas with flags at half-mast, honoring its cocreator. Salsbury's death had terrific impact on Cody. He had lost a dear friend, astute financial advisor, and show business genius as a trusted partner. Complicating matters, his debts were mounting. He had invested heavily in the Oracle Gold Mine in Arizona, and his irrigation project in the Big Horn Basin, aside from his multiple investments in the region, had cost a fortune. Some historians theorize that the ever-optimistic Cody had been duped into investing in the Oracle mine by "seeding," one of the oldest of tricks in mining communities. Con men would display very rich ore which they claimed came from the mine, when, in fact, they had nothing but hopes for an expensive hole in the ground. Ever eager for cash, Cody would have been an easy mark for such a confidence game. He estimated that, in addition to running the Wild West, he employed over four thousand men.

Will Cody had been a community builder from the very beginning of his career on the Great Plains. Cody, Wyoming, stands today as an abiding monument to his vision of a community in the Big Horn Basin. He poured his phenomenal energy into the creation of the community of Cody the same way he did into everything else; in addition to his TE Ranch, the Irma Hotel, and the irrigation project, Buffalo Bill financed *The Cody Enterprise* newspaper and planned to open a military college and academy of "Rough Riders"; he also built the "Wapiti Inn" and purchased spectacular property, which he named "Pahaska's Tepee," high in the Absaroka Mountains near Sylvan Pass, which is the eastern gate to Yellowstone National Park. Anticipating the modern phenomenal flow of automobile traffic that pours into the park annually, Buffalo Bill created a line of stagecoaches linking his holdings along the "Cody Road" into the Yellowstone. Renowned for his robust appetites, Cody was equally vigorous in his support of the religious community in both North Platte and in Cody. As mentioned earlier in this text, Cody paid the annual salaries of ministers of five churches in North Platte. The story of the origin of the Episcopal Church lingers in the mythology of the town of Cody even today. The story goes that George Beck, Tom Purcell, and William F. Cody were playing poker in Purcell's saloon. When the jackpot grew to $500 the players decided that the man who won the jackpot would contribute it toward building a church. When the jackpot reached $550, Beck won the game and stipulated that the Episcopal church receive the money.[15]

During the performance season, Cody often promised to limit his drinking to three glasses of whiskey a day but had the liquor served to him in oversized beer mugs. Even while he basically remained true to his vow to Salsbury and rarely drank during performances, Cody's off-season binges are legendary. When the season ended, Cody would promptly head for Omaha, where he would begin drinking and reminiscing with old cronies. From Omaha he would head to North Platte, picking up more old friends and comrades en route and the "tanglefoot-jollification" would continue to grow as it approached the Big Horn Basin and the town of Cody. Cody pioneers maintained that because he had to stop at every ranch house it took Buffalo Bill two days to drive in from the railroad to the town of Cody. In 1996, I interviewed a lifelong resident of Cody, Francis Purvis, a delightful ninety-eight-year-old woman, who told me that when Buffalo Bill returned from his tours with the Wild West, he never failed to stop at her father's ranch to bring presents for her and her siblings. Once actually in the town of Cody, Buffalo Bill would find the four saloons packed with so many reception committees that it would take him a week or so to finally reach his TE Ranch. The TE Ranch would be jammed with as many guests as the house would hold and they were each invited to stay as long as they wished and drink with him, and listen to his well-worn stories."[16]

Aside from attracting those who wanted to join the continual party that followed Cody, many were drawn to the showman to take advantage of the flow of money that he spread in his wake. Cody's spending habits matched his drinking habits. Except for his sumptuous wardrobe, however, Cody was not extravagant or self-indulgent. Nevertheless, he did thoroughly enjoy being rich enough to be able to respond to any appeal for help. He was a fountain of money and no one, least of all Buffalo Bill, ever knew how much money he went through in his forty-year career in show business. When the Wild West was the world's premier entertainment attraction and making millions annually he spent money "as if he were trying to give it away faster than he earned it." After the show Cody would go to the box office, fill his pockets with money and hit town. The entourage of open-handed dreamers, schemers, drinkers and beggars would begin to gather at the box office and grow as Cody stepped out into the night. Cody bought every drink at every bar and usually drank everyone under the table.[17]

Louisa deplored Will's generous and rambunctious behavior from the beginning of their relationship. Where they seem to have maintained some semblance of genuine affection for one another, and the intensity displayed in their very public conflicts implies a molten core passionately united them, gregarious Cody increasingly avoided his antisocial wife as his success took him to the far corners of the globe and he became capable of embracing life even more vigorously. Even though he supported Lulu in grand style in North Platte, Will grew more distant with each personal career accomplishment. A virile, romantic, and handsome man, powerful, wealthy, and generous, but in an unhappy marriage, it was inevitable he would attract women. Some genuinely adored him, while others used him merely as a stepping-stone to further careers. When he was bored, lonely, worried, ill, or drinking, he sought out interesting women. He hated to go home and wished he could get away from Lulu for good.[18]

Many of Buffalo Bill's companions believed that his community building in the Big Horn Basin had more to do with getting away from Louisa's negativity than anything else. Early in the relationship Cody had considered divorce, but, since his career took him away from her for long periods of time, natural separation essentially resolved the issue. During his second tour of England, however, he fell in love with Katherine Clemmons and decided to pursue a divorce from Lulu. With terrible ironic timing, upon his return to North Platte from England and Miss Clemmons' affections, Lou-isa served her husband cold salmon that had gone bad, nearly killing him with food poisoning.[19]

Cody was convinced Lulu had tried to poison him with "dragon's blood," a gypsy love potion. Louisa admitted that she had put a drug in his coffee, but insisted, rather than poison, it was a potion to cure him of his enormous ability to consume alcohol.[20]

From this point forward Cody's affections for Lulu shifted dramatically. Throughout his career he had regularly written affectionate letters to his wife, but after the food-poisoning incident, communication effectively ceased. Adding insult to injury, Bessie Isabell, an attractive young woman, also began traveling with the Wild West during this period. Mrs. Cody jealously accused her husband of employing Miss Isabell for no apparent reason, yet Buffalo Bill, in spite of Arizona John Burke's presence, maintained she was a press agent.

The food poisoning incident must have triggered Cody's deeper concern about his health as well as his marriage. The fainting incidents could not be ignored and certainly indicated something was not right physically. As his natural vigor faded, Cody had spoken repeatedly of "nervousness" attacks. He had confided to Johnny Baker that he was not sure he could go on much longer and wanted him to be prepared to take his place in the show.[21]

Furthermore, Cody's position in the Wild West had been severely undermined as Bailey rose to greater power with Salsbury's death. To begin with, the hundred thousand dollars Cody owed his partner had been transferred to James Bailey when Salsbury's estate sold his stock in the Wild West to the circus promoter. Gaining control of the Wild West, Bailey promptly booked the show on the Ringling Brothers' circus circuit in Europe for four years in order to take it out of competition with his circus tours in America. There is also reason to believe that Bailey believed that because of the appeal of the "exotic" and romantic elements of the Wild West to European tastes, the show was actually better suited for European than American audiences.

Edward had become King of England and with his old friend on the throne, Cody enjoyed enduring popularity in Great Britain. In early April, 1903, however, fate dealt Cody another cruel blow when his horse stumbled and fell, throwing Cody and injuring him so badly that he could not return to the saddle for three weeks. Terrible weather delivered the knock-out punch and pursued the Wild West throughout the tour of England and by October, when the show was housed in winter quarters, Cody returned to America "in ugly humor."[22]

Aside from the strain on his nerves with the Wild West and his huge financial burden, Cody's wife had given him reason to be in a nasty mood. Throughout his life Cody had taken care of his sisters and remained very close with each of them. Lulu's meddling into his affairs in Wyoming, however, had caused trouble between Will and one of his sisters: Cody had given his sister Helen a piece of property which Lulu refused to sign over. Will and Helen argued over the situation and the disagreements had become so intense that in his letters to Julia he asked her to make sure Helen was out of Cody when he returned.[23]

Cody's bad mood also provoked him to take the step he had long pondered and he sued Lulu for divorce under the grounds that they were incompatible and she had attempted to poison him. His actions, however, were met with immediate, unforeseen disaster: Will and Louisa's daughter Arta proclaimed her heart "broken" over her father's divorce suit and died three days later. Suffering terrific grief with Arta's sudden death, Lulu accused her husband's divorce suit of killing their daughter. This insensitive remark naturally only created more hostility between the grieving couple; when Lulu offered a reconciliation at Arta's funeral in Rochester, New York, Cody angrily refused and returned to England to continue Bailey's tour. When he returned to America in 1905 the divorce suit came to trial.[24] The Codys' 1905 divorce trial before Judge Charles Scott in Cheyenne, Wyoming, was arguably the most public at that point in American, if not world, history. Mrs. Cody maintained throughout the trial that she had been a loyal wife and portrayed her husband as generous to a fault while also accusing him of habitual drunken behavior and infidelities with numerous women—in her wildest moments implying those dalliances included Queen Victoria. Cody accused his wife of attempting to poison him and his dogs and of being inhospitable to his friends and guests. On March 23, 1905, after the embarrassment of publicly airing the most private aspects of their marriage, Judge Scott ruled in Mrs. Cody's favor and dismissed the suit.

With the loss of the divorce suit, Cody had two years remaining of Bailey's four-year tour of the Wild West throughout Europe. He left America immersed in the bad luck that had dogged him since the turn of the century. By the time the tour entered France, glanders broke out among the horses, forcing Cody to supervise the destruction of the entire herd of the Wild West.[25] The loss of his beloved horses was only a small part of Buffalo Bill's troubles. His finances were about to take yet another tumble towards disaster. Cody insisted that Bailey had made an oral promise not to call upon him for any part of the losses that might be incurred in Europe, but before the tour ended, Bailey died and his estate forced Cody to pay.[26]

Being forced to pay the Bailey estate hit Cody hard financially, yet, perhaps of even greater importance, Bailey's death put Cody and the Wild West in a very precarious administrative situation. Bailey's primary purpose in booking the Wild West for such an extended European tour had been to avoid competing with his circus business in America. Moreover, Bailey controlled the touring routes of the Ringling Brothers throughout Europe and he logically speculated that audiences there would be attracted to seeing Buffalo Bill for a series of "farewell" tours. Bailey also reckoned that after a prolonged absence in Europe that the Wild West would be able to attract very large audiences for similar farewell tours in America. With Bailey's death, however, Cody's debt had been passed from the estate of Nate Salsbury to the estate of James Bailey. If the hundred thousand dollars he now owed the Bailey estate were the only debt on his slate, Cody would have been able to clear it in one good season. His many other debts were, however, multiplying faster than he could manage. Of greater importance, Bailey's death served to undermine Cody's core control over the Wild West. Salsbury had initially contracted Bailey as a booking agent for which he would receive for his services a percentage of the Wild West's profits. With Salsbury's death, however, Bailey had assumed a much more important role, eventually even pushing Arizona John Burke into the background of the marketing of the show. Bailey's death meant the loss of his vitally important contribution to the booking and administration of the Wild West. Now, when he needed a managerial genius more than ever, Cody was forced into administrating the Wild West himself. As financial and administrative stress consumed Cody, Johnny Baker and John Burke loyally drew even closer to the star, the only two who began with the Wild West and stayed with it until the end, never failing in their devotion to their chief. The two old men and their young friend held together and endured the blows of fate. And Buffalo Bill was the most valiant of them all as he swung into the saddle for the opening of Madison Square Garden in the spring of 1907—sixty-one and still with his foot in the stirrup.[27]

Burke and Baker tried to absorb most of the managerial burden of the Wild West, but the strain of the show continued to negatively effect Cody. Fluid movement of such a large body of people and livestock was a constant nightmare. Coordinating the railroad schedules alone was a full-time chore; extraordinary advance logistical planning was required to simply insure that the Wild West would arrive in a town on schedule, with enough time to set up its huge canvas tents, arrange and conduct a promotional parade, perform a matinee and evening show, strike the tents and move the entire operation on to the next town. As a result of the increased administrative stress and his advancing years, Cody's nerves were shattered. This condition naturally affected Cody's performance as a marksman, causing him to frequently miss shots in the show. Commenting on every missed target, fickle newspaper reporters called attention to the number of glass balls the old scout failed to hit, rather than acknowledging the fact that he was still in the arena in his late sixties riding, targeting, and hitting anything at all. Late in 1908 Wild West alumni Major Gordon "Pawnee Bill" Lillie, came to his old employer's rescue and offered much needed assistance. Lillie had procured Pawnees for the Wild West's initial seasons and had acted as an interpreter for the group of Indians. Early on, however, Lillie had left the Wild West to create his own competitive exhibition which, after initially stumbling, had prospered as *Pawnee Bill's Far East*. Pawnee Bill had been frugal with his money and was prepared to invest some of his fortune in helping Cody return to glory. Angered by the Bailey estate's attempts to remove Johnny Baker and Arizona John Burke from the Wild West, Lillie bought the Bailey estate's interest and became the sole owner of the show. He gave Cody the canceled Bailey note, declined the opportunity to claim interest on the additional notes he had assumed purchasing the Wild West, and offered Cody the opportunity to earn equal ownership of his show back by working in their combined exhibition. The duo immediately planned another series of "farewell" tours throughout the United States and Canada. Aside from his generosity toward Buffalo Bill, Major Lillie had pulled together a wonderful bargain for himself. With Buffalo Bill's desire to retire so apparent, he could lovingly facilitate the old scout's wishes, portray himself as Cody's successor, and complete the transition of becoming America's premiere western impresario while making money with Buffalo Bill's retirement tours.

When it came to spending money Major Lillie could hold his own with Cody. Unlike Cody, however, he did not have a continuous record of success in show business. Even with Annie Oakley in his first production in 1888, the show failed. In 1890 and 1893 he tried again with a show titled *Pawnee Bill's Historical Wild West, Mexican Hippodrome, Indian Museum, and Grand Fireworks Exhibition.* Lillie advertised three hundred men and women and two hundred horses in the production, but was threatened with foreclosure before the 1895 season opened. A backer came to his rescue, however, and that season Lillie was successful, paid off his debts and firmly established himself in the business. Like Cody, Lillie was an entrepreneur and community builder; parallel with Cody's development of Cody, Wyoming was Pawnee Bill's involvement in the town of Pawnee, Oklahoma, where he was president of a bank, donor of a $55,000 schoolhouse, head of the school board, and investor in many enterprises.[28]

Apparently, audiences believed they were being given a last chance to see Buffalo Bill and, for the 1909–1910 season, the "Two Bill's Show," as it was called, prospered. Unfortunately, attendance for the 1911–1912 season fell dramatically and the one-hundred-thousand dollar profits were not nearly enough to meet the demands of Cody's creditors.[29] Facing such low profits, Buffalo Bill offered to sell Lillie Scout's Rest Ranch for $30,000 debt to Major Lillie. The $10,000 balance was covered by a transfer of the mortgage on the Irma Hotel. Through these transactions with Major Lillie, Cody was actually half-owner of the show at the end of 1911.[30]

Most of Cody's financial problems stemmed from his expensive gold mines in Arizona and his efforts to create a community in the Big Horn Basin. His numerous debts were so old, large and varied, however, that many swindlers confronted the scout with bogus claims because they realized that Cody, thinking he had forgotten the debt, would succumb to their extortion; sadly, more often than not, Cody paid the fraudulent claims. Cody's Arizona mines provide a perfect example of the origin of most of his financial woes: Visiting one of them, Johnny Baker had found only four men working where there were thirty-six names on the payroll.[31]

Cody had dropped half a million dollars into those Arizona mine shafts during the year of 1912 alone. A fraction of that investment would have saved him from catastrophe in 1913. Scout's Rest Ranch, the development of Cody, and even the Arizona mines would appear to be sound investments, yet they were all expensive and made him no money. He made fortunes in show business, but none of his investments outside of show business ever paid off.[32] Indeed, Cody was simply ahead of the times with most of his major investments. Buffalo Bill would beam with pride to see the fruit of his "plausible" investment in modern day Cody, Wyoming. Nevertheless, in 1912, when Cody's world was rapidly falling apart, it was impossible to foresee the enduring legacy his vision in the Big Horn Basin would produce.

While visiting his sister in Denver early in 1913, Cody was introduced to H. H. Tammen, who, with his partner Fred Bonfils, owned the *Denver Post* and the Sells-Floto Circus. In the course of the conversation, Cody told Tammen he needed twenty thousand dollars to settle his debts. Tammen offered to loan Cody the money if he would give him a six month note on the show's property as collateral. Having helped the old scout out of a jam, Tammen then pressed Cody to leave Pawnee Bill at the end of the season and to appear with the Sells-Floto Circus the following year. Against his better judgment, Cody reluctantly agreed.[33]

Cody's irrational decision to leave Pawnee Bill after the 1913 season was the beginning of the end of the Wild West. Cody's desperate need for more and more money had perhaps clouded his judgment to the point that he concluded that with his ownership in the "Far East/Wild West" combined with the Sells-Floto Circus he would essentially be earning money from two shows at once. More likely, however, Cody naively assumed he would come up with the money to pay Tammen back and that, upon repayment, the newspaper man would release him from the agreement to perform in the Sells-Floto Circus. Major Lillie naturally assumed that Cody had betrayed him and was furious. That Lillie quietly assumed Cody's "starring role" in the show indicates that he was preparing himself and his business for the inevitable split.

As if to hurry their partnership's demise, Cody and Lillie made the terrible mistake of touring the south for the 1913 season. Cody and Lillie had hoped the region would be blessed with better climate than in the north or midwest, but soon discovered themselves in unseasonably cold and wet weather. Freezing rains kept the grounds flooded and crowds away. High winds blew the canvas tents down several times in one week. Adding to the awful weather conditions, cotton prices plummeted. The loss of the region's cash-crop meant that no one had the money to spend on anything but the essentials. On one particularly bad day the total receipts amounted to only seven dollars and fifteen cents; the show lost money for one hundred successive stands.[34]

Saying "My medicine is rotten," Cody urged his foster son Johnny Baker to move on with his own career in show business.[35] Defining his condition with very obvious Plains Indian rhetoric, the old scout's language indicates that he knew something had shifted in his life force and his ability to direct his own course of direction. Baker and Burke believed Cody's "good medicine" would return. Nevertheless, the strain and sense of betrayal was too much for Major Lillie to endure. Aware that Cody was leaving him at the end of the 1913 season, it became senseless for him to spend anymore of his fortune on helping Cody deal with his financial problems. Disheartened, Lillie left Cody to the mercy of Harry Tammen.

It is doubtful that mercy was a concept Harry Tammen understood. A lifelong newspaper journalist himself, Don Russell describes Tammen and his partner, Frederick Bonfils, as "probably the most amoral and unscrupulous partners ever to publish a newspaper." Born in Baltimore, Tammen went to work at the tender age of seven as a beer porter. By the age of twenty-one, he was the head bartender at Palmer House in Chicago. Cody probably first met him when he worked as the head bartender at the Windsor in Denver. Eventually Tammen quit bartending and opened a free museum and curio shop. Later Tammen met Fred Bonfils on a visit to Chicago. Bonfils had made a large sum of money in an illicit lottery and the pair used it in 1894 to purchase the *Denver Post*. Within a decade, with skillful use of tasteless, contemptible headlines, Tammen and Bonfils's rag had the most circulation and profits of any newspaper in Denver.[36]

Tammen literally entered show business with a dog and pony show. He named his show the Floto Dog and Pony Show after the *Denver Post*'s sports editor, Otto Floto, because he thought the name had a circus "sound" to it. After buying the rights to the name of one William Sells in order to mislead the public and imply an involvement with the four Sells Brothers of circus fame, he entered the major leagues with a donnybrook with the big boys. Since, after the customary circus "war," the Sells Brothers had been incorporated into the Ringling Brothers, Barnum and Bailey conglomerate, Tammen's use of the name "Sell" brought out the lawyers. In 1909, Ringling Brothers, Barnum and Bailey, sued Tammen and Bonfils to pre-

vent their use of the name Sells. The court decision which enjoined the
Sells-Floto Circus from the use of the portraits of the four Sells Brothers
cost Tammen and Bonfils $260,000, but they had established themselves as
an entity to be reckoned within the entertainment world.[37] Major Lillie certainly underestimated Tammen when he unwisely booked the Wild West
into Denver after an attempt to recoup some of the money he and Cody
had lost in the Deep South. Lillie admitted that he was forewarned of the
danger of appearing in Denver so near to the July 21 due date of Cody's
note, but the Major was apparently so angry with Cody that he did not care
what happened to his old friend. This was the reaction Tammen had
counted on from Lillie: Tammen had purchased a note from Denver's
United States Printing and Lithographing Company, to whom the Wild
West owed $60,000 for posters, programs, and other materials. Lillie had
not foreseen that Tammen was willing and able to use this note to foreclose
on the Wild West and destroy it in order to get Buffalo Bill totally under
his control.[38]

Cody was one of the first to see the sheriff's men on the lot of the Wild
West. He hurried his assistant, Thomas Smith, to the box office in an attempt to get the day's receipts, with which he hoped to pay his performers
one last time. Unfortunately, Smith was unable to get to the treasury
wagon before the sheriff's men and every penny was seized. More than
anything else, Cody seems to have been genuinely shattered at the thought
of not being able to provide his loyal company with the means to get
home. The man who had filled so many open hands was heartbroken to see
Indian performers being forced to sell their costumes to have the money to
return to Pine Ridge.

Meanwhile, Major Lillie hurried to New Jersey to file a bankruptcy petition, but his effort was obstructed when Denver attorneys filed an invol-
untary bankruptcy petition for two creditors claiming $340 for merchan-
dise and $36 for stock feed. Next, Tammen used the *Denver Post* to very
effectively attack Lillie for not affixing his interests in Cody's North Platte
property and the Hotel Irma to the show's debt. Driving the final wedge in
between the partners, Tammen persuaded Cody to sue Lillie for an ac-
counting and demand that their partnership be dissolved. When Tammen
attached the show for Cody's $20,000 note Lillie was checkmated. The im-
presario was able to salvage much of his personal fortune, but was never
able to make a comeback in show business.[39]

Having seized the Wild West, Tammen delivered the "*coup de grace.*" He
auctioned the Wild West to the highest bidders in a sheriff's sale. Watch-

ing his life come apart piece by piece broke Cody's heart. Beaten and severely wounded, Pahaska retreated to his TE Ranch in Cody.

Wyoming seemed to realize her favorite son needed healing. Cody had never seen his ranch in the summer and he discovered the TE in full blossom. His livestock was healthy and his crops were abundant. The Irma Hotel was holding its own and, reviewing the books, Cody was actually hopeful it might produce a profit within the coming year. Will and Lulu's children had secretly arranged a meeting between the feuding couple in which they had remarkably arrived at a genuine truce and buried the hatchet. Lulu had moved to Cody and she and her husband settled into the bucolic summer at TE Ranch.

Nurtured by Wyoming's blessings and new offers for work coming his way, Cody's optimism returned with stunning speed. Vaudeville agents immediately began to present him work proposals but he refused all offers. He briefly entertained an invitation to return to England to perform for $2,500 a week for himself, a female rider and a marksman but finally rejected it, demanding a minimum of $5,000 a week to mount such a show. Eventually, with "love and good cheer," there arrived at TE Ranch an offer from Harry Tammen to appear in a motion picture. Cody understandably rejected Tammen's offer; the proposal, however, triggered one of the worst ideas of Cody's career—one which would severely threaten to undermine the integrity of his life-long relationships with Indians.[40]

Cody began to consider going into the movie business himself, perhaps even developing the TE ranch as a headquarters for producing western films. After considering many topics such as his duel with Yellow Hand and the death of Sitting Bull, Cody finally decided to attempt a film based on Wounded Knee Massacre, filmed at Pine Ridge with Indians and soldiers who had actually participated. Cody was certain his friend General Miles would be glad to participate.[41]

With this surge of creative energy, Buffalo Bill's vitality returned, and he promptly headed to Denver to ask Tammen and Bonfils to help him with the idea of creating a film of the Wounded Knee Massacre. Coincidentally, the Secretary of War happened to be visiting in Denver at the time and Cody was able to use his influence to get himself appointed to the reception committee. His charm intact, Cody returned from the reception with permission to use the regular cavalry in his film. Upon learning that the Secretary of Interior was in Colorado Springs, Cody went there next and secured permission to hire Indians for his film. Tammen, yet again attaching himself to Cody's coattails, introduced the scout to his associate,

George K. Spoor, a partner in the Essanay Film Company of Chicago. Essanay assisted Buffalo Bill in structuring his new company: The Colonel W. F. Cody Historical Pictures Company.

Combining the initials "S" from Spoor, who began making and exhibiting films in Denver in 1895, and "A" from Gilbert M. Anderson, who directed the historic *The Great Train Robbery*, Essanay Films was certainly well-qualified to help Buffalo Bill enter the motion picture business. Anderson's *The Great Train Robbery* was the first movie to actually have a story and also the first "western." It had amassed a cult following, being shown along with variety shows on the vaudeville circuit, and risen to great popularity just as Nickelodeon tents, announcing the beginnings of the motion picture industry, were popping up all over the country.

Gilbert Anderson and George Spoor became partners in 1907. At their studios in Chicago Anderson took male leads, directing and producing the films as he went. When he took a company on location in Wyoming he became the very first of the western film stars—Bronco Billy Anderson. Anderson made over six hundred Bronco Billy movies in Wyoming and in Niles, California and, in the process, created much of the legend of the glamorous movie cowboy.[42]

In the fall of 1913, only three months after the auctioning of his Wild West, Cody arrived at Pine Ridge with General Miles and three troops— over six-hundred men—of the Twelfth Cavalry. Also present were Generals Frank Baldwin and Jesse M. Lee, as well as Colonel Marion P. Maus. Cody had also managed to convince Lakota's Short Bull, No Neck, Woman's Dress, Flat Iron and many other Ghost Dancers who had been in the Wild West to participate in the filming.[43]

Lakotas, believing the site of mass burial to be hallowed ground, considered a reenactment of the massacre at the sacred location to be a discretion of their ancestors' spirits and were extremely hesitant to become involved in any way with the film. Cody's adopted son, Johnny Baker, however, went to the Lakotas through Wild West alumnus Iron Tail, who convinced his kinsmen that their ancestors would be proud of the film as it would set the record straight about what really happened there on that fateful day. Soon tepees were ringed all along Wounded Knee Creek and Lakota children were playing on the stone monument over the mass grave of over 150 of their murdered ancestors. A merry-go-round was even brought in to the delight of both Lakota children and adults. As the calliope music churned, veteran Lakota warriors took surrealistic rides on garish carnival horses at the site of the worst massacre in American history.

None of this went down well with some of the younger warriors, who began to urge their comrades to load their weapons with bullets instead of blanks in order to turn the staged film fight into a real one. When Cody learned of this plan he called a midnight meeting of the Lakota headmen. Rather than discussing the ethics of filming a reenactment of the massacre, Cody explained pragmatically that it would do no good for the Lakota to create an incident because the government would simply hunt down those responsible for making trouble and punish them. Once again he assured them he would attempt to tell their version of the tragedy. From that point forward the dissidents were calmed.[44] Nevertheless, before this incident, whether in war or peace, Cody had never attempted to use his power to influence Plains Indians to do something they did not wish to do. He was fully aware of the Lakotas' spirituality and had always, whether as friend or foe, respected their religious belief system. The only excuse that can be offered is that Cody had allowed his debt to cloud his judgment in spiritual matters and, in the process, done serious damage to his relationship with Lakotas. Having so recently suffered the loss of his life's work to the sheriff's auction, it might be argued that Cody was minimally in the throes of clinical depression if not suffering from a complete nervous breakdown.

Cody had nearly as much trouble on the film set from General Miles as he did from the Lakota warriors who opposed filming at Wounded Knee. Miles took his job with the film seriously and insisted on everything being interpreted literally. The general would not allow any incident to be depicted which had not actually been part of his 1890 campaign. Since he had commanded eleven thousand troops in the field during the campaign, Miles insisted on all eleven thousand being seen on film. In order to appease the general, the troops Cody had at his disposal were marched past the camera forty times. After the first few passes of troops Cody instructed the photographer to close his lens and Miles never knew the difference.[45]

In spite of all the difficulty, Cody completed filming of the *Massacre at Wounded Knee* and held high hopes that he would be able to use the film to create a lecture circuit for himself, introducing and discussing the movie and his colorful career. Having produced his first motion picture, Cody went out for the 1914 season with the Sells-Floto Circus. He was paid $100 a day plus 40 percent of box office receipts over $3,000. Buffalo Bill introduced the show from the saddle for this salary, but did nothing else. His role was basically a promotional one, courting important local and regional personalities, speaking at Masonic Temples and Elk's Lodges and doing interviews with newspaper reporters. Even while he boasted of good health in public, however, in mid-October in Texas after the last show of the season, Cody "went to pieces" and, very ill, retreated to sister Julia's in Denver.[46] Sadly, this behavior had become Cody's pattern: At the end of each season, his health and nerves shattered, he would retreat to Julia's to spend his winters recuperating and plotting ways to somehow stay ahead of creditors. When his health recovered he would head to Cody and prepare for the next season. During his convalescence of 1914 at Julia's—against doctor's orders—Harry Tammen was able to corner Cody and convince him to return to Sells-Floto for the 1915 season. Cody was in such a weakened state that he failed to notice that Tammen had raised the box office amount from $3,000 to $3,100, which required him to earn an additional forty percent of the gate.

The 1915 Sells-Floto season was a disaster. Bad weather cursed the performances and Cody counted only four days of sunshine during the first forty-five days of the season. He had good reason to count: Poor attendance meant that Cody could not claim his percentage of box office profits. When Cody complained about the weather's negative effect on his percentage clauses, Tammen and Bonfils appeased him by raising the ticket price from twenty-five to fifty cents. This naturally encouraged Cody to believe that he would finally make extra money to fend off creditors. Tammen and Bonfils indeed raised the ticket price to fifty cents, but, defrauding customers, they also continued using old publicity posters which advertised the ticket price at a quarter. Unsuspecting people arrived at the box office surprised to learn that tickets were twice the advertised price. Upon learning of this disgraceful behavior Cody was furious, calling this practice "graft and robbery." He had spent a lifetime in show business creating a sterling professional relationship with the public and the media and was not about to allow Tammen and Bonfils' unethical practices to ruin his reputation overnight. He warned Sells-Floto press agents and promotion men not to use his name or image in connection with such fraudulent advertising.

When Cody and Salsbury had been in full command of the Wild West, the organization was highly disciplined, utterly professional, and thoroughly proud to be a creative American role model. Aside from Cody and Salsbury's brilliant logistical and impresarial talents, an outstanding characteristic of the professionalism of the Wild West was its creator's genuine concern for the personal welfare and entertainment of each and every member of the audience. Increasingly, Cody came to realize that Tammen and Bonfils' only concern was money. Cody loved earning money as much as any other show business producer. Tammen and Bonfils, on the other hand, sought to spend very little on production and take as much money as possible for their cheap efforts. This cutting of costs was most evident in the type of person working on the crews of the Sells-Floto Circus and Buffalo Bill Show. Cody was made painfully aware of the lack of character of the roustabout crew which now supported his performance when the show arrived in Fort Madison, Iowa and the "Big Top" tents were set up near a swamp. As the show began a thunderstorm suddenly struck. With stunning speed, the swamp rose until two feet of water swept into the tent, endangering the lives of a thousand women and children. Four hundred circus crewmen bolted in panic before Cody and a few brave men were able to calm them and prevent an audience stampede; the cowardly roustabouts quickly fled while Cody and only five men of the crew remained to help women carry children to evacuate. The incident made Cody completely conscious of how far he had fallen; to begin with, sensitive to the peculiar changes in weather, his roustabouts would have never set up so close to a swamp. More importantly, however, the conscientious men of his Wild West crews would have never abandoned women and children in panic. After this debacle with the Sells-Floto crew, Cody became increasingly worried about the danger he faced with the unethical Tammen and Bonfils' control over his life. He noticed the Sells-Floto tent was old and all the ropes were rotten. He became concerned that if the tent collapsed on an audience, being an experienced showman, he would be held libel. He threatened to leave the show if Tammen and Bonfils did not create a safe environment for audiences. When Cody issued his ultimatum, Tammen hit the old scout with yet another legal punch. The newspaperman claimed that after the auction of the Wild West Cody still owed him $20,000! Tammen informed Cody that he would be taking the money from Cody's $100 per day salary.[47] Cody reacted like a cornered, wounded animal to Tammen's legal ploy:

> . . . the Colonel was writing wildly to old friends seeking help—and even Pawnee Bill tried to aid him, although a suit against Lillie in Cody's name was still pending in the courts—Tammen saw that he had stirred up more than he had bargained for. Cody did not have to go to Denver; Tammen came to Lawrence, Kansas, to see Cody— and when he got there, he was afraid to go in the Colonel's tent. And well he might have been, for there was fire in the old scout's eye, and

he had written to a friend, "This man is driving me crazy. I can easily kill him but as I avoided killing in the bad days I don't want to kill him. But if there is no justice left I will."[48]

While it is true that Cody never was a gunfighter or killer he had certainly survived the glory days of such types. Remarkably, even when dog drunk in the midst of such a violent society as that of the western frontier, Cody's life history is strikingly peaceable. It is a sad but vivid testament to Tammen's manipulative treatment of him that at age sixty-nine he could stir Cody into such a rage.[49]

Tammen had aroused Cody's profound concern for the welfare of his audience. This anger and anxiety brought Cody's inherent courage and dignity back to the surface. Cody suddenly began to act like the wasichu chief he was and now forced Tammen to come to him to negotiate. A clear indication of the return of Cody's power is the fact that it took Tammen awhile to muster the courage to face the great man he had so skillfully tormented. Cody's intrinsic power was returning but he was still subject to the overwhelming weight of his debt; the result of the meeting between the pair was a strained compromise: The newspaperman dropped all claims against Cody's salary and the scout agreed to remain with the show until the end of the season. Tammen, however, refused to drop the $20,000 debt he claimed Cody owed him and also threatened to sue Cody if he pulled out of the show before the season's end. Cody, ever true to his word, held on until the end of the tour. On October 14, 1915, at the annual Sells-Floto farewell dinner in Fort Worth, Texas, Cody boasted that after nearly 17,000 miles and 366 shows in 183 days he had not missed one single performance. As the show had done very well financially toward the close of the season, according to Buffalo Bill's calculations, Tammen owed him $18,000 on his percentage of box office profits. He declared himself free from Tammen.

On February 11, 1916, Cody embarked with his Wounded Knee film from New Rochelle, New York upon a lecture tour. Arriving in Manhattan on March 5, the experience clearly disappointed him; immediately after the conclusion of his lecture tour Cody sold his interest in the Indian War films.[50]

Acting as his own agent, Cody went immediately about creating new sources of income for himself. He planned a big game hunt in Wyoming which never materialized, but he was able to structure a deal with publisher William Randolph Hearst to write his memoirs of a career in show business. This accomplished, he went searching for backers for a new Buffalo Bill show.

Once again Cody's instincts were on target. The First World War was entering its second year and, struggling to remain neutral, President Woodrow Wilson was finding it increasingly difficult to keep the United States out of the conflict. Buffalo Bill joined the growing numbers of Americans urging Wilson minimally to be "prepared" to enter the war. Cody conceived of a new production, "A Pageant of Preparedness," and presented the idea to U.S. Army Chief of Staff, Major Hugh L. Scott. The major quickly approved the proposal and agreed to allow Cody to use pieces of artillery and troops.

Cody had been watching with obvious interest the development of the Miller Brothers Ranch 101 Show. The Miller Brothers, featuring Kansas cowboy-turned-heavyweight championship boxer, Jess Willard, had enjoyed a most successful 1915 tour. Cody learned the Miller Brothers had paid Willard one-hundred thousand dollars at the end of the tour, but, even more attractive, he also learned that he could purchase the Ranch 101 Show for sixty-five thousand dollars. He immediately began to try to raise the money to buy the Miller Brothers show with hopes of developing it into his "Pageant of Preparedness."[51]

L. G. Moses describes the differences between the Miller Brothers and Buffalo Bill:

> In some ways the Miller Brothers were opposites of Buffalo Bill Cody and his Wild West. With the fortune Cody had made with his Wild West show between 1883 and 1903, he bought land, invested in mines, and involved himself in town building and real estate. With the farming, ranching, oil refining, and mercantile empire created by their father, Colonel George Washington Miller, and added to by their own labor, the Miller Brothers, J.C. or Joe, Zack and George, founded the 101 ("Hundred and One") Ranch Real Wild West. It boasted not only an authentic western ranch to inspire the show and serve as its headquarters, but also real cowboys and real dispossessed Indians from the tall-grass prairie of northeastern Oklahoma Territory. The Miller Brothers' ranch chewed up the better part of four counties, 110,000 acres or 172 square miles.

> In June 1905, in something reminiscent of the Old Glory Blowout, the Miller Brothers staged a roundup for the National Editorial Association. The organization naturally spread news of the success of the combination Wild West show and roundup. Ranch workers per-

formed what Cody's organization years before had dubbed "cowboy fun," but would eventually be known as rodeo.[52]

When Tammen learned that Cody was seeking investors for a new "Buffalo Bill" show he warned the scout that he now owned the name and intended to continue using it. Tammen callously informed Cody that for a fee of $5000 he could license the name "Buffalo Bill." If Tammen had a genuine claim to the name, however, it was certainly worth more than $5000, so it is probable that he realized Cody could have fought him and whipped him in the courts for the right to use his name and he was most likely attempting to squeeze one last penny from his cash cow.[53] Whether valid or not, Tammen's claim to the name "Buffalo Bill" served to thwart any investor interest in backing Cody's dream of a new Wild West. Ironically, Buffalo Bill was hired by the Miller Brothers for the 1916 season and, indicating that Tammen literally swapped Cody for the boxer, Jess Willard signed to tour with the Sells-Floto Circus.[54] At the age of seventy-one, Cody once again was racing on horseback shooting glass balls.

In spite of the circumstance of riding and shooting at his advanced age, Cody was jubilant over being free from the tentacles of the parasitic Harry Tammen. He failed to negotiate a share of the Miller Brothers' show, but he made a deal with them which provided him with $100 a day and one-third of the profits over $2,750 each day. From this relationship, when the Miller Brothers' show did well, Cody earned as much as $4,163[55] in one week. Reuniting his loyal core team, Cody also persuaded the Miller Brothers to hire Johnny Baker as his arenic director and Major John Burke as his personal publicity director. The crushing debt Cody faced remained even after Harry Tammen departed, however, and creditors continued to hound him. In spite of his prosperity with the Miller Brothers' show, Cody was soon signing away his prospective share of profits to speculators offering cash-in-hand. Perhaps best portraying how desperate Cody had become for money, the old scout heard that each holder of the Congressional Medal was entitled to a dole of ten dollars a month. He wrote to the adjutant-general:

I am a Congressional Medal of Honor man I need that ten dollars a month in my business. As it rains all the time. How do I go about to get it? Will you please send me a blank application. Very truly yours, William F. Cody, Bill Cody of the old army.

Even as Cody wrote his desperate letter, a board of officials was preparing to remove the names of all civilians from the list of Medal of Honor winners. No reply came to Cody's request for the $10 monthly dole and fortunately the old patriot never learned his name had been removed from the list of those honored.[55]

This continual anxiety concerning money finally drained Cody's phenomenal energy dry. Cody's complete health suddenly foundered. His nerves had become so frayed with the strain of struggling with his enormous debt and the exhausting responsibility of his gigantic production that it could be argued that he was often working while simultaneously suffering a series of nervous breakdowns. Aside from enduring painful bouts with rheumatism and neuritis, Cody also had major problems with his heart and with his prostate. His failure to have a simple corrective operation had caused the prostate condition to worsen to the point that it was impossible for surgeons to help him.[56] As his health collapsed he became increasingly anxious that he would die in the arena. Loyal to the very end, foster-son Johnny Baker would help Cody struggle painfully into the saddle, where the old scout would slump in agony, waiting for his cue to ride into the arena. When Baker would shout, "Ready, Colonel," he would pull himself into his characteristic perfect posture. Richard Walsh and Milton Salsbury complete the picture:

> In the noble pose that molded him to his horse he rode out to face his audience as gaily as ever, to lead the march, to shoot the glass balls, to flourish his sombrero in parting salute. Still holding the pose, he reined his horse backward through the parted curtains, the centaur still. But as the curtains swung between him and the crowd, he fell forward with a groan, and Baker would be there to catch him and help him to the ground. Day after day it happened so. He held out to the last.[57]

Rain continued to keep audiences away from the Miller Brothers 101 Ranch Show throughout the summer. By July an epidemic among children also tore into the show's core following. Financially, attendance no longer mattered to Cody anyway; as the season ended November 4 Cody had already sold all his shares of the show's profits to speculators and barely had the train fare to get to home. Suffering from a disabling cold, he made his last public appearance in Portsmouth, Virginia on November 11, 1916 and headed to Cody. Having given up on raising money for a new Wild West show from his multitude of wealthy friends and associates, Cody was forced to resort to a new tactic: en route to Denver, the showman stopped in Chicago for a meeting with a professional fund-raiser who, for ten percent commission, promised to find him the money to start again. Cody was able to make the meeting, but was too weak and sick transact any business. Exhausted and extremely ill, Cody made the journey to younger sister May's in Denver to recuperate. Buffalo Bill had hoped to find in the Big Horn Basin the peace and quiet he required for writing his memoir for William Randolph Hearst. By the time he arrived in Denver, however, May was stunned to realize the state of her brother's health. She begged him to stay with her and seek medical help, but he declined, feeling it better for him to get to Cody and the therapeutic powers of the Yellowstone country.

As always, Absaroka brought restoration to Buffalo Bill. After a few weeks convalescence at the TE Ranch Cody's strength returned to the point that he was able to attend a dinner held in his honor at the Irma Hotel. Even the Yellowstone country's recuperative energies were not enough for Cody now, however; at the testimonial dinner, some of his longtime friends observed the look of death in his eye. Even though his old friends in Cody urged him to slow down and allow himself a period of time to recover, the showman insisted upon traveling to Denver to do business. By the time Cody arrived in Denver, however, he was in the first stages of uremic poisoning; May immediately brought Dr. J. H. East to her brother's bedside. Dr. East ordered Cody to cut down on smoking which immediately improved Cody's equally threatening heart condition. Dr. East also referred Cody to Dr. W. W. Crook, a physician at the mineral baths at nearby Glenwood Springs, whom he felt might be able to help his famous patient.

On January 3, with hopes of miracles in the mineral waters, Cody traveled to Glenwood Springs. On January 5, however, he suffered a complete nervous collapse and was brought back to Denver. Harry Tammen's *Denver Post* quickly began a series of barking headlines of Cody's hovering near death. In spite of the newspaper stories, Dr. Crook informed the press that if Buffalo Bill's condition improved, he would return to his home in the Big Horn Basin. Crook told reporters that the scout had told his friends he wanted to die in Wyoming, and had selected a specific gravesite location on Cedar Mountain overlooking the town of Cody as well as the entire Big Horn Basin.[58] Sell and Weybright write:

When he was in New York City a decade before he had drawn up a will. The second clause read, "It is my wish and I hereby direct that my body shall be buried in some suitable plot of ground on Cedar Mountain, overlooking the town of Cody, Wyoming, in order that my mortal remains shall lie in close proximity to that fair section of my native country which bears my name and in the growth and development of which I have taken so deep and loving an interest, and to which wheresoever and whatever parts of the earth I have wandered I have always longed to return . . .

"I further direct that there shall be erected over my grave, to mark the spot where my body lies, a monument wrought from native red stone in the form of a mammoth buffalo, and placed in such a position as to be visible from the town, in order that it may be a constant reminder to my fellow citizens that it was the great wish of its founder that Cody should not only grow in prosperity and become a populous and influential metropolis, but that it should be distinguished for the purity of its government and the loyalty of its citizens to the institutions of our beloved country. I give to my said executors the sum of ten thousand dollars for the cost of the monument and its erection and to carefully keep the ground about it in proper order."[59]

Surrounded by his adoring family, Cody's condition improved enough for him to give one last interview. Chauncey Thomas, a well-known writer for the magazine *Outdoor Life*, and son of one of Buffalo Bill's old friends, W. R. Thomas, was permitted to visit briefly with the last of the great scouts. Cody spoke in detail with Thomas of his relationship with Wild Bill Hickok and Major Frank North, and of his early days on the Great Plains with other legends such as Custer, Sheridan, Carr, and Crook. The old scout also spoke with Thomas of scores of lesser-known scouts, soldiers and other such characters of the frontier. Cody spoke frankly with Thomas about the changes he had witnessed. Sell and Weybright continue:

He called for Dr. East. This is the physician's account of the interview as he told it to the Cody Enterprise:

"Sit down, Doctor, there is something I want to ask you. I want you to answer me honestly. What are my chances?"

"There is a time, Colonel," said Dr. East, "when every honest physician must commend his patient to a higher power."

Colonel Cody's head sank. "How long?" he asked.

"I can only answer by telling you your life is like an hourglass.

The sand is slipping gradually, slowly, but soon the sand will be gone. The end is not far away."

Cody roused himself and called for his brother-in-law, Lew Decker, who inquired what the doctor had said.

"Let's forget about it," said the old scout, "and play high-five."[60]

On January 8, the Cody family officially announced to the world that Buffalo Bill was dying. *Pahaska*, Colonel William Frederick "Buffalo Bill" Cody, held on for two more days before dying at 12:05 PM on January 10, 1917. Lulu and Irma were present as the last of the great scouts crossed the Great Divide. Cody had hoped that he would see Johnny Baker one last time, but his foster-son had been in New York, as usual, hustling for money and deals to cope with the colonel's debt. Upon learning his mentor's time had run out, Baker rushed to Denver, arriving to late to see Buffalo Bill before he died. Six weeks later in Washington a broken-hearted John Burke dropped dead.[61] Cody's body was taken to the rotunda of the Colorado capitol, where it laid in state awaiting funeral ceremonies. It was estimated that 25,000 people passed Buffalo Bill's coffin to offer their final respects to the fallen hero. Tributes from the high and mighty began to be published immediately as the world mourned its first true celebrity. President Woodrow Wilson, Theodore Roosevelt, and Generals Nelson Miles and Hugh Scott were the first to issue statements eulogizing Buffalo Bill. Roosevelt remarked that:

> Buffalo Bill was one of those men, steel-thewed and iron nerved, whose daring progress opened the great West to settlement and civilization. His name, like that of Kit Carson, will always be associated with old adventure and pioneer days of hazard and hardship when the great plains and the Rocky Mountains were won for our race. It is eminently fit to commemorate his gallant, picturesque and most useful career by such a monument as you propose. He embodied those traits of courage, strength and self-reliant hardihood which are vital to the well-being of our nation.[62]

The monument to which Roosevelt referred was Harry Tammen's attempt, even—or especially—in death, to attach himself to Buffalo Bill's destiny. Immediately at Cody's death, the *Denver Post* announced its sponsorship of a nationwide campaign encouraging schoolchildren to collect pennies to erect a monument for Buffalo Bill on Lookout Mountain in

Denver. Upon departing the Buffalo Bill gravesite at Lookout Mountain, in fact, the visitor is still given the opportunity to deposit loose change into a Victorian-style urn placed there by none other than Harry Tammen. The money goes toward maintaining the grounds. *The Post*, though, mentioned nothing about Cody's will detailing his personal wishes to be buried on Cedar Mountain in Cody. Louisa Cody, however, produced a second will with a later date in which everything of her husband's estate was left to her. Lulu's document had been witnessed and signed in Cody, Wyoming, not long after her reconciliation with Cody in 1910. The *Denver Post*, of course, insisted that Cody himself had expressed wishes to be buried on Lookout Mountain. The town of Cody, aware of its creator's wishes, was furious. Even though Mrs. Cody was later forced to sign a document denying published reports that she refused the erecting of monuments to Cody's memory anywhere but in Denver, the rumor persists to this day that Harry Tammen paid Mrs. Cody ten thousand dollars for the rights of selecting Buffalo Bill's burial site. Whatever deals went down behind the scene, Mrs. Cody and Cody's foster son, Johnny Baker, supported Tammen's efforts to bury the scout on Lookout Mountain and the decision was complete.

The location Tammen eventually selected was not available as roads had not been built up the side of Lookout Mountain. As a result, Cody's many friends in the Masonic and Elk's Lodges performed a series of eulogies, memorials, and funeral services in Denver before Cody's body was taken to Olinger Funeral Home and placed in a crypt, where it waited for a spring burial.[63] On June 3, 1917, thousands of vehicles crept past the budding spring alpine flowers as the funeral procession slowly wound up Lookout Mountain. Twenty-five thousand people attended the graveside services as Pahaska was finally laid to rest.[64]

Annie Oakley traveled and performed with Cody and the Wild West for nearly two decades. At one point, she and Buffalo Bill argued and parted company only to reunite later. From her unique perspective, "Little Missy," when asked in 1917 by the *Cody Enterprise* to write her memories of Buffalo Bill, offered perhaps the most personal and eloquent description of the man who was Will Cody:

> He was the kindest, simplest, most loyal man I ever knew. He was the staunchest friend. He was in fact the personification of those sturdy and lovable qualities that really made the West, and they were the final criterion of all men, East and West. Like all really great and

gentle men he was not even a fighter by preference. His relations with everyone he came in contact with were the most cordial and trusting of any man I ever knew.

I traveled with him for seventeen years—there were thousands of men in the outfit during that time, Comanches, cowboys, Cossacks, Arabs, and every kind of person. And the whole time we were one great family loyal to him. His word was better than most contracts. Personally I never had a contract with the show after I started. It would have been superfluous.

. . . it may seem strange that after the wonderful success attained that he should have died a poor man. But it isn't a matter of any wonder to those who knew him and worked with him. The same qualities that insured success also insured his ultimate poverty. His generosity and kind-hearted attitude towards all comers, his sympathy and his broad understanding of human nature, made it the simplest thing possible to handle men, both in his show and throughout the whole world. But by the same token he was totally unable to resist any claim for assistance that came to him, or refuse any mortal in distress. His philosophy was that of the plains and the camp, more nearly Christian and charitable than we are used to finding in the sharp business world he was encountering for the first time. The pity of it was that not only could anyone that wanted a loan or a gift get it for the asking, but he never seemed to lose his trust in the nature of all men, and until his dying day he was the easiest mark above ground for every kind of sneak and gold-brick vendor that was mean enough to take advantage of him.

I never saw him in any situation that changed his natural attitude a scintilla. None could possibly tell the difference between his reception of a band of cowboys and the train of an emperor. Dinner at camp was the same informal, hearty, humorous, storytelling affair when we were alone, and when the Duchess of Holstein came visiting in all her glory. He was probably the guest of more people in diverse circumstances than any man living. But a tepee or a palace were all the same to him, and so were their inhabitants. He had hundreds of imitators but was quite inimitable.

His heart never left the great West. Whenever the day's work was done, he could always be found sitting alone watching the sinking sun, and at every opportunity he took the trail back to his old home. The sun setting over the mountain will pay its daily tribute to the resting place of the last of the great builders of the West, all of which you loved and part of which you were.[65]

In November, 1917, the writer Zane Grey, in the epilogue to Helen Wetmore Cody's biography, offered this summary of William Frederick Cody's incredible life and his burial on Lookout Mountain:

It was not the place he had hoped to go to his last sleep, but, nevertheless, it is indeed a fitting grave for the last of the great scouts. He would have chosen a lonelier grave, far from the crowd. In the years to come his resting place will be visited by thousands; and that will be well. The coming generations ought to have memorable appreciation of the man who so faithfully served the West.

Every hunter and plainsman and scout loved the solitude and loneliness of the wilds. This is what made them great.

The sunset, the descending twilight, the sweet silence of the hills, the brightening star, the lonely darkness of the night—these things Buffalo Bill loved. And these things he will have.

His life was full to the brim. He will not be forgotten. He represented the onward movement of a race. Surely he will rest in peace there on the rocky height where the wind will moan and the day will break solemn and grand and the night fall to the end of time.[66]

NOTES

INTRODUCTION

1. I later became friends with Arthur Kopit, and we even sat together on a symposium panel in a theatrical workshop in 1983 at Creighton University in Omaha, Nebraska.

2. The full-company musical of *Seekers of the Fleece* debuted in June 1988 in Cody, Wyoming, in a little "sweat-box" on Twelfth Street just north of the Irma Hotel. The drought that plagued Wyoming that summer resulted in the historic Yellowstone Fires, which turned Cody into a "ghost town" and caused the production to suffer major losses. In 1989 the production moved outdoors to the Robbie Pow Wow Gardens at the Buffalo Bill Historical Center and ran each summer there until 1994.

PROLOGUE

1. Frank Waters, *Time and Change, A Memoir* (MacMurray and Beck, 1998), 132–133.

2. Raymond J. DeMaille, *The Sixth Grandfather: Black Elk's Teachings Given To John G. Neihardt* (Lincoln: University of Nebraska Press, 1984), 249.

3. Don Russell, *The Lives and Legends of Buffalo Bill* (Norman: University of Oklahoma Press, 1960), 331.

4. Frank Waters, *Time and Change, A Memoir* (MacMurray and Beck, 1998), 131.

5. ibid, 139–163.

6. Raymond J. DeMaille, *The Sixth Grandfather: Black Elk's Teaching Given To John G. Neihardt* (Lincoln: University of Nebraska Press, 1984); and, John G. Neihardt, *Black Elk Speaks* (Lincoln: University of Nebraska Press), 1979.

7. Vine DeLoria, Jr., *For This Land* (New York: Routledge, 1999), 157.

8. Eric Sorg, *Buffalo Bill: Myth and Reality* (Ancient City Press, 1998), 151.

9. John G. Neihardt, *Black Elk Speaks* (Introduction by Vine DeLoria, Jr.) (Lincoln: University of Nebraska Press, 1979), 12–13.

10. Luther Standing Bear, *Land of the Spotted Eagle* (Lincoln: University of Nebraska Press, 1978), 68–69.

11. Kay Graber, editor, *Sister To The Sioux, The Memoirs of Elaine Goodale Eastman* (Lincoln: University of Nebraska Press, 1978), 16–18.

12. Luther Standing Bear, *Land of The Spotted Eagle* (Lincoln: University of Nebraska Press, 1978), 72–73.

13. John G. Neihardt, *When The Tree Flowered* (New York: Macmillan Company, 1951), 151–181; and Ron Goodman, *Lakota Star Knowledge: Studies In Lakota Stellar Theology* (Mission, South Dakota: Sinte Gleska University Press, 1992), 25–28.

14. Dr. Charles Eastman, *The Soul Of The Indian* (Lincoln: University of Nebraska Press), 157–158.

15. Stanley Vestal, *Sitting Bull, Champion of the Sioux*, (Norman: University of Oklahoma Press, 1956), 119.

16. Cecil Alter, *Jim Bridger* (Norman: University of Oklahoma Press, 1962), 82.

17. Stanley Vestal, *Jim Bridger, Mountain Man* (Lincoln: University of Nebraska Press, 1970), 237.

18. ibid, 238.

19. ibid, 239.

Chapter One. THE RAINBOW TRAIL

1. Robert G. Athern, *The Mythic West in the 20th Century* (Lawrence: University of Kansas Press, 1986), 231.

2. Frederick Turner, *Beyond Geography, The Western Spirit Against the Wilderness* (New Brunswick: Rutgers University Press, 1983), 295.

3. William F. Cody, *The Life of Honorable William Frederick Cody* (Lincoln: University of Nebraska Press, 1978), 26.

4. Lewis Paul Todd and Merle Curti, *The Rise of The American Nation* (Harcourt, Brace, and World, 1966), 341.

5. Henry Blackman Sell and Victor Weybright, *Buffalo Bill and The Wild West* (Signet, 1959), 19.

6. William F. Cody, *The Life of Honorable William Frederick Cody* (Lincoln: University of Nebraska Press, 1978), 41–42.

7. ibid, 46.

8. ibid, 39.

9. Sell and Weybright, *Buffalo Bill and The Wild West* (Signet, 1959), 30.

10. William F. Cody, *The Life of Honorable Wm F. Cody* (Lincoln: University of Nebraska Press, 1978), 66–69.

11. ibid, 39.

12. Don Russell, *The Lives and Legends of Buffalo Bill* (Norman: University of Oklahoma Press, 1960), 25.

13. William F. Cody, *The Life of Honorable William F. Cody* (Lincoln: University of Nebraska Press, 1978), 66.

Chapter Two. THE SCOUTS

1. William F. Cody, *The Life of Honorable William F. Cody*, (Lincoln: University of Nebraska Press, 1978), 30.

2. ibid, 30.

3. ibid, 37.

4. Helen Wetmore Cody, *Buffalo Bill, Last of the Great Scouts, The Life of Colonel William Frederick Cody* (Grosset and Dunlap, 1918), 40.

5. Mark Twain, *Roughing It* (Harper and Brothers, 1913), 310.

6. William F. Cody, *The Life of Honorable William F. Cody* (Lincoln: University of Nebraska Press, 1978), 69.

7. George Armstrong Custer, *My Life On The Plains* (New York: Citadel Press, 1960), 68–69.

8. Sell and Weybright, *Buffalo Bill and The Wild West* (Signet, 1959), 42–44.

9. Helen Wetmore Cody, *Buffalo Bill, Last of the Great Scouts, The Life of Colonel William Frederick Cody* (Grosset and Dunlap, 1918), 32.

10. William F. Cody, *The Life of Honorable William F. Cody* (Lincoln: University of Nebraska Press), 1978, 72.

11. ibid, 73–74.

12. Don Russell, *The Lives and Legends of Buffalo Bill* (Norman: University of Oklahoma Press, 1960), 35–36.

13. William F. Cody, *The Life of Honorable William F. Cody* (Lincoln: University of Nebraska Press, 1978), 78.

14. William F. Cody, *The Life of Honorable Wm F. Cody* (Lincoln: University of Nebraska Press, 1978), 79–80.

15. ibid, 89–90.

Chapter Three. THE PONY EXPRESS

1. Fred Reinfield, *The Pony Express* (Lincoln: University of Nebraska Press, 1973), 29–31.

2. ibid, 32–40.

3. ibid, 40.

4. ibid, 9.

5. William F. Cody, *The Life of Honorable William F. Cody* (University of Nebraska Press, 1978), 91–92.

6. ibid, 27.

7. Don Russell, *The Lives and Legends of Buffalo Bill* (University of Oklahoma Press, 1960), 42.

8. William F. Cody, *The Life of Honorable William F. Cody* (University of Nebraska Press, 1978), 98.

9. ibid, 101.

10. ibid, 103–104.

11. Mark Twain, *Roughing It* (Harper and Brothers, 1913), 63.

12. Don Russell, *The Lives and Legends of Buffalo Bill* (Norman: University of Oklahoma Press, 1960), 49.

13. Mark Twain, *Roughing It* (Harper and Brothers, 1913), 69–70.

14. William F. Cody, *The Life of Honorable Wm F. Cody* (Lincoln: University of Nebraska Press, 1978), 104.

15. ibid, 105.

16. Mark Twain, *Roughing It* (Harper and Brothers, 1913), 70–71.

17. William F. Cody, *The Life of Honorable William F. Cody* (Lincoln: University of Nebraska Press, 1978), 105–106.

18. Dee Brown, *Bury My Heart At Wounded Knee* (Bantam, 1970), 68.

19. George E. Hyde, *Red Cloud's Folk* (Norman: University of Oklahoma Press, 1937), 70–76.

20. William F. Cody, *The Life of Honorable William F. Cody* (University of Nebraska Press, 1978), 106–107.

21. ibid, 107–108.

22. ibid, 109.

23. ibid, 110.

24. ibid., 116–117.

25. ibid., 117–118.

26. Mark Twain, *Roughing It* (Harper and Brothers, 1913), 79–80.

27. Fred Reinfield, *The Pony Express* (Lincoln: University of Nebraska Press, 1973), 113.

28. ibid, 113–114.

29. ibid, 114–116.

30. ibid, 117.

31. Don Russell, *The Lives and Legends of Buffalo Bill* (Norman: University of Oklahoma Press, 1960), 46–47.

32. Fred Reinfield, *The Pony Express* (Lincoln: University of Nebraska Press, 1973), 119–120.

Chapter Four: DESTINY

1. Sell and Weybright, *Buffalo Bill and The Wild West* (Signet, 1959), 46.

2. William F. Cody, *The Life of Honorable William F. Cody* (Lincoln: University of Nebraska Press, 1978), 125–126.

3. Don Russell, *The Lives and Legends of Buffalo Bill* (Norman: University of Oklahoma Press, 1960), 56.

4. William F. Cody, *The Life of Honorable William F. Cody* (Lincoln: University of Nebraska Press, 1978), 127.

5. Don Russell, *The Lives and Legends of Buffalo Bill* (Norman: University of Oklahoma Press, 1960), 59.

6. William F. Cody, *The Life of Honorable William F. Cody* (Lincoln: University of Nebraska Press, 1978), 135.

7. Helen Wetmore Cody, *Buffalo Bill, The Last of the Great Scouts, The Life of Colonel William Frederick Cody* (Grosset and Dunlap, 1918), 114–115.

8. Don Russell, *The Lives and Legends of Buffalo Bill* (Norman: University of Oklahoma Press, 1960), 62.

9. Lewis Paul Todd and Merle Curti, *The Rise of the American Nation* (Harcourt, Brace, and World, 1966), 374.

10. William F. Cody, *The Life of Honorable William F. Cody* (Lincoln: University of Nebraska Press, 1978), 136.

11. ibid, 136.

12. Don Russell, *The Lives and Legends of Buffalo Bill* (Norman: University of Oklahoma Press, 1960), 69.

13. ibid, 70–72.

14. William F. Cody, *The Life of Honorable William F. Cody* (Lincoln: University of Nebraska Press, 1978), 143.

15. ibid, 143.

16. Helen Wetmore Cody, *Buffalo Bill, Last of the Great Scouts, The Life of Colonel William Frederick Cody* (Grosset and Dunlap, 1918), 146–147.

17. Sell and Weybright, *Buffalo Bill and The Wild West* (Signet, 1959), 58.

18. Don Russell, *The Lives and Legends of Buffalo Bill* (Norman: University of Oklahoma Press, 1960), 76.

19. William F. Cody, *The Life of Honorable William F. Cody*, University of Nebraska Press, 1978, 145.

20. ibid, 146.

21. Don Russell, *The Lives and Legends of Buffalo Bill* (Norman: University of Oklahoma Press, 1960), 90–91.

22. Paul Fees, *The Flamboyant Fraternity*, Buffalo Bill Historical Center Newsletter.

23. William F. Cody, *The Life of Honorable William F. Cody* (Lincoln: University of Nebraska Press, 1978), 148.

24. ibid, 148.

Chapter Five. THE INDIAN WARS

1. Sell and Weybright, *Buffalo Bill and The Wild West* (Signet, 1959), 59–60.

2. ibid, 221.

3. Ron Goodman, *Lakota Stellar Theology* (Mission, South Dakota: Sinte Gleska University Press), 1992.

4. George E. Hyde, *Red Cloud's Folk* (Norman: University of Oklahoma Press, 1937), 38.

5. Francis Parkman, *The Oregon Trail* (Penguin Books, 1985) 150–151.

6. Dee Brown, *Bury My Heart At Wounded Knee* (Bantam, 1970), 40.

7. George E. Hyde, *Red Cloud's Folk* (Norman: University of Oklahoma Press), 1937, 102.

8. ibid, 103.

9. Dee Brown, *The Fetterman Massacre* (Lincoln: University of Nebraska Press, 1971), 16.

10. Dee Brown, *Bury My Heart At Wounded Knee* (Bantam, 1970), 73.

11. ibid, 75.

12. ibid, 79.

13. ibid, 83.

14. ibid, 85.

15. ibid, 85.

16. Dee Brown, *The Fetterman Massacre* (Lincoln: University of Nebraska Press, 1971), 14.

17. ibid, 14.

18. ibid, 26–27.

19. ibid, 147.

20. ibid, 150.

21. ibid, 174.

22. John G. Neihardt, *Black Elk Speaks* (Lincoln: University of Nebraska Press, 1979), 11–13.

23. Stanley Vestal, *Jim Bridger, Mountain Man* (University of Nebraska Press, 1970), 286.

24. ibid, 286.

25. Dee Brown, *Bury My Heart At Wounded Knee* (Bantam, 1970), 133.

Chapter Six. PAHASKA BECOMES BUFFALO BILL

1. Tom McHugh, *The Time of the Buffalo* (Alfred Knoff, 1972), 263.

2. William F. Cody, *The Life of Honorable William F. Cody* (Lincoln: University of Nebraska Press, 1978), 162.

3. Don Russell, *The Lives and Legends of Buffalo Bill* (Norman: University of Oklahoma Press, 1960), 90.

4. ibid, 89.

5. William F. Cody, *The Life of Honorable William F. Cody* (Lincoln: University of Nebraska Press, 1978), 157.

6. Don Russell, *The Lives and Legends of Buffalo Bill* (Norman: University of Oklahoma Press, 1960), 86.

7. Tom McHugh, *The Time Of The Buffalo* (Alfred Knopf, 1972), 2.

8. John G. Neihardt, *Black Elk Speaks* (Lincoln: University of Nebraska Press, 1979), 56–57.

9. Francis Parkman, *The Oregon Trail* (New York: Penguin Books, 1985), 280.

10. George Armstrong Custer, *My Life On The Plains* (New York: Citadel, 1960), 80–82.

11. Luther Standing Bear, *My People The Sioux* (Lincoln: University of Nebraska Press, 1975), 64–65.

12. Tom McHugh, *The Time Of The Buffalo* (Alfred Knopf, 1972), 285.

13. ibid, 14.

14. ibid, 15.

15. Michael S. Sample, *Bison: Symbol of the American West* (Falcon Press, 1987), 12.

16. Don Russell, *The Lives and Legends of Buffalo Bill* (Norman: University of Oklahoma Press, 1960), 91.

17. ibid, 173.

18. William F. Cody, *The Life of Honorable William F. Cody* (Lincoln: University of Nebraska Press), 1978, 171.

19. ibid, 173.

20. ibid, 173–174.

21. Sell and Weybright, *Buffalo Bill and the Wild West* (Signet, 1959), 86.

22. ibid, 83.

23. ibid, 80.

24. ibid, 83.

25. Don Russell, *The Lives and Legends of Buffalo Bill* (University of Oklahoma Press, 1960), 100.

26. Dee Brown, *Bury My Heart At Wounded Knee* (Bantam, 1970), 158.

27. Don Russell, *The Lives and Legends of Buffalo Bill* (Norman: University of Oklahoma Press, 1960), 101.

28. Dee Brown, *Bury My Heart At Wounded Knee* (Bantam, 1970), 237.

29. William F. Cody, *The Life of Honorable William F. Cody* (Lincoln: University of Nebraska Press, 1978), 186.

30. ibid, 186.

31. ibid, 187.

32. Don Russell, *The Lives and Legends of Buffalo Bill* (Norman: University of Oklahoma Press, 1960), 103.

Chapter Seven. CHIEF OF SCOUTS

1. William F. Cody, *The Life of Honorable William F. Cody* (Norman: University of Nebraska Press, 1978), 207–208.

2. Don Russell, *The Lives and Legends of Buffalo Bill* (Norman: University of Oklahoma Press, 1960), 107–108.

3. Cecil Alter, *James Bridger* (Norman: University of Oklahoma Press), 1962, 311.

4. Dee Brown, *Bury My Heart At Wounded Knee* (Bantam, 1970), 102–103.

5. Cecil Alter, *James Bridger* (Norman: University of Oklahoma Press, 1962), 312.

6. ibid, 313.

7. ibid, 314.

8. Stanley Vestal, *Jim Bridger, Mountain Man* (Lincoln: University of Nebraska Press, 1970), 240.

9. Cecil Alter, *James Bridger* (Norman: University of Oklahoma Press, 1962), 315.

10. Richard O'Connor, *Sheridan* [Konecky and Konecky (Bobbs-Merrill), 1953], 302.

11. William F. Cody, *The Life of Honorable William F. Cody* (Lincoln: University of Nebraska Press, 1978), 212.

12. ibid, 215.

13. ibid, 215–216.

14. ibid, 216–217.

15. Don Russell, *The Lives and Legends of Buffalo Bill* (Norman: University of Oklahoma Press, 1978), 109.

16. ibid, 110.

17. Richard O'Connor, *Sheridan* [Konecky and Konecky (Bobbs-Merrill), 1953], 305.

18. Wm F. Cody, *The Life of Honorable William F. Cody* (Lincoln: University of Nebraska Press, 1978), 222.

19. ibid, 222.

20. ibid, 226.

21. ibid, 226.

22. Don Russell, *The Lives and Legends of Buffalo Bill* (Norman: University of Oklahoma Press, 1960), 112–113.

23. William F. Cody, *The Life of Honorable William F. Cody* (Lincoln: University of Nebraska Press, 1978), 227.

24. ibid, 229.

25. Don Russell, *The Lives and Legends of Buffalo Bill* (Norman: University of Oklahoma Press, 1960), 116.

Chapter Eight. THE TRAIL TO SUMMIT SPRINGS

1. Ron Goodman, *Lakota Star Knowledge, Studies in Lakota Stellar Theology* (Mission, South Dakota: Sinte Gleska University Press, 1992), 2.

2. Stanley Vestal, *Sitting Bull, Champion of the Sioux* (University of Oklahoma Press, 1956), 83–84.

3. Frederick Turner, *Beyond Geography: The Western Spirit Against The Wilderness* (New Brunswick: Rutgers University Press, 1983), 129.

4. ibid, 130.

5. John D. Unruh, *The Plains Across: The Overland Emigrants and the Trans-Mississippi West, 1840–1860* (University of Illinois Press, 1979), 327.

6. ibid, 127–128.

7. William F. Cody, *The Life of Honorable William F. Cody* (Lincoln: University of Nebraska Press, 1978), 246–247.

8. ibid, 247–248.

9. Don Russell, *The Lives and Legends of Buffalo Bill* (Norman: University of Oklahoma Press, 1960), 122.

10. William F. Cody, *The Life of Honorable William F. Cody* (Lincoln: University of Nebraska Press, 1978), 249.

11. Don Russell, *The Lives and Legends of Buffalo Bill* (Norman: University of Oklahoma Press, 1960), 122–123.

12. William F. Cody, *The Life of Honorable William F. Cody* (Lincoln: University of Nebraska Press, 1978), 249.

13. Helen Wetmore Cody, *Buffalo Bill, Last of the Great Scouts: The Life of William Frederick Cody* (Grosset and Dunlap, 1918), 327–328.

14. William F. Cody, *The Life of Honorable William F. Cody* (Lincoln: University of Nebraska Press, 1978), 250.

15. ibid, 251–252.

16. ibid, 252.

17. ibid, 256.

19. ibid, 260.

20. ibid, 260–261.

Chapter Nine. DIME NOVELS

1. Sell and Weybright, *Buffalo Bill and the Wild West* (Signet, 1959), 96–97.

2. Don Russell, *The Lives and Legends of Buffalo Bill,* (Norman: University of Oklahoma Press, 1960), 150.

3. William F. Cody, *The Life of Honorable William F. Cody,* (Lincoln: University of Nebraska Press, 1978), 263.

4. ibid, 264.

5. Don Russell, *The Lives and Legends of Buffalo Bill,* (Norman: University of Oklahoma Press, 1960), 159–160.

6. William F. Cody, *The Life of Honorable William F. Cody* (Lincoln: University of Nebraska Press, 1978), 266–267.

7. William Goetzmann, *Exploration and Empire: The Explorer and the Scientist in the Winning of the American West* (New York: Random House, 1966), 425.

8. ibid, 425–426.

9. William F. Cody, *The Life of Honorable Wm F. Cody* (Lincoln: University of Nebraska Press, 1978), 278–280.

10. Don Russell, *The Lives and Legends of Buffalo Bill* (Norman: University of Oklahoma Press, 1960), 167–168.

11. William F. Cody, *The Life of Honorable Wm F. Cody* (Lincoln: University of Nebraska Press, 1978), 270.

12. ibid, 271.

13. ibid, 275.

14. Don Russell, *The Lives and Legends of Buffalo Bill* (Norman: University of Oklahoma Press, 1960), 165–166.

15. William F. Cody, *The Life of Honorable William F. Cody* (Lincoln: University of Nebraska Press, 1978), 278.

16. Don Russell, *The Lives and Legends of Buffalo Bill* (Norman: University of Oklahoma Press, 1960), 170.

17. William F. Cody, *The Life of Honorable William F. Cody* (Lincoln: University of Nebraska Press, 1978), 282.

18. Don Russell, *The Lives and Legends of Buffalo Bill* (Norman: University of Oklahoma Press, 1960), 171.

19. Sell and Weybright, *Buffalo Bill and the Wild West* (Signet, 1959), 100.

20. Don Russell, *The Lives and Legends of Buffalo Bill* (Norman: University of Oklahoma Press, 1960), 173.

21. Sell and Weybright, *Buffalo Bill and the Wild West* (Signet, 1959), 103.

Chapter Ten. MAGICIANS FROM MYTHOLOGY

1. William F. Cody, *The Life of Honorable William F. Cody* (Lincoln: University of Nebraska Press, 1978), 296.

2. ibid, 297.

3. ibid, 298.

4. Don Russell, *The Lives and Legends of Buffalo Bill* (Norman: University of Oklahoma Press, 1960), 177.

5. George Armstrong Custer, *My Life On The Plains* (New York: Citadel, 1960), 360–361; 145.

6. William F. Cody, *The Life of Honorable William F. Cody* (Lincoln: University of Nebraska Press, 1978), 301.

7. Don Russell, *The Lives and Legends of Buffalo Bill* (Norman: University of Oklahoma Press, 1960), 179.

8. ibid, 179.

9. William F. Cody, *The Life of Honorable William F. Cody* (Lincoln: University of Nebraska Press, 1978), 307–308.

10. ibid, 308.

11. Don Russell, *The Lives and Legends of Buffalo Bill* (Norman: University of Oklahoma Press, 1960), 181.

12. Sell and Weybright, *Buffalo Bill and the Wild West* (Signet, 1959), 111.

13. William F. Cody, *The Life of Honorable William F. Cody* (Lincoln: University of Nebraska Press), 1978, 311.

14. ibid, 311.

15. Don Russell, *The Lives and Legends of Buffalo Bill* (Norman: University of Oklahoma Press, 1960), 183.

16. Sell and Weybright, *Buffalo Bill and the Wild West* (Signet, 1959), 111–112.

17. ibid, 112.

Chapter Eleven. TRODDING THE BOARDS

1. William F. Cody, *The Life of Honorable William F. Cody* (Lincoln: University of Nebraska Press, 1978), 313–314.

2. Don Russell, *The Lives and Legends of Buffalo Bill* (Norman: University of Oklahoma Press, 1960), 187.

3. ibid, 187.

4. William F. Cody, *The Life of Honorable William F. Cody* (Lincoln: University of Nebraska Press, 1978), 315–316.

5. Don Russell, *The Lives and Legends of Buffalo Bill* (Norman: University of Oklahoma Press, 1960), 190–191.

6. ibid, 192.

7. William F. Cody, *The Life of Honorable William F. Cody* (Lincoln: University of Nebraska Press, 1978), 320.

8. ibid, 321.

9. ibid, 321.

10. Don Russell, *The Lives and Legends of Buffalo Bill* (Norman: University of Oklahoma Press, 1960), 189.

11. William F. Cody, *The Life of Honorable William F. Cody* (Lincoln: University of Nebraska Press, 1978), 323–324.

12. ibid, 326–327.

13. ibid, 327.

14. Don Russell, *The Lives and Legends of Buffalo Bill* (Norman: University of Oklahoma Press, 1960), 195.

15. ibid, 196.

16. Sell and Weybright, *Buffalo Bill and the Wild West* (Signet, 1959), 126.

17. Don Russell, *The Lives and Legends of Buffalo Bill* (Norman: University of Oklahoma Press), 1960, 197.

18. Lewis Paul Todd and Merle Curti, *The Rise of the American Nation* (Harcourt, Brace, and World, 1966), 297.

19. William F. Cody, *The Life of Honorable William F. Cody* (Lincoln: University of Nebraska Press, 1978), 328.

20. Don Russell, *The Lives and Legends of Buffalo Bill* (Norman: University of Oklahoma Press), 1960, 201.

21. ibid, 202.

22. Sell and Weybright, *Buffalo Bill and the Wild West* (Signet, 1959), 128.

23. Don Russell, *The Lives and Legends of Buffalo Bill* (Norman: University of Oklahoma Press, 1960), 202-203.

24. William F. Cody, *The Life of Honorable William F. Cody* (Lincoln: University of Nebraska Press, 1978), 329.

25. ibid, 329.

26. Sell and Weybright, *Buffalo Bill and the Wild West* (Signet, 1959), 131.

27. William F. Cody, *The Life of Honorable William F. Cody* (Lincoln: University of Nebraska Press, 1978), 331.

28. ibid, 133.

29. ibid, 334–335.

30. ibid. 336.

31. ibid. 339.

Chapter Twelve. THE DUEL WITH YELLOW HAND

1. Frederick Turner, *Beyond Geography: The Western Spirit Against The Wilderness* (New Brunswick: Rutgers University Press, 1983), 153.

2. Dee Brown, *Bury My Heart At Wounded Knee* (Bantam, 1970), 271.

3. Stanley Vestal, *Sitting Bull, Champion of the Sioux* (Norman: University of Oklahoma Press, 1956), 16.

4. ibid, 9–10.

5. ibid, 9–10.

6. ibid, 20–21.

7. Frederick Turner, *Beyond Geography: The Western Spirit Against The Wilderness* (New Brunswick: Rutgers University Press, 1983), 273–274.

8. Stanley Vestal, *Sitting Bull, Champion of the Sioux* (Norman: University of Oklahoma Press, 1956), 138.

9. ibid, 139.

10. Dee Brown, *Bury My Heart At Wounded Knee* (Bantam, 1970), 272.

11. Stanley Vestal, *Sitting Bull, Champion of the Sioux* (Norman: University of Oklahoma Press, 1956), 140.

12. Don Russell, *The Lives and Legends of Buffalo Bill* (Norman: University of Oklahoma Press, 1960), 218.

13. Dee Brown, *Bury My Heart At Wounded Knee* (Bantam, 1970), 273–274.

14. Stanley Vestal, *Sitting Bull, Champion of the Sioux* (Norman: University of Oklahoma Press, 1956), 141.

15. ibid, 144–145.

16. George Armstrong Custer, *My Life On The Plains* (New York: Citadel, 1960), 165–166.

17. ibid, 219–220.

18. William F. Cody, *The Life of Honorable William F. Cody* (Lincoln: University of Nebraska Press, 1978), 340.

19. Eric Sorg, *Buffalo Bill: Myth and Reality* (Ancient City Press, 1998), 25.

20. John G. Neihardt, *Black Elk Speaks* (Lincoln: University of Nebraska Press, 1979), 95–96.

21. ibid, 98.

22. Stanley Vestal, *Sitting Bull, Champion of the Sioux* (Norman: University of Oklahoma Press, 1956), 150.

23. ibid, 151.

24. Dee Brown, *Bury My Heart At Wounded Knee* (Bantam, 1970), 276–277.

25. George E. Hyde, *Red Cloud's Folk* (Norman: University of Oklahoma Press, 1937), 265.

26. William F. Cody, *The Life of Honorable William F. Cody* (Lincoln: University of Nebraska Press, 1978), 341.

27. George E. Hyde, *Red Cloud's Folk* (Norman: University of Oklahoma Press, 1937), 272.

28. William F. Cody, *The Life of Honorable William F. Cody* (Lincoln: University of Nebraska Press, 1978), 342.

29. Don Russell, *The Lives and Legends of Buffalo Bill* (Norman: University of Oklahoma Press, 1960), 225.

30. ibid, 225.

31. William F. Cody, *The Life of Honorable William F. Cody* (Lincoln: University of Nebraska Press, 1978), 343–344.

32. Don Russell, *The Lives and Legends of Buffalo Bill* (Norman: University of Oklahoma Press, 1960), 236.

33. ibid, 230.

34. ibid, 244.

35. Alexander B. Adams, *Sitting Bull* (Barnes and Noble, 1973), 319–320.

36. Don Russell, *The Lives and Legends of Buffalo Bill* (Norman: University of Oklahoma Press, 1960), 247.

Chapter Thirteen. GRANDMOTHER'S LAND

1. Stanley Vestal, *Sitting Bull, Champion of the Sioux* (University of Oklahoma Press, 1956), 188.

2. ibid, 188.

3. ibid, 191–192.

4. ibid, 192.

5. ibid, 195.

6. Stanley Vestal, *Sitting Bull, Champion of the Sioux* (Norman: University of Oklahoma Press, 1956), 183, 201.

7. Dee Brown, *Bury My Heart At Wounded Knee* (Bantam, 1970), 289–290.

8. Alexander B. Adams, *Sitting Bull* (Barnes and Noble, 1973), 245–246.

9. Joseph Manzione, *I Am Looking To The North For My Life: Sitting Bull, 1876–1881* (Salt Lake City: University of Utah Press, 1991), 26.

10. Dee Brown, *Bury My Heart At Wounded Knee* (Bantam, 1970), 294.

11. Joseph Manzione, *I Am Looking To The North For My Life: Sitting Bull, 1876–1881* (Salt Lake City: University of Utah Press, 1991), 47.

12. ibid, 48.

13. ibid, 49–50.

14. ibid, 74.

15. ibid, 81–82.

16. Stanley Vestal, *Sitting Bull, Champion of the Sioux* (Norman: University of Oklahoma Press, 1956), 215–216.

17. ibid, 216–217.

18. ibid, 218.

19. ibid, 228.

20. Joseph Manzione, *I Am Looking To The North For My Life: Sitting Bull, 1876–1881* (Salt Lake City: University of Utah Press, 1991), 118.

21. ibid, 129.

22. ibid, 130.

23. Stanley Vestal, *Sitting Bull, Champion of the Sioux* (Norman: University of Oklahoma Press, 1956), 225.

24. ibid, 232.

Chapter Fourteen. THE WILD WEST

1. Eric Sorg, *Buffalo Bill: Myth and Reality* (Ancient City Press, 1998), 45.

2. Robert G. Athern, *The Mythic West in the 20th Century* (Lawrence: University of Kansas Press, 1986), 272.

3. Eric Sorg, *Buffalo Bill: Myth and Reality* (Ancient City Press, 1998), 48.

4. Don Russell, *The Lives and Legends of Buffalo Bill* (Norman: University of Oklahoma Press, 1960), 266.

5. ibid, 272.

6. Sell and Weybright, *Buffalo Bill and The Wild West* (Signet, 1959), 153.

7. William F. Cody, *The Life of Honorable William F. Cody* (Lincoln: University of Nebraska Press, 1978), 362.

8. Don Russell, *The Lives and Legends of Buffalo Bill* (Norman: University of Oklahoma Press, 1960), 261.

9. Sell and Weybright, *Buffalo Bill and The Wild West* (Signet, 1959), 159.

10. Richard Walsh and Milton Salsbury, *The Making of Buffalo Bill* (Bobbs-Merrill, 1928), 219–220.

11. ibid, 221–222.

12. Don Russell, *The Lives and Legends of Buffalo Bill* (Norman: University of Oklahoma Press, 1960), 285.

13. L. G. Moses, *Wild West Shows and the Images of American Indians, 1883–1933* (Albuquerque: University of New Mexico Press, 1996), 12.

14. ibid, 13.

15. Sell and Weybright, *Buffalo Bill and The Wild West* (Signet, 1959), 161.

16. Richard Walsh and Milton Salsbury, *The Making of Buffalo Bill* (Bobbs-Merrill, 1928), 224.

17. ibid, 225.

18. Sell and Weybright, *Buffalo Bill and The Wild West* (Signet, 1959), 164.

19. ibid, 165.

20. Don Russell, *The Lives and Legends of Buffalo Bill* (Norman: University of Oklahoma Press, 1960), 313.

21. Stanley Vestal, *Sitting Bull, Champion of the Sioux* (Norman: University of Oklahoma Press, 1956), 250.

22. L. G. Moses, *Wild West Shows and the Images of American Indians, 1883–1933* (Albuquerque: University of New Mexico Press, 1996), 27.

23. ibid, 27.

24. ibid, 27.

25. Sell and Weybright, *Buffalo Bill and The Wild West* (Signet, 1959), 178.

26. ibid, 179.

27. Don Russell, *The Lives and Legends of Buffalo Bill* (University of Oklahoma Press, 1960), 316–317.

28. Stanley Vestal, *Sitting Bull, Champion of the Sioux* (University of Oklahoma Press, 1956), 250–251.

29. ibid, 251.

30. L. G. Moses, *Wild West Shows and the Images of American Indians, 1883–1933* (Albuquerque: University of New Mexico Press, 1996), 31.

31. Richard Walsh and Milton Salsbury *The Making of Buffalo Bill* (Bobbs-Merrill, 1928), 260–261.

32. Sell and Weybright, *Buffalo Bill and The Wild West* (Signet, 1959), 180.

Chapter Fifteen. GRANDMOTHER ENGLAND

1. Sell and Weybright, *Buffalo Bill and The Wild West* (Signet, 1959), 186.

2. L. G. Moses, *Wild West Shows and the Images of American Indians, 1883–1933* (Albuquerque: University of New Mexico Press, 1996), 38.

3. ibid, 61.

4. Luther Standing Bear, *Land of the Spotted Eagle* (Lincoln: University of Nebraska Press, 1978), 250–251.

5. Dee Brown, *Bury My Heart At Wounded Knee* (Bantam, 1970), 397.

6. L. G. Moses, *Wild West Shows and the Images of American Indians, 1883–1933* (Albuquerque: University of New Mexico Press, 1996), 62.

7. Luther Standing Bear, *Land of the Spotted Eagle* (Lincoln: University of Nebraska Press, 1978), 251.

8. L. G. Moses, *Wild West Shows and the Images of American Indians, 1833–1933* (Albuquerque: University of New Mexico Press, 1996), 39.

9. Luther Standing Bear, *Land of the Spotted Eagle* (Lincoln: University of Nebraska Press, 1978), 245.

10. L. G. Moses, *Wild West Shows and the Images of American Indians, 1833–1933* (Albuquerque: University of New Mexico Press, 1996), 40.

11. Don Russell, *The Lives and Legends of Buffalo Bill* (Norman: University of Oklahoma Press, 1960), 327.

12. John G. Neihardt, *Black Elk Speaks* (Lincoln: University of Nebraska Press, 1979), 218–219.

13. L. G. Moses, *Wild West Shows and the Images of American Indians, 1833–1933* (Albuquerque: University of New Mexico Press, 1996), 43.

14. Sell and Weybright, *Buffalo Bill and The Wild West* (Signet, 1959), 193.

15. ibid, 198.

16. ibid, 194–195.

17. L. G. Moses, *Wild West Shows and the Images of American Indians, 1833–1933* (Albuquerque: University of New Mexico Press, 1996), 48.

18. ibid, 49.

19. Don Russell, *The Lives and Legends of Buffalo Bill* (Norman: University of Oklahoma Press, 1960), 329.

20. Sell and Weybright, *Buffalo Bill and The Wild West* (Signet, 1959), 200.

21. Don Russell, *The Lives and Legends of Buffalo Bill* (Norman: University of Oklahoma Press, 1960), 330.

22. Ray DeMallie, *The Sixth Grandfather: Black Elk's Teachings Given To John G. Neihardt* (Lincoln: University of Nebraska Press, 1984), 249.

23. Don Russell, *The Lives and Legends of Buffalo Bill* (Norman: University of Oklahoma Press, 1960), 331.

24. Sell and Weybright, *Buffalo Bill and The Wild West* (Signet, 1959), 209–210.

25. Don Russell, *The Lives and Legends of Buffalo Bill* (Norman: University of Oklahoma Press, 1960), 337.

26. Ray DeMaille, *The Sixth Grandfather: Black Elk's Teaching Given To John G. Neihardt* (Lincoln: University of Nebraska Press, 1984), 251.

27. Walsh and Salsbury, *The Making of Buffalo Bill* (Bobbs-Merrill, 1928), 273–274.

28. Don Russell, *The Lives and Legends of Buffalo Bill* (Norman: University of Oklahoma Press, 1960), 342–343.

29. ibid, 343.

30. ibid, 344.

Chapter Sixteen. ARROWS OF LIGHT

1. Stella Adelyne Foote, *Letters From Buffalo Bill* (Foote Publishing, 1954), 22.

2. John G. Neihardt, *Black Elk Speaks* (Lincoln: University of Nebraska Press, 1979), 228.

3. Stella Adelyne Foote, *Letters From Buffalo Bill* (Foote Publishing, 1954), 35–36.

4. Don Russell, *The Lives and Legends of Buffalo Bill* (Norman: University of Oklahoma Press, 1960), 352.

5. Sell and Weybright, *Buffalo Bill and The Wild West* (Signet, 1959), 216–217.

6. ibid, 217.

7. ibid, 218.

8. Luther Standing Bear, *My People The Sioux* (Lincoln: University of Nebraska Press, 1975), 263–264.

9. ibid, 260–261.

10. Robert G. Athearn, *The Mythic West in the 20th Century* (Lawrence: University of Kansas Press, 1968), 186.

11. L. G. Moses, *Wild West Shows and the Images of American Indians, 1833–1933* (Albuquerque: University of New Mexico Press, 1996), 98.

12. ibid, 101.

13. Luther Standing Bear, *My People The Sioux* (Lincoln: University of Nebraska Press, 1975), 249.

14. L. G. Moses, *Wild West Shows and the Images of American Indians, 1833–1933* (Albuquerque: University of New Mexico Press, 1996), 103.

15. ibid, 103.

16. Dee Brown, *Bury My Heart At Wound Knee* (Bantam, 1970), 397.

17. Stanley Vestal, *Sitting Bull, Champion of the Sioux* (Norman: University of Oklahoma Press, 1956), 252.

18. ibid, 239.

19. ibid, 240–242.

20. Dee Brown, *Bury My Heart At Wounded Knee* (Bantam, 1970), 400.

21. Stanley Vestal, *Sitting Bull, Champion of the Sioux* (Norman: University of Oklahoma Press, 1956), 255.

22. ibid, 249.

23. ibid, 262.

24. ibid, 264.

25. ibid, 271.

26. ibid, 271–272.

27. Jack Utter, *Wounded Knee and the Ghost Dance Tragedy* (National Woodlands Publishing Company, 1991), 12.

28. Stanley Vestal, *Sitting Bull, Champion of the Sioux* (Norman: University of Oklahoma Press, 1956), 272.

29. Robert Utley, *The Lance and The Shield* (Henry Holt and Company, 1993), 286.

30. Dee Brown, *Bury My Heart At Wounded Knee* (Bantam, 1970), 409.

31. Jack Utter, *Wounded Knee and the Ghost Dance Tragedy* (National Woodlands Publishing Company, 1991), 15.

32. Stanley Vestal, *Sitting Bull, Champion of the Sioux* (University of Oklahoma Press, 1956), 277.

33. ibid, 278.

34. Don Russell, *The Lives and Legends of Buffalo Bill* (Norman: University of Oklahoma Press, 1960), 359.

35. James McLaughlin, *My Friend The Indian* (Lincoln: University of Nebraska Press, 1989), 210.

36. Don Russell, *The Lives and Legends of Buffalo Bill* (Norman: University of Oklahoma Press), 1960.

37. Richard Walsh and Milton Salsbury, *The Making of Buffalo Bill* (Bobbs-Merrill, 1928), 286.

38. Stanley Vestal, *Sitting Bull, Champion of the Sioux* (Norman: University of Oklahoma, 1956), 281.

39. Walsh and Salsbury, *The Making of Buffalo Bill* (Bobbs-Merrill, 1928), 287.

40. James McLaughlin, *My Friend The Indian* (Lincoln: University of Nebraska Press, 1989), 211.

41. Stanley Vestal, *Sitting Bull, Champion of the Sioux* (Norman: University of Oklahoma Press, 1956), 252–253.

42. ibid, 253.

43. ibid, 254.

44. ibid, 300.

45. ibid, 300.

46. ibid, 301.

47. ibid, 301.

Chapter Seventeen. ABSAROKA

1. Don Russell, *The Lives and Legends of Buffalo Bill* (Norman: University of Oklahoma Press, 1960), 363; Robert Utley, *The Lance and The Shield* (Henry Holt and Company, 1993), 313.

2. Jack Utter, *Wounded Knee and the Ghost Dance Tragedy* (National Woodlands Publishing Company, 1991), 20–21.

3. Jack Utter, *Wounded Knee and the Ghost Dance Tragedy* (National Woodlands Publishing Co., 1991), 20–24; Dee Brown, *Bury My Heart At Wounded Knee* (Bantam, 1970), 413–419.

4. John G. Neihardt, *Black Elk Speaks* (University of Nebraska Press, 1979), 259.

5. ibid.

6. Don Russell, *The Lives and Legends of Buffalo Bill* (Norman: University of Oklahoma Press, 1960), 366.

7. ibid, 367.

8. ibid, 368.

9. L. G. Moses, *Wild West Shows and the Images of American Indians, 1883–1933* (Albuquerque: University of New Mexico Press, 1996), 108–109.

10. Don Russell, *The Lives and Legends of Buffalo Bill* (Norman: University of Oklahoma Press, 1960), 369.

11. ibid, 370–371.

12. Richard Walsh and Milton Salsbury, *The Making of Buffalo Bill* (Bobbs-Merrill, 1928), 293–294.

13. Don Russell, *The Lives and Legends of Buffalo Bill* (Norman: University of Oklahoma Press, 1960), 425.

14. Stella Adelyne Foote, *Letters From Buffalo Bill* (Foote Publishing, 1954), 40–41; Walsh and Salsbury, *The Making of Buffalo Bill* (Bobbs-Merrill, 1928), 307–309.

15. L. G. Moses, *Wild West Shows and the Images of American Indians, 1883–1933* (Albuquerque: University of New Mexico Press, 1996), 111.

16. ibid, 114–115.

17. ibid, 115–116.

18. ibid, 118.

19. Stella Adelyne Foote, *Letters From Buffalo Bill* (Foote Publishing, 1954), 37.

20. ibid, 37.

21. Walsh and Salsbury, *The Making of Buffalo Bill* (Bobbs-Merrill, 1928), 298.

22. Don Russell, *The Lives and Legends of Buffalo Bill* (Norman: University of Oklahoma Press, 1960), 374.

23. L. G. Moses, *Wild West Shows and the Images of American Indians, 1883–1933* (Albuquerque: University of New Mexico Press, 1996), 130–131.

24. ibid, 133.

25. ibid, 134–135.

26. Don Russell, *The Lives and Legends of Buffalo Bill* (Norman: University of Oklahoma Press, 1960), 375.

27. L. G. Moses, *Wild West Show and the Images of American Indians, 1883–1933* (Albuquerque: University of New Mexico Press, 1996), 137.

28. Sell and Weybright, *Buffalo Bill and the Wild West* (Signet, 1959), 233.

29. Don Russell, *The Lives and Legends of Buffalo Bill* (Norman: University of Oklahoma Press, 1960), 375.

30. Walsh and Salsbury, *The Making of Buffalo Bill* (Bobbs-Merrill, 1928), 302–303.

31. Don Russell, *The Lives and Legends of Buffalo Bill* (Norman: University of Oklahoma Press, 1960), 375.

32. L. G. Moses, *Wild West Shows and the Images of American Indians, 1883–1933* (Albuquerque: University of New Mexico Press, 1996), 126.

33. Walsh and Salsbury, *The Making of Buffalo Bill* (Bobbs-Merrill, 1928), 304.

34. ibid, 305.

35. Don Russell, *The Lives and Legends of Buffalo Bill* (Norman: University of Oklahoma Press, 1960), 433; Walsh and Salsbury, *The Making of Buffalo Bill* (Bobbs-Merrill, 1928), 305–306.

36. Helen Wetmore Cody, *Buffalo Bill, The Last of the Great Scouts: The Life of Colonel William F. Cody* (Grosset and Dunlap, 1918), 252–253.

37. Walsh and Salsbury, *The Making of Buffalo Bill* (Bobbs-Merrill, 1928), 309; Don Russell, *The Lives and Legends of Buffalo Bill* (Norman: University of Oklahoma Press, 1960), 378–379.

38. Don Russell, *The Lives and Legends of Buffalo Bill* (Norman: University of Oklahoma Press, 1960), 379.

39. ibid, 427.

40. ibid, 426.

Chapter Eighteen. PAHASKA HAD A STRONG HEART

1. Richard Walsh and Milton Salsbury, *The Making of Buffalo Bill* (Bobbs-Merrill, 1928), 311.

2. ibid, 313.

3. Don Russell, *The Lives and Legends of Buffalo Bill* (Norman: University of Oklahoma Press, 1960), 418.

4. ibid, 416–417.

5. Richard Walsh and Milton Salsbury, *The Making of Buffalo Bill* (Bobbs-Merrill, 1928), 317–318.

6. Don Russell, *The Lives and Legends of Buffalo Bill* (Norman: University of Oklahoma Press, 1960), 417–418.

7. ibid, 418.

8. Richard Walsh and Milton Salsbury, *The Making of Buffalo Bill* (Bobbs-Merrill, 1928), 318–319.

9. ibid, 319.

10. Henry Blackburn Sell and Victor Weybright, *Buffalo Bill and The Wild West* (Signet, 1959), 249.

11. ibid, 257.

12. Richard Walsh and Milton Salsbury, *The Making of Buffalo Bill* (Bobbs-Merrill, 1928), 320.

13. Don Russell, *The Lives and Legends of Buffalo Bill* (Norman: University of Oklahoma Press, 1960), 420.

14. Stella Adeline Foote, *Letters From Buffalo Bill* (Foote Publishing, 1954), 49.

15. Henry Blackburn Sell and Victor Weybright, *Buffalo Bill and The Wild West* (Signet, 1959), 271.

16. Richard Walsh and Milton Salsbury, *The Making of Buffalo Bill* (Bobbs-Merrill, 1928), 323–324.

17. Henry Blackburn Sell and Victor Weybright, *Buffalo Bill and The Wild West* (Signet, 1959), 264–265.

18. ibid, 266.

19. ibid, 266–267.

20. Richard Walsh and Milton Salsbury, *The Making of Buffalo Bill* (Bobbs-Merrill, 1928), 325.

21. ibid, 327.

22. ibid, 331–332.

23. Stella Adeline Foote, *Letters From Buffalo Bill* (Foote Publishing, 1954), 56–58.

24. Richard Walsh and Milton Salsbury, *The Making of Buffalo Bill* (Bobbs-Merrill, 1928), 331.

25. ibid, 332–333.

26. ibid, 330.

27. ibid, 333.

28. Don Russell, *The Lives and Legends of Buffalo Bill* (Norman: University of Oklahoma Press, 1960), 446–447.

29. Richard Walsh and Milton Salsbury, *The Making of Buffalo Bill* (Bobbs-Merrill, 1928), 336.

30. Don Russell, *The Lives and Legends of Buffalo Bill* (Norman: University of Oklahoma Press, 1960), 451.

31. Richard Walsh and Milton Salsbury, *The Making of Buffalo Bill* (Bobbs-Merrill, 1928), 339.

32. Don Russell, *The Lives and Legends of Buffalo Bill* (Norman: University of Oklahoma Press, 1960), 426.

33. Henry Blackburn Sell and Victor Weybright, *Buffalo Bill and The Wild West* (Signet, 1959), 285.

34. Richard Walsh and Milton Salsbury, *The Making of Buffalo Bill* (Bobbs-Merrill, 1928), 341–342.

35. ibid, 344.

36. Don Russell, *The Lives and Legends of Buffalo Bill* (Norman: University of Oklahoma Press, 1960), 452.

37. ibid, 453.

38. ibid, 455.

39. ibid, 456–457.

40. Richard Walsh and Milton Salsbury, *The Making of Buffalo Bill* (Bobbs-Merrill, 1928), 344; and, Don Russell, *The Lives and Legends of Buffalo Bill* (Norman: University of Oklahoma Press, 1960), 456; also see Vine DeLoria's, *The Indians.*

41. Richard Walsh and Milton Salsbury, *The Making of Buffalo Bill* (Bobbs-Merrill, 1928), 344–345.

42. Don Russell, *The Lives and Legends of Buffalo Bill* (Norman: University of Oklahoma Press, 1960), 457.

43. ibid, 457–458.

44. Richard Walsh and Milton Salsbury, *The Making of Buffalo Bill* (Bobbs-Merrill, 1928), 345–346.

45. ibid, 346.

46. ibid, 348.

47. Don Russell, *The Lives and Legends of Buffalo Bill* (University of Oklahoma Press, 1960), 459–460.

48. ibid, 460.

49. Richard Walsh and Milton Salsbury, *The Making of Buffalo Bill* (Bobbs-Merrill, 1928), 353.

50. Don Russell, *The Lives and Legends of Buffalo Bill* (Norman: University of Oklahoma Press, 1960), 461.

51. ibid, 463.

52. L. G. Moses, *Wild West Shows and the Images of American Indians, 1883–1933* (Albuquerque: University of New Mexico Press, 1996), 176–177.

53. Don Russell, *The Lives and Legends of Buffalo Bill* (Norman: University of Oklahoma Press, 1960), 461.

54. ibid, 463.

55. Richard Walsh and Milton Salsbury, *The Making of Buffalo Bill* (Bobbs-Merrill, 1928), 357.

56. Henry Blackburn Sell and Victor Weybright, *Buffalo Bill and The Wild West* (Signet, 1959), 292.

57. Richard Walsh and Milton Salsbury, *The Making of Buffalo Bill* (Bobbs-Merrill, 1928), 358.

58. Henry Blackburn Sell and Victor Weybright, *Buffalo Bill and The Wild West* (Signet, 1959), 294–295.

59. ibid, 295.

60. ibid, 297.

61. Richard Walsh and Milton Salsbury, *The Making of Buffalo Bill* (Bobbs-Merrill, 1928), 360.

62. Henry Blackburn Sell and Victor Weybright, *Buffalo Bill and The Wild West* (Signet, 1959), 298.

63. ibid, 298–299.

64. ibid, 299–300.

65. ibid, 277–281.

66. Helen Wetmore Cody and Zane Grey, *Last of the Great Scouts ("Buffalo Bill")* (Grosset and Dunlap, 1918), 332–333.

INDEX